MILWAUKEE'S JESUIT UNIVERSITY

MARQUETTE, 1881-1981

MILWAUKEE'S JESUIT UNIVERSITY

MARQUETTE, 1881-1981

BY

THOMAS J. JABLONSKY

MARQUETTE
UNIVERSITY

PRESS

URBAN LIFE SERIES

NO. 3

THOMAS J. JABLONSKY, SERIES EDITOR

LIBRARY OF CONGRESS CATALOGING-IN-PUBLICATION DATA

Jablonsky, Thomas J.
  Milwaukee's Jesuit University : Marquette, 1881-1981 / by Thomas J. Jablonsky.
  p. cm. — (Urban life series ; no. 3)
  Includes bibliographical references and index.
  ISBN 978-0-87462-080-1 (hardcover : alk. paper) — ISBN 978-0-87462-082-5 (pbk. : alk. paper)
  1. Marquette University—History. 2. Universities and colleges—Wisconsin. I. Title.
LD3231.M542J33 2007
378.775'95—dc22

2007007472

© 2007 Marquette University Press
Milwaukee, Wisconsin 53201-3141
All rights reserved.
www.marquette.edu/mupress/

♾The paper used in this publication meets the minimum requirements of the
American National Standard for Information Sciences—
Permanence of Paper for Printed Library Materials, ANSI Z39.48-1992.

MARQUETTE UNIVERSITY PRESS
MILWAUKEE

The Association of Jesuit University Presses

CONTENTS

DEDICATED TO ALL MY STUDENTS, 1970-2007

ACKNOWLEDGMENTS

Authors always take the time—rightly so—to recognize the invaluable contributions of associates who helped to make a book possible. In the case of non-fiction, these expressions of appreciation are often far more numerous.

From the outset, the unflinching support of Reverend Robert A. Wild, SJ, has been especially vital. He made it clear from the outset that this volume was my study and that he did not feel the need to be updated on its contents. He maintained this position of trust throughout the process and, for that in particular, I will be always grateful. For the others who helped shape the environment in which this history would be written, specifically Father Pat Burns and Dr. Jerry Viscione, another round of thanks. And to the committee members who first determined that Marquette University deserved a new accounting of its role in Milwaukee and the Midwest, my acknowledgment as to how important your conclusions were to this effort.

Any success this volume may have in the future will be the result of reliable support from the University Archives staff, specifically Matt Blessing, Michelle Sweetser, and Susan Stawicki-Vrobel. Especially when I was out of state writing, they graciously clarified confusing details, double-checked fuzzily written citations, and even uncovered previously forgotten sources. You are a great team, a wonderful set of colleagues, and I can only hope that this volume compensates for the barrage of phone calls that I have made over the past few years. Also from the library, Dean Nick Burckel, a fellow historian, and Michael Pate were wonderful in providing work space for my research team even as construction of the Raynor Library unfolded around us. Our working environment was perfect due to your abiding consideration.

Ordinarily, an author must extend cautious appreciation to anonymous readers hired by the publisher to evaluate a manuscript. Their suggestions lift the original draft, often dowdy and parochial, into a crisper and more expressive final product. It has been my good fortune that from the beginning I knew the names of those who had devoted too much time and attention improving this volume. Any failures to act upon their recommendations is entirely my fault. Father Paul Prucha, SJ, Father Gerald McKevitt, SJ, Father Anthony Kuzniewski, SJ, Dr. Philip Gleason, and Dr. Ralph Weber read all or portions of this work, sharing insights from their careers as accomplished historians. My thanks for their honesty and wisdom. A double share of thanks is consequently due to Father Steven Avella, my good friend in Marquette's history department, and to Dr. Ed Perkins, my former colleague and poker-playing companion at the University of Southern California. They had the misfortune of reading the manuscript twice. My condolences and deepest appreciation.

In the production phase of the project, I required more hours than were justified from the manuscript's always-caring copy editor, Dr. Rhoda Sherwood, and the director of the Marquette University Press, Dr. Andy Tallon. How kind they were in keeping up with the pace that we maintained near the end and how virtuous they were in putting up with the ravings of a deadline-obsessed author. Truly, my thanks many times over.

To my wife, Pam, my gratitude for her patience for the hours and days and weeks and months and years during which this project imposed itself upon our household. Now, maybe, we can go somewhere without the laptop in tow!

Finally, my deepest gratitude goes to the research assistants who spent so many hours committed to this study. It is a pleasure to recognize John McCarthy, Christopher Miller, Ed Schmidt, and Brigitte Charaus for their loyalty and dedication. They understood my ambitions for this project from the outset and provided a level of conscientiousness in their attention to detail worthy of their alma mater. I wish them the best in their own nascent careers as historians. These four remarkable individuals are part of a stream of students who have assisted me in fulfilling my vocation as an educator. To all my students since 1970, I dedicate this book. My best wishes to each, whether our paths crossed at Don Bosco Technical Institute in Rosemead, California; California State University, Los Angeles; the University of Southern California; or Marquette University. Thank you for making every workday a holy day.

PREFACE

Late in 1997, Marquette University's senior administration charged a committee to review the options available for a new university history, one that would succeed Father Raphael Hamilton's monumental *Marquette University*, published in 1953. The committee included representatives from Memorial Library, the Marquette University Press, and the Department of History. On the distant horizon lay the 2006-07 celebration of Marquette's 125th anniversary.

After months of work, the committee concluded that the university had three alternatives: a coffee table volume, heavy with memorable photographs but short on interpretation and documentation; a middle-ground publication with a few, short, original essays accompanied by a copious display of photographic images; or finally, a scholarly tome, based on an entirely new reading of the tens of thousands of pages of primary sources, a study that would offer a completely new perspective of the university's evolution. The committee settled upon the last of these options.

The final decision rested with Fathers Robert A. Wild, university president, and Patrick Burns, corporate vice president, as well as Dr. Jerry Viscione, executive vice president. In the end, they enthusiastically embraced the committee's recommendation. Without their conviction that Marquette deserved a serious accounting of its maturation into one of the most important Catholic universities in the country, the challenges encountered along the way might have buried this project. The commitments of these three individuals became more personal after they accepted my offer to take on this assignment.

The research started slowly because of administrative duties, but I did have the opportunity over the first few years to meet various members of the Marquette family: the Association of Marquette University Women, the Parents' Association, graduates returning for their golden jubilees, and current faculty, staff, and students. It became abundantly clear that no writer could fairly represent their abiding memories of this institution because these experiences were so intimate. Realizing that I might not meet their expectations was troubling. I knew that I was writing for each of them as well as for the institution at large. In an earlier project on Chicago's Back of the Yards neighborhood during the 1920s and 1930s, I tried to craft a community history, the details of which provided some understanding of everyday life for thousands of working class Chicagoans. Trying to get that story right was also personal because the residents under study included all four of my grandparents as well as my parents. But the size of the Marquette community—thousands of people who had deep concerns over what was said about their alma mater or their place of employment—made this effort far more intimidating. Everyone wanted to ensure that Marquette's story was told correctly.

Ultimately, these sentiments could neither determine the book's content nor steer its interpretive conclusions, even as the intensity of their feelings underscored the point that history always touches upon genuine human emotions. Even if the objects of a study are deceased and quite forgotten (unlike, for instance, John Raynor and Al McGuire), they must be honored with accurate representations. In the end, historians are obligated to their professional consciences: to a thoroughness in collecting the evidence, to a fair and representative reading of the documentation, and to the framing of substantiated interpretations. Beyond the details of Marquette's own record, there were other contexts that had to be addressed, including the history of the Jesuits, the history of the Roman Catholic Church, the history of American higher education, and the histories of Milwaukee and the United States of America. Marquette University has always been part of something larger. Yet at the same time, it has served as an institutional tapestry upon which thousands of individual lives are intimately recorded. A historian's balancing act requires that members of the Marquette community see themselves in the overall narrative though, perhaps, not with the same words that they would have chosen to tell their stories to thousands of strangers.

I always saw three themes shaping this project: an administrative history of the university, complete with power brokers and their stern-minded decisions; the development of student culture, a series of lifestyles created over ten decades by thousands of alumni who proudly called themselves Hilltoppers or Warriors; and finally, Marquette in Milwaukee, the story of a vital Catholic institution with its roller-coaster relationship with the city and region that surrounds it. The first theme—administrative history—opens most chapters because I came to believe that the physical, demographic, and curricular conditions imposed by university presidents, senior administrators, and (sometimes) the faculty provided the environment in which most student experiences took place. Whether Marquette admitted medical students or women, whether a science center or a student union existed, whether tuition rates increased annually or once every quarter-of-a-century were all decisions made in administration hall. These choices subsequently molded the everyday world in which first-year students eventually aged into alumni. Most of these presidents, academic vice presidents, deans, and faculty are deceased, but their decisions—enlightened or otherwise—molded the institutional landscape in which others learned or worked. Within these curricular and morphological settings, Marquette students formed their character, plotted their future, and constructed scrapbooks of memories.

Although these three themes shaped the narrative's organizational flow, the central thesis focuses upon the issue of control, of the forces (most from inside but some from outside the university) that determined the school's destiny. Who was responsible for the fulfillment of its loftiest goals: the students, the faculty, the Jesuits? Who shaped its policies and procedures: church authorities, boards of trustees, the North Central Association, the American Medical Association, the National Collegiate Athletic Conference?

When Marquette opened in 1881 as a college/high school on the northwest corner of Tenth and State streets, fewer than a dozen Jesuits controlled everything but the institution's financial future. In the absence of a lavish endowment—or any endowment, for that matter—every tuition-paying student played a tiny part in the institution's fiscal well-being. After Marquette affiliated with the Milwaukee Medical College, purchased two proprietary law schools, and created an engineering college, decisions regarding courses, staffing, and even student behavior began to slip, imperceptibly at first, out of the hands of the black robes and into the hands of men and (ultimately) women who were often neither Jesuits nor Roman Catholics. A long transition, one that is still unfolding, had begun.

Whatever adjustments the university's student body and academic leadership have undergone over the decades, the central mission of Marquette remains essentially unchanged: the salvation of one's soul through a life of learning. The institution continues to educate individuals who epitomize faith, excellence, service, and leadership. Responsibility for holding true to that legacy has now devolved upon a new generation of leaders. Tomorrow, yet another set of guardians will embrace this obligation. Godspeed to them all in their preparation for this mighty task.

Thomas J. Jablonsky
March 2007

JESUITS AND MARQUETTE IN MILWAUKEE, 1855-1981

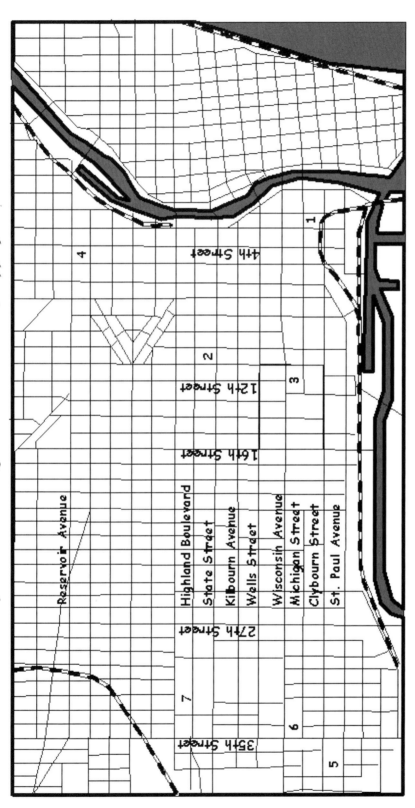

#1 St. Gall's Church and School
#2 Original site of Marquette College (Hilltop)
#3 Church of the Gesu
#4 Marquette School of Medicine, 1913-32
#5 Marquette football stadium
#6 Marquette University High School
#7 Lisette Lodge/Highland Boulevard residences

Main Campus
Streets
Railroads
Rivers/Canals/Lake

Cartography by Christopher Miller.

THE JESUITS COME TO MILWAUKEE
1844-1880

I t was August 15, 1880, the feast of the Assumption of the Virgin Mary into heaven. Every member of Milwaukee's Catholic community seemed to have trudged up the steep slopes northwest of the city center to witness the laying of a cornerstone for Marquette College. Placed within that cornerstone were photographs of Pope Leo XIII, Archbishop John Martin Henni (Milwaukee's prelate), and Father Stanislaus Lalumiere (the local Jesuit superior); pictures of St. Ignatius Loyola and St. Aloysius (another Jesuit saint); various medals and coins; a list of principal churches in the diocese; and, finally, the latest map of Milwaukee.

The religious mementos captured the day's sacred purpose. But the final item, a simple spatial representation of the city, hinted at another emotion stirring within the throng. A quiet, patriotic energy infused the proceedings—quiet, that is, until it found a voice during the keynote address. Father Leonard Batz, the Milwaukee diocese's vicar general, spoke in German and explained how Catholic boys required monitoring even after graduation from the city's twelve parish schools. At Marquette College, Milwaukee's young men would learn how to save their souls through, in his words, "the science of salvation," a mainstay of any Jesuit institution. Batz concluded his speech with a curt dismissal of what he suspected some in the audience felt about this new school: that it would "be little German, too much Irish." Rather, he exclaimed, it would be "Catholic American. We are proud to live in this land and we shall make it the object of our lives to be people who are ready to give our property and shed our blood for our faith and American citizenship. All hail Milwaukee. All hail Wisconsin. All hail the United States of America."[1]

Contents from the cornerstone of the original Marquette College building, opened in 1970. File 887

A DREAM IS BORN

Milwaukee's center for "the science of salvation" originated neither with an American nor with a son of St. Ignatius Loyola. It sprang instead from the dreams of a Swiss immigrant who probably knew nothing about the shores of Lake Michigan when he first arrived in North America. John Martin Henni, born in 1805, began to study for the priesthood at the tender age of ten. While taking theology classes in Rome, he came upon a priest from Cincinnati, a river town in the newly formed United States of America. This visitor was recruiting clergymen for missionary work in the New World. Inspired by such a calling, Henni accompanied another seminarian in 1827 to what he envisioned a frontier outpost. He carried with him a single ambition: to become a priestly advocate for German-language immigrants in America's heartland.[2]

John Henni spent his first two years in the United States at a seminary in Bardstown, Kentucky, completing his theological training before ordination in 1829. The city of Cincinnati, to which he was assigned, may not have been an ancient metropolis like Rome but it was hardly as rough-hewn as the young priest first imagined. Located at a bend in the Ohio River, the Queen City served as a gateway to the American West early in the nineteenth century. The settlement became a bustling port, nurturing a robust steamboat industry and providing a marketplace for the region's agricultural riches. Cultural improvements came with economic success, as music schools opened and book and magazine publishers gave the city a reputation for learning. There was even a Catholic college by 1831. Streams of immigrants, many from Germany, joined ambitious transplants from the Atlantic seaboard states to make Cincinnati a city on the move. In 1836, after seven years of routine priestly duties, Henni was named pastor of Holy Trinity Church in the Over-the-Rhine neighborhood. Under his leadership, Holy Trinity became a "model ethnic church," according to historian Steven Avella. For example, within a year of his arrival, Henni organized an orphanage for German children and set up a German Catholic newspaper. In 1838, he became vicar general for the Cincinnati diocese, the local bishop's right-hand man. With a growing resume in both parish and diocesan administration, Henni was appointed the first bishop of Milwaukee in November 1843 by Pope Gregory XVI. The new prelate arrived in Milwaukee seven weeks after his consecration on March 19, 1844. The geographical dimensions of his diocese were daunting, for they included what four years later became the State of Wisconsin as well as the Minnesota Territory east of the Mississippi River. Henni had only four priests to care for 20,000 Catholics. Undeterred, he set out to familiarize himself with his far-flung congregants.[3]

Whoever became the first bishop of Milwaukee would have found his surroundings fresh and unfamiliar because everything *was* new in Milwaukee, Wisconsin, and, indeed, throughout the upper Midwest. In 1835, Wisconsin became the last corner of the Old Northwest Territory to be opened to settlement. Within a year, founding fathers Solomon Juneau, Byron Kilbourn, and George Walker had attracted nearly a thousand brave souls to join them along the western shores of Lake Michigan. These three developers vied over every newcomer, conniving to get each potential property

Archbishop John Martin Henni. Henni Biographical File

owner to settle in "his" section of town (Juneau on the east, Kilbourn on the west, and Walker on the south). Competition was so keen between Juneau and Kilbourn that they set up rival newspapers and offered land for a county courthouse. When residents of Juneautown tried to build a bridge to the west bank of the Milwaukee River, rivals in Kilbourntown dismantled it. Those who saw their future in Milwaukee usually came from the East by way of the Erie Canal, followed by a steamer trip across the Great Lakes. Most exciting for the community's new bishop, Milwaukee soon rivaled Cincinnati and St. Louis in attracting German immigrants.[4]

Agriculture was the mainstay of the local economy. In 1835, during the first year of land sales, eighty-two schooners and lake steamers arrived in town. One thousand vessels visited the port ten years later, as wheat, barley, leather, and timber were exported. By 1843, the year before Henni's arrival, Milwaukee's population approached 6,000. For Catholics, the first Mass was celebrated in 1835 in the home of Solomon Juneau. The first church was built four years later on land donated by Juneau. The rivalry among Juneautown, Kilbourntown, and Walker's Point eased sufficiently by late

1845 to allow these settlements to jointly petition for municipal incorporation. By the end of 1846, Milwaukee boasted 9,500 residents, with nearly 6,000 more scattered across the rest of the county. The German influence grew apace, with German-born Milwaukeeans outnumbering American-born residents by 1850. This balance would shift during the following decade, but at the end of the American Civil War, a majority of the city's inhabitants could still claim German ancestry. This ethnic concentration made the choice of John Martin Henni as the first bishop of Milwaukee appropriate and fortuitous.[5]

As fast as Milwaukee may have grown during the 1830s and 1840s, the diocese was still unprepared for at least one of their new bishop's visions. Not long after his arrival, Henni decided to complete the cathedral church, a building whose foundation sat unfinished. As the bishop's church, the cathedral represented the regional stature of the Catholic Church—and the local prelate. That objective was attainable, if expensive. However, Henni's second goal, the establishment of a Catholic college, proved far more improbable given the circumstances. Milwaukee's new bishop may have been spoiled by the rapid maturation of Cincinnati. In 1831, two years after Henni began his priestly duties in the Queen City, the diocese of Cincinnati opened the *Athenaeum*, "the first Catholic institution of higher learning in the Northwest Territory." Nine years later, the school encountered hard times following the financial panic of 1837. A new bishop convinced the superior general of Jesuits to take control of the *Athenaeum*, which was subsequently renamed St. Xavier College. Henni, therefore, had witnessed what could be done with the proper combination of vision and support. But the notion that Milwaukee—without paved streets, a library, or even a high school—could sustain a college was unrealistic. This gap between dream and reality was underscored when the Norbertine, Dominican, and Benedictine orders all declined Henni's solicitations to manage "his" college. The bishop came to realize that the recruitment of a religious sponsor faced two serious obstacles: first, funds were needed to cover the real estate and construction costs and, second, a sufficient number of priests and brothers must be available to handle the student load.[6]

THE JESUITS ARRIVE

Thwarted, Henni turned to a strategy that American bishops had successfully employed for years. He headed to Europe to raise funds among sympathetic Catholics for missionary work in America. In his case, Milwaukee's prelate sought support to complete the Cathedral of St. John the Evangelist and to underwrite an institution of higher education. His trip lasted through the winter of 1848-49. Incredibly, the bishop settled the issue of his college through two serendipitous encounters. First, the prelate met Father Anthony Minoux, superior for the Jesuit province of Upper Germany whose confreres had been exiled from Henni's Swiss homeland in 1847. Many of these displaced Jesuits had been sent to St. Louis, headquarters for the Missouri vice province of the Society of Jesus and, like Cincinnati and Milwaukee, a center of German migration to America. Henni urged the German provincial to consider assigning his homeless—and penniless—charges to the increasingly Teutonic-rich city of Milwaukee with the intention of building a college.[7]

While Minoux thought about this offer, Henni addressed the financial needs of his new school through a chance meeting with Monsieur Guillaume Joseph DeBoey, a "legal agent" who had attained some wealth and status in his native Antwerp, Belgium. DeBoey had dedicated himself to the philanthropic work of the Jesuits in Europe and the Church in general. In recognition, the Holy See appointed DeBoey to the Order of the Knights of St. Gregory. Impressed by the work of Jesuit and fellow Belgian Peter Jean DeSmet among Native Americans in the Oregon Territory, DeBoey promised Henni 75,000 francs ($16,000) to assist in the establishment of what had become, almost over night, a Jesuit college. Although he did not expect to receive the money for years, Henni was emboldened and pressed Father Minoux to dispatch his confreres to Milwaukee. The provincial demurred, citing an unfamiliarity with the circumstances in mid-America. Instead, he turned over the final decision to the superior of the Missouri vice province, Father John A. Elet, who was looking after the displaced Swiss Jesuits.[8]

Father Elet mistrusted Bishop Henni at first. The two priests had undoubtedly crossed paths in Cincinnati in 1840 when the Jesuits assumed control of the former *Athenaeum*. Elet was the first Jesuit president of what became St. Xavier College. Henni was vicar general of the Cincinnati diocese at the time. Something in this experience soured Elet on the man who three years later became the first bishop of Milwaukee. When Father Minoux passed along Henni's invitation to have the Swiss Jesuits develop a college in Milwaukee, Elet characterized the Milwaukeean as an individual who did not have the best interests of the Society of Jesus in mind. The vice provincial scoffed at the backwardness of Milwaukee and at the inadequacy of DeBoey's $16,000 ($398,000 in 2005 dollars) to support a college. Moreover, the Jesuits had just taken over St. Joseph's College in Bardstown in 1848. Staffing this school as well as colleges in Cincinnati, Louisville, and St. Louis strained the vice province's capacity to provide faculty. But everything changed after Father Elet made a trip to Milwaukee to meet with the bishop and after Father Jan Roothaan, superior general of the Jesuits, asked the vice provincial to consider relocating the displaced Swiss Jesuits to Milwaukee. Father Elet reversed himself, assigning two Swiss priests to work in Wisconsin.

Fathers Anthony Anderledy and Frederick Hubner came to Milwaukee in August 1849. This latest appearance of Jesuits in the Badger State (following, as they did, in the footsteps of seventeenth-century missionaries such as Rene Menard and Claude Allouez) took on a sad note when Hubner died shortly after his arrival, becoming the first priest interred in the city. Father Joseph Brunner soon replaced him and joined Anderledy in consultation with Bishop Henni over a prospective college. Drawings were prepared, but staffing beyond these two Jesuits presented a problem. Moreover, the two priests turned out not to speak English. So Bishop Henni assigned them to a German-speaking parish in Green Bay. Anderledy, in poor health, returned to Europe the following year. Later, he became superior general of the Society. Now alone, Father

Brunner spent his time in the Manitowoc area, until he too was recalled to Europe. Much to Bishop Henni's dismay, his first attempt to found a Jesuit college in Milwaukee had failed. Despite the cash the prelate now controlled due to Monsieur DeBoey's unexpected death in early 1850, patience was required.[9]

ST. GALL'S PARISH

Three years passed before another set of Jesuits came to town to preach a mission and to conduct a retreat for diocesan priests. This brief visit in 1853 provided a window of opportunity for Bishop Henni to once again pursue his college plan with Father Elet's successor as vice provincial, Father William S. Murphy. Like Elet, Murphy opposed the idea of a college in Milwaukee. But his provincial advisors in St. Louis as well as a new superior general in Rome, Father Pieter Beckx, favored the idea. Hence, in 1855, the vice provincial dispatched two priests to Milwaukee with instructions to cooperate with John Henni. Fathers Francis X. DeCoen and Peter DeSmet (the same missionary whose work in the Pacific Northwest Guillaume DeBoey so admired) arrived in mid-September. To keep these clergymen occupied until they could open a college, Henni directed them to administer Milwaukee's newest parish, St. Gall's. (It was common practice in the United States for bishops to provide the first members of a religious order with a pastoral assignment until a school could be opened.)

St. Gall's had been established in 1849 and was named after Henni's Swiss canton of birth and his original seminary in Switzerland. The church building, two blocks west of the Milwaukee River, was a simple, wood-frame structure, ninety-four feet by forty-six feet rising to the modest height of twenty-four feet. It was located on the southwest corner of Second and Sycamore (today's Michigan) streets, a footprint later occupied by the "greatest [street]car barn in the world," the Public Service Building. Alongside the church was a primitive rectory that routinely flooded during spring meltdowns and summer downpours, leaving behind an assortment of amphibians to cohabit with the clerics.[10]

In the years before and after the Civil War (1861-65), grain elevators, brick warehouses, small factories, storage facilities, and loading docks sprouted up along both banks of the Milwaukee River. Scattered among these workplaces south of Spring Street (today's Wisconsin Avenue) were one-story houses and primitive shanties filled with Irish immigrants. Although Milwaukee's principal Irish community in the nineteenth century blossomed east of the river in the Third Ward, on the west bank where St. Gall's was located, the Fourth Ward experienced its own distinctive evolution, featuring Irish homesteads set amidst bustling streets, noisy railroad lines, and varied industries. In this section of town, the Jesuits became part of Milwaukee's Irish history. In the nearly forty years between the arrival of Fathers DeSmet and DeCoen and the closing of St. Gall's, some fifty-six Jesuits served the congregation, contributing to a heritage that remains unbroken into the twenty-first century.[11]

These first Jesuits were handed a difficult assignment, one that required considerable diplomacy. Bishop Henni believed the Jesuit's management of St. Gall's was a temporary expediency. He understood that the sons of St. Ignatius needed somewhere to live and somewhere to work before opening "his" college. In contrast, the Jesuits saw their task as the spiritual well-being of the faithful at St. Gall's. For the Society of Jesus, parish work took priority, with an institution of higher education a distant eventuality. The geographical boundaries of this parish were extensive, made more difficult by the church's peculiar location in one corner of its territory. The parish's northern border was one block north of the church at Spring Street. The eastern border was two blocks away at the Milwaukee River. In contrast, the western border stretched five miles into the Town of Wauwatosa and the southern border reached for miles into unsettled stretches of Milwaukee County.

Prior to the permanent arrival of the Jesuits in 1855, the faithful at St. Gall's suffered under remarkably unstable administrations, going through perhaps as many as fourteen pastors in fewer than six years. The laity had grown distant from the clergy; religious practices among the nearly 1,000 members had become irregular at best. For example, fewer than two dozen confessions were heard during an ordinary week. The church building's humble appointments never generated the sense of place—and pride—that could be found so readily in immigrant neighborhoods in other cities. There were no soaring church spires, no hand-worked wood paneling, no marble altars that defied the faithful's everyday lives of poverty. St. Gall's church looked as forlorn as its lineup of transient pastors. Yet Father DeCoen and his associates worked with such earnestness that within the first year, forty hours devotions, the way of the cross, and pieties to the Virgin Mary became part of the parish's liturgical routine. Within eighteen months after the arrival of the Jesuits, Bishop Henni proudly came to the small church to bestow the sacrament of confirmation upon eighty-four soldiers of Christ. A new rectory more than half the size of the old church was built within two years. As a result of these early successes, a modest step was finally taken toward the creation of a Jesuit college in Milwaukee.[12]

ST. ALOYSIUS ACADEMY

Much to John Martin Henni's delight, two additional Jesuits arrived in September 1857 to establish a school—alas, a preparatory school, not a college. One newspaper was ecstatic: "'The Jesuits … will teach all branches of a commercial, classical, scientific and philosophical education. They are the most renowned educators in the world.'" Father Stanislaus Lalumiere and Mr. Cornelius O'Brien, a scholastic (that is, a Jesuit in training), opened their fledgling operation in the leaky, former rectory that had been moved a block west to Third and Everett. This flimsy, frame structure was raised ten feet, a quality foundation was installed, and a new first floor was constructed beneath the original building, which was subsequently lowered to become the second floor of St. Aloysius Academy. (St. Aloysius was the second Jesuit saint whose image was placed in the cornerstone of the original Marquette College building in 1880.)

Administration of the school was assigned to Father Lalumiere who, over the next three decades, earned the affection of every Milwaukeean he met. Among those who crossed Lalumiere's path even before he joined the Society of Jesus was a frontier lawyer charged with evaluating young Stanislaus when he applied for admission to the Illinois state bar. The examiner's name: Abraham Lincoln. The future priest and the future president remained friends through the years, with the Jesuit fondly reminiscing over the rail splitter's sense of humor. After being admitted to the bar, Lalumiere served as deputy clerk for the U.S. Court in Springfield, Illinois, and for the circuit court in St. Louis. He then shifted careers, entered the seminary, and was ordained in 1857 at the age of thirty-five. Milwaukee was his first—and longest—assignment: the former attorney served as principal at St. Aloysius from 1857 to 1859 and as pastor at St. Gall's from 1861 to 1889. In the latter role, he turned his parish into an "important center for English-speaking Catholics." As pastor, Lalumiere recruited the Little Sisters of the Poor to open a facility for the elderly poor. He helped establish the House of the Good Shepherd for "wayward girls," (pregnant, unmarried young women). During these years, Lalumiere often returned to his first career when assisting widows and orphans with probate and other legal matters. From the richest men in town (including magnate

Alexander Mitchell) to the poorest Irish immigrant in the Fourth Ward, Lalumiere won their respect for his openness and sincerity. From 1887 to 1889, he served as president of Marquette College. His departure from the city featured a farewell proclamation whose gushing contents must have embarrassed this aging giant of Milwaukee religious history. He then moved to Cincinnati where, despite poor health, he ministered to jail inmates. He returned to Milwaukee only once, to witness the laying of the cornerstone for the Church of the Gesu. His failing health and eventual death in March 1895 was closely covered by Milwaukee newspapers.[13]

Nearly thirty years earlier, upon his arrival at St. Gall's in 1857, the thirty-five-year-old Lalumiere could hardly have envisioned such a glorious career. For the moment, all he could see was a situation that warranted neither a college nor even an academy (high school). Consequently, he and his Je-

Father Stanislaus Lalumiere. Lalumiere Biographical File

suit companion created a hybrid institution that, while it officially carried the name St. Aloysius Academy, operated as an awkward combination of elementary and high school. It opened in the fall of 1857 with fifty students. Their ages ranged from six to twenty-five, a distinctive if not unusual circumstance for early nineteenth-century academies. At the conclusion of the first year, Lalumiere described the academy to his superiors as "'a humbug.'" Simply put, St. Aloysius did not warrant the considerable talents of Stanislaus Lalumiere. Accordingly, in 1859, the Jesuits turned over control of the academy to the lay faculty despite rising enrollments and Lalumiere was reassigned to St. Louis. Yet he returned as pastor in 1861 and Jesuit management of the school resumed. In 1864, Lalumiere directed construction of a sizable brick schoolhouse at Third and Sycamore streets, a facility that was given a name more suited to its role

St. Aloysius Academy. File 15

in the neighborhood: St. Gall Academy. In the same flush of energy, a glorious new church was erected in 1868 at the cost of $100,000. Said to be one of the largest and most costly churches in the state of Wisconsin, the Byzantine-style structure, also located on Sycamore Street, could hold 1,000 worshipers. The original church building was subsequently remodeled to accommodate a school for girls, directed by the School Sisters of Notre Dame. Enrollment at the boys' academy climbed to more than four hundred, with Jesuit and lay faculty working side by side. Then, in 1872, the provincial office in St. Louis announced that no additional scholastics—the mainstay of the teaching staff—would be assigned to Milwaukee; they were needed at other schools in Missouri, Kentucky, Illinois, and Ohio. St. Gall Academy closed, ending its brief history as the educational incubator for prominent Catholics throughout the city.[14]

THE HILLTOP

As beneficial as these pastoral efforts may have been for the faithful of St. Gall's, they did not move the Milwaukee community closer to Bishop Henni's dream of a Jesuit college. From the prelate's perspective, St. Gall's was simply a lure to get Jesuits to come to Milwaukee until they took steps to open his long-anticipated college. As early as 1849, Henni had drawn upon the promise of DeBoey's money to purchase a brick house and eight lots near the cathedral to serve as a site for the college. Within a short time, however, these properties were deemed inadequate, so in 1850 (following DeBoey's death), Henni used the remainder of the bequest ($11,000) to acquire half of the square block between Tenth and Eleventh streets, Tamarack to Prairie (today's State and Highland respectively). These lots represented a prime piece of property, set back slightly from prominent bluffs that overlooked downtown. The bishop conveyed use (but not ownership) of this land to the Jesuits in 1856 through a deed of trust. By that action, Henni accomplished two objectives: he fulfilled part of his promise to Monsieur DeBoey to establish a Jesuit college in Milwaukee and he imposed upon the Society of Jesus an obligation to use the hilltop for Marquette College.[15]

As early as 1850, Henni had preemptively referred to the school as *Marquette College* in correspondence with the Jesuits. Whatever titles he may have employed when speaking to other religious orders about a Catholic college in Milwaukee, Henni quickly turned to the heritage of Père (Father) Jacques Marquette in his conversations with the Society of Jesus. Born in Laon, France, on June 1, 1637, Jacques Marquette yearned to travel to the New World as a missionary from his first days in the seminary. He journeyed to New France (today's Canada) after his ordination in 1666 despite frail health. Evangelical work among the indigenous peoples followed. In 1673, Marquette and Louis Joliet set out on an adventure that took them through central Wisconsin by way of the Fox and Wisconsin rivers. They journeyed down the Mississippi River south of St. Louis and then returned north to Lake Michigan by way of the Illinois and Chicago rivers, imprinting their names upon cities, counties, buildings, parks, and streets throughout the region. Marquette undertook a second voyage in late 1674. On this trip, he camped along the banks of the Milwaukee River for several days, thereby linking himself forever to the area's history. In naming his college after this great priest, Bishop Henni sought to bind the Jesuits even more firmly to his plan.[16]

In August 1868, twelve years after executing the hilltop's deed of trust, Bishop Henni signed over complete ownership of the land, as well as that of St. Gall's parish, to the Jesuits. Despite this gesture, the prelate remained doubtful that he would ever see his dream fulfilled. His heartbreak at the endless delays was never more evident than in an exchange he had with Father Lalumiere in 1872: "'Are you disappointed in the Society in regard to education'" asked the lawyer-turned-priest. Henni responded: "'Altogether so.'"[17]

Father Lalumiere had his own disappointments. After Bishop Henni turned over use but not ownership of his hilltop lots to the Jesuits in 1856, the local Jesuit superior (in this case, the pastor at St. Gall's) became responsible for this land. During the mid- to late-1860s, the Jesuits acquired those portions of the square block (commonly referred to in its day as Block 199) not already owned by Henni. Consequently, when the bishop surrendered ownership of his portion in 1868, the entire block came under the control of a single investor: the Missouri Province of the Society of Jesus, with Stanislaus Lalumiere as its local representative.[18]

That rather cold, secular designation—local representative for an absentee landowner whose corporate offices were in St. Louis—illustrates a serious duty that Lalumiere bore as the landowner's agent: property taxes. The land on which St. Gall's church, rectory, academy, and girls' school rested was exempt from taxation because of its religious uses. The land at Tenth and State, however, was appraised as a speculative investment by the county assessor, to be taxed as though it were owned by any other private developer. The significance of this financial burden can be seen by comparing the tax bills that have survived. In February 1858, two years after gaining use of the hilltop, the Jesuit community was responsible for Henni's eight lots (half of the entire block). Seven of these lots were appraised at $400 with the remaining site at $450 for a total valuation of $3,250. With a city tax rate of 5 percent and a state, county, and school tax rate of 2 percent, the tax bill came to $226.68 ($5,356 in 2005 dollars). Twelve years later, after the Jesuits had purchased the rest of Block 199, Father Lalumiere paid $322.95 in taxes for all sixteen lots (as well as one piece of property in the Walker's Point neighborhood). By this time, tax rates had dropped appreciably to 1 percent for the city and ward, and .69 percent for the state, county, and school taxes (plus an unexplained "Special Tax" of .1 percent).

Lower tax rates were offset by rising property values. As the city of Milwaukee matured during the 1860s, the valuation of Henni's original eight lots increased to $10,500 in 1870, more than three times their original appraisals. Whereas the Fourth Ward property (St. Gall's) was listed on the 1870 tax notice without a tax charge, Block 199 was still assessed for its investment potential. Lalumiere attempted to get around this annual burden by using his legal expertise. In March 1864, he incorporated Marquette College through an act of the Wisconsin Legislature. From that point until a reincorporation of Marquette University in 1969, ultimate authority over this legal entity resided in a board of trustees that always consisted of three Jesuits. But these first trustees made the fateful decision in 1864 to delay construction of the college (according to their handwritten minutes) because of the high cost of materials and labor during the Civil War. Unstated influences on this decision may have included a shortage of Jesuits to staff the school as well as a shortage of qualified students. With an educational institution in name only, Lalumiere's real estate gambit failed because the county tax office continued to view Block 199 as undeveloped property. Consequently, tax bills arrived like clockwork.[19]

A NEW CHURCH—AND A NEW SCHOOL

As America recovered from the Civil War, Milwaukee blossomed from its frontier status built upon the entrepreneurship of Solomon Juneau and Byron Kilbourn into a vital Great Lakes port city. Its factories and processing facilities were linked by railroads to other Midwestern industrial centers as well as to the fertile fields of rural Wisconsin. By 1873, Milwaukee had become the wheat capital of America with the importation of twenty-eight million barrels from its vast hinterland and an exportation worldwide of twenty-five million barrels. Although that may have been the high point for Milwaukee's prominence in the national grain market, an entirely new sector of the economy developed after Eber Brock Ward opened his Milwaukee Iron Company in the Bay View district in 1868. The city subsequently joined the age of industrialization, an era that transformed the United States into the world's manufacturing leader. Pittsburgh grew upon the sturdy frame of steel production, and Chicago became the hog butcher to the world as well as the nation's railroad center. Milwaukee blossomed through diversification: brewing, meatpacking, leather processing, steel production, and metal fabricating, becoming in historian John Gurda's words, "Machine Shop of the World." In 1870, 8,433 Milwaukee employees (40 percent of the labor force) worked in manufacturing. Twenty years later, this number had grown to 43,423, constituting 58 percent of the labor force—an all-time high. By the early twentieth century, companies such as Edward P. Allis, Pawling and Harnischfeger, Chain-Belt, Nordberg, Kearney and Trecker, A. O. Smith, Falk, Allen-Bradley, and Harley-Davidson were redefining the legacy of their host city. Much of this development took place in Walker's Point and in the Menomonee River Valley, districts within walking distance of the Fourth Ward's Irish laborers.[20]

For parishioners at St. Gall's and the Jesuits who served them, this shift in employment patterns meant the landscape around the parish was changing dramatically. Sec-

St. Gall's Church at Second & Michigan. Milwaukee Road station to the left. File 1205

ond and third generation Irish-Americans moved west into neighborhoods such as Tory Hill and Merrill Park as they followed their jobs into the western half of the Menomonee Valley. Downtown Milwaukee, once so unremarkable, became headquarters for financial and governmental institutions that shepherded this growth. Just a stone's throw from St. Gall's rose one of the two most important railroad stations in the city: the Chicago, Milwaukee, and St. Paul depot on Everett Street. This station, with at least five sets of tracks curving north from St. Paul Street onto Clybourn Street and then west into the depot, sat in the church's backyard. Every day, dozens of trains and hundreds of freight and passenger cars rumbled by the church and, until it closed, St. Gall Academy. The presence of these religious institutions squeezed between a rail yard and a major commercial district along the Milwaukee River forced the Jesuits to look for a more propitious location for their ministries, one that might get the Tenth Street property off the tax rolls and might bring Marquette College into reality.[21]

Holy Name of Jesus Church—a small, wooden structure, half the size of the still relatively new St. Gall's Church—was erected in 1875 at the southwestern corner of Block 199. Included in the rough sketches for this church was a second building labeled the "Marquette School." Funding for Holy Name came from loans obtained locally and from East Coast insurance companies. The financial stipulations agreed upon by the Marquette College Board of Trustees called for a loan of $15,000 for four years at the rate of 9 percent per annum, with the property and buildings at St. Gall's as collateral. Later, the trustees obtained a second loan, using the hilltop as security in order to fund the college building at Tenth and State.[22]

Work on Marquette College began five years after completion of Holy Name Church. Bishop Michael Heiss presided over the blessing of the college's cornerstone in August 1880. He had been named coadjutor with right of succession only three months earlier after seventy-five-year-old John Martin Henni's physical and mental health worsened. More than three decades had passed since Henni first enticed Swiss Jesuits to move to Milwaukee. An archbishop since 1875, the one-time immigrant and missionary probably could not hear the sacred chants and throaty cheers emanating from Block 199 on that special day in August, but the ambition that he had first shared with Monsieur DeBoey in 1849 was now twelve months away from fulfillment. In the New World, dreams really could become reality.[23]

A JESUIT LIBERAL ARTS COLLEGE
1881-1906

Whether earned in nineteenth-century Milwaukee, Cincinnati, Rome, or Calcutta, an education at a Jesuit-run college was predicated upon a carefully honed tradition. For centuries, Jesuits abided by an educational philosophy first defined during St. Ignatius's lifetime and then crystalized into a worldwide system of learning following his death in 1556. Geography did not matter. Often, time did not matter. What mattered was the *Ratio Atque Institutio Studiorum Societatis Jesu* (or the *Ratio Studiorum*), the Society of Jesus's plan of studies, which systematized Jesuit education over time and space. It produced an intellectual branding that marked its offspring forever.

THE PRINCIPLES BEHIND MARQUETTE COLLEGE

The *Ratio Studiorum*, finalized in 1599, ran some two hundred pages. Its origins could be found in principles and practices that St. Ignatius codified in the light of his personal experience at universities and his subsequent work with educational institutions, most notably the Jesuit college at Messina, Italy, during the 1550s. These principles and methodologies became blueprints that survived largely intact into the twentieth century. Over decades and then over centuries, the Society acquiesced to certain refinements, with a thorough update completed in 1832. By that time, two Jesuit colleges (Georgetown and Saint Louis) were operating in the United States. Fifteen additional schools were established before Marquette opened in 1881 and each adhered to the 1832 edition of the *Ratio*. Since the *Ratio* was officially promulgated, its details assumed a doctrinal air, although circumstantial adjustments seeped in over time. The original *Ratio Studiorum* had been personally handed to the Society of Jesus by its founder, amidst the turmoil of the Protestant Reformation. It was a valued legacy, crafted at a critical juncture in Church history and subsequent generations of Jesuits feared that situational concessions might diminish this precious gift. For this reason, the most fervent defenders of the *Ratio* treated its curricular order as though it were inflexible when, in fact, Ignatius clearly preferred an adaptable set of rules.[1]

The *Ratio Studiorum* was introduced into the United States when the Jesuits assumed control of Georgetown College in 1806, during a particularly stressful period in the Society's history. Beginning in Portugal in 1759, Jesuits became the target of royal suppression in major European nations, including France and Spain. A powerful alliance of European monarchs succeeded in pressuring Pope Clement XIV in 1773 to suppress the Society, banning the order not only in Europe but around the world. (Russia's Catherine II was among the handful of rulers who refused to recognize the papal decree.) In North America, Jesuit ministries were closed in locations such as Maryland, Baja California, and the Great Lakes area. To secure the order's possessions and properties for possible use in the future, ex-Jesuits reassembled in Maryland under a legal rubric known as the Corporation of Roman Catholic Clergymen. This secular (non-canonical) association came under the protection of America's first bishop, John Carroll of Baltimore, who, by virtue of the suppression, was himself a former Jesuit. Eventually, the Maryland group reestablished its official ties to the Society of Jesus through the Russian province that Catherine II had protected. In 1814, Pope Pius VII restored the Society, although the Jesuits continued to engender resistance from political authorities in places such as Sicily (1860) and Germany (1872).

Fifteen years after Pope Pius VII restored the Society, Saint Louis College introduced its educational traditions to the American Midwest. Across the vast expanses of America, Jesuit institutions sprang up over the next half century: several in the 1840s and 1850s, only one during the disruptive decade of the Civil War, and then half a dozen in the 1870s. From New York City to San Francisco, from Boston to Mobile, seventeen Jesuit colleges dotted the American landscape before Marquette opened in 1881. In most instances, local bishops aggressively recruited Jesuits because of their world-renowned pedagogy. For local prelates, a Jesuit school was more than a matter of prestige; it was a guarantee of excellence. For the Jesuits, this recruitment pattern gave their educational ministry a decidedly urban flavor, a characteristic that suited the traditions of St. Ignatius.[2]

In the original design of the *Ratio*, a boy's education could begin as early as the age of five and conclude fourteen years later, running through three clearly delineated segments of five, three, and six years respectively. The presence of very young boys did not interfere with this formation because a carefully crafted training sequence (a ladder in one depiction) took the students through each phase of their intellectual and moral development. By the time Marquette was founded, the American version of this system included a preparatory program ("Rudiments" at some schools) that started at the age of ten. At most American Jesuit colleges (though not Marquette), this included a boarding system. (In St. Ignatius's original terminology, *colegio* actually referred to a residence, not a center of study.) Each college also welcomed day students.

Some Jesuit institutions in the United States offered a six-year instructional program after the preparatory phase. Others, like Marquette, provided a seven-year "classical course" which, in turn, was subdivided into a three-year "academic" department and a four-year "collegiate" department. Throughout the classical course's seven years, students honed their skills in Latin (and, to a lesser extent, in Greek) while mastering the wisdom of classical civilizations. Before 1907, Marquette students set off on this long road at the age of thirteen or fourteen by entering the academic department, a program that titled its years of study in a descending order, that is, third academic was followed by second academic and then first academic. These three years provided the linguistic, literary, and grammatical grounding in the classical languages necessary for the second phase: the collegiate course. At Marquette, the academic and collegiate phases were a seamless unit, seven years of a step-by-step education, each year distinctive for its content, each year progressively moving a boy toward a maturation in the power of reasoning. Since the greater glory of God and a young man's salvation were the objectives of all Jesuit education, annual classes in Christian doctrine (which was taught as catechetics, not as theology) were integral to this training.[3]

When Marquette opened in 1881, its curriculum included an instructional option outside the mainstream of the *Ratio Studiorum*, a concession in the minds of some Jesuits to the American preoccupation with money-making. When they first enrolled at thirteen years of age, Milwaukee teenagers had two tracks to choose from. Students could enter the academic portion of the classical course which would ultimately lead to the collegiate program (this was the preferred choice among Jesuits), or they could enroll in the commercial program which took three years to complete but did not lead to college classes.

The commercial program was a Jesuit response to the industrialization of America in the late nineteenth century. Since parents increasingly preferred that their sons' education provide for a livelihood, Jesuit colleges reluctantly created a work-related option alongside the classical course. In the United States, Jesuit schools did not have their ancestral roots tied to sixteenth-century society nor to a landed aristocracy as in Europe. Latin and Greek had never been the language of the streets, the language of civil society, nor except for Catholics, the language of faith. Even for American Catholics, Latin was the language of priests, not the laity. By the late nineteenth century, it was no longer the language of law and medicine. The commercial course at Marquette offered local employers competent and reliable trainees for mid-level management. It provided adolescents who could not attend college at Marquette (because they had not completed the academic course) with an education suited for the business world. Classes in penmanship and bookkeeping blended with classes in history, geography, mathematics, and literature. A commercial certificate from Marquette verified a rigorous education, but one whose content did not differ greatly from that of public high schools (even though no Jesuit would ever admit that the commercial course was a version of what was taught at secular schools). In California, Santa Clara College took this concern for contemporary needs to the next level when it created a very popular bachelor of science degree (no Latin and Greek at all) as early as 1858. Administrators at Marquette College did not go that far and even discouraged the commercial program for high school-age boys, describing it as "necessarily inferior" because of the absence of training in classical cultures. At the completion of their studies, commercial students received certificates, not diplomas or degrees.[4]

The commercial program was a concession to the times and *concession* was not a word that fit comfortably with the *Ratio Studiorum*. Jesuit traditionalists insisted that St. Ignatius had not worked on the Society's *Constitutions* (Part Four being the source of the *Ratio*'s principles) during his last years so that a young Milwaukeean could slip into a job at Northwestern Mutual Life Insurance Company or with the Chicago, Milwaukee, and St. Paul Railroad. At one brief point, the Jesuit school in Philadelphia

(Saint Joseph College) refused students who were not inclined to complete the seven-year classical course. It was all or nothing. Most Jesuit schools in the United States, being tuition-dependent, did not have the financial luxury to be so discriminating. Nonetheless, their mission—the mission of Marquette College—was to provide an Ignatian education predicated upon the genius of the *Ratio Studiorum*, not upon a hastily improvised response to economic exigencies. Through a firm foundation in Latin and Greek, in classical literatures, scholastic philosophy, and always, Christian doctrine, a young man was provided the intellectual wherewithal to save his soul. After all, a "science of salvation" was one way to understand the *Ratio Studiorum*'s intent.

St. Ignatius's devotion to the propagation and defense of the Catholic faith imbedded itself in the classical course through a ceaseless emphasis upon written and oral communication. Through literature, pupils encountered a tapestry of human foibles. Through elocution, students acquired a command of public issues and confidence in addressing those issues, whether in the seventeenth century or the twentieth. During the early years of the academic course, students recited passages from classical literature or from the Fathers of the Church. Daily recitals of essays, poems, orations, sermons, and commentaries from the past provided students with repetitious exposure to virtues and vices as well as God's redeeming grace. Along this instructional path, students gained the self-assurance to motivate audiences of varying sizes—and receptiveness. This was how Marquette graduates experienced their faith—in the public arena. The ability to think on one's feet became a hallmark for alumni from hundreds of Jesuit schools scattered around the world.

From the outset, Marquette's three-year academic department served as a foundation for the collegiate department's four-year sequence. The tight integration between the academic and collegiate programs was underscored by the fact that, during its first twenty-five years, Marquette College only recognized recipients of college degrees and of commercial certificates. When a student completed his third year in the academic department (called the first academic), he simply moved on to his next year's work in the collegiate department. There was no fanfare, no ceremony, no graduation. Although the full, seven-year classical program superficially resembled the American system of four years of high school and four years of college, Marquette's seven-year sequence had its own three-hundred-year-old history. Any similarity between the American system and the Jesuit system only made the latter's eventual accommodation to the former that much easier. Marquette College students may have often seen the academic course as a Jesuit version of high school, but their instructors knew better.

One indication of just how different the goals of the American and Jesuit systems were in 1881 is illustrated in the relevance of a Marquette student's course work to his career plans. According to historian Helen Lefkowitz Horowitz, a post-Civil War college education "turned the boy into a man prepared for success in the competitive world of American business." At a Jesuit college, the bachelor of arts degree had nothing to do with earning a living. An individual who completed the classical course was not prepared for *a* career. Rather, he was prepared for *any* career through "a thorough knowledge of the classics" and of philosophy. The formation of a student's mind in the Jesuit system prepared him to handle life's challenges regardless of which career he later entered. Each student was taught reasoning, observation, industry, and ultimately, imagination, not job skills. By absorbing "abiding and universal values," graduates of a Jesuit education developed "standards by which to appraise not only works of arts and of literature but also social and political theories and movements." And they acquired these advantages through an intense indoctrination into classical languages and civilizations.

The collegiate course at a Jesuit institution did not use modern terminology to depict the four years of college. There was no freshman year followed by sophomore year and so on. Instead, each of the four years in the collegiate course bore a title that captured the topical focus of those nine months. During the first year (humanities year) of college, the student was preoccupied with narrative and descriptive composition. The second year (poetry year) exposed a student to a particularly reflective articulation of the human experience, and the third year (rhetoric third), imparted "a close criticism of literature and the precepts of oratory." Finally, in the last year, philosophy courses trained "habits of correct reasoning and … sound principles of morality." At the same time that composition, poetry, literature, and philosophy were foremost on the students' minds, they also took classes in mathematics, science, and history, but these had a distinctly secondary emphasis—filling out the curriculum, not defining it. The Jesuits wanted their students to be prepared for the unpredictable circumstances that adults confront during their lifetimes, the unseen future that no one can envision at eighteen. After college, Jesuit graduates could choose from a smorgasbord of career options, but they would undertake those careers bolstered by a thorough grounding in philosophy, literature, poetry, and composition—the liberal arts as seen from Ignatius's sixteenth century.

At Jesuit schools, students were guided to find those manifestations of God's grace by which individually they could testify to God's glory and thereby save their souls. (In Jesuit parlance, this is referred to as *magis*.) These talents might reveal themselves in careers as a lawyer, doctor, scientist, politician, soldier, colonial bureaucrat, corporate magnate, or priest. Throughout their adult lives, graduates of Jesuit institutions could rely upon their understanding of human nature developed through years of careful study of ancient civilizations, especially Greek and Roman. *Magis* calls for one's love of God to be evidenced through service to others. The offspring of a Jesuit education were expected to be leaders, to direct the various groups they would encounter in a lifetime: families, clients, patients, political constituents, regiments, employees, or congregations. Graduates of Jesuit schooling could assume leadership positions in a divinely designed universe because they had been taught to ingest ideas, deconstruct them into their constituent parts, and then reformulate them in the future by the light of the past. The technical skills and expertise needed as a doctor or dentist, lawyer or businessman could come later with specialized training after leaving the Jesuit incubator. But first students had to learn the order of God's creation, whether in the sixteenth century or in the nineteenth, whether in Africa or in Milwaukee. The moral firmness to cope with good and evil, change and stability, justice and avarice was expected after seven years in the classical course. There was something elevating about the promise of a Jesuit education, an experience that could not be matched in any other course of study, Catholic or secular. Some American colleges might offer versions of this training in the classics, but few insisted upon comparable rigor or relied upon a spiritually based rationale.[5]

THE DOORS OPEN

How the *Ratio Studiorum* would be implemented in the State of Wisconsin was outlined in the *Milwaukee Sentinel* three months before Marquette College opened. As much promotional as informational, the article outlined the "departments" that would be available in September 1881. Three tracks—commercial, academic, and collegiate—were anticipated as well as a preparatory program for youngsters who were not quite ready for either of the first two. Discipline, which established a receptivity for learning, the article explained, was to be "mild rather than severe" but matters of "punctual attendance, strict obedience, assiduous application and blameless conduct" were required. Not only were Catholic students urged to apply, so were "pupils of every denomination … provided they [were] willing to conform, in a respectful manner, to the ordinary exercises of daily prayers." This sense of tolerance was typical of Jesuit colleges in America, but was decidedly less so for other faith-based institutions of the same era. Nationalistic divisions, even among American Catholics in the late nineteenth and early twentieth centuries, often created embarrassing conceits among church leaders (including those in Milwaukee) and these petty rivalries were nothing compared to prejudices manifested between different Christian denominations. The inclusiveness of Marquette College was particularly well-received in a community already divided between German and Irish Catholics as well as Catholics, Lutherans, Jews, and freethinkers. The *Sentinel* article also noted that this superb education was available for the sum of sixty dollars year, payable in quarterly installments. It urged readers to obtain further information from the college's first president, Father Joseph F. Rigge, or from the city's old friend, Father Stanislaus Lalumiere, who was still at St. Gall's.[6]

The home for Marquette College was a new three-story, red-brick building on the northwest corner of Tenth and State streets. The first construction contracts were let in July 1880, a month before the cornerstone ceremony. Edward Townsend Mix, Milwaukee's most prominent architect, designed the building. James Quinn served as senior carpenter (for $10,379) and Dennis Trainor was the mason contractor (for $12,300). Extra expenses included grading of the property, plumbing, sheet-metal work, and installation of gas fixtures for lighting. Intended to accommodate 450 students, the building was 60 feet wide facing State Street and 140 feet deep along Tenth Street. Windows, especially those along the east and west sides, augmented the building's gas lamps and provided the only ventilation during warm weather. A kitchen, dining area, and storerooms were located in the basement, guaranteeing that aromas from meal preparation would slowly waft upward into fourteen classrooms, a 400-person assem-

Marquette College at Tenth and State streets. Holy Name Church to left. File 885

bly hall, and the Jesuit chapel and apartments. On August 15, 1881, exactly one year after the cornerstone had been laid, the building was dedicated. Local clergy joined the Jesuits in a procession from the Church of the Holy Name to the assembly hall, already crowded with laity. The usual assortment of sermons and speeches followed, this time with one keynote in German and another in English.[7]

Although there were seventeen Jesuit colleges and universities in operation before Marquette, in 1880 there were only 85,000 college students in the United States, less than 2 percent of the country's 18- to 21-year-olds. Yet the opening of each institution created a special moment in their host towns. With barely suppressed anticipation, three Jesuits moved into their new accommodations in late June, before the building was completely furnished. When fully assembled, the community consisted of three lay brothers, three scholastics, and three priests, including one whose primary responsibility was the pastorship of Holy Name Church. (The men jokingly remarked that the school should be named "Trinity College" given the fact that three individuals representing each of the three ranks of the Jesuit order lived at Marquette.) After floors had been swept of construction dust and blackboards installed, registration day, September 5, finally arrived. Staff members were as nervous as the students, according to a first-hand account. The doorbell rang for the first time at 7:30 a.m. Visitors were greeted, registered, and passed on to the prefect of study for an evaluation of each student's competency. Book distribution followed. Registrants came from the Third and Fourth wards near St. Gall's; from the Tory Hill neighborhood, the new Irish enclave six blocks away; from the Silver City area of Milwaukee's south side; and from as far away as Hales Corners. The staff's excitement led them to anticipate at least one hundred students, perhaps even one hundred and fifty. Within the first ninety minutes, twenty-eight young men enrolled.

Then a lull set in. And it continued for the rest of the day. By nightfall, only seven more youngsters registered. The disappointment was almost palpable: thirty-five students and six instructors! Worst yet, only a small (but unknown) number of these students had the credentials necessary for college work. School officials made the difficult decision to refuse admission for these potential collegians and to begin the most advanced level of instruction at the first year of the academic sequence (third academic). This choice must have been particularly painful for those unidentified individuals who were, in fact, prepared for the collegiate course but in numbers insufficient to warrant a full program. Meanwhile, younger applicants wandered in during the next few months, a behavior typical of the nineteenth century. By school year's end in June, seventy-seven students were in attendance, although eighty-nine names appeared on the registration rolls. Of the seventy-seven, twenty-three had been assigned to the academic department, thirty-two to the commercial, and twenty-two to the preparatory. In the next school year, 1882-83, this number grew to 139, but once again no college classes were offered.[8]

It may have been just as well that Father President decided to delay college-level instruction until 1883 because discipline among nineteenth-century teenagers was no easier to enforce than in contemporary society. Handwritten diary notes left by Jesuit administrators indicate regular student assemblies wherein rules of conduct were repeated once again, conduct marks were announced, and the rules of dress for special events reinforced: "hair nicely combed, shoes blackened, necktie and white collar Sunday suit." Some youngsters had trouble following these guidelines, requiring consultations with their parents. At times, the parents could be just as difficult as their offspring, leading to the dismissal of their boys from Marquette. In one instance, the college actually hired a private detective to look into unexplained allegations of misconduct at the home of a student. This child was subsequently dismissed. The faculty formalized their response to chronic disciplinary problems in November 1885 by establishing Marquette's version of the traditional after-school punishment known as "Jug" (Justice Under God, according to one explanation). Miscreants had to stay after school in a study hall from four to five o'clock. Five years later, trouble developed over snowball fights that interfered with streetcar traffic on State Street. Rules had to be formalized, requiring snowballs to be thrown only in an east-to-west direction between the college building and Holy Name Church, not north and south toward State Street.[9]

The most memorable disciplinary challenge during these early years came a week before Christmas in 1881, only three months after the school opened. Word reached the prefect of study that "parish roughs" from St. Gall's and some Irish lads from Marquette College were badgering their German classmates after school, when the latter tried to return to the south side across the Sixth Street Viaduct. At 8:45 the next morning, the entire student body assembled before the faculty and the neighborhood watchman. After administrators reviewed the rules of conduct and decried the shame that these tussles brought to the school's still-evolving reputation, they called out three youngsters who were "severely strapped." For the next week, this trio was required to meet with the prefect after school for "another warming up." On the same day as the assembly, the president, Father Rigge, headed over to St. Gall's parish school, where he singled out another group with a warning that they should never apply for admission to Marquette College. A policeman was stationed at the bridge and the ethnic haranguing ended—for the moment. By the next year, a specific admonition in the college catalogue warned that any "gross violation of gentlemanly conduct on the streets" could lead to dismissal. On college property, chewing tobacco, smoking, and profanity were forbidden. While other public and private institutions may have honored similar rules only in the breach, each member of the Marquette College student body needed to understand that wherever he might be in Milwaukee and whatever he might be doing, he was potentially under the watchful eyes of St. Ignatius's sons. As with eternal life, actions had consequences.[10]

COLLEGE CLASSES

By Marquette's third year, administrators had addressed the first round of behavioral challenges presented by the preparatory program's eleven-year-olds' mingling with nineteen-year-olds. There were 118 preparatory, academic, and commercial students at Marquette in September 1883. Most important, twelve others had completed the academic course and were now eligible to begin their first (or humanities) year of the collegiate phase. Eight individuals from this original dozen advanced to their second (or poetry) year in 1884, six to the rhetoric year in 1885, and five to their philosophy year in 1886. By the time these five graduated, thirty-three other college students were following in their footsteps; thirty-nine youngsters were enrolled in Marquette's academic department, seventy-five in the commercial, and twenty-nine in the preparatory. In September 1886, Marquette College finally had students enrolled in each of the seven years of the classical course as well as respectable numbers in both the commercial and preparatory programs.[11]

With one exception, the college's daily routine followed the pattern found at other Jesuit institutions. Early in the first year, the superior of the Missouri Province met with President Joseph Rigge and the senior Jesuit in town, Father Lalumiere, to discuss the expectation of mandating daily attendance at mass, a tradition at Jesuit schools. Father Rigge was strongly opposed and, for his one year as president, won his point. By the next September, with a new chief executive on board, daily mass became a requirement for all Catholic students. Monthly confession and communion were also mandated. A typical day started with a voluntary study hall at 7:15 a.m., followed by mass at 8:30. The school day ran from 9:00 to 4:00, with an hour and forty-five minutes for lunch (apparently the students went home for lunch or brought food with them). Instructors administered tests every month, with the results posted for public scrutiny. Splendid work was openly recognized, as much to shame their classmates as to honor the high achievers. In the Jesuit system, emulation was a pedagogical tool used to prod youngsters to do their best. Parents received quarterly reports and were advised that two or three hours of study per night was expected. Class sessions lasted from thirty to sixty minutes, usually five days a week. Thursday was "recreation day," whereas Saturday was a regular class day. The reasoning behind this schedule was that it avoided a long, distractive interruption from Friday afternoon to Monday morning. Most Milwaukee fathers probably worked at least half a day on Saturdays (if not nine or ten hours), making it easier to treat that day as a regular school day. Thursday remained a recreation day for twenty-eight years, until the fall of 1910.[12]

Like pupils everywhere, Marquette College students loved their free days. Lengthy holiday breaks were unknown in the 1880s. After a single day off for Thanksgiving, classes resumed on Friday. Christmas breaks began around December 23 and ended on January 2 or 3. With no summer school until 1909, the college building was quiet from graduation day in late June until classes resumed in early September. Of particular importance to Marquette students were special appearances by religious superiors such as the archbishop of Milwaukee and Baltimore's Cardinal James Gibbons as well as, predictably, the provincial's annual visit. Inevitably, a student delegation approached these guests, requesting a holiday—an appeal that the college president seemed obliged to honor. Election days were usually half-day holidays. The most unusual cause for celebration in Milwaukee was the annual circus parade. The yearly invasion of clowns, animals, stunt performers, and the big top captivated the entire city, especially Milwaukee's young people. In Marquette's first year, the faculty tried to hold classes even as the parade tramped by within earshot of the students. Attendance dropped precipitously that day. By the next year, when the parade marched within a block of the campus along Ninth Street, the staff conceded this point, quietly canceling classes after 9:30.[13]

In an age when famous personages were names in newspapers and not familiar faces on television, their arrival in town could cause a stir. Two U.S. presidents visited Milwaukee in the school's first thirty years, in each case disrupting the school's daily schedule. In 1899, students were allowed to delay the start of school in order to watch William McKinley's procession along Grand (Wisconsin) Avenue on his way to the Soldiers' Home, west of the city. Ten years later, on September 17, 1909, President William Howard Taft actually entered the college building, spent some time with the faculty in the parlor, and spoke for about ten minutes. Two years later, Taft motorcaded past the college; this time, he had his automobile slow down so he could salute the students by doffing his cap. Milwaukee's harsh winters did not win the students many holidays. The prefect of studies often recorded temperatures down to twenty degrees below zero in his diary. Occasionally, morning mass had to be moved from the Church of the

Holy Name to the Jesuit community's private chapel because heating the larger building was impractical. But only once, on February 10, 1904, with the temperature at its coldest in a quarter century, did the younger children at the parish school benefit from a snow day. The college students did not receive a similar consideration even though, in these early years, every student—regardless of age—was a commuter who used the streetcar or trudged on foot through the snow each morning and afternoon.[14]

STUDENT LIFE

Although tuition at Marquette College remained sixty dollars per year for more than a quarter of a century, expenses to attend school remained a challenge for young Milwaukeeans. Unlike most American Jesuit colleges, Marquette enrolled only day students. Not until Alumnae House opened in 1938 did the university directly control the residential life of its students. Most Hilltoppers commuted from home during the late nineteenth century. Out-of-town students, whose numbers increased with time, rented rooms in nearby boarding houses. Only in the mid-1920s did the dean of students begin to intervene, where possible, in the private housing market, distributing a list of rental units whose landlords promised to act, in cooperation with the university, *in loco parentis*. Before then, college officials rarely stepped into this corner of a student's life, unless there was a serious moral question at stake.

Marquette men covered tuition costs as well as room and board through part-time jobs during the school year and full-time jobs, when possible, during summers. A 1905 survey of student employment noted that "a sufficient amount of pluck and self-reliance" would earn a young man between thirty and forty dollars per month, an income that was described as suitable for the average student. A surprising number of students picked up work igniting gas lamps along the city's major streets. Between eighteen and twenty-three dollars per month could be earned by caring for eighty to one hundred lamps per day. Except during winter storms, when the work became more arduous, these gas company jobs did not interfere with classroom attendance. Still, most students needed to find summer employment in order to handle tuition as well as unexpected costs.[15]

With the obligation to make their own way through college, Marquette students of this era viewed extracurricular activities as luxuries. Yet student organizations made their mark as early as the conclusion of the first semester. In January 1882, one local Jesuit organized Marquette's chapter of the Sodality of the Immaculate Conception of the Blessed Virgin Mary to promote "the cultivation of a religious spirit." Every Jesuit college had a form of this sodality and at most schools, membership was a distinction. At Marquette, at least in the beginning, every Catholic student was automatically a member. The sodality became so successful that within a dozen years it was divided into junior and senior divisions, and in 1904 the junior division was further divided. A list of confraternity officers published at the conclusion of the 1883-84 school year indicates that three of the college's first five graduates (from 1887) held positions of responsibility in the sodality. For generations, this organization epitomized Marquette's commitment to Catholic spirituality.

The arrival of the collegiate program in 1883 seems to have inspired other student organizations. The earliest clubs favored academic themes: the Marquette Literary Society offered practice in debate and public speaking, and the Reading Room Association at first encouraged readings in "standard English works and choice periodicals" and later cared for the college's library room. Some groups popped up and then disappeared just as quickly. Others became fixtures, including the German Literary Club (two incarnations), the St. John Berchman Acolytical Society, the Apostleship of Prayer, and the *Marquette College Journal*. The St. Cecilia Society was established in April 1884 to serve as an outlet "to improve its members in vocal music," but it was short-lived. Not until January 1901, did instrumental music find its voice in the Mandolin Orchestra, which featured forty-six members: twenty-six on mandolins, eleven on guitars, two on banjos, five on violins, one on a violoncello and one on the flute. Two-and-a-half years

Mandolin Club, 1904. Oversized images, File K-2

later, the orchestra included clarinets, cornets, a French horn, and timpani. A glee club was organized in the same year as the Mandolin Orchestra to promote "vocal music" among the students.[16]

An informal athletic society appeared at the opening of the school's second year when a Jesuit scholastic gained permission from Father President to use the school yard west of the college building for an hour each afternoon. A ten cent per month fee paid for the equipment. At first, the Jesuits approved only handball and baseball. Later students

Athletic field, looking southeast toward Tenth and State. File 885

began to play a type of football whose rules forbade touching the ball with one's hands except when catching it on the fly. One enthusiastic participant insisted that the object of this game was "to kick the opponents' shins." College officials established the Athletic Association of Marquette College in 1883 "to promote the physical development of its members by manly games and healthful exercise" and to foster a "college spirit." For more than a decade, baseball dominated organized sports at Marquette College. Then, in 1892, the school approved a high school-level football team. It played a three-game season that year, with one victory. Admission cost ten cents. When these teams were finally allowed to travel, the faculty (meaning the Jesuits) insisted that student-athletes could be absent for no more than one day. The school's first permanent coaching staff, hired in 1902, introduced college football to Marquette. These early teams did rather well in the helter-skelter schedule available to them, winning five of seven collegiate games in 1902 and six of seven in the following year. Encounters with the University of Wisconsin's eleven, however, proved the immaturity of Marquette's program, as evidenced by 33-0 and 29-0 losses to the Badgers in 1904 and 1905.[17]

The college administration took a rather dim view of organized sports, preferring an intramural program that involved every student regardless of talent. Football at Marquette was actually banned in 1897 because of its violent, unsportsmanlike character. It was not restored until 1900, the same year that track joined the list of approved sports. Three years later, Father President reminded students that "athletics were only a means to an end … [that is] to develop the body and give self-control." In contrast, he

Handwritten record of 1895 baseball season. File 39

praised the influence of music through the groups such as the mandolin and glee clubs. The Jesuit faculty's insistence that football undermined rather than enhanced student life may have been softened somewhat in 1906 after a code of conduct was developed for intercollegiate play in southern Wisconsin and northern Illinois. According to these guidelines, faculty supervised athletics at each school, professional coaches were forbidden, participants could not use their knowledge of the game for financial gain, no student taking fewer than ten hours of class work was allowed to participate, and any student who was "guilty of brutality in any contest [would] be debarred from the game, and the team penalized twenty yards."[18]

The most celebrated sporting event at Marquette in the late nineteenth century was the school's annual Field Day, which later became a two-day activity because of its success. Track and field events occupied most participants, although in 1896 the college's baseball team featured a gifted third baseman by the name of Herbert C. Noonan, who three days later delivered the valedictory address at graduation. Nineteen years later, he returned to campus as Father Herbert C. Noonan, university president. The most common form of athletic activity at Marquette consisted of pick-up games played on the cinder-covered lot between the Church of the Holy Name and the college building. The field slowly evolved into an authentic athletic site with low-rise wooden stands snuggled against the college hall; later a matching set on the west side of the field was added. When Holy Name's school building located behind the church was abandoned in 1899, Marquette alumni raised funds to refurbish the two-story structure and develop the school's first gymnasium. The school's first floor was completely gutted, creating a cavernous space for the gym. On the ground level, the alumni built a running and bicycle track sixteen feet wide and one-sixth of a mile in length. They also provided $350 worth of equipment, purchased from the Spalding Company. The second floor of the building was subsequently converted into the Marquette College library, setting up an interesting auditory contest.[19]

GAINING THE CITY'S ATTENTION

The first student to complete his studies at Marquette College received neither a diploma nor a degree. In June 1884, Thomas W. Smith earned a commercial course certificate, after developing a remarkable reputation: the Best in Arithmetic honor in 1882 and the Catechical Essay Gold Medal the following year. (Later, he joined the Society of Jesus.) College degrees were not conferred until three years after Smith received his certificate and six years after the school opened. Despite the absence of graduates per se, the college still scheduled literary "Exercises" in both February and June 1882, the school's first year of operation, to showcase the benefits of a Jesuit education. They provided free advertising for Milwaukee's newest cultural center. Six hundred invitations were sent out for the mid-year event. Parents, clergy, Catholic and public school teachers, and friends of Marquette filled the third-floor assembly hall on February 17, 1882. Two dialogues, two songs, one oration, and one discourse spotlighted the school's best students. One Milwaukeean was so struck by these presentations that he offered this unusual affirmation: the "college is to be complimented in not debarring students of other denominations than its own, from attending the recitations and lectures—for this betokens a praiseworthy freedom from all narrow-minded prejudice." Future mid-year exercises featured orations on great moments in American history, recitations in Latin and Greek, serious dramas, classical musical performances, and the dreaded question-and-answer sessions. More than anything else, Q & A sessions terrified students because the audience was free to challenge the panelists with whatever

Four of the five first recipients of a bachelor of arts degree & the college president. File 590

inquiries they wished. Students viewed it as the third degree, never knowing whether they might face nonsensical questions such as "How high is up?" or serious questions on science or law posed by specialists in the audience.[20]

Marquette's first year drew to a close with a second exhibition. (The term "commencement" was not used until the following year.) At eight o'clock on June 28, 1882, the assembly hall's four hundred seats were filled; as many as one hundred additional on-lookers stood in the aisles and stairways. The city's most prominent citizens watched the students file in with "gentlemanly behavior." Among the presentations were a free-hand drawing of the State of Wisconsin on a blackboard with colored chalk, an essay on Wisconsin, an oration entitled "Let My Actions Speak," and a lecture by the afore-mentioned Thomas Smith on "Theory and Practice, With Experiments." Gold and silver medals as well as "handsomely bound volumes" were awarded to the best student in each arithmetic class. One medal was given for excellence in Christian doctrine and manly piety. The college also recognized any student who achieved a cumulative grade of eighty or better (out of one hundred points).[21]

The real testament to a Jesuit education finally came on June 29, 1887, when Francis X. Bodden, John I. Drew, Charles Gaffney, Henry F. Millman, and James D. O'Neill received their bachelor of arts degrees. The first three were in the original third academic class of 1881-82. Two years after receiving his bachelor's, Bodden was awarded Marquette's first Master of Arts degree, after an undetermined amount of advanced reading. In the interim, he taught at the lower levels, becoming the college's first lay instructor. Bodden later served as the first president of the Marquette College Alumni Association as well as a vice president at Marshall & Ilsley Bank. John Drew became city treasurer of Milwaukee. James O'Neill studied for the priesthood in Baltimore and subsequently held a pastorship in Highland Park, Illinois. Henry Millman, who graduated at seventeen, left behind a distinguished record when he departed Marquette to become, eventually, a purchasing agent for Geuder, Paeschke and Frey in Milwaukee. He started at Marquette in 1881, two classes behind his colleagues but caught up to them within twelve months. In his second year, he won the gold medal for excellence in the classical department, the silver medal in mathematics, and a premium (cash award) in German. In 1886, a year before his college graduation, Millman took on the best Latin scholars from the Missouri Province's five colleges. Judges awarded him the gold medal for his essay, *Laus Sancti Joannis Chrysostomi* ("In Praise of St. John Chrysostom").[22]

The college's assembly hall hosted the first three commencements, but by 1885, these events had moved to auditoriums around the city, including the Grand Opera House, Bijou Opera House, Davidson Theater, and Pabst Theater. Featured speakers from outside the college community eventually replaced student performances at graduation. The search for such a speaker in 1902 brought Father President to city hall where he intended to ask Mayor David Rose to assume this responsibility. Recognized as one of Milwaukee's most popular (five two-year terms) and most corrupt chief executives, Rose made the Jesuit wait for two and half hours. Still, he agreed to speak and "promised not to curse," a pledge he honored when heralding small colleges over large universities.[23]

In addition to highlighting student talents through exhibitions and commencements, the college also sponsored public demonstrations showcasing the faculty's scholarly prowess. At the conclusion of the school's first year, "'it was deemed necessary to do something which might bring the school before the attention of the people.'" Thus in May 1882, Father President, Joseph Rigge, delivered a memorable lecture, "The Wonders of Sound." He spoke of the microphone, the phonograph, and the telephone, praising the genius of Thomas Edison. The day's most memorable moment came when a piano being played at the Church of the Holy Name school could be heard by the audience in the college hall a block away through the magic of a telephone. Some years later, the Jesuit faculty scheduled a weekly public lecture series, covering everything from "Acoustic Waves" and the "American Classic" to "Genesis and Geology" and "Jesuitism."[24]

Other strategies employed to bring Marquette to Milwaukee's attention included an appeal from Archbishop Michael Heiss in 1884 to "the Rev. Clergy and Beloved Laity of Milwaukee." He emphasized the importance of "higher training," given the "supreme influence of education." The prelate also lauded Marquette College's curriculum which, he noted, matched those from "some of the best colleges of larger and more pretentious cities." It guaranteed Milwaukee boys the religious and secular training necessary for them to enter "the more honorable walks and higher pursuits of life." To broaden its impact, this appeal was translated into German, Polish, and Bohemian. The college administration was so pleased with this effort that it reprinted Archbishop Heiss's letter verbatim in the 1884-85 *College Catalogue*. Later college presidents sent their own letters to Milwaukee-area pastors, appealing for help in the recruitment of first-rate students. Jesuits reminded their clerical brothers that "Catholic boys cannot lead unless they are fitted for leadership by a good education." By the early 1890s, similar appeals appeared in local newspapers, including German and Polish language publications. Late each summer, just before registration, these notices ran for as many as four consecutive weeks. This was the college's principal recruitment tool in the late nineteenth century.[25]

FISCAL MATTERS

Although the principal motivation for public displays of student and faculty talents was the enlistment of new students, a less-recognized ambition addressed the school's financial condition. Some public demonstrations—but never the mid-year and commencement exhibitions—charged a modest admission price. These events supported specific projects, such as purchasing laboratory equipment. Construction of Holy Name Church in 1875 and Marquette College five years later left the Milwaukee Jesuit community with more than $40,000 of debt—more than two-thirds of this charged to the college. (While this sum may not appear significant to contemporary eyes, it translated to an obligation of $759,675 in 2005 dollars.) Moreover, the notion of long-term debt was new and more than a little tainted for Jesuits. St. Ignatius had wanted the Society's schools to open with endowments that permitted them to choose students based on potential, not ability to pay. His was to be a meritocractic system. And so it went in Europe. But in the United States, endowed Catholic colleges were fiscally impractical. They were seen as aristocratic and therefore un-American. Consequently, long before

Marquette was established, administrators at Georgetown and Saint Louis colleges had pleaded with superiors in Rome to waive the endowment requirement. They refused. Anxious to recruit Jesuit colleges to their dioceses, American bishops then appealed to the Holy See. The Vatican intervened and American colleges received dispensations permitting them to charge tuition. For the nineteenth century, that charge was typically $50 to $60 dollars per year. Both Creighton and Saint Joseph colleges briefly held endowments that permitted them to operate as "free schools," but most Jesuit administrators borrowed to build.[26]

Marquette College was founded without an endowment and without the expectation of an endowment. It was tuition-dependent from the outset. With tuition set at $60 a year for more than a quarter of a century, administrators struggled to meet each year's expenses while trying to pay off old obligations. As early as 1885, the school's finances became so shaky that provincial officers in St. Louis discussed closing the college. (A similar discussion took place regarding St. Xavier College in Cincinnati in both the 1850s and 1860s.) However, the assistant to the superior general for English-speaking provinces came to Marquette's rescue by encouraging the provincial consultors to support the Milwaukee school. Only two years later, a different set of superiors in St. Louis briefly entertained the idea of inviting German Jesuits from Buffalo, New York, to take over the Society's work in Milwaukee. An icy reaction from Marquette Jesuits put an end to this trial balloon. As a consequence, Milwaukee Jesuits tended to keep their financial woes private, until a very unusual statement was published on page twelve of the 1898-99 catalogue. It explained that the institution's debt remained at $25,163.33, nearly the same amount as in 1881. The statement pointed out that Marquette did not even receive the revenue that its student numbers suggested because each year "needy but deserving" young men were admitted free. Thus, for the first time, a direct appeal went out for scholarship support: $60 a year for annual scholarships or permanent scholarships for a one-time donation of $1,000. There is no record of how the Catholic community responded to this request, although a follow-up appeal in the following catalogue (1899-1900) indicated that the school's debt had been reduced by nearly $5.000.[27]

These long-term obligations had to be satisfied at the same time that the college met annual operating expenses. Insurance bills, furniture and book purchases, coal supplies, a choir director ($100 per year), chairs for the college hall (250 @ 35 cents apiece), and the ubiquitous property tax charges (reduced to 10 percent of earlier sums when most of Block 199 was used for religious activities) created recurrent headaches for Father President. In the summer of 1885, for example, in anticipation of another Milwaukee winter, the Jesuits ordered ninety-five tons of coal for the college, twenty tons for the grammar school at Holy Name, and fifty tons for the church. The bill totaled $1,055.61. Insurance premiums for $5,000 policies on each of these three buildings ran $75 apiece annually. When the parish decided to open a girls' grade school across the street from Holy Name Church, local Jesuits purchased this land for $9,000, with a third down and a note for the balance. Just as tuition income never covered the college's expenses, Sunday collections at Holy Name failed to make a dent in the church's debt. Short-term loans up to $1,000 from financial institutions and private parties became routine. In one instance, the college president borrowed money from his mother. Most often, these personal loans covered an interest payment on some larger debt, thereby creating yet another obligation.[28]

Without question, Marquette College's fiscal survival depended upon the vow of poverty taken by members of the Society of Jesus. With the exception of a very small number of lay faculty who taught primarily preparatory and commercial students, the faculty consisted of Jesuits. These religious received no salary; their living expenses were simply charged to the college budget. Every expense was recorded, from $5 for a pair of boots to $1 for a pair of slippers to $5.25 per week for four bottles of Mass wine. Handwritten accounts of the Jesuit community's expenditures from September through November in 1885, January through March in 1886, and May through July in 1887 provide a glimpse into how little these priests and scholastics cost the college. For a dozen individuals, the Jesuit community spent between $4 and $13 per month in 1885 for butter, between $5 and $9 for eggs, and up to $6 for pears, but only 20 to 40 cents per month for the streetcar and—once in that span of three months—30 cents for candy. Two years later, over a three-month period, chickens cost between $1.80 and $13.00 per month, tomatoes from $1.30 to $9.50, and beans and peas up to $10.10 in a given month. Unusual charges included 25 cents for a necktie, 90 cents for a baseball and bat, and 25 cents for medicine; in June of 1887, $13 was set aside for pipe tobacco and cigars. The self-sufficiency of the Jesuit community was singled out years later when a local insurance agent conceded that the Jesuits took care of their own and consequently injuries or illnesses did not come at any expense to insurance companies. Therefore, he noted, "the insuring company has no right to ask you [the college] to pay any premium on the value of maintenance for the Jesuit fathers."[29]

CHURCH OF THE GESU

A decision to consolidate St. Gall and Holy Name parishes complicated the financial condition of Milwaukee's Jesuit ministries. In February 1889, the college's board of trustees offered their property at St. Gall's to the U.S. government, which was looking to build a new post office in the downtown area. Negotiations with federal officials went nowhere, however. Nonetheless, expansion of Milwaukee's central business district into the Fourth Ward complicated the quality of life around St. Gall's. The dangers inherent in a commercial or industrial landscape were realized on October 29, 1892, when the most destructive fire in the city's history roared through the adjoining Third Ward, wiping out sixteen blocks and 440 buildings and leaving two thousand residents homeless. Many Third Ward Irish did not to return to their old community. Instead they joined an in-progress migration to the near west side neighborhoods of Tory Hill and Merrill Park.

The unassuming Church of the Holy Name at Eleventh and State served these transplants, but it was never intended to be the principal worship center for the Jesuit's west side pastorate. It had been seen as only a modest first step. Consequently, even before the Third Ward fire, Jesuit administrators began to search for appropriate properties on or near Grand Avenue. In 1891, they purchased two sizable parcels from Winfield Smith and John L. Mitchell on the south side of the avenue, across from the old state fairgrounds where Abraham Lincoln once delivered an address. They took out additional mortgages on Block 199 to fund these acquisitions. In December of the same

Church of the Gesu, circa 1901. Science/Marquette Hall will be built on the lot to the right. File 590

Gesu Parish School, facing Thirteenth Street. File 618

year, the priests borrowed $55,000 from Northwestern Mutual Life Insurance Com-
pany with interest at five percent. About the same time, the college president, who was
religious superior for Milwaukee's Jesuits, summoned the congregations of St. Gall's
and Holy Name to outline his plans for a new church and a new college building on
Grand Avenue at Twelfth Street. In encouraging their generosity toward the parish-side
of this project, he promised that their contributions would not be used to pay for costs
related to a college building.[30]

Two months after this meeting, the Jesuits reached an agreement with developer
Ephraim Mariner for the sale of the property and buildings at St. Gall's for $237,300.
As part of the deal, Mariner was required to alter the exterior of that church so that
passers-by would never recognize the building as a former place of worship. The two
parties also promised to keep their arrangement a secret until a later date. Meanwhile,
the Jesuits quietly purchased additional plots near Grand Avenue, including a house
intended to serve as a future rectory. The new church was allocated 147 feet of front-
age on the avenue whereas the college was assigned 138 feet. Contracts for excavation
work were let in the summer of 1892. By the fall, discussions turned to land needed for
parish grade schools. The cornerstone for the Church of the Gesu, named after the site
in Rome where the body of St. Ignatius of Loyola rests, was laid on May 21, 1893. As

with the college's cornerstone ceremony in 1880, hundreds of Catholic societies sent representatives; Archbishop Frederick X. Katzer officiated. Seventeen months later, a final religious service closed St. Gall's and the building was demolished in 1899.

On December 16, 1894, Milwaukee's archbishop dedicated the glorious new center of worship. The church's two steeples (250 feet and 215 feet high) flanked the main entrance; it had interior dimensions of 125 feet by 160 feet; its aisles were 18 feet wide and 65 feet long; and it contained 5 altars. The first pastor, Father James D. Foley, was assisted by two priests who ministered to nearly seven hundred families. They came from the Fourth Ward, from the area surrounding Holy Name Church, from Tory Hill, and from elite Catholic families whose mansions helped define Grand Avenue. A large school was built in 1899 to the southwest of the church building. The sale of the property at St. Gall's paid for the development of the Gesu parish project, but no funds remained to develop the college property east of the church. This land remained vacant for another dozen years.[31]

AN ALUMNI ASSOCIATION

One potential source that might have helped get a new college hall off the drawing boards was the college's graduates. Jesuit colleges in America were remarkably slow in organizing their graduates, even for non-fundraising events such as religious services, lecture series, smokers, or reunions. At Saint Joseph College in Philadelphia, alumni established an informal club only forty-five years after the school's founding in 1851. A formal alumni association was not organized until 1915, sixty-four years after the school opened. At St. Xavier in Cincinnati, it took forty-eight years. Marquette College was a bit more assertive. Three years after the first baccalaureate degrees were conferred, a group of alumni gathered for an informal reunion in late August 1890. Providing financial assistance to the college was not their intention. Instead, they organized a lyceum for the following fall term. The aim of this semi-monthly session was "development of an active Catholic spirit; the cultivation of a taste for philosophical, literary, and scientific studies; and the formation of ready and able writers in defense of Catholic truths, especially in their bearing on civil society." During the inaugural season, which ran from early November to late May, presentations included "Religion—the Essential Basis of Society," "History of the Tariff," "The Catholic Church and Science," "A Phase of Socialism," "Humor," and "What Our Rivers Have Accomplished." Three of the five collegiate graduates from 1887 (Bodden, Gaffney, and Millman) contributed original papers.

A more serious effort to establish an association of Marquette College alumni came in June 1893, at the instigation of Father E. J. Gleeson. Over sixty individuals decided to create a formal organization and selected Francis X. Bodden as their first president. A committee spent the year working on a constitution and by-laws, before submitting them to the membership at their next meeting the following June. The object was "'to preserve and strengthen the traditions of Marquette College; to maintain a fellow feeling among the former students of the institution; to further the interests of higher

Catholic education, [and] to promote the welfare of Marquette College, the Marquette College Alumni Association and its members.'" Although the alumni held smokers on a regular basis, the highlight of each year was a banquet, generally scheduled for late spring or early summer. The menu at these events was truly impressive: little mac clams, mock turtle madere, filet of sole, cutlet of young chicken, tenderloin of beef larded with mushrooms, asparagus, drawn butter, new potatoes, a watercress salad, and then vanilla ice cream and assorted cakes.[32]

Just how vital this group could be was soon apparent. The Capitol building in Washington, D.C., houses what is called the Statuary Hall Collection, statues depicting distinguished personages, up to two per state. In 1885, a proposal was made to have a statue of Father Jacques Marquette become Wisconsin's first entry in this collection. The state legislature concurred in 1887. Nine years passed before completion of the statue. At the last minute, one legislator in Madison introduced a bill intended to block its placement in Statuary Hall. In a decade filled with anti-immigrant, anti-Semitic, anti-black, and anti-Catholic prejudices, allies of Marquette College viewed this parliamentary maneuver as nothing short of religious bigotry, one preventing the image of a cross-bearing defender of the papacy from representing the state of Wisconsin.

Only three years old at this point, the alumni association rose to the challenge. They prepared a strongly worded remonstrance, decrying the insult to their alma mater's namesake. They sent letters to every parish in the state, urging congregations to submit their own petitions of protest; many did. The alumni also helped organize a committee of prominent Catholic businessmen, led by Patrick Cudahy, to direct this fight. Representatives of the alumni association and the Cudahy-led committee met with state legislators. When the anti-Marquette measure was finally put to a vote in April 1896, the original author could enlist only two additional supporters; his resolution failed seventy-eight to three. The U.S. Senate accepted the statue quickly, but the House of Representatives delayed a vote, perhaps because of its reluctance to include a Catholic priest within a pantheon heralded by Ethan Allen, John Winthrop, Sam Adams, James A. Garfield, and Daniel Webster. The alumni association worked with Congressman Theobald Otjen to get the House's acceptance. It took years. Not until January 29, 1904, did the House of Representatives welcome the statue of Père Marquette into the hall. Today, the Statuary Hall Collection includes representations of George Washington, Henry Clay, Robert E. Lee, Jefferson Davis, Brigham Young, Sam Houston, Will Rogers, Dwight Eisenhower, and the Badger State's second entry, Robert F. La Follette. Congress's brushes with anti-Catholicism eased over time for the statue of Père Marquette was eventually joined by sculptures of Father Junipero Serra (California) in 1931 and Father Damien (Hawaii) in 1969.[33]

ADMINISTRATIVE DEVELOPMENTS

Displays of loyalty by the alumni reflected the school's evolving self-image as it moved toward the college's silver jubilee in 1906. Some of this confidence arose from pivotal figures. In its first twenty-five years, the college went through ten presidents. Joseph

Rigge, the first chief executive, lasted one year, stepping aside to serve on the faculty. He was replaced for a two-year period by the amiable Isidore J. Boudreaux. Father Boudreaux had been one of the two Jesuits to come to Milwaukee to preach the priests' retreat in 1853 and, in the process, helped revive Bishop Henni's contacts with the Missouri vice province. He served as master of novices in Florissant, Missouri, for

Statue of Father Marquette, Washington, D.C. File 1053

twenty-three years (1857-80) and later assisted Father Lalumiere at St. Gall's. He was also an early "explorer" on the hilltop. After Bishop Henni made this property available to the Jesuits, Father Boudreaux took a carriage ride to examine the site. On the uneven terrain, his buggy overturned, throwing him to the ground. Uninjured, the Jesuit jokingly remarked that he "'had [just] taken possession of the soil'" for the Society of Jesus.

After Father Boudreaux, Thomas S. Fitzgerald became president. Before ascending to the top post, he taught natural science for a year. Fitzgerald served as president for three years (1884-87) and officiated at the first college graduation. One distinctive mark of his term was a more forceful articulation of Marquette's religious mission. A new paragraph entitled "Religious Training" in the 1884-85 catalogue declared that the "Catholic Church is professedly regarded as the only true one." Furthermore, the "Catechism is a text book in all the classes." Like his predecessor Father Rigge, Fitzgerald stayed on after leaving the presidency, in his case to serve as prefect of study (effectively, the vice president). He moved on to head the Jesuit colleges in Omaha and Chicago (Creighton from 1889 to 1891 and St. Ignatius from 1891 to 1894). Reserved and meditative, Father Fitzgerald grew anxious when placed in administrative assignments and was clearly more comfortable in his later assignment as pastor of Gesu parish.[34]

Aging but still a beloved figure across the city, Father Lalumiere was briefly president from July 1887 to November 1889 when he was reassigned to Cincinnati, much to the dismay of Milwaukee Catholics. Over the next four years, Joseph Grimmelsman, Rudolph J. Meyer, and Victor Putten served as president in quick succession. Meyer prepared for his two-year term by spending time as prefect of study. Later as provincial, he introduced the intercollegiate Latin competition among Midwestern Jesuit schools, the event at which Henry Millman won a gold medal. Father Putten arrived in Milwaukee in 1885 to serve as college treasurer and to teach a special Latin class. He fulfilled these responsibilities for many years, both before and after his brief time as what was, in effect, acting president.

Father Leopold Bushart followed Father Putten. Like John Martin Henni, as a seminary student in Europe Bushart became captivated by stories of Father Peter DeSmet's work with the Indian missions in the western United States. Although Bushart's evangelical ambitions brought him to the New World, his administrative talents prevented him from ever reaching the west coast. He served as president at St. Xavier (1871-74), Saint Louis (1874-77), and as Master of Novices in Florissant, Missouri (1880-82), as well as five years (1893-1898) as president of Marquette. In 1898, he was replaced by William B. Rogers, who stayed in Milwaukee for only two years before carving out an impressive career at Saint Louis University. Rogers served in Missouri during the same span of time as his Marquette successor, Alexander Burrowes: 1900 to 1908. Visionary educators, these two men completely redid the academic programs at their respective institutions, elevating both institutions to positions of prominence within Midwestern Catholicism. In fact, so blessed was Marquette during its first quarter of a century that at some point Burrowes, Bushart, Meyer (twice), Fitzgerald, and Grimmelsman each

Marquette presidents in the late nineteenth & early twentieth centuries. File 885

shouldered the heavy burden of serving as provincial. Between 1882 and 1919, these five men headed the Missouri province for twenty-nine of those thirty-seven years, a testimony to their stature in the Midwestern fraternity of Jesuits.[35]

CURRICULAR DEVELOPMENTS

Among these early presidents, Fathers Grimmelsman and Meyer were noted for their unflinching loyalty to the *Ratio Studiorum* in its most traditional form. Meyer had a reputation for not just resisting specific refinements, but for rejecting *any* discussion of change. A singularly brilliant student, he (like Grimmelsman) had been selected by his superiors to undertake a very rare public examination in the entire field of theology known as the "Grand Act." (There were only three such defenses—including Meyer's—among Jesuits in the United States between 1874 and 1903; Grimmelsman made his in France.) Meyer moved on to a remarkable career in administration, serving as provincial twice (1885-89 and 1907-12) and as president at St. Xavier College (1879-81) and Saint Louis University (1881-85) in addition to Marquette. He was also assistant to the superior general for English-speaking provinces from 1892 to 1906. As provincial in 1887, he ordered a review of academic programs throughout the Missouri province. His aim was to insure uniformity through a strict adherence to tradition. A course of study was promulgated, requiring every college within his canonical jurisdiction to abide by the same curriculum. The classical course was to be not only the central offering at each school, but also preferably the only option. The classical course would always consist of a three-year academic sequence followed by a four-year collegiate course (a practice maintained at Marquette since its opening). The names for each year of study (humanities, poetry, rhetoric, and philosophy) were to be uniform (a situation already in place at Marquette). There were no electives. This course of study prescribed a standard list of readings and exercises for every class year. "Evidences of Religion" joined Latin, Greek, English, and philosophy as crucial subjects; other fields, including history, mathematics, and the natural sciences, were considered subsidiary branches.

Two years later, in 1889, before Meyer became Marquette's president, the superior general in Rome selected him to investigate "the state of Jesuit affairs in California." Among Meyer's concerns was what he thought might be sloppy implementation of the *Ratio Studiorum* at Santa Clara College. After all, the school's president had already earned a stern rebuke from the superior general for deviating from the *Ratio*. (This superior general was none other than Andrew Anderledy, one of the Jesuits who came to Milwaukee in 1849 but had been reassigned to Green Bay because of his poor command of English). In the wake of Meyer's visitation to California, new instructions stipulated that the *Ratio* was to be followed with diligence, including assigning Latin and Greek first place. Particularly troubling for the visitor-general was the popularity of Santa Clara's commercial course among high school students. Students who had no intention of pursuing the collegiate course favored this option because they could bypass the classical languages. Meyer insisted that Santa Clara explain itself to the superior general. Ultimately, the California school retained its commercial program but only by requiring more hours in literature and rhetoric. About the same time, across the continent, Canisius College, the Jesuit school in Buffalo, New York, discontinued its commercial program. Tradition, for the moment, held fast.[36]

Meyer, Grimmelsman, and like-minded confreres struggled against what they considered to be educational fads, a distinctly American penchant for chasing the trendy and contemporary. They understood that this defense of the *Ratio* would involve continuing skirmishes over curricular and pedagogical refinements. What worried Meyer about the current uproar was its emphasis upon materialism and its devotion to scientific inquiry. This led to what he labeled "absolutism." For Meyer, religion was the foremost interpreter of the visible world. To him, interest in contemporary science, technology, literature, and art glorified human accomplishments. To prevent a breach in the walls of righteous learning, traditionalists insisted that the *Ratio* remain unaccommodating to newer lines of inquiry. As Jesuit historian William B. Faherty has remarked, Meyer was "repressive and inflexible" because "even a minor change seemed to endanger the entire mechanism." Very little in modern thinking—regardless of the field—belonged in the classical course. It was extraneous to what a young man needed to save his soul. These Jesuits received encouragement when the Society of Jesus's 25th General Congregation in 1906 agreed not to rewrite the *Ratio Studiorum*, although this action sprang from a realization that worldwide standardization was increasingly impractical.

To traditionalists, one particularly ominous novelty threatened American higher education. A growing number of non-sectarian colleges allowed young people to select their own courses through a new procedure called electives. From the traditionalist point of view, this was idiocy. How could eighteen-year-olds know what was right for them to study? How could they select what they did not understand? For Jesuits, the *Ratio Studiorum* reflected an authentic translation of the Latin root for the word *education*. *Educare* means to "draw out," as in "to develop" in contrast to "fill up" with information—no matter how captivating this information may be. The *Ratio Studiorum* maintained that there were keystones to any student's mental and spiritual training that could not be left to the whimsical musings of youth, a reasonable point given the tender age at which many Jesuit students around the world started their studies. Whether this same admonition applied to college students in America was the question at hand. At Marquette—and elsewhere in the Jesuit world—this reluctance to trust the preferences of undergraduates meant that wiser, black-robed adults safeguarded centuries of learning for young American Catholics.[37]

At large public universities and prominent private institutions such as the University of Chicago and Johns Hopkins University, however, an American interpretation of *educare* was favored. *Electivism* was a genuine challenge to Jesuit traditions, especially in the United States, where a national culture steeped in democratic principles—if not always accompanied by democratic practices—allowed students to make their own choices. Deference to the inherent wisdom of a superior class (even if it consisted of clergymen) was antithetical to American culture. Elites who acted as though, by birthright, they knew more than ordinary folk met resistance in American politics and fared no better in areas such as education. The *Ratio Studiorum*'s value, the by-product of thousands of dedicated educators laboring over centuries, now competed in a buyer's market predicated upon notions of freedom and equality. The preferences of tuition-paying college students from Milwaukee and Wisconsin would be the real test as to which system of learning might prevail in the twentieth century.

One measure of how the *Ratio Studiorum* might sustain its relevance could be found in the experiences of Marquette College graduates after they left the hilltop. Because the *Ratio* did not provide career training in a nineteenth-century frame of reference, employment after graduation was not the first—or even second—priority of a Jesuit education. However, the growth of industries and cities redefined the United States after the Civil War. White-collar occupations called for increasingly complex job skills. (Converting skilled artisans from the colonial period into twentieth-century assembly line workers suggests that the opposite process was underway in the blue-collar sector of the economy.) Simple literacy mixed with some practical experience and perhaps a dash of physical strength was no longer sufficient to address the needs of a technologically sophisticated society. Railroad trestles spanning the Mississippi River, subways tunneling beneath Manhattan Island, water and sewer systems serving millions of urbanites, electrical power systems delivering wonderful conveniences over great distances, and horseless carriages bumping along cow paths at thirty miles per hour demanded heightened levels of design, quality, organization, and management. Failure could be catastrophic for thousands. These rising expectations demanded advanced training in fields such as civil engineering and industrial design. It even applied to older professions such as law in which an aspirant no longer could simply "read" with an individual attorney, as Father Lalumiere had done in the 1850s. For-profit schools in medicine, dentistry, pharmacy, law, and engineering came under pressure from newly created accrediting agencies to integrate their professional training into a broader curriculum. Every type of educational institution, from grade to graduate school, became subject to external evaluation and review. If Jesuit education in America was to survive, it had to place itself within this competitive framework. Parents with disposable incomes cared less in 1900 about classical languages than about laboratory sciences. Jesuits had to look no further than the popularity of their own commercial classes to prove this point.

Competition in a marketplace of higher education was tested in the last decade of the nineteenth century by a series of events unfolding eight hundred miles east of the hilltop. In 1893 Harvard University Law School barred graduates from any college not found on its select list of institutions. Not a single Jesuit or Catholic was included in the original draft of that list. After protests by Catholic spokesmen, including the president of Georgetown (the oldest American Jesuit college), Harvard added three Jesuit institutions: Georgetown, Boston College, and the College of the Holy Cross. Four years later, without explanation, the last two were dropped. Charles Eliot, the president of Harvard, added fuel to this controversy in a magazine article in which he dismissed the pertinence of a Jesuit education in the modern age. He added bigotry to insult by comparing what he saw as the religious straitjacket of a Jesuit education to the stifling influence of the Koran in Muslim societies. In 1895, amid this controversy, the regents of the State University of New York questioned preparation levels of Fordham and Georgetown graduates for professional education in law and medicine. Non-Catholic authorities openly challenged Jesuit higher education: was a thorough grounding in the classical languages with a capacity to contrast Aristotle's and Aquinas's notions of free will sufficient for graduate work in law, medicine, engineering, economics, or sociology? Mention of these last two subjects speaks to the ascending importance of the social sciences in American higher education. Universities increasingly took the position that contemporary societies warranted as much scholarly attention as ancient civilizations. Subjects such as economics or political science were absent from the *Marquette College Catalogue* through the nineteenth century. Even a course in education (or pedagogy, as it might have been called) could not be found. Could reading Cicero's poetry in his original language compete with course work that, in the not-too-distant future, would unravel the mysteries of Chicago's street gangs or child-rearing in the South Pacific? With only a few after-school electives in modern languages, with no majors per se, no laboratory-based science courses, and no courses addressing contemporary social sciences, could Jesuit schools survive for very long? The mismatch of undergraduate preparation at Marquette and graduate study at the University of Wisconsin or the University of Chicago became as disruptive for the individual consumer (student) as railroad tracks with different gauges: you could not get from here to there without disembarking and leaving one system behind.[38]

Father Alexander Burrowes faced this watershed in American Jesuit education when he arrived at Tenth and State in 1900. During its first twenty years, Marquette College undertook only minor adjustments in its programs because the *Ratio Studiorum* eliminated any need for academic assessments. There was no need for a curriculum committee or a committee on academic policies and procedures. The rules had been set. Only enforcement was necessary. At the end of the 1891-92 academic year, the administration discontinued the preparatory program, removing the youngest boys from the college building. By the college's silver anniversary in 1906, the commercial course, an American innovation, had dwindled to a single certificate recipient in 1903, three in 1904, and four each in 1905 and 1906. The academic department remained the largest division of Marquette College because it provided the finest high school education in the city. Even if the Jesuits saw the academic program as a mandatory prerequisite for the collegiate course, Milwaukee parents increasingly viewed it as a de facto high school.

Enrollment at Marquette and other Jesuit colleges proved this point. In the beginning, the number of bachelor of arts degrees awarded each year at Marquette College grew by a reassuring margin. In 1887, the first 5 college students graduated. A decade later, 20 students received a B.A. at commencement. But in five years time, by 1902, that number dropped to 4—less than the first graduation class. By the silver jubilee in 1906, the numbers stabilized at 13, hardly a promising output after twenty-five years of labor by the Jesuit faculty. Similar stagnation beset other Jesuit institutions. In the first fifty years of Loyola College in Baltimore, only 15 percent of its 2,600 students enrolled in the college portion of the program and only one-half of this 15 percent completed its collegiate program. At Santa Clara College, in the thirty-four years before 1891 (when the bachelor of science was discontinued in the aftermath of Father

Meyer's visit), only 21 percent of the graduates completed the bachelor of arts program with its mandatory training in Latin and Greek. Most individuals preferred the B.S. option. At Marquette, its troubling graduation numbers reflected problems with overall enrollment. A cohort of 12 students constituted the first college class in the fall of 1883. By 1896, the number of undergraduates peaked for this era at 78. It dwindled to 56, a 28 percent drop, by the time Father Burrowes arrived in 1900. Milwaukee parents clearly valued the academic department (a high school to them), but the college program was struggling. Parents, students, employers, and nonsectarian universities all seemed to question the pertinence of the classical course in the modern age.[39]

Marquette's vice president, Father Henry Spalding, sought to substantiate this trend during the fall of 1904. He sent letters to nearby universities, asking about the admissibility of Marquette alumni when they applied for graduate studies. The responses from Northwestern, Chicago, Wisconsin, Michigan, and Minnesota essentially said the same thing: each student would be evaluated individually. There would be no blanket recognition of a bachelor of arts degree from Marquette, with its unusual concentration of Latin, religion, and philosophy. Northwestern University indicated Marquette graduates would be required to complete an extra year's work before undertaking advanced studies. At Wisconsin, they would, in most instances, need a fifth year of work before receiving their second bachelor of arts degree with a major in either Latin, Greek, mathematics, or philosophy. Only then could they begin graduate studies. This also applied to the University of Wisconsin's teaching program, which made sense because Marquette did not offer a single education class. (For locals who wanted to become teachers, the state normal system opened its Milwaukee branch at Eighteenth and Wells in 1885, four years after Marquette began operation in a three-story building designed by the same architect. Today, the Milwaukee Rescue Mission occupies this building.) Only the UW school of law (not a graduate program per se at this time) provided uniform acceptance of transfer students from Marquette: admission as juniors after attending Marquette for one year. The implications of these responses explain some of the motivations driving Burrowes, Spalding, and their allies to renovate Marquette's undergraduate curriculum.[40]

As Father President, Burrowes was not about to renounce his Jesuit heritage, but he had a reputation for not ignoring the need to adapt. Years later, as provincial, he reminisced before a group of young Jesuits:

> We realized … that this … was a moment that might pass and never come again. So, though, we had neither money nor resources, though we were inexperienced in the university forms, we built and annexed and ventured into new fields. We … had to act fast, courageously, and sometimes apparently against sound judgment and prudence. Now you have Jesuit universities; what will happen to them is yours to decide.

Burrowes had first evidenced this determination as president at Xavier College during the mid-1890s when he introduced an evening graduate program, opening the doors to an entirely new type of student. At Marquette, he incrementally adjusted the undergraduate curriculum between 1901 and 1907, retaining the classical course while providing additional instruction in the social and natural sciences. He introduced electives, but they were extras added to the traditional core. Changes appeared as early as his second year in Milwaukee. At one level, it was symbolically reflected in the college's adoption of the cap and gown at graduation. Even this concession to American styles was accepted only "after considerable deliberation."

More significantly, the 1901-02 *Marquette College Catalogue* introduced language that reflected American nomenclature on higher education. Instead of opening the "Course of Study" section with the traditional list of authors and books studied in the philosophy year followed by the rhetoric, poetry, and humanities years, the bulletin started in chronological order with the first year of college now titled the "freshman" year. It still listed the authors and books studied in Latin, Greek, English, and literature classes but also mentioned in distinctly smaller typeface "Accessory Branches" that were available to the students: history, elocution, voice, physics, chemistry, and modern languages. While the reference to accessory branches resembled the tone of Father Meyer's 1887 course of study, including non-traditional subjects was a start. In addition to the freshman year, the second year was now labeled sophomore year instead of poetry year. Also in this catalogue came a discussion of the philosophy year*s*, suggesting that more time was to be spent on this major subject. (The rhetoric year disappeared entirely.) The term *humanities* was now used for the last year in the academic department—what most readers would have taken to mean the fourth year of high school. Up to this moment, the academic department had been completed in three years. Now it was expanded to four, matching the timetable for American high schools.[41]

In the following school year, 1902-03, the terminology found in the *Marquette College Catalogue* went a step further. The last year of college was now described as both the "Class of Philosophy" and as "Senior Year." Almost as a counter to the bulletin's proto-Americanization, the "Prospectus" section (which always opened the catalogue by discussing specific policies regarding grading, punctuality, politeness, and holidays) now included a new entry, four-and-a-half pages in length, organized around three pedagogical themes: guiding principles in education, scope of Marquette College, and what kind of an education it gives. This rather wordy narrative presented a passionate defense of the college's traditional course of studies, without making it sound too old-fashioned. It emphasized "a drawing out rather than a putting in" and "branches of study" that were "mind-developing" and "character-building" rather than the "imparting of information." Electivism and specialization, hallmarks of the new American system, were fine for some schools, the essay admitted—and this was a significant concession— just not for Marquette. Readers of the prospectus (who were more likely to be parents than teenagers) were warned that "young students are not the proper judge of studies essential in life." "Such freedom of selection," while available at other schools, could be "injurious rather than beneficial to unformed youth." The essay concluded by elucidating the intellectual treasures of the *Ratio Studiorum*—but never mentioned it by name. Nor, curiously, was the word *Jesuit* ever used. The commentary did admit, however, that "an acquaintance with sociology, political science, and economic laws … [and] the constitution of the United States" was now part of the instructional program. It concluded with the observation that Marquette's "unwillingness to adopt extreme views with regard to electives, specialties, novelties and fads might more properly be urged as a proof that we have studied to some purpose the science of education."[42]

This essay remained in Marquette catalogues for years. Despite its unapologetic defense of traditional Jesuit education, this statement did not preclude curricular responses to newer fields such as the social sciences. By the next catalogue, the long-established habit of delineating the books and authors students studied each year was discontinued. Instead, the bulletin now outlined nineteen subjects that students studied during their four years at Marquette, including philosophy, physical culture, geology, and instrumental music. The emphasis was no longer upon the intensive, self-contained material of a given year (rhetoric year, for instance), but on exposures to nineteen different subjects over four years. Moreover, at the opening of the degree requirements paragraph in the 1903-04 catalogue, the phrase "unit hours of work" was mentioned for the first time, with seventy units mandated for the only degree available: a bachelor of arts. There were still no majors, but the subjects that students studied were presented as discrete intellectual exposures—as history, as physics, as geology—rather than themes (such as historical issues) touched upon while students concentrated on poetry for an entire year. This introduction of a broader array of exposures expanded when the unit hours of work grew from seventy in 1903 to one hundred and thirty in 1905 to one hundred and forty in 1906. In 1904-05, the conversion of the names of the four years of college to American designations was complete; students now proceeded from freshman to sophomore to junior to senior years. There were still no majors, however. Students still took years of Latin and studied classical literature, but the regime also included natural and social science classes as well. Even a "Teachers' Course" was added after being approved by the state board of examiners—a secular, governmental agency—in January 1905. And the pre-collegiate training was now referred to as "Academic or High School" rather than simply as "Academic." By 1906, traditional designations for the four years of high school as third academic, second academic, first academic, and humanities also disappeared, although the schedule of classes stilled referred to its hourly breakdown as "Recitations," suggesting that the instructional format remained quite traditional.[43]

This marriage of the Jesuit past with an emerging American present took place on different schedules at Jesuit colleges across the land. Marquette was in the vanguard of this change, as was its sister school in St. Louis under the direction of former Marquette president, William Banks Rogers. In Milwaukee, Alexander Burrowes and his able assistant, Vice-President Henry S. Spalding, engineered this revolution with a deft touch. (Spalding moved on to Loyola University in Chicago, where he established the sociology department and published a number of problem-oriented studies on social problems.) They accomplished this union of the *Ratio Studiorum* and an American style of higher education with little heartache and, remarkably, no acrimony—a style of leadership Burrowes later employed as provincial. Father President accomplished this reformation amidst preparations for the college's silver jubilee. At the same time that hundreds of friends and graduates assembled in Milwaukee to celebrate their pasts, Burrowes was retooling their alma mater's future. And it never interfered with their celebrations.[44]

THE SILVER JUBILEE

Marquette College's silver jubilee commenced with a pontifical high Mass in the Church of the Gesu at 10:30 a.m. on Monday, June 18, 1906. There followed a luncheon for about eighty clergy. The alumni later gathered at the Pabst Theater for an evening's entertainment. The Federation of Alumni Associations of Jesuit Colleges in the United States, representing eighteen institutions, scheduled their annual meeting to coincide with Marquette's jubilee. Tuesday was largely spent with federation matters, except for the fourteenth annual alumni banquet at the Pfister Hotel at 8:00 p.m. The following morning, a requiem Mass was held to memorialize deceased faculty, students, alumni, and benefactors. An elocution contest at the Gesu auditorium that evening recalled academic exercises from days gone by. The jubilee's final day opened with another Mass, followed by graduation ceremonies at the Pabst. By all accounts, the turnout for every event was magnificent. Local pride—a sorely desired commodity—was never more evident. In capturing the flavor of this moment, Father John Copus, future founder of the School of Journalism at Marquette, modestly characterized the first twenty-five years at Marquette College as "thorough but unostentatious work for the city of Milwaukee and the state of Wisconsin." In his two remaining years as Marquette's president, Alexander Burrowes took on the task of converting "thorough but unostentatious" into something more eye-catching: Marquette *University*.[45]

GREAT TRANSFORMATIONS
1906-1916

The most critical phase in the evolution of American higher education came, arguably, in the fifty years following the Civil War. Unprecedented demands were made upon post-secondary education by a nation transforming itself from a log cabin past to an urban-industrial future. Tax-supported universities offered dynamic alternatives to the older, smaller, undergraduate colleges built largely by religious denominations. Passage of the Morrill Land Grant Act in 1862 provided federal incentives for states to establish comprehensive universities whose missions differed markedly from those of faith-based schools. With a panoply of undergraduate and graduate programs as well as professional schools, public universities threatened to overshadow denominational colleges. Moreover, a handful of heavily endowed private institutions such as Johns Hopkins and Chicago elevated research to a prestigious status in the world of learning. Ivy League schools, including Harvard and Princeton, replaced their religious roots with updated ambitions more attuned to those of Hopkins and Chicago. Even smaller schools such as Wesleyan, Rochester, and Drake left their denominational origins behind as they identified with fresher conceptualizations of higher education.

For Catholic colleges—of more recent vintage with fewer resources than either land grant schools or heavily endowed, private universities—the 1871 observation of University of Michigan President James B. Angell (a firm advocate of "Christianity on campus") rang ominously true: "'In this day of unparalleled activity in college life, the institution which is not steadily advancing is certainly falling behind.'" With nearly five hundred Catholic students at Harvard and at least three hundred at the University of Wisconsin by 1907 (in a student body of nearly 3,000), the theologically wrapped cocoon provided by a Catholic college no longer served an increasing number of Catholic families whose incomes permitted their offspring to indulge in post-secondary education. The demise of Catholic higher education was not a certainty as the twentieth-century unfolded, but its slippage into a second-rate status became a possibility.

By the end of the nineteenth-century, America's university system championed service to contemporary society, emphasizing applied education for students and research for faculty. The natural and social sciences came of age during the late nineteenth century, whereas theology, once the mainstay of a collegiate education, was increasingly relegated to specialized departments or pushed off campus into seminaries. In an industrial and commercial age, professional programs in medicine, law, engineering, business, journalism, social work, and education focused on the workplace. Furthermore, American schools were influenced by the emphasis on faculty scholarship, first cultivated at

German universities. Unfettered inquiry into scientific mysteries governed by natural law, not divine intercession, became central to a university's mission by the early twentieth century, as "facts" became separated from "values." Whether in agriculture or sociology, university faculty pursued questions whose profundity seemed limited only by the scholar's intellect—and his or her laboratory equipment. Unraveling the wisdom of western culture through the memorization of specific canon (church-based or classically rooted) was challenged by contemporary learning styles that captured students' imaginations because new "truths" seemed to unfold before their very eyes. To engage in medical or metallurgical investigations required sophisticated training, outside the circumscribed boundaries of faith. Graduate study was now marked by tough-minded inquiry based on relentless research.

In the face of these developments, late nineteenth-century Catholic higher education was not steadily advancing. There was no such thing as applied Catholic instruction in electrical engineering, macroeconomics, veterinary medicine, or periodontal dentistry. Church teachings certainly informed medical education and scholasticism instructed twentieth-century morality, but doctrinal proscriptions tended to require compliance, not encourage originality. Depending upon the religious authorities who administered a particular college, these proscriptions might become so restrictive that they forbade what growing numbers of Americans embraced as legitimate lines of inquiry. Moreover, according to historian William Leahy, during the mid- to late-1890s a "spirit of repression" ran through the American Catholic Church, captured in Pope Leo XIII's encyclical "warning against erroneous ideas on faith and religious life." The modern collegian's inclination to ask whatever questions came to mind frequently encountered clerical admonitions. As historian George Marsden has sagely noted with regard to the survival of the Protestant faith at late nineteenth-century American campuses, the enemy of educational reformers was not so much theology as clerical authorities. As part of Catholic education's establishment, Jesuits were not alone in trusting Counter-Reformation pedagogies to instruct youth who zipped about in Model Ts.

In 1907, Pope Pius X condemned "modernism" and placed limits on some forms of scientific research. By the same year, only 53 percent of the 18,400 Catholics in American higher education attended Catholic colleges and universities. Whether they wanted to study bugs or marriage, these young Catholics found the lecture halls of non-Catholic universities, staffed with mostly non-Catholic faculty, addressing topics that captivated their minds or, at a minimum, promised them jobs. From where would the new century's Catholic intellectuals come? Bishop John Spalding from Peoria, Illinois, in his homily before the Third Council of Baltimore in 1884, boasted that when "'the first writers and thinkers of the day'" were Catholic, Church apologists would no longer have to prove that their faith was not at war with intellectual excellence. But what if those Catholic writers and thinkers graduated from non-Catholic universities? What kind of Catholic thinkers would they be when they reached intellectual maturity? If Harvard and Wisconsin were the destinations of young Catholic professionals, where did that leave Marquette College?[1]

Fortunately for Milwaukee's Jesuit university, Alexander Burrowes not only grasped what was transpiring in American higher education in the late nineteenth century, he had a strategy to involve Jesuit higher education in professional education and delivered on that plan during the same years that he was rewriting the *Marquette College Catalogue*. Burrowes did not, admittedly, have the prescience to address the role of academic research at a Catholic college. Another half-century of heartache and disagreement passed before that matter was adequately handled. Yet thanks to Father Burrowes, it was Marquette University—not Marquette College—that would tackle this next conundrum.

FIRST, A COLLEGE BUILDING

For Marquette, this transformation began amid the school's silver anniversary, at a time when people usually exult in the past, not plot the future. For more than a year before this jubilee, rumors circulated that the school was considering expanding into law, science, and, perhaps, medicine. Whatever tomorrow's academic plans might be, first something had to be done with the physical plant. Crowded hallways filled with more high school teenagers than undergraduates—with behavior frequently sinking to the youngest common denominator—forced senior administrators to revisit earlier plans to build a separate hall for the collegians. When the 1881 building was originally designed, blueprints included two companion structures that in combination created a quadrangle facing State Street. But the property between Holy Name Church and the college was filled with grandstands and playing fields, not classrooms. In 1893, property to the east of the Church of the Gesu had been set aside for a college building, but limited resources kept this vision from becoming a reality. By 1906, the university still owed $11,000 on its hilltop building and, after twenty-five years, still charged $60 a year for tuition. As many as twenty students (out of 106 in 1905-06) received free educations. (In contrast, Creighton University, the Jesuit school in Omaha, had been blessed with an endowment of $500,000 and therefore for a time permitted students in its classical course to attend free of charge in the true Ignatian tradition.) Alexander Burrowes, now in his sixth year as president (the longest in Marquette history to this point), sensed that the silver jubilee might provide the up-beat occasion to underwrite a new college hall. What alumnus or benefactor would refuse to contribute toward a magnificent structure to stand alongside the Church of the Gesu?[2]

As forward-looking as he may have been, Father Burrowes had no experience in directing capital campaigns. In fact, no one at Marquette knew how to acquire money other than borrowing it. Yet Burrowes intuitively understood that he needed to develop some kind of momentum to be successful at raising the $85,000 he needed for a college hall. Just as contemporary capital campaigns go through a "silent" phase during which the institution banks a substantial foundation of donations, Burrowes solicited $20,000 in February 1906 from an unidentified patron. Burrowes hoped others might emulate this generosity. The secret donor was described as a prominent Catholic who

Grand Avenue, looking west, circa 1881. Cross street at end of median is Eleventh Street. File 952

lived along Grand Avenue and—here the veil of secrecy slipped a bit—whose son was a Jesuit.

Within a short time, it became evident that this noble soul was Robert A. Johnston. Born of Scottish immigrants and to a father steeped in public service in early Milwaukee (including a stint as alderman and as city treasurer), Robert had served as an altar boy at St. Gall's and graduated from St. Aloysius Academy. In adulthood, he transformed his family's bread, crackers, and candy business into a baking goods empire that put him in a position to help create Nabisco (the National Biscuit Company). His wife, Ellen Story, came from an even more distinguished family, one whose ownership of a local quarry warranted naming a Milwaukee neighborhood and a parkway in their memory. Ellen received her schooling at Rockford College in Illinois, before marrying Robert in 1873 at the age of twenty-three. Thirteen years later, she converted to Catholicism after a lifetime as a Congregationalist, with a Marquette Jesuit serving as her spiritual guide. Founding members of the Gesu parish, the Johnstons lived eleven blocks west of the spot where Marquette College's new building would stand. Their son, Robert S. Johnston, graduated from Marquette before joining the Society of Jesus. With the Johnston family's gift in hand, Father Burrowes sought permission for a new college hall from the superior general in Rome as well as the provincial in St. Louis.[3]

Marquette's new structure was intended from the outset for undergraduates, not high school students. In the 1870s, this land to the east of Gesu consisted of dense woods, "traversed by a narrow cow path and a wagon trail" (eventually, Eleventh Street). To the north lay Camp Scott where Wisconsin soldiers trained during the Civil War. As early as January 1905, a year before the first Johnston family donation, school officials had sketched a rough floor plan for the new building. The local press saw these plans as an obvious move toward converting Marquette College into a university. The formal announcement of Robert and Ellen Johnston's offer came in February 1906. Months passed without news of additional gifts. Then, in early June 1906, local newspapers trumpeted details of Marquette's new edifice, a structure whose price tag had climbed to $110,000. Excavation could start any day. Although Father Burrowes had secured permissions from his religious superiors, fund-raising languished, unaffected by the school's silver anniversary. Held with great fanfare, the jubilee failed to spark the financial outpouring that Burrowes and Johnston anticipated.[4]

A strange quietude hung over the college throughout the summer and deep into the fall as some excavation took place. The college trustees amended the articles of incorporation to reflect that Marquette was now located broadly in "the City of Milwaukee," not necessarily "on Block One Hundred and Ninety-nine, in the Second Ward" as the original charter had stipulated. But no donor stepped forward to follow Robert Johnston's lead. Then, on Christmas day 1906, Milwaukee newspapers announced that a month earlier Robert and Ellen Johnston, in the name of their Jesuit son, had secretly presented Father Burrowes with two certified checks totaling $110,000, the entire amount needed to erect a college hall. In appreciation, the trustees offered to rename

Johnston Hall, with Mackie house on left. File 750

the institution *Johnston College* (not unlike what happened in Omaha at Creighton). Flattered, the family declined this honor. So the trustees named the building after Mr. Johnston.[5] Construction restarted. Additional properties were purchased south of the project site. By mid-May 1907, the new hall was far enough along to warrant an informal reception, with Mrs. Johnston in attendance. Unfortunately, Mr. Johnston was too ill to attend. The four-story structure included an attic and an astronomical observatory. Made with concrete floors (instead of the wooden frame of the old college building), Johnston Hall used an expansive array of windows to introduce natural light into the classrooms. Offices for administrators and a residence for the Jesuits occupied some of the first floor. A library dominated the second floor, with classrooms and laboratories for physics on the third floor and chemistry on the fourth. In the basement, a lunchroom adjoined a small gymnasium. Sadly, Robert A. Johnston did not live to see the fruit of his kindness. On August 15, 1907, just six weeks after the Jesuit community moved into their new quarters and a few weeks before students christened the new hall, the second great benefactor of Marquette College (after Bishop Henni) died at his Lake Beulah summer home in nearby Waukesha County. A funeral mass followed four days later. Some years later, his portrait was hung on the first floor of Johnston Hall as a reminder of the merchant's munificence to what, by the time of his death, had already become a university.[6]

A "NEW" MEDICAL COLLEGE

Marquette's conversion from a single-degree, liberal arts college to a multi-college university unfolded with remarkable ease. It did so because the institution's medical and dental departments did not have to be built from the ground up. In the spring of 1906, just weeks before the silver anniversary, an attorney representing Dr. William H. Earles, president and principal owner of the Milwaukee Medical College (MMC), visited Father Burrowes. The lawyer proposed a collaboration between the two institutions, though it was unclear exactly what that meant and how it might be implemented. For the moment, Father Burrowes failed to attend to this matter, probably because he was deeply involved in the jubilee and busy trying to raise funds for the new college hall. A college of medicine would have to wait.

A few months later, Father Henry Spalding (the college vice president) got together with a new friend, Henry Banzhaf (dean of dentistry at MMC), at a downtown restaurant. During their meal, Banzhaf once again raised the idea of the medical college's "affiliating" with Marquette. Rumors about Marquette opening programs in law, engineering, architecture, and medicine had been bandied about in the press for at least two years. The administration was clearly receptive to these ideas. Timing was critical. Spalding brought Banzhaf's proposal back to Father Burrowes. Within a short time, the superior general in Rome and the provincial in St. Louis provided canonical approval for Burrowes's plan. (As early as the 1840s and 1850s, both Saint Louis and Georgetown universities had sponsored medical schools, setting precedents upon which Marquette now drew.) With the silver anniversary behind him and the second

Johnston family gift in hand, Father Burrowes became receptive by early 1907 to a discussion of health care education.[7]

The Milwaukee Medical College (MMC) was a privately owned, for-profit corporation. It trained doctors, dentists, pharmacists, and nurses. Opened in September 1894 with ninety-six students, the medical college awarded its first seven MD degrees the following year. Graduation numbers ranged from four in 1899 to forty-three in 1903. Admission required a four-year high school education. Dr. Earles used two buildings that he owned on the southeast corner of Ninth and Wells streets, just three blocks southeast of the hilltop and another three blocks northeast of the fast-rising Johnston Hall. A five-story classroom building fronted onto Wells Street, and the second building, operated as Trinity Hospital, faced west onto Ninth. A member of the Association of American Medical Colleges, MMC struggled to maintain its professional licensure amid the rising standards in health care education. Every medical institution came under pressure to upgrade its faculty, classroom pedagogies, laboratory experiences, and clinical training. Heightened standards demanded greater financial investments, obligations that left MMC's minority stockholders dissatisfied. This situation was likely to get worse if the University of Wisconsin used taxpayers' dollars to open a medical program in the near future. (It did so in 1907.) The only viable option for MMC was an affiliation with Marquette. The question remained: what did *affiliation* really mean?[8]

Negotiations between Marquette and the medical college moved so quickly during the spring of 1907 that this question was never fully resolved. By May 4, the three priests who constituted Marquette's board of trustees voted to approve a change in the name of the institution and to adopt "proper resolutions for receiving the Milwaukee Medical College as a branch of [their] institution." The first action changed Section 1 of the 1864 charter to remove the words *Marquette College* and substitute *Marquette University*. In addition, the power of Marquette's trustees to grant "literary honors and degrees" was expanded to read degrees in "art, literature and science as … are usually conferred in similar institutions."[9]

As to the matter of affiliation, a second resolution designated the Milwaukee Medical College as "a branch" of the new university and urged formal contracts to effect this union. Ten days later, on May 14, 1907, officials from both institutions signed two agreements. The first outlined operational details for an affiliation. The president of Marquette became a member of the medical college's board of directors, but all property and appurtenances of the college remained under the care and control of MMC's owners. Marquette University was to have no financial control or responsibility for the conduct of business at the medical college, although the university president could advise on those issues. Marquette's president and its board of trustees in cooperation with the medical school's board of directors would "prescribe and lay out the courses of studies to be pursued in said Milwaukee Medical College." However, it was stipulated that "atheism, materialism, agnosticism, the non-existence of the rational soul, abortion, craniotomy, and onanism [masturbation] shall not be taught." Both boards could "nominate professors and teachers," although "physicians or surgeons known to practice abortion or craniotomy shall not be allowed to teach." In recognition of the large number of non-Catholics at the college, it was agreed that no "religious exercises shall be conducted at any of the annual commencements of said Milwaukee Medical College nor at any other exercises or functions of said College."

These agreements were binding for ten years; with appropriate warning, they could be terminated at an earlier date. Moreover, for the consideration of one dollar, the buildings occupied by the medical college's schools of medicine, pharmacy, and dentistry as well as Trinity Hospital remained available for purchase by Marquette at an amount to be determined five years after September 1, 1906. Marquette could, before September 1, 1911, extend that time frame for another five years if it wished. (On August 15, 1911, the university president did just that, preserving the school's interest in the property.) As a sign of the good will that permeated these discussions, on May 11, 1907, three days *before* the agreements were signed, Marquette trustees approved degrees in medicine, dentistry, and pharmacy for the students of the Milwaukee Medical College branch of Marquette University. Three days later, on the day of the signing, university officers hosted a graduation banquet at the Plankinton Hotel. Father Spalding welcomed these first graduates of Marquette University as they savored a banquet of chicken gumbo de Orleans, fillet of sole, sirloin, roast spring chicken, potatoes, green peas, olives, radishes, salad makings, vanilla ice cream, lady fingers, cheese, toasted wafers, and coffee.[10]

Almost overnight, Marquette College with its one hundred students became a university with more than three hundred students—most of them probably non-Catholic. The school now operated at two locations: Johnston Hall (which opened four months after the MMC-Marquette agreement) and the medical college buildings at Ninth and Wells. Father Burrowes had arranged this metamorphosis for the price of one dollar. During their negotiations, the two sides had conducted a detailed appraisal of the medical college and Trinity Hospital. Its equipment, including classroom seats, laboratory supplies, dental stations, and drugs for the pharmacy program, was valued at $27,920. The buildings with their various wings, a power plant, elevators, and fixtures totaled $153,532. Finally, the land itself (upon which today rests the north wing of the Milwaukee Public Library) was valued at $29,650, bringing the total to $211,102 (over $4,000,000 in 2005 dollars). In the entire state in 1907, only the University of Wisconsin had a curriculum and a student body that exceeded Marquette's.[11]

The next step rested with attorneys who needed to file the amended corporation papers with the Wisconsin secretary of state. University administrators had their own task: adopt a seal for Milwaukee's first university. A final design came together as quickly as the school's affiliation with the medical college. The seal's upper right-hand corner features a pair of wolves to either side of a kettle; this image represents the paternal side of St. Ignatius of Loyola's heritage. The Spanish word for wolf is *lobo* and for pot is *olla*. When contracted, *lobo y olla* forms the family name, Loyola. From his mother's side, the house of Onaz is represented by bars of red across a field of gold, creating seven stripes; this honors seven members of the Onaz family who fought against the French

Seal of Marquette University. File 1232

at the battle of Beotibar in 1321. The words *Numen Flumenque* ("Deity and the River") are linked to the image on the left side of the seal; there explorer Jacques Marquette is depicted pointing toward the Mississippi River. Alongside him is an American Indian. The speed with which the seal design and the medical school affiliation were completed allowed the June 1907 bachelor of arts graduates to applaud the seal at their commencement and claim the distinction as Marquette *University*'s first graduates—the same claim made by the MMC graduates a month earlier.[12]

TWO "NEW" LAW SCHOOLS

The harmonious manner of Milwaukee Medical College's affiliation with Marquette set the tone for subsequent expansions. Timothy Hannan, an 1895 Marquette graduate, approached Father Burrowes shortly after the MMC merger concerning a similar affiliation between his second alma mater, the Milwaukee Law School, and Marquette. Preliminary discussions moved so rapidly that the last page of the 1906-07 Marquette catalogue (printed in those days during the summer after the conclusion of a school year) carried a two-sentence paragraph alerting students to the likelihood that the law school and Marquette would effect a union before the upcoming fall term. The local press picked up this story, claiming that Lynn S. Pease, president of Milwaukee Law School, and Father Burrowes had already agreed to the final arrangements.[13]

Both the press and the catalogue were premature. The law school, like the medical college, was a proprietary corporation, although its brief history offered little hope of turning a profit. It represented the first, formal legal training program in Milwaukee. Up to this point, any individual who dreamed of practicing law "read" or "clerked" with an established attorney before taking the state bar exam. The law school provided systematic instruction to a larger body of students. In the beginning, it arranged for reputable lawyers and judges to offer lectures and supervise readings. After incorporation in 1895, the school scheduled formal classes at night, permitting attendees to retain their daytime jobs. By 1907, its directors sought to upgrade their program through an affiliation with the city's only university, hence Timothy Hannan's visit to Father Burrowes. But just as a merger seemed about to become reality, the directors had second thoughts. Over the next year, repeated inquiries by Marquette led nowhere.

Then, in the spring of 1908, these directors informed Father Burrowes's successor that although they were no longer interested in an affiliation, they were willing to sell their company for $6,000. Marquette administrators hesitated only because of the price. They had already obtained appropriate permissions from St. Louis and Rome. Unlike the medical college, the law school owned neither a library nor property. Its only value to Marquette rested in its reputation, developed over sixteen years. After considering their options, the university's board of trustees agreed to purchase the law school on two conditions: the law school's directors had to promise not to establish a competitor for a minimum of five years and the second installment of $3,000 would not be paid until at least fifty students were enrolled in the university's newest department. Both parties approved the sale in May 1908. The law students simply stood up one day, exited their rented classrooms on Grand Avenue, and marched over to Johnston Hall. As part of the final agreement, any previous graduate of the Milwaukee Law School who had passed the state bar exam was retroactively eligible to receive a LLB (bachelor of law) from Marquette University—and nearly everyone chose to. So at its June 1908 commencement, the university conferred degrees in the arts, law, medicine, dentistry, and pharmacy. Graduation ceremonies became so time-consuming that the long-standing tradition of student performances was soon discontinued.[14]

University administrators spent the summer of 1908 recruiting United States Circuit Judge James G. Jenkins to serve as law school dean, deciding how much money to spend on a law library (estimates ranged from $2,500 to $10,000), and considering whether the night school schedule of the Milwaukee Law School should be expanded to include a day program. This last suggestion caused consternation among some of the law faculty. Nonetheless, university authorities moved ahead with day classes, scheduled from eight in the morning until noon. Special lectures by "eminent members of the legal profession" were held at five in the evening to accommodate both sets of students. Then just before the beginning of the fall 1908 term, a *second* proprietary law school became available if the university paid $40 for the students and $175 to cover this school's advertising bill from its summer session. Marquette's discussions with officials from the Milwaukee University Law School (which had opened in 1905) were concluded in a single day. The law school's eleven students moved into Johnston Hall the next day. As with its medical school branch, Marquette University created a viable school of law without having to labor through the academic birthing process. For $6,215, Marquette had acquired two cohorts of law students. The biggest problem was where to put them.[15]

The crowding of high school students with collegians had forced Marquette administrators to construct Johnston Hall. Now, mixing day and night law students with students from arts and sciences (as well as engineering) proved unsatisfactory. In the fall of 1908, seventy-three law students squeezed in among bookshelves holding the Jesuit community's reference volumes. Clearly, Johnston Hall was already overcrowded. In 1910, the board of trustees eased this problem by renting the former residence of Dr. William Mackie, located on the corner of Eleventh and Grand, east of Johnston Hall. A friend of the university purchased the two-story house from Dr. Mackie's widow for $30,000 and agreed to lease it to Marquette. He also offered to sell the building to the Jesuits at their convenience for $500 more than he had paid. The university completed this purchase in 1912.[16]

By the time these law school negotiations concluded in the late summer of 1908, Father Burrowes was already in Chicago, having been named president of St. Ignatius College. Within a year and half, he transformed this liberal arts school into Loyola

Mackie House, circa 1920. File 881

Father Alexander J. Burrowes. Burrowes Biographical File

University, with programs in law and medicine as well as arts and sciences. And a new campus on the city's north shore was about to open. After his time in Chicago, Burrowes moved on to Saint Louis University for two years, stepping down in 1913 to become superior of the Missouri Province. Although Alexander Burrowes's name is not familiar to current administrators, faculty, students, and alumni, it ought to be. He may have been the most instrumental visionary ever to manage the university's curriculum. Burrowes thoroughly renovated Milwaukee's unpretentious hilltop college. With a timely assist from Robert and Ellen Johnston, he put Marquette on Grand Avenue. He crafted a re-articulation of the collegiate course (renamed the College of Arts and Sciences following the medical college merger). And he negotiated his way through a thicket of conversations to add medicine, dentistry, pharmacy, nursing, law, and engineering to the school's curriculum. During his stewardship, the institution's student body grew from 56 students to 503 in eight years. By the fall of 1908, Marquette was on the verge of competing with the University of Wisconsin within the Badger state and with Notre Dame across the upper Midwest.

Taking the reins from this gifted educator was Father James McCabe, who had arrived as vice president in September 1907, five months before his elevation to the presidency. McCabe had served at St. Mary's College in Kansas City, first as vice president for seven years and then as president for eight years. At Marquette, McCabe unabashedly followed Father Burrowes's lead—and then proceeded to best his confrere by introducing coeducation to Catholic higher education.[17]

MORE NEW PROGRAMS

James McCabe became president of Marquette University on February 10, 1908. Sixteen days later, following a recommendation from Father Burrowes, the board of trustees authorized a Department of Applied Science and Engineering to open the following fall. Tuition was set at one hundred dollar per year, forty more than that charged arts and sciences students, because specialized equipment was required. The preliminary plan called for a two-year engineering program, with students transferring to the University of Wisconsin for their final two years. To head this new unit, Father McCabe followed his predecessor's advice and looked to Cornell University for a dean. After an exchange of correspondence with Cornell's president and with several candidates, McCabe settled on Dr. John C. Davis. Almost two dozen students enrolled during engineering's inaugural semester. Their courses took place in whatever space was available in Johnston Hall, with arts and sciences and law receiving first priority. Drafting, for instance, was taught in the basement. The success of that first year generated so much enthusiasm among local manufacturers and prospective students that the administration changed its mind and initiated a full four-year engineering program in 1909.[18]

Shortage of space was the engineering faculty's biggest challenge because they needed laboratories in addition to classrooms. Renovations were made to the hilltop building on State Street to accommodate these students, but the real answer rested in a separate building. The first year's successes led the administration to consider plans, complete with design specifications, for an impressive $200,000 structure west of Gesu (where Marquette Hall now stands). The estate of Miss Elizabeth Plankinton had sold this property for $27,500 in July 1908. Sketches depicted a blocky building that was somewhat larger but less elegant than Johnston Hall (even though they were both designed by the same architect). Rumors circulated regarding a new law building on the same site. Instead, the trustees spent $25,000 to purchase a duplex and an adjacent Chinese laundry behind Gesu on Sycamore (Michigan) Street. At the conclusion of the 1909-10 school year, engineering students and their faculty, including Dean Davis, demolished the western half of the duplex as well as the laundry and in their place erected a three-story, brick and concrete structure. Six years later, the eastern half of the

Bellarmine Hall. File 115

duplex was leveled and a matching section added to the 1910 wing. Named Bellarmine Hall after the famous Jesuit theologian and cardinal of the Counter-Reformation, this building housed the College of Engineering until 1941. Subsequently, Bellarmine hosted the U.S. Navy, the graduate school, *Teatro Maria*, and, most recently, the Gesu Parish Center.[19]

From the outset, practicality was a key to Marquette's engineering program. University officials turned to experts in industry (Allis-Chalmers, for instance) and in education (Milwaukee Trade High School) to determine whether an on-campus laboratory program or an off-campus shop approach was preferable. Late in its first year, engineering students took to the field when they laid out new baseball and athletic grounds at the hilltop. In 1912, the college installed an automobile testing plant in Bellarmine Hall. Four years after the program opened, its first nine graduates received degrees in civil and electrical engineering. They came from as far away as British Guiana and Hungary and as close as the Gesu parish school. The engineering faculty made their mark on Milwaukee as well as upon their students. For example, John Davis, the first dean, later became director of the city's municipal research bureau and his successor, J. C. Pinney, had served as city superintendent of buildings and bridge construction before coming to Marquette.[20]

The university's academic expansion paused only briefly before adding three more departments in 1910 and 1911. A School of Business Administration within a College of Economics was inaugurated in September 1910 at the urging of a board of corporate advisors created by Father McCabe. These industrialists and businessmen wanted young, well-trained, mid-level managers for their factories and offices. Faculty arrived with expertise in finance, accounting, banking, fire insurance, water transportation, life insurance legislation, boiler insurance, traffic problems, and fire prevention. Gustave Pabst and J. E. Uihlein (from Schlitz) lectured on the brewing industry. Recruited from the University of Chicago, the first dean, Dr. William C. Webster, quickly made connections with the local community. During the school's first year of operation, it received a $2,000 donation from the daughter of Samuel Marshall (a founder of Marshall & Isley Bank) for a library to be named in her father's honor. In recognition, Samuel Marshall's portrait joined Robert A. Johnston's in Johnston Hall. Meanwhile, the Johnston family continued its generosity toward Marquette, leading the administration to rename this new unit the Robert A. Johnston College of Economics.[21]

Creation of the economics college provided a serendipitous opportunity for yet another initiative, fostered this time not by powerful industrialists, but by a little-known, black-robed member of the faculty. Born in Surrey, England, John E. Copus went through three careers during his lifetime. As a public school teacher in England, he had the honor of meeting Charles Dickens. Copus launched his second career after becoming a Catholic in 1876 at the age of twenty-one. He moved to Canada to become a journalist, at first working for his brother. Later, Copus spent nearly a decade with the *Detroit Evening News* until, in 1888, he entered the Society of Jesus, his third career. As a working journalist, John Copus was repulsed by the propensity of his colleagues to fake stories and felt that the public's insistence on sensationalistic articles (arising from the era of the "yellow press") was undermining his profession's ethics. He maintained that "'the press, next to the pulpit, is the most powerful influence for good.'" To regain its footing, journalism needed an academic base within an urban setting, making Milwaukee a perfect venue for this redemption. Moreover, he insisted that Marquette's Catholic mission would benefit the journalistic profession and the public alike. Even during his years as a Jesuit, Father Copus maintained a rigorous writing schedule, making a mark for himself in fiction for young boys. Here he spun morality lessons within adventurous storylines.[22]

After John Copus persuaded Father McCabe to open Catholic higher education's first journalism program, the new school offered three courses of study: a two-year program leading to a diploma, a three-year program leading to a bachelor of journalism degree, and a four-year program leading to a bachelor of arts in journalism. As dean, Copus sought to combine the Jesuit tradition of classical studies with professional training. During their opening semesters, journalism students occupied themselves with liberal arts classes such as English, literature, and American political history. Later, they turned their attention to professional instruction in news writing, ethics, and the theory and practice of journalism. Seventeen students enrolled in the first year, a number that doubled by the second. As leader of the new journalism school, John Copus was so admired by local journalists that his lengthy battle with throat cancer in late 1914 and early 1915 was covered by the press with daily updates. (Incredibly, it snowed on the day of his funeral: June 14, 1915.)[23]

The final piece in Marquette's revamped academic mosaic came in the fall 1911 when the university opened a conservatory of music under the leadership of Liborious Semmann. The university had affiliated with the Wisconsin Conservatory of Music during the 1910-11 school year, but subsequently decided to build its own program with classes in public school music, vocal culture, violin, piano, mandolin, banjo, guitar, and selected brass instruments. Befitting the traditional Jesuit emphasis upon elocution and performance, school officials added a dramatic arts option to the conservatory's offerings. In its early years, the music program worked out of a rooming house (said to be haunted) on Tenth Street, a half-block south of the original college building. During its two decades as part of Marquette, the conservatory specialized in music lessons for children and young adults, drawing students from throughout the metropolitan area. It also offered college-level classes and in 1912, Anton Bumbalek became the first recipient of a bachelor of music degree. Conservatory commencements, other than for those receiving university degrees, were typically held at the Plankinton Hall Auditorium. They attracted large audiences. Also drawing crowds were the conservatory's operatic performances when this program was available in the 1910s. The music program moved on campus in 1918, occupying one of the Plankinton mansions off Fifteenth Street. The College of Music closed in 1930, a victim of the Great Depression.[24]

Expansion of Marquette's curricular offerings during the first decade of the twentieth-century was not unique among Jesuit colleges. The University of Detroit opened

Students of the Marquette Conservatory of Music, circa 1917. File 970

programs in engineering, law, and business during the same period. Creighton University provided professional training in medicine, law, pharmacy, and dentistry. Saint Louis University revived its medical school in 1903 and on the east coast, Fordham opened law and medical schools in 1904. In Cincinnati, Xavier College's new chief executive, remembered for his "great energy," established first a school of commerce, accounts, and finance and then a school of journalism and advertising, followed by a school of law. Given their shaky financial situations, Jesuit institutions had to consider what they could afford and what roles these new departments would play within their respective metropolitan areas. Loyola College in Baltimore did not add its school of business until 1937, whereas Canisius College in Buffalo did not establish a similar school until 1958, during Dwight Eisenhower's second administration. Thanks to Father Burrowes's resolve, Marquette was able to expand with haste, little expense, and remarkable harmony. This last attribute would be sorely missing during the university's next adventure.[25]

WHAT TO DO WITH THESE (WOMEN) STUDENTS?

For hundreds of years, the *Ratio Studiorum* had operated within a single-sex environment. From pre-adolescence through young adulthood, students at Jesuit institutions never encountered females as classmates and seldom as instructors. (Creighton did have a female instructor in the rudiments—preparatory—course when it opened in 1878.) Essentially, there were no female peers or authority figures for the boys, and the Society of Jesus never needed to apply the *Ratio Studiorum* to a gender-inclusive academy or college. No operational manuals explained how to monitor hundreds of young women and men as they passed each other in hallways and classrooms. At St. Gall's, Holy Name, and Gesu parishes, boys and girls were separated in different elementary schools, one taught by the Jesuits and another by an order of nuns. Because they worked at single-sex institutions, most American Jesuits did not interact with women on a daily basis. Although Oberlin College in Ohio had introduced coeducation to American higher education in 1833, by the time Marquette College was established, the trend leaned toward women's colleges such as Wellesley and Smith, not coeducational institutions.

The American Catholic Church separated males and females in parish schools, in the Holy Name and altar and rosary societies, and (for young people at least) at different sides of the communion rail. Theological beliefs as well as practical considerations drove these divisions. In the Catholic faith, both sexes had divinely assigned roles in human society. The path to salvation for females centered upon the family, upon childbirth and mothering. This was the way God intended the human species to operate. Thus, it should come as no surprise that the first college degrees awarded to women at a U.S. Catholic college did not come until 1899. On the eve of the twentieth century, six women graduated from the College of Notre Dame in Maryland. Two decades later, there were still only a handful of Catholic colleges for females, with estimated enrollments of 1,500 students. In addition to distinctive paths to heaven, church leaders also feared the proximity of serious sin in every encounter between males and females. Keeping young boys and girls apart was not only easier to administer, it was morally preferable.[26]

When Marquette College abided by the dictates of the *Ratio Studiorum* during its first twenty-six years, no one questioned its male-only world, just as no one questioned this practice at schools directed by the Dominicans, Augustinians, or Christian Brothers. But the same document that converted Marquette from a college to a university (its affiliation with the Milwaukee Medical College) carried the potential for trouble—or change. On page eight of the 1907 *General Announcement* (catalogue) for the medical branch of Marquette University, published within weeks of the affiliation, the mission of this department read: "the object of the school is to give such professional training to men *and women* that will make them successful in the actual practice of medicine." (Italics added.) This same inclusive term also applied to dentistry and pharmacy. The medical branch's nurse training option, a non-degree program, was of course entirely female at this time. Clearly, the care of female students (about half a dozen in the medical program alone) now fell under the administrative purview of Marquette, but for the moment at least, they attended classes at Ninth and Wells Streets, two and a half blocks from Johnston Hall. Female students never used the arts and sciences building. Georgetown, Creighton and Saint Louis universities had made similar allowances, over the years, in either their law or medical programs.[27]

The reality of coeducation could no longer be finessed, however, following Marquette's acquisition of the Milwaukee Law School which, because of its for-profit status, was open to both sexes. On the day the final purchase agreement was signed, law students left their rented classrooms at Eighth and Grand and moved into Johnston Hall. Within that cohort was at least one female student, Katherine R. Williams. Females were no longer two and a half blocks away at the medical school complex. They were inside Johnston Hall. Williams completed the 1907-08 school year in the main college building and apparently attended classes there for the next two years, although she may not have entered the facility until evening because she attended the night program. In June 1910, Williams received an LLB, perhaps the first women ever to receive such a degree from a Jesuit-run university. She proceeded to work for the state of Wisconsin. A devout Catholic, she was a member of the National Council of Catholic Women (eventually president), the Milwaukee Archdiocesan Council of Catholic Women, and the Catholic Instruction League. Before Williams completed her studies though, four other women had graduated from Marquette. In June 1909, Jennie A. Lambach, Maud Pratt, and Martha A. McCullough earned their MD degrees, and Daisy Grace Wolcott received a bachelor of science degree, all from Marquette's medical branch. (Four years later, Wolcott received her medical degree from Marquette University's newly reorganized School of Medicine.)[28]

What these firsts might have meant in the long run remains unclear because an even more daring step was taken the same month that Lambach, Pratt, McCullough, and Wolcott completed their course work at medical branch—and thus at Marquette

University. This other move, as audacious as it was, forced Marquette to become a role model for other Catholic institutions. Father James McCabe had arrived in Milwaukee after many years in college administration at St. Mary's College in Kansas City and he was no stranger to difficult decisions. Early in 1909, McCabe received a report from a Jesuit, Father Cornelius Shyne, who foresaw an impending crisis in Catholic elementary and secondary education in Wisconsin. Not a single, four-year Catholic women's college existed in Wisconsin. Religious women, the instructional bulwark of parochial schools, could not earn college degrees in the Badger State. Shyne predicted that in the near future Catholic schools might be overwhelmed by the academic superiority of public education. Only die-hard Catholic parents would send their children to schools staffed by ill-prepared teachers. Furthermore, there was no university in Wisconsin where the handful of sisters who had earned baccalaureate degrees from out-of-state schools could obtain advanced degrees so that they might become college instructors for the next generation of parochial school teachers. Once again, the superior resources of secular schools threatened Catholic education.[29]

President McCabe acted with resolve. From September to June each year, Johnston Hall was overcrowded with male students from law, engineering, and the arts and sciences. After commencement day, however, these young men scattered to the winds, leaving the building empty except for a handful of Jesuits who used the residential quarters. Father McCabe had already planned a unique undertaking for the summer of 1909: the first summer session in the history of Catholic higher education, to begin on June 28. These classes were intended for "deserving [male] students who [found] it impossible to attend the regular courses of our colleges and universities" because they had to "work during the day or during a part of the ten months usually devoted to school tasks." The curriculum promised instruction in German, French, Latin, general chemistry, analytic and organic chemistry, physics, mathematics, drawing, and history. The staff consisted mostly of laymen, including Dean John Davis of engineering. Suddenly, without the sanction of his religious superiors, Father McCabe expanded the phrase *deserving students* to include religious sisters and lay women. The doors to Marquette University had been unexpectedly thrown open to females, including Sister Generose Cahill, OSF, who successfully completed a course that summer on the short story and novel taught by Father Copus. To stop what he perceived to be a gross breach of tradition and protocol, Father Rudolph J. Meyer—head of the Missouri Province, a former president of Marquette College, and a champion of conservatism—demanded that Father McCabe cancel what remained of the summer session. Instead, Marquette's president proceeded along his chosen path, appealing the provincial's directive to the superior general in Rome. (There may never have been a better example of the witticism: "It is easier to ask forgiveness than permission.")[30]

Bureaucracies often take an interminable amount of time to arrive at momentous decisions, and such delays can cause great anguish for those who wait. In Marquette's case, time benefitted inclusiveness. The summer of 1909 ran its course without word from Rome. When no guidance was received from father general by June1910, Father

McCabe approved another co-educational summer program. In the following fall, the School of Journalism opened its doors. Dean John Copus had long supported female journalists. He felt that they could aid a profession sorely in need of ethical cleansing. As classes started in September 1910, Copus admitted women to the first "J-School" at a Catholic university although, it must be conceded, journalism held its classes in the evening, when most arts and sciences students were not present. At the conclusion of the 1910-11 academic year, a third summer school session took place, with a robust mixture of nuns, lay women and at least sixteen men. By the fall 1911, the university added the Conservatory of Music, another female-intensive program taught at a remote location. Marquette now enrolled a growing contingent of female students, although many did not actually take classes inside Johnston Hall.

Finally, in the spring of 1912, nearly three years after Father McCabe's original request, Rome responded to his appeal. Permission was granted for the inclusion of "'ladies and even nuns to attend'" Marquette's summer session. By the following summer, at least forty-three sisters attended classes with nearly two dozen men. Within another four years, these summer session students even included three Jesuit scholastics. Course offerings now included Greek, English, philosophy, and education, the first three requirements for a bachelor of arts degree. In 1913, Sister Mary Remi, BVM, received a bachelor of science degree, the first nun to graduate from Marquette. The following year, she and two other nuns earned bachelor of arts degrees, the signature achievement at a Jesuit university. Six nuns received undergraduate degrees in 1915; seven in 1916; and ten in 1917. One year later, Sister Mary Stanislaus, SSND, became the first woman to receive a master's degree at Marquette. By the end of the twentieth century's second decade, more than three dozen nuns had been awarded baccalaureate degrees from Milwaukee's Jesuit university. Within a short time, a handful of other Catholic schools (including Catholic University) followed Marquette's lead.[31]

Differences over the propriety of coeducation deeply divided the Marquette Jesuit community. Questions were also raised among the Milwaukee faithful. Throughout the spring of 1911, leaders among the area's Catholic women deliberated over a women's college, either as a free-standing institution or as one affiliated with Marquette. Katherine Williams, with her recently minted law degree, was an outspoken proponent of such a college. The model for these women was Radcliffe College's association with Harvard University and Barnard College with Columbia University. But when the cost for such an undertaking climbed to $150,000, supporters hesitated. About the same time, the Sisters of Charity from Dubuque, Iowa, wrote the rector at Catholic University asking for assistance in developing an accelerated program whereby a few of their sisters might become college instructors in time for the opening of a Milwaukee women's college in 1912. Archbishop Sebastian Messmer endorsed these conversations. He was decidedly uneasy about coeducation at Marquette and he opposed a Catholic women's college under lay management because he did not trust its moral and religious content. The prelate preferred that a single order of nuns run a college that would have an association with Marquette. Despite the genuine enthusiasm for this project, nothing came of it. For the moment, the education of Catholic women in Wisconsin remained Marquette's responsibility.[32]

The only disappointment in this story was the absence of Father McCabe. During the summer of 1911, before Rome's final decision was handed down, McCabe was replaced after only three years. The Jesuit House records suggest a suddenness and a sadness to this move: "The change is not made with much festivity. We are sorry to lose Fr. McC...." Jesuit presidents could be reassigned at a moment's notice. On any given day, a stranger (of sorts) might suddenly occupy the rector's chair in the Jesuit refectory. Throughout his time in Milwaukee, McCabe had battled health problems. He may have been excused simply to provide a respite. However, it is also possible that those who opposed him on the coeducation issue may have had a hand in his early depar-

Father James McCabe. McCabe Biographical File

ture, especially since Father Meyer remained provincial until 1912. McCabe himself remained unapologetic. Later, as president of Xavier University, he opened the door for nuns and laywomen to pursue course work for a bachelor of arts degree.[33]

The institutional adjustments imposed by this unplanned presence of female students at Marquette can be considered from several perspectives. Milwaukee newspapers tended to focus upon the distinctiveness of Marquette's "girls." For example, one paper singled out Gabriella Tomkiewicz for her pharmacy studies in a 1908 piece entitled "Polish Girl Is Druggist." Four years later, Frances Mertes, daughter of a drug store owner, was described as "the only girl graduate" and as the first "Hartford [Wisconsin] girl ever graduated as a Pharmacist." In the same graduation class, Anna H. Burmeister had a long article devoted to her life story from Waukesha County to Marshall Field's in Chicago and, finally, to Marquette's School of Dentistry, with plans to later pursue a degree in medicine. "'I did no more than other girls would have done or can do,'" she explained. "'All that is required is determination.'" A more substantial depiction of a female student from Marquette appeared in a 1912 clipping heralding her first-place finish in a competition among nine leading dental schools. Six years later, note was made that the only woman to pass the Wisconsin bar exam that year was a graduate of the Marquette University School of Law.[34]

Student publications rarely rose above stereotypes when depicting female peers. A 1912 article in the *Marquette University Journal* described the women in pharmacy as "seven young ladies" who offered "a very good representation of the fair sex." Four years later, the same publication ran an essay, entitled "Marquette Loves Its Women." This piece highlighted the female staff members in Marquette's first fund-raising campaign. Yet the adjoining photograph depicted a curly-haired little girl in her Sunday finery. By the mid- to late-1910s, the *Marquette Tribune* routinely ran features such as "Is Woman Cautious?" "Co-eds Satisfied with Marquette," and "Marquette Co-eds in Definition of Ideal Man Give Him Leeway in Personal Habits." Even basic human necessities, such as a restroom for women, warranted sexist remarks: "A box of powder, a powder puff, and a mirror. The girls are happy." The student yearbook was no different. The only woman graduating from pharmacy in 1915 was described as "distinctly feminine" because "she never hesitates to tell what she knows." The only woman graduating from the College of Economics was spoken of in a positive light because after "marked attention on the part of some [male] students," she "announced her intention of specializing in household economics rather than in business economics."[35]

However light-hearted and innocent these remarks may have sounded to the male ear, they reflected the uncertain status of women on campus. Were they full-fledged Marquette students or temporary anomalies? No model existed for Milwaukee's Jesuit university, no pioneer to emulate. Marquette was the first Catholic university in the world coping with males and females in the same classrooms and hallways. The Catholic Church's teachings limiting the role of women outside of marriage and its even more adamant exclusion of women from liturgical roles did not help Marquette authorities find balance in their day-to-day choices. By 1916-17, the university had attracted almost one hundred women, including forty in nursing, seventeen in journalism, twelve in economics, nine in music, six in law, and smaller numbers in the health sciences. (This does not include as many as 290 females in non-credit music classes.) By early 1917, there were enough women at Marquette to warrant steps being taken to form a club for "co-eds." For the moment, organizers chose to keep their plans a secret—perhaps because of the dismissive or sarcastic remarks they might have received from male colleagues.[36]

But what must have felt like two steps backward for every step forward could not have been further from the truth. Whatever time it took to find a measure of acceptance, the fact is that Marquette was at the forefront of Catholic education worldwide. Xavier University in Cincinnati did not admit nuns and laywomen to its non-degree summer session classes until 1914; three years later, its Saturday extension classes, leading to a bachelor of arts degree, became coeducational (at Father McCabe's direction); and in 1918, religious women finally graduated from the university. At Detroit, the turning point came in 1911 when a series of popular psychology lectures taught by a Jesuit were opened to women; the commerce and finance program admitted females when it was established in 1916; women graduated from the university's law school for the first time in 1917; and Saturday and evening extension classes became coeducational in 1925, with the summer session opening its doors to both sexes that following summer. In Buffalo, Canisius College opened its summer school and extension program to nuns in 1919. Saint Louis University began training female teachers in 1925; two years later, Loyola in Baltimore did the same. Santa Clara and Saint Joseph's did not admit women until after World War II.

At Marquette, any improvement was progress. After all, the U.S. Constitution did not guarantee woman suffrage until eleven years *after* Father McCabe forced the issue of coeducation. In 1910, Marquette's College of Economics, with its business administration and journalism departments, opened with gender-inclusive admission policies. On paper, every academic unit at Marquette but one was now coeducational. (Although the College of Engineering did not enroll a single female until World War II, it did not openly exclude women.) Marquette's one male-only unit was the College of Arts and Sciences. It remained so until 1926.[37]

RETAINING THE JESUIT TRADITION

The College of Arts and Sciences epitomized Jesuit traditions at Marquette (including the matter of male-only admission). In bringing aboard dentistry, law, engineering, and the other new programs, Fathers Burrowes and McCabe had taken on the task of converting these professional programs into Jesuit products. They were missionaries, not in a foreign land but in foreign subject areas. Through the revision of course requirements and course content, through faculty development and student activities (such as the sodality), these presidents pledged to instill a Jesuit imprint onto the study of medicine, law, engineering, and other professions. This was a mighty task, with few examples on how to accomplish it.

However, there was no such question regarding the bachelor of arts program. The newest programs could disappear overnight, but as long as the liberal arts remained, Marquette would be a Jesuit institution—a financially troubled institution perhaps, but faithfully Jesuit. Eliminate the bachelor of arts curriculum and there might be a licensed corporation bearing the name *Marquette University*, but it would not be a Jesuit university. These subtleties were lost on almost everyone at the university outside of the Jesuit community. No matter how Catholic in faith or how committed as educators, the lay faculty were not prepared to deliver a Jesuit education. Even if they were graduates of Marquette College, they did not have adequate formation to complete the school's Jesuit mission. Burrowes and McCabe had committed this institution to find a way whereby *every* professional school, in conjunction with arts and sciences, could represent the future of the Jesuit past.

At the Milwaukee Medical College complex on Ninth and Wells, health science education was so far beyond the expertise of Marquette Jesuits that university administrators allowed the medical college personnel to operate what became essentially an unsupervised satellite. As for law, engineering, business, and journalism, certain Jesuits characterized them privately as "vocational schools," that is, something distinctly different from—and lesser than—arts and sciences. Still these professional schools were now part of Marquette University, so the Jesuits needed to provide them with some exposure to the *Ratio Studiorum*, while conceding that most of their curricula had to be taught by lay professionals, not Jesuits. Whenever possible, liberal arts courses in rhetoric, literature, history, or philosophy became requirements for professional degrees. When possible, the university assigned Jesuit instructors to these classes. In addition, priests and scholastics taught the Christian doctrine classes. Marquette Jesuits were often overworked because, beyond their academic responsibilities, they also had pastoral obligations such as weekend confessions and Sunday Masses. Meanwhile, the lay faculty in law, engineering, and business had no idea how to make their classes live up to the promises of a Jesuit education. For this reason and others, the Jesuit community came to believe that the instructional standards among lay faculty in these professional programs left something to be desired. Could this explain why as late as 1911, the College of Arts and Sciences used only four non-Jesuits: two in contemporary foreign languages and two in chemistry?[38]

In expanding Marquette's academic offerings so quickly, Burrowes and McCabe may have been influenced, in part, by the need to survive financially, although the record is not clear on this point. The number of students enrolling in the collegiate course would not have sustained the school indefinitely after 1900. In 1883-84, college classes began with twelve students. Three years later, the number of collegians on the hilltop rose to thirty-eight. It stayed in the thirties until 1891-92 when it climbed to fifty-two. Nineteenth-century enrollment peaked at seventy-seven in 1896, before dropping back to fifty-five the following year. This number remained stagnant over the next decade, climbing to ninety-three in 1909-10 and then falling off to fifty-five the next year—the same total as 1897. Each fall, administrators awaited September registration, wondering how many graduates of the academic course might move on to the collegiate course. If twenty or so new college students enrolled, it was time to smile; if only half that number, anxiety set in.[39]

Meanwhile, the university's overall enrollment soared, with 292 new Marquette students taking classes at the medical department alone in the 1907 fall term. Two law schools in the fall of 1908 added another 127 students—49 more than arts and sciences had that year. Whereas the liberal arts enrolled 55 in 1910-11 (its thirtieth year of operation), the medical college had 452 students, law 125, and engineering 88. That same year, the College of Economics alone (with 108 in business administration and 14 in journalism) more than doubled enrollment in the arts and sciences. The same dilemma appeared at other Jesuit schools. At Fordham in 1911-12, for example, there were 160 students in the collegiate course, but 164 in medicine and 255 in law. At Loyola in Baltimore, the high school financially underwrote the college program.[40]

What the Society of Jesus believed to be the heart of Marquette University (or any Jesuit institution) was being overtaken by hundreds of students who were not adequately trained in the arts and sciences, were not Roman Catholic, and were, in some instances, female. It was evident that teenage boys in Milwaukee in the early twentieth century did not want to submit to a high school curriculum that emphasized classical languages and literatures. However, without this background, they were not eligible for the bachelor of arts program. This forced many Milwaukee high school graduates into Marquette's professional schools. Even those who did attend Marquette University Academy or High School were not enthusiastic about pursuing a classical education during their college years. Because it was almost impossible for women to study classical languages and literatures at girls' high schools, they too were ineligible to enter the College of Arts and Sciences (even if there had been a willingness to admit them). With a lack of interest in Latin, Greek, and philosophy among males and a lack of opportunities for the study of Latin, Greek, and philosophy for females, how could the *Ratio Studiorum* survive at Marquette? And how could the university remain Jesuit without a viable bachelor of arts program?

One way to keep the collegiate course vital would have been to recruit from outside the pool provided by the university's own high school. As the years went by, the administration stepped up its advertising in the local press, promoting the professional programs as well as liberal arts. Notices appeared in more than a half-dozen English-language newspapers as well as in the German- and Polish-language presses. Over time, these promotions took on a high-sounding tone, boasting of Marquette's importance in Milwaukee and describing the school as a local "asset." These ads often employed the phrase "Milwaukee's university." Out-of-town newspapers picked up this story of how a small, local college had blossomed into a complex university. By 1908, administrators were becoming more creative. Three thousand letters were sent to high school graduates across the Midwest. Of 380 responses received, 220 asked about engineering, 80 about law, and 40 about arts and sciences. Clearly, the public did not favor the one college dearest to every Jesuit. Scholarships provided a final but insignificant recruitment tool. There were only five, full-tuition scholarships, given to male graduates from local parish schools: four scholarships supported studies at the academy and one supported a young man through both his academic and collegiate courses.[41]

If the professional schools drew the largest share of student attention, then the administration had to insure that these programs remained under Jesuit tutelage. The average Jesuit priest was not trained to be a dean of medicine or engineering. So Marquette presidents turned to a familiar Jesuit strategy to guarantee that there was at least one senior Jesuit in every college: they appointed a *faculty regent* to every unit without a Jesuit dean. With the College of Arts of Sciences under the control of a Jesuit until the late twentieth century, only professional schools required regents. In theory, this priest collaborated with the lay dean. In practice, each faculty regent served as the eyes, ears and, if necessary, mouth of the president. Sometimes, the faculty regent was familiar with the professional curriculum, the faculty culture, and student life. More often, it was a bit of a stretch. Father Henry Spalding, the university's vice president, became the first such regent, appointed to the law school in 1908. Until the 1950s, this type of assignment remained a vital marker of Marquette's Jesuit identity.[42]

Commencement for School of Pharmacy and Nurses' Training Program, Davidson Theater, 1911. File 400

LEADERSHIP CHANGES

The word *regent* took on an additional meaning in January 1909, when Father McCabe appointed a board of regents (mentioned earlier in relation to the origins of the College of Economics). These lay advisors, whose actual influence fluctuated depending upon the president, were intended to create a "bond of union or connecting link between the University Faculty [meaning the Jesuits] and the citizens of Milwaukee." The board was "to advise with the Faculty of the University as to the best means and methods for meeting the higher educational requirements of the city, and to represent to the public-spirited citizens the ways and means by which they may render the activities of the University efficient for the best interests of the community." Because Marquette wanted "to give to the people of Milwaukee, and to others of the surrounding towns and cities of the middle West, the advantages of a complete and up-to-date University" and because the Jesuits had worked "without salary … for more than twenty-five years," McCabe hoped that "the funds necessary for such a development [might] in large part be furnished by the public-spirited citizens."

This reference to giving suggests that fund-raising was a central obligation for the board of regents, although such a conclusion would be misleading. Father McCabe wanted Marquette to become the equivalent for Milwaukee of what the University of Chicago was to its host city. A great city, according to his reasoning, demanded a great university. Upon their graduation from Marquette, young professionals assumed vital positions locally in medicine, dentistry, law, engineering, and journalism. These freshly certified experts were the offspring of a great university. A twentieth-century education prepared young men for their entrance into a diversified job market. (Father McCabe still saw the world in terms of a male workforce.) To assist the university in preparing these young leaders, the school turned to its board of regents. Who better to represent the university before political officials, corporate executives, and industrial supervisors? Yet they were decidedly not decision-makers. Not until the days of President Albert Fox in the mid-1920s could these regents regard themselves as anything more than experts-on-call.[43]

Nonetheless, a remarkable list of local leaders served on the first board. Dr. Gerhard Bading, then health commissioner and later mayor of Milwaukee from 1912 to 1916, joined Patrick Cudahy, General Otto H. Falk, Judge James G. Jenkins (first dean of the law school), Harry S. Johnston (a son of Robert A.), Gustav Pabst, and Archbishop Sebastian Messmer as well as senior executives from Gimbel Brothers, Allis-Chalmers, and The Milwaukee Electric Railway and Light Company. There were twenty-four regents in all. The list included Protestants as well as Catholics—and, not long thereafter, Jews. The local press became fascinated with the non-sectarian nature of the board, speaking with amazement at the mixing of people of different religions at a faith-based enterprise. For its part, Marquette had a role to fulfill. One of the board's first members, publisher William George Bruce, explained how Milwaukee had "its promotional bodies … 'to foster, protect and advance the commercial, industrial and civic interests'" of the city. "Marquette University must become a potent factor in that movement. It must labor for a greater Milwaukee industrially, commercially and numerically; for a more beautiful Milwaukee, physically and externally; a better Milwaukee morally and educationally. It must become an organized and intimate part of the [city's] life." This link between Marquette and its host city—the same relationship emphasized in recruitment ads—meant a great deal to the regents. The board aimed to position Marquette as a more prominent player in the life of the city, which may explain its promotion of a business college in 1910.[44]

This intensifying connection between Marquette and Milwaukee's civic leadership was evidenced in October 1911 at a dinner welcoming a new president to the university. In July, Father Joseph Grimmelsman, president of Marquette from 1889-91, replaced Father McCabe. On the evening of October 7, two hundred guests representing the professional, industrial, political, and educational elite of the city, county, and state gathered at the Pfister Hotel. An assembly of this magnitude—of Catholics and non-Catholics, of members from the Marquette community, and those who had no ties to the institution—was unprecedented. It reflected the university's ascending prestige locally, a stature tied to the new professional programs. In the past, the laying of cornerstones and the dedication of buildings attracted every Catholic club in the area. But the 1911 inaugural banquet was a first. It included speeches from not only the board of regents, faculty, and alumni, but also from Wisconsin Governor Francis E. McGovern (labeled "a renegade Catholic" in the Jesuit community diary) and Charles R. Van Hise, president of the University of Wisconsin. Judges and retired military officers attended as did tannery magnates Charles F. Pfister and Gustav J. A. Trostel. In his response, Father Grimmelsman took a very blunt tone, noting that Marquette had not received as much financial support as it deserved (except from the Johnston family). He did not, however, press his point. In an editorial published two days later, the *Evening Wisconsin* lauded "Milwaukee's Great University." About the same time, Marquette published a twelve-page brochure using the same designation: "Marquette: Milwaukee's University."[45]

A SCHOOL OF MEDICINE

During his second stint at Marquette, Joseph Grimmelsman faced two great challenges. The first arose from a combination of previous administrations' inadequate oversight of the medical branch and a general stiffening of national standards in medical education. In May 1907, without a ripple of concern, the Milwaukee Medical College had affiliated with Marquette University. On the surface, these two institutions maintained a harmonious relationship for the next few years—at least as regards financial concerns. But with regard to the department's academic standing, it was a different matter altogether. Anxious to force substantial improvements in American medical education but cornered by an ethics code that forbade physicians from criticizing one another, the American Medical Association recruited the Carnegie Foundation for the Advancement of Teaching to undertake a thorough evaluation of the country's medical colleges. In a scathing report published in 1910, the author of this evaluation, Abraham Flexner, condemned the state of medical education across America in general and in Wisconsin in particular. After visiting Marquette's medical branch in February 1910, he dismissed the laboratory facilities as "meager," with the bacteriological lab consisting of "several wire baskets of dirty test tubes." The clinical facilities were said to be "extremely weak," with the school's dispensary being "ill equipped." In conclusion, Flexner described the two medical schools in Milwaukee as "without a redeeming feature."

So it was no surprise that in 1912, the American Medical Association's Council on Medical Education threatened to downgrade Marquette's medical branch to a Class C rating unless it made specific improvements. When these changes were not forthcoming, students worried that they would soon be attending a third-rate institution whose diminished credentials would place them at a disadvantage in the job market. Preparing for the worst, a group of medical students asked the Wisconsin College of Physicians and Surgeons (WCPS), located on the north side of downtown Milwaukee, to consider their admission. A private institution owned by Dr. A. Hamilton Levings, the city's second medical school was in no better shape than the Milwaukee Medical College, according to the Carnegie foundation. Its bacteriology laboratory was "poor and very disorderly" and its anatomy lab was "very poor," without a complete skeleton. There was not a single full-time faculty member in 1910. Consequently, the American Medical Association undertook to investigate Levings's college as well as Marquette's.[46]

Meanwhile, the troubled dean and faculty at Marquette's medical branch faced an unsympathetic accreditation agency and a disgruntled student body. As for the university administration, according to the original affiliation agreement, the Milwaukee Medical College's financial management had been left to its founder and his co-investors. After Dr. William H. Earles died in 1908 (about a year after his college's affiliation with Marquette), one of his sons assumed control of the college's assets in the name of his mother and siblings, but did so from out-of-town. Its shareholders spent as little as possible to maintain the institution's three buildings, its equipment, and the instructional program. The Carnegie foundation considered the medical college "nominally" under university supervision. Father McCabe recognized the seriousness of this situation, even before the AMA's threat. In early 1911, he instructed the university's lawyers to draft resolutions proposing that Marquette lease the medical college's property (and presumably its equipment) and take over complete oversight of the instructional program. Nothing came of this effort, however, perhaps because of the succession of university presidents. Father Grimmelsman took a different tack, appointing Father Charles Moulinier as faculty regent at the medical college in late 1911. He gave Moulinier authority to review all student applications, to review the participation of medical students in the university's varsity athletic program (which the administration believed had become the chief recruitment tool for the medical college), and to work with the college dean "to stop all *hazing* and very especially all '*cutting*' of classes … as far as possible." The department's academic troubles remained essentially unaddressed.[47]

By late 1912, the refusal (or inability) of the medical college dean to address the American Medical Association's demands meant that a Class C rating was imminent, a classification that insured Marquette medical degrees would not be recognized by twenty-seven state licensing boards. (The most important licensing board of all, the Wisconsin Board of Medical Examiners, was considering action to become the twenty-eighth state to treat Class C schools in a similar manner.) Rumblings of a possible student walkout grew throughout November. Rumors swirled in the local press that Marquette would soon take over the Milwaukee Medical College and that the Wisconsin College of Physicians and Surgeons would likely follow. The university's board of trustees warned the Earles family that Marquette might refuse to award degrees to the medical college's seniors. Every player in this crisis, including the Council on Medical Education, held meetings during the last months of 1912 to consider the situation. At one point, the medical college threatened to dismiss any student who spoke to reporters. At eighteenth- and nineteenth-century colleges, student riots, including damage to property and assaults on faculty, were commonplace, but the December 4, 1912, walkout at Marquette's medical branch was unprecedented. En masse, students marched from their college buildings at Ninth and Wells to the Wisconsin College of Physicians and Surgeons at Fourth and Reservoir. When the Wisconsin College's dean accepted the Marquette enrollees, his school grew in a matter of hours from eighty to three hundred and thirty students. A month later, in mid-January, the AMA's Council on Medical Education acted on its threat, downgrading *both* the Milwaukee Medical College and the Wisconsin College of Physicians and Surgeons to Class C schools. Confusion reigned.[48]

Telephone wires began to hum. Everyone wanted to discuss the matter with other sides of this controversy. The problem was there were at least six sides: the owners of the Milwaukee Medical College, its administration, the owner and administrators of the Wisconsin College of Physicians and Surgeons, the university, the students, and the American Medical Association. The dean at the Milwaukee Medical College resigned. The son of the original owner of this medical college returned to town to handle matters in person. The Marquette University Board of Trustees met nearly every other day in the weeks before Christmas 1912. Into this chaotic mess stepped the dean of the dentistry program at Milwaukee Medical College. Dr. Henry Banzhaf, a former Milwaukee school board member who was once talked about as a candidate for mayor, had maintained a private practice before assuming the deanship at Milwaukee Medical College in 1902. Administrators and lawyers from the two medical colleges as well as Father Grimmelsman now turned to Banzhaf to save the situation. As for the dean, it was a simple matter of saving the medical college's dental program, an endeavor he had devoted himself to for more than a decade.

Amid this swirling mayhem, Banzhaf negotiated two settlements. The first involved the university's purchase of the Milwaukee Medical College's equipment for $7,000 and a lease of the latter's buildings: Trinity Hospital, the adjoining classroom building on Wells Street, and the nurses' residence across from the hospital on Ninth Street. In the second agreement, Marquette agreed to purchase the Wisconsin College of Physicians and Surgeons, whose history went back to the 1893. Dr. Levings had originally asked for $55,000, an offer that Banzhaf turned down. The sides subsequently agreed to a price of $35,000. To pay for this acquisition, Father Grimmelsman sent the dental dean to brewing executive Joseph Uihlein. The latter graciously lent the entire $35,000 through his family's Second Ward Savings Bank in installment payments suitable to Marquette's chief executive. As a questionable reward for his role as intermediary, Dr. Banzhaf was appointed superintendent of Trinity Hospital, now renamed Marquette University Hospital, even though he also stayed on as dean of dentistry. Banzhaf immediately left for the Mayo Clinic in Rochester, Minnesota, and later for New York City, where he underwent months of intensive training as a hospital administrator. Unbeknownst to him and his family, this was only the beginning of an extraordinary career at Marquette.[49]

Medical students at both schools cheered Banzhaf's resolution to this crisis. They now attended what was titled the Marquette University School of Medicine. They moved contentedly into the Wisconsin College of Physicians and Surgeons building at Fourth and Reservoir, where extensive renovations were made over the next year and half. Modern classrooms replaced two amphitheaters whose design represented an older style of medical education. The upper two floors of the five-story building housed the anatomy department. A floor below were laboratories for pathology and bacteriology. A chemistry lab occupied most of the second floor. The physiology laboratory used space on both the first floor and in the basement, near a 3,000-volume library. Clinical training sites were expanded from St. Joseph and Trinity hospitals to include St. Mary and Miserecordia hospitals as well as St. Vincent's Home and the Milwaukee Infants' Home and Hospital. Free public dispensaries operated at both the Reservoir and the Wells Street sites. The "medics" (as the yearbook referred to them) stayed at the Wisconsin College of Physicians and Surgeons until a new structure was built on campus in 1931. The fruits of Banzhaf's and Grimmelsman's efforts were realized in February 1915 when the Council on Medical Education awarded the Marquette University School of Medicine a Class A rating. The following year, the university was recommended for membership in the American Medical Colleges Association.

At the same time, the dental, pharmacy, and nursing programs took over the Milwaukee Medical College buildings. Dentistry students appreciated the university's efforts, promising "hearty co-operation in striving to make this a school of which we may all justly be proud." Within a few years, this department became one of the first dental programs in the country to switch to a four-year curriculum. Nursing students saw their clinical opportunities expand when arrangements were worked out to assign them to Mount Sinai and Emergency hospitals as well as the university hospital. Remodeling of the latter permitted four new wards to be opened, including an eye, ear, nose, and throat facility on the second floor, and a maternity and nursing center on the fifth floor.[50]

FISCAL WOES

The sizable debts incurred during the founding of Marquette's school of medicine precipitated the second great trial of Father Grimmelsman's presidency because these new obligations placed an untold burden upon the university budget. Every extra expense worsened an already serious situation. On the main campus, a space shortage had developed within a year of Johnston Hall's opening. This moved the administration to buy the duplex on Michigan Street for the engineering students. University officials also leased and then purchased the Mackie house for law students. Then the journalism and music programs opened. University administrators also felt obliged to address the question of athletic facilities for the intramural program. Students had raised the issue of a gymnasium for years. The most common suggestion called for a gym to replace the hilltop building once the academy moved to the land west of Gesu Church (the property previously promised to engineering and law). Financing all these projects weighed heavily upon McCabe and Grimmelsman. Furthermore, the lingering embarrassment felt over the failure of the alumni and other university supporters (beyond the Johnston family) to respond to the informal capital campaign of 1906 remained on the minds of senior administrators.

Late in McCabe's presidency, the university became surprisingly forthright in admitting its financial woes to the public. The *Marquette College Journal* openly called for help in April 1911. It cited the shortage of space for the law and engineering programs, and spoke of the students' desire for club rooms, reading rooms, and a large gymnasium. Two months later, the president startled everyone by using a significant portion of his time at the podium during commencement to bemoan the fact that he was "unable to announce any bequest or foundation of such large amounts as the University needs at the present time to carry out the program for developing Marquette University and making it such an institution as the people of Milwaukee may feel proud of." He acknowledged the "generous assistance" of $6,000 from the estate of Mrs. Herman Kroeger, $2,000 from Elizabeth Marshall for the economics college library, and yet another beneficence ($3,000) from the Johnston family. The president also singled out the alumnus who had purchased the Mackie mansion specifically for use by the law school. Gifts were usually noted in each issue of the *Marquette College Journal*. In the fall of 1914, for example, modest donations were received from Charles F. Pfister ($250), Gustav Pabst ($250), Fred Vogel ($125), and Herman and Otto Falk ($125). The university also recognized "a friend" who wiped out a $657 deficit in the college of economics. The university's relentless budgetary woes were even mentioned in a newspaper article that praised Marquette's rapid growth over the past few years. Late in his narrative, the author suggested wealthy individuals might consider making Marquette the beneficiary of their wills.[51]

The need for additional classrooms and for a student union or gymnasium may have contributed to Father McCabe's health problems. They certainly worsened Father Grimmelsman's. It did not help that Jesuit authorities in St. Louis added to this burden. They wrote: "Don't you think it is high time for the payment of your debt to the Province, i.e. … the interest on loans to Marquette University and the Gesu Church? We have large outlays and other heavy obligations have to be met very soon and our available funds are low." When Grimmelsman first replaced McCabe in mid-

Marquette buildings after 1913, clockwise from top left:
Nurses' dormitory was located on the southwest corner of Ninth and Wells (current Wisconsin Club parking lot);
Conservatory of Music was on Tenth Street, behind current County Courthouse;
School of Medicine was at Fourth and Reservoir;
College of Law was housed in the Mackie house;
College of Engineering occupied Bellarmine Hall;
Schools of Dentistry and Pharmacy (& Trinity Hospital) were situated on the southeast corner of Ninth and Wells;
the Administration building (to right) is Johnston Hall;
Marquette Academy (High School) athletic field looking northeast toward Pabst Brewery. File 245

1911, it is likely that the new chief executive had been advised to slow the pace of institutional change. This would have certainly been consistent with Grimmelsman's disposition and reputation. In 1915, for example, he authorized sections of the arts and sciences entry in the catalogue to be rewritten so that they now resembled traditional conceptions of the bachelor of arts degree found in the *Ratio Studiorum*. With the exception of the medical school episode, Father Grimmelsman's second term in office was marked by curricular stagnation and fiscal crisis. Enrollment in arts and sciences stumbled along, unchanged. The new professional programs brought in hundreds of new students but increased expenditures for facilities, faculty, equipment, and library acquisitions. Overall, budgets were so tight during Grimmelsman's second term that the university could not afford to publish catalogues in 1913 and 1914. Students with outstanding bills were excluded from classes in the middle of the spring 1916 semester. The central administration threatened to discontinue the junior prom and the new yearbook until they could prove their fiscal viability. Several attempts by Grimmelsman to solicit financial support came up empty.

Suddenly, in early 1915, while in Europe for the election of a new father general, Grimmelsman suffered a stroke that left him paralyzed. For days, the Jesuit community in Milwaukee was kept in the dark regarding his condition. When he finally returned to Milwaukee in a weakened condition, Grimmelsman took things easy. He failed to attend to many presidential responsibilities, as he and the Jesuit community awaited the appointment of a successor. Finally, on September 1, 1915, the new executive arrived, brimming with confidence. Father Herbert C. Noonan knew Marquette, having graduated from the college in 1896. He had earned a master's degree from Saint Louis University and a PhD from the Gregorian University in Rome. Only forty years of age, Noonan understood that the first task facing him was the issue of undercapitalization.[52]

THE UNIVERSITY'S FIRST CAPITAL CAMPAIGN

Two months after taking the reins from Grimmelsman, Father Noonan moved in a direction never seen at Marquette. He signed an agreement with Frederick C. Barber, a New York fund-raiser, to direct a $300,000 short-term, capital campaign. The university had already received pledges totaling $123,000 from a group of donors, including the Knights of Columbus and the Catholic Order of Foresters. Railroad magnate James J. Hill had offered $25,000, tied to certain conditions. In an unusual move, the administration also sought support from secular organizations, including the Carnegie Foundation for the Advancement of Teaching. The chief fund-raiser was promised a 5 percent commission on all contributions beyond these initial pledges. By the time this campaign officially kicked off in mid-March 1916, the university's aspirations had grown to $500,000, with the focus clearly upon a building fund. But ill will developed between the hard-nosed university president and his distracted fund-raiser. At the same time that Barber was running the Marquette effort as an out-of-town "director general," he was also involved in a one million dollar campaign for Occidental College in Los Angeles. Moreover, Barber criticized both Marquette's stature within the local community and the businessmen who backed this campaign. Barber resigned just before he was fired. Another New Yorker, Mrs. Elizabeth Rudyerd Currier, was brought in as the new campaign director. She earned high marks for her work over the next few months.[53]

In the spirit of the ongoing war in Europe, Currier divided hundreds of university supporters into seven "divisions," each headed by a "field marshall." A division had five "teams" under the direction of "captains." Within each team were as many as ten "corps" (workers), matched in pairs. And this was just the local "army." Another division handled statewide solicitations and an executive council oversaw general operations as well as donations involving more substantial sums. Noted civic leaders headed committees on speakers, outdoor displays, headquarters, finances, news publicity, and advanced pledges. Mrs. Currier prepared an instruction pamphlet, detailing every step of the process for field workers. It explained how daily updates should be handled, how good prospects must be cultivated with second and third calls, and how not to use the telephone among the general population because it allowed potential subscribers to decline to make a donation without embarrassment. Every team that raised $5,000 could "bestow a [$60] scholarship" in the "Liberal Arts Department."[54]

Two days before the kickoff dinner, more than a thousand students, assembled by college and department, marched in a torchlight parade despite a heavy snowfall. Flanked by a path of green and red lights, they moved down Grand Avenue from Johnston Hall, crossed the Milwaukee River, circled the city's financial district, and paraded back up Grand toward the university. A local dealer loaned the parade-organizers nine automobiles. On their way, the crowd passed a giant, clock-like tote board on the east wall of Gimbel's Department Store, overlooking the river. The board recorded the campaign's successes in $1000 increments. The kickoff dinner itself was a glorious affair with words of encouragement from the university president, from Mayor Bading (who served on the board of regents), and from Archbishop Messmer who, in light of the Lenten season, lifted the abstinence laws for the entire two-week campaign.[55]

The first full day of work was Tuesday, March 14. Over the next twelve days, subscriptions arrived at headquarters in every amount possible. A newsboy turned over a quarter to one member of the executive council, explaining that was all he could afford. A janitor at the academy offered $5. Senior medical students chipped in $1,255, the pharmacy seniors $225, and the journalism students a similar amount. The Boston Store offered $1,000, a confectioners' club $100, a dental supply outfit $500, a dairy $250, and the men's club and women's club of Marshall & Ilsley Bank jointly contributed $338.75. From Marquette College's first graduating class, Francis X. Bodden contributed $200. In the middle of the campaign, former president William H. Taft visited Milwaukee, offering encouragement and guaranteeing the campaign's success because, as he said, "'You have a woman at the head of the movement.'" The governor of Wisconsin also provided verbal support, although it is unclear whether his encouragement included a material expression. The Uihlein family offered $10,000, the largest gift until Mrs. Robert A. Johnston raised her total contribution to $75,000. The Miller Brewing Company subscribed for $5,000 and the Pabst Brewing Company for $2,000. The wealthiest merchant in Wisconsin, Charley Toy (whose Wells Street mansion the university eventually purchased) offered $500. *The Marquette Campaigner*, a daily newsletter written and printed by the journalism students, kept the army of volunteers inspired with stories of generosity and with financial updates. The local press in Milwaukee lavished the campaign with free publicity through headlines, articles, and features. Every part of Milwaukee joined in the spirit of the moment but one. Only the alumni association, in the words of one Jesuit, remained "far from loyal" and "largely ungrateful." Otherwise, it was a special time for Marquette.[56]

The civic aspirations for this unprecedented effort were revealed in a campaign pamphlet. It explained how Marquette had recently grown into a large institution that served the "civic, social, educational and business" interests of the city through the $1 million that the university, its students, and faculty spent annually in Milwaukee; and how 31,000 "needy persons" received assistance from the school's two free dispensaries and the dental school's infirmary. This was the first time that the university had ever drawn attention to the services it provided within the local community. Other campaign literature reminded Milwaukeeans that new buildings, erected on the strength of this endowment, would serve a non-denominational student body, especially in the professional schools where over two-thirds of the students were non-Catholic. After all, the piece hailed, Marquette "belongs to the entire city."

In the end, this superb effort collected almost $550,000, an unbelievable sum for this era. Congratulations flooded in. Father McCabe sent a warm letter, lauding "the grand triumph." (He also observed that he had doubted whether such a success was possible given the "religious prejudices in Wisconsin.") The students responded in the *Marquette University Journal* proclaiming "$500,000 as an Eye Opener." In the fall of 1916, Father Noonan noted the increased attention Marquette had received from potential faculty members. Within a month of the campaign's conclusion, a senior administrator boasted that plans were underway to make Marquette the "largest institution of its kind in the world." Perhaps the university had been too successful, for within days of this boast four doctors were indicted in Chicago for issuing fraudulent medical diplomas bearing the name of Marquette University.[57]

STUDENT LIFE

When President Grimmelsman had sent Father Moulinier to the Milwaukee Medical College as faculty regent in 1911, two of the three problems this Jesuit intended to remedy concerned student life: the role of football as a recruiting tool for the medical college, and the excesses of hazing and cutting of classes at that branch. A college-level football program, initiated in 1902, had replaced baseball as the most popular varsity sport at Marquette within a decade, much to the dismay of the Jesuits. The central administration resisted the fans' fascination with the gridiron, whose popularity at Marquette mirrored national tendencies. College football was building momentum toward its golden era in the 1920s. Yet in the first decade of the twentieth-century, executives in higher education and even as manly a politician as Theodore Roosevelt raised concerns over the level of violence associated with college football. In October 1911, when a thousand Marquette students gathered for a football rally in an orderly manner, the Jesuit community diary actually voiced relief that the event had not become unruly. Three years later, another Jesuit disapproved of the "vulgar songs and personal remarks" that erupted at a Marquette football game. The vice-president was instructed to renounce such behavior.

Physical exercise was a tradition at Jesuit institutions. But the priests favored intramural, not varsity sports. With its stress upon advanced skill levels, varsity athletics eliminated a majority of the student body from the benefits of physical competition. In issue after issue of the university catalogue, the only athletic body listed among approved student organizations was the Marquette College/University Athletic Association, which emphasized all-student facilities, not varsity sports. Baseball remained an important springtime activity, whereas basketball and track struggled to gain attention. It is ironic, then, that the first Marquette athlete to participate in the Olympic games was broad-jumper John Joseph Brennan in 1908.[58]

Already strapped for funds, university administrators committed very few dollars to the football program. They simply maintained "Marquette Field," the cinder-covered lot west of the old Marquette College building. Because this field was also used for baseball and track, a six-foot fence rimmed three sides to prevent loose balls from interfering with streetcar traffic or threatening pedestrians. Neighbors protested, claiming that the fence lowered property values. (Among these neighbors was the Pabst brewery, north of the field across Prairie—later Highland—Avenue.) After the alumni converted the former boys' school at Holy Name into a gymnasium and library in 1899, the university encouraged students to use this facility. But it quickly deteriorated without routine upkeep and was razed in 1908. Father McCabe heard the student demands for an authentic gymnasium and, years later, so did the ex-baseball star and now Marquette president, Herbert Noonan.[59]

Nothing bothered the central administration more about football than its cost. In 1909, the program ran a deficit. When losses reoccurred three years later, the Jesuit faculty abolished athletics for a minimum of one year. Upon news of this action, the students staged a protest, first at the medical college and later, in conjunction with the alumni, at the Gesu parish auditorium. Fans promised to work down the $15,000 deficit through fund-raisers such as a theater party held in April 1913. The administration relented. Student efforts paid off during the following season when the football program earned its first substantial surplus ($500) in history. The creation of a single, unified alumni association in 1915 may have been hurried along by the administration's refusal to provide greater support to the football team. In creating this association, Marquette alumni followed the lead of peers at other institutions in becoming sponsors for athletics in general and football in particular.[60]

In addition to concerns over the misuse of football at the medical college, Father Moulinier also attended to hazing. For years, freshmen at Marquette had been required to wear blue "beanies" with a yellow button. A feature of American college life throughout the nineteenth and twentieth centuries, hazing was an activity that easily got out of hand. At Marquette, this point was reached in 1915. The previous year, "the Student Council ruled that all Freshmen in the University be obliged" to wear the beanies. During the fall 1914 term, upperclass students in dentistry praised the loyalty of their freshman for faithfully wearing their "gold-lettered 'Skullcaps.'" Arts and sciences students received compliments on their "pretty blue" caps. But everything soon went overboard because in late October 1915, Dean Henry Banzhaf suspended the dental school's *entire* junior class for hazing a first-year student. On the day in question, what was described as "a dappily-attired" freshman strutted past the junior "dents" as they exited their building on Wells Street. The first-year student apparently failed to demonstrate a proper sense of humility toward his elders who, in turn, chased him for several blocks onto the college athletic field. When caught, this unfortunate freshman was dumped, fully clothed, into a locker room shower. Father Coagley, the principal at Marquette Academy, ended the assault. All sixty-three juniors in dentistry were implicated. Each was required to report to Dean Banzhaf.

When confronted by challenges from the administration and faculty, nineteenth century American college students maintained a "code of honor," in Helen Lefkowitz Horowitz's phrase. They preferred expulsion over the ostracism that would result if one student informed on another or failed to stand united against institutional discipline. Accordingly, in a letter dripping with insolence, the junior "dents" at Marquette delivered a resolution signed by all but two of their classmates. They promised "to act as a body and as a class in any further action taken by the Faculty." If the intention of the faculty was "to make an example of one or two or three members of our Junior Class by way of expulsion, then let it be further resolved that we as the Junior Class do and will act in a body and claim the privileges and share the burden of expulsion." They refused to "tolerate disgrace to be heaped upon anyone, two or three of [our] members." This bold challenge came, ironically, only eighteen months after the dental students had promised their unfailing loyalty to Marquette following the central administration's rescue of the Milwaukee Medical College and the Wisconsin College of Physicians and Surgeons in January 1913. In marked contrast to the juniors, the freshmen (on behalf of their "dappily-attired" comrade) sent a letter of "regret" to the dean, promising henceforth to be "sincere, faithful and obedient student[s]." They admitted that in the past their class spirit may have been too riotous and apologized for "cutting" classes "without permission of the Dean or Registrar." Father Noonan was beside himself, insisting that the defiant letter from the juniors was "'too ridiculous to answer.'" The last newspaper accounts covering this episode reported that four juniors and, strangely, the victimized freshman were suspended.[61]

The relative orderliness of a small liberal arts college on the hilltop had been shattered with the addition of two medical colleges and two law schools as well as engineering, business, journalism, and music programs in only four years. In fact, the audacious challenge of the junior dentistry students in 1915 suggests just how much things had changed within a short time. The priestly authority of Marquette administrators was tested by the addition of hundreds of new students, most of whom had not faced the disciplinary regime typical of Catholic grade and high schools. An average Marquette student's willingness to submit to a religious authority figure in 1915 differed markedly from that of a previous generation. These adjustments in the makeup of Marquette's student body help explain the declining membership in organizations whose roots could be traced back to the origins of Marquette College. The sodality, the library association, the glee club, and the mandolin club remained fixtures at the university, but their relative importance waned. At times, the sodality's numbers diminished so dramatically that Jesuits and students alike sought to revitalize an association that could be found at every Jesuit institution. In 1912, Catholic students from across the campus considered creating a new organization that would "bring about a closer religious and social relation between these respective departments."

In the place of the more traditional associations, newer organizations appeared. A few such as the acolythical society (which provided servers for liturgical events) had a religious mission. Most resembled the *Marquette Journal* (the principal student publication in the days before a campus newspaper or a yearbook) and the engineering association, organizations centered upon professional training. In 1915, the journalism school undertook to distribute a yearbook, the *Hilltop*, and on September 30, 1916, a group of journalism students published the first 500 copies of the *Marquette Tribune*. This first edition sold $300 worth of advertising, a matter of some concern since the students had put up their own money the previous summer to purchase the printing equipment and a Stonmetz cylinder press. By the third issue of the *Tribune*, they were cranking out the paper in the southeast corner of Johnston Hall. A consistent outlet for student opinions—at least supervised opinions—was now part of the university culture. For its part, the Jesuit community struggled with not only the matter of coeducation, but also a growing student body whose backgrounds, attitudes, expectations, and ambitions differed strikingly from those of the smaller, more homogeneous groups of the previous century.[62]

A striking example of how twentieth-century student life differed at Marquette from an earlier era could be seen in the weekly schedule of dances and smokers. Students assembled after hours, on their own, in organized leisure activities, often with both sexes present. This was not their fathers' social calendar. Change was in the wind when a prom, hosted by the law, medicine, dentistry, and engineering students, was scheduled for Milwaukee Auditorium's Juneau Hall on March 31, 1910. A year later, this event climaxed a full week of activities. Father Charles Moulinier's participation on the planning committee for the prom provides an interesting insight into the Jesuit's reaction to the development of a university-based social calendar. It suggests the administration's willingness to tolerate, if not encourage, activities involving both male and female guests. By the 1915-16 school year, dentistry, economics, engineering, law, pharmacy, and journalism each sponsored their own dances. Most dances took place in the early winter or late spring in order to avoid abstinence restrictions during Lent. Male-only smokers were especially popular. Departments, professional and local fraternities, and the alumni association all sponsored gatherings where the emphasis was upon camaraderie, card-playing, billiards, cigarettes and cigars, and (if appropriate) alcohol. In the autumn of 1915, for instance, Alpha Gamma Phi sponsored a smoker on October 6, Alpha Kappa Kappa gave one on October 11, Phi Beta Pi did the same the following night at the Blue Mound Club, and Alpha Chi wrapped up the week on October 13.[63]

By the end of the 1915-1916 academic year, Marquette University had concluded the most momentous decade in its history. In 1906, Marquette College stood ready to celebrate twenty-five years as a small, liberal arts college, operating within the well-stated tradition of the *Ratio Studiorum* and housed in the tight confines of a three-story building on land purchased by Bishop Henni more than a half-century earlier. Over the next decade, its location changed; its name changed; its seal changed; the presidency changed three times; it successfully executed its first full-fledged capital campaign; its academic programs increased by ten times and its student body by eight times; and most significantly, with coeducation the future direction of Catholic higher education was altered forever.

No single individual attending the silver jubilee could have envisioned this transformation. Father Burrowes may have understood how the Americanization of the *Ratio Studiorum* might transform Jesuit education. Father McCabe might have anticipated the importance of coeducation. But no one could have perceived all this plus what the affiliation with the Milwaukee Medical College and the development of law, engineering, business, and journalism programs would mean to the mission of Marquette, to its role in Wisconsin, to the stability of the university budget, and to the size of the school's physical plant. In time, more attention would be paid to facilities and to the university's management style. But first Marquette—and the nation—confronted an overseas war, an event that took male and female students from "Milwaukee's University" to the battlefields of Europe.

4

MILWAUKEE'S UNIVERSITY
1917-1928

World War I erupted in August 1914, dividing Europe into two alliances: Great Britain, France, Russia, and Italy represented the allied side; Germany, Austria-Hungary, and Turkey constituted the axis powers. The United States remained neutral at first. In fact, President Woodrow Wilson asked the American people to remain neutral in thought as well as action, a difficult assignment in an immigrant-rich city such as Milwaukee. The area's German-American community earnestly supported its ancestral homeland. Rallies and fund-raising for the axis powers became weekly events during the war's early years. For Tory Hill Irish, the choice was simple: who opposed Great Britain, the hated occupier of the Emerald Isle? The south side Polish asked: how quickly would the Austrian-Hungarian empire topple so an independent Poland might once again influence the fate of central Europe? In Milwaukee, everyone had a viewpoint and neutrality was an illusion.

As time passed, Germany's aggressive use of submarines, epitomized by the sinking of the Lusitania in 1915, nudged public opinion toward the allied cause. Once the United States enlisted on the British and French side in early April 1917, Marquette's president, Herbert Noonan, made loyalty a trademark of his alma mater. He had unabashedly supported military preparedness before the war. Once his country committed itself to making "the world safe for democracy," Noonan personally directed the university's war effort. Yet as the casualty lists grew, the mood at Marquette shifted from bravado to resolve. When Germany became America's sworn enemy and the murderer of its dough boys, Milwaukee's German Americans had to adopt a lower profile, even changing the names of organizations such as the Deutscher Club (a neighbor of Marquette) to the Wisconsin Club.

In a prewar speech, Father Noonan had once linked what he viewed as one great evil—pacifism—with a second evil—socialism. His advocacy of prewar preparedness demonstrated his readiness to confront the first of these dangers. From his perspective, the second evil already occupied the mayor's office after the election of Daniel Hoan in 1916. Moreover, Victor Berger, another socialist and an opponent of America's participation in World War I, held one of Milwaukee's congressional seats. The nation's enemies seemed to be everywhere. So when war actually came, Noonan threw his full support behind groups such as the Marquette University Loyalty League, intended to guarantee 100 percent student participation in bond drives. During the Third Liberty Loan campaign in April 1918, nearly 100,000 Milwaukeeans lined Grand Avenue from Thirty-third Street to east of the Milwaukee River. Forty bands, hundreds of soldiers and marines, the American Motor Corps from the National League for Women's

Services, a female troop of Polish war workers, and a large contingent of Hilltoppers marched before the cheering throng. Each university "department" participated. Business students entertained the crowd with snake dances and law students carried a service flag with stars representing each student in uniform.

"Wheatless" bread and "candyless" days as well as "pieless," "cakeless," and "meatless" meals served as civilian contributions to the war effort. A few weeks after Congress authorized America's participation, editors at the *Marquette Tribune* redesigned the paper's masthead to feature an oversized, fierce-looking eagle flanked by American flags. William McAdoo, the U.S. secretary of the treasury, visited the campus to promote loyalty. Faculty incorporated war-related themes into their courses. The university scheduled radio classes in the evenings to make them convenient for training members of the Aero Squadron and the Signal Corps. Out-of-town students registered for the draft on campus. The administration cancelled the prom in 1917 for two reasons: in recognition of the nation's war footing and because the previous year's dance had incurred a deficit. Deans worried that voluntary enlistments and later the draft might disrupt university enrollments—and, therefore, the school's fragile financial condition. However, when the fall 1917 term rolled around, most academic programs were unaffected. By the following fall, administrators once again became concerned after the draft age was lowered to eighteen.[1]

Even before Congress declared war, six seniors from the medical school class of 1917 had responded to the navy's call for volunteers to serve in its hospital corps. Once their country entered the fray, other Hilltoppers volunteered or were drafted into the armed services. Marquette students serving in the army's engineering corps came under live fire within six months of the war resolution. Weekly updates on stateside training and battlefield experiences appeared in the *Tribune*. The sinking of the troop ship *Tuscania* in February 1918 drew everyone's attention because four Hilltoppers were on board. By this time, at least 47 members of the Marquette community were already in France; 170 medical students were in the service by May 1918; and a month later, over 700 Marquette alumni were in the active service, with nearly double that number in the reserves. The *Tribune*'s articles assumed an added solemnity as the fall 1918 term opened. During the previous summer, at least four members of the Marquette community had been killed, including E. Genevieve Mullen, a former vocal instructor at the conservatory. She was caring for allied soldiers in a Paris church when enemy artillery shells took her life.[2]

The 1918 *Hilltop* (published in late spring) opened with twenty pages of photographs (four-to-eight snapshots per page) depicting Marquette alumni, faculty, and students who were in the armed services, whether overseas or stateside. A six-page Marquette Honor Roll (about seventy-five names per page) listed every Hilltopper in the military. At least twenty of those names were women assigned either to camp hospitals in the United States or to Red Cross units with the American Expeditionary Force in Europe. Released seven months after the armistice, the 1919 *Hilltop* was dedicated to those who died in this "world struggle." Short obituaries with photographs reminded stu-

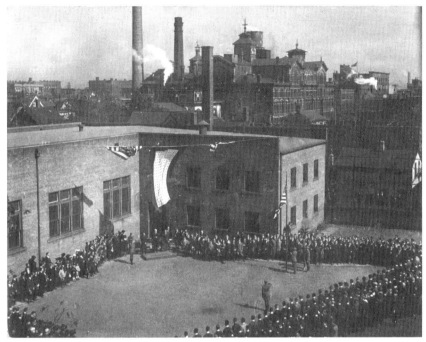

SATC activities. File 722

dents of the ultimate sacrifice made by classmates and alumni. Every professional college at the university was represented in this memorial. Of the twenty-four members
of the Marquette community who died while in uniform, most succumbed to disease
or influenza. The great Spanish influenza pandemic swept the globe throughout 1918
and into 1919, killing as many as twenty million people. Particularly susceptible were
military personnel who lived in large common barracks where the contagion spread
swiftly. The epidemic also struck the Marquette student body, sickening at least one
hundred and fifty by late October 1918.[3]

The war's most visible reminder on campus was a Students' Army Training Corps
unit (SATC). On October 1, 1918, at 525 campuses across the country, 140,000 college students entered a special unit of the United States Army. Seven hundred and
fifty Marquette men enlisted. Although only a handful of naval units were established
nationwide, Marquette had sixty students training as deck officers. These young men
could continue their educations while receiving an introduction to military life. The
army hoped to identify officer material as it prepared for a lengthy campaign overseas.
Student-soldiers received a private's pay ($30 per month) along with board, lodging,
and tuition. They received eleven hours per week of military training, sixteen hours of
classroom work, and five hours of instruction in international and military law. En-
listees bunked at a local laundry, a nearby restaurant, a church hall near the medical
school, and in the Gesu parish auditorium. The government built a mess building for
the cadets on university property at Sixteenth and Clybourn. Recruits were required
to break all contact with their fraternities while in uniform and a saloon-free zone
was enforced within a half-mile radius of any SATC facility (including the barracks),

cramping entertainment habits at the Schlitz Palm Garden, the Hotel Wisconsin, and the Eagles Club. By the war's end, a majority of Catholic participants in the corps came from Jesuit colleges and, among Jesuit schools, Marquette had the largest contingent with 825 volunteers, 765 with the army and 60 with the navy. Within a month of the armistice (November 11, 1918), the Army began to disband the university's SATC unit.[4]

The strongest opinions about World War I on campus emanated from the president's office. Father Noonan had come of age during the presidency of Theodore Roosevelt and tended to view his university position as a "bully pulpit." From this platform, he addressed audiences large and small, urban and rural, Catholic and non-Catholic, in Milwaukee and across Wisconsin. Like many American bishops, he viewed World War I as an opportunity to prove once again the patriotism of Catholics, just as Boston's

Father Herbert C. Noonan. Noonan Biographical File

Irish had weakened years of ethnic hatred through their blood-stained bravery on Civil War battlefields. Marquette's leadership in the Students' Army Training Corps was just one example of Noonan's determination to tie his religion to his citizenship, Catholicism to patriotism.

The president's outspokenness did not stop with war-related matters. When discussing "the woman question" (as women's rights were then known), Noonan urged faithfulness to traditional roles and caution on political equality even though he hoped that women in the public arena might save America from what he saw as impending doom. He was an unapologetic defender of Irish independence from Great Britain. As for prohibition, the university president decried legalized dryness and after the passage of Prohibition, the government's use of students as "spies" to identify lawbreakers. But he was equally fierce in condemning cheap, accessible wine at Italian saloons in the Third Ward.

Public oratory came as second nature to Herbert Noonan. He was a throwback to the days when public speaking was one of Marquette's most distinguishing features. For example, in 1922, Noonan delivered a speech on February 6 in Burlington, Wisconsin, addressing "The Goal of Education." The next day, he spoke at the Blue Mound Sanitarium on "Happiness." Three days later, he offered his thoughts on "Education and Democracy," and forty-eight hours later, he presented three talks, two on "Christian Education" and one on "Education Adrift." Noonan even announced his political preference in the 1920 presidential contest: Republican Senator Warren G. Harding of Ohio. He chose the Republican ticket, Noonan explained, because their Democratic rivals supported the League of Nations, which the Marquette president dismissed as "'rooted in injustice.'" (The Jesuit may have taken this stance because President Wilson's Fourteen Points did not require Irish independence.) Despite his disagreements with President Wilson, Noonan permitted the first wartime *Hilltop* to be dedicated to the nation's chief executive. Patriotic honor came first, a point he emphasized in urging his faculty to "set an example in patriotism." As a clergyman, he lectured male students concerning the morality of infectious (venereal) diseases when encountering "scarlet wom[e]n." In recognition for his work, the French government named Father Noonan an Officer of Public Instruction in the Republic of France.[5]

Herbert Noonan may have been the most self-assured president in the history of Marquette. He did not favor fine distinctions, preferring to confront controversies colored in black and white. In the words of university historian, Raphael Hamilton, Noonan "gloried in a good, clean fight." His self-assuredness applied to campus concerns as well as public affairs. In November 1919, shortly after a difficult capital campaign to endow the School of Medicine, about a dozen part-time instructors at Marquette's medical school protested university rules regarding therapeutic abortions. They felt these guidelines were excessively sectarian and jeopardized their academic freedom as medical educators. The disgruntled faculty had unfavorably compared the situation at Marquette "with that of non-sectarian medical schools" where "freedom of investigation and of teaching" were not subject to "a one-man interpretation of ethical principles."

In his handwritten response (carefully scripted along the margins and between the lines of a copy of the protest these instructors had sent to the president), Noonan dismissed each complaint and the premise upon which it was predicated. There was no such thing as academic freedom, he observed, if it became a license to do what God forbade, "including 'Thou shalt not kill.'" The School of Medicine was non-sectarian only in the sense that it derived its principles "from the Commandments which are *not sectarian.*" He dismissed the notion that the faculty determined ethical standards at this medical school. Not only was the instructional staff not responsible for the institution's medical ethics, neither were the school's board of administration and its board of directors. Only one man defined ethics at the Marquette University School of Medicine: Father President. The potency of these sentiments was demonstrated two years later when the Carnegie Foundation for the Advancement of Teaching, which had invested more than a third of a million dollars in the medical school's endowment, requested an explanation regarding the 1919 disturbance. The university simply reissued Noonan's defense of his presidential powers. One outcome of this imbroglio was a mandatory set of lectures for all medical students titled "The Sacredness of Human Life." At times, Marquette's Jesuits may have been required to accede to the regimen of the American Medical Association, but Herbert Noonan was more than happy to clarify when these accommodations would cease.[6]

A RUSH OF CONSTRUCTION

As stern as Father Noonan appeared on public issues, he was remarkably solicitous on behalf of students. As a former Marquette undergraduate, the president was particularly sensitive to the socio-spatial disconnectedness that the university's city-rich location produced for students. Classes were scattered among three detached locations separated by busy streets and rapidly evolving commercial and residential landscapes. The absence of a college gymnasium was a particular sore point for students. The old, makeshift gymnasium that the alumni had funded in the old Holy Name parish school was long gone by the time Noonan returned to the university as president. Marquette's sports teams competed with parish teams for practice time in the Gesu auditorium. The entire campus community agreed that the absence of a basketball tradition at Marquette could be explained by the lack of an athletic facility.[7]

Early in 1916, Father Noonan met with Henry Banzhaf, dean of the dental college and university intermediary during the medical college negotiations three years earlier. The president proposed a confidential investigation into the availability of the Plankinton estate, a very large piece of land situated between Fifteenth and Sixteenth streets, Grand Avenue to Clybourn Street. Three years earlier, a member of the board of trustees had written William Woods Plankinton, asking him to consider donating the family estate to the land-needy university and thereby become as noble as Robert A. Johnston had been in 1906. Nothing came of this request. So in 1916, Henry Banzhaf contacted friends in the real estate community regarding the Plankinton property. He discovered that it was for sale, but not to Marquette because the university was "a

Catholic corporation." The university retained a real estate agent to keep an eye on the situation, but time passed. Suddenly at the June 1918 commencement, Father Noonan revealed to thunderous cheers that Marquette had purchased the entire 313-foot by 847-foot estate for $163,000. Because differences arose between the sellers and

John Plankinton residence, facing Grand Avenue.
Home to the music conservatory at first and later to the school of speech. File 1116.

William Plankinton residence, facing Sixteenth Street. Home to the eye, ear, nose, and throat clinic at first and later to the athletic department. File 1340.

Marquette over what items could be removed from the property, court action briefly delayed the university's use of the buildings.[8]

The origins of this valuable plot of land date back to land developer James H. Rogers who in the 1850s had purchased 160 acres between Spring Street (Grand Avenue) and the Menomonee River, and Twelfth and Twenty-first streets. On the portion that Marquette later acquired, Rogers had built an elegant house, completed in 1858 at the

Gymnasium on Clybourn Street. File 655

breathtaking price of $60,000. The two-story structure with a distinctive Queen Anne-style tower sat amidst seven acres of formal landscaping, with a fountain and four stone lions guarding the entranceway. John Plankinton, Milwaukee's premiere meatpacker and perhaps its wealthiest resident at the time, bought the property in 1864, and ten years later, following his engagement to his second wife, he renovated the residence in her honor. At one point, its worth reached $200,000, and it was said to be the finest home in the entire Midwest. Plankinton later built an adjoining house for his son, William. By the second decade of the twentieth century, however, the entire estate had gone on the market and Father Noonan made his move.[9]

Once the court battles concluded, the music conservatory moved into John Plankinton's former residence and the Eye, Ear, Nose and Throat Annex of Marquette University Hospital occupied his son's house. In late 1918, the university offered the southwestern corner to the Students' Army Training Corps for a mess hall. Father Noonan finally announced in early 1921 that he intended to construct the long-anticipated gymnasium on the site of that mess hall, using some of the building's original footings. The new 90-foot by 160-foot athletic facility was to be joined, one block to the north, by a building for the dentistry program. In combination with the two Plankinton houses, these structures constituted what became known as the "upper campus."[10] Within another year, Noonan initiated preparations for two additional projects that would be authorized and completed during his successor's term: a three-story structure for the law school on the footprint of the Mackie house and a four-story science build-

School of Law, after 1938. Observatory visible on roof of Johnston Hall. Portion of Tory Hill neighborhood on upper left.
File 800

ing on the empty lot west of Gesu, property that had been sitting idle since 1908. The first building was estimated to cost $60,000, and the second $175,000. In addition, the university announced improvements to the school of medicine on Reservoir Street and to Johnston Hall. Administrators also made plans to renovate two residences south of Johnston Hall purchased in April 1920 for $33,000. General Frederic C. Winkler (a founder of the Deutscher Club) had resided in an attractive brick house set back from Eleventh Street behind a large, sloping lawn. The general subsequently built a second residence in his side yard for his son-in-law, Dr. Harry Hitz. The university originally used the Winkler residence as a law school annex, although over the years this facility housed many departments, including the College of Hospital Administration. The Hitz house, subsequently renamed Drexel Lodge, became one of the most beloved buildings on campus, serving as the women's student union from 1923 to 1953.[11]

The final construction project from this era was, like the gymnasium, long overdue. For years, the students and faculty of Marquette University High School had endured the physical limitations of the hilltop's original college building. Few improvements had been made to this forty-year-old structure. During the 1916 building campaign, Ellen Story Johnston had provided $100,000 for a new high school. This money was placed in an endowment. Then, following her death in 1923, Mrs. Johnston's will

Science Hall. File 890

*Winkler residence to right; became Lalumiere Hall, Administration Hall, and then O'Hara Hall.
To left, Hitz house; later Drexel Lodge.* File 515

bequeathed to the Jesuits securities worth approximately $450,000. With the original gift, land was purchased at Thirty-fourth and Grand, more than two miles west of Johnston Hall. Construction for a new high school was completed by the fall of 1925, with space for nearly one thousand students. It included twenty-four classrooms, two laboratories, and a gymnasium with a "gridiron." In recognition of Mrs. Johnston's lifetime of generosity to the university, to Gesu, and to Milwaukee's Jesuit community, the main building at the high school was named in her honor. (The family's tradition of giving was later carried on by her son Harry, whose financial gifts over time totaled at least $100,000.) The last step in this massive overhaul of the Jesuit properties in Milwaukee required disposal of the hilltop. The generosity of Ernest Miller, a one-time Marquette Academy student and son of the founder of Miller Brewing, permitted the Capuchins, a Franciscan order, to purchase Block 199 for $150,000 in order to expand their programs on behalf of the city's African American community.[12]

A PRESIDENTIAL SUCCESSION

The Jesuit community in Milwaukee, like counterparts around the world, was directed by a priest who carried the titles of both rector and president. In America during the nineteenth century, this first designation was typically used to identify a religious superior whereas in the twentieth century, the second became increasingly more common. A rector guided the spiritual and material lives of each priest, brother, and scholastic at Gesu, Marquette University High School, and the university. As president, this same individual oversaw every detail of the university, including budgets, hirings, and curriculum. He was usually assisted by a vice president, who also served as dean of arts and sciences. This vice president was subordinate not only by virtue of his *vice* presidency but also by virtue of the overwhelming authority wielded by the rector. One man, as Father Noonan would have reminded us, was ultimately responsible for Marquette University, whether he was called Father Rector or Father President.

In the summer of 1919, the provincial reassigned Father Noonan to the presidency and rectorship of Saint Louis University. Senior Jesuits in Milwaukee sent their superior in St. Louis a respectful protest, pleading for Noonan to stay at Marquette until at least the end of the year. They made this request for two reasons. First, the school of medicine was in the midst of a capital campaign that was not going very well; the president's departure at this crucial juncture would guarantee the failure of this vital endeavor. Second, the private colleges and universities of Wisconsin, in a unique collaboration of faith-based and non-sectarian institutions, were undertaking their own statewide fund-raising campaign; Noonan was a pivotal figure in this drive. The provincial agreed to his confreres's request, delaying Noonan's departure for St. Louis until the end of the calendar year. A further appeal by Father Noonan himself won over the provincial who then decided to appoint another priest as president of Saint Louis University. The Marquette chief executive could now stay in Milwaukee and fulfill his various obligations.[13]

As land acquisitions escalated and construction plans flourished during the next few years, Jesuit authorities in Rome (and perhaps in St. Louis) began to question both the methods used to finance these projects and whether proper permissions had been obtained in each and every instance. These same officials also became uneasy over the fact that Father Noonan was heading into his seventh year as president and rector, beyond the new canonical limit of six years. As a consequence, the provincial appointed Father Albert Fox as vice president in January 1922, after a tenure as president of Campion College in Prairie du Chien, Wisconsin. Fox was an ascending figure in American higher education, having served as president of the Catholic Educational Association's department of colleges and secondary schools. A devoted proponent of change, Fox was considered "the most prominent Jesuit exponent in the United States of the new standards of education that had developed after World War I."[14]

In addition to being vice president, Father Fox was named rector of the Jesuit community, an appointment that university historian Raphael Hamilton calls unprecedented in American Jesuit history up to that point. Father Noonan remained president but in a subordinated role that gave him responsibility for the university but not over matters pertaining to the Jesuits in Milwaukee. Moreover, when this information was conveyed to the religious community, Fox placed a note on the Jesuit bulletin board stating that as vice president, he would shape the university's "educational policies" and guide it in "educational matters." What did this mean? Who had the final authority at Marquette University? In private correspondence, Noonan asked: what powers does a vice president possess if the president is not in charge? This divisive arrangement limped along until late in the summer of 1922 when Noonan was reassigned once again, this time to Loyola University in Chicago. In his private papers, Noonan made clear his sense of betrayal over Father Fox's behavior, even though the latter was apparently fulfilling the wishes of their religious superiors. Months after his reassignment, Father Noonan defended himself to the superior general in a two-page, single-spaced letter written in Latin. In a note to Henry Banzhaf, the Jesuit thanked the business manager for all he had done "to lighten my load at Marquette during the past seven years and to encourage me 'to carry on.' Now that I am away I can tell you more easily how much I appreciated your loyalty and your splendid spirit of self-sacrifice." Noonan conceded that leaving Milwaukee "was much harder than [it] appeared on the surface." For his part, Fox was relieved that he no longer had to mask his real authority. Despite this bitterness, the two priests exchanged cordial words at a farewell dinner held in Noonan's honor in September 1922. The outgoing president spoke movingly of how much he would miss Milwaukee. Before five hundred guests, the two men kept their differences under wraps for at least one evening.[15]

FOX'S FISCAL TROUBLES

If one of Father Fox's specific assignments had been to get control of construction costs at Marquette, that task was greatly aided by his predecessor's authorization of the university's first professional audit, prepared during the summer of 1921. Reilly, Penner and Benton, C.P.A., opened a "new set of general books." Until this time, the university's financial records were informal accounts kept in handwritten notebooks maintained by the university treasurer, a Jesuit who usually served on the board of trustees. When the professional audit was completed in 1921, it revealed that $175,000 remained from the 1916 building campaign, with $42,000 still owed in outstanding pledges. Beyond this combined sum of $217,000 from 1916, the university had accumulated only $17,231 in additional endowment—seventeen thousand dollars to show for forty years of service to Milwaukee![16]

The school's liabilities in 1921 totaled a little under $500,000, most of it tied to specific buildings and came in the form of notes to banks and individuals. These liabilities soon grew, as the gymnasium, dental, law, and science building projects moved forward. By the end of the 1922 fiscal year, the university's debts jumped $800,000 to $1.3 million. A year later, they grew modestly to $1.5 million. But by 1924, with new facilities for law and the basic sciences nearly completed, the debt climbed to $2.1 million. Finally, by July 31, 1925, with work on a new high school underway, Marquette's liabilities came to $2.6 million dollars—a growth in the school's debt obligations of 500 percent in only four years.[17]

The oddest item in this ledger referred to obligations owed to the Northern Michigan Land Company. This financial albatross bedeviled five successive university presidents from 1919 until the late 1940s. The saddest part of this story is that the debt originated with a promising opportunity. In May 1917, efforts to get the Carnegie Foundation for the Advancement of Teaching to participate in Marquette's 1916 building campaign had belatedly culminated in an unexpected challenge grant: the foundation would award a third of a million dollars to the university's school of medicine if it could raise twice that sum, thus establishing a $1 million endowment. This invitation came just fourteen months after the 1916 campaign, but afraid of missing out on the largest gift in school history, Father Noonan made a fateful decision to accept this challenge. The foundation's original deadline of July 1918 was later extended to September 1, 1919, because of World War I. Carnegie's interest in Marquette came from a favorable review of the medical school's curriculum, which was held to be "'solid in fundamentals, while many other universities were drifting away from fundamental principles.'" The offer was flattering, but the wisdom of accepting it was soon called into question.[18]

Even before fund-raising could begin, Father Noonan decided in October 1917 to separate the school of medicine from the university. A new corporation, with its own board of directors, would then control the expanded endowment. The president may have been driven to this decision by the foundation's rule against aid to schools that taught religion. An independent medical school, not legally tied to university proper, could sidestep the mandatory religious instruction of Catholic students that guided the rest of the institution. (The evidence on this point, however, is sketchy.) The provincial had already approved Noonan's proposal in July 1918. The new medical school corporation existed exclusively for "educational, benevolent and charitable purposes." Its board of directors (which university publications repeatedly—and confusingly—referred to as a board of trustees) consisted of the university's board of trustees, the faculty regent of the medical school, and fifteen additional members, among whom in the beginning were the medical dean, his associate dean, a judge, an attorney for Northwestern Mutual Life Insurance Company, and several industrialists and physicians. It also included the president of the Carnegie Foundation for the Advancement of Teaching.[19]

"A Million for Marquette!" became the slogan for the challenge grant's campaign, which started its quiet phase at the end of 1917. A fifty-page pamphlet outlined the nature of medical education in Milwaukee, the administrative structure that would oversee the endowment, the role of Marquette's dispensary, and the impact of World War I upon the region's and the nation's needs for medical personnel—thereby assigning a patriotic theme to gift-giving. The campaign's main energy was exerted between July 22 and July 30, 1918. At the end, the goal of $666,666 was short by at least $200,000. Into the breach stepped donors with names such as Cudahy, Vogel, Trecker, and Johnston. Other supporters included the Knights of Columbus and the Gesu Parish Married Ladies Society. The Northern Michigan Land Company promised over $100,000. The university's board of trustees telegraphed the Carnegie foundation on August 31, 1919, one day before the second deadline, that they had met the challenge. In October, the foundation delivered a check for a third of a million dollars.[20]

The frantic effort to create an endowment for the school of medicine (which without these funds might have closed) led Father Noonan and the board of trustees into a costly but unforeseen blunder, an entanglement that turned Marquette University into a land developer. To fill the initial shortfall of $200,000, Father Noonan contacted C. A. McCann, a prominent member of the Knights of Columbus from St. Paul, Minnesota, and a relative of Harry Johnston. McCann was president of the Northern Michigan Land Company, a development corporation that was preparing to issue $900,000 in bonds on 300,000 acres of land scattered across six counties in the Upper Peninsula of Michigan. The company intended to sell land to small farmers at $10 per acre. In exchange for a cash commission of $175,000 (most of which would go toward the medical school), the university promised to guarantee $400,000 of the bonds. The Marquette-underwritten bonds sold so quickly that the university increased the value of its share. The non-Marquette bonds, however, did not sell very well. Furthermore, some of those who bought the non-Marquette bonds did so under the impression that the university stood behind those sales as well. To make matters worse, World War I destabilized the bond market. Sales dropped off. Individuals with liens against the company's land began to squeeze the guarantors. In 1922, a lengthy list of aggrieved parties filed a law suit that took six years to wend its way through the courts of Michigan and in the end produced mixed results for the university. Meanwhile, McCann had died. In his absence, the land company dissolved, leaving the university as the sole representative of this debacle.[21]

Marquette dutifully paid the interest coupons and later redeemed the Northern Michigan Land Company bonds with their own bonds. The university also foreclosed on what remained of the land company in order to obtain title to all the property. Some acreage was lost over time through random foreclosures and tax delinquencies. The bondholders who mistakenly thought they had purchased Marquette-guaranteed paper deluged the president's office with complaints, decrying what they perceived to be fraud and threatening law suits. University presidents patiently wrote each complainant, explaining why Marquette was not liable for their bonds. In addition, the university's business manager dutifully paid annual property taxes on this empty land. In 1927, as an example, taxes came to $11,407.14 from thirty-four townships scattered across Schoolcraft, Mackinac, Chippewa, Luce, Marquette, and Alger counties. Marquette officials struggled over what to do with this land and eventually turned over management to the Banzhaf family through a trusteeship. University representatives renegotiated vaguely worded timber contracts originally signed by the Northern Michigan Land Company. They explored various uses for the properties, including potato farming, peppermint farming, silver fox production, and peat moss harvesting for plastics. Discussions centered on magnesium ore that might be used for the war effort in 1943. Large tracts near Manistique were literally under water. The university hired crews to bulldoze these bogs and dig drainage ditches in an attempt to make the land productive. At one point, specialists recommended a College of Forestry for Marquette with an Upper Peninsula campus. By the early 1940s, the university was still negotiating with the United States Forest Service and with Michigan's Department of Conservation to sell what remained.[22]

A CORPORATE STYLE OF MANAGEMENT

Father Albert Fox did not want to spend his presidency dealing with mint farming, angry bondholders, and timber contracts. He preferred spending his time working on an administrative framework that would efficiently address Marquette's traditional problems as an institution of higher education. Fox constantly spoke of "systems" and "policies of management." He envisioned the perfect alignment of positions and managers. His rhetoric suited the corporate-mindedness of the 1920s.

His first goal was to clarify the role of the university business manager. In February 1921, Father Noonan had created this post for Henry Banzhaf. Three years earlier, in the winter of 1918, the board of trustees had offered Banzhaf a long-term contract as dean, a six-year agreement at one-and-a-half times his previous salary. They made this offer in appreciation for his services to presidents Grimmelsman and Noonan. When the role of business manager was added to his portfolio in 1921, his 1919 salary was doubled. Moreover, this unprecedented appointment was "for as long as he shall live." (His salary, large by 1921 standards, was never expected to change—a sore point decades down the line.) Dean Henry Banzhaf became the highest-ranking layperson in Marquette history up to that moment, with responsibility for the university's day-to-day fiscal decisions, its construction projects, *and* oversight of the dentistry school.[23]

During the brief, awkward period when Father Fox was rector and Father Noonan was president, Banzhaf reported to the latter, who after all had appointed him, was his friend, and held the title *president*. The business manager also tried to intercede with the provincial on Noonan's behalf, while carefully avoiding any denigration of the newcomer. This confused state of affairs led Fox to reprimand Banzhaf in July 1922: he insisted that

> all authority and all responsibility at Marquette is in my hands despite the mask I have worn for the last six months before the public. I shall, therefore, ask you henceforth to deal with me directly and exclusively regarding all financial questions and money matters ... If I see fit to confer with or consult Father Noonan on any point I shall do so at my own discretion. Of course, as long as matters remain as they now are, he will have to sign papers for the University, but even this is to be done through me."

Chastened and probably confused, Banzhaf delivered a summary of the construction schedule to Fox ten days later and had the outside auditors reissue the year's accounting summary to the rector. Despite this shaky start, Father Fox retained Banzhaf as business manager, a post he faithfully executed until his retirement in 1947.[24]

Fox's preoccupation with organizational management occasionally led to disasters, as evidenced by his first administrative recruitment. The president hired alumnus Philip Grau in 1923 to be director of organization for a two-year period at the princely sum of

$18,000 per year (at the same time, the director of the Central Bureau of Information and Statistics, a woman, received $3,000 annually). Fox compared Grau's new position to that of corporate executives "whose duty it is to so thoroughly inter-organize the various branches and activities of their plants that there is no overlapping of effort. This means greater efficiency." Within nine months, Grau submitted his resignation because he never figured out what he was supposed to do. He and the president exchanged letters, sorting through this confusion. But Grau's insistence that certain things "'must be done in my way'" triggered a reminder from Fox that only the president could make such a claim. Fox was particularly angered because his director of organization had explored, on his own, the possibility of founding a correspondence school at Marquette. In addition, Grau's ill-defined role, according to Fox, had encouraged "disgruntled students and contriving faculty members" to approach the director of organization rather than the president on certain matters. And it did not help that Grau was Father Noonan's good friend. Within a short time, Father President reversed his original offer to Grau, maintaining that budgetary circumstances required a cut in his salary. The two sides parted company.[25]

A far more successful appointment came with the hiring of Edward A. Fitzpatrick, brought aboard in the summer of 1924 as a professor of education. He was also hired to serve as dean of the graduate school, an office established by Fox two years earlier even though Marquette had awarded advanced degrees as early as 1889. Within two years of his arrival—and with Father President's acquiescence—Fitzpatrick became deeply involved in renewed efforts to establish a Catholic women's college in Milwaukee.

The 1910 campaign to create a female-only affiliate to Marquette had gone nowhere and in 1921, a distinctly different vision of coeducation at Marquette also failed. In the case of the latter, the Marquette Woman's League and the Archdiocesan Council of Catholic Women approached Archbishop Sebastian Messmer, asking him to use his influence to insure that "all departments at Marquette University … be opened to women and that full degrees be given in all departments instead of in a limited number." In particular, these women wanted members of their sex to be admitted to the College of Arts and Sciences, the heart of a Jesuit university. Up to this time, female students had enrolled in liberal arts classes only as majors in journalism or business. The women's league and its associate wanted these restrictions removed because the "number of college women in our country is multiplying marvelously each year." They noted: "Woman's place in the public life of America is much larger than in the public life of Europe … . Whether they want it or not, Catholic women have to get into this public life to defend their homes, their ideals and their country from the errors with which so many non-Catholic women in public life are infected." However, they added, no "matter how good their intentions and how strong their faith, Catholic women with an inferior education can at best make a sorry showing against the better training of their non-Catholic sisters." The two groups implored the archbishop to use his authority to convince the Jesuit superior general to grant permission for the enrollment of "our daughters" in the arts and sciences college. They failed to understand that a

Milwaukee prelate had no influence over the superior of a religious order headquar-
tered in Rome, so in the end, their campaign went nowhere.[26]

The intentions evidenced in 1910 and again eleven years later did not disappear,
however. By 1926, Father Fox himself took up this matter. On April 18, the Marquette
president met with two nuns from Iowa to discuss staffing a women's college. He spoke
of his alarm at "the problems arising from having [a growing number of] women
and girls at the University with little or no provision for discipline, supervision, etc."
Buoyed by this meeting, the women returned to their convent and drafted a plan of action that included administrative guidelines and even a list of courses for a Marquette-
affiliated college. But like its predecessors, this initiative foundered.

At the same time, Fox was also exchanging notes with Sister Mary Eugene, head of
St. Mary's College in Prairie du Chien, an institution run by the School Sisters of Notre
Dame. Sister Eugene, who may have known the Marquette president from his days at
Campion College, sought to relocate her school to Milwaukee as a branch of Marquette University. She did not care if it was as a four-year institution on the Barnard
and Radcliffe models or as a two-year junior college. Even though he was in consultation with another congregation of nuns at the same moment, Fox was quite sincere
in his remarks to Sister Eugene. He warned the nun that not all of Marquette's female
students could be required to transfer to St. Mary's if it moved to Milwaukee. A third
of these female students were Protestant, and Fox did not believe their parents would
acquiesce to a mandatory transfer of their daughters to a Catholic women's college,
even one affiliated with Marquette. Clearly, female students had become so important
to the university that Fox did not wish to jeopardize their enrollment. When their conversations failed to move St. Mary's to Milwaukee, Fox took the unprecedented step of
making the College of Arts and Sciences coeducational, an astonishing move given the
centrality of this unit to the tradition of Jesuit higher education. (This may have been
the earliest admission of women to an arts and sciences college among Jesuit schools.
Saint Louis University delayed the direct enrollment of women in liberal arts classes for
two decades by directing them to the school of education after 1925. In this way, the
university could honestly report back to superiors in Rome that "'There are no women
in the [arts and sciences] College.'")[27]

St. Mary's College finally relocated to Milwaukee in 1929, becoming Mount Mary
College, but by that time, the enthusiasm for an affiliation with Marquette had waned.
Both schools officially encouraged cooperation between faculty, but the physical distance between the institutions precluded a close association. The chancellor (and later
president) at the transplanted Mount Mary College was none other than Edward A.
Fitzpatrick, who remained dean of graduate studies at Marquette. This incredible arrangement—which Father Fox clearly approved—troubled Fox's successor, Father William Magee. He insisted upon clarifying Fitzpatrick's dual roles, in part because the
new Marquette president became annoyed with members of the Mount Mary community, believing that persistent rumors ("mischievous misrepresentations" in his words)
of Marquette's discontinuance of coeducation emanated from either the faculty at or

the alumni from Mount Mary. Because he firmly backed the admission of women to Marquette, Father Magee threatened "to give to all the papers of the city a formal statement of denial." Despite his doubts, Father Magee permitted Fitzpatrick to remain as chancellor at Mount Mary College as well as dean at Marquette.[28]

THE SCHANDEIN INCIDENT

Albert Fox's most difficult experience as president and perhaps the university's most distressing experience in its first one hundred years had nothing to do with personnel matters or coeducation; instead it had to do with the Milwaukee County Board of Supervisors and the Ku Klux Klan. The lease that Marquette had signed in 1913 to use the Milwaukee Medical College's three buildings at Ninth and Wells ran for six years. In 1919, the university invoked a stipulation in the original agreement offering a four-year renewal. But in 1922, a year before the second lease was due to expire, business manager Henry Banzhaf advised Father Noonan that an extension of the agreement (which by now cost $9,500 per year) was financially prohibitive. The hospital building was dilapidated and a fire risk, hospital operations and the nurses' program were running deficits, and the instructional building on Wells Street would soon be empty after the dental students moved to their new facilities on Sixteenth Street. Moreover, the City of Milwaukee had its eye on the Wells Street property, intending to build an addition to the public library. Banzhaf urged the administration to let the lease expire, an action that would effectively close Marquette University Hospital and the nurses' training program. (The School of Medicine remained in place at the former Wisconsin College of Physicians and Surgeons building on Fourth and Reservoir.) Persuaded by these arguments, Noonan wrote the hospital chief of staff on June 1, 1922, that "since the primary function of this University is educational, and since the facilities for taking care of our present student enrollment are inadequate," he was not going to waste the school's limited funds on a new lease. The hospital was to close on August 31, 1922.

Father Fox disagreed. Upon his elevation to the presidency in July 1922, he revoked these instructions and ordered the hospital to stay open for another year. A few months later, Banzhaf submitted a second report, again outlining the losses expected from the hospital's continued operation. He warned the president that the doctors who used the university hospital were so disappointed by his decision to keep the facility open that they were likely to refuse to send their patients to the center. This would incur additional losses. Moreover, the new lease price was likely to run $16,500 a year, so Banzhaf restated his recommendation to close the hospital.[29]

Father Fox devised a solution for this problem in 1924 when he recruited the Franciscan Sisters from Little Falls, Minnesota, to take over management of the hospital. Marquette authorities remodeled the space vacated by the dental students into residential quarters for the nuns and the medical school's dispensary on Reservoir was relocated to the university hospital to help with the latter's balance sheet. (The eye, ear, nose, and throat dispensary in the former Plankinton house was unaffected because it was not running a deficit.) In everyone's mind, this new arrangement was purely a stop-gap measure; the real solution was a new hospital. In 1925, the *Marquette Tribune* revealed plans for such a facility. Father Fox envisioned a $2 million complex housing a hospital, a nursing program, and the university's new College of Hospital Administration (the first of its kind in the country).[30]

The County of Milwaukee also had an interest the area's health care system. In 1918, it established a committee of leading medical experts to look into this matter. Dr. Louis F. Jermain, then dean of Marquette's School of Medicine, served on the committee, which recommended the construction of a 500-bed hospital, open to both paying and partial-paying patients. (Whether for-pay patients could be admitted to such a hospital was not clarified until mid-1921 when the district attorney ruled that the size of any county-operated hospital could be based only on the needs of "indigent and destitute persons," thereby excluding cash customers.) At the same time, the county had purchased the Schandein estate, a square block stretching from Twenty-fourth to Twenty-fifth streets, Grand Avenue to Wells Street with the thought that it might use this land for a new health care center. County officials had designs for a new hospital prepared and the state legislature loosened restrictions on paying patients at county hospitals. In 1923, another citizens' committee repeated the earlier call for a centrally located hospital within the city limits. Yet within two years, political support for this proposal evaporated. Instead, the county proposed a new hospital on land it owned in the western suburb of Wauwatosa, and in late 1926, the board of supervisors' judiciary committee took steps to act upon this alternative suggestion.[31]

As soon as Milwaukee County abandoned plans for a hospital on the Schandein property, Father Fox stepped forward. At a university dinner honoring the now retired Dr. Jermain, Fox announced that Marquette intended to build its own 500-bed hospital for all the needy citizens of the city "irrespective of color, race, creed or political affiliation." He asked the board of supervisors to sell the Schandein block (where only remnants of a mansion remained) to the university for the same $110,000 price that the county had paid for the property nearly a decade earlier. To promote its case, Marquette initiated a petition-signing campaign, requesting that "some arrangement [be] made by the County of Milwaukee for the purchase of said site by Marquette University." A pamphlet, titled "22 Direct Questions Directly Answered," was also prepared. Alumni received copies of the petition. The Eagles Club jumped onto this bandwagon, hoping that Marquette's smart-looking hospital would add prestige to their new clubhouse across Grand Avenue from the Schandein block. Father Fox delivered speeches before Catholic and non-Catholic groups. As the time neared for the county board's decision, the university claimed to have obtained 34,000 signatures endorsing the president's proposal.[32]

On February 28, 1927, a public hearing was held in Circuit Judge John J. Gregory's courtroom. Supporting the university were Edward Fitzpatrick and William George Bruce, a longtime friend of the university and a deeply admired civic leader. Arrayed against the plan were the head of the county dispensary (who expected to move his operation to the Schandein property if the county hospital was built in Wauwatosa), a representative of the area's Methodist churches, the reform-minded City Club, the city's fire fighters union, and Ray O. Twinning of the Ku Klux Klan. Just two weeks earlier, a different Klan spokesman ("the Exalted Cyclops of Milwaukee County Klan No.1, Realm of Wisconsin") had urged the city's common council to reject a resolution approving the transfer of former city land from the Milwaukee Children's Hospital Association to the Milwaukee Catholic Home for the Aged. Now the Klan sought to block the exchange of other public land to a second Catholic institution. Twinning may also been seeking revenge on Father Fox, who two years earlier had denounced the Klan shibboleth of "100% Americanism."[33]

On March 8, a week after this hearing, the Milwaukee County Board of Supervisors rejected the university's request to buy the Schandein property for $110,000. The vote was seventeen to three against the proposal. The majority insisted that the county still had plans for the Schandein property, specifically a small emergency hospital and dispensary. This made Marquette's project superfluous. The three supervisors who backed the university's ambitions included representatives from the Marquette neighborhood and the area north of the campus as well as Lawrence J. Timmerman from a district northwest of the university. The county's rejection of his plan stunned Father Fox, who never envisioned defeat. How could county officials dismiss such a wonderful enhancement to the area west of downtown? Fox may have overestimated the impact that 34,000 signatures would mean in the face of reputable (Methodist clergy) and disreputable (KKK) opposition. Fox himself did not testify because he considered it undignified and because he feared his presence might incite even more anti-Catholic sentiment. His reaction was to press ahead. Five weeks after the supervisors' vote, he released an architectural rendering of Marquette University Hospital for public examination. The sketch depicted a massive, towering structure built in the collegiate gothic style, with a landscaped entranceway facing Grand Avenue. But this dream was not to be. Even though Fox's successor continued to campaign for a university hospital near the campus, the outcome had already been determined through a curious combination of political and religious differences.[34]

A BOARD OF GOVERNORS

Father Fox's most meaningful response to the Schandein episode could be found in his alliance with a group of executives whose advice he especially valued. Having been defeated by Milwaukee's political establishment represented by the county board, Fox turned to the region's business elite as the university's new guardians. Under Father Noonan who preferred his own counsel, the lay board of regents first established by Father McCabe had fallen into disuse. In contrast, Fox convened a different group, a board of advisors, in March 1924. He named presidents of three banks as well as the leading executives from Wisconsin Telephone, Allis Chalmers, Kearney Trecker, Boston Store, Robert A. Johnston Company, and the Wisconsin Press Association. Milwaukee's Archbishop Sebastian Messmer was also included. Father Fox insisted that he recruited these men for their business acumen, not their financial generosity. The

Sketch of proposed Marquette University Hospital, 1927. File 610

following year, Fox quietly sought legal counsel regarding a possible reconstitution of the one body that held ultimate control over the corporation known as Marquette University: the board of trustees, which by charter consisted of three Jesuits.[35]

In the end, Fox was not prepared to go quite that far. But within six months of the Schandein incident, he moved Marquette closer toward the corporate management style he favored, privately inviting six individuals in late August 1927 to serve with him on a board of governors. He introduced this board to the public in mid-September (along with yet another version of the board of advisors, although this last group never played a real role at the university). The board of governors included (in addition to Fox) Archbishop Sebastian Messmer; General Otto H. Falk, president of Allis Chalmers; Albert C. Elser, vice president of the Second Ward Savings Bank; Frank Sensenbrenner, vice president of the Kimberly-Clark Paper Company; Dr. Charles E. Albright, special representative from Northwestern Mutual Life Insurance Company; and Harry S. Johnston, president of his family's baking company. The powers delegated to this body were astonishing for its day, nearly identical to the authority exercised by the current board of trustees. The governors were assigned responsibility for all university investments, for annual audits and budgets, for the approval and supervision of all construction, for all salaries and conditions of employment for non-academic personnel, for the salary scale of all faculty, for approval of all new academic areas (including affiliations with outside institutions), for all tuition charges, for the establishment of a student loan program, for policies regarding student dormitories (of which there were none at that time), and for a "system of pensions and retiring allowances for members of faculties whenever the University resources permit."[36]

Fox's initiative was not an empty gesture. Correspondence between him and Frank Sensenbrenner, for example, reveals the genuine respect that Fox held for the Neenah manufacturer, even before the board of governors was established. In turn, Sensenbrenner was frank and forceful in his advice, especially his annoyance regarding the Northern Michigan Land Company fiasco. Father Fox wanted Sensenbrenner and his associates on the board to give the university direction as well as to provide a powerful public face to the local community. This was aptly illustrated in a strongly worded document produced in 1929, a year after Fox was replaced as president. Entitled "Why Marquette" and issued under the name of General Falk, a leader among Milwaukee corporate giants, this declaration made the case for Marquette University's financial and educational roles in southeastern Wisconsin. It reminded readers of the urgent need for a teaching hospital in a city as prominent as Milwaukee and challenged the local citizenry to match the sizable gifts donated to other private institutions during 1929 (the opening year of the Great Depression): $8 million to Northwestern, $3 million to Yale, and $2 million to Harvard. To have the governors comparing Milwaukee's Jesuit university to Ivy League schools was audacious, to say the least.[37]

The breadth of power that Father Fox originally assigned to this board drew national attention from other Catholic administrators. Only a few schools had tested similar waters by the late twenties. In early 1929, not long after Father William Magee replaced

Fox, the National Catholic Welfare Conference asked Marquette for advice when an unnamed Catholic university proposed giving "the laity a share in [its] financial administration." Conference representatives came to Milwaukee because they assumed Marquette was "a Catholic college or university under the control of a religious order that has transferred any or all of its power in financial affairs to a lay board of governors or trustees." Father Magee, who did not hold the board of governors in quite the same esteem as his predecessor, explained that the board of governors constituted the "financial agent of the Board of Trustees," while the board of trustees retained complete "control over the educational and internal policies of the institution." The governors had been recruited, Magee offered, because Marquette "could not hope to get effective lay co-operation unless we gave the laymen concerned an active interest in the affairs of the university." The role of Fox's board of governors may have been futuristic for its time, but it demonstrated his visionary style of university governance.[38]

OUTSIDERS LOOKING IN

One motivation behind Fox's preoccupation with finding the proper organizational structure to guide Marquette's future was the growing influence of outside agencies. The American Medical and the American Bar associations represented one type of this oversight. Another came from within the national Jesuit community. Proponents of reform among American Jesuit universities—Albert Fox among them—saw their schools in the postwar period as "inadequately staffed, underfinanced, and unevenly administered." In 1920, they convinced the U.S. provincials to establish an Inter-Province Committee to discuss a broad agenda of improvements. Fox became a key figure in the committee's brief decade of work. He hosted the first meeting in March 1921 at Campion College; he was elected the group's first chair. At that session, delegates endorsed the creation of academic departments within colleges, the creation of majors and minors, the treatment of Greek as an elective not a requirement for a bachelor of arts, and the separation of the high schools from the colleges. Future meetings pushed for updates in administration, curriculum, publicity, endowments, libraries, and graduate education. The committee also advocated improved relationships with regional accrediting bodies and won the provincials' approval for a prefect of studies in each province to promote these refinements. So when Father M. J. O'Connor, an instructor in the early years of Marquette College, visited Milwaukee as the newly appointed "general director of studies for all Jesuit colleges and universities in the Missouri Province," he was cordially welcomed. O'Connor aimed to introduce "standardization of study in all [the province's] institutions, which is to be similar in many respects to the work done by the North Central association and like regional institutions." Faculty scholarship as an emblem of Jesuit ideals was a particular focus for Father O'Connor. No one could have been a more fervent advocate of O'Connor's causes than Albert Fox.[39]

A similar push toward standardization and assessment came from the North Central Association of Colleges and Secondary Schools. In 1913, when the association released its first list of approved schools, Notre Dame was the only Catholic school represented in the Midwest. For the better part of a century, Catholic educators had been wary of government support of church-sponsored education because they preferred that public funds come with no strings attached—an awkward position at best. In the twentieth century, this cautionary stance applied to accrediting bodies as well. Yet Father Noonan recognized the power of these agencies to bring good (offering third-party evaluations of an educational product) as well as harm (forcing faith-based institutions to surrender their distinctiveness). In 1920, he applied to have Marquette accredited. MU was neither the first nor the last Jesuit institution in America to seek accreditation. In 1916, the University of Detroit had applied to North Central, whereas Loyola University in Maryland did not ask for a visit from its regional body until 1929 and Santa Clara University was not accredited by its respective association until 1932. The North Central Association was unable to handle all the requests it received in 1920 and therefore delayed "without prejudice" its visit to Milwaukee for one year.

Finally, on March 7, 1921, the chairman of the Commission on Institutions of Higher Education met with the Marquette president, the deans, and senior administrators, including the registrar. (This inspection did not apply to medicine and dentistry because they were already accredited by their own professional organizations; the music college and the high school were also excluded as academic anomalies.) The visitor attended classes and examined the laboratories and libraries. The university performed remarkably, given the fact that the association's standards were still evolving and Marquette had no experience in preparing for such an inspection. Teaching at Milwaukee's Jesuit university was deemed "better than average." Its standards for admission and graduation were acceptable, except in the College of Economics which, in general, did not do well. (This may explain the elimination of the three-year bachelor of commercial science degree less than two months after the accreditation visit.) The financial condition of Marquette did not trouble the visitor, although seventeen Jesuits "serving without pay" warranted a special notation. The visitor depicted the academic buildings as adequate but overcrowded, a condition soon addressed by Father Noonan's building spree. The future of the arts and sciences college raised some concerns because its exclusion of women and its requirement of high school Latin guaranteed that enrollments would not expand in this core unit. Father Fox addressed this concern in 1926 by making the college coeducational.[40]

A LIBRARY

Marquette fared remarkably well in this first encounter with secular authorities (beyond earlier visitations by professional accreditation teams). This was a testament to the education provided by the Society of Jesus, regardless of whether strangers were looking over their shoulders or not. The reviewer's report did observe that the university technically failed the association's standard on libraries, which was described as "a negligible quantity." This deficiency was overlooked "because the great city library is within one block of the University campus." For years, the Milwaukee Public Library and Museum had been spoken of by university representatives as if they were departments at the school. And given the way students and faculty used those facilities, they might very well have been. With 250,000 volumes, the public library functioned "to a considerable extent as a college library," boasted the city librarian. In 1924, he wrote to Father Fox urging greater cooperation between the faculty and his office. As soon as a professor required a set of readings or recommended some verse, the librarian explained, students rushed to Ninth and Grand to claim the library's circulating copies. The less fleet of foot were simply out of luck. If the faculty would simply notify the library staff ahead of time, he advised, an appropriate number of copies could be put on reserve. His letter carried the tone of an internal memorandum addressing an intra-organizational inefficiency. There was not the slightest hint that library administrators resented this role. But it was apparent to everyone at the university, including Father Fox, that while this arrangement might have worked in 1881 or even 1910, it was not acceptable in the mid-1920s. This public facility had undoubtedly saved Marquette thousands of dollar over the years, but an authentic university library was imperative. The path to this library, however, had a peculiar curvature.[41]

In early 1925, as part of his organizational overhaul, Albert Fox ordered a thorough review of the university's publicity efforts. In the absence of a central office to handle advertising, student recruitment was haphazard, relying as much upon word of mouth among parish priests as upon notices in local newspapers. A faculty committee proposed hiring an advertising firm at the cost of $36,000, a suggestion that Fox and Banzhaf quickly brushed aside. Annoyed, Fox appointed a member from the board of trustees to leaven the deliberative process. However, he saw some wisdom in another of the committee's ideas: the creation of a "Central Agency of Information." In late 1925, Fox hired Irma Hochstein, former chief reference librarian of the Wisconsin Legislative Library, to head the new Central Bureau of Information and Statistics. Hochstein was charged with coordinating the publication of university catalogues and pamphlets, collecting statistics on Marquette students, their parents, and the faculty, and reorganizing the university library—such as it was.[42]

On the hilltop, Marquette College's classrooms and hallways had been filled with books owned by the Jesuit community. They were lent on an as-needed basis to individual students. Later, the faculty established a reading room, although it lacked a book collection. Eventually, a library was opened on the second floor of the former Holy Name parish school, with the school's first gymnasium one floor below. Yet this facility was still more of a study hall than a circulating library. Only the medical and law schools received funding for library materials; their accrediting bodies insisted upon this. Individual academic units, with little oversight or support from the central administration, maintained their own collections. By the time Father Fox hired Hochstein in 1925, what was called the "university library" had been moved to the first floor of Johnston Hall where it remained under "lock and key by Father Librarian." It consisted of several thousand volumes. There were no regular hours and most of the titles could not be used outside the reading room.

Within a year of her arrival, Irma Hochstein made remarkable progress. She brought library science students from the University of Wisconsin to work with a few enthusiastic Marquette undergraduates. They classified and arranged nearly a thousand books and set about identifying out-of-date reference materials. For example, one of the most popular encyclopedia sets was twenty-five years old, absent most of the European conquest of Africa, the arrival of the automobile and air flight, and World War I. In her first annual report on the library, Hochstein recommended the appointment of a full-time, professionally trained librarian and urged tuition scholarships to pay for student assistants who would help keep the facility open from 9:00 a.m. to 9:00 p.m. every school day. The next three years were spent calling in the books traditionally housed in individual departments, a process that must have required a consummate diplomat. By 1927, an interlibrary loan system was in place for faculty. Finally, in 1928, the university hired a full-time librarian and added a professional cataloguer the following year. The staff introduced the university to the Dewey Decimal classification system. By 1930, the main library's holdings had grown to 30,000 volumes.[43]

IMPOSING STANDARDS ON GRADUATE EDUCATION

Progress toward a genuine university library (with both medicine and law continuing to oversee their own collections) was critical to Marquette's academic advancement. In 1889, two years after the first baccalaureate degrees were awarded, Francis X. Bodden had received a master's degree. For the next thirty-three years, supervision of course work for master's degrees (and later for doctoral degrees) remained a departmental prerogative and, consequently, was irregular at best. By the early 1920s, this lack of oversight by a central university authority deviated from the national movement toward precisely defined, measurable standards for all academic programs and especially professional and graduate degrees. So Father Fox created an new office, appointing Father George A. Deglman as the first dean of the graduate school in 1922. Its role was to insure uniform standards across disciplines. Fox, with his reputation for innovations in higher education, contended that the quality of graduate education at a university was a bellwether of its intellectual stature. But Deglman's reassignment to another Jesuit post forced Dr. James O'Gorman to become graduate dean in 1923. The following year, Fox finally brought in the man he wanted, Edward A. Fitzpatrick. His principal objective was to improve the instructional program through a thorough upgrade in the instructional staff. To accomplish this, Fitzpatrick issued guidelines that outlined who would be allowed to teach graduate courses, although final authorization still rested with the dean. Faculty status alone no longer guaranteed access to graduate students. Fitzpatrick also limited fields of study, based upon which departments in his mind possessed qualified faculty. Research, heretofore not a mandatory obligation for faculty at Marquette, became "a factor in determining promotion only second to the direct teaching service." For the first time, graduate assistantships (both instructional and research) became available. They provided free tuition and a $600 to $800 annual stipend. His campaign to standardize graduate education extended to degree requirements as well. All master's degrees now required thirty credits and each student had to take a twelve-unit major and two six-unit minors along with six units of thesis work.[44]

Enrollment in graduate studies at Marquette reflected the improved state of instruction. In 1922, the graduate school's first year of operation, fourteen students were working on post-baccalaureate degrees. By the time Fitzpatrick arrived in 1924, 38 students were registered. This number tripled to 115 by the spring of 1927. In total, 265 graduate students with baccalaureate degrees from sixty-two institutions registered at Marquette between 1924 and 1927. Half had received their undergraduate diplomas from either Marquette or the University of Wisconsin. The other half came from institutions such as the University of Illinois, Catholic University, Columbia University, the University of Notre Dame, and the University of Chicago. Master's degrees—the terminal degree for most college faculty in those days—were now available in history, education, English, philosophy, Latin, German, economics, chemistry, and physics.[45]

OTHER NEW ACADEMIC VENTURES

Improvements in the library and graduate education during the mid-twenties supported other academic initiatives. In an address before the Milwaukee Rotary Club in the fall of 1924, Father Fox promised four additional areas of study in the coming years: schools of architecture, pharmacy, library science, and social service. It was no coincidence that all four focused upon service professions. In his speech, the president reflected upon Marquette's relationship with Milwaukee, how it needed to resemble the role that Harvard had played in the development of Boston. However, of these four professions, only social work became a reality at Marquette many years later. One promising, service-oriented addition that had a glorious but fleeting appearance (1924 to 1928) was the College of Hospital Administration. Father Charles Moulinier, SJ, head of the Catholic Hospital Association, developed a program that trained executives, technicians, dietitians, and social workers. Its offices were in General Winkler's old residence, then known as Lalumiere Hall. By the college's second year, the course of study Moulinier had introduced became the national standard, adopted by the American Hospital Association. The ubiquitous Edward Fitzpatrick served as the college's educational (curriculum) director. However, Father Moulinier's preference to have the Catholic Hospital Association located in Cincinnati removed his guiding hand from Milwaukee. Without him, Father William Magee (Fox's successor) closed the hospital administration program in early 1928 at the first sign of budgetary troubles. The failure to obtain the Schandein property and build a teaching hospital made this decision that much easier.[46]

Among the successful initiatives from this era were several that relied heavily upon specialists recruited from secular institutions. In the case of education, Father Fox hired James M. O'Gorman away from the State University of Idaho in 1923 to take the reins of a new department then housed in the College of Arts and Sciences. The following year, Edward Fitzpatrick arrived to assist O'Gorman. Together, they developed a very popular after-hours curriculum that drew hundreds of teachers from the Milwaukee public schools. With a similar tilt toward the needs of the local community, Marquette opened a one-year dental hygiene program in 1923, following the Wisconsin legislature's decision in 1921 to license these professionals. Until 1919, Marquette's Department of English maintained oversight over all instruction in elocution. Father Noonan then established a Department of Public Speaking (perhaps the first independent speech department at a Catholic university) that also assumed responsibility for the dramatic arts classes, previously supervised by the music conservatory. Three years later, William R. Duffey arrived at Marquette from the University of Texas to open a speech clinic. In 1926, with Duffey as its first dean, Father Fox upgraded the speech department to a School of Speech. William Lamers succeeded Duffey three years later, by which time the school also offered a speech correction option, managed the radio station, and supervised the debate program. Its offices were on the fifth floor of Johnston Hall until 1928, after which time it shared space with the music program in the former John Plankinton residence. With the closing of music in 1930, this once-magnificent mansion at Fifteenth and Wisconsin became synonymous for a generation of Marquette undergraduates with their core classes in speech.[47]

Another significant advancement promoted during Albert Fox's time in Milwaukee was his mandate that students in the professional colleges attend classes in the College of Arts and Sciences for their first two years. This was Fox's way of imprinting a Jesuit education upon students regardless of their majors. He insisted undergraduates have a minimal exposure to literature, composition, language, history, and philosophy—a practice now synonymous with general education or the core. Thus, the new five-year program in dentistry (designed by Henry Banzhaf) required two years in arts and sciences before students could advance to specialized training. Likewise, the law school mandated two years of preparation in arts and sciences before students began their legal education. Albert Fox characterized arts and sciences as the "'hub'" around which the rest of the university revolved; nothing was more important. He made it clear to each dean that, except for some basic technical training, studies in the College of Arts and Sciences must preface other collegiate course work.

To better express this elevated role for a unit that had been called the College of Arts and Sciences since 1907, Father Fox changed its name to the College of Liberal Arts. He also authorized a bachelor of philosophy degree (which did not require two years of Latin) to complement the traditional bachelor of arts program. All liberal arts students, regardless of degree objective, took fifteen units of philosophy, sixteen units of modern languages, six in history and six in mathematics. Previously non-Catholic student had been exempt from the requirement of eight units of "Evidences of Religion" (one unit per semester for four years). Fox now added religion classes for all liberal arts students, as well as four units of "gymnasium work" and two units in public speaking. For Catholic students, although "the core of apologetical and doctrinal courses continued to be part of the curriculum for freshmen and sophomores," upper class students could now take courses on sacred scripture, the life of Christ, and the history of the Church.[48]

MILWAUKEE'S UNIVERSITY

From the day he first arrived in town, Albert Fox held that Marquette was grossly underappreciated across Milwaukee and throughout Wisconsin. For this reason, he persistently promoted Marquette as "Milwaukee's University," using this phrase, for example, when introducing his Schandein plan. Well-known nationally among Catholic educators, the president presented a broad view of American higher education when he discussed the contributions of great universities such as Chicago, Columbia, and Marquette to their host cities. He developed this theme at length in a paper titled "University's Vision of the City." The essay detailed the civic partnership that needed to exist between a top-flight educational institution and its home town. Fox worried, however, that Milwaukee's Jesuit university tended to engender suspicion, if not outright opposition, because of the area's religious prejudices.

Some of the loudest, and certainly the most insistent, opposition to the Society of Jesus came from the region's dominant political party, the Social Democratic Party (SDP). Socialists in Milwaukee controlled the mayor's office from 1910 to1912, and again, from 1916 to 1940. The party also maintained a powerful, if not commanding, presence on the common council and on the county board of supervisors. These politicians tangled with a Catholic Church that was unified in its opposition to socialism, both as a theory and as a system. Various popes, Milwaukee archbishops such as Sebastian Messmer and Samuel Stritch, and Jesuits such as Alexander Burrowes and Herbert Noonan all took turns condemning socialism. In retaliation, the SDP's daily newspaper, the *Milwaukee Leader*, seemed to take vociferous exception to almost everything the Jesuits did in Milwaukee, sarcastically objecting to one university proposal after another. In his history of Marquette, Father Raphael Hamilton characterized the newspaper as "pugnaciously anti-clerical." To make matters worse, university administrators found fault with the *Milwaukee Journal* (a leading daily without the slightest tilt toward the left) for not being more appreciative and supportive of Marquette.[49]

Whereas Father Noonan had taken his bully pulpit on the road across Wisconsin, his successor preferred to use the offices of the university to make his case. Father Fox treated the student newspaper as if it were *the* official organ of Marquette University and released major announcements through the student paper rather than the city press. The *Tribune* reprinted his speeches and provided front-page coverage of the university's contributions to the community through the medical school's dispensaries, the dentistry school's clinics, and the engineering college's collaborations with local manufacturers. When the dean of engineering designed a new viaduct over the Milwaukee River at North Avenue, it was headline news—in the *Tribune*. When Alderman John Koerner hailed Marquette's impact upon the Milwaukee economy ($6 million in 1922), the *Tribune* gloried in this admission. Fox also directed his new Central Bureau of Information and Statistics to tabulate the public funds that taxpayers saved through Milwaukee's Catholic school system. And in 1925, Fox initiated an annual civic convocation at which the university recognized outstanding local leaders. Among the early recipients were corporate executive Charles Pfister and publisher William George Bruce, both devoted friends of Marquette.[50]

Recognition for the university from outside the Marquette community came largely through symbolic gestures. The Chicago, Milwaukee and St. Paul Railroad named a Pullman coach car after Father Marquette in 1927. The following year, the new Schroeder Hotel named one of its dining rooms for the priest-explorer. Soon thereafter, *Marquette* was designated an exchange prefix by the Wisconsin Telephone Company at the initiative of senior executives who were alumni. About the same time, the common council considered a proposal to have Cedar and Biddle streets (the same street, but with different names on opposite sides of the Milwaukee River) retitled for the university's namesake. Father William Magee, Fox's successor, declined this offer, fearing that it would trigger a fight (presumably with local anti-Catholics or with the socialists) and wondering "if it would be worth the fight when it was done." The thoroughfare was ultimately named for one of the city's founding fathers, Byron Kilbourn.[51]

WHO WERE THESE MARQUETTE STUDENTS?

When Herbert Noonan replaced Joseph Grimmelsman as president in 1915, enrollment at the university stood at 878, more than eight times what it had been a decade earlier when the institution offered only a bachelor of arts degree. During World War I, the size of Marquette's student body did not drop as precipitously as it would twenty-five years later during the next war, but it did not grow much either. Between the fall of 1918 (when the armistice was signed) and the fall of 1919, enrollments rose by 37 percent, and by an additional 28 percent between 1919 and 1920. Marquette enrolled 2,847 students during the fall term of 1922. Six years later, at the end of Albert Fox's term, the student body had grown to 3,505. The summer school program, gateway to coeducation, surpassed a thousand registrants by the mid-twenties. A 1927 survey of ten Jesuit colleges and universities in the Midwest had Marquette trailing only Chicago's Loyola University in total enrollment. Among these institutions, only Marquette had programs in such fields as business administration, dental hygiene, hospital administration, journalism, music, and speech.[52]

Father Fox's insistence that undergraduates, regardless of religious affiliation, complete eight units of religion reflected the religious diversity at Marquette. No longer were only a handful of its students non-Catholic. Fewer than three out of five students were Roman Catholic by 1924. By college, these figures ranged from a high of 80 percent Catholic in the College of Journalism to a low of 46 percent in the School of Dentistry. Protestants students made up 44 percent in dentistry, but only 13 percent in music. For Jewish students, who numbered 155 in total, the percentages ranged from a high of 22 percent in journalism to a low of 3 percent in business administration. By denomination in 1927, there were 215 Lutherans, 85 Methodists, 85 Presbyterians, 76 Congregationalists, 42 Baptists, and smaller numbers from 21 other sects. Faculty figures from across the university for 1925-26 revealed 155 non-Catholic teachers versus 154 Catholics.[53]

In 1926, 47 percent of the university's students hailed from Milwaukee (probably meaning the metropolitan area) and another 35 percent resided elsewhere in the state. For those from out of state, 167 students came from Michigan, 110 from Minnesota and 108 from Illinois. In total, the university's student body drew from thirty-four states, thirteen nations, and three U.S. territories. For the first time, the Central Bureau of Information and Statistics identified the occupations of the students' parents and guardians. The largest number fell into a category labeled "Business-Miscellaneous" (469 students), followed by "Business-Mercantile" (403), "Skilled Laborers" (327), and "Agriculturists" (275). Less than 10 percent of the parents were designated as "Profession[al]," which included medicine, law, teaching, military, and ministry.[54]

COEDUCATION: PART TWO

The central bureau's statistics revealed two sets of numbers that showed just how diverse the student population had become. When Herbert Noonan returned to his alma mater in 1915, female students constituted almost 9 percent of the total enrollment. By the end of the Noonan-Fox era, females made up nearly 25 percent. Eight hundred and sixty-nine women were enrolled at Marquette in1927. This included an astonishing total of 194 females as full-time students in the College of Liberal Arts (until recently, arts and sciences), an academic unit that had been opened to women only one year earlier. (A request to the provincial and to the superior general four years before to admit nuns full-time to liberal arts had been firmly denied, much to Father Fox's disappointment.) Elsewhere on campus, there were eighty-nine female students in nursing and sixteen in dental hygiene, both all-female programs. Women made up 94 percent of the students in the College of Hospital Administration, 89 percent in the Conservatory of Music, 61 percent in the Graduate School, 29 percent in the College of Journalism, and 13 percent in the College of Business Administration. Only the College of Engineering remained male-only, as it would until World War II.[55]

The greatest adjustment in the practice of coeducation at Marquette came not so much in the numbers of female students as in the way Jesuits viewed these women. When Alexander Burrowes, who had transformed Marquette College into a university, visited Milwaukee in early 1918 while provincial, he endorsed his successor's decision to add "girls," although he still preferred the more expensive proposition of separate Catholic women's colleges. In contrast, when Father Noonan returned to the campus in 1928 to see Father Fox's successor installed, he gloried in the fact that the "fight for co-education is just about over in Jesuit universities ... Marquette was the pioneer in co-education and I am very glad to say that it was during my term that woman students began to come here in any great numbers." Noonan could also claim credit for appointing the first female administrator, registrar Catherine Foley, in 1918.[56]

Noonan's successor was even more outspoken and proactive regarding gender equity. In the fall of 1921, his last autumn at Marquette, Father Noonan had recognized the growing importance of extracurricular activities when he established the position of dean of men. Two years later, Father Fox insured at least some parity when he appointed Mathilda Steinbrecher (a Marquette graduate, a former school teacher, and a science instructor in the dental school) as the first Supervisor of Women. In an address before one hundred and fifty female students, Fox made it clear that he did not care if the women were in male-dominated programs such as law and dentistry or female-dominated programs such as music and nursing: they were all Marquette students who, he hoped, would take an active part in all school functions. He needed them to have a "good influence on the student body in general—a good influence which they should exercise to the fullest extent." He advocated women in higher education, the president explained, because if men and women were to solve the nation's social, economic, and domestic problems, schooling was imperative. He demonstrated just how strongly he felt on this issue when he authorized distribution of a pamphlet titled "Opportunities for Women." This document highlighted the traditional female fields of music, dental hygiene, nursing, and journalism, but it also reminded readers that law, medicine, and dentistry were available to women at Marquette. A material expression of Fox's concern was shown in his renovation of the Hitz house on Sycamore Street after the men's union vacated the building. Fox turned the former residence into Drexel Lodge, "official headquarters for the coeds."[57]

Fox also demonstrated his support for Marquette women when he encouraged the establishment of the Marquette University Alumnae Association. At their first general meeting in Drexel Lodge on November 24, 1924, the alumnae turned their attention to the availability of morally and physically safe housing for female students. In March 1926, a committee investigated the feasibility of a women's dormitory. Housing was on everyone's mind. The dean of women, Margaret Harrington, announced in 1926 that "'women students of Marquette University shall not live in unchaperoned apartments'" after January 3, 1927. She condemned lodging houses where both males and females could rent rooms. Instead, the dean preferred sororities because of the presence of house mothers. Harrington also warned her charges against frequenting road houses (outside the city limits) where students could obtain illegal liquor. The central administration backed Harrington's efforts. The university business manager looked into the possibility of purchasing property at Fourteenth and Wisconsin for a dormitory in 1924. Even the *Marquette Tribune* got into the act when it made "recognition of the needs of the coeds for better housing and meeting facilities" one of its planks in a Program for a Greater Marquette.[58]

The slowly evolving world of Marquette women included, finally, a partial answer to the question first raised by the *Marquette Tribune* in 1918: what about female athletics? One response was the gymnasium requirement imposed upon all first-year students, female as well as male. A second response came when the Marquette women followed the nursing students' lead and organized an athletic association in 1923. During its first year, this group sponsored a basketball team that played local competitors such as Holy Angels Academy, Milwaukee Normal College, and the Young Women's Christian Association. This innovative program gained official status the following year when Frances Baker, a graduate of Barnard College, became the first women's athletic director. Through Baker's efforts, the university approved the Marquette Women's Athletic Association (WAA) which, in turn, affiliated with the American Conference of Athletic College Women. The WAA promoted "interest in gymnastics and athletics and [sought] to present these activities in the light of their highest ideals to the women students of the University." Membership was open to all female students, although active status was contingent upon the accumulation of at least 100 points to be earned in four categories: sportsmanship, leadership, scholarship (75 points for a C average in all classes with no failures), and physical activities (gym credit as well as involvement in team and individual sports). Individuals who earned more than a 1,000 points (later raised to 1,200) received a white varsity sweater (with an "M" on it) and thereby became members of the "M Club." An impressive list of team and individual sports became available over the next few years: soccer, basketball, baseball, track, tennis, golf, swimming, bowling, and ice hockey. By 1929, there were three female ice hockey teams: a varsity, a freshman, and a nurses' team.[59]

RACIAL DIVERSITY

Although gender inclusiveness registered some noticeable advances during the twenties, international and racial diversity proceeded at a slower pace. As noted a few pages earlier, the university attracted only a small number of students from other countries at this time, even though the school had been approved by the federal government as "a school for immigrant students." By the fall of 1926, thirty-eight students from thirteen countries attended Marquette. The largest number (ten) came from Canada. By college, engineering attracted sixteen, liberal arts eight, and dentistry five. In 1929, Marquette offered a handful of scholarships to foreign students who were sponsored by the Maryknoll Fathers, a missionary order working in China, Japan, and Manchuria.[60]

Until 1924, university records regarding the demography of its student body ranged from sketchy to non-existent, except for enrollments. It is, therefore, unclear when the first student of color was admitted. The first contacts Jesuits made with African Americans in Milwaukee came through their parish ministries. In 1886, a group of black Catholics attended services at St. Gall's. This number grew to perhaps as many as 140 worshiping at Gesu, although black parishioners were relegated to the gallery. The first mention of an African American student at the university came in 1912 when Eugene W. Scott, "a negro student" in law, presented a lecture titled "'The Prince of Self-Made Men'" (Abraham Lincoln) at the Masonic Hall in Bay View before an audience of four hundred people. A year later as a junior, Scott was a finalist in the law school's oratorical championship. His subject had a familiar ring to it: "'The Self-Made Man.'"[61]

The introduction of yearbooks in 1915 finally allows the use of photographic evidence to identify students of color, although grainy reproductions of somber-looking students enshrouded in black caps and gowns make conclusive identifications difficult. Thomas A. Boger, an African American, received a doctor of medicine degree that year and over the next fifteen years, a steady but small number of black men graduated from the School of Medicine. One African who attended Marquette for two years but did not complete his program in Milwaukee was A.B. Xuma, president of the African National Congress from 1940 to 1949. He completed his basic science courses at Marquette's medical school between 1921 and 1923, before transferring to Northwestern University for financial reasons (Northwestern cost about $75 less). He received his medical degree at the Evanston school. Also noteworthy was the small but steady stream of black students at the School of Dentistry beginning after World War I. Most years, at least one African American student received a doctor of dental surgery degree. In 1918, three dental graduates were African Americans. In 1923, Elijah Williams, identified as the fastest man in Kansas, enrolled in dentistry while running track. For his contributions on the defensive line of an undefeated (once tied) team in the fall of 1922, Rollie McMahan (the "Kansas Cyclone") became the first black athlete showcased in either the *Marquette Tribune* or the yearbook. The next year, he received a bachelor of science in electrical engineering, after varsity experience in football, track, and hockey. The first African American woman to complete a program may have been Sarah Louise Brewer, from Cleveland, who in 1928 received a certificate in dental hygiene.[62]

As for the university's central administration, there is nothing in the recruitment materials, the student handbook, or administrative correspondence to suggest any institutional policies based upon race. Father Fox blasted racial and religious discrimination as twin evils endangering American life in a speech at a union hall meeting in 1924. (This may have been the address in which he denounced "100% Americanism," thereby earning the enmity of the Ku Klux Klan.) With a black population of only 2,229 in Milwaukee in 1920 (compared to Chicago's 109,458), discussions of race relations rarely appeared in the *Marquette Tribune* during this decade. In a 1927 editorial, the paper decried protests by white students against the integration of a high school in Gary, Indiana. It took note of the literary and musical successes of the Harlem Renaissance and concluded (prophetically) that "race troubles" in the North were likely to linger longer than in the South because racial prejudice could not be "adjusted in a day." Fifteen months later, another editorial sought to explain to its readers how self-respect lay behind the reluctance of local African Americans to attend downtown performances of the play *Porgy*. The *Tribune* interviewed seven men and women from the Milwaukee Urban League's settlement house for their reactions on the poor turnout. The editorial did notice the fact that the venue had a segregated seating policy. (The light opera version, *Porgy and Bess* by George Gershwin, did not appear until eight years later.)

In both 1921 and 1922, vaudeville productions presented during Marquette's prom week included white students wearing black face. As evidenced by Al Jolson's donning of black face in the 1927 talkie, *The Jazz Singer*, white society clearly did not find anything inappropriate about this practice during the roaring twenties. However, the fact that black face did not appear in yearbooks after 1922 raises the possibility that Father Fox may have taken his opposition to racial and religious discrimination out of the union hall and into Gesu Auditorium where most campus shows took place. It is also worth noting that during this same time period (1914 to 1938), Catholic University in the District of Columbia denied admission to African American students, reversing its inclusive policy that dated back nearly two decades.[63]

STUDENT LIFE

The orderliness that Father Fox brought to the central administration applied to student life as well. He oversaw production of the first student handbook. Sixty-four pages in length, it detailed a host of policies at Marquette: a semester hour (fifty minutes of "recitation" per week during an eighteen-week semester), graduation requirements (128 units), admission exams (by the College Entrance Examination Board), registration procedures in the gymnasium, registration limitations on freshman (sixteen units), rules on "cuts" (none), physical education classes for freshmen (required), smoking in classrooms and corridors (forbidden), boarding house guidelines, and eligibility for varsity athletics.

The new handbook revisited a troublesome issue from the past: hazing. Since the school's earliest days, Marquette upperclassmen had adopted the well-developed collegiate tradition of requiring first-year students to wear beanies. Jesuit administrators did not have a problem with this particular indignity, so much as with what usually followed. In the early twenties, freshmen were forced to march down Grand Avenue with their pants legs rolled above their knees and their jackets turned inside out. In the 1922 yearbook, one photograph depicts a young man with his pants pulled down around his ankles and a group of upperclassmen whacking him with a stick; in the background, others wearing beanies wait their turn. The following fall, upperclass women required newcomers to wear green arm bands with blue and gold ribbons. Administrators imposed limits on this behavior, and when those restrictions failed, they became sterner. In 1924, the first dean of men, Father Simon J. Nicolas, banned the practice of "subjecting fellow students to indignities of any character." Even mingling with a crowd "engaged in hazing [would] be considered to be participation in hazing," warned the dean. For a short time, the issue was brought under control, only to reappear once again.[64]

One new university office that students found useful was a health center. In October 1924, Father Fox asked the Committee on Student Health and Hygiene to report within one month on the suggestion of a student health service. Two months later, the committee proposed using Marquette University Hospital's dispensary at Ninth and Wells. Senior medical students could assist resident physicians; special provisions were made for examinations of female students. Henry Banzhaf, the business manager, delivered a model budget to the president in early January 1925 with revenues for this office generated by a six-dollar annual fee. No university funds would be needed in this plan. Behind this initiative was a growing concern about the student body's ignorance of health issues as well as the health dangers present in fraternity houses and private boarding houses. The university's imposition of mandatory medical inspections for all incoming students in the fall of 1923 helped force the issue. Given the university's tight finances, administrators must have been delighted at the financial success of their efforts, for in the first two years of operation the student health service produced a positive cash flow of $10,172.[65]

A (MALE) STUDENT UNION

For male students at least, the most important "office" opened during the 1920s was the Marquette Union. Its origins rest with the students themselves or, more precisely, one assertive undergraduate. Peter A. Brooks was a veteran of World War I, a junior in arts and sciences, and president of the Marquette Honor Society. During the first week of May 1920, this young Hilltopper (who subsequently became president of Marquette) attended a convention of student representatives scheduled around the dedication of a $1 million facility at the University of Michigan. Within days of his return, Brooks drafted an article for the *Marquette Tribune* heralding the benefits that a central facility would hold for Marquette's (male) students who were scattered about town at Fourth and Reservoir (School of Medicine), Ninth and Wells (School of Dentistry) and Eleventh and Grand (everyone else). With Father Noonan's blessing, Brooks called the men together for a mass meeting in the Gesu school auditorium. The president suspended all university activities during this assembly and personally led the deans and faculty into the auditorium. After Brooks addressed the audience, it authorized by a unanimous vote a $5 charge per (male) student for the maintenance of a center to house student activities. Noonan "was greeted by cheers that shook the roof" when

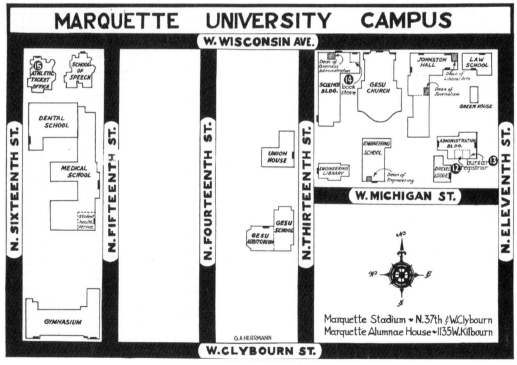

Marquette campus, circa 1940. File 260

he offered to provide the former Hitz house on Sycamore Street as a temporary home for the Marquette Union, a name that came to signify both the organization and its headquarters.[66]

Within a month's time, Peter Brooks asked Charles Cobeen, a friend who soon graduated from the College of Business Administration, to serve as secretary and manager of the union. (Cobeen held this position for twenty-seven years, until he succeeded Henry Banzhaf as university business manager in 1947.) By September 1921, the union board had purchased a site for a new building one block west of the Hitz house. Three years of plans and counterplans created a blizzard of blueprints and design sketches before the union was completed at the cost of $65,000. To pay for it, the Marquette Union took out a $50,000 loan, after becoming a non-stock corporation in early 1923. Dedication came during homecoming week in 1924. The two-story structure occupied seventy feet along Thirteenth Street, to the depth of one hundred and thirty-two feet. On the first floor, a cafeteria seated 150 and served, except on Sundays, three meals a day. Also on the first floor were a two-chair barbershop and meeting rooms. On the second floor was a lounge with chairs, tables, and divans as well as a banquet room and dance hall that could accommodate sixty to seventy couples. The union was open from seven in the morning to eleven at night, with the exception of Sunday when it closed at seven. Female students were allowed in the building only during the prime cafeteria hours of 11:30 a.m. to 1:30 p.m. and from 5 p.m. to 7:30 p.m.[67]

HOUSING AND STUDENT EXPENSES

One of the first issues tackled by the men's union was the same problem that the alumnae association addressed at its first meeting: student housing. In an early blueprint, the Marquette Union had three floors, with the top level consisting of private rooms for rent. The "dormitories will be the greatest feature of the new Union" trumpeted the *Marquette Tribune*. The student paper repeatedly bemoaned the shortage of student housing as well as the cost incurred in the private market. Expanding enrollments only aggravated this problem. Even Father Noonan conceded that the university needed dormitories. Accommodations in the local rental market varied greatly. One landlord complained in 1920 that female students caused trouble because they wanted their rooms swept and dusted, while the men did not care about such fine points. On the other hand, students accused landlords of price gouging. In a 1921 survey conducted by students of a Jesuit sociology professor, most Marquette students indicated they paid between three and four dollars a week for a room. The survey suggested that landlords made between 11 and 30 percent in profits. By 1927, room and board (in contrast to the rooms-only survey in 1921) was running $10 to $12 per week. Inflation drove prices higher throughout the twenties, including tuition which reached $180 for liberal arts students in 1927, three times the traditional $60 charge that had stood for decades.[68]

Students met their college expenses through part-time employment. Finding work was not difficult, given the vitality of Milwaukee's economy. Moreover, the students established an employment bureau, which the Marquette Union later supervised. A May 1919 listing of positions procured through the bureau included five slots in inventory work at Cutler-Hammer, two elevator and bus boy jobs at the Hotel Aberdeen, five clerkships in the post office during Christmas rush, five positions as streetcar conductors, four as sweepers at the Eighth Street school, three as insurance agents, and one man to tend a furnace and shovel sidewalks. In a *Tribune* article published five years later, the student newspaper listed "hash slinging" as one of the "most popular and numerous" occupations. A 1927 column repeated some of the old favorites such as clerking and restaurant work but also added magician, undertaker's assistant, professional baseball player (during the summers, of course), ice cream packer, taxi driver and, for medical students, first-aid assistant in industrial plants.[69]

THE SOCIAL CALENDAR

Although the Marquette Union served as the favorite hangout after classes for men—and Drexel Lodge, with fewer amenities, for women—the most popular student activity in the 1920s involved a hectic week of dancing. The number of social events was almost as staggering as the list of organizations sponsoring them. Father Noonan imposed a limit of no more than one per college or school annually during World War I, with the junior prom receiving an automatic exemption if it paid for itself. Once the war was over, Marquette's social calendar stretched across the entire school year, with some groups hosting as many as three events. In the 1920-21 school year, there were seventy-nine official dates on the "Marquette Social Calendar." It started with the arts and sciences smoker on October 13 in the Gesu club rooms. A week later, journalism held its dinner-dance at the Hotel Blatz. The same venue hosted the following week's Sigma Alpha smoker, and the month concluded with three events on the 29th: the co-eds' club dancing party, the Psi Omega "hallowe'en" party, and the nurses' "hallowe'en" party. Banquets, dinner-dances, and smokers took place nearly every weekend until two fraternity banquets topped off the season at the hotels Medford and Astor. By academic unit, nursing sponsored three events, journalism two, economics two, engineering two, and dentistry, commerce, law, and medicine at least one each. And this did not include those scheduled by the fraternities and sororities. During Father Fox's regime, the student handbook tried to limit all university-approved dances to Friday and Saturday nights.[70]

Junior prom week was the highlight of each year. In 1924, this special week began with the formal prom on Wednesday, February 27, at 9 p.m. Private motor cars and taxis pulled up in front of what on any other day would have been the Marquette University gymnasium and discharged those who on any other day would have been ordinary college students. But on this night, these young adults were transformed into elegant men dressed in tuxedos and beautiful women bedecked in floor-length dresses, coiffed and accessorized in styles reflecting the roaring twenties. Athletic equipment was carefully hidden, leaving gold and blue bunting and Virginia creeper vines to mask the upper floor of the gym. A ten-piece orchestra greeted the guests. Each gentleman

1924 prom in the MU gymnasium. File 1143

received a black leather cigarette case embossed with the university seal, and each lady was presented a combination card case and pocketbook. At 10 p.m., the grand march began and dinner was served from 11 p.m. to 1 a.m., with dancing until 2:30 a.m. The following evening, festivities shifted to the Pabst Theater for the vaudeville show, with nearly every fraternity offering a skit. On Friday, it was back to the gym for the informal prom dance, "the most popular and democratic event" of the week, where the music of fox trots and waltzes filled the night air. With Ash Wednesday came Lent and, with Lent, a complete shutdown of the social calendar for forty long days. American college life had become, if not equal parts social and intellectual, at least noticeably less cerebral. The head-shaking among some older Jesuits can only be imagined.[71]

FRATERNITIES, SORORITIES, AND CLUBS

Fraternities originated at Marquette University through the Milwaukee Medical College. By the time the medical college affiliated with Marquette in 1907, several professional fraternities had been established. The first was Psi Omega, a national dental fraternity in 1897; it was followed by three national medical fraternities in 1900, 1903, and 1907. Twenty years later, students in most of the professional colleges (journalism, economics, engineering, and law) had fraternities available to them. Moreover, there were four national Jewish fraternities (two professional and two social) at Marquette by 1928. The first social fraternity approved by the university was Alpha Gamma Phi in 1908 and the first sorority, Kappa Beta Gamma, was launched in 1917. The second sorority was Alpha Beta Pi, authorized in 1920, followed by a dental hygiene sorority in 1925. Alpha Sigma Nu, the national Jesuit honor fraternity, originated at Marquette in 1915 and was the university's first honor society. With his penchant for rules, Father Fox insisted upon guidelines to govern panhellenic organizations. Developed in 1922, these rules required each fraternity and sorority to have a constitution and by-laws, and to register each year in order to sponsor social events. Activities were banned for first-semester freshmen. In addition, the faculty had to approve the location of each group's house and each pledge's candidacy.[72]

The Greek experience remained remarkably unchanged over the course of the twentieth century. Every fraternity and sorority sponsored social events such as dances and smokers. They organized a panhellenic bowling league and later a basketball league. The latter became so competitive that a *Marquette Tribune* columnist urged self-control after angry protests led to a censure of the coaches. The pledge process also had familiar contours. A Kappa Gamma pledge in the mid-1920s was required to vacate the sidewalk when encountering an active member. At this point, the pledge was required to acknowledge her deference: "'I, scum of the earth, bid thee, Miss _____, good morning or good afternoon.'" A pledge was denied rouge, powder, and lipstick, and had to keep her hair in a straight style. She was forbidden to date or even to have conversations with members of the opposite sex during her probationary period. She was obliged to carry a scroll containing the sorority's rules to every class—along with a grapefruit. Finally, each noon, the pledge reported to Red Arrow Park at Eleventh and Grand with a bag of marbles for a tournament. Under no condition were the rules to be revealed to those outside the sorority.[73]

Department, fraternity, and sorority socials filled a student's weekend just as other student organizations filled weekday evenings. The sodality strove to improve each member's Christian character, while the apostleship of prayer sought to turn daily actions into moments of prayer. A menorah club drew those who wished to study Jewish life and religion. A Lutheran club, started in 1923, provided for students of that faith. The lecture bureau and the debating society continued long-held traditions at Jesuit schools whereas the Marquette Players and the harlequin club were new organizations that collected the school's thespians. After World War I, an all-university American Legion chapter was established for those who had served in uniform. A few years later, the gun and blade club was established, also for veterans.

For those with an academic bent, there was the liberal arts association, the classical club, the Spanish club, the literary club, the Schiller club, the French club, and the Aristotelian society. In the professional schools, there was the American Society of Mechanical Engineers, the American Institute of Electrical Engineers, the American Society of Civil Engineers, the engineering club, the press club, the commerce club, and for nursing students, the Edith Cavell club. The Marquette orchestra made a comeback in 1926 after nearly a decade of neglect. There was also the university band, and both a men's and a women's glee club. The men's group toured Wisconsin, including stops in Green Bay and Marinette. There were state clubs for those who came from Iowa, Kansas, Michigan, Minnesota, and North Dakota as well as school clubs for graduates of North Division High School and Campion College, the Jesuit school in Prairie du Chien. Polish students organized a Joseph Conrad club to propagate "the spirit of Marquette among the Poles of Milwaukee and elsewhere," even though the club's namesake spent most of his life in England.[74]

THE UNIVERSITY RADIO STATION

One activity that reached out from the campus into the local community was WHAD, the Marquette radio station. It began in 1921 as a university-owned 100-watt station, with a 70-foot-high four-legged tower behind Johnston Hall. During its first year, programming focused on speeches, sermons, and concerts. The glee club presented the first concert. The energy behind this undertaking came from Father John B. Kremer, chairman of the physics department. Kremer built most of the early equipment himself but left the programming to others, although as faculty advisor he remained responsible for over-the-air content. When Science Hall was completed in 1924, the station moved from Johnston Hall. WHAD occupied two rooms in the new building, a broadcast studio in the tower and a room for its generators and batteries in the basement. By 1925, the station was generating 500 watts. It became the most powerful station in Milwaukee, with a signal picked up occasionally in Boston and San Francisco.[75]

Originally, programming was available only on Wednesday nights. After the university entered into an operational partnership with the *Milwaukee Journal*, WHAD broadcast from studios on campus and from remote locations such as Washington Park, the Milwaukee Athletic Club, and Marquette University Stadium. News, weather, sports, dance music, dinner music, and religious programming were heard across the state. Weekly entertainment from the Wisconsin Theater was broadcast using thirteen microphones. Ceremonies honoring the golden anniversary of the Milwaukee Archdiocese were broadcast live from the Marquette University Stadium. Reminiscent of President Ronald Reagan's nascent broadcasting career, a WHAD staffer relayed an Associated Press teletype of the 1925 World Series for (nearly) up-to-the-moment play-by-play. Traditionally, Sunday was a silent night for the station, but other nights featured Marquette football games, Wisconsin theater organs, and the Athletic Club's dance band. In late 1926, the potential of this new medium was demonstrated when four hours of music from the National Broadcasting Company studios in New York City was broadcast by WHAD and twenty others select stations across the country. But after only three years of affiliation, Father Fox startled the *Milwaukee Journal* by ending the broadcasting partnership in 1927, much to the latter's "amazement and dismay." For the university, publicity had become a key justification for continuing to invest in the radio station. By 1929, programming featured faculty members discussing the musical history of nations, personal deductions allowed on income taxes, conditional

W H A D

Established October, 1921

HILLTOP STUDIO
1217 WISCONSIN AVENUE

Telephone Grand 8100 (day), Grand 1237 (night)

MARQUETTE UNIVERSITY
MILWAUKEE, WISCONSIN

SUPPLEMENT OF THE MARQUETTE TRIBUNE
Vol. XII.   Number 16.   January 26, 1928.

1110 KILOCYCLES
2701 METERS
500 WATTS

✄✄✄

"CARRIER of news and knowledge, instrument of trade and industry, promoter of mutual acquaintance, of peace and good will among men and nations."

✄✄✄

REV. A. H. POETKER, S.J., Director
EDWIN L. CORDES, Operator
CYRIL C. FOSTER, Program Manager
HARRY A. FRIEDMAN, Announcer

Wednesday, February 22
3:30-4:00—Prof. **Wm. M. Lamers**, Correct English, (Common Errors). Music.
Prof. **James M. O'Gorman**, Washington, The Leader.
7:30-8:00—**George M. Niedecken**, Good Taste in Home Furnishing
John Holland, Violin.
Dr. **J. D. Logan**, Songs at Twilight; by the Marquette Poets.

Thursday, February 23
3:30-4:00—Rev. **J. Vincent Kelly**, Ethics, (The Social Animal). Music.
Prof. **Wm. M. Murphy**, Fields of Inquiry to Determine Feeble-Mindedness.
8:15 P. M.—Basketball, **Marquette vs. Notre Dame.**

Friday, February 24
3:30-4:00—Dr. **Wade R. Plater**, Prevention of Dental Decay in Children. Music.
Prof. **R. N. Bauer**, The Location of Wells.
4:30-5:00—Children's Half Hour, Academic Students, College of Music.
7:30-8:00—**Walter Bender**, Forests and Flood Control.
Victor Moreau, Vocal.
Rev. **Edw. F. Garesche**, The Fool of the House and the Master of the House.
8:00-9:30—Musical Program, **D. J. McKenna**, flute; **Victor Hamm**, piano; **Frank Sage**, tenor; **Rose Bink**, soprano.

Sunday, February 26
4:30-5:00—**John Leicht**, Organ Recital

Monday, February 27
3:30-4:00—Prof. **Anthony Bumbalek**, Lecture Recital, (Polonaise, Seguidilla, Tango).
7:30-8:00—Dr. **Joseph Lettenberger**, Heart Disease and Sudden Death.
Max Kreisler, Violin.
Dr. **Stewart Scrimshaw**, Economic Individualism vs. Collectivism.

Tuesday, February 28
3:30-4:00—Prof. **J. L. O'Sullivan**, Question Box. Music.
Mrs. **Miriam G. Robertson**, Readings of Modern Poetry.
7:30-8:00—Prof. **Daniel J. McKenna**, How the Law Grows.
Marion Raison, Vocal.
Ted Carpenter, Hilltop News Notes.

Wednesday, February 29
3:30-4:00—Prof. **Wm. M. Lamers**, Correct English, (Common Errors). Music.
7:30-8:00—Dr. **D. E. W. Wenstrand**, Art for the Amateur.
Margaret Schmit, Cornet.
Dr. **J. D. Logan**, Songs at Twilight; by the Marquette Poets.

Portion of 1928 WHAD programming guide. File 1160

sale contracts, and the history of the West as well as sports programming highlighting the school's hockey and basketball teams.[76]

UNIVERSITY ATHLETICS

The importance of Marquette varsity athletics to WHAD's programming schedule reflected the rise of sports (both college and professional) across America during the 1920s. Boxing fans point to the popularity of Jack Dempsey. Baseball historians see the twenties as a golden age, saved from the ignominy of the Black Sox scandal by the feats of Babe Ruth and his New York Yankee teammates. The National Football League was organized during the twenties, at the same time college football devotees heralded an era replete with stars such as Red Grange of Illinois and coach Knute Rockne at Notre Dame. One hundred and twenty-three thousand fans filled Chicago's Soldier Field in 1929 to watch the Irish take on the West Coast's football powerhouse, the University of Southern California. This same wave of sport mania washed over Milwaukee and Marquette. For Hilltoppers, this energy culminated in the development of two sports centers, physical monuments to the spirit then coursing through the student body and alumni.[77]

Ever since the explosion in Marquette's enrollment during the presidencies of Fathers Burrowes and McCabe, it had become clear that a university of this size and stature required an indoor athletic facility that could serve both the general student body and an intercollegiate sports program. At times, the student voice on this matter could be deafening. After a dismal basketball season in 1918, a *Marquette Tribune* article bewailed the absence of a gymnasium. It ended with a fervent declaration: "IT NEEDS A GYM …WE WANT A GYM." In the same issue, Charles R. Atkinson, dean of the Robert A. Johnston College of Business Administration, sympathized, although he tended to blame the team's poor performances on irresponsible athletes and a selfish student body. He agreed that "the decentralized character of the University [had] much to do with an apparent lethargy and lack of spirit on the part of the students." "We do not know each other," the dean lamented, even as he dreamed for a "better day when Marquette [could] get together and get acquainted."

That "better day" arrived when Father Noonan announced plans for a gymnasium at Sixteenth and Clybourn. When the facility opened in 1922, the university began to require freshmen to take "physical training." Handball nets, horseshoe lanes, and volleyball courts were located in the basement of the new building and basketball courts were on the first floor, with a track looping the balcony. Boxing and wrestling contests were scheduled on the main floor. Father Fox soon found a second use for the building: as a place to "get together" in the words of Dean Atkinson. On November 22, 1922, the first general convocation in Marquette history was held, with 2,000 students and 150 faculty members in attendance. Father Fox urged his audience to "'gain a spirit and a bearing, which will mark you out among men, and gain for you their trust, and love and confidence. We want you to acquire a spirit which will compel people to say "a student of Marquette, is a man who can relied upon."'" Thereafter, convocations became a regular feature of campus life, as university presidents delivered an annual state of the university address. The building was also used for a variety of special events, such as the conferral of an honorary doctor of music degree upon John Philip Sousa in 1923. Classes were dismissed for the 10:00 and 11:00 a.m. hours so that students could witness this memorable moment. In gratitude, Sousa wrote a special anthem in honor of Marquette University.[78]

If the gymnasium took on the task of unifying the student body, a second athletic center heralded a new era for varsity sports at Marquette. For decades, the school's teams had played a dangerous brand of baseball and football on a sun-baked, rock-hard, cinder-covered field alongside the old college building. According to one reminiscence, "it was an ideal place for one to remove large chunks of his anatomy if he should by chance happen to hit the ground with any degree of abruptness." Rickety wooden stands lined the east and west sides of the field (whose north end opened toward the Pabst brewery). A tragedy proved the dangers of this makeshift construction. On a Saturday afternoon in October 1917, Father Leo J. Lyons, a young, popular Jesuit was killed in what was called at the time "the saddest accident in the history of Marquette." A three-foot-high barrier atop the bleachers collapsed when students rushed to see a fight that was taking place at ground level. As Father Lyons arrived to disperse the crowd, the railing gave way, catapulting a dozen individuals to the ground, including him. He was rushed to Trinity Hospital three blocks away but never regained consciousness. He died that afternoon.[79]

An indoor sports facility took priority over an outdoor arena, and for that reason, the gymnasium came first. That did not keep journalism students from routinely voicing their opinions. They wanted an outdoor stadium to match those at Ohio State, Wisconsin, Yale, and Stanford. Henry Banzhaf actually looked into purchasing land for a football stadium. In May 1922, during his last weeks on campus, Noonan received a report that listed five possibilities, including an old brickyard near Washington Park, a site opposite Calvary Cemetery, and another one in the Menomonee Valley where Milwaukee County Stadium would be built thirty years later. The most affordable space could be found on the western edge of what was known as the "old circus grounds." West of Thirty-fifth at Clybourn was a large piece of property on which the Barnum and Bailey and Ringling Brothers circuses had camped for years. The city of Milwaukee had acquired this twenty-four-acre tract for $125,000 with plans for a park and a playground, but with the understanding that a portion could be sold to help finance the recreational center. (It is interesting to note that this tract was not even within the city limits at the time but remained in the jurisdiction of the town of Wauwatosa until 1925.) In early 1923, the Marquette University Alumni Association purchased an eight-acre slice of the circus grounds for $40,000. One-third of this sum was raised in cash by students and alumni, with the balance met through a $26,000 mortgage. Confident that full funding could be found, the alumni moved ahead with plans for a steel and concrete stadium designed by Alexander Eschweiler Jr, an early donor to the project. His blueprints called for a horseshoe-shaped stadium with an ultimate seating

To the Faculty and Students of The Marquette University of Milwaukee, Wis.

Marquette University March

Piano Acc.   JOHN PHILIP SOUSA

Written by John Philip Sousa in gratitude for 1923 honorary degree. File 105

capacity of 48,000. For the time being, the capacity would be 20,000, with bleachers flanking the east and west sides of the playing field. Marquette University Stadium opened on October 18, 1924, when the Hilltopper eleven triumphed over a team from John Carroll University (a Jesuit sister school in Cleveland) by a score of ten to three. The first phase of stadium construction was completed the following year.

Unfortunately, the first phase became the stadium's final phase. Seating in an oval behind the north end zone never became necessary. Forty-eight-thousand rabid fans remained a pipedream. In fact, the alumni association could not handle the mortgage and the construction loan, so they surrendered ownership and fiscal responsibility for both to the university, forcing the institution to take out 6 percent bonds totaling $250,000 to pay these debts. Suddenly faced with these unexpected burdens, Father Fox hoped that the athletic program could earn enough each year to cover what was

Marquette Stadium looking south. File 1255

due on the bonds. Instead, the football program continued to incur deficits. In fact, by 1927, the stadium's fourth season, attendance still failed to fill the original 20,000 seats. Fearful that the administration might shut down the football program, undergraduates organized a campaign to put football on a "higher paying basis." Unbeknownst to the Marquette community, the stadium's largest bond maturities would come due in 1933, 1934, and 1935— at the height of the Great Depression.[80]

The stadium had been built for two reasons. First, during college football's golden age, any institution that wanted to be thought of as a sports powerhouse needed a modern stadium to hold its thousands of rabid spectators. Father Fox wanted Marquette to be a "player" in a national network of Catholic universities. Second, the Marquette alumni and students finally had football teams worthy of their admiration. Football became a collegiate sport at Marquette in 1902 when the school's teams started to play exclusively college-level opponents, which meant teams from Ripon, Carroll, and Lawrence colleges as well as normal schools at Oshkosh and Whitewater. But the go-

First Touchdown In New Stadium Made By Gerlach.

File 595b

ing was tough. The 1905 team scored only twenty-three points all season and was shut out in four of six matches. The following year, it was scoreless in the first six games before breaking out for eight points in the finale against their soon-to-be classmates, the Milwaukee Medical College. However, during the 1907 and 1908 seasons, the Marquette defense turned things around, permitting the opposition only four points the first year and twenty-one points the second. The year 1908 also featured the first in a short series of annual games against Notre Dame. Marquette lost that first year (six to zero) and then played three straight ties, including two scoreless games. A sixty-nine to zero thumping at the hands of the Fighting Irish in 1912 put a damper on the series for a time. The war and the worldwide influenza epidemic limited the 1918 season to three games. The postwar teams, however, won the hearts of every fan. These squads plowed through their opposition with a single defeat in 1919, two losses each in 1920 and 1921, and undefeated seasons in 1922 and 1923 (giving up three points in the first and twelve in the second). In recognition, a New York writer assigned the nickname *Golden Avalanche* to Marquette's team in 1923, following successive Saturday victories over Boston College and the University of Detroit.[81]

The success of these football teams swept up Marquette fans and even the central administration. The popularity of football inspired an expanded homecoming celebration in 1921 that included a parade, complete with floats, along Grand Avenue. In its early years, control of the athletic program had fallen to Father John Danihy, John Copus's successor as dean of journalism. Later, an athletic board oversaw the running of "clean athletics," with the specific charge not to allow expenses to harm the institution. Typically, two alumni served on the board along with a single student appointed by the president. They were joined by two faculty members, including in most instances the Jesuit who headed the College of Arts and Sciences. Athletics clearly had a place in the modern Marquette landscape, but it was a limited role, as Father Noonan reminded students and alumni: "I regard athletics as a department of the University and as such they should be as much in the hands of the faculty as Law, Medicine or any other course." By 1926, a successful intercollegiate program and a burgeoning physical education program forced Father Fox to do something he thoroughly enjoyed: develop another administrative office, in this case, the director of athletics. Conrad Jennings, who had revived the university's track program, was given this new assignment. He immediately hired Kay Iverson from the University of Wisconsin to coordinate the expanding intramural program. The athletic board still retained ultimate authority over financial and other administrative decisions. Ice hockey, tennis, and golf joined football, track, and basketball as varsity sports during the twenties, although the university delineated minor sports (the first three) from major sports (the last three). After decades as the school's most popular sport, baseball was relegated to pick-up games and intramural competition. Basketball had been around nearly as long as Marquette College, but it did not become an officially sponsored activity until the winter of 1917. The first game was a thirty-five to twenty-six victory over Whitewater Normal College on January 13. This sport, like football before it, struggled during its first decade of intercollegiate play.[82]

Physical improvements and administrative adjustments characterized the years between 1917 and 1928, following the previous era's curricular revolution. Herbert Noonan bought or developed six buildings: Lalumiere Hall, Drexel Lodge, Science Hall, the dental and law buildings, and the gymnasium. The Marquette Union was put on course during his watch. He supervised the school's first two capital campaigns in less than three years' time. Through his speech-making, Noonan gave the Marquette presidency regional stature. His successor, as a powerful voice in Catholic higher education, provided the university a national presence. Father Fox conceded that one man could no longer manage every aspect of a truly complex institution, although he gladly reminded all that there was still just one man—Father President—who could insist on doing things his way. Enrollments reached four-figures and then doubled and tripled in a matter of years. Students spoke to the nation by way of WHAD and interacted with peers across the land through social organizations as well as the Marquette Union. The school's football team was potent enough to attract the attention of the national news media. The decade's biggest stumble came in the Schandein fiasco. Not long thereafter, the nation took a tumble of its own, experiencing the greatest economic crisis in its short history. And then came another world war. For Marquette in 1928, there was no warning of what the short-term future held, a future that ultimately tested the very existence of the institution.

TROUBLED TIMES
1928-45

Atwo-ocean war on the heels of economic tribulations thoroughly derailed the institutional momentum achieved at Marquette in the 1920s. Basic tasks such as balancing the budget consumed university officials during the Great Depression. There was neither time nor money for innovation and then just as the depression loosened its grip, World War II threw the university into organizational bedlam. Hundreds of male students departed, either to serve in the military or to take jobs in the regional workforce, a dislocation that severely damaged the income stream that kept an endowment-poor institution in business. Were it not for Marquette's female students, the university's future might have been in jeopardy. During two traumatic decades, Marquette University went through three presidents, lost several degree programs as well as its doctoral studies option, and became a year-round classroom for the armed forces. *Adjustment* was the watchword on a campus besieged by uncontrollable external forces.

PRESIDENTIAL SUCCESSION

Father William Magee replaced Albert Fox as president of Marquette University on the evening of January 18, 1928, with a suddenness typical of reassignments in the Society of Jesus. In the presence of the provincial, Magee rose from his usual seat at the refectory's head table and reseated himself at the center chair assigned to Father Rector. The new president, a native of Chicago, had arrived in Milwaukee five years earlier, only two years after his ordination. He rapidly rose through the ranks, serving as a faculty member in psychology, regent for the College of Business Administration, and dean of the College of Liberal Arts—the latter a pivotal responsibility at any Jesuit university. Before coming to Marquette, the young Jesuit taught Latin and Greek at St. John's College in Toledo, Ohio, where he also oversaw the athletic program, a facet of college life in which he took particular delight. Named university president at the age of forty-three, Magee was unusually young for such a post, an asset that proved invaluable during nine stressful years as the school's senior officer.[1]

A two-day inaugural, an event without precedent at Marquette, welcomed the new president. On Sunday, April 22, an academic procession into the Church of the Gesu preceded Archbishop Sebastian Messmer's sermon and a concluding benediction service. Delegates from across the country attended a reception on the following morning. Harvard, Yale, Princeton, Columbia, Saint Louis, Canisius, Detroit, Notre Dame, St. Norbert, and DePaul, among others, sent representatives. The president of the University of Wisconsin and the vice president of the University of Notre Dame presided over an educational symposium that same afternoon. Later, the board of governors hosted a dinner at the Pfister Hotel, an event that preceded the inaugural ceremony at the Milwaukee Auditorium where General Otto Falk, chairman of the board, symbolically "inducted" Father Magee. The new president directed his remarks toward the true meaning of a Marquette education: training of the mind and the soul so that a graduate was prepared for this world and the world to come. Magee drew upon his recent term as dean of liberal arts to drive home the importance of history, literature, and philosophy in the lives of cultured individuals. He cited a contemporary scholar when making the point that education was not the filling in of what had previously been a void, but the shaping of absent behaviors. The long day concluded when the university bestowed four honorary degrees and two distinctive civic service awards.[2]

As for Father Magee's predecessor, Albert Fox departed Milwaukee with more equanimity than his predecessor six years earlier. Five hundred dinner guests feted the outgoing executive at a farewell banquet. Heartfelt expressions of appreciation eulogized his hard work in promoting Marquette's advancement. Religious and civic leaders (including the city's leading rabbi, the governor, and the mayor) rained tributes upon the obviously flattered priest. The following morning, Fox quietly boarded a train for a month's vacation in Florida. On his wrist was a new watch, a symbol of the previous night's accolades. The former president subsequently became dean of liberal arts at John Carroll College, the Jesuit school in Cleveland. He died only six years later at the age of 56.[3]

BEGINNINGS OF A *GREAT* DEPRESSION

Late in October 1929, the New York Stock Exchange began a long, disastrous sell-off that lost fortunes and portended the opening round of the Great Depression. The seeds for this crisis rest within the booming economy of the 1920s. Key sectors of the economy, such as coal mining and agriculture, struggled throughout the decade, whereas other indicators, including the stock market, promised endless bounty. Overblown assurances of relentless growth transfixed the country's educational leadership as much as they did the rest of the nation. And when disaster set in, the educational sector was just as likely to pay the price for its giddy optimism.

In Milwaukee, "Machine Shop to the World" according to historian John Gurda, the Great Depression arrived somewhat later than in other northern industrial cities. Standing orders for turbines, mining drills, and bulldozers continued to be filled even as new orders slackened off. The area's varied economy (from agricultural exports and leather goods to tractors and precision electrical controls) seemed to provide a guarantee against future catastrophes. Not until 1931 and 1932 did the true implications of the depression hit home in Milwaukee. One newspaper, the *Sentinel*, spoke reassuringly in 1930, noting that the city "'was one of the few bright spots on the nation's business map. Here is a market immune from peaks and panics. Industrial diversification is a sure stabilizer of steady progress.'" Yet within a short time, an avalanche of unemployment (and its sibling, underemployment) shattered the city's complacency. By 1933,

Milwaukee County experienced a 44 percent decrease in the number of wage earning positions, falling from 117,658 jobs in 1929 to 66,010. As primary wage earners lost incomes, families at first turned to relatives and friends for assistance and then, embarrassingly, to taxpayers. At a low point in 1935, nearly a fifth of Milwaukee County's population (40,176 families) was receiving public aid. More than half of the city's property taxes went unpaid. The municipality issued scrip (promissory notes) instead of paychecks to its employees. Southeastern Wisconsin mirrored the nation's hardship. In March 1933, one-quarter of the nation's work force was unemployed and an equal portion was underemployed. United States Steel had 225,000 full-time workers in 1929 and zero on April 1, 1933. A homeless New York family found shelter in a Central Park cave and unpaid teachers in Chicago fainted from malnutrition. Economic calamities overwhelmed American workers, whether in Philadelphia or Milwaukee or Oakland.[4]

With a tuition-dependent budget, Marquette felt the impact of the Great Depression sooner than the city at large. After only six months on the job, Father Magee was informed by Henry Banzhaf in July 1928 that the business manager had "reduced" the following year's anticipated deficit to $171,575 in the preliminary budget. Most of this shortfall could be explained by $179,144 in interest payments owed to lenders and bondholders. Banzhaf reasoned that gifts from friends would be needed to cover this gap if the school wished to avoid additional borrowing. By the conclusion of the 1930-31 fiscal year, the school's operating deficit remained about the same as Banzhaf had anticipated two years earlier: $170,723. A year later, however, the shortfall climbed to $209,800. A close examination of these accounts reveals that the academic departments actually produced a profit of $33,834 that year; athletics, on the other hand, incurred a deficit of $10,534. The real villain, however, was the interest owed on notes, loans, and mortgages. It now totaled $235,000 annually.[5]

The university's trustees turned to a familiar, if risky, alternative in February 1930: issue new bonds, totaling one million dollars. They were scheduled to come due in September 1939, a date far enough in the future to seemingly guarantee a more robust economy. In asking for permission from the provincial and the superior general to issue these bonds (the latter was particularly reluctant to approve additional obligations), Marquette administrators emphasized that this additional indebtedness would be used only for ordinary expenses, not new initiatives. Of course, the annual interest on these bonds—which were unsecured—subsequently contributed to each year's budgetary stresses. But given America's relentless optimism that the country's economic downturn would end any day, the trustees (three Jesuits including Father President) sought to buy time, an approach endorsed by the businessmen who dominated the board of governors.[6]

CLOSURES AND OTHER CUTBACKS

Upon recommendations from the board of governors and Henry Banzhaf, university trustees also adopted a second strategy to deal with the school's fiscal woes: discontinue selected academic programs. In one of his last acts as president, Father Noonan had ordered Marquette University Hospital to be closed. Father Fox overturned this decision and, after lengthy negotiations, turned over management of the hospital to the Franciscan Sisters of Little Falls, Minnesota. In exchange for staffing the hospital and supervising the nursing program, these nuns received expenses, living quarters, board, laundry, and an annual payment of $500 per sister. In general, this arrangement satisfied both parties, although there were the usual disagreements that can arise between physicians and nurses or a central administration and its departments.[7]

In practical terms, however, the aging, undersized facility at Ninth and Wells guaranteed future headaches. One problem was an admissions policy that welcomed partial- as well as full-paying patients. Between 1913 (when the university took control of the hospital from the Milwaukee Medical College) and 1922, the hospital experienced only a single deficit in any budgetary year. After 1922, however, the record became spottier, with losses totaling $42,192 during the two-year period of 1926-28. With the medical school some distance away at Fourth and Reservoir and with fewer than 50

beds, Marquette University Hospital had a diminished value except for the nursing program. Moreover, the city purchased the hospital land in 1926, and although municipal authorities permitted Marquette to use the former Milwaukee Medical College buildings for the time being, they threatened to forge ahead with plans to build on the land, a plan that would require demolition of the university hospital. Its uncertain future distracted university presidents throughout the 1920s.[8]

By the end of that decade, the depression's earliest effects forced Marquette administrators to consider alternatives. The Schandein proposal was still fresh in everyone's mind as was the county board's decisive rejection of Father Fox's vision for a new hospital. In the winter of 1928, the university briefly considered purchasing old St. Joseph's Hospital on the city's east side. Although a former dean of the medical school backed this proposal, Henry Banzhaf saw it as a losing proposition: trading one aging facility for another.

Dr. Henry L. Banzhaf. Banzhaf Biographical File

Moreover, he feared that this deal would confuse the Carnegie foundation, which the university intended to approach for funding to underwrite a new medical building at Fifteenth and Wisconsin (formerly Grand) Avenue. In addition to the St. Joseph's Hospital option, the university briefly entertained the idea of having the Franciscan Sisters help build a new hospital. The two parties went so far as to draft a preliminary agreement. The nuns would "provide the necessary nurses, supplies, and superintendence to operate the said hospital." Ultimately, both proposals went nowhere.[9]

Not long after becoming president, Father Magee approved a six-page white paper that outlined the competing needs of a medical teaching facility and of a neighborhood hospital. Magee clearly favored something akin to the Schandein proposal—a teaching facility within a hospital environment. He believed that the educational and financial benefits Marquette brought to Milwaukee warranted public support for a university-run, community-centered hospital. But as unemployment grew, hopes of reversing the county supervisors' decision on the original Schandein project evaporated. Yet something had to be done with Marquette University Hospital. Time was critical. In January 1930, the university business manager presented Father President with a dispassionate review of the situation. Only 30 out of 48 admitted patients at the hospital were full-paying. In addition, "overhead expenses are entirely out of proportion to the volume of business being done at this time," Banzhaf warned. The city once again threatened to develop the property at Ninth and Wells. The lease was due to run out within three months and the annual rent had climbed to nearly $13,000, while operating deficits at the hospital during August to November of 1930 were anticipated to approach $12,000.[10]

Within weeks, the board of governors acted. It recommended that the hospital be closed, the Marquette University Eye, Ear, Nose, and Throat Dispensary (which operated at a profit) be moved from the hospital grounds to other university property, and a new teaching hospital be constructed. The board of trustees approved the first two suggestions. The dispensary was relocated to the former William Plankinton residence at 1533 W. Wisconsin. (Seven years later, a fire severely damaged the dispensary. The city building inspector reluctantly permitted the university to use the damaged structure, but not as a medical clinic. Instead the athletic department began to use the patched-up Victorian.) As for the hospital, its closure ended the university's brief partnership with the Franciscan Sisters and the university's well-established nursing program. The trustees did not stop there. In his January 1930 report, Banzhaf had hinted at another move: discontinuing the College of Music. The trustees endorsed this recommendation, effective July 31, 1930. Marquette had never fully embraced the music program. For most of its life, the college operated largely as a conservatory, training hundreds of Milwaukee youngsters on a fee-for-lesson basis. Its non-collegiate nature, coupled with budget deficits ($2,263 during the 1928-29 fiscal year), made music an easy target during the first round of cuts.[11]

MAKING BUDGETS BALANCE

Even the closure of unprofitable programs did not bring the university's accounts into balance. More had to be done. Student enrollment dropped precipitously between 1930 and 1933. By April 1933, student tuition payments were $30,000 in arrears. With revenues dwindling, the administration's hand was forced. The main library in Johnston Hall slashed its periodical subscriptions by 33 percent during the 1931-32 school year. Additional cuts came the following year and their effects lingered. As late as 1938, the Graduate School still received only $855 of funding per year for new books and periodicals. Administrators initiated a rigorous campaign aimed at turning off ceiling lights in empty classrooms and laboratories, and they scaled back equipment purchases in every academic unit. Tax-delinquent land in the upper peninsula of Michigan was sold to the government for $11,000. Half of this sum was used to pay overdue property taxes and the other half as operating revenue.[12]

Ultimately, budget cutting led to salary reductions. In April 1932, the university sliced incomes for 250 employees by ten percent, explaining that other institutions had already taken this step. Deans, faculty, librarians, athletic department personnel, student health center staff, and members of the central administration received notices. With deans earning between $3,100 and $8,000 and faculty earning between $2,300 and $3,000, the cumulative savings came to $42,000. A second review of the 1932-33 budget revealed that it would still not be in balance. Therefore, on June 9, 1932, the board of governors authorized Father Magee to consider further reductions in salaries and personnel. Six days later, Henry Banzhaf submitted a draconian package of proposals that promised to save $68,000. He recommended not filling certain staff vacancies, canceling all library purchases for individual colleges, discontinuing the Marquette Press including the *Tribune* and *Hilltop*, eliminating all university advertising, closing the School of Speech building, removing some office telephones, enforcing mandatory two-week unpaid vacations, and imposing a second set of 10 percent salary cuts on those who earned more than $1,200. Three weeks later, on July 5, 1932, Banzhaf announced the second set of salary reductions. The administration hoped that a quick turnaround in the national economy might permit a restoration of these cuts, but in 1943, some faculty claimed they were still earning less than they had thirteen years earlier.[13]

In supporting Father Magee's frantic campaign to slash expenses, the board of governors came upon an interesting idea: ask the archbishop of Milwaukee for help. The relationship between Milwaukee's prelates and the city's Jesuit community had been cordial, if somewhat distant. Neither religious superior held sway over the other's sphere of authority, although Jesuit superiors always maintained a respectful tone toward the local prelates. Bishops were appointed by the pope, cared for the faithful of their dioceses, and usually had their hands full with parishes, schools, and social service agencies. Father Rector, on the other hand, oversaw Milwaukee-based Jesuits at the university, the high school, and the Church of the Gesu. He reported to the head of the Missouri Province of the Society of Jesus and through him to the superior general in

Rome, not to the local bishop. Communication between these independent wings of the Catholic church was ordinarily on an as-needed basis. In Milwaukee, this distancing was enhanced by Archbishop Sebastian Messmer's many illnesses and his dislike of Marquette's coeducational program.

Trite as it may sound, desperate times called for desperate measures. Milwaukee's bishop, Samuel Stritch (who later became a cardinal while heading Chicago's archdiocese), received a detailed report on the university's fiscal troubles in early 1933. He was under no obligation to do more than acknowledge receipt of this communication. However, Stritch was "a quondam intellectual" who had worked with the Jesuits in Toledo during a previous assignment. He was also a former school superintendent who favored collegiate education for teaching nuns. In this regard, Marquette served a vital function in his archdiocese. Moreover, the archbishop's residence at the former Pabst mansion along Wisconsin Avenue was within walking distance from Marquette, and for a time, Gesu had served as a surrogate cathedral following the fiery destruction of the Cathedral of St. John the Evangelist. Consequently, despite his own financial headaches, Stritch responded with sympathy to the university's contact. He offered some thoughts on how to cope with the bond maturities that were coming due. Six months later, in a magnanimous gesture, he issued a three-page appeal to the faithful of Milwaukee, asserting Marquette's "value to the christian life of our State in our day when neo-paganism has been widely dominant cannot be adequately estimated." Noting that the university had been entrusted "with consecrated lives," not "stocks of money," Stritch ordered a special collection on behalf of the university. Although there is no record of the final amount that was gathered at the Masses on July 30, Father Magee did send a letter of appreciation to each pastor.[14]

The president's final, untapped resource—approached with the greatest reluctance—was the alumni. It is not clear why he took so long in asking for their help. Historically, Marquette had treated its graduates gingerly when it came to fund-raising. If individuals wished to assist their alma mater, that was perfectly fine, but as a group they were seldom contacted regarding the school's ongoing problems. Annual giving had not become a habit for the alumni. In addition, university administrators understood that a great many graduates faced their own problems during this economic downturn. But fiscal pressures mounted to the point that Father Magee broke with tradition by mid-1933. He mailed a carefully worded, inoffensive appeal, explaining how the university had avoided taking this step for five years, knowing that Marquette alumni had their own difficulties. The president reminded them that their alma mater was not an endowed institution and that a majority of the students took part-time jobs to pay at least a portion of their tuition. On behalf of these Hilltoppers, Father Magee asked for five dollars a year, starting the following month. Once again, the archives do not reveal the full extent of the alumni's response, although there is at least one reply in the presidential correspondence that blasted Magee's request for being "so naive" and "deserving of an emphatic No.[15]

Looming in the background was the $3 million General Mortgage and Refunding Bond issued in the late twenties, with interest payments starting to come due in 1933 and the principal due in 1939. In early 1933, Marquette administrators began to consider reissuing these bonds, hoping to delay full payment until 1949. The university asked Archbishop Stritch for his advice as well as permission to use his name if the bond payments had to be delayed. Again, Stritch was supportive, reassuring the president that he was making an honest effort to protect the university's interests. Father Magee sent a three-page letter to all Marquette University bondholders on May 26, 1933. After explaining the steps already taken to reduce costs (including lowering living expenses for the Jesuits and drastic cuts in the salaries of laymen and laywomen), the president asked bondholders to sign off on an extension of all maturities until September 1, 1939, at an interest rate lowered from 5 percent to 3 percent. Much to the president's relief, by February of the following year, 86 percent of the bondholders had approved these new bonds.[16]

In his nine long years as president, Father Magee rarely had an idle moment during which he could dream of innovative reforms at the university. Instead, he seemed to spend every waking hour trying to keep the institution fiscally afloat. He had few distractions, one being the football team's practice sessions. He also liked to stroll around the neighborhood. As he ambled along Wisconsin Avenue (so named after 1926), it was clear that with one notable exception his tenure was not going to be one crowned, like those of his two predecessors, with towering structures made of stone and brick. If new classrooms and laboratories would not be his legacy, then maybe another, relatively unacclaimed, decision might serve as a marker of his time in office.

In early August 1929, amid the relative calm preceding Wall Street's Black Tuesday, Father Magee invited Henry Banzhaf to consider whether Marquette University should pull up its roots as a "city University" and look ahead fifty years to being a "campus university" in the suburbs. It is not clear why the president posed such a weighty question at this particular moment. In a thoroughly developed response, however, Banzhaf took an unequivocal position, one that Father Magee found convincing and probably confirming. Tradition, said the longtime dean of dentistry, bound Marquette University to the city. Through the specializations attendant to each professional school (which he discussed in detail), Marquette served the region in ways that no other Wisconsin school could match. Only the College of Liberal Arts and a potential fine arts college, he proposed, could intellectually endure the absence of crowds and businesses. The professional schools needed the dynamism and demands of the city to survive and grow. Marquette had become intricately linked to its downtown location. Twice in his remarks, once at the beginning and again near the end, Banzhaf warned of the negative impact that any relocation would have upon the "poor" students at Marquette. By endorsing Banzhaf's depiction of Marquette's place in southeastern Wisconsin, Father Magee established an institutional position upheld by his successor, Father Raphael McCarthy, a decade later after a donor suggested the university move to land that he promised to provide in rural Kenosha County. In his response to this kind offer, Father

Marquette in Milwaukee: looking east along Wisconsin Avenue from Fourteenth Street in 1939. Gas station at far left is on the site of the lawn in front of today's Jesuit Residence, with Varsity Theater to its east. Biltmore Apartments is the second building from far right. File 1373

McCarthy explained that it would be "unwise for us to think of transferring Marquette from Milwaukee, no matter how attractive an offer might be made to us." Despite the hard times, Marquette would remain Milwaukee's Jesuit university.[17]

CHANGING OF THE GUARD

Father Magee's reward for enduring these trying times was an extension of his term beyond the canonical guideline of six years. In January 1934, as Magee approached completion of a normal term, the *Marquette Tribune* gleefully celebrated the provincial's decision to allow the president to stay for an indefinite period. When this grace period continued into the fall of 1935, the *Tribune* congratulated the university community on its "fortune." Finally, on November 29, 1936, after nearly nine years in office, Father Magee listened quietly to an instruction from the superior general, stood up, and shook hands with the man to his right at the refectory table, the Reverend Raphael Charles McCarthy, SJ.[18]

In a statement released to the press that same day, Father McCarthy revealed a terse, uncompromising persona. "'I haven't much patience,' he remarked, 'with the tendencies of modern education that give more concern to training for mechanical ability and even professional skill than to the development of a person's cultural side.'" In a reference that might have made Father Fox cringe, McCarthy went on to highlight

Father Raphael McCarthy. McCarthy Biographical File

two errors afflicting American education: "'the principle that everyone can profit by a university education and that we have introduced big business methods into it.'" Born in Marquette, Michigan, in 1889, Raphael McCarthy joined the Jesuits in 1906, receiving a doctoral degree in psychology from the University of London in 1925. He served in several capacities at Saint Louis University before coming to Milwaukee. In his first speech before the university community, three weeks after his appointment, the new president warned of the modern world's shortcomings. He "decried modern 'catchword' philosophies" and warned that the greatest evil of the moment was not the economic crisis but the "'forgetfulness of the principles of God.'" Greed, lust for power, and human selfishness had replaced charity and love for God and our neighbor, advised the new Father Rector. McCarthy urged students and faculty to seek the "'kingdom of God and His justice. Do not stoop to the cheap, the tawdry that deceives the crowd. You go forth from this school with our hopes pinned upon you. In whatever community or station of life you shall be, practice, fearlessly the principles of Marquette—the principles of God and Christ.'"[19]

As for Father Magee, he was honored at a farewell dinner in the Crystal Ballroom of the Schroeder Hotel. With Henry Banzhaf serving as honorary chairman for the night, Magee received the adulation of seven hundred friends. They championed him as a man whose "'star will shine in the greatest constellation of past presidents of Marquette.'" The former executive thanked his friends for their support and admitted that he was grateful to be relieved of the financial challenges that had plagued him throughout his tenure. After a brief period of rest, Magee was appointed president of John Carroll College in Cleveland and later served as head of the Chicago Province.[20]

A FEW NEW STRUCTURES AFTER ALL

In his 1929 white paper on the "city University," Henry Banzhaf had referenced both a hospital on Wisconsin Avenue and a medical school building on Sixteenth Street. The first of these never became a reality, despite how dear this dream was to Fathers Fox and Magee. The second, however, became the only structure—and a sizable one at that—constructed during William Magee's years as chief executive. Not long after assuming office, Magee determined that a teaching facility was more important to the medical school than a hospital. Facilities at Fourth and Reservoir had become an embarrassment, and once again, the medical school was in danger of losing its Class A rating with the American Medical Association. The president concluded that the new county hospital in Wauwatosa and a new St. Joseph's Hospital on Burleigh Street would suffice for the school of medicine's clinical needs. An instructional facility, however, would be Marquette's responsibility.

Raising funds for medicine's instructional center was impeded, curiously, by one the university's own friends: General Otto Falk, chairman of the board of governors. Magee felt that Marquette's governors needed to serve as role models, proffering substantial contributions to the capital campaign and only later soliciting gifts from friends and associates. The medical school's goal was set at $500,000. In correspondence with

Frank Sensenbrenner, a board member, Magee revealed his frustrations at the costly delays incurred by the Falk's reluctance to launch a campaign. Even after the project was publicly announced, progress was slow. In February 1930, the *Marquette Tribune* mentioned a medical school building on Wisconsin Avenue (where an engineering building was eventually located), but design plans were still being discussed months later. As a separate corporation legally detached from the university, the school of medicine was required to proceed on its own. In the end, the capital campaign never took place. Instead, funding came from an endowment established through Mrs. Harriet L. Cramer's $1 million estate gift. Widow of the founder of the *Wisconsin Evening News*, Mrs. Cramer stipulated that a portion of her gift provide free medical care, with special attention to the blind. (This was in memory of her late husband who had been sightless during the last decades of his life.) Coupled with funds from the 1919 Carnegie endowment, Mrs. Cramer's gift allowed the university to move ahead with a facility that was named, appropriately, in her honor. The university leased land on Fifteenth Street to the Marquette University School of Medicine from July 1, 1931, until June 30, 1982, for purposes of erecting "a new medical school building at the cost of no less than $250,000."[21]

Ground was broken in October 1931. The Great Depression actually provided a boost for the project by creating a large pool of job-hungry construction workers whose labor permitted the building to be finished with astonishing speed, opening in time for the 1932-33 school year. The four-story building ran for 260 feet north to south along Fifteenth Street, with wings at either end stretching 160 feet to the west. Its collegiate gothic style architecture blended perfectly with the neighboring dental school. A two million cubic-foot facility, costing $363,000, was dedicated on January 4, 1933. It included an auditorium with a capacity of five hundred, space for the student health service, and an eye clinic in respect for Mrs. Cramer's intentions. The former Wisconsin College of Physicians and Surgeons building was subsequently sold in 1944 for $5,500.[22]

If Father Magee only had this single building to represent his time at Marquette, his successor did not fare much better. As noted earlier, in 1920 Father Noonan had purchased two residences south of the law school. Dr. Hitz's house, facing Michigan Street, first hosted the Marquette Union and later became Drexel Lodge, named for Mother Katharine Drexel following her visit to the campus. (Her canonization in 2000 makes this nun the only Church-recognized saint to have walked the grounds of Marquette, although Mother Theresa of Calcutta, with a visit to the university for its centennial in 1981, may some day join that list.) The adjoining structure facing Eleventh Street—where, the story goes, Theodore Roosevelt once slept—was renamed for Father Lalumiere in 1923. Over the years, the former residence of General Winkler was used for law, language, mathematics, religion, and Latin classes as well as by the short-lived College of Hospital Administration and the graduate school. Shuttered by 1931, plans were in the works for its demolition. Yet four years later, a handful of Jesuits had moved back in, residing in its rickety upper floor while carpenters repaired

Sketch of Cramer Hall, facing Fifteenth Street. File 940.

classroom chairs in the basement. As the 1938-39 school year opened, Father McCarthy announced an anonymous gift of $100,000 to renovate Johnston, Science, and Lalumiere halls. In Johnston, the attic became living quarters for the Jesuits, including those displaced by work on Lalumiere. In the latter, the rear wall was removed and a two-story addition constructed. The front entrance of Lalumiere, once graced with twin stairways, was simplified into an unpretentious doorway without a porch. In 1939, the president, registrar, bursar, and business manager moved into what was temporarily called Administration Hall. Subsequently, Father McCarthy designated it O'Hara Hall, after Charles O'Hara, father of a Marquette Jesuit and a member of the board of governors whose generosity provided for the building's renovations.[23]

The structural crown jewel of Raphael McCarthy's eight years in office was a long overdue facility for the College of Engineering. Housed briefly in Johnston Hall, engineering moved to Bellarmine Hall (appropriately nicknamed the "engine house") in 1910. Always cramped for space, engineering taught classes in satellite locations across the campus, including the dental and speech buildings as well as the basement of Lalumiere Hall. In the early twenties, the college adopted a cooperative style of instruction in which students worked at local factories and businesses during the last three of their five years. (They alternated months in the classroom and at their placements.) The depression shrank the number of student assignments, but by 1939-40, training opportunities abounded as military-related production brought Milwaukee's economy out of its doldrums. Once again, engineering graduates were in demand. But out-of-date facilities in Bellarmine (built to handle 200 students when enrollment had climbed to over 500) concerned faculty and the area's industrialists alike. With service to Milwaukee's manufacturing community at the core of the college's mission, its standing in the world of engineering education was jeopardized. No matter how inauspicious the timing, something had to be done to save this vital division of the university.[24]

Henry Banzhaf had advised the Milwaukee Association of Commerce as early as 1937 that it needed to play a central role in raising funds for any new teaching center. In spring 1939, the board of trustees authorized a New York firm to formulate plans for a capital campaign. The idea was to raise $1 million, half for the construction of a new building and half for an endowment to maintain it. (A maintenance endowment was an entirely new concept for Marquette.) Solicitation letters went out in mid-1939. Father William Grace, dean of the faculty, and Professor William Hebard of engineering headed the campaign. By that fall, engineering had put together an advisory board that included representatives from Nordberg Manufacturing, Falk Corporation, Allis Chalmers Manufacturing, Wisconsin Electric Company, the Milwaukee Road, and the state highway commission. By the year's end, pledges totaled more than $350,000. Having learned from past experiences, Father McCarthy refused to break ground until at least $300,000 was in hand. (By the time the building opened, $391,510 had been collected, with costs having risen to $389,181.) A site for the building was finally chosen in February 1940: along Wisconsin Avenue between Fifteenth and Sixteenth

Streets. As excavation work commenced later that year, Dean Franz A. Kartek began soliciting new equipment for the structure's thirty-six laboratories and classrooms. After its completion, Father McCarthy spoke rather proudly of the facility's depression-era plainness: its lack of "architectural frills," its cinder block walls, and its industrial ambiance. With the walls still unpainted, 5,000 donors, civic and industrial leaders, faculty, students, and alumni attended open houses held in December 1941. The scheduling of these events was timely because they began two weeks after the "date that will live in infamy," the day of Japan's attack on Pearl Harbor. The engineering college's mission during wartime required not only first-rate facilities but a remarkably flexible approach to instructional routines.[25]

ACADEMIC STANDARDS AMIDST HARD TIMES

Marquette survived the battering of the Great Depression through decisive management, the student body's commitment to work twice as hard to pay its tuition bills, and the dedication of faculty and staff who endured severe salary cuts. Evidence of just how effectively these constituencies handled the crisis came when the North Central Association of Colleges and Secondary Schools (NCA) sent an evaluator to Marquette for a periodic assessment. Over two days during the winter of 1939, he examined every undergraduate program. (Law, medicine, and dentistry were excluded.) Despite desperate times, the examiner reported that the university's admissions standards had not been compromised. Applicants still had to come from accredited high schools or be ready to take a standardized entrance exam. Applicants still had to have letters of recommendation from their principals. Undergraduates in the College of Liberal Arts were required to complete one major and one minor with no grade below a C, and at least three-quarters of their course work during their last two years had to be taken at the upper-division level. Hundreds of years of Jesuit tradition lived on because each bachelor of arts recipient still completed fifteen units of Latin. (However, by 1937, over 90 percent of the liberal arts majors pursued a bachelor of science or a bachelor of philosophy, largely because neither required a classical language.) The examiner lauded Marquette as "deserving of congratulation that it still is able to hold so much of its 'cultural' program." This was most evident, according to the visitor, in the requirement of fifteen hours of philosophy for all undergraduates. The North Central Association's representative also commented favorably on the high quality of the instructional staff and of the regular visits to classrooms by department heads and the dean of the college. He also acknowledged annual reviews by the Missouri province's prefect general of studies. This visit proceeded smoothly, in contrast to the bumpy relationship between the NCA and the Catholic educational community during the thirties over endowments and the fiscal accounting of instructors from religious communities.[26]

Among improvements in the university's curricular offerings during the thirties was a resurrected nursing program. In March 1936, six years after the first program had been disbanded upon closure of the university hospital, Father Magee approved an affiliation between Marquette and St. Joseph Hospital's well-established training school for

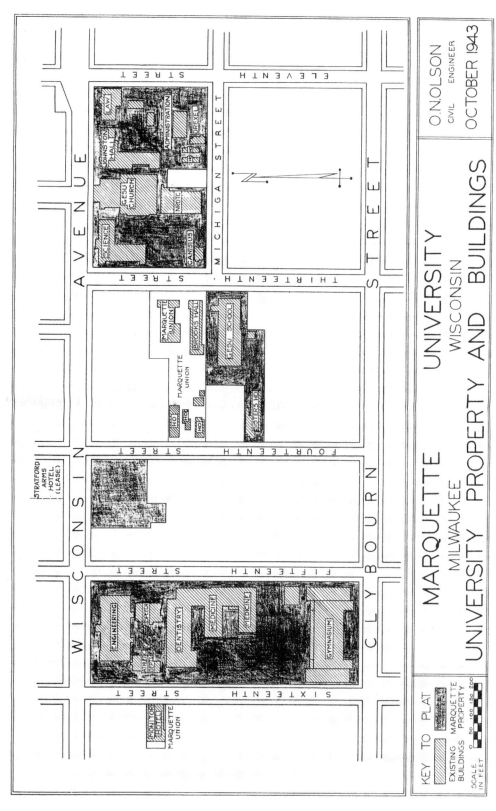

University leased the Monitor and Stratford Arms hotels to house military personnel. The Marquette Union owned property along Fourteenth Street that would later become the site of Brooks Memorial Union. Two small structures to the west of Drexel Lodge are Lalumiere and Jogues halls. Canisius Hall served as the engineering library and later was used by the navy during World War II. File 264a

nurses. The latter's three-year diploma program was soon replaced by a four-year bachelor of science in nursing degree and three years later augmented by a master of science in nursing education. For their first two years, nursing students attended classes on the main campus, an opportunity not afforded years earlier to students at the Milwaukee Medical College. Professional training during the third and fourth years took place at the hospital. The Franciscan Sisters who managed St. Joseph's nominated Sister Mary Berenice Beck, OSF, to be dean of the new College of Nursing. The elevation of nursing to the status of a college was another indication of just how integral female students had become to Marquette.[27]

Less than two months before America's entrance into World War II, the administration established a "Labor College" within the business college's Institute of Industrial Relations. The labor college offered eleven classes to union members who wished to receive training that might be pertinent to their work in Milwaukee's factories. Courses were available in labor ethics, labor legislation, parliamentary procedure, public speaking, and social justice. Instructors contributed their services free of charge, with additional operating expenses relying upon contributions from the students and the general public. Father Thomas Divine, a professor of economics in the College of Business Administration, directed the program. Nearly two hundred Milwaukee workers jumped at the chance to participate. Educational backgrounds did not matter; workers with grade school diplomas sat alongside college graduates. Three-quarters of the participants were union members, 70 percent married, two-thirds Roman Catholic, and 14 percent female.[28]

Both the labor college and the Institute of Industrial Relations represented a national commitment by Jesuits to address labor relations in light of tensions arising from the Great Depression. (As an example, Saint Louis University organized an "Institute of Social Order.") Class warfare had raged across industrial America during the1930s, from the rise of the Congress of Industrial Organizations, to factory sit-downs in Flint, Michigan, to the deadly violence at Chicago's Republic Steel Works. In 1934 alone, Milwaukee experienced 107 strikes involving 27,000 workers in the tanning, garment, and steel industries. Union membership in Milwaukee County jumped from 15,000 to 100,000 between 1929 and 1939. Getting employers and workers to talk to one another rather than throttle one another seemed appropriate for the area's leading academic institution. The volatility of labor politics during this era was evident in the case of a business professor who, after a decade of service at Marquette, lost his job in 1936, allegedly for having trade unionists speak to his class on labor problems and for having joined his wife at two meetings of the local communist party (not to be confused with the socialist party). This professor was said to "have become ... a liability for Marquette University." Father McCarthy's willingness to punish this instructor reflected the Catholic Church's determined opposition to communism, a position reinforced the year after this incident in Pope Pius XI's encyclical *Divini Redemptoris*. On the other end of the political spectrum, the chancellor of the Milwaukee Archdiocese questioned another faculty member's essay in the oddly titled *Social Justice*, an anti-Semitic, anti-

New Deal periodical edited by Father Charles Coughlin, a controversial priest from the Detroit area. In a 1937 letter to Father McCarthy, the diocesan administrator opined: "It is a mistake for your professor to publish articles in this paper for fear that it may be understood that the University in some way approved the editorial policy of Social Justice." The university president assured the chancellor that the faculty member had promised never to repeat this mistake.[29]

One other academic achievement of this era was the School of Law's much-delayed victory in achieving professional parity with the University of Wisconsin. For nearly two decades, Marquette officials had objected to the fact that its graduates were forced to take the state bar examination after spending "the same number of years" studying the "same case books" during the "same number of hours of law" as students in Madison. The University of Wisconsin's "diploma privilege," as it was called, remained an irritant for Marquette faculty and students although Father Fox had advised the university community against becoming "bellicose about this matter." He felt that the matter would take care of itself. The *Marquette Tribune*, in contrast, endlessly campaigned for equal treatment. Finally, in 1933, the state legislature extended the diploma privilege to Marquette law graduates.[30]

The founding of a credit union for all employees in October 1933 marked a small improvement during difficult times. After payment of a 25-cent membership fee, each participant had to deposit five dollars before he or she could apply for a loan. The interest rate on these loans was 1 percent. In its first year of operation, the credit union made fifty-four loans totaling $5,682. Half of the loans (worth $3,297) had already been paid back, allowing the board of directors to declare a dividend of 4 percent for 1934. As the national economy regained some stability by early 1941, Father McCarthy approved the university's first hospitalization plan. For single-person coverage, an employee paid seventy-five cents per month; subscribers with dependents paid $1.50 per month to cover spouses and all their children. Up to twenty-one days of hospitalization included a semi-private room, meals, general nursing services, an operating room, anesthesia, surgical dressings, ordinary drugs, and maternity care. The program charged a patient half of the costs for laboratory and x-ray services, electrocardiograms, and physical therapy. One benefit that did not become available until the end of World War II was a university-sponsored retirement program. In addition, the university still lacked tenure and promotion policies, a condition typical of Catholic colleges across the country as revealed in a 1941-42 national study. Yet the McCarthy administration did look into the advisability of creating rules for tenure and promotion. University officers recognized how much this situation affected the recruitment of senior faculty.[31]

TROUBLES IN THE GRADUATE SCHOOL

Senior faculty were critical to the quality of graduate education at Marquette. When Edward Fitzpatrick had taken over the university's nascent graduate school in 1924, he brought an administrative style that mirrored the corporate style preferred by Father Fox. Both men, well-respected figures in American Catholic higher education, ran their respective offices with a uni-directional management style: top-down. In the graduate school, Fitzpatrick laid down rules that he expected students and faculty to follow and he weeded out instructors who failed to meet his standards in teaching and scholarship. This vigilance triggered a number of unpleasant episodes with students and, on at least one occasion, with faculty who sought flexibility in some of his rules. In Fitzpatrick's schema, the board of graduate studies was appointed by the dean, had its agenda defined by the dean, and ultimately approved the dean's recommendations. The dean maintained a fierce territoriality over his office, insisting that he had final authority over graduate matters in the professional schools as well as in the liberal arts. Fitzpatrick also controlled the subject areas available for graduate study. By 1939, graduate degrees were offered in twenty disciplines. Nine areas, however, enrolled fewer than ten students. The largest enrollments were in Fitzpatrick's home department of education (138 students). Milwaukee-area teachers attended evening classes and a summer program that led to a master of education degree. Education also offered a special clinic on contemporary social and economic problems for social science teachers. (As if he did not have enough to do, Edward Fitzpatrick served as facilitator for this clinic.) Religious women continued to sustain Marquette's summer programs as evidenced by the

Father William Magee, on right, greeting recipient of honorary degree, Right Reverend Monsignor James H. Ryan, president of Catholic University. On left is Dr. Edward Fitzpatrick. File 400

fact that in 1938, of forty-two master's and doctoral theses approved by the graduate school, twenty-three were authored by nuns.[32]

By the end of the thirties, however, winds of change swirled around the appointment of the graduate school's second Jesuit regent, Father Edward McGrath. His predecessor had admired Fitzpatrick's "'great fertility of mind as well as his broad grasp of affairs and his capacity for administration.'" As the president's personal representative to a college or school, the faculty regent could either be an aide to the lay dean or a weighty impediment. Under Father McGrath, parallel administrations unfolded in the graduate school. Differences in styles and ambitions led to the preparation of a damning report at the conclusion of the 1937-38 school year. It detailed directives that Father McGrath had handed down either behind Fitzpatrick's back or, in some cases, to his face as if the Jesuit were the final authority in graduate school matters. Father McCarthy had clearly intended to end Fitzpatrick's one-man rule when he appointed Father McGrath. Eventually, the president became "'sick of the whole business.'" So did the disgruntled Fitzpatrick, who left at the end of the following year after more than fifteen years of service. Father Raphael Hamilton, a member of the history department and future historian of the university, replaced Fitzpatrick as dean.[33]

The graduate school's troubles did not end there, however. In 1926, Father Fox had Marquette apply for admission into the Association of American Universities (AAU), an organization whose endorsement guaranteed recognition of an institution's degrees, including its graduate degrees. The association delayed action on Marquette's application, causing some in the administration to worry that it did not respect the university. For its part, the AAU insisted that too many schools had asked for admission at one time. In the interim, it urged Marquette to have its alumni develop a deeper track record at AAU-recognized graduate schools. The association also expressed concern over the possible departure of Father Fox. After years of impressive achievements with Fox at the helm, the AAU wondered if Marquette could sustain this progress in his absence. The university was finally accepted into the Association of American Universities in late 1931, five years after its application. This status, distinctive if not unique among Catholic universities, was heralded in the opening section of the 1935 *Hilltop*.[34]

But within the AAU's letter welcoming Marquette into the inner circle rested a hint of trouble. The association singled out the classics department as understaffed for the number of classes offered. Fiscal pressures at Marquette after 1931 worsened similar situations within other departments. Salary cuts and hiring freezes blocked the recruitment of accomplished senior faculty, despite Dean Fitzpatrick's best efforts. Overworked and underpaid faculty epitomized institutional shortcomings, particularly in graduate education. This was why Father McCarthy considered at one point establishing a formal tenure and promotion system. Somehow the university had to strengthen the quality of its senior faculty. Maybe the enticement of tenure would compensate for below-market salaries.

Suddenly, on November 25, 1940, the Association of American Universities informed Father McCarthy that it had decided Marquette University was "overextended" in its graduate offerings. Following a campus visit by two members of the AAU's Committee on Classification of Universities and Colleges, the association concluded that the graduate school's ambitions exceeded its "resources" and its "number of students." (This did not apply to the professional schools.) The evaluators recommended that school officials review each master's program, reduce the MA options to a handful of programs in which offerings could guarantee excellence, and most important, terminate all doctoral programs no later than mid-1943. The association also insisted upon specific improvements in the library and in the registrar's office. The shock in O'Hara Hall was palpable. Reactions varied. Some tried to take the notification letter at face value. Others saw the influence of Edward Fitzpatrick who, upon his departure from Marquette, had asked the North Central Association to look into lapses in the graduate school's enforcement of its rules and regulations. (Whether Fitzpatrick had a role in the AAU visit was pure speculation because there is no evidence of his involvement.) A private meeting between Father Hamilton, the graduate dean, and the secretary of the AAU's classification committee failed to provide alternatives to the dismantling of the institution's doctoral programs.[35]

At the university's request, a second AAU representative visited the campus in June 1942. The timing could not have been worse. World War II had decimated student enrollments at Marquette. Faculty followed employment opportunities in industry and the government. Class schedules were in a constant state of flux to accommodate new training programs for the military. The outcome of this second visitation failed to alter the AAU's position: Marquette needed to discontinue its doctoral programs. The association then dropped Marquette from the list of approved institutions and cited an "utter lack of agreement between the Committee and the University concerning requirements and standards for graduate work." Father McCarthy fired back, expressing surprise at the finality of this decision and amazement at the notion that an "attitude" separated the two sides. Privately, the president revealed his and the graduate dean's take on the matter: anti-Catholic prejudice contaminated the second visitor's recommendation. The priests were particularly bothered by the second evaluator's inquiries regarding the faculty's sense of scholarship in their lives as college teachers. The AAU representative had also asked whether Marquette authorities had barred subjects such as evolution from instruction and research because of church teachings. Throughout the 1930s, the role of research at Catholic universities—whether unfettered inquiry was appropriate at faith-based schools—had preoccupied Catholic educators, especially Jesuits. How could Catholic institutions encourage the search for unrevealed truths (the essence of scholarly investigation) if all significant truths were already revealed through the church and its teachings? Scholars could certainly become more familiar with these truths, but could they—should they—seek to uncover new revelations? And how much authority should a secular agency hold over the instructional content of a Catholic institution? This last point grated on McCarthy and Hamilton. At the center of this explosive controversy rested the futures of Marquette's graduate students.

Thanks to the intervention of the Jesuit Educational Association, this standoff was brief. Several months after the AAU removed Marquette from its list, a three-man committee representing the Jesuits conducted its own on-campus survey.. These visiting priests acknowledged the graduate school's good intentions and the quality of the faculty. But they also endorsed the AAU's recommendation that Marquette shut down its doctoral programs, even in stronger departments such as history. The absence of promotion guidelines, an excessive teaching load in many departments, and a weak salary structure for senior faculty persuaded these visiting Jesuits to back the AAU's position.[36]

Advice from within the Society of Jesus was far easier to accept, even if the outcome was the same. So, the board of graduate studies voted on April 13, 1943, to discontinue all PhD programs "at least for the duration of the war." Father McCarthy and Hamilton were still smarting from the abruptness of the AAU's demands and from the second visitor's alleged lack of respect for Catholic and Jesuit traditions. The inadequacies of the university library, however, could not be ignored. This specific issue—the weakness in the library's book collection in particular—became the administration's public explanation for its decision to discontinue the doctoral programs. A year later, Father Peter Brooks replaced McCarthy as president, and early in his term, he replaced Father Hamilton as graduate dean with Father Edward Drummond. The new executive then wrote the AAU's Committee on Classifications in October 1944, introducing Drummond as a scholar who had earned his doctorate from the State University of Iowa and as a "man with a most sincere interest in the objectives of graduate study and research." Brooks assured the AAU of the university's "complete cooperation." Six months later, Dean Drummond quietly met with the classifications committee chair, the same individual who had investigated Marquette in 1942. They agreed that the previous administration had over-reacted, precluding a meeting of minds. The two men also agreed that Marquette should not resume doctoral studies until it had accepted national standards in terms of faculty quality, scholarly production, library facilities, and student residency. Responsibility for change rested with the university and nearly two decades passed before doctoral programs were reintroduced. Yet the sincerity of Brooks's and Drummond's cooperation with the AAU was rewarded in October 1945 when Marquette was "restored to the accepted list of the Association of American Universities" because the "Committee was impressed by the vigorous and constructive way in which the University has met the criticisms of its program."[37]

A RESURGENCE OF CATHOLICISM

Father McCarthy's dismay over the AAU's decertification was understandable, but his belief that anti-Catholicism lay behind the association's intentions raises some questions. Why assume, as one administrator observed, that the evaluator was "typically protestant, totally unfamiliar with Catholic concepts … honestly and unintentionally, bigoted?" Why not accept the conclusion that the library and certain faculty members were unprepared to support a palette of doctoral programs, especially when so many faculty had only master's degrees?

McCarthy's and Hamilton's defensiveness may have sprung, in part, from the battering the university had taken from the local socialist press and from occasional anti-Catholic episodes, including the Schandein controversy of 1926. Throughout the twenties, religious as well as racial bigotry had permeated the American landscape. Between 1915 and 1925, the second coming of the Ku Klux Klan featured a hatred of Catholics, Jews, foreigners, and modernists (liberals) as well as African Americans. Indiana, from whence the second AAU evaluator hailed, topped the nation in Klan membership, with nearly a quarter of a million true believers. Klan-backed officials held the Indiana governorship and controlled the state legislature following the 1924 election. Early that year, a violent confrontation had unfolded in South Bend between the Klan and students from the University of Notre Dame. The 1924 Democratic convention in New York City collapsed into gridlock as Klan-sympathizers blocked the nomination of the Catholic governor of New York, Alfred E. Smith. In Milwaukee, despite the region's heavy German, Polish, and Irish traditions—or perhaps because of them—Klan membership grew to 4,400, with headquarters only a mile from Marquette at Twenty-fourth and Kilbourn. The height of national anti-Catholicism came in the fall of 1928 after Governor Smith won his party's nomination for president of the United States. With religious white heat, some Protestant groups decried the thought of a papist residing in the White House. In the end, Herbert Hoover's landslide victory smashed Smith's dreams of becoming the first member of his faith to serve as the nation's chief executive.[38]

In light of these events, the reaction of Marquette administrators was not as outlandish as it might first appear, although there was no reason to automatically mistrust the judgment of an AAU evaluator from Indiana. In fact, this suspicion of secular authorities who questioned the role of Church teachings in American universities may have been intensified by dynamics within the Society of Jesus itself. In 1915, Father Wlodimir Ledochowski, an Austrian, had been elected superior general of the Jesuit order. Born to the aristocracy and raised within an anti-democratic tradition both at home and within the Church, he was never "at ease with the American political system and [was only] superficially acquainted with the development of the Catholic Church in the United States." He "feared that the American tendency to improvise and innovate, even to accommodate, would in the end dilute the Ignatian goals of Jesuit education." Ledochowski's suppositions that American culture distorted the judgment of Jesuit educators deepened following an embarrassing meeting with a senior Vatican official in early 1927. The latter shared accusations that American Jesuit universities were insufficiently Catholic, if not non-Catholic. Father general's shame at these suggestions by a ranking member of the Curia fueled a campaign to rid Jesuit schools of questionable practices. In 1928, he summarized his thoughts in a dispatch to the American provincials. Henceforth, his letter read, the presence of non-Catholic students at Jesuit universities could be tolerated but was not desirable. A non-Catholic presence of 7 percent or less among faculty was tolerable but not desirable. Deans must be Catholic; this was not a matter for discussion. And coeducation might be necessary, but it was not to be encouraged. This included religious women attending summer session classes.[39]

Hypersensitivity toward Marquette's Catholic identity during the presidencies of Fathers Magee and McCarthy may have, therefore, derived from a mixture of regional and national politics as well as Society-based influences. Both presidents aggressively promoted the school's faith-based traditions. Their vigor may have also been energized by what some perceived as an underemphasis of the school's Catholic mission during Father Fox's administration. University publications during Fox's tenure tended to downplay the denominational character of Marquette. Brochures from that period emphasized the "strictly non-sectarian" nature of the professional schools and the openness of Marquette to "men and women of all religious faiths." Advertisements in local newspapers characterized the school as non-denominational (sometimes twice within a single ad). A university official, while traveling across New York soliciting donors, had been advised to keep in mind that non-Catholic students outnumbered Catholic students on campus (2122 to 2025) and that only 33 percent of the faculty were Roman Catholic. Had the university been willing to trade its financial advancement for the diminution of its religious heritage?[40]

Early in his administration, Father William Magee made it clear that the Catholic culture of Marquette would no longer be understated. In a 1928 letter to Professor Jeremiah O'Sullivan, Magee admonished the venerable dean of journalism, indicating that he never wanted to be referred to by his surname only in student publications because the absence of "the title 'Father' [was] an impropriety." At the same time, Magee criticized the *Marquette Tribune* for running an advertisement that promoted a shoe store's "best dressed girl" contest, an activity that Father President considered to be tasteless at a Catholic university. From that point forward, Magee offered, presidential approval would be required for similar ads. Earlier, when serving as dean of the liberal arts, Magee had scolded Henry Banzhaf for the frequent use of *undenominational* to describe Marquette. This practice had proven "very distasteful to Catholics and has, so far as I can discover, had little or no effect in removing prejudices of non-Catholics." Furthermore, Magee wanted religious instruction at the dental school to be displayed among its regular course listings, not relegated "to the obscurity of a foot note." By the mid-thirties, recruitment brochures at the university routinely featured a section titled "Catholic Atmosphere." Despite troublesome fluctuations in enrollments, Marquette stood as a "Catholic University" whose mission was to foster "Catholic ideals of character and conduct and to strengthen the Catholic student in his devotion to his faith."[41]

Nearly two years after Father Ledochowski's 1928 admonition to the American provincials, Father Magee's successor as dean of liberal arts prepared a memorial explaining how the issues of Catholicity were being addressed in his college. It underscored the dean's commitment to recruiting Catholic faculty "if possible." The dean spoke of instructors—including Edward Fitzpatrick—who produced textbooks with a "Catholic view-point." But when it came to the hundreds of nuns on campus, the dean backed

Students in procession at Forty-Hours Devotion, 1935. File 999

away from Ledochowski's instructions, explaining how religious women improved Marquette's campus culture. He described the nuns as being "among our most earnest and successful students" and as having "an uplifting influence on the other students." This willingness to rely on their own judgments to override the superior general's wishes was exactly the problem with Americans, according to Father Ledochowski.[42]

In 1929, perhaps at the initiative of the superior general's edict to the American provincials, the university compiled a report, listing the rank, religious affiliation, and marital status of all Marquette faculty members. To Jesuits, the college of liberal arts remained the university's instructional center, and for this reason, students in the professional programs took their first two years of classes in that college. Their professions were secondary to the foundational education that they received in philosophy, history, literature, and religion. Therefore, the liberal arts faculty needed to set an example for the rest of the institution. Of the forty-eight liberal arts faculty listed in the February 1929 report, fifteen were either non-Catholic or listed with the designation "not given." At 31percent, this threshold of non-Catholics was well above the 7 percent standard set by Father Ledochowski. By the time Father Magee left Marquette during the 1935-36 school year, the percentage of non-Catholic faculty within the liberal arts college had dropped to 26 percent. By the middle of World War II when Father McCarthy left office, this percentage had risen to 34 percent.

In terms of deans, Marquette did not have a sterling record when implementing the superior general's "zero tolerance" policy. In 1929, the dean of business administration was a member of the Methodist Episcopal Church; the dean of dentistry (Henry Banzhaf) was Episcopalian; the dean of law, a Quaker; and the dean of music, Lutheran. Roman Catholics headed engineering, journalism, medicine, speech, and the graduate school. Clearly evident in these statistics was the difficulty Marquette presidents faced in finding Catholics suited to direct the university's many professional schools. As for the presence of Jesuits on the instructional staff, they constituted only thirteen (including the dean) of forty-eight faculty members (27 percent) in the college of liberal arts in 1929. By the time Father McCarthy was elevated to the presidency in 1936, they had slipped to 23 percent of the liberal arts staff. Moreover, not a single Jesuit was teaching in business administration, journalism, or speech; only two were in engineering and one each in law and medicine.[43]

Neither Father Magee nor Father McCarthy ever intended to discriminate against non-Catholic students and faculty. From its opening day, Marquette had welcomed people of all faiths. With Father Fox's approval, clubs for Lutheran and Jewish students were established in the 1920s. For his part, Father McCarthy encouraged a Kenosha man in a 1937 letter to "inform your non-Catholic friends that they would be welcome at Marquette and would experience no discrimination because of their religious beliefs." Tolerance of religious diversity, however, should not be confused with indifference toward Catholic students' violating church teachings. In 1942, the *Milwaukee Journal* aggressively covered a Marquette student's expulsion just days before his graduation because he "persisted in marrying a Protestant girl." The hint of religious intolerance reflected in the Journal articles perturbed Father McCarthy. In a series of letters defending his decision, Marquette's president insisted that if this student had simply followed his faith's precepts and had received a dispensation for a mixed marriage, nothing would have happened to him. However, by flaunting his disregard for the Church's teachings on interdenominational marriages days before his graduation, this student had forced the university's hand: ignore sinful behavior or uphold Church teachings. As a member of the Jesuit community later recalled: "If a Catholic dared to marry a non-Catholic in a Protestant ceremony, that was the end of the line for him[;] he just got thrown out." Intervention by the university president in marital matters such as the one described above was hardly unique to these times. Father Fox had received a solicitous letter in 1923 from a young Catholic school teacher in upstate Wisconsin who did not trust her social skills to interpret the sincerity of a Marquette student's romantic intentions. She pleaded for the president's advice. Fox ordered and received a very detailed report on the student's character and behavior. In his reply to the young woman, the president listed the man's pluses and minuses with vivid specificity, including his penchant for ingratiating himself with his teachers. In matters of both the faith and the heart, Marquette presidents routinely served as father figures.[44]

For Catholic students at Marquette, the annual lenten retreat provided a vital encounter with their faith. (Non-Catholic students were warmly invited to participate.) The retreat was intended to "furnish time for mental stock-taking," to remove "all thoughts of dances, parties, and other functions," and to invite students to reflect on their "duties to God and his fellowmen." Attendance at the three-day exercise had been mandatory in the school's earliest days; later, it became "expected" of all Catholic students. One distinct aspect of this spiritual exercise was its weekend schedule. Typically, it opened on Friday morning and concluded on Sunday afternoon. Mornings started with Mass at 8:30 followed by instruction, spiritual readings, and an examination of conscience. Afternoons began with stations of the cross followed by more instruction (from a visiting Jesuit of note) and, finally, benediction. The university scheduled similar retreats for female students, beginning at their own request in 1921. Both the upper and lower churches of Gesu were used, as was the chapel in Johnston Hall. The rigid separation of men and women—in fact, for a time, the retreats were held on different weekends—moderated by 1932 to allow both sexes to come together for the rosary and benediction in Gesu's upper church. An annual faculty retreat in March replicated the students' exercises.[45]

The most spectacular testimonial of Marquette's Catholic mission came in 1937 with the three hundredth anniversary of Father Jacques Marquette's birth. The United States Senate declared June 1 Marquette Day. In Milwaukee, American flags flew along city streets, but that, strangely, was the extent of the city's participation. In contrast, ninety miles to the south, a high Mass drew members of the Chicago city council and was followed by a motorcade to the site of Father Marquette's 1674 encampment near the Wrigley Building for the dedication of a tablet commemorating his visit. Weeks earlier President Franklin D. Roosevelt had sent a letter to the *Marquette Tribune* characterizing Father Marquette as "one of those dauntless pioneers whose faith sustained him in the face of all obstacles." The chief executive added: "The very name of your University therefore should inspire all who pass through its halls with something of the intrepid spirit of the great missionary in whose honor it was established." The university held its memorial on May 12, 1937. The main address was delivered by the new president

of John Carroll University, Father William M. Magee, sixteen months after his departure from Milwaukee. Musical selections by Marquette's band and chorus included
the French national anthem. Later several individuals received honorary degrees. Four
years later, the Society of Jesus celebrated its own birthday: the four hundredth. A
student novena in May 1940 inaugurated six months of activities. They were capped
off with a solemn High Mass on November 21, with Milwaukee Archbishop Moses E.
Kiley as celebrant; former Milwaukee archbishop (and fiscal angel of the university)
Samuel A. Stritch delivered the sermon.[46]

ENROLLMENTS AND RECRUITMENT

The university's renewal of its Catholic roots undoubtedly made a difference in the lives
of individual students, but it probably had little impact on just how many students
attended Marquette during a decade of hard times. Marquette's enrollment had set an
all-time record of 3,657 in September 1929, but dropped 6 percent in the following
fall, nearly a year after the stock market crash. The decrease among female students was
23 percent, suggesting that a daughter's education may have been among a family's
first concessions to the oncoming depression. Female enrollment dropped another 17
percent between the fall terms of 1931 and 1932, and again between 1932 and 1933.
By 1933, only 636 females attended Marquette, the nadir for women at Marquette;
the numbers rose every year thereafter (except two) until 1947. In fact, the resurgence
in female enrollment meant survival for the school during the darkest days of World
War II.[47]

   The number of male students at Marquette dipped, briefly, even before the stock
market crash, falling by 499 students in September 1929 from a high of 2,932 one year
earlier. Then, inexplicably, male enrollment climbed between fall 1929 and fall 1931,
after which it declined steadily over the next three years. Male enrollment reached a
low point in 1934 when only 2,414 men attended, the lowest since the fall of 1921.
Liberal arts and engineering took the hardest hits, losing 9 and 11 percent of its male
students between 1932 and 1933. Business administration, dentistry, law, and medicine experienced slight declines in the early years of the depression, with the medical
school actually rebounding after Cramer Hall opened in 1932. By 1935, the medical
school had the luxury of refusing 90 percent of its applicants.[48]

   In practical terms, each student lost to the Great Depression made it more difficult for
the university to balance the budget. The loss of two hundred students between the fall
of 1931 and the following September, for example, produced a revenue shortfall of at
least $40,000. When the university suffered a similar decline of two hundred students
by the fall term of 1933, it lost another $40,000 in revenue—a total of $80,000 in just
two years. As noted earlier, these shortfalls led to salary reductions for the faculty and
staff, and to the closing of academic programs such as nursing and music. In the face of
such challenges, the administration attended to recruitment and retention as never before. In early 1935, Father Magee ordered a survey of every college and school in order
to demonstrate that the university "has in no way been impaired in the past year, and

that—if this is a fact—there have been numerous improvements in range or quality of services." To evaluate educational efficiency, fifty-seven "high spots" were measured, including the "character of recent appointments to the faculty," health conditions in each unit, and student discipline. Although the need to prove Marquette's value was distasteful to some in the Jesuit community, it harkened back to the faculty's scientific demonstrations in the early 1880s when the faculty sought to showcase the benefits of a Marquette education. Fifty years later, salesmanship was still a necessity.[49]

One of the questions in Father Magee's 1935 survey inquired as to "educational guidance of students." On campus, this included a new "Freshman Welcoming Program." Presentations by the dean of men, the director of athletics, and the secretary of the Marquette Union were bundled together along with a bus trip across the city to introduce Milwaukee to students from outside the area. Later the university added a series of seventeen compulsory lectures (one set for men and one for women) spread across the first semester to facilitate the transition from high school. Directed by the Faculty Committee on Educational and Vocational Guidance, these orientation activities inspired an outreach campaign through a new university office, the Department of Vocational Guidance. It dispatched faculty speakers to high schools throughout Wisconsin, to address matters such as "What Shall I Be?" and "Choosing a Vocation during Depression Times." The university responded to 281 of 310 requests for speakers in 1939. Thirty-three schools in the state received two visits from university representatives and additional presentations were made before Kiwanis, Rotary, and Lions clubs. Newspaper ads invited high school graduates to use the Department of Vocational Guidance to receive career counseling. The success of these efforts persuaded Father McCarthy to establish a permanent guidance office in September 1940. One member from the three-person staff counseled Marquette students on personal matters, another assisted those with academic difficulties, and the third guided undergraduates in their career choices. Even in a time of cutbacks and reductions, administrators had to invest in student services to stem enrollment losses.[50]

STUDENTS STRUGGLE WITH THE DEPRESSION

When undergraduates arrived on campus during the deepest trough of the depression (1932-34), they faced about $700 in expenses per year. Annual tuition ran $200 in the fall of 1932. Additional fees covered matriculation, graduation, and laboratories. Enrolled students received free admission to football and hockey games as well as all basketball games except those played at the Milwaukee Auditorium. School supplies ran about $10 per term except in the professional schools where students had to invest in what was characterized as the "tools" of their trade. Books ran $20 to $35 a year. Until the alumnae opened the first dormitory in the late thirties, students found their own living accommodations. Two-person rooms rented for $2 to $4 per week; singles for $2.50 to $5. Deflationary effects over the first two years of the depression did help, dropping prices by 20 percent. The university's *in loco parentis* obligations required the central administration to maintain a certain amount of vigilance over landlords and their policies. To oversee the moral behavior of students in this private housing market, the university hired an assistant dean of men to work with managers of nearby apartments and boardinghouses. For students who did not get meals with their rooms, restaurants cost between $6 and $7 per week; the Marquette Union (which was open to women only during the lunch hour) could save a person a few pennies, costing around $5.50 per week. The most desperate students spent only a couple of dollars per week on food.[51]

To finance their college years, undergraduates worked at any jobs they could find. When the first effects of the economy's downturn were felt in 1930 and 1931, about 20 to 30 percent of Marquette students held part-time jobs. These included "waiting on tables, playing in orchestras, ushering at the theaters, clerking in shoe stores, department stores, or drug stores, running taxicabs, acting as conductors or motormen on the street cars, and tending furnaces." One student cut down Christmas trees on his family's property in northern Wisconsin to sell in Milwaukee. On campus, a handful of fortunate students worked in the gymnasium, assisted at registration, or served as secretaries to the faculty. Even individuals from well-connected families found it difficult to obtain summer employment because rules in the work place gave preference to married men with families over single college students. The Marquette Union continued to operate its employment bureau, but it attracted more job seekers than placements. In 1937, the university invited alumni to participate in a placement council that assisted recent graduates in landing their first full-time positions. The real healing in Milwaukee's job market came, however, with the boost in industrial production following the outbreak of war in Europe in 1939.[52]

Very little help came from student scholarships. In 1926, Marquette offered twenty undergraduate scholarships and provided only three graduate fellowships. The latter increased to six by the early thirties, each paying $600 per year. Marquette was a tuition-dependent, endowment-poor institution, so the paucity of financial aid was not surprising. In a survey of Jesuit universities taken in the late thirties, Marquette reported only seven scholarships compared to twenty-one at Boston College, twenty-five at John Carroll, twenty-eight at Canisius, and thirty-six at Fordham. Of the seven undergraduate awards at Marquette, three went to male graduates of Pio Nono, Messmer, and St. John's Cathedral high schools and another three to female graduates of Mercy and Holy Angels high schools (the latter at Twelfth and Kilbourn), and St. Mary's Academy. The Knights of Columbus provided an annual gift of $2,000 to support nuns who attended summer school. The State of Wisconsin offered a few dollars through its office of vocational rehabilitation which assisted disabled students suffering from polio, amputations, or deafness. For a handful of needy juniors and seniors, the university maintained the Father Noonan Loan Fund. And the bursar's office provided a part-time payment schedule for students unable to pay their full tuition at the outset of a semester.[53]

The most important source of financial assistance for depression-era students was government-supported employment through the New Deal's Federal Emergency Relief Administration (FERA) and later the National Youth Administration (NYA). In February 1934, the FERA's student employment project assigned $3,510 to Marquette to assist two hundred and thirty-three students. Each participant earned between $10 and $20 a month for work on campus, and the government required that the ratio of males and females in this program match the school's gender balance. Professor William Hebard, who later chaired the engineering building campaign, managed Marquette's FERA program. Within its first week, Marquette received between five and six hundred applications for the two hundred and thirty-three positions. University officials kept recipients under constant review, with students whose financial situation improved being replaced by needier peers. As the 1934 fall term began, over one thousand students applied for approximately three hundred part-time positions. Charles Cobeen, still secretary of the Marquette Union, replaced Professor Hebard as senior administrator. By government edict, at least half the recipients had to be newcomers who could not have enrolled without this help. The idea was to keep young people in school and out of the depleted job market. On-campus work for FERA participants included research and typing for various departments, stenography, printing, filing, library work, and painting. Sensitive to criticism that some of the work was "'trifling, or that they [the student workers] are not held to a faithful performance of their tasks'," a steering committee consisting of deans O'Sullivan (journalism) and Kartak (engineering) as well as Cobeen and Hebard insisted that supervisors be diligent in their oversight. By the fall of 1936, after two and a half years of operation, the National Youth Administration (which continued the FERA program) had not increased its monthly allocation to the university, leaving fewer than three hundred student jobs. A few participants now worked off-campus with the West Allis Youth Club, the Y.M.C.A., and the U.S. Forestry Service. The NYA shut down in early 1942, with the country fully engulfed in a world war and unemployment no longer a consideration.[54]

The Great Depression not only affected the personal finances of students. It also threatened student publications. In the fall 1932, the Marquette Press announced that it might be forced to discontinue the yearbook because the previous issue had incurred a deficit. It needed eight hundred subscriptions to insure the *Hilltop*'s survival. Five weeks of campaigning secured only half the required subscriptions. Somehow this break-even figure was reached, providing for a 1933 edition. During the following school year, the Marquette Press reduced the sizes of the *Marquette Tribune* and the oldest student publication on campus, the *Marquette Journal*. The *Marquette Engineer* abandoned plans to become a monthly and publications for the drama society, the Aristotelian Society, and the Classical Club disappeared altogether.[55]

Also vanishing in 1934 was WHAD, the university's beloved radio station. About the same time that Father Fox had cancelled the station's agreement with the *Milwaukee Journal* in 1927, the Federal Radio Commission imposed limits on college-owned frequencies, requiring them to broadcast educational and cultural programs only. Thus programming during the 1927-28 academic year consisted of performances by students and faculty from the School of Music, spiritual sermons, lectures by faculty, and broadcasts of football and basketball games as well as university convocations, the baccalaureate Mass, and commencement. During the following year, the station added a weekly children's half-hour. This schedule retained a strong academic flavor through 1930-31 with seventy-two faculty members offering commentaries and lectures. One philosophy professor delivered forty-nine talks; a representative from the alumni spoke forty-seven times. The station was on the air for only twelve to fourteen hours a week. To strengthen its programming, WHAD affiliated with the Columbia Broadcasting System in 1932. But operating costs and competition for air space created more headaches than administrators could tolerate. During the last quarter of 1932, the station incurred a debt of nearly $4,000. With a sense of urgency, the university sold its rights and its equipment in the spring of 1934 to WISN, the Wisconsin News station, an affiliate of the Radio Division of Hearst Enterprises. Thus an important regional outlet for the university became another victim of the Great Depression.[56]

STUDENT LIFE SURVIVES

The hardships that students endured during the depression years were balanced by the benefits they anticipated from a Marquette education. The university undertook a survey of first-year students in the fall of 1938, seeking to understand why they attended Marquette. The most common response was the school's "Catholic auspices" (32 percent of respondents) followed by "Convenient location." Father McCarthy must have been delighted to see that Marquette's Catholic mission attracted so many young people. A year later, Wenonah Eis (who later became the first housemother at Alumnae House) conducted her own survey of first-year women (except those in dental hygiene and members of religious orders) as part of her Master of Education thesis. Eighty-seven percent of her 166 respondents came from Wisconsin, 64 percent lived at home, 20 percent had fathers who had graduated from college and, surprisingly, only 31 percent had graduated from Catholic high schools although 73 percent were Catholics. (This last discrepancy may have reflected the unacceptable costs of a parochial education during an economic downturn.) The motivations that brought them to Marquette varied: 47 percent were impressed by the "rating of [the] school," 44 percent by its location, and 38 percent by its Catholic identity. These women came to college with serious intentions: two-thirds planned a career or at least a job following graduation. Nearly everyone said she enjoyed watching college football and basketball. Two-thirds played basketball themselves and 39 percent enjoyed swimming. Forty-two percent chose ping-pong as her favorite indoor sport. Typical of the era's young women, nearly three out of four enjoyed dancing; only one-third said the same about homemaking. As for their larger view of the college experience, 65 percent said they liked Marquette "very much;" an additional 23 percent liked it "sometimes." Only 15 percent had considered quitting school.[57]

The enthusiasm that these women exhibited for dancing reflected a depression-era social behavior that defied class and location. Whether in the immigrant neighborhoods of this country's cities or at the nation's colleges, dance halls beckoned young adults, especially young women. If a union or parish hall had enough room to hold a few dozen dancers, it held the promise of an entertaining evening. Big band music entranced Hilltopper crowds at the homecoming dance, department shindigs such as the "engineers' domino dance" and the "medicals cut-up dance," inter-fraternity dances at the Wisconsin Club, the holly ball (where women initiated the choice of dance partners), and of course the prom. With Lent just around the corner, February was special, filled with all sorts of activities. Every event sponsored by a university organization fell under review of the committee on student life (CSL). One of its rules required that dances take place on weekends; others determined where they took place. The university gymnasium was the committee's preferred site—and the last choice of students. More enticing locations included the Eagles Clubhouse, the Milwaukee Athletic Club, and the Plankinton, Pfister, Shorecrest, Schroeder, and Astor hotels, although students could use only the latter's Roof Room because its Venetian Room was too close to the bar. By the late thirties, the committee on student life had relaxed a stipulation that went back to Father Noonan's day, a rule restricting fraternities, sororities, and departments to no more than two events a year. The two-dance limit now applied to each semester instead of the entire school year.[58]

The hours that Marquette students spent traversing Milwaukee's near west side streets helped shape a type of university town. The Grand Avenue of the nineteenth century with its mansions and expansive lawns underwent a steady transformation in the early twentieth century. Gas stations, eating establishments, and hotels sprang up amid a smattering of residences from the horse and buggy era. Along Clybourn, Wells, Kilbourn, and State, three- and four-story brick apartment buildings, with commercial storefronts on the ground floor were interspersed among Victorian-era frame houses. Local residents and students alike became enthusiastic consumers—when they had the money. The Weigle-Schewe Pharmacy (later the University Pharmacy), on the north side of Wisconsin Avenue across from Gesu, became a popular spot for undergraduates to gather between classes. In a letter published in the September 24, 1931, issue of the *Marquette Tribune*, owner Henry G. Schewe expressed a hope that his store might become an all-purpose center for students. Schewe described how, during his days at Marquette, he had missed the conveniences that his new shop aimed to provide. It cashed checks, sold stamps, checked parcels, made free pharmacy deliveries, and provided an array of pencils, pens, and loose-leaf notebooks. It featured the Varsity Room, where lunches, sodas, phosphates, and malted milks were downed amidst a thick, blue-gray cloud of cigarette smoke. Students bought quick, convenient meals at the Ardmore Pharmacy, the Ardmore Restaurant, the Monitor Restaurant, the Marquette Union cafeteria, the Campus Kitchen (in the LaSalle Hotel), and the Stratford Arms Hotel Restaurant. The Abbot Crest Hotel, a few steps west of the drug store, featured a dining room, a shoe repair shop, and its most popular enterprise, a billiard parlor. In the fall of 1930, a splashy, five-story, terra cotta office building rose on the northwest corner of Eleventh and Wisconsin, across the street from the law school. Managers of the Franklin State Bank building (currently Marquette's 707 Building) promised that

Sixteenth and Wisconsin, 1939. Note Walgreens Drug Store in same building as today and gas station on southwest corner of intersection. File 280

Hopkins Hall on south side of Wisconsin, west of Thirteenth Street (Also known for time as Duffey Hall and used by speech clinic). Note stairway to pedestrian tunnel under Wisconsin Avenue. File 693

its tenants were all professional men who were "Marquette Minded." Attorneys, physicians, real estate brokers, and a dentist invited students to make use of their services. In a *Tribune* advertisement, management urged overworked students to relax at the rooftop miniature golf course which featured "new Turftex greens." The course was open from nine in the morning (just an hour after classes began) until midnight.[59]

The average student's sense of place—developed amidst an urban landscape of hotels, retail stores, diners, gas stations, union offices, and taverns—intensified with each passing semester. In an 1936 editorial the *Marquette Tribune* commiserated with freshmen who arrived to find no centralized campus and no means of connecting with other students outside the slow process of joining clubs or hanging around drug stores and diners. The essay commented unfavorably on the deplorable conditions of the sidewalks along Wisconsin Avenue as well as on the university's walkways. Every student became a "mudder," coping with "mud-caked heels and soggy trouser cuffs." The city finally addressed the dangers created by automobile traffic along the "Avenue," especially for youngsters who attended the Gesu parish school, when it constructed a pedestrian tunnel beneath Wisconsin, from the west side of Thirteenth Street to the front of the Grandmora Apartments. Stairways leading into this underground subway became a favorite meeting place for Marquette students of both sexes.[60]

The Marquette Union was busier than ever during the thirties because male students sought inexpensive ways to occupy their evenings As its business manager, Charles Cobeen became part social director, part landlord, and part housefather. Although the cafeteria was open to women, the union board did not allow women into the Smokey Blue Room with its juke box until 1945. Drexel Lodge remained the center of the female campus, although the building's layout as a former residence restricted the types of events and the number of women who could gather at any one time. The use of the hall's third floor by religious sisters contributed to these limitations.[61]

ORIGINS OF STUDENT HOUSING

For female students at Marquette, the most innovative advancement of the 1930s came at the instigation of Mabel Mannix McElligott, the beloved dean of women. She assembled five hundred graduates at the Astor Hotel on February 12, 1938, to organize the Marquette Alumnae Association (later the Association of Marquette University Women). The association immediately went to work addressing the desperate need for respectable housing within walking distance of the university. McElligott recommended that the group borrow $10,000 from the Jesuit community and use $4,000 to sign a ten-year lease on an apartment building at 1135 West Kilbourn Avenue. The remainder was used to refurbish the four-story building during the summer of 1938. Volunteers sewed 130 pairs of new drapes, waxed floors, applied fresh paint, and accumulated bargain-priced furniture. The last was unceremoniously dumped on the lawn by a disgruntled delivery man, so husbands and family members completed the task of moving the beds, chairs, and dressers into the building. On September 15, 1938, Alumnae House opened for business. Its eighty-five residents provided their own blankets, towels, bedding, and personal effects. Rent for two- and three-person rooms ranged between $260 and $300 per year, breakfast and dinners included. A year later, the alumnae association purchased the building outright for $25,000, and in 1944, it

Brooks Hall, first men's dormitory, on left, was previously Waverly Club and after 1953 was renamed Noonan Hall. On right is Marquette Union, later Carpenter Hall. Photo taken in early 1940s. File 150

Lisette Lodge. File 865

Alumnae House, 1965. File 26

received the adjoining lot and house as a gift from George J. Meyer, Sr., the original owner of the Alumnae House property.[62]

The association's assertiveness in addressing the residential options available for female Hilltoppers broke a logjam regarding university involvement in student housing. Although apartment rentals remained the preferred domicile for most students, momentum built for university-sponsored quarters. Two years after Alumnae House was dedicated, the first men's dormitory opened in the former Waverly Club. Adjacent to the Marquette Union on Thirteenth Street, this three-story, freshman dormitory was named after Peter Brooks, the undergraduate who had inspired the union and the Jesuit who at that moment headed the Missouri province. Brooks Hall was outfitted with thirty-eight single rooms and forty-two doubles. University administrators had design sketches prepared for a grander, five-story structure (shrewdly labeled Alumni Hall), but World War II obliterated that proposal. The university did purchase the 1920s-era Monitor Hotel on Sixteenth Street in 1943 and leased the Stratford Arms Hotel on Wisconsin Avenue, both to house naval students. The university also received a magnificent $100,000 mansion at 3200 Highland Boulevard through the generosity of Mrs. Lisette Miller, widow of the founder of the Miller Brewing Company. Marquette reopened the structure in 1944 as Lisette Lodge, a residence hall for two dozen women.[63]

INTRAMURAL AND VARSITY ATHLETICS

Another popular hangout was the university gymnasium. Except for undergraduates who dedicated two years to the band, chorus, glee club, or orchestra, every student completed two semesters of physical education classes, ordinarily during the freshman year. By the early 1940s, a well-rounded program that included archery, badminton, bowling, fencing, riding, riflery, ping-pong, and swimming replaced the old-fashioned physical education courses, dominated by calisthenics. The university added a Bachelor of Science in Physical Education to the curriculum in 1929, with courses in camp craft, first aid, and playground and community center management. Also using the gym, the school's intramural program featured teams from the fraternities, class years, and colleges. Intramurals grew from 600 participants in the late twenties to 1,700 a decade later. Graduate students, those in special adult classes, and undergraduates were all eligible to participate in handball, wrestling, indoor baseball, and the distinctive activity of that era, boxing. A different "sport" from this era (and one that remains popular into the twenty-first century) involved changing the school's nickname. The *Marquette Tribune* took the position that *Hilltopper* referred to the school's ancient location at Tenth and State streets. (In a related topographical matter, engineering students proudly employed their surveying skills to confirm that the "medics," "dents," and engineers occupied the *upper* campus—13.5 feet higher at their end of Wisconsin Avenue—compared to the *lower* campus five blocks to the east where most undergraduates took classes.) In the spring of 1941, the Marquette Union held a nickname contest, arguing that the *hilltop* reference was antiquated and the *Golden Avalanche* moniker, adopted briefly during the mid-1920s, no longer fit sport teams that wore all-white uniforms. What might have come of this campaign will never be known since the attack on Pearl Harbor in December 1941 made nicknames trivial.[64]

While financial constraints imposed by the depression forced an average student to find inexpensive distractions such as intramural sports, the varsity athletic program also struggled, weighed down with its own budgetary burdens. The athletic department's most serious challenge involved the football stadium's bonds, responsibilities inherited from the alumni. When the bonds came due in 1933 ($25,000), 1934 ($25,000), and 1935 ($110,000), the university sought to delay these obligations by extending their maturity dates and lowering the interest rate. Despite hard times, the bonds were reissued with reassuring ease, much to the university president's delight.[65]

The athletic board faced other financial pressures, as evidenced by its elimination of the bowling team in 1929 and its discussion of possibly discontinuing golf and tennis. It carefully scrutinized the track and field program because of a $12,000 operating deficit. The football team was certainly not exempt from these considerations. The board restricted the size of the squad to as few as 35, which helped keep uniform and travel costs under control. It is also managed the sports programs beyond fiscal oversight. At one point, the board reprimanded the football coach for "carping from the bench during the games." At another time, it ordered the coach to insert a particular player and to work out a more efficient combination in his backfield. The athletic director received instructions to direct the student body to stop booing when scores of other games were announced. The university suspended twenty-one students from varsity athletics because of grades during the spring of 1931. When the athletic director tried to get the football coach released from his obligation to teach political science courses, the board reproached him with the reminder that, after all, the coach was a teacher and therefore had academic obligations to fulfill. The board maintained tight controls over athletic events during the Lenten retreat as well as during examination periods. Its vigilance extended to players who contacted a sexually transmitted "Social Disease" ("ease the student out of the University without delay"), and to married men (forbidden to play varsity sports). The board also restricted female spectators to contests held in the gymnasium or the stadium, with no picture-taking allowed.[66]

The era's highlight for varsity sports came on January 1, 1937, with the unexpected choice of Marquette's football team to take on Texas Christian University in the first Cotton Bowl game. The university found out about its selection only two weeks before the game, which was scheduled for Dallas, Texas. Less than a week after receiving this exciting news, the team departed Milwaukee by train. What may have been the university's finest gridiron eleven in history—alumni from the early 1920s would undoubtedly contest this point—ended an otherwise fabulous season with a sixteen to six loss to TCU and its star player, "Slingin' Sammy" Baugh.[67]

The presence of Marquette's most gifted athlete in its history also added luster to this decade. Born in Atlanta, Ralph H. Metcalfe prepped at Tilden Tech on Chicago's south side. He came to Milwaukee in the fall of 1930 and stayed through the spring of 1936, with time spent at the 1932 Olympics. Metcalfe earned a bachelor of arts degree from the College of Liberal Arts and briefly attended law classes. He was chosen treasurer of the men's sodality and elected president of the senior class. He was also the first African American selected for membership in the National Jesuit Honor Society, Alpha Sigma Nu. After leaving Marquette, Metcalfe served as track coach and athletic director at Xavier University in New Orleans until he was called into the army during World War II. Just before his military service, the former Hilltopper received the prestigious James J. Hoey Award for Interracial Justice. The citation referred to his conversion to Catholicism while at Marquette, his making the sign of the cross in front of an obviously displeased Adolf Hitler at the 1936 Olympics, and his devotion to soldiers of every race through involvement in the USO. After the war, Metcalfe became an alderman in Chicago and later served in the United States Congress. He died in 1978.[68]

Metcalfe's exploits on the cinder track began during his teenage years in Chicago. While at the university, this gifted speedster held the Amateur Athletic Union and the National Collegiate Athletic Association titles in the 100-meter and 200-meter events for three years (1932-34), and the AAU's 200-meter title in 1935 and 1936. He was frequently matched against Eddie Tolan of Michigan and Jessie Owens of Ohio State. In the Olympics, Metcalfe won a gold medal in 1932 as part of the 4 by 100-meter relay, and silvers in the 1932 and 1936 games in the 100-meter, losing in the latter event to Owens by less than a yard. The Hilltopper earned a bronze medal at the 1932

Olympics in Los Angeles, although a mistake in the chalking of the lanes may have deprived him of the gold. Because his American teammates Eddie Tolan and George Simpson also received medals, Metcalfe did not challenge the judges' decision. His devotion to sports ran so deep that Metcalfe served as water boy for the football team for three years. He brought such prestige to this lowly assignment that when he stepped away from the role in 1934, the university held a campus-wide recruitment for his successor: the water boy who replaced the "world's fastest man."[69]

More than his athletic prowess, Ralph Metcalfe's election to class office and his participation in the sodality and Alpha Sigma Nu demonstrated the improving conditions for African Americans at Marquette. Ten African Americans attended the university in 1939: eight undergraduates and two graduate students. Only two were Roman Catholic. Their membership in the sodality, Alpha Sigma Nu, the Holy Name lecture bureau, the *Marquette Tribune*, the sociology club, and the chemical club demonstrated a participatory pattern not witnessed in earlier decades. In a related vein, the *Marquette Tribune* became increasingly outspoken on racial issues. For example, a March 1933 editorial blasted the student council at Kansas State Teachers College for depriving three seniors of social privileges for "dancing with Negro girl students at a 'social hour' sponsored by the Y.M.C.A." The *Tribune* editor asked why interracial dancing should constitute a "'problem in discipline'" and concluded by wondering if young minds shouldn't be "freed from the restraint of bigotry" through their involvement with higher education. A decade later, at the height of World War II, *Tribune* articles covered visitors who came to speak on racial equality. One unattributed column bemoaned racial flare-ups in Detroit and New York during the summer of 1943, at a time when the nation was in a deadly battle with those who upheld "Fascist race hatred." "To the Catholic college student falls the duty to combat [racism's] pernicious doctrine," advised the young journalist. A similar concern was sounded in an April 1944 editorial: "Christ left us no leeway in this matter; His word on this subject can be interpreted but one way: that we must, if we wish to obey God, treat everyone in the same manner in which we would treat Christ Himself."[70]

At the administrative level, progress was glacial. Several times during his term as president, Father McCarthy expressed caution when discussing the admission of unmarried black women to Marquette. He framed his hesitation in terms of the segregated conditions that black females faced in Milwaukee, not in terms of any reluctance to admit African American women. In fact, when a black teacher who was married asked to attend evening classes at Marquette in 1941, the president encouraged her to apply. McCarthy made it clear that African American men were admitted on an equal basis with other applicants, except in one instance: the medical school. This policy arose, he explained, from local prejudices "against Negro physicians." Father McCarthy felt that in the absence of a hospital for African Americans and in the absence of a university hospital, black interns would not be able to complete their training in the local area. However the Labor College, when it opened in 1941, proudly declared that it did "not discriminate as to religious beliefs or races." One other positive sign was a brief

Ralph Metcalfe. Peter Murphy Collection

exchange between the dean of liberal arts and a new university president during the summer of 1945 regarding the recruitment of a black faculty member. Their remarks focused entirely upon matters related to his qualifications and not to the propriety of such a hiring.[71]

WARTIME

Marquette's slow, steady return to institutional normalcy was abruptly interrupted by America's entrance into World War II. The school's first "casualty" was the enrollment, the school's fiscal lifeline. In the fall of 1929, at the outset of the depression, the university had set an all-time record with 3,657 students. Over the next four years, the student body dropped by 17 percent, triggering layoffs, salary cuts, and program reductions. By the mid-thirties, enrollments started to rebound, with modest growth for the rest of that decade. By the fall of 1941, 4,393 students attended Marquette, a new all-time high. But as the semester drew to a close, Japan attacked Pearl Harbor. Within days, the United States declared war on the aggressor and, in turn, Nazi Germany declared war on the United States. Between students who volunteered for duty and those who responded to orders from the selective service, the male population at the university dropped 39 percent in two years. By fall 1943, only 1,920 males remained, compared to 3,147 two years earlier. The School of Law suffered the greatest decline: from 275 students in 1940 to 85 in 1942. One factor permitted the institution to survive these dramatic losses: the steady enrollment of women. Rumors abounded that the administration was about to take drastic actions because of its dwindling student body. To counter this hearsay, Father McCarthy issued a calming statement at the annual Parents' Day banquet in November 1942 and later in a letter to each student. He reassured his audiences that any concerns over the future of law, journalism, speech, and the liberal arts were unwarranted. Female students alone, he reasoned, could keep the university fiscally afloat until peace returned—a stunning admission considering the grief that coeducation had brought Father McCabe. Amid these chaotic times came another first: a female transfer student from Northern Illinois State Teachers College enrolled in chemical engineering in the fall of 1943, shattering that college's men-only tradition. One segment of the student body whose numbers would certainly not recover for the duration were international students. Marquette was down to twenty-three students from overseas by the fall of 1942, with only two from outside the Western Hemisphere.[72]

To meet wartime demands, Marquette reinvented the way it did business. Medicine, dentistry, and engineering set the example as the university catered to a new type of student: men (and a few women) in military uniforms. A year before America entered the war, Marquette received government approval to become the first Catholic university to host a naval ROTC unit. By September 1941, the program's 203 cadets occupied Bellarmine Hall, the former engineering building, and used the gymnasium for drill practice. After war was declared, Marquette began cooperating with the U.S. Army to recruit aviation cadets to the campus. The School of Medicine switched to a trimester, year-round schedule in July 1942, so that its traditional four-year curriculum could be compressed into three. The rest of the university, except for the graduate school, followed suit a year later. Ninety-two seniors in engineering had their course work accelerated in the spring of 1942, permitting those already commissioned in the army, navy, or marines (about half of the total) to graduate two months early. Within a year, the university became deeply committed to two major service programs: the Army Specialized Training Program and the Navy College Training Program (known as V-12). In spring 1943, the trustees accepted responsibility for 1,000 naval personnel. Marquette's close relationship with this branch of the armed services was recognized in

May 1945 with the christening of the S.S. Marquette, a Victory-class (an upgrade of the Liberty-class) ship. At 10,730 tons, the 455-foot vessel was dedicated with a tribute singling out "one of America's distinguished institutions of higher learning, Marquette University, located in Milwaukee, Wis." Father President was represented at the ship's launching by Leonard Pruski, a 1941 graduate who had developed a distinguished service record as a naval aviator.[73]

By the first anniversary of Pearl Harbor in December 1942, more than 700 Marquette men were in active service and six had already given their lives for the cause of freedom. In mid-July 1943, the army called all 320 medical and dental students who had been in the reserves to active service. By that time, nearly half the male students on campus were either in the military or in reserve status and, therefore, subject to military discipline. For example, naval students who used the library in Johnston Hall at night did so under orders of silence. In the summer of 1943, a U.S. Cadet Nurses Corps reserve unit was commissioned at Marquette. Eight Marquette Jesuits eventually joined the cause, enlisting as military chaplains. For those who remained civilians, the *Marquette Tribune* urged them find defense jobs with the Red Cross Canteen Corps, decontamination squads, or the air-raid warden program. Science Hall served as a training site for the last. The "coed chapter" of the Red Cross assumed responsibility for recruiting blood and plasma donations from the student body.[74]

The Catholic identity of the university shone through as members of the Marquette community participated through their faith. Students and faculty organized a multi-denominational "victory and peace" prayer movement. Law students recited the rosary. As the fall 1942 term opened, the student newspaper called for a "Week of Prayer" on behalf of classmates in the military. Servicemen on campus formed their own "Apostleship of Prayer" under the direction of Father George Ganss, who became military chaplain at Marquette. The golden anniversary of the Church of the Gesu in December 1943 provided an opportunity for prayers to be offered for the safe return of all military personnel and for an eventual end to the conflict. Hectic training schedules even forced concessions in devotional regulations. First Friday Masses were now offered in the afternoon as well as the morning to accommodate enlisted men. Only servicemen could receive communion at the afternoon liturgy; civilians still had to receive the Eucharist at the morning services. The university reduced the annual retreat for women to a single day to accommodate the trimester class schedule. A capacity crowd filled the gymnasium and offered prayers on April 19, 1945, during a special memorial service to honor President Franklin D. Roosevelt who had died a week earlier.[75]

Once war was declared in December 1941, Father McCarthy followed Father Noonan's example in 1917 by throwing himself completely behind the nation's effort. McCarthy called upon students to support every liberty loan campaign and they met his challenge. Within a month of Pearl Harbor, organizers from every college and school urged students to "do 'their bit with two-bits'" in the first drive. A twenty-five cent contribution earned the donor a pin; earnings from these bonds went into a scholarship fund. A survey of nearly 900 students conducted a few months later revealed that 691 had purchased defense bonds and stamps, 213 had pledged blood, 148 were involved in civilian defense activity, and 250 had enlisted or intended to enlist in the armed services. As the 1942 school year opened, sororities cancelled all formal balls for the duration, with money that would have been spent on dresses, shoes, and hair appointments going to the next bond drive. During that school year, students raised nearly $40,000, an average of more than $3,000 per month. Fund-raising campaigns tended to acquire nicknames. For instance, the 1943-44 slogan was "Mark It For Mark-ette" with "Mark" being a symbolic serviceman representing Milwaukee's Jesuit university. By early 1945, students, families, and friends had raised $537,497.25 in various bond drives.[76]

The decision to cancel all sorority dances after the fall of 1942 reflected the general mood on campus: distractions could wait. Only five formal, all-university dances remained on the schedule during the war years. In 1943, the committee on student life added a military ball to the list. Food rationing became necessary as the Marquette Union and Alumnae House adjusted to shortages of tomato and orange juice, spaghetti, and sauerkraut (which, unlike the practice during World War I, was not renamed "liberty cabbage"). One government mandate (Law 85 from the Office of Price Administration) proposed making shorter and narrower skirts to save fabric for the war effort, a campaign patriotically endorsed by *Marquette Tribune*.[77]

The greatest sacrifices were made, of course, by those in the service. The first Hilltopper to lose his life in the armed forces was a 23-year-old, former football player from the College of Engineering whose training plane crashed in a New Mexico rainstorm early in 1942. The *Tribune* kept its readership posted on the whereabouts of students and alumni with a weekly column summarizing wartime assignments. When announcing deaths in action, deaths in the line of duty, prisoners of war, or those missing in action, the student newspaper reported each event with a somberness befitting the tragedy. A front-page column noted the passing of the 100th Marquette casualty in April 1945, just a month before hostilities drew to a close in Europe. The university erected a billboard in front of Johnston Hall during the fall 1943 bond campaign with the theme "You've Got a Bill To Be Paid." Attached to the billboard were the names of twenty-seven deceased servicemen. A final accounting sent to Father President in December 1945 (four months after V-J Day) listed 138 deaths among Marquette students and alumni, with twenty-five still missing. Nearly seven thousand members of the larger Marquette family had served in the armed services. As hundreds of veterans returned to campus in the postwar years, they brought home to the university community the seriousness of the epoch they had just survived.[78]

Amid this turmoil, Father McCarthy was replaced in February 1944 by Father Peter Brooks. Born in Watertown, Wisconsin, Brooks had worked for a number of years before entering Marquette as an undergraduate in the fall of 1916. The young man became a role model, personifying Father Noonan's passion for the American cause during World War I by leaving school and enlisting in the coastal artillery. After serving in France, the veteran had returned to his classes in the fall of 1919, won the Jesuit

Marquette Army and Navy units in gymnasium during World War II. Image of Father Peter Brooks superimposed. Brooks Biographical File

Intercollegiate English Essay contest, inspired the student body and administration to create a (male) student union at Marquette, and entered the Jesuit order following graduation. While serving as superior of the Missouri Province from 1937 to 1943, Brooks repeatedly prodded Saint Louis University to consider dropping its ban on African American students. When returning to his alma mater in 1944, Brooks advised his audience: "I do not have to be in any sense an innovator. The Jesuit system of education is over 400 years old and has proved its substantial worth through times of peace and times of crises." He reminded students that the university offered "a philosophy of life" through "the discovery and dissemination of truth—and the first truth is that man is created in the image and likeness of God." With these reassuring words, Father Brooks set a course for the postwar period, an era characterized by freely adopted changes, not harried adjustments wrought by the frightening onslaughts of the Great Depression and World War II.[79]

Navy V-12 dance during World War II. File 975

6

POSTWAR ADJUSTMENTS
1945-54

Coming out of World War II, the Marquette community craved nothing more than normalcy—even boredom would suffice. For a decade and a half, the university had been buffeted by powerful national and international forces. America's most trying economic crisis, longer in duration than anyone ever dared to imagine, had been followed by the greatest military epoch in world history. War-weary Americans sought contentment in a loving marriage, healthy children, a steady job, an unassuming house, and an operating automobile. Yet they were haunted by a fear that the nation could quickly slip back into the grips of the Great Depression. The dangers of a cold war with the Soviet Union only escalated these anxieties. At Marquette, university administrators anticipated budget constraints similar to those in the thirties. Upgrading the physical plant and expanding academic programs were pipedreams that had vanished amid the chaos of recent times. The mundane never looked so good. But instead of facing either heartache or boredom, Marquette encountered its largest student body, a host of costly new buildings, and a strategic plan that ultimately propelled the school into the lead among Catholic universities.

ENROLLMENT SURPRISES

The most notable departure from custom during the immediate postwar period was a startlingly upswing in enrollment. Students of every age and background flooded the campus in numbers never witnessed in Milwaukee. In the fall of 1943, deep in wartime, registrations at Marquette had sunk to their lowest point since the Great Depression: just over 3,000 students. The following fall—only three months after the invasion at Normandy and when victory by Christmas seemed within reach—enrollment had edged upward to 3,772. One year later in September 1945—a month after V-J Day—this number had crept up another thousand to 4,752. But that was nothing compared to September 1946 when registrations reached 7,296. A jump of 1,119 by the subsequent fall brought the student body to yet another all-time record: 8,415. Enrollment finally peaked at 8,603 in 1948, before slipping to below 7,500 by 1951. A new growth spurt then began in 1954. Emblematic of these remarkable throngs of students was the introduction in the fall 1951 of plastic-coated photo-identification cards. Distribution of these badges was delayed, however, when a spot-check revealed excessive falsification of birth dates.[1]

Startled by this landslide of students, administrators scurried to accommodate the overflow, even though each solution was tempered by a caution that these new Hilltoppers might be only a temporary bump in Marquette's popularity. What would happen if enrollment levels dropped precipitously in a few years? Consequently, the administration's first steps were modest and inexpensive. In early 1946, two barrack-style buildings (not technically Quonset huts), each 120 feet long and 20 feet wide, were erected behind Science Hall for $16,000. They provided seven classrooms for 400 liberal arts, business, and journalism students. According to these undergraduates, heat in these prefabricated structures during Milwaukee winters was nothing but a rumor. Other barracks were installed on Sixteenth Street behind Cramer Hall. Regular classrooms were filled to capacity as was the library in Johnston Hall. Basements and storage areas, never intended for instructional purposes, were transformed into makeshift classrooms. Full-time faculty took on heavier workloads and part-timers handled extra sections. Classes started at 7:30 in the morning and concluded at 10:00 at night. The university even considered Saturday classes.[2]

The discharge of military veterans fueled this transformation. Male enrollment jumped by 86 percent between fall 1945 and fall 1946, from 2,911 to 5,429. The following year, it increased another 21 percent. According to one report, by the fall of 1946 Marquette had experienced the largest increase of male and female students among all the private universities in the United States since 1939: 95 percent among males and 90 percent among females. What drew thousands of ex-servicemen to college campuses across the country was, of course, the GI and Veterans Rehabilitation bills of 1944. A grateful nation promised to pay educational expenses at accredited

Crowded classroom, 1946-47. File 170

Thirteenth Street barracks, late 1940s. File 255

institutions. During the spring term of 1944, six veterans were enrolled at Marquette; by the summer, this number had grown to 37. In November, there were more than 200 vets on campus, with the largest number in the liberal arts. Two months earlier, these ex-servicemen had organized the Marquette Veterans' Brigade to help its members ease into civilian and academic life. The university had already established a Veterans' Guidance and Counseling Service wherein faculty from the Department of Education met with ex-servicemen on a regular basis regarding their progress in school. Early in 1945, a Marquette Rehabilitation Center opened on the sixth floor of the county courthouse to test and counsel all veterans seeking government benefits. The speech clinic assisted those who suffered speech problems after leaving the service. Father Peter Brooks, an ex-serviceman himself, charged a university committee to provide the institutional response to the needs of veterans. To welcome all these newcomers, the *Marquette Tribune* ran a regular feature titled "The Veteran's Viewpoint."[3]

The number of ex-service personnel increased from 206 veterans (including two women) in November 1944 to over 300 by the end of the 1945 summer session, about the time the war ended. From that point on, veterans deluged the campus, with 1,899 (including 39 women) enrolled by the spring 1946 term. (This does not include 363 navy trainees still housed at the Stratford Arms Hotel and 114 at Brooks Hall.) When a new all-time enrollment was achieved in 1948-49 (8,603), the registration of veterans also peaked at 4,820.[4]

Even before the declaration of war in December 1941, uniformed personnel could be spotted on campus. During the war, academic departments had learned to handle the trainees' ever-changing schedules. Students in uniform had become a familiar part of the campus culture, and thus within months of the war's end, Father Brooks sought to make this relationship long term when he applied for a permanent naval ROTC unit. Meantime, most wartime training programs slowly disbanded. Brooks Hall, the former freshman dormitory, returned to civilian use in summer 1946. About the same time, the cafeteria in the Marquette Union brought back its non-military menu. Even though new distractions tempered wartime memories, the campus community acknowledged those who had lost their lives. As their predecessors had done in 1919, yearbook editors in 1946 honored 147 individuals from the university who had died in World War II.[5]

Next to classroom space, housing was the university's biggest challenge. The demand for apartments strained a rental market whose volume had stagnated since 1929. At one point, the university considered using Sunday sermons to ask local Catholics to make extra rooms available to struggling students. The school also floated the idea of turning its gymnasium into a dormitory. Married students had the greatest difficulty. First, they had the almost impossible task of finding family housing. Then at home, they faced their children's simple but pointed question: "Why, Daddy?" when fathers poured themselves into their studies instead of playing with their offspring. The federal government provided between $65 and $90 per month for living expenses, a sum that forced many vets to find part-time jobs. In 1947, the veterans' brigade decided to help their members fight inflationary prices by establishing a cooperative store in the basement of the athletic building (one of the former Plankinton houses). At first,

Male students fill the Marquette Union, late 1940s. File 1360

the co-op's shelves stocked a single brand of canned milk or beans, but as time went by, the store began to sell baby food, typewriters, refrigerators, and even "'hot rod' accessories." (It closed for lack of interest in 1951.) The veterans' brigade also ran a textbook exchange from inside the law school. A great many ex-servicemen encountered difficulties with the abrupt adjustment from fox holes to term papers, so their supporters implored the faculty to respond with patience and flexibility. To keep the focus on what those in uniform had endured for the good of the nation, the veterans' brigade created Vet's Day, in February 1946. It began with a Mass at Gesu, followed by a parade down Wisconsin Avenue. A ball in the evening topped off the memorial. In its second year, the parade featured a fly-over of planes from the Glenview, Illinois, naval air base. Lending support to this celebration, Father Brooks canceled classes in the afternoon so that students could attend a free movie at the Varsity Theater.[6]

UNPLANNED SUCCESSION

At the center of everything dealing with veterans was Peter Brooks. No previous president had a more varied career than Brooks. His time as a second lieutenant in the coastal artillery, his cheerleading for a Marquette Union, his ordination in 1931, his years as a faculty member at Saint Louis University, and his nearly seven-year term as head of the Missouri Province had created a confident man, a man who like Herbert Noonan became energized by his posting in Milwaukee. Brooks was a familiar sight around the campus, eagerly joining students at the Marquette Union for a meal. His priestly advice was delivered in a gentler, less sermonizing tone than that of his predecessor. He resurrected the long-established tradition of an annual all-university convocation in 1947, after a six-year absence. At this gathering of faculty and students, Brooks trumpeted the "'tremendous influence for good the student body of Marquette university'" could be. He encouraged his audience to reach high, saying "'You are not afraid of work, you have high ambitions and ideals, you are hopeful of the future.'" Brooks exuded pride in his alma mater at every event and in every presentation. In early 1947, he appointed his old friend "Charley" Cobeen to replace Henry Banzhaf as university business manager. The latter had resigned as dean of the dental school in 1942, ending thirty-five years as an academic administrator at Marquette. Five years later, Banzhaf agreed to step down as business manager, ending twenty-six years in that capacity. (Marquette's first great lay administrator, he died four years later on March 6, 1951.) Cobeen, now working alongside his former classmate in O'Hara Hall, remained Brooks's closest associate.[7]

On the evening of May 16, 1948, Cobeen arrived at the Jesuit residence in Johnston Hall to accompany the president to the annual Alpha Sigma Nu dinner. When Father Brooks failed to answer the bell in his room, a confrere went upstairs to discover that the rector had died of a heart attack. He was fifty-five. The campus community was thunderstruck. For months, student publications memorialized Brooks, speaking of his passing with dismay. A special student Mass was offered prior to the funeral service; fourteen hundred students filled the upper church at Gesu. They formed an honor

Funeral for Father Peter Brooks, 1948. Brooks Biographical File

guard from Gesu to the Milwaukee Road train station as the body of the father of the Marquette Union was taken to Missouri for burial. Father Max Barnett, university vice president, became acting president until a successor could be chosen.[8]

Whoever followed Peter Brooks was facing an awkward situation, given the abruptness of his death and the heartache that his passing had caused the university community. Father Joseph Zuercher, the provincial, may have had that in mind when he selected an individual whose background made him, in one way, the perfect choice to succeed Brooks and, in another way, a very curious selection. Edward Joseph ("Red," because of his hair color) O'Donnell grew up literally in Marquette's backyard. Shortly after his birth on May 11, 1909, the family moved into a three-story, mixed-use apartment (with a tavern on the first floor) at 1229 West Clybourn, on the southeast corner of Thirteenth and Clybourn. The eldest of seven children, O'Donnell graduated from Marquette University High School in 1927 and from the university four years later. His earliest ambition was to become a lawyer. Instead, he joined the Society of Jesus, spending formation time in Florissant, Missouri, before continuing his studies at Saint Louis University and St. Mary's College (in Kansas). O'Donnell was ordained in 1942. As a scholastic and later after ordination, O'Donnell spent time at St. John's College in Belize, British Honduras. In fact, after heading the teacher-training college in Belize for several years, he was about to be named rector of the Jesuit community there when he received the surprising summons to return to his alma mater. Given his familiarity with Marquette and Milwaukee, O'Donnell was a perfect replacement for Father Brooks. But as a university president, he was an unlikely choice because he had never held a collegiate appointment in the United States—neither as a faculty member nor as an administrator. Yet at the tender age of 39, he became the youngest president of Marquette University and its seventeenth chief executive.[9]

FUND RAISING WITH A PLAN

A peculiar event greeted Edward O'Donnell when he returned to his hometown. On October 19, 1948, a tribute to Father Brooks was combined with a welcoming banquet for O'Donnell at the Hotel Schroeder. The board of governors, the alumni association, and the Milwaukee business community greeted the neighborhood-youngster-turned-university-president. An impressive array of local executives attended: Michael Cudahy, Harold Falk, Edmund Fitzgerald, William Grede, Walter Harnischfeger, Joseph Heil, Walter Schroeder, and Robert Uihlein.[10]

The presence of so many powerful Milwaukee corporate leaders at this dinner illustrated Father Brooks's success in building bridges to the area's economic elite during his short time in office. As one example of his popularity, in January 1946, the university president had been selected Man of the Month by the Milwaukee Sunday Morning Breakfast Club. Brooks's close ties with local businessmen contrasted with the distance that his two predecessors had maintained. Father Albert Fox had created a board of governors in 1927, with Otto Falk as chairman. In the aftermath of the Schandein debacle, Fox intended to generate some clout for Marquette through Milwaukee's business community, if the institution could not obtain respect from the area's elected officials. In the earliest days of the Great Depression, Father Magee followed in his predecessor's footsteps, drawing guidance from these business leaders when addressing the university's fiscal woes. They had urged him to close the university hospital and to cut employee salaries by 20 percent, actions that Magee had taken. But as time progressed, both Magee and his successor, Raphael McCarthy, backed away from the board as a whole, preferring to rely upon private relationships with individuals such as Harry Johnston and Frank Sensenbrenner. Both presidents relied upon Johnston's frequent financial assistance and Sensenbrenner's savvy advice. (Sensenbrenner, in particular, always spoke his mind but seemed unfazed if the president chose to go in a different direction.) Both Jesuits sought this kind of consultancy in contrast to the jumble of personalities at board meetings. Father Fox had granted the governors wide discretion in 1927, but neither Magee nor McCarthy ever permitted these laymen to exercise the full extent of their stated powers. Instead, they gathered advice as needed and otherwise managed the university without interference. Unfortunately, their ineffective use of the governors' clout in the local community had hindered Marquette's funding efforts.[11]

In 1938, as the depression's most troublesome effects moderated a bit, Father McCarthy had initiated a reordering of the board of governors. He pushed Falk into calling a meeting to welcome two new appointees: Matthew H. Carpenter, president of a family-owned baking company, and Charles M. O'Hara, whose generosity had funded the renovation of Johnston and Lalumiere halls. When General Falk died two years later, O'Hara replaced him as chairman. Then in October of 1943, Father McCarthy asked the Jesuits on the board of trustees to revise the governors' statutes. Their powers to direct all finances, appointments, and academic initiatives were replaced with a shorter list of reduced powers. Now the board would "advise and assist" the president and the board of trustees in the construction of new buildings and on the "means to securing adequate funds, by way of gifts, bequests, and otherwise, with which to assure a well balanced budget." In turn, the governors were to receive "regular and comprehensive reports … on all aspects of the institution, physical, financial, and educational, and to make appropriate recommendations to said authorities regarding same." The purpose of this revised board of governors was clear: advice and assistance only.[12]

Despite America's deep involvement with a world war, Father McCarthy wanted to kick off a capital campaign intended to underwrite an authentic university library. Still smarting over the closure of Marquette's doctoral programs, McCarthy conceded that the school could never take its rightful place among Catholic universities until it operated a first-class library. Marquette's dependence upon the public library down the street had to stop. Since 1937, the university had been using one of the public library's main conference rooms for morning classes, as long as "no controversial subject" was taught (meaning religion and philosophy). In 1940, Father McCarthy had pleaded with Mayor Carl Zeidler, a Marquette alumnus, not to cut the library's funding so that it would have to close at 5:30 in the evening. This would seriously disadvantage the university's graduate students, the president explained. When Peter Brooks took on the presidency in 1944, he endorsed McCarthy's library campaign and had a three-page compendium of criticisms made by the Association of American Universities, the Jesuit Educational Association, and the North Central association prepared to delineate the current library's shortcomings as well as its future needs. Brooks energized the board of governors by appointing several new members, including Michael Cleary (president of Northwestern Mutual Life Insurance Company), Charles Coughlin (president of Briggs and Stratton), and Walter Geist (president of Allis-Chalmers Manufacturing Company). Although the governors backed the library plan, some in the Marquette Jesuit community tried to steer the campaign toward a new liberal arts building to replace Johnston Hall. Instead on August 1, 1944, the board endorsed Frank Sensenbrenner's suggestion to keep the library in mind but to move forward with a broader ambition, one that emphasized university needs in light of the impending return of military veterans. Patriotism became a subtle theme for what was designated the Marquette Fund. Moreover, the first phase of fund-raising was to be quiet, reaching out only to "industrial concerns." Later, perhaps, the general public would get involved. That same day, the board of trustees endorsed the governors' revised proposal.[13]

The new campaign officially opened on October 19, 1944, with a dinner for thirty industrial leaders. Each member of the board of governors was assigned three-to-seven companies to approach, based on the governor's area of strength. Therefore, Robert Uihlein contacted Froedtert Grain and Malting, Miller Brewing, and Pabst Brewing. Harold Falk handled Bucyrus-Erie and Cutler-Hammer, and Walter Geist of Allis-Chalmers took responsibility for Chain Belt, Heil, and the Falk Corporation. The outcome of these efforts was impressive. Despite the war, the Marquette Fund received pledges of almost $500,000 by January 1945 and $577,620.50 by the end of that year. Gifts of $10,000 or more came from Milwaukee's best known businesses and from the university's strongest supporters: Allis-Chalmers, Mrs. William Bonifas, Boston Store, Briggs and Stratton, Cudahy Brothers Company, Falk Corporation, First Wisconsin National Bank, Gimbel Brothers, Harnischfeger Corporation, Heil Company, Harry S. Johnston, Kearney and Trecker Corporation, Nordberg Manufacturing, Charles O'Hara, Pabst Brewing, Joseph Schlitz Brewing, Frank Sensenbrenner, and A. O. Smith Company. Because the initial phase of fund-raising focused on industrial Milwaukee, the alumni portion of the campaign faltered, totaling only $32,561 by December 1945. But when the appeal reached out to the general public in 1946, this sum nearly quadrupled to $124,000 in two years. Students became more involved after they learned about the details regarding a library, classroom buildings, and a men's dormitory (designated Alumni Hall). Rumors of a new student union generated even more excitement among students and alumni. Father Brooks encouraged these sentiments, hoping that a successful completion of the Marquette Fund might inspire a subsequent effort to replace the increasingly obsolete Marquette Union.[14]

But Brooks passed away just as the public phase gained momentum. Fund-raising languished while the provincial selected Brooks's successor. And once Father O'Donnell was on aboard, the campaign became only one of many concerns pressing upon his time. O'Donnell found that Brooks had no "grand plan," although the provincial director of studies, who had conducted a visitation a year earlier, provided detailed notes suggesting steps that Marquette should take to realize its quest for excellence. Members of the Jesuit community, on the other hand, advised O'Donnell to move slowly and "not make too many changes to start."

Brooks had left a list of buildings he wanted to construct and some money to fund these projects, most notably the library. Within a short time, O'Donnell had a sketch of a futuristic campus prepared, showing the location and general details of various new buildings. Although he did not leave a detailed blueprint for future construction, Brooks did make it clear that what Marquette needed was elbow room. Space for large instructional buildings was at a premium. Twenty-year-old apartment houses, forty-year-old single-family residences, and clusters of churches, hospitals, and public buildings hemmed in the university on all four sides. Blocks of residential and commercial landscapes separated the upper campus near Sixteenth Street from the lower campus near Gesu. What the university really needed first, before a library or science labs, was land on which to build its new facilities. In time, O'Donnell brought his own approach to this problem. For the moment, the Marquette Fund had sufficient capital to start some construction. As of January 31, 1949, the library portion of the fund had

$665,478 on hand. Mrs. William Bonifas, whose husband had advised earlier university presidents on disposing of the Northern Michigan properties, left an estate bequest of $250,000. Moreover, the sudden stream of tuition dollars from thousands of post-war students produced cumulative surpluses of $400,000 by June 1949. O'Donnell now had over $1.4 million at his disposal for special projects.[15]

A NOVELTY: BUILDING WITH CASH IN HAND

Father O'Donnell's first step in pushing forward with the revitalized capital campaign was to retitle it, the Marquette Fund II. Its slogan, "A Greater Marquette in a Greater Milwaukee," appeared on billboards across the city. The university brought potential benefactors to campus in June 1949 for a tour of older facilities such as Science Hall. Donors heard about plans for a central library, for classroom buildings, and for a men's dormitory. These appeals were strikingly straight-forward: $100,000 earned naming rights for a building and $10,000 a dedicated classroom; a faculty office could be furnished for $150. Sketches of the proposed buildings helped supporters visualize what the last half of the twentieth century would look like at Marquette University. Brochures depicted overcrowded conditions in the library, cafeteria, and classrooms and how the new facilities would benefit returning veterans. Placed in charge of this publicity was Ted Carpenter, head of the university news bureau, and Frank Casey. Father O'Donnell had personally recruited the latter to become, in effect, the university's first director of development. Casey had served for many years as executive director of the civic powerhouse known originally as the 1948 Corporation and later as the Greater Milwaukee Committee. The president relied upon Casey and Carpenter to assist him in canvassing Wisconsin during this campaign.[16]

At the same time, the central administration and the board of governors finally narrowed their choice for the vaguely designated classroom building. In early 1949, they decided to invest in the College of Business Administration. The governors had been adamant that funds raised specifically for the library could be used for that project only, so the president was forced to find other support to provide for the business college. A budget surplus of $400,000 during the 1948-49 school year offered a start and donations from local firms quickly brought in another $120,000.[17]

The university announced a construction schedule in May 1949. The site chosen for this new building was the northeast corner of Thirteenth and Michigan, diagonally across from the Gesu parish school. Canisius Hall, a once-elegant residence that had fallen into severe disrepair by this time, housed naval students at first and later an overflow of books from the Johnston Hall library. On January 10, 1950, a raw and windy day, ground was broken. Nine months later, a formal clerical procession, accompanied by the pealing of Gesu's bells, preceded the laying of the cornerstone for the business college's new home. By the middle of May 1951, the sparkling new tower hosted its first classes. With its modern glass and stone exterior, and a design that sported a horizontal look, the new building contrasted with the collegiate Gothic tradition of Marquette's other buildings. The cost came to $625,872, half of which was funded

Canisius Hall, on northeast corner of Thirteenth and Michigan. File 281a

Business Administration building, completed in 1951.
Note BusAd building is only half of its current size and Thirteenth Street barracks to left. File 175

through donations and half through operating surpluses. A six-story wing along 13th Street housed the college's central offices and twenty-five faculty offices; a five-story wing along Michigan Street provided twenty up-to-date classrooms. Relocation of the business faculty into this new facility permitted the Department of Education's staff to consolidate in Science Hall, the political science and sociology programs to move into education's former space in Bellarmine Hall, and the philosophy and religion departments to each gain one office in Johnston Hall (although in the case of the last, eight Jesuits shared four desks per office).[18]

Most people on campus expected a new library to be next in line. Instead, Mabel Mannix McElligott, the dean of women, announced that the Association of Marquette University Women (AMUW) was moving ahead with its plans to address the shortage of student housing. In 1945, the association had purchased an apartment building at 1717 Wisconsin Avenue, which was subsequently renamed Merritty Hall after Thomas E. Merritty, a retired department store executive whose will assigned over $100,000 to Marquette upon his death in 1946. In combination with Alumnae House, this new residence provided for fifty first- and second-year students by 1950. Juniors and seniors squeezed into Bonifas Hall on Fifteenth Street, Nicolas and Rigge halls on Eighteenth Street, and the Highland Boulevard complex (four residencies, including Lisette Lodge). Nursing students lived at 3058 N. Fifty-first Street on the grounds of St. Joseph's Hospital. The need for a central residence was obvious. Together Nicolas and Rigge halls occupied enough land to support development of a new dormitory that would hold 350 students. Despite restrictions on building materials during the Korean War, the women's association moved ahead in 1950 with its $1 million project on Eighteenth Street. The first residents moved into a finished portion of the building in February 1952, with full occupancy the following fall. Encouraged by the federal Housing Act of 1950, Marquette approached Washington for a building loan, the first request for direct federal aid in school history. To be eligible to receive a loan (through which the federal government provided 90 percent of the construction costs), Marquette needed to own the development site. With marvelous generosity, the Association of Marquette University Women surrendered the Eighteenth Street properties, although not before the group decided to name the hall after Father O'Donnell. In yet another gesture, the AMUW made Alumnae House available as a male dorm after O'Donnell Hall opened. The first men to move into Alumnae House noted its benefits (such as curtains) and its shortcomings (such as the absence of outlets for electric shavers). In June 1953, the women's association officially ended its pioneering work in student housing when the organization transferred ownership of Alumnae House and Merritty Hall as well as their investment in O'Donnell Hall to Marquette University, assets valued at half a million dollars. In return, the university pledged to establish a Chair in Humanistic Studies, an endowed faculty chair to be filled by a woman. The association then proceeded to raise the $1.5 million to fund this position.[19]

In 1920, Peter Brooks had attended the dedication of a new student union at the University of Michigan. This trip inspired, in turn, a comparable organization, if not

Merritty Hall, 1717 W. Wisconsin Avenue. File 950

Residential space in Nicolas Hall. File 982

facility: the Marquette Union. In fall 1945, another Marquette delegation traveled to Madison for the opening of the University of Wisconsin's new union. This contingent of Hilltoppers also returned to Milwaukee filled with envious ambitions. The burgeoning enrollment of the postwar years triggered dreams of improved facilities, including a new union, among students, alumni, and administrators. Father Brooks and Charles Cobeen (as the principal contact with the alumni) did nothing to dampen this enthusiasm. They did stress, however, that funding for a union—which from the beginning was understood to be coeducational—would have to come from the alumni and the students.[20]

This campaign commenced in spring 1948, just months before Father Brooks's death. Its goals were $100,000 from past graduates (each alumnus was asked to contribute a dollar a month for a year), $100,000 from the Marquette Union, and an unspecified sum from current students. This total represented less than third of the $800,000 needed for such a building. Organizers hoped that once the first phase of the fund-raising had been completed, additional donors would step up or that business loans might become available. (The site on Fourteenth Street was already owned by the university.) But by the spring of 1950, two years after the campaign began, only $60,000 had been raised. By the end of that same year, this figure edged upward

O'Donnell Hall Lounge. File 1020

to $106,000, one-eighth of the necessary funding. Despite this gap, on May 1, 1951, ground was broken at an event where, in Father O'Donnell's words, the spirit of Father Brooks was "still abroad." A stream of problems, from a nationwide steel shortage to a building trades strike, delayed construction. Costs rose to nearly $1.5 million. At least $500,000 in loans was necessary and no bank was willing to provide such a large sum to a student organization whose leadership fluctuated year to year. So in January 1953, the Marquette Union dissolved itself, turning over its assets to the university. In turn, Marquette assumed responsibility for what was designated the Father Peter A. Brooks Memorial Union. An open house was finally held on April 7, 1953. It drew visitors to the grill, cafeteria, lounges, meeting rooms, and the ballroom. Don McNeill, a 1929 alumnus, broadcast his nationally syndicated *Breakfast Club* show from the union during its inaugural week. Charles Cobeen was officially named "Father of the Marquette Union."[21]

A ripple-effect of reassignments followed. Marquette Union was renovated, with an entrance whose limestone exterior matched the stone on the business administration building across the street. Renamed Carpenter Hall in honor of the recently deceased member of the board of governors, the onetime union now housed a new Army ROTC unit on the first floor, and five classrooms and the Psychology Department's testing

Brooks Memorial Union, completed in 1953. File 155c

labs on the second. Next door, the freshmen dormitory (formerly Brooks Hall) was renamed for the university president who had sanctioned the original Marquette Union, Father Herbert Noonan.[22]

Brooks Memorial Union's neighbor across Fourteenth Street, a university library, remained a work in progress. Marquette's standing among Catholic universities suffered immeasurably from the absence of such an essential facility. In 1949, Father O'Donnell explained in a letter to the common council how the area's colleges relied upon the main public library and how "its value to the educational programs of our schools can hardly be over-emphasized." The main piece of property needed for Marquette's own library had been provided many years earlier through a gift from Miss Paula Uihlein. Additional properties, occupied by six- and eight-family apartment buildings, had been purchased in 1946 and then cleared. For years, the board of governors discussed designs, architects, and contractors. Deadlines for the first phase of construction were established and then forgotten. Finally, the board approved the blueprints for a three-story building, running 202 feet along Wisconsin Avenue. With a 65-foot north-south wing at the center, it resembled a cross (a Maltese cross, according to some) from the air. Its price was set at $1,428,000—50 percent higher than the original figure from a decade earlier. Ground was broken in July 1951, with a twelve-to eighteen-month construction schedule. Twenty-nine months later, the library opened after suffering the same setbacks that the student union had encountered. When it came time to transfer the university's library collection from the second floor of Johnston Hall, volunteers used intricate hoists to remove these volumes before they were placed in bins and rolled down Wisconsin Avenue to their new home. The dedication was spread over five days in December 1953. At the main event, Monsignor Frank M. Schneider, rector of the Milwaukee diocese's St. Francis Major Seminary, struck a responsive chord among the thousands of on-lookers, saying "'Thank God for this library.'"[23]

The postwar's final expansion addressed the needs of the medical and dental schools. Father Clarence J. Ryan, faculty regent to the alumni, headed fund-raising for both projects. With incredible ambition, he set out to contact all 2000 alumni of the medical school. In the end, he traveled 13,000 miles and visited every state over a five-year period. Of the first 400 individuals he approached, 215 offered contributions averaging $1,000. Originally, the university planned to spend $600,000 to add two wings to the Cramer building. One portion was designed as a library to serve both medicine and dentistry. This phase received a jump-start through an estate gift from Mrs. Eben Carey, widow of the former medical school dean. In April 1951, promises were made that construction would begin in June; in March 1952, it was scheduled for the following month. Ground for the school of medicine wings was broken in May 1952. As with the student union and library, construction ran into delays. The two wings were completed in May 1954. Two years later ground was broken for the dental school addition which, when it was first conceived, had been expected to cost about $500,000. (The health science additions totaled $1.4 million, nearly $300,000 over original estimates.) With its greatest concentration of professionals in the upper Midwest (75

Memorial Library under construction. Note former Plankinton residence, home of the School of Speech, to the left of the engineering building. File 835

percent in Wisconsin alone), the Dental School Alumni Association created its own touring company of speakers who traveled to every medium-sized city across the region seeking support.[24]

Raising significant sums of money for all these projects, one after another, forced the university to refine its policy regarding the naming of buildings. On July 10, 1953, Father Raymond McAuley, dean of men, informed Father O'Donnell that he had just posted a notice on the Jesuit bulletin board asking members of the community to participate in renaming university buildings after what he referred to as "important benefactors." A name, the dean noted "is perpetuated throughout the years and the name becomes synonymous with Marquette University and all that the University stands for." McAuley added that two likely candidates to have buildings named for them presented problems: Frank Sensenbrenner because of the length of his name and Charles O'Hara because his son who was a Jesuit remained a member of the Marquette community.[25]

In the immediate postwar period, Marquette University buildings carried the names of Jesuits (Bellarmine, Canisius, Copus, Lalumiere, Nicolas, and Rigge), notable donors (Johnston, Cramer, and Merritty), or academic specialties (dentistry, law, and science). The O'Donnell administration's willingness to recognize significant contributions to the Marquette Fund II through naming rights had already been laid out. As an outcome of Father McAuley's appeal to the Jesuit community, a "Names Committee" recommended changes. The law school building honored long-time advisor and university benefactor, Frank Sensenbrenner (despite the length of his name) and the former Marquette Union was renamed for Matthew Carpenter, a late member of the board of governors. Among suggestions never implemented were renaming Science Hall for Patrick Cudahy, the dental school for the Pabst family, and Monitor Hall for Bishop John Henni.[26]

ACADEMIC LIFE AND CURRICULAR CHANGES

This latest expansion of Marquette's instructional facilities relied largely upon individual donors, corporations, alumni, and even students. But it also drew upon a most unusual revenue stream: operating surpluses. In 1939, a relatively stable year between the worst moments of the Great Depression and the irregular times created by wartime, the university completed the fiscal year with a surplus of $50,945. With enrollment records being set annually, the institution achieved surpluses of $607,578 in 1946, $1,139,160 in 1947, and $929,215 in 1948. In managing these surpluses, Fathers Brooks and O'Donnell chose to address the present, rather than the future. They applied this money to immediate needs such as the library, not to the university endowment.[27]

O'Donnell seemed to understand that, by definition, halcyon days are fleeting, a point underscored as the university's reserves dwindled steadily following construction of the aforementioned buildings. O'Donnell faced two key budgetary problems during his years in office. In 1945, the cost of teaching a liberal arts student was calculated to be $209; in the College of Business Administration, it was $135 and in engineering, $405. In medicine, however, it was $588. Ten years later, expenditures to educate a liberal arts student had more than doubled to $486; in business administration, it had more than tripled to $494, but in engineering had risen modestly to $534. Medical education, on the other hand, now cost $2,219 per student. In one year alone, between 1954 and 1955, this price had grown by 32 percent. Forty years of surpluses in the School of Medicine's annual budget came to an abrupt halt in the 1950s as a string of deficits pressed upon the administration. One positive force in this era was the expanding role of the federal government in medical education. To ensure that Marquette's medical school could take advantage of this support, the school's senior administration would be forced in the future to make a fateful decision.[28]

The second budgetary knot that pestered the president was faculty compensation. From 1939 to 1945, the average annual salary for full-time, lay faculty had increased by a total of $341. In terms of real income, these instructors suffered a 12 percent decline. For lay men and women who had been on the staff since the early thirties, the consequences of the salary cuts in 1932 continued to linger. Below-average salary levels had drawn the attention of the Association of American Universities when it criticized Marquette's doctoral programs in the early forties. How Peter Brooks might have addressed this concern will never be known because of his untimely death. He apparently recognized how far Marquette had slipped in contrast to public colleges and universities. In 1946, he urged the board of governors and the board of trustees to initiate a retirement trust fund for administrative, instructional, and clerical employees. Northwestern Mutual Life Insurance Company managed this plan. Four years later, the trustees finally agreed to join the nation's social security system, expanding the retirement options of employees.[29]

As he moved into the president's office, Father O'Donnell recognized that the university's compensation history threatened the premise upon which he had built the new library. The president understood that the engine for excellence rests not in bricks and mortar, certainly not in the prowess of its sports teams, but in the quality of its faculty—in their brilliance in the classroom and their scholarly careers. Teaching had been Marquette's hallmark since its days on the hilltop. Jesuits were trained as educators from their first days at the novitiate, even if they ultimately labored in other ministries. They learned about Ignatius's quest for excellence and how that ambition had been realized in thousands of schools over hundreds of years. Each Jesuit was trained to appreciate education as a path toward salvation. But in the post World War II era, lay faculty replaced Jesuits at an accelerating rate. Doctorates from secular institutions such as the University of Wisconsin, the University of Toronto, and the University of Minnesota became routine among Marquette faculty members. These lay instructors arrived with promising resumes but often without the slightest familiarity with Jesuit traditions. If they were ever to comprehend what it really meant to be part of a Jesuit ministry, they had to acquire this understanding on the job—a notoriously inefficient instructional mode. There was no education for mission because the Jesuits were only slowly coming to realize that the lay faculty *were* the future of Jesuit schools. And given the male hegemony of Catholic higher education, the growing number of female faculty made this training for mission more tenuous because Marquette and its sister schools were not prepared to treat women as equals, either intellectually or organizationally. Father O'Donnell realized that he had to develop a salary structure that could attract and retain gifted teacher-scholars of both sexes who valued the Marquette mission. In the end, salary matters were far easier to address than the mission issue. To fund competitive salary scales, the president turned to regular tuition increases, a strategy that his predecessors could never have envisioned.[30]

Father O'Donnell also faced market pressures from postwar students who were more attuned to the workplace applications of professional schools than to the intellectual insights of the liberal arts. Father Fox had insisted that two years of liberal arts preface all professional training. He thereby insured at least a passing exposure to the *Ratio Studiorum* for every Marquette student. Yet the growing popularity of the professions in postwar America threatened to drive a wedge between the liberal arts and the rest of the institution. Every academic department saw itself as vital to the success of the institution. This democratization of subject areas had elicited a chorus of protests within the College of Liberal Arts as early as the mid-1930s. Jesuits in particular bemoaned the diminished emphasis upon language, literature, history, and philosophy. Catholic colleges across the nation appraised this slippage in the liberal arts, frustrated that a diminished respect undermined the "imparting of Catholicism as a total 'culture.'" At Marquette, the liberal arts faculty, laymen and Jesuits alike, worried that the distinctiveness of Marquette University (in contrast to the University of Wisconsin or Milwaukee State Teachers College) was in danger of becoming diluted because the liberal arts were becoming little more than "a feeder to the professional schools." They feared that "the gradual encroachment of the physical and social sciences" came "at the expense of the humanities, philosophy, and religion." At their faculty retreat in 1936, the liberal arts staff was reminded that its college was "the heart of the organism," "the very basic purpose, scope, and aim of education." Four years later, the philosophy department's Father Gerard Smith spoke of the "relatively unimportant place of natural sciences and education" and the "major place which theology, philosophy and the ancient and English classics should occupy" in the lives of students—*all* students. Even Marquette undergraduates came to the aid of liberal education after a North Carolina congressman insisted that "'all the educational institutions [in] the country which are teaching philosophy, Latin and sociology and such bunk'" be converted into wartime training sites for the military. The *Tribune*'s response explained that the notion of freedom was inextricably tied to the heritage of Western culture, the homeland of philosophy and the classics.[31]

Defense of the liberal arts—and by extension, of the Jesuit heritage at Marquette— usually fell to the dean of that college who, for nearly the entire twentieth century (until 1988), was a Jesuit. In 1945, the new dean of liberal arts, Father Max Barnett, addressed the entire university when he explained that the "'pronounced objective of

Jesuit education [was] to teach students how "to live.""" His successor, Father Virgil Roach, echoed these thoughts, warning that modern society had a penchant for emphasizing how to make "a living rather than the living itself." To reorder these two priorities into a suitable sequence, a thorough grounding in the liberal arts was necessary to provide a "solid foundation in … intellectual and moral makeup." Only then could a student indulge in the "superstructure of further vocational, scientific or professional training." Only with this comprehensive education could every Marquette graduate confront "life's problems on the basis of principles rather than expediency." This positioning of the liberal arts before professional education updated the *Ratio Studiorum* for twentieth-century students. To Dean Roach, the essence of a Jesuit education remained (almost) the same in 1950 as it had been in 1881: "the classical and modern languages, the sciences and mathematics, history, philosophy, literature, [and, curiously] manual arts."

Consequently, he abolished the bachelors of science in medicine and dentistry in 1951 because these programs allowed undergraduates to bypass their final year in the liberal arts and begin professional training in the fourth year of college. Roach replaced them with a more generic bachelor of general studies for "students whose abilities [lay] in the practical rather than in the theoretical order." There were no majors or minors, only two emphases. One concentrated on classes in business administration and the liberal arts, and the other on courses in literature and the social sciences. The following year, Roach dropped the bachelor of philosophy degree, that early twentieth-century creation for students who lacked sufficient training in Latin to earn a bachelor of arts. Henceforth, students with appropriate credits in Latin earned a bachelor of arts; everyone else would receive a bachelor of science degree. In another move responsive to the times, Father Roach established a Department of Political Science in early 1954. As America's confrontations with the Soviet Union took on worldwide implications, matters related to democracy, capitalism, communism, subversion, the United Nations, and decolonization warranted, in the dean's mind, the elevation of government classes to the status of a separate department. By the end of the department's first year, there were fifty-five majors.[32]

This anxiety over the application of Jesuit pedagogy in the middle of the twentieth century became entangled with the status of female instructors in the College of Liberal Arts. In 1938, Father McCarthy made it clear that there was no "place for women on the philosophy faculties of Jesuit colleges. The traditions are not in favor of such appointments and usually we are better supplied with our own men." Eight years later, the aforementioned defender of liberal arts, Father Gerard Smith, challenged this policy when he hired two alumnae as instructors in philosophy, an action clearly sanctioned by the new president, Peter Brooks. A fixture in the philosophy department since 1929, Smith served as chair from 1944 to 1966. Always ready to tangle with academic superiors (who were, after all, fellow Jesuits), Smith saw great promise in undergraduates Beatrice Zedler and Lottie Kendzierski. He convinced them to give up their studies in English and become philosophy majors. Upon completion of their

Registration in gymnasium, late 1940s. File 1180

bachelor's and master's degrees, the two women left Milwaukee for Fordham University where they completed their doctorates. In New York, Dr Elizabeth Salmon became their mentor. The two young scholars learned that "'philosophy definitely requires use of the human reason" and "a woman can be as capable in using her power of reason as can a man.'" Thanks to Father Smith, Zedler and Kendzierski joined the Marquette faculty in 1946 and moved through their probationary years as assistant professors. Eventually someone—in this case their chairman—had to ask the obvious (if, for him, somewhat tongue-in-cheek) question: since no women had ever been granted tenure in the department, when should we dismiss these instructors?[33]

When it came time to provide an answer, Smith wrote an impassioned letter to his dean in which he warned that the departure of these two instructors would further damage an academic unit that was already struggling. The women, he said, were "excellent teachers," "first-rate scholars," and "productive." Smith conceded that he could find two males to replace the women—only these men would not be their equals. For some time, Father Smith had been concerned about the shaky record of scholarship among his colleagues. Now he hit this point hard. He claimed that one of Zedler's publications was "the only piece of impressive research *which has ever issued from our department*" other than Professor Anton C. Pegis's work in the 1930s. Realizing that he was inviting the abandonment of yet another tradition, Smith pointed to the promotion of women at other Jesuit universities, specifically Fordham, Saint Louis, and Creighton. Father O'Donnell finally weighed in on this discussion in November 1950 with a simple comment: "I do not think we would seriously consider letting them go." And so they stayed. In March 1952, Zedler and Kendzierski (with Smith's support) arranged for their Fordham mentor, Elizabeth Salmon, to become the first woman ever invited to deliver the acclaimed Aquinas Lecture, a series that had previously featured the likes of Mortimer Adler, Jacques Maritain, Robert M. Hutchins, and Anton Pegis.[34]

Among this era's other academic successes was the Marquette University Labor College, established by Father Thomas Divine in 1941. During the Cold War, the labor college became an invaluable forum for measured conversations between capital and labor. It received spiritual encouragement from the Jesuit Superior General's 1949 letter encouraging all Jesuit communities to reassess their outreach to the world's workers who suffered under the conflicting tensions of atheistic communism and "liberal materialism." Divine, from his position as dean of business administration, recruited instructors from business, journalism, law, speech, and the liberal arts. Classes met twice a week on the third floor of Science Hall. The ten-week program offered thirteen classes in all. At first there had been no charge for participants; later a one-dollar registration fee was imposed.

The courses closely followed the teachings of the Catholic Church regarding work, workers, and labor unions, with an aim to "'offer to working men and women of Milwaukee an opportunity to improve themselves as individuals and as members of organized labor by demonstrating the place of organized labor ... within the framework of

American democracy.'" As the years went by, classes shifted from general topics such as industrial ethics to more refined matters such as time-motion studies and alcoholism in industry. At the end of course work, participants received a certificate awarded by the university president. In 1952, graduation day consisted of a spaghetti dinner at Pius XI High School, and in a throwback to Marquette's earlier commencements, the evening concluded with a series of dramatic skits. The business college also established a night school baccalaureate in 1949 and four years later a master of business administration degree in response to demands raised by the local community. Community pressure also persuaded the graduate school to rewrite its guidelines for a master of arts degree in 1949 so that high school and junior college teachers who had no interest in pursuing a doctorate could complete their MA without a thesis and mastery of a foreign language. Instead, these students took extra classes to strengthen their command of the subject area.[35]

In the health sciences, longstanding clinics continued to provide for the Milwaukee community. During the 1946-47 school year, the speech clinic became the largest in the country when it treated 1,200 patients. Every private and public school in the metropolitan area was invited to use the clinic if it lacked a therapist. Marquette enrolled more students in speech therapy than any other Catholic college in the United States. Similarly, the dental clinic became one of the four largest in the country in 1954 when it treated over 8,200 patients. In early 1950, both dentistry and medicine turned their attention to cancer when the former offered a non-credit cancer symposium and the latter established a low-fee cancer diagnostic center at Twenty-fourth and Mitchell. In the fall of 1952, the school of medicine initiated a degree in physical therapy in "'response to community demands.'" Other local forces prompted the medical school's first contacts with the Milwaukee County Hospital. Hard feelings had lingered ever since the failed Schandein proposal in 1927. This situation finally changed in 1946, following "charges of mismanagement and lack of patient care brought by disgruntled residents and interns." Confidential conversations were held to consider the possibility of Marquette's taking on certain management duties at the hospital. Church-State legalities kept the status quo in place until 1948, when the Milwaukee County Board of Public Welfare voted to establish a direct affiliation with the medical school "as a participating associate." Given twenty years of icy relations, this was a significant step for the university at a time when the costs related to training medical students were escalating.[36]

POSTWAR CATHOLICISM

National and international affairs impinged upon university life beyond initiatives such as the labor college and the political science department. Marquette students constantly debated aspects of America's role in the postwar world. Philosophy professor Father Edward A. McGrath evaluated the morality of the atomic bomb only a month after its use in Japan in 1945. Five years later, the hydrogen bomb, with one hundred times the destructive potential of its predecessor, became the topic for discussion. Because the nascent United Nations was such a keen topic, the business college's commerce club sponsored several visits by representatives of the Chicago Council on Foreign Relations. The Current Affairs Institute, established in 1948 by the alumni association, sponsored regular presentations on race relations, municipal planning, and Milwaukee history. In one of its many articles addressing the Cold War, the *Marquette Tribune* warned against "hysteria" in the government's battle against internal subversion, after legislation in Washington threatened civil liberties. In a piece published in November 1950, five months into the Korean War, a reporter carefully argued that "Christian Social Reform" should not be ignored just because it might be slapped with the label "socialist." He reminded his readers that socialism's denial of God was its most serious shortcoming, not its attention to the "idea of a national child welfare program that insures proper natal care and constant supervision of health for all American children." Father Brooks joined the conversation when, in his 1947 convocation address, he warned students that honoring democracy was achieved through "Christ-like living." Father O'Donnell offered a slightly different spin on this theme of democracy two years later in his own graduation address. He decried the secularization of American higher education, a process he characterized as "an atheistic importation." "Education for democracy has come to mean in our day," he explained "education without religion, without God." Only by fulfilling the "obligations of our faith," the president concluded, could we "save ourselves."[37]

Reminders that a vigorous spiritual life was necessary to combat evils found overseas and at home became a routine part of Marquette's religious culture after 1945. Student Masses were celebrated every Sunday morning in Gesu's lower church. Confessions were heard daily as well as on Saturday afternoons and evenings. Devotions to the Sacred Heart were held every Friday at midnight. The Mass of the Holy Ghost still heralded the beginning of each school year. Student retreats remained an obligation for each Catholic student, although by 1948 weekend retreats in small groups could be substituted for the all-university exercises. Faculty retreats, held since 1922, also continued. After 1947, the sodality's devotional schedule became the responsibility of a coeducational central committee. As undergraduates, Catholic students (74 percent of the entire student body) still completed eight units of religious instruction, with classes in apologetics and Christian morality for those who had attended Catholic high schools, and Christian origins and Catholic family life for those who had not.

Matters of faith could threaten students' standing at the university as well as their access to certain types of reading materials. In 1951, the university threatened one individual with expulsion (a far more serious offense than dismissal) if she did not voluntarily withdraw, following accusations she had participated in local communist activities. She was subsequently accused of apostasy (rejecting her faith), a much more serious charge, after she denied her interest in communism but refused to return to her obligations as a Catholic. A year later, another student was dismissed for "a violation of Catholic principles" following his divorce and remarriage. Church rules also applied to "forbidden books." Because the canonical authority of local bishops controlled access to such literature, the university sent a list of students who needed to examine such materials to the Milwaukee archbishop, by semester in the case of undergraduates in specific classes and for the "duration of their work at Marquette University" in the case of graduate students and faculty. As Father O'Donnell clarified for a fellow Jesuit president: "Since the Bishop's ordinary faculties do not permit him to grant permission to read books which are professedly obscene or books which professedly attach with argument the foundations of the Christian religion, we do not ask permission for students to read such books."[38]

During the forties and fifties, a vital sign of a rich Catholic life on campus could be found in the presence of professed religious attending classes, especially during the summer. In the summer of 1949, for example, 327 sisters representing forty religious communities enrolled. Benedictine Sisters from Yankton, South Dakota, joined members of the Congregation of the Most Holy Rosary from St. Catherine, Kentucky, and Sisters Adorers of the Most Precious Blood from Wichita, Kansas, and Sisters of Mercy from Bethesda, Maryland. They came in groups as large as thirty-six (Sisters of Charity) and as small as one (an Ursuline nun). To better serve these women and to confirm their ties to Marquette, the university established a master of arts in theology in 1953, one year after that department expanded its mission when changing its name from *religion* to *theology*. Until 1958, the master's program ran during the summers only, at a time when its principal pool of students (nuns) could attend classes and when additional instructional staff could be recruited from the Jesuit theologate at St. Mary's, Kansas.[39]

Marquette's Jesuit identity was similarly stamped upon the university by the constant presence of scholastics and priests—some as students, most as staff members. In 1939, twenty-nine Jesuits were assigned to the university (while seven served the Gesu parish). This number rose to fifty-two in 1953. About half a dozen Jesuits were usually assigned to administrative duties, with the remainder working in the classrooms. As the Jesuit community grew, housing became an issue. Johnston Hall and Regis Hall (on Michigan Street) could not hold both the high school and university staff, so in 1950 a new residence at Thirty-fourth and Michigan was approved for those assigned to Marquette High. In January 1951, Father O'Donnell announced that the high school, a division of the university since 1881, was now a separate corporation. Later that year, O'Donnell had the burden of serving as both president and rector lifted from his shoulders after the provincial appointed an assistant to the rector. These two roles were further delineated in 1953 when a "Dependent Superior" was named to provide for the spiritual well-being of university-based Jesuits. For twenty years, the Jesuits had experimented with implementation of father general's 1934 instruction suggesting different individuals direct the educational corporation and the religious community. Had they been in place, these new governance rules might have averted the ugly conflict that arose between Fathers Noonan and Fox in 1921-22, a situation encountered at other Jesuit institutions.[40]

The impact of hundreds of religious women and men moving about the campus can be measured by the number of Marquette students who chose follow in their footsteps. During the years after World War II, about a dozen men from the university went on to diocesan seminaries annually; a slightly larger number entered religious congregations other than the Society of Jesus; and twenty or so typically chose to follow St. Ignatius. About half a dozen young women entered various houses of formation each year. Between 1948 and 1954, nearly 250 Marquette students left the campus either before or after graduation to become priests, brothers, and sisters. The roots of Jesuit ministries in the upper Midwest had so deepened by the summer of 1954 that the superior general authorized the creation of a Wisconsin vice-province. After a century as part of the Missouri province, Jesuits in Wisconsin, Minnesota, North and South Dakota, Nebraska, and Iowa now reported to a regional superior in Milwaukee.[41]

STUDENT LIFE

Among the many Jesuits who had a marked influence upon the formation of under-graduates during this period was Father Claude Heithaus, a man who bridged the students' new-found fascination with public affairs and the school's Catholic roots. He taught in the sociology department at Marquette, although he was a classical ar-chaeologist by training and practice. During his many years at Saint Louis University, Heithaus had served as the first managing editor of the student newspaper when an undergraduate and later played a critical role in the creation of the school's museum. His most famous moment, however, came on February 11, 1944, when he openly con-fronted the university's exclusionary policies. At a student Mass, Heithaus astonished and then awed the congregation when he evoked the faithful to witness the presence of African Americans in the Mystical Body of Christ, asserting that "'Some say that if the Society of Jesus gives Catholic Negroes the Catholic education which the Church wishes them to have, our white students will walk out on us... I challenge the whole world to prove that even one of our Catholic students will desert us when we apply the principles for which Jesus Christ suffered and died.'" He asked everyone to stand, ask forgiveness for past racist offenses, and pledge to do all they could to prevent them in the future. Even though the university president reluctantly agreed to admit African Americans, he insisted upon strict segregation in social matters. Heithaus's condemna-tion of this continuing evidence of institutional racism earned him a reprimand and a reassignment.

In Milwaukee, he inspired the postwar generation of Hilltoppers to confront Ameri-ca's own iron curtain: the separation of white from black, whether by law in the South or by everyday practice in the North. Inspired by a 1949 letter from the superior gen-eral urging greater solidarity with the poor and working classes, Jesuit communities around the world examined how their apostolates reached out to those who suffered from "'inequitable condition[s].'" In the New Orleans province, for example, this self-reflection led to the fateful decision to discontinue the practice of racial discrimination in all institutions, including schools, parishes, and the order itself. At Marquette, since wartime, a distinct subset of students had been torn by the hypocrisy of battling totalitarianism overseas and tolerating racial bigotry at home. Milwaukee's African American community was forced to live in a confined, deteriorating neighborhood a few blocks northeast of the campus. Father Heithaus recruited directors from the Milwaukee Urban League, the Friendship House (Chicago's interracial center), the Community Jewish Center, and even other Marquette students to serve as guides for exploring the city's racial barriers. In 1945 and 1946, Charles L. de Lay, a graduate student in journalism, provided background for several articles in the *Tribune*. As an African American and as the publicity director at Xavier University in New Orleans (the first Catholic college for American blacks, established by Mother Katharine Drexel), de Lay spoke of what America's racial divide meant to devout Catholics.[42]

For years, Heithaus moderated the Inter-racial Study Club, an organization whose original sponsorship by the sodality bound faith to social action. With the *Tribune*'s open support, the inter-racial club proposed a survey in1947 to examine racial discrimination in Milwaukee high schools. Three years later, the group applied its academic curiosity to the campus when it approached the university to "audit interracial matters at Marquette" including "housing, hiring, health service, [and] awarding scholarships." The committee on student life sanctioned an evaluation of "recreational activities involving campus student groups only." Later, the interracial club examined racial clauses in the membership rules of Marquette's fraternities and sororities, asking whether discriminatory bans imposed by national headquarters were being enforced in Milwaukee. Another confrontation arose in 1949 when the club challenged Marquette's athletic director regarding allegations of segregation on the football and basketball teams, a charge that he vehemently denied. Father Heithaus himself delivered a five-part lecture series in 1947 titled "Catholicism and White Racism." In his last lecture, five local black leaders joined Heithaus at a well-attended session held in the moot court room of the law school. The following year, his presentations became part of the alumni association's Current Affairs Institute. And in 1949, he became involved in an incident of alleged racism by a sorority. Over time, the students that he affected joined with like-minded peers from Mount Mary College and Cardinal Stritch College after Marquette joined the Wisconsin Regional Interracial Commission, an offshoot of the National Federation of Catholic College Students. This preoccupation with racial justice in the postwar period was notable both for its intensity and for its sustained presence. Never before had Marquette students so passionately connected the instructional side of their lives as college students with a moral issue of national importance.[43]

A heightened level of seriousness could likewise be found in the changing world of student government. In 1946, the men's union and the Women's Student Club (made permanent in 1939 and better known as the coed board) agreed to consolidate once a new union building became available. As Brooks Memorial Union moved toward completion during the 1952-53 school year, they fulfilled their promises of unification. On January 13, 1953, members of the Marquette Union voted 2,675 to 4 to dissolve their corporation, turning over their possessions—including the union building—to the university. The coed board dissolved its association on the same evening. Within months, the two groups drafted a plan to reorganize into a single body. As the spring term concluded, however, their proposal failed to elicit a response from O'Hara Hall. When by the following fall they still hadn't heard anything from the administration, they formally asked the committee on student life to approve the consolidation. Senior administrators, however, preferred to move slowly, seeking to understand all the implications of a unified student government. After all, oversight of so many activities, from Varsity Varieties (an offshoot of Vaudeville Day) and Dad's Day (which returned to the schedule in 1952 after a twenty-year absence) to the Holly Ball and homecoming would fall under the jurisdiction of the new student government. This was more authority than had ever been granted to students at Marquette. Eventually, the dean of men, Father Raymond McAuley, proposed a revised plan that ultimately prevailed. In April 1954, the administration finally approved a constitution for this new student senate.[44]

Meetings of this group were held in Brooks Memorial Union, a building that became the socio-spatial anchor for students outside of class time. From the moment Father O'Donnell blessed this stylish building on April 12, 1953, it—and the student activities building, a sagging, two-story frame house next door—became second homes for Marquette students. Within weeks of its opening, the senior prom was held in the union's spacious ballroom. So was the communion brunch on graduation day. The union became so popular that an old problem soon reappeared: the amount of cafeteria space occupied by cardplaying afficionados. They confiscated lunch tables for hours, just as they had in the Marquette Union. To combat this problem, the administration handed down an edict in 1952 forbidding cardplaying in *any* university building and reminded students of the long-standing prohibition against gambling. This ban was not well-received. Students complained about the sweeping nature of this order. By 1953, the administration reversed itself, although the battles for table space carried over into the new union.[45]

The drive for a normal social life, after years of economic tribulation and war, was evidenced by the busy dance card students kept. For example, in the fall of 1946, the Marquette Union and the coed board sponsored the year's opening mixer for freshmen. A few days later came the "medical dance," the first in long line of college and school functions. Journalism, business, liberal arts, dentistry, engineering, and nursing all had their nights. The Veterans' Brigade scheduled its dance for late in the school year. The following school year, 1947-48, the law school and the inter-racial club joined this list of sponsors. For women, the dress codes presented a bit of a problem. Before 1945, women were forbidden to wear slacks at any time, even when walking, hiking, or riding. School officials acknowledged that female students avoided this rule by rolling up their pant legs and wearing a coat until they reached their destination, a practice that could be exceedingly uncomfortable during Milwaukee summers. In April 1945, the committee on student activities and welfare modified the rule so that slacks were permitted "for active sports" but not allowed when students gathered in other areas of the campus. Five years later, the committee issued another reminder that slacks and blue jeans could be worn "at girls' functions and for participation in outdoor sports but they [could] not be worn at mixed parties." The committee took the public behavior of female students very seriously. In 1954, it placed a woman on probation for participating in a "marathon kiss that lasted six and a half minutes on television." Her conduct was characterized "by viewers as vulgar."[46]

The prom, an event timed to occur on the eve of Lent, remained the most prominent date on the school's social calendar. The first formal prom had been held in 1911, with the governor of Wisconsin and his wife in attendance. Fifteen years later, the journalism fraternity began to publish a midnight edition of the *Tribune* in order to showcase the evening's gowns and decorations. In 1931, celebrating the university's fiftieth anniversary, nearly 1,300 couples attended. A decade later, the not-yet-famous Perry Como performed, just before the prom went into hiatus during wartime. It returned in 1947. Yet habits were changing in the years after the war. Several times in the immediate postwar period, the *Marquette Tribune* noted how difficult it was for some organizations to sustain membership when students were distracted by so many activities. There was even a call for dissolving groups such as the Chicago, Rockford, and Minnesota clubs

Junior Formal Prom, February 1950. File 1143

Sigma Phi Delta house during Homecoming, 1948. File 680

because they pulled students in too many directions. Early in 1954, the union grill in Brooks Memorial cancelled its Sunday night dances when student interest waned.[47]

Like the prom, homecoming never lost its luster—especially the parade. First held in 1921, the parade drew the entire city to Wisconsin Avenue with its size, color, and excitement. Sometimes it proceeded east from the university toward the lakefront. Other times, it marched west from downtown toward the stadium. In 1949, the parade conflicted with Milwaukee's special weekday shopping night (Thursdays) and was relocated to Kilbourn at the request of Wisconsin Avenue merchants. The students were irate, so the following year, the parade returned to Wisconsin Avenue but on a Wednesday to accommodate downtown businesses. The homecoming dance, originally held on Fridays, was moved to Saturdays so that Marquette's (presumably) victorious gridiron warriors could attend. Although the last parade before wartime (1941) was dampened by a shower so heavy it was impossible to judge the floats, Mayor Carl Zeidler still took the time to march alongside thirty departmental, fraternity, and sorority entries as well as six bands. By 1952, one hundred floats, cars, and marching units entertained the crowds. Awards were assigned in four categories of floats: departments, clubs, fraternities, and sororities. The weekend's events always started with a high Mass at Gesu Church. For Milwaukee's elite, the university president hosted a luncheon. Gracing these invitation lists were names such as Bradley, Cudahy, Falk, Froedtert, Harnischfeger, Heil, Kohler, Sensenbrenner, Uihlein, and Vogel.[48]

ATHLETICS

The target of the enthusiasm surrounding homecoming, the university's football team, did not fare well in the postwar period. Tom Stidham had the unfortunate luck of serving as head coach during wartime when his best players came and went dependent upon military assignments. In February 1946, the athletic board replaced Stidham after a season of five wins, five losses, and one tie (and an overall record of twenty wins, twenty-two losses, and two ties). He was replaced by the coach everyone "knew" would bring a renaissance to the hilltop: Frank Murray. As Marquette coach from 1922 to 1936, Murray had directed undefeated teams in 1922, 1923, and 1930. His teams genuinely earned the "Golden Avalanche" sobriquet. His 1935 team played in the first Cotton Bowl. In his fifteen years at the helm, Murray etched a 90-32-6 record in the books before he moved on to the University of Virginia. By 1946, he was ready to return to the Midwest at the same moment Marquette was looking for inspiration on the gridiron. However, Thomas Wolfe's lament that you "can't go home again" was never truer. Murray's teams in 1946 through 1949 stumbled to an unimpressive record of twenty-four wins and twenty-three losses. Concerned for his health, the athletic board even tried to keep him off the field during games, urging his son to intervene. The board reassigned Murray for 1950, the final year of his five-year contract. Line coach Lisle Blackbourn moved into the top spot. During this coach's four-year stay through 1953, the football team won twenty-four, lost thirty, and tied four. Mediocrity reigned. Even a new practice field, purchased through the generosity of alumnus Victor McCormick, failed to help.[49]

The university's other sports teams also had their woes during this decade, including a basketball team led for two years (1951-53) by Tex Winter, who subsequently became a coaching legend at Kansas State. Disappointing sports teams caused the *Marquette Tribune* to question school spirit, once referring to "'cheerless' cheering" because the students were unacquainted with the yells. The athletic board repeatedly questioned programs that struggled to stay afloat financially. When suggestions were offered to elevate baseball, boxing, wrestling, and hockey to intercollegiate status, it took the board only minutes to reject such notions. For a single game in 1949, the Marquette hockey team skated on the ice at the State Fair Coliseum—just long enough for outside sponsors to complain about the small crowd.

The athletic board employed a variety of strategies to attract fans. In 1947, the business manager for athletics mailed 15,000 football schedules to create area-wide interest. In the same year, sixty local business firms agreed to encourage their workers to attend a battle between Marquette's gridiron eleven and a team from the University of Detroit. In 1947 and 1949, the basketball and football teams respectively began to broadcast selected games through the new medium of television. The former still played most home games in the old gymnasium, although prominent opponents (such as the University of Wisconsin) justified incurring costly rental fees at the newly built Milwaukee Arena. When two Jesuits schools dropped football in 1952 (bringing the total of Jesuit schools without that sport to eighteen of the twenty-seven colleges and

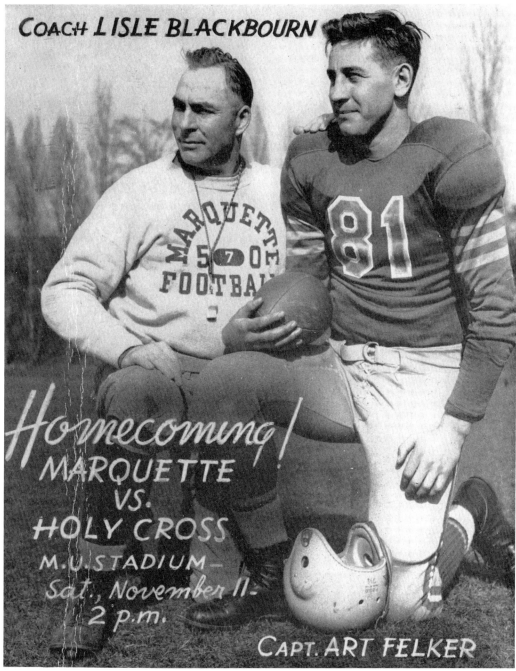

1950 Season. File 680

universities), longtime athletic director Conrad Jennings maintained that Marquette would never abandon its team. He insisted that Hilltopper football was in sound financial shape. The athletic department repainted the stadium every other year, hoping to lure fans into its seats, and in 1949 it installed new light towers for night games. Whatever the record of Marquette's sports teams in the postwar years, Jesuit administrators still viewed athletics as distinctly secondary to the academic contests that took place in Johnston Hall, Science Hall, or Memorial Library. Father Brooks made this point when, in 1946, he expanded the athletic board from five positions to nine, giving the faculty a majority of five appointments and leaving three for the alumni and one for current students.[50]

SPECIAL MOMENTS

If the university's sports teams did not bring fame to Marquette in the postwar period—beyond mournful coverage in the local press—there were other avenues to raise the school's visibility. Since 1908, Marquette had annually awarded honorary degrees to individuals who earned distinction in education, church ministry, or philanthropy. Just as the student body's engagement with international issues grew after World War II, so too did the range of individuals honored by the university. Recipients still included church leaders such as Archbishops Francis Spellman of New York (1945) and Richard Cushing of Boston (1948), but they also included government leaders such as J. Edgar Hoover (1950), director of the Federal Bureau of Investigation and one of America's leading anti-communists. The most memorable recipient from this era, however, was General Douglas MacArthur, honored on April 26, 1951. Head of the country's military forces in the Pacific during World War II, MacArthur oversaw the American occupation of Japan after August 1945. At the moment that he was chosen to receive a degree from Marquette, the general commanded United Nations troops in South Korea against invading forces from communist-controlled North Korea. However, between the time that MacArthur agreed to accept this honor and his arrival in Milwaukee, President Harry S. Truman dismissed the general for insubordination. MacArthur became an instant hero among groups that already considered Truman and his fellow Democrats soft on communism. Much to its chagrin, Marquette was suddenly at the epicenter of a political whirlwind, looking as though it was championing the anti-Truman wing of American politics.[51]

Caught in an awkward position, the administration decided to move ahead. Father George Ganss served as master of ceremonies, with assistance from Frank Casey and Ben Barkin, a local public relations expert who helped handle the crush of photographers. Classes were cancelled. Schools and businesses in Milwaukee closed for the day. Thousands greeted the career military man as he made his way from Mitchell Field to the Marquette University Stadium. On an extraordinarily damp and chilly day, a warmly dressed (but not capacity) crowd of 22,000 welcomed the controversial general. In his opening remarks, Father O'Donnell drew attention to MacArthur's role in accepting the unconditional surrender of Japan on September 2, 1945, an occasion during which the general had warned that if the world did not "'devise some greater and more equitable system than the destructiveness of war, Armageddon will be at our door. The problem is basically theological and involves a spiritual recrudescence and improvement of character.'" Father Edward Drummond, dean of the graduate school, conferred a doctoral degree upon the general. As MacArthur approached the microphone to express his gratitude, the audio system suddenly failed. Members of the engineering college rushed forward to correct the situation. In his brief response,

General Douglas MacArthur at MU stadium, 1951. Oversized Photograph Files, Box 3.

a fatigued MacArthur reminded listeners that the "university tradition is one of the greatest bulwarks of modern civilization…. It represents a symposium of science, art, culture, and divinity." He concluded by expressing his great pride "in having my name scrolled on your tablets as an honorary alumnus." To many at Marquette, this was the most memorable moment in the school's history, surpassing the day that President William Howard Taft had stopped by in 1909.[52]

Among notable alumni seen on campus during the thirties through the fifties was movie star Pat O'Brien, who was born in the same building on Clybourn where Father O'Donnell had been raised. The actor frequently returned to Milwaukee for homecoming. In the early forties, Mayor Carl Zeidler, a Marquette law graduate, appeared with regularity. A handsome, blond-haired bachelor, Zeidler was blessed with a wonderful voice that thrilled student audiences. (Tragically, in late 1942, a short time after resigning from office to serve in the military, Zeidler's ship disappeared off the coast of South Africa.) Even the presence of Lawrence Welk's daughter as a freshman in journalism warranted a column in the *Marquette Tribune*. But during the postwar period, Marquette's most newsworthy graduate captured international headlines, not local attention. United States Senator Joseph McCarthy, a Grand Chute native, enrolled at Marquette in 1930, completing two years in engineering before switching to law. McCarthy participated in intramural boxing and later directed the program for a year. He was narrowly elected class president in his first year in law school. Like his classmates during the depression, the future celebrity took whatever jobs he could get, including yard work, short-order cook, flypaper salesman, and window caulker. He sold his blood to hospitals at least a half dozen times. Six months after graduation in 1935, McCarthy successfully ran for district attorney in Outagamie County. In 1939, at the age of 28, he was elected as the youngest circuit judge in state history. After military service in the Pacific during World War II, "Tail-gunner Joe" became the junior senator from Wisconsin in 1946, initiating a brief but consequential career that inserted his surname into the lexicon of American politics.

The senator's contacts with his alma mater were curiously restrained and businesslike. In one instance, he even responded to an inquiry from a university official with a form letter. For its part, the university maintained a certain distance, especially after McCarthy began his freewheeling crusade against domestic communism in February 1950. Before his public image became too controversial, however, the university allowed him to attend a business college fraternity dinner only to find him denouncing the U.S. State Department's incompetence in fighting communism, once again linking Marquette to anti-Truman activities. After his tactics were called into question, the committee on student life turned down a request to have him speak on campus in 1952, explaining its rule against candidates for office appearing at the university. McCarthy was censured by his senate colleagues in late 1954 and died in May 1957.[53]

What Fathers Brooks and O'Donnell sought in the years after World War II was an interlude of fiscal stability and healthy enrollments. They were blessed with both. Even the routine of student life remained rather unremarkable in that returning veterans, who constituted such a sizable portion of the student body, wanted nothing more than unimpeded advancement toward their degrees. Missing from this checklist of achievements, however, were measurable enhancements of the university's academic programs. Marquette University was on the verge of becoming the largest Catholic university in the country and yet it lacked an academic blueprint to guide its future. Recognizing this deficiency, Father O'Donnell set out during the second half of his tenure to prepare his alma mater for an elevated position in American Catholic higher education.

TRANSITION TO PROMINENCE
1954-62

Improved finances during the postwar period allowed Marquette to undertake a physical expansion reminiscent of thirty years earlier. In the 1920s, however, every decision to construct another building, create a new department, or codify student rules into a handbook originated in the president's office. Albert Fox's dreams for Milwaukee's Jesuit university not only prevailed, but were usually implemented without consultation. By contrast, during the fifties—a "quiet and tame" time according to Father O'Donnell—the central administration embraced a collegial style in planning the school's future. Together, Jesuits and laity shaped an institution that welcomed a generation of young adults who increasingly viewed college as an expectation, not an exception. Higher education in this country no longer prepared an elite cadre of "learned men" who went on to command America's economic, political, and religious systems. Democratization of higher education, a phenomenon that Father Raphael McCarthy had once dismissed as outlandish, transformed the meaning of college for a student population that now included men and women from every social class and soon from every race. Marquette's pace-setting self-analysis coupled with historic opportunities to refine the academic programs permitted the institution to fulfill its ambitions as one of America's premier Catholic universities.[1]

SEVENTY-FIFTH ANNIVERSARY

On May 6, 1948, the *Marquette Tribune* published a special edition celebrating both the centennial of Wisconsin statehood and the 275th anniversary of Jacques Marquette's 1673 voyage across the upper Midwest. In a message posted on page one, Father Peter Brooks (only a week away from his untimely death) tied Wisconsin's progress during the previous one hundred years to Marquette's maturation as the state's largest private university. According to Brooks, these two great enterprises—one secular and political, the other religious and educational—benefitted from each other's refinements over the decades. The president reminded his readers that Père Marquette's statue represented the Badger State in Statuary Hall. The school's defensiveness, so evident in the early twentieth-century, had vanished by the postwar period and Marquette was now as much a part of the state's educational scene as the University of Wisconsin.[2]

Marquette's own anniversary, its seventy-fifth, personified this self-assurance. The golden jubilee in 1931 had been muted in the shadow of the Great Depression. So in the mid-fifties, Father O'Donnell had no intention of suppressing the festiveness of this moment. He wanted each event in 1955 and 1956 to showcase his alma mater's past achievements as well as its potential greatness. But he also approached this memorable year with intentions similar to those of Alexander Burrowes in 1906: exploit the attendant optimism to lay the groundwork for transformational change. Father Burrowes had secured funding for a majestic new building along Grand Avenue that cleft the college program from the high school. He also laid the groundwork for the introduction of professional education one year later. His first move changed the physical face of Marquette College whereas the second redefined the school's role in Milwaukee and Wisconsin. A half-century later, Father O'Donnell wanted the campus community to reconsider the university's academic trajectory and its administrative structure in anticipation of the next twenty-five years. O'Donnell handpicked the theme for this celebration ("The Pursuit of Truth to Make Men Free"), intending to dramatize Marquette's responsibility to save souls by creating a better world.

During the summer of 1953, Father Clarence Ryan, vice president of public relations and development, wrote a letter to the faculty detailing the proposals already under consideration for the anniversary and inviting them to suggest additional ideas. To direct the jubilee, O'Donnell turned to a layman instead of a Jesuit. Professor Robert Kidera from the School of Journalism received a year's sabbatical leave to serve as the anniversary's executive director. Thirty-eight thousand invitations were mailed out. Thirty-four thousand individuals were estimated to have visited the campus during twelve months of activities. There were nights of chamber music, jazz, and big bands (including an appearance by former Hilltopper Woody Herman in the union ballroom). As many as 13,000 may have participated in the two-week Festival of the American Arts. The grandest of these events highlighted Marquette's community of scholars. In June 1955, five hundred industrialists, economists, and educators attended a two-day conference titled "The Power and Problems of the Expanding American Economy." Similar sessions followed: "From Disorder to World Order" in November; "International Cooperation for the Improvement of Our Health and Welfare" in January 1956; "Problems of Communication in a Pluralistic Society" in March 1956; and "The Role of the Independent School in American Democracy" in May. Special institutes examined the St. Lawrence Seaway, persecution of the Church, and the nature of Jesuit education. By the year's end, 286 scholars either delivered papers or offered commentaries at one of these events.[3]

Starting with a preview dinner in June 1955, the administration kept the faculty fully informed and encouraged departments to sponsor meetings of their professional organizations in Milwaukee. Fathers Edward Drummond and Gerard Smith wrote signature essays on the anniversary's central theme. The biggest extravaganza came with a special convocation on April 16, 1956. The president of the University of Illinois addressed seven thousand students, faculty, and guests at the Milwaukee Auditorium. Representatives from more than two hundred colleges, universities, and academic societies attended, including sixteen presidents. Political leaders such as Mayor Frank Zeidler, County Board Chairman Lawrence Timmerman, and Governor Walter B. Kohler offered citations of congratulations. Pope Pius XII sent his regards. The evening was topped off when Father O'Donnell presented the first Père Marquette Awards to nine individuals "'who … exemplified the qualities which the University cherishes.'" Among the religious figures, business executives, and public servants so honored was Henry Millman, the only surviving member of Marquette College's first graduating class in 1887. For Father President, the crowning moment came two months later when Chancellor Konrad Adenauer of West Germany traveled to Milwaukee to receive an honorary degree.[4]

REFLECTION FOR CHANGE

Father O'Donnell envisioned the seventy-fifth anniversary as "the end of one era and the beginning of another." On April 3, 1954, more than a year before the jubilee's kickoff, he assembled one hundred faculty members for a full-day session at which he announced a sweeping self-analysis. (Self-survey and self-study were also terms used to describe this undertaking.) O'Donnell wanted the entire university to participate in this assessment, an endeavor that the president foresaw as "one of the most important things the university has ever done." Topics from the optimum size of Marquette's student body to the school's civic responsibilities in Milwaukee were considered. There was no hidden agenda. Unbiased self-reflection was the only objective. Lay faculty dominated the project's eleven committees. On the objectives (or mission) committee, laymen outnumbered Jesuits, six to two. On the administration committee, there were six laymen to three Jesuits. Admittedly, these committees remained a layman's prerogative, with only one woman on each of the curriculum, instruction, and libraries committees, and two each on committees dealing with student services and institutional studies. To handle this sizable undertaking, O'Donnell recruited the chair of Loyola University's education department, Dr. William Conley, to serve as "Educational Assistant to the President." An educational economist by training, Conley was a noted expert in American Catholic education and later in 1963 became the founding president of Sacred Heart University. At Marquette, he handled day-to-day responsibilities of the self-analysis in collaboration with the academic vice president. A budget of $65,000 was set aside for the entire project.[5]

By January 1955, committee reports on the current status of the university were completed. The second phase involved drafting plans for the next twenty-five years. Organizers hoped to have this work done by June 1956. Behind the scenes, however, differences arose over how the Catholic mission of Marquette was being characterized and how the traditions of St. Ignatius were being used to guide this moment of institutional introspection. In the case of the latter, Conley distributed an essay interpreting Ignatian pedagogy to every member of the eleven self-analysis committees. However, a leading Jesuit at the university objected to the slant taken by the essay's author, another prominent Jesuit on campus. Moreover, before a final draft of the self-analysis could be approved, working drafts were surreptitiously sent to Jesuit superiors in Rome. These authorities instructed Father O'Donnell to address questions raised by their scrutiny of the leaked drafts. In his reminiscences, the president openly acknowledged distress over these leaks, although he did not impugn the sincerity of the whistle-blowers. He was

Aerial view of Marquette neighborhood, looking north, 1955. Oversize File.

Aerial view of Marquette neighborhood, looking northwest, 1955. Oversize File.

particularly upset that differences of opinion had not been ironed out locally and that what was leaked did not necessarily reflect the final conclusions of the self-analysis. He regretted interference from Europe, arguing that "authorities in Rome should not be expected to solve all local problems." In O'Donnell's own words: "we were hemmed in by strictures that were outmoded and out of keeping with educational developments at Marquette."[6]

As if nothing were amiss, in November 1955, the academic senate (only an administrative council at this time) examined responses from a student questionnaire produced as part of the self-analysis. Not until two years later was the senate informed that a "formal implementation of the Self Survey as rapidly as the President had hoped and all of us had planned" could not proceed because misunderstandings "had arisen in the minds of some Jesuit officials about the intent and content of the Self Survey." University authorities admitted that the process might take "a little while" longer than originally planned.[7]

Thwarted on one front, O'Donnell moved in a totally different direction. Father Drummond informed the senate that Father O'Donnell decided to use "data from [the self-analysis] to solve problems and situations facing him. Thus, indirectly and informally, a number of recommendations of the Self Survey [had already] been carried out." In light of Rome's doubts about the self-analysis, the senate was advised that the president wished to have the information about his implementing the study treated as confidential. Moreover, O'Donnell did not want the university community to know that distant powers were blocking the hard work of eleven committees. Instead, he was prepared to take the blame for any delays. Four years later, in March 1961, a summary report from the self-analysis was distributed to senior administrators with the warning that its contents were still "not for outside circulation." In his memoirs, O'Donnell conceded that the rest of the university community probably thought that these delays were his fault, that their efforts had been wasted. However, the president admitted that he had found ways, both "indirectly and informally," to carry out a number of recommendations.[8]

To move things along, Father O'Donnell created a second group, the president's advisory council, in November 1957. Members of this body came from outside the university and included Milwaukee-based industrialists, businessmen, and professionals. Their task was to examine "the more urgent of the current problems confronting Marquette University." The group held fifteen meetings during 1958. Their report ran 157 pages in length, examining the university's "programs, operations, and goals." In its comments on the student body, their report noted that more than a third of the Marquette students came from outside Wisconsin, a trend that suggested the admissions office retool its recruitment strategies. Moreover, although enrollment had topped ten thousand in 1958, Marquette's percentage of the total college population in the United States had grown only fractionally since 1940. Thus while there were two-and-a-half times more students at Marquette than thirty years earlier, administrators needed to operate from the premise that the university was only keeping pace with the

competition, not moving ahead. As for the university's efforts to increase the proportion of faculty with doctoral degrees, the figure of 42 percent placed Marquette in the
upper third of major universities in the North Central region and only 1 percent behind public universities in the Midwest. However, faculty salaries and their effect upon
retention of accomplished scholars continued to plague the administration. Senior
faculty at Marquette earned only two hundred dollars a year less than their colleagues
at other private universities, but two thousand dollars less than professors and associate professors at the region's public universities. Linked to this issue was the matter of
released time for research among the senior faculty.[9]

COMMUNICATIONS AT AN EDUCATIONAL CORPORATION

The attention paid to faculty welfare in the advisory council's report underscores the
status that Father O'Donnell envisioned for the laity in Marquette's future. The president's lack of experience in higher education may have contributed to his calmness
regarding the expanding role of lay faculty and administrators. He never seemed teth-
ered to the past, perhaps because he was so new to university management. O'Donnell
understood that he was in charge of an operation that was far too complex for one
individual to oversee. Delegating authority, even outside the Society of Jesus, seemed
crucial to Marquette's well-being.

His first step in bringing the faculty into university governance involved sharing information. In his early years in O'Hara Hall, Father O'Donnell distributed open letters
to the faculty, updating them on routine matters such as fund-raising and construction
schedules. In October 1953, the *Marquette Report* was created to keep parents and
benefactors "informed of important campus news, developments and personalities."
However useful the *Report* may have been for these important constituencies, the four-
page quarterly was far more significant for the faculty and staff because it was their
everyday lives that were being highlighted: the awarding of grants and promotions,
faculty publications, special activities on campus, the creation of new university offices,
and the dedication of new buildings.

The flow of information throughout the university community preoccupied this administration. In 1955, the academic senate spent hours discussing what was referred
to as the university's "systems of communication," arguing that pronouncements from
O'Hara Hall were "too casual and informal." In one session, William Conley pointed
out that communication across a university was more complex than in the corporate
world. The latter needed speed in delivering data, but decision-making was simple:
top-down, with no questions asked. With university faculty serving as far more than
hired help, information had to be exchanged, had to move up as well as down. When
the *Marquette University Magazine* was created in 1960 (seven years after the *Marquette
Report*), the glossy quarterly continued to "publish reports on the work of the university—[that is], teaching, research, the publication of scholarly materials and the sponsorship of public and semi-public institutes, seminars and conferences where theory
and practice confront each other as men scrutinize and debate the great issues of the

day." O'Donnell wanted the *Marquette Magazine* to highlight "the work of the university through the people of the university—that is, through the teacher, the student, the researcher, the administrator."[10]

In showcasing the faculty as they executed Marquette's academic mission, Father O'Donnell touched upon a question that was constantly on his mind: who was responsible for what university operation? He worried about this when making administrative assignments and he worried about it regarding faculty appointments. Consequently, in early 1957, a draft of what later became the first faculty handbook circulated for comment within the academic senate. As these types of manuals go, the final version, published in 1960, was relatively simple, with one- or two-sentence descriptions of each administrator's responsibilities, from the president down to the department chair. Appointments, promotions, and tenure were discussed with the broad language of a constitution rather than the legalistic detail of an insurance policy. The section on academic freedom, the longest, confirmed the university's acceptance of the 1941 Statement of Principles, endorsed by both the Association of American Colleges and the American Association of University Professors (AAUP). The latter had been concerned with the personal rights of faculty members since World War I. For example, could an instructor be a pacifist when the nation was at war? Columbia's president, Nicholas Murray Butler, had said no in his 1917 commencement address, a position that subsequently forced a nationally respected scholar to leave Columbia for embracing what Butler viewed as a disloyal position. Later, on the eve of World War II, the AAUP revisited this matter and revised its statement on academic freedom and tenure, adopting policies that Marquette came to endorse twenty years later in its first faculty handbook. Henceforth, in the words of the AAUP, when a faculty member spoke as a citizen, "he should be free from institutional censorship or discipline" although this individual should "remember that the public may judge his profession and his institution by his utterances." Critical for those entrusted with the care of Milwaukee's Jesuit university, the AAUP held that "limitations of academic freedom because of religious or other aims of the institution should be clearly stated in writing at the time of the appointment."[11]

The faculty handbook inspired a matching set of guidelines for administrators. In early 1959, the academic senate considered a revision of the statutes affecting the offices of president, vice president, and dean. The senate clarified responsibilities, authority, and lines of reporting, with specific mention of their relationships to public relations and development. Created after 1947 when the university council had been "democratized," the academic senate in 1958 consisted of central administrators and deans. That year, it took under advisement a proposal to add a faculty voice at Marquette's policy-formation level, although one dean warned: "Democratization should not be carried to extremes." Three years of review led Father Edward Drummond, the academic vice president, to announce in 1961 that "three or four senior members of the full-time teaching faculty" would join the academic senate whose task henceforth would be to "formulate major academic policies." The senate was to serve as an advisory body for the academic vice president whenever discussion and evaluation might be "useful or necessary."

Six months earlier in a speech at the annual Père Marquette dinner, Father O'Donnell had announced formation of a committee on faculty (COF). This committee consisted primarily of faculty members (in contrast to the senate) because up to now, in Father Drummond's words, faculty members had not been "sufficiently involved in the formulation of policy." The administration had quietly conducted a survey among similar institutions, including the University of Notre Dame, Catholic University, Saint Louis University, and Northwestern University. At Catholic schools, faculty membership in bodies such as the academic senate averaged about half elected and half appointed. In May 1964 (three years after being established), the committee on faculty was reorganized to tip the balance of power toward elected members (seven) over appointed members (six). Faculty governance was being put to the test because the committee's responsibilities came to include matters such as tenure, appointments, faculty welfare, advancement in rank, conditions of faculty service, and long-range planning for faculty development.[12]

IMPLEMENTATION OF THE SELF-ANALYSIS

Father O'Donnell and his key ally, Father Edward Drummond, expected this overhaul in governance procedures to be a model for other academic improvements. From early 1957 through 1959, the requirements for majors in the College of Liberal Arts were thoroughly rewritten, beginning with philosophy in March 1957. In response to a survey of similar departments at other Catholic schools, the requirements for a Marquette philosophy degree were raised from twenty-four to thirty units and for a minor from eighteen to twenty-one. Philosophy requirements for all liberal arts students were also revised. A year later, political science, a relatively recent addition, redid its course offerings, as did sociology. History did the same in 1959, just as an undergraduate major in theology was added. (For theology, a university's usual sequence of development was reversed because its master's degree program preceded the undergraduate major.) Smaller adjustments included a merger of the botany and zoology curricula in the biology department (1959) and a merger of the classics department with foreign languages (1963).[13]

Curricular enhancements also involved an intriguing agreement between the Layton School of Art and Marquette. The plan was to make Layton's fine arts classes available to Marquette's liberal arts students and to make the university more diverse curriculum available to Layton's students. In the fall of 1956, Layton offered courses in pictorial composition, analysis of nature forms, applied aesthetics, basic drawing, and sculpture laboratory. Sixty-five Marquette undergraduates took advantage of these opportunities; nearly an equal number of art students enrolled for course work at the university. In late 1958, the self-analysis prompted the start of a university honors program, with the Superior Student Program. By the following fall, the dean of liberal arts planned to invite the top 5 percent of first-year students (approximately fifty individuals) to take advantage of individualized classes, a series of special lectures and colloquia, and advising by a handpicked team of faculty. After a few years of insufficient progress, Dean Eugene Korth, SJ, started a campaign to develop a more elaborate "Honors Program for Superior Students," with a half-time director, a programmatic budget, and physical space set aside for these select students. He fired off memorandum after memorandum, asserting the importance for Marquette of attracting superior students. By this time, Father O'Donnell was no longer president, having been reassigned to the new position of chancellor. Yet the former president took up Korth's cause, presenting its possibilities to a potential donor. Finally, in the fall of 1963, a formal honors program was initiated, with special sections in English, history, and theology.[14]

Other curricular changes in the late fifties included a new Asiatic Studies Institute in fall 1956, about a year after the first classes were offered in Japanese and Korean. Instruction in Korean was precipitated by the Wisconsin province's intentions to help establish a Jesuit university in Seoul, only three years after the unsettled conclusion of America's "police action" in Korea. According to Father Drummond, Marquette hoped that the Asiatic Studies Institute would "'serve as an orientation for those who wish to teach, do missionary work or carry on business in the Far East.'" Academic minors in Latin American, Slavic, and German Studies followed between 1957 and 1959. Even more memorable was the end of the fifteen-unit Latin requirement for a bachelor of arts degree. Pressure from outside the university, specifically the Jesuit Educational Association, drove this decision after several Jesuit colleges in the western United States dropped their Latin requirements. This action removed the last distinctive remnant of Marquette College's original curriculum. Since 1952, when the bachelor of philosophy option had been abolished, liberal arts students who did not complete enough units in the classical languages received a bachelor of science degree, regardless of their area of emphasis. In 1959, this changed, with majors in the humanities and social sciences receiving a bachelor of arts of degree and majors in the natural sciences receiving, typically, a bachelor of science degree.[15]

For a time, improvements in Marquette's undergraduate offerings overshadowed refinements at the graduate level. Yet as early as 1950, senior administrators had quietly considered a restoration of doctoral studies in philosophy. The chair, Gerard Smith, assured Father Drummond (who was then dean of the liberal arts) that the cost of a doctoral program would be insignificant if the number of students was kept to a minimum. Drummond had a personal stake in this issue because as the newly appointed dean of the graduate school in 1944, he had completed the dismantling of the university's doctoral programs. He had also negotiated a reconciliation with the Association of American Universities, allowing Marquette's master's programs to be reinstated in 1945.

First as dean and later as academic vice president, Father Drummond spearheaded the return of the PhD to Marquette, fully aware of the AAU's original criticisms from the early 1940s. In the spring of 1953, the university administration released a document titled "The Principles of Marquette University on Scholarship and Research." It identified the "pursuit of truth" as the primary obligation of the institution. The "possession, communication, and enlargement of knowledge" was central to the university's operation. To achieve the intellectual stature expected of every Marquette graduate, the faculty—their mentors—had "to grow in greater intellectual competence." This was accomplished through scholarship, of which there were three types: pure research that was theoretical, not applied; applied research done out of a commitment to "the enlargement of the truth for the commonweal"; and instructional research, which furthered teaching. Every faculty member was required to engage in at least one style of research. The end result—the pursuit of truth by Marquette students—thereby served the cause of human liberty as well as the enhancement of American intellectual life, both of which had a spiritual value. In this manner, a Marquette education provided a path to service and to salvation.[16]

By the fall of 1954, inspired by the still unfolding self-analysis, the graduate school board revised its objectives for graduate work at Marquette. The board used criteria prepared by the Jesuit Educational Association. Each department with a master's program was instructed to evaluate its efforts in light of the association's standards. Three years later, on September 21, 1957, Father O'Donnell proudly announced that the university would begin, once again, to offer doctoral degrees. The initial degrees would be in philosophy and the general area of biological sciences, with concentrations in botany, zoology, anatomy, biochemistry, microbiology, pathology, pharmacology, and physiology. According to the president, the issues originally raised by the AAU (faculty preparation and quality of the library) had been resolved. Restoration of doctoral studies was seen as a "natural development." Over the next six years, seven doctoral degrees were awarded: two in philosophy and five in the biological sciences. By January 1964, 42 students were enrolled in doctoral programs: 13 in philosophy, 23 in biological sciences, and six in the newest option, theology (added in 1963).[17]

Doctoral programs were certainly the era's most glamorous academic initiatives, but this renewed attention to graduate education also extended to the master's programs. Early in 1957, one of the newer departments, psychology, requested permission to offer a master of science degree. Approval was granted in the fall of 1958 as part of six new programs: political science, Spanish, electrical engineering, oral surgery, dental materials, and psychology. This brought the total number of master's level programs at Marquette to twenty-eight. To fill these classes, the vice president of student affairs announced a program in early 1959 to counsel Marquette seniors to consider graduate studies and to help them obtain grants and scholarships. The approval of degrees in psychology and political science in 1958 as well one in sociology two years later reflected Father Drummond's advocacy of the social and natural sciences. He felt that new degree programs had to fit with the university's growth areas, disciplines that prepared Catholic laymen to successfully engage "a pluralist society." Drummond's outspoken support for the social sciences was also evident in his push to have professional colleges such as engineering become fully integrated with the College of Liberal Arts. In the fall of 1959, the College of Engineering switched from a quarter system to a semester system, allowing its first- and second-year students to attend classes in the liberal arts, speech, and journalism.[18]

The introduction of new degrees and departments depended upon a growing staff of lay instructors. In the fall of 1955, sixty-five new lay faculty and three Jesuits were hired; the next year eighty-eight lay people and seven Jesuits joined the faculty. The annual recruitment of new, full-time professors brought nearly fifty individuals to campus per year between 1957 and 1962; then, in the fall of 1963, seventy-eight were hired. The outcome of having so many non-Jesuits on board threatened the institution's religious mission. Every Jesuit college in the United States faced the same dilemma: more students meant more faculty, but who could guarantee their acquiescence to the Ignatian traditions of each institution? The Jesuit Educational Association addressed this matter bluntly in May 1958, writing: it "is obvious that the number of laymen in strictly professional schools will outnumber Jesuits. This may be true also, but to a lesser degree, in colleges… But wherever laymen are employed, they should be those whose character and educational background are such as to make them apt members of a team striving for the aims of Jesuit education. To assure this unity of spirit, a program of indoctrination in the history, aims, and methods of Jesuit education should be provided for lay members of our faculties."[19]

In recognition that a team, not just Father President, was now responsible for Jesuit education at Marquette, Edward O'Donnell initiated an annual Père Marquette Day dinner to provide an evening in mid-May (on or near the anniversary of Father Marquette's death) when he could offer an inspirational reflection on the state of the university and when selected faculty could be recognized for their work as teacher-scholars. The intent was to reaffirm the team's commitment to the university's goals. At the first gathering on May 18, 1959, four hundred faculty members assembled in the Brooks Memorial Union ballroom to watch John F. Douglas from engineering and Gerard Smith from philosophy receive teaching-excellence awards. The audience also heard Father O'Donnell announce a new theme for the university. Replacing the seventy-fifth anniversary slogan of "The Pursuit of Truth to Make Men Free" was "Marquette University—Commitment to Intellectual and Moral Excellence." This newest motto quietly moved away from the Cold War rhetoric of its predecessor to one that linked learning with salvation, the quintessential Jesuit value.[20]

FINANCING IMPROVEMENTS

Hiring so many new faculty members and raising faculty salaries (a point to be discussed shortly) placed a tremendous burden on the institution's chief executive. Other private colleges and universities often had endowments that underwrote innovations. Marquette presidents never had this luxury. In his president's report of November 1955, Father O'Donnell lamented the inadequacies of the school's income, observing that it hampered the "University's continued aspirations for excellence." Every new project had to be subsidized through unscheduled gifts, fund-raising, or risky ventures such as the Northern Michigan Land Company. As early as the spring of 1953, the president started to set aside certain donations to fund specific improvements. For example, an annual gift honoring Michael Carpenter, founder of the Carpenter Baking Company, and special gifts from Fred Pabst and from the Schlitz Foundation were earmarked for faculty development programs. The administration's efforts to upgrade faculty scholarship paid off with an increase in external research grants. In 1956, university researchers received ten grants from outside agencies. Three years later, this number jumped sixfold. These sixty grants, totaling $200,000, came largely from the National Science Foundation, the U.S. Public Health Service, and the Atomic Energy Commission. Marquette faculty were now competing with peers on a national stage. To promote this cause, O'Donnell established a vice presidency for development and public relations. Father Clarence Ryan was charged with soliciting business firms, foundations, and individuals to underwrite faculty research as well as student scholarships.[21]

In the earliest years of the O'Donnell presidency, Marquette's income exceeded its expenses, producing the most favorable balance sheets in history. Eventually, new buildings and new faculty took their toll on revenues. In 1950, the university produced a surplus of $469,000; by 1955, this positive balance dwindled to $23,000. From 1957 to 1962 (when Father O'Donnell stepped aside), the university experienced two budgets with surpluses and four without. The worst shortfall came in 1960: $491,380. The 1957-58 budget revealed just how tuition dependent the institution had become: 68 percent of school's income came from tuition and 5 percent from "Jesuit-contributed services." Only 8.5 percent of the school's annual income came from gifts and a minuscule 1.1 percent from the endowment.[22]

Marquette's notoriously uncompetitive salary structure was a prime target for enhancement during the O'Donnell years. Between the 1959 and 1960 fiscal years, for example, faculty remuneration in the liberal arts, journalism, and law increased an average of nearly 6 percent. Salaries in the College of Business Administration grew by 6.3 percent and in engineering by 7.4 percent. Instructional costs were not the only drain on the university's finances. The athletic department encountered deficits in 1954, 1956, and 1957. Athletic scholarships cost $128,400 in 1953, with only a small portion actually paid through department revenues. By 1957, the athletic scholarship program had grown to $180,000, although the department now paid more than 50 percent of this bill. One of the university's more unusual expenditures was the "provincial tax," paid to the regional headquarters of the Society of Jesus. This charge grew by 21 percent between 1956 and 1957. And student scholarships rose during the same period by 26 percent to $298,507. General administrative costs rose 21 percent to nearly two-thirds of a million dollars.[23]

These figures did not include what was happening in the School of Medicine. Although the medical school was a separate corporation, university officers felt responsible for its fiscal integrity. In the 1955 fiscal year, the School of Medicine's deficit was more than $270,682. The next year's shortfall grew to $299,254. In 1959, it was $242,200. Projections through the mid-sixties promised more of the same. The accumulated debt was daunting, despite gifts of every sort. The Milwaukee Braves baseball club donated

$25,000 for an electron microscope in 1954; the March of Dimes provided $85,364 in 1957 for a rehabilitation instruction program; and the Ford Foundation contributed more than $1.5 million between 1956 and 1957. But nothing seemed to stem the flow of red ink at the medical school. In answer, Dean J. S. Hirschboeck (who succeeded Eben J. Carey in 1947) prepared a report whose conclusions echoed those of Father Albert Fox in 1927: Marquette needed its own hospital where the faculty could carry on their private practices and where the medical school could access new revenue streams offered by the federal government. The cautious relationship established in the late 1940s between Marquette and the Milwaukee County Hospital was welcomed but insufficient to deal with the medical school's most serious financial problems. Constant nitpicking over assignments and jurisdictional matters between county and university officials did not bode well for a lasting relationship. The cumulative effect of the medical school's fiscal woes began to wear upon the administration.[24]

One way the central administration coped with rising costs was through tuition increases on a scale never witnessed at Marquette. For decades in the late nineteenth and early twentieth centuries, tuition at Marquette College/University had held steady at $60 a year, a symbol of the Jesuits' desire to have a free school where expenses never kept a worthy student from its doors. Tuition increases had always been imposed with the greatest reluctance. In 1945, general tuition was $250, with a student body that was approaching 4,400. By 1950, tuition had increased to $350; five years later, another one hundred dollars was tacked on, bringing the total to $450 a school year (and affecting nearly 9,500 students). Tuition rose at the rate of $50 a year for the next two until it reached $650 in 1958, at which time a new approach was introduced: increases every other year. These nearly automatic increases violated certain Jesuit traditions. During discussions regarding a tuition increase for the 1958-59 school year, the academic senate considered the consequences of these adjustments for each college and school. The liberal arts dean, Father Kochanski, worried that his unit would wind up "attracting the wealthy students" and shutting out "some of the students who are even now at Marquette." The dean of nursing believed that earlier increases had already cost her college to "lose some girls … to other institutions." Father Drummond countered with the warning that a tuition increase twice as large as the one under consideration might be necessary in order to balance an expected drop in enrollment. Tuition alone could never fund a university the size of Marquette. The central administration knew this. Gifts from individual donors such as Faye McBeath and agencies such as the Ford Foundation were critical but unpredictable. McBeath's beneficence of $300,000 in 1960 endowed the Lucius W. Nieman Chair of Journalism and the foundation awarded Marquette more than $1.3 million for the improvement of faculty salaries. This money, delivered in 1956 and 1957 (not to be confused with the foundation's gifts to the medical school), was put in an endowment to fund salary increases over the next decade, after which the principal could be used at the university's discretion. But more was needed.[25]

THE MARQUETTE PLAN

Father O'Donnell engineered the physical and academic expansion of Marquette during the fifties and early sixties by authorizing a series of capital campaigns, burdens that he embraced with admirable grace because he believed fund-raising had become the principal responsibility of university presidents. Although his successor later insisted O'Donnell was not comfortable asking people for money, the truth was that he had a remarkable facility for getting potential contributors to talk about how they wanted to help the university. His difficulty seems to have been in closing the deal. He came into office during the postwar push to build a library, a classroom building and, perhaps, a student union. This first campaign, titled the Marquette Fund, was subsequently re-christened the Marquette Fund II after Father O'Donnell expanded it to include the medical and dental school expansions. Then in November 1955, the university announced its Seventy-fifth Anniversary Plan, with a goal of $5.5 million. At the direction of the board of governors, this campaign was to be brief and intense. Indeed, it reached nearly 80 percent of its goal by August 1, 1956. Three-quarters of this $4 million had been donated by corporations ($2,827,750), with foundations contributing another $377,000. Alumni chipped in with $308,000, and private individuals provided $367,000.[26]

The success of the Marquette Fund II and the Seventy-fifth Anniversary Plan, modest by contemporary standards, encouraged Father O'Donnell to undertake his most audacious project. In November 1960, he announced The Marquette Plan, a capital campaign of unrivaled proportions at Milwaukee's Jesuit university. Conceived over three years, this plan sought to raise $45 million over ten years. A third of that would come from a combination of government loans and annual faculty research grants (now approaching $1 million a year). The remaining $30 million would be raised in two phases of $15 million each: 1960 to 1965 and 1965 to 1970. The 1960-65 phase had two allocations of $7.5 million each. In the first allocation, $3 million apiece would be earmarked for faculty salaries and for the university endowment, with the rest directed toward student aid. The second allocation of $7.5 million would focus upon buildings, specifically, a life sciences building, a communications complex for journalism, a center for legal research, a central classroom building, a Jesuit residence, and additional land acquisitions and renovations. The 1965-70 phase, as envisioned in 1960, was understandably vague. Its $15 million was also going to be divided into halves, with the first portion assigned to the endowment, faculty, library, and scholarships, and the second half toward yet another group of buildings for physics, chemistry, fine arts, engineering, education, business administration, and physical education/health clinic/ROTC.[27]

A select audience witnessed a confidential presentation explaining why Marquette deserved nearly $50 million. The university had "arrived at one of these critical stock-taking moments in its history," explained Father O'Donnell. Technological breakthroughs, exploration of outer space, an increasing student population, and the international threat of Marxism demanded "a commitment to intellectual and moral

Mixing fund-raising with homecoming, 1954. File 8900

excellence." As of 1960, the university was prepared to take on this challenge with ten thousand students, one thousand full- and part-time faculty, fifty-five Jesuits, thirty-six master's programs, eight doctoral programs, sixty-eight buildings, forty-three acres, and a $12 million operating budget. One of every three teachers in the public and private schools of the Milwaukee area had attended Marquette; half the students receiving medical degrees in Wisconsin each year were Marquette graduates; four out of five dentists in the state were alumni; and 80 percent of the presiding judges in Milwaukee County had taken classes at the law school. Good faculty cost money; Marquette faculty at the rank of professor received only 88 percent as much as their peers at Big Ten schools. The university was not looking to increase its enrollments. A steady state was desired, not expansion. Already more than 50 percent of Marquette students worked at least part-time and 8 percent of full-time undergraduates were receiving scholarships by 1959. Excellent schools "'are not accidents,'" the president insisted, they "'are the result of careful planning and foresight, of years of arduous effort.'"[28]

In the eyes of some, Father O'Donnell set out on this road without sufficient expertise and personnel. At a meeting of the administrative committee on April 20, 1961, John D. Wellman, who as vice president for development and public relations was nominal head of The Marquette Plan, warned that the university lacked the leadership for such a large undertaking. In October, he returned to this point, complaining about the declaration of a major campaign without the appointment of a full-time director. Although Milwaukee's largest business firms had been evaluated for their potential support, he noted, regarding the alumni, "we do not know enough about them yet." An IBM computer was used for the first time to organize information on the university's graduates, but this technique was only in its earliest stages of development a year after the plan was announced. At one point, Wellman urged the Jesuit community to help beyond "the benefit of prayer." He asked the Jesuits to use their contacts around town and among the alumni to discuss Marquette's needs and the ongoing development fund.[29]

New staff was added to the development office, and after three years, $5.5 million had been raised, a third of the goal for the 1960-65 period. Corporations had donated the largest share: $3,234,000. Offering support were the Allen-Bradley Corporation (a $300,000 pledge), American Telephone and Telegraph, Gimbel's, Kimberly-Clark, and Wehr Steel Company. The alumni had contributed just over a million dollars. Foundations had provided $500,000, about the same that the development office had raised through wills and bequests. With $3,630, the faculty portion represented the poorest showing.[30]

LAND AND BUILDINGS

The Marquette funds I and II, the Seventy-Fifth Anniversary Plan, and The Marquette Plan (later to become the Greater Marquette Plan) redefined the role of university president at Marquette, just as Edward O'Donnell had anticipated. Yesterday's Father Rector, the stay-at-home master of all university matters, was transformed into a jet-setting (or train-hopping) solicitor. In the past, a president had been absent only long enough to attend convocations of Jesuit superiors in St. Louis or Rome. Otherwise, he was in his office, although not always visible to the students and faculty. In the future, however, an absentee president would oversee university affairs through layers of lieutenants. This growth of fund-raising into an educational business produced a second consequence for Marquette. In 1952, the university received the largest sum of money from a single source in the school's history: $1 million from the U.S. government. These federal funds underwrote construction of O'Donnell Hall. Within a short time, Washington provided a second grant, this time $1.2 million for a men's dormitory. Since the days of Father Brooks, a Gothic-style Alumni Hall had been bandied about by the central administration. But other necessities—a classroom building for business, a library and a student union—had first claim on the university's dollars. The dormitory project languished, without a central funding source. Then the federal government stepped forward.[31]

To develop the men's dorm, the university needed to accumulate a large piece of property. So in January 1954, it purchased two homes and two businesses on the southwest corner of Thirteenth and Wells for $85,000. These lots provided 144 feet of frontage along Thirteenth and 150 feet along Wells. They abutted other university land (192 feet of frontage, 150 feet deep) to the south. By late 1955, blueprints for an eight-story residence hall that would house 606 students were nearing completion. But by the time these drawings were finalized, construction costs had more than doubled to $3 million. When the second federal loan was finally approved, however, the government agreed to increase its share to $2.8 million. Ground was broken on April 14, 1956. A year and a half later, Walter Schroeder Hall opened. A member of the board of governors, Schroeder offered experience as head of Wisconsin's largest hotel chain that had proven invaluable in developing of what was, for the moment, the largest structure on campus.[32]

Nearly every piece of property acquired during Father O'Donnell's tenure was purchased in painstaking increments: a frame residence here, a brick commercial building there. In the spring of 1958, O'Donnell offered an update on campus development since 1950. Of the thirty-five properties listed in his report, fourteen buildings had been demolished. Others had been adopted for university use. For example, in 1955, the Marquette Women's League (founded by Father Charles Moulinier in 1910) donated its clubhouse on North Prospect Avenue to the university. Following the example set with Alumnae House, the administration turned the clubhouse into a women's residence. The university also bought two apartment houses along Fifteenth Street to use as dormitories. The Drexel Apartments, at the corner of Clybourn Street, became a men's residence. The second apartment complex, near the new library's rear entrance, became Bonifas Hall, first a men's dormitory and later a women's residence.[33]

Additional housing became available when the university leased three floors of the Knights Tower Hotel at Eleventh and Wisconsin. Forty rooms housed eighty women beginning in September 1956. Four years later, in June 1960, the Jesuit community was informed that confidential negotiations between the Catholic Knights Insurance Company and the university had led to Marquette's purchase of the entire 16-story, 188-room structure for nearly a million dollars. Two commercial lessees, the Consolidated Savings and Loan Association and the Tower Tavern/Restaurant would have to be eased out before the women could move in. The Jesuit community was invited to suggest names for the new residence hall. When it opened as a university facility the following fall, it bore the name M. Carpenter Tower, in honor of three benefactors from the Carpenter family: Matthew H. Carpenter, former member of the board of governors, his sister, Mary A. Carpenter, and their father, Michael Carpenter. (For a time, then, Matthew Carpenter had two buildings named in his honor: the Tower as well as the former student union on Thirteenth Street.) The Stratford Arms Hotel at 1404 Wisconsin Avenue, originally leased during World War II to house military personnel, was acquired in 1962. When it opened as a student residence, it was named for Dr. John A. Heraty, a 1914 graduate of the School of Medicine who had left a $450,000 bequest to the university and Gesu Church.[34]

Sorely in need of office space for the faculty, Marquette purchased the Grandmora apartment building on Wisconsin Avenue in March 1957. This four-story, thirty-six unit structure had been owned by the Cudahy family since the 1880s. As university property, it housed the English, history, philosophy, and theology departments. Two

Tower Hall, later M. Carpenter Tower Hall. File 305.

blocks to the northwest, the Charlie Toy mansion at Fourteenth and Wells as well as the adjoining Ruby's Dinette and Camel's Tap along Wells were purchased in the summer of 1957. Toy had been one of the earliest Chinese immigrants to Milwaukee, eventually becoming a highly respected restaurateur. The "House of Toy," a stone building with a distinctive turret, was used as an academic support facility for a brief time until its demolition provided for a small parking lot. The dinette and bar were gutted and turned into the Teaching Materials Center. One block south, the Varsity Theater was leased for use as a large classroom and a special events hall beginning in the fall of 1959.

Although dormitories, offices, and support programs could use structures originally intended for other purposes, university administrators preferred new buildings for classrooms and laboratories. As early as 1956, a steering committee considered three separate but related buildings, one for each of the basic sciences: biology, chemistry, and physics. Another project with roots in the mid-fifties was a joint facility for the College of Journalism and the School of Speech. Over time Journalism used Johnston Hall, Copus Hall, and Alumnae House. Since the 1920s, speech had used John Plankinton's former mansion on Fifteenth Street. One planning committee, established in the fall of 1955, discussed a communications building. In January 1957, a second committee prepared the building's design. Years later, when a structure was finally erected north of Clybourn Street, it housed the foreign languages department. Journalism eventually moved back to Johnston Hall, its original home in 1910.[35]

One major revision of the local landscape not under university management was the Central Expressway Interchange (later the Marquette Interchange). By 1962, the east-west expressway approached downtown Milwaukee from the west, terminating at Clybourn near Thirteenth. With the north-south expressway then running only south

Commercial property on Wells Street that later became the Teaching Materials Center. At the right is Charlie Toy's residence. File 1303.

from a proposed interchange, the Tory Hill neighborhood remained, for the moment, a vital but eclectic mixture of aging frame and brick homes, taverns, union offices, repair shops, and industrial plants—a true urban community. Its primary open space was Red Arrow Park, east of Sensenbrenner Hall. The northern edge of Tory Hill along Wisconsin Avenue was distinguished by a row of churches west of Eighth Street: St. James Episcopal, Calvary Presbyterian, First Methodist, and Gesu. The university's position, then and later, was that these expressways and the future interchange would create natural boundaries for the school and not harm the area's general environment.[36]

ADMINISTRATIVE REORGANIZATION

The onslaught of academic innovations and capital projects weighing down upon Father O'Donnell during the 1950s never altered his genial exterior, but it did damage his health. While traveling in Germany for a conference of American and German Catholic educators in the summer of 1960, he suffered a mild heart attack and spent twelve days in a German hospital before returning to Milwaukee for the fall term. O'Donnell regained his characteristic color and enthusiasm, but these health problems reinforced what was already evident: one man could no longer be responsible for the spiritual well-being of the Jesuit community (now approaching sixty members), be the everyday master of all faculty and staff hires and promotions, oversee curricular developments in ten colleges and schools, be the key university contact for thousands of donors, and manage land acquisitions and construction schedules for new buildings. No individual could handle so many activities on a single day, let alone month after month. But by tradition, the president had the final say on each facet of Marquette's operation. In a moment of candor in 1954, Father O'Donnell had admitted that he "attend[ed] too much to certain details" and needed "to rid himself of as much confining work as possible." He understood that public relations was his primary duty and that no one could better represent his institution than the president. His task was to help others know the school "so they will help it develop and grow in excellence." If his time was to be spent at off-campus meetings, everyday routines had to be turned over to trusted lieutenants. But in his 1954 remarks, Father O'Donnell acknowledged that "replacements are difficult to secure among Jesuits." Perhaps that is why he continued to carry a disproportionate burden leading up to his 1960 heart attack.[37]

He did approve of the reallocation of responsibility when it pertained to his Jesuit confreres. As mentioned in Chapter 6, the provincial had appointed an assistant to the rector in 1951 to help handle routine permissions within the Jesuit community. In the fall of 1953, Father O'Donnell delegated even more of his duties as rector to Father Albert C. Zuercher, a recent provincial, who was named dependent superior of the Marquette Jesuit community, freeing the president of, in his words, "domestic responsibilities." For the moment, the president retained the title of rector and members of the religious community were free to approach him about personal matters, but under normal circumstances, they would contact Father Zuercher. Adjustments in the oversight of Marquette's Jesuit community foreshadowed the creation of a Wisconsin vice province during the summer of 1954. This separation of Jesuit ministries in Wisconsin, Iowa, Minnesota, Nebraska, and North and South Dakota from the Missouri province was completed a year later in August 1955 when a Wisconsin province, boasting 630 members, was established as one of sixty such administrative units around the world.[38]

As president, Herbert Noonan had come to trust Henry Banzhaf and Peter Brooks had found a confidant in Charles Cobeen. "Red" O'Donnell relied upon a team of specialists. Roy O. Kallenberger had joined the university in 1948 as Cobeen's assistant business manager and over the next decade gained the president's confidence. By 1960, O'Donnell had appointed Kallenberger director of the physical plant, allowing him to supervise campus development. In turn, Kallenberger recruited Seb Helfer as his assistant. Helfer eventually became the university's representative at city hall, working with the mayor, his aides, and the common council as well as with federal officials in town and at their regional offices in Chicago. Under O'Donnell's successor, Father William Kelley, Helfer negotiated crucial urban renewal agreements with the city of Milwaukee and the U. S. government. Kelley relied so heavily upon Helfer's public relations genius that he met with the mayor only to sign final documents. Helfer took care of the rest.[39]

Other members of the central administration included William Conley, Max Barnett, and Edward Drummond. Conley's primary task as the president's educational assistant was to direct the self-analysis under the supervision of the academic vice president, Father Drummond. On the eve of the self-analysis in 1954, Father O'Donnell realigned the Jesuits who served him directly. He reassigned Father Max Barnett to the new position of executive assistant to the president. Barnett had first arrived in Milwaukee in 1943. Two years later, he was named dean of liberal arts and, in 1948, academic vice president. With Father Brooks's sudden death, Barnett had stepped in as acting president until O'Donnell's appointment. Barnett then returned to his former post as academic vice president until elevated to the role of executive assistant in 1954, in essence, the president's chief of staff. During the summer of 1955, O'Donnell upgraded Barnett's position to executive vice president, a post that gave him responsibility for the university's everyday academic and administrative matters. With Barnett's promotion, Father Drummond became academic vice president. Drummond had joined the English department in 1942 and two years later was promoted to the graduate school deanship during the awkward months when the university was forced to terminate its doctoral programs. In his capacity as vice president, Drummond implemented recommendations from the self-analysis. A dedicated planner, he nurtured the reworking of liberal arts majors in departments such as philosophy, history, and political science, directed the development of new masters programs in psychology, sociology, and electrical engineering, and plotted the reintroduction of doctoral studies.[40]

Father O'Donnell maintained that his principal job was as the public face of Marquette. To assist him with this task, the president constantly tinkered with the public relations side of his staff. Edmund Carpenter had directed the news bureau since its inception in 1923; by 1951, he bore the title, publicity director. Then he became director of public relations. Two years later, he was named director of public information. By that time, Carpenter reported to a new division of the university overseen by a vice president of public relations and development, Father Clarence Ryan. Also reporting to Ryan was Frank Casey, the public relations executive whom Father O'Donnell had personally recruited in 1949. Until his untimely death in December 1953, Casey served as director of university relations, handling, for instance, the press corps during General MacArthur's visit to the university. O'Donnell so valued Casey's savvy that he had also named him secretary to the board of governors, making Casey the president's principal contact with the board's corporate executives. After Casey's passing, O'Donnell turned to a friend from the Jesuit community. Father Charles O'Hara, whose father had underwritten renovations in the administration building in 1938 and had served as chairman of the board of governors up to his death in 1950, was given the awkward designation of "assistant to the president for university interest outside of Milwaukee." This responsibility put O'Hara on the road developing civic committees among donors in Wisconsin and neighboring states, thereby saving Father O'Donnell a great many medium-range trips. In fact, O'Hara was gone so much that no one realized that he had lain dead in his room at the Jesuit residence for perhaps as much as two days in late1962. Yet another sad passing was that of Charles Cobeen. He retired from his position as university business manager in May 1963 after a remarkable forty-two years of service. Father O'Donnell honored Cobeen at the time of his retirement with the Père Marquette Award. A few months later, "Charlie" Cobeen died of cancer.[41]

STUDENT LIFE: ADMINISTRATION AND SPIRITUALITY

Father O'Donnell's proclivity for tinkering with staff assignments spilled over into the student affairs office as well. In the summer of 1952, Father Raymond R. McAuley, an instructor in theology, was appointed dean of men, the university's senior appointment in student life. He supervised student housing, health, dances, religious retreats, Greek life, and student organizations. The list grew even longer after the Marquette Union board was dissolved in 1953, leaving management of the student union and events such as homecoming to the dean of men. As a consequence, Father O'Donnell completely reworked the administrative side of student life in 1956, creating the post of vice president of student affairs. (For the moment, athletics remained under the athletic board which, in turn, reported directly to the president.) Henceforth, the deans of men and women reported to the vice president of student affairs, with their responsibilities focusing largely upon student conduct. Mabel Mannix McElligott soon resigned as dean of women, after twenty-three years, to become assistant to the vice president for public relations and development. Her subordinate, Mary Alice Cannon, moved up to the deanship.[42]

Father O'Donnell's penchant for tinkering with institutional offices led to yet another new position in 1953: coordinator of spiritual activities, a person who also chaired the new "permanent committee on spiritual welfare." To insure the spiritual well-being of every student, priest-counselors were assigned to each college and school at Marquette. In the past, the assignment of a non-teaching Jesuit to law, dentistry, engineering, or the graduate school usually meant a faculty regent, that sometimes controversial representative of the president who assisted lay deans in their fulfillment of the university's mission. The priest-counselors, however, directed their attention to the spiritual lives of students, not the administrative practices of the deans. These priests were advised to mingle with students, to "endeavor to show an interest in them and their interests, and thus to win their good will and confidence." They were also "to see to it that the personalized spiritual care of the students which St. Ignatius desired to be characteristic of Jesuit education" reached each student. Because "spiritual problems are usually woven into domestic, financial, social, academic, and other human problems," the priest-counselors were asked to look after students when they were sick or hospitalized, and to maintain contact with parents when "special care" was required. Counselors maintained offices in their respective colleges and kept regular office hours so that students could reach them as needed rather than be forced to search them out at one of the Jesuit residences. The student handbook provided each counselor's name. Working with the permanent committee on spiritual welfare (five-to-seven Jesuits appointed by the president), the coordinator of spiritual welfare oversaw every religious activity at the university, from Sunday and Baccalaureate Masses to First Friday communions and annual retreats.[43]

Retreats continued to provide an interlude for spiritual reflection. The *Marquette Tribune* and student handbooks periodically reminded students that those "who fail to fulfill their retreat obligation can be suspended from school." The upper Gesu church hosted the men's retreat; the women's retreat used the lower church. Exercises completed at private retreat houses, an option gaining favor among students, could also fulfill this obligation. Lent was another time of the year during which students immersed themselves in the Catholic identity of Marquette. Food services at the student union provided meatless meals on Mondays through Thursdays as a part of Lenten abstinence rules. In addition, the student social calendar went on a hiatus for the forty days of Lent. By 1957, the committee on spiritual welfare maintained a special liturgical schedule at chapels in the dental school and in Johnston Hall, in

MEN'S RETREATS

1955

February 11-13 - Fr. Markoe
February 18-20 - Fr. Verdieck
February 25-27 - Fr. Ganss
March 18-20 - Fr. McEvoy
March 25-27 - Fr. Maddigan

SIGN UP NOW!

at the Dean of Mens' office in the Union Building

File # 1186

residences such as O'Donnell and Schroeder halls as well as in the Church of the Gesu. The Marian Chapel, on the grounds of Lisette Lodge, served female students who were

Mass in Johnston Hall chapel, mid-1950s. File 750.

housed nearly three miles northwest of the campus at the Highland Boulevard dormitories.[44]

One manifestation of Marquette's religious mission briefly caused a flap in the College of Liberal Arts during the mid-fifties when the dean proposed starting each class period with a prayer. Father A. J. Kochanski asked non-Catholic instructors to allow a Catholic student to lead the students in the recitation of the "Our Father" if the professor did not feel comfortable doing so. A group of Catholic students had requested mandatory prayer because, they said, "'there is a lack of Catholic spirit in the University.'" Their observation can be challenged, however, in light of the steady stream of Marquette students who chose to follow a religious vocation. Between 1948 and 1961, more than 500 students entered the religious life, the largest number among American Catholic universities. One hundred and twenty-one women joined 41 different congregations; 106 men joined 28 religious orders and congregations; 120 men left to become priests in 22 dioceses; and 150 men decided to follow St. Ignatius.[45]

In addition to the presence of Jesuit priests and scholastics on campus, hundreds of nuns attended what was now the nation's largest Catholic university. The first recipients of the new master of arts in theology in 1958 were five sisters representing four congregations. That same year, four other nuns received health science degrees at commencement: one a doctor of medicine degree and three doctor of dental science degrees. During summer sessions, when their numbers increased significantly, sisters served on the student newspaper and populated the Gesu bowling lanes on Fourteenth Street. In the mid-sixties, as vocations reached all-time highs across America, several religious congregations and even private developers proposed year-round residences to house the nuns, brothers, and priests attending Marquette University. The Carmelites actually purchased an apartment building on Seventeenth Street for their confreres who attended Marquette.[46]

STUDENT LIFE: HEALTH AND PARKING

The university's self-analysis included a comprehensive assessment of student life, drawing upon a survey of daytime undergraduates. In May 1955, faculty were asked to leave their classrooms so that students might complete a sixty-four-point questionnaire. The first part of this survey covered basic information such as major, grade point average, religious affiliation, income level of parents, number of hours of employment during a school term, and expenses during a routine school year. Next came questions regarding motivational influences, such as a student's reason for attending college and for attending Marquette. Female students were asked about their satisfaction with the education given to women at the university. Students were also quizzed on their reactions to the faculty, to the library, to the freshmen orientation program, and to the student union. They were asked their "pet peeves" about Marquette. The results revealed that an overwhelming number of students identified themselves as Catholic (90 percent of the women and 80 percent of the men). For men, location followed by religion topped their reasons for coming to Marquette, whereas women offered the

Five religious orders are represented by these 1954 summer session students. File 995.

same reasons but in reverse order. Only 20 percent of the fathers of these students were college graduates. (The same question was not asked about their mothers.) Regarding their socioeconomic backgrounds, there were distinctive clusters among professional occupations (17 percent), business executives (14 percent), and factory workers (16 percent). As for student services, freshmen and sophomores were more content with what the university provided than juniors and seniors.[47]

Collecting this data was not a perfunctory undertaking. The administration genuinely sought student opinion, especially in the service areas of student life. In late 1956, fiscal pressures forced the student health center to discontinue the extraordinary privilege of consulting with private physicians at university expense. In addition, free hospitalization was cut from two weeks to one, although home visits by health center doctors were still available. To compensate, the university established a campus infirmary in the fall of 1958 to handle illnesses that could not be cared for by the walk-up clinic. Administrators discussed a student health insurance program as early as 1957; implementation came in 1959. For a fee, students received health coverage at home, during the summer, and while traveling. For single students, the cost was $20.50 a year.[48]

On a daily basis, students cared far more about university's parking problems than health issues. During the decade after World War II, automobile registrations in the United States skyrocketed, setting new records as Americans happily put the depression and wartime in their rear view mirrors. In the Milwaukee area between 1945 and 1953, "automobile and truck ownership expanded by 61 percent in the city and 66 percent in the county." Traffic within the city doubled during roughly the same period. As they embraced the increasingly affordable automobile, Milwaukeeans abandoned old-fashioned forms of transportation, prompting students in business administration to conduct a survey in 1954, asking residents why they no longer used public transit. Hundreds of Marquette students from southeastern Wisconsin as well as Illinois and Indiana were inconvenienced in 1958 when the North Shore Railroad discontinued service to Milwaukee, forcing out-of-towners to consider the automobile a college necessity. As early as 1950, the student newspaper complained that faculty were not using parking spaces assigned them on Fourteenth and Fifteenth streets; as many as one hundred slots were wasted, wailed the *Tribune*. As the university purchased and then demolished older structures in the neighborhood, these vacant properties frequently became makeshift parking lots until new halls could be built. Thus, the shabby residence west of Hopkins (Duffey) Hall, the barracks south of Science Hall, and the Toy mansion on Wells Street were all replaced by small, often unpaved, and ultimately inadequate parking lots.

With the increase of automobile traffic in the Marquette neighborhood, Milwaukee police injected themselves into campus life by periodically cracking down on jaywalking. Crossing Wisconsin Avenue in front of Johnston Hall or Thirteenth Street between the business administration building and Carpenter Hall (a key roadway leading into the Menomonee Valley) elicited two-dollar municipal tickets "for 'obstructing the free flow of traffic.'" In March 1956, a speech instructor produced "Confusion on 13th Street." This film highlighted the dangers facing drivers and pedestrians between Wisconsin and Michigan Avenues. In the tradition of academic decision-making, a committee was appointed "to investigate the parking problem on the Marquette campus." To reduce the number of automobiles parked along Thirteenth Street, the university installed an electronically operated gate at the faculty lot that replaced the old barracks south of Science Hall. Implemented in March 1957, this was the first campus activity controlled by a plastic card. Nothing came of this effort. By the following fall, city hall was again bombarded by complaints about students jaywalking across Thirteenth. Just how serious this problem could be became evident in October 1958, when a nun from the nursing program was killed and another sister seriously injured while crossing Wisconsin Avenue in front of Gesu Church. The driver's first explanation was that the women had darted into traffic while trying to catch a bus. Later he explained that his vision was obscured by another vehicle as he turned from southbound Twelfth Street to eastbound Wisconsin. Fourteen months later, the city installed "walk" lights in front of Gesu and four-way traffic lights at Eleventh Street.[49]

STUDENT LIFE: CONDUCT

Historians have characterized American college students during the 1950s as the "silent generation," in marked contrast to their decidedly louder siblings of the late sixties. In the postwar decade itself, the *Marquette Tribune* agreed with this depiction, referring on occasion to student "apathy" and of a need to shatter the "silence" of their peers. From the perspective of the student affairs office, the behavior of Marquette undergraduates was certainly subdued in the decade after 1954. For example, in late 1963, the committee on student conduct released a report of misconduct violations during the previous school year. With roughly twelve thousand students, the student affairs office handled only 101 violations among males. Fifty were for alcohol-related matters, nineteen for residence hall violations, and a similar number for off-campus housing infractions. Among women, there were only thirty-eight violations: thirteen for possession of false identification cards and ten regarding residence hall issues. In addressing these 139 incidents, one student was expelled, twenty suspended, and the rest received some term of probation.[50]

Rules regarding student housing were clearly the most difficult for undergraduates to follow. In a concession to the times, the university removed curfew restrictions in the men's dorms on an experimental basis in May 1957; more flexible hours at the women's dorms came a year later. Yet problems remained. "Public displays of affection" at the front doors of female residence halls drew the ire of the dean of women. To avoid "bringing discredit" to the students' families, the dean ordered housemothers to prevent loitering at entrance ways and vestibules. Another trouble point involved unapproved housing. With the growing size of the student body, the institution's control over housing for male students was shaky at best. In addition, landlords no longer cared to serve as chaperones on behalf of the university. As a token guideline, the administration forbade residence in nearby hotels, including the Abbott Crest, Ardmore, La Salle, Stratford Arms, and Tower. (In time, the university acquired all but the Ardmore.)

Underage drinking bedeviled the student affairs office during these years. The Madison police embarrassed Father O'Donnell in 1955 by complaining about the "conduct of the Marquette students" at the annual Badger-Warrior football games. In response, the committee on student life denied permission to female students to be away from their residence overnight on the weekends of these games and threatened any student who rented a room in Madison with dismissal. It also warned Marquette students that anyone who was arrested would face "severe disciplinary action." The behavior of the 1960 homecoming crowd at the Marquette stadium triggered a deeply perturbed editorial from the *Tribune*. It criticized those who insisted on "watching Marquette football through the bottom of a tilted whiskey glass." Because Father O'Donnell had been overwhelmed during his halftime speech by "a din of slushy-mouthed shouting, organized nonsense cheers and other halftime hilarities," the editorial demanded action from university authorities. By 1961, both municipal and university officials began to change their "boys will be boys" approach to the use of false "IDs" at neighborhood bars. Judge Christ T. Seraphim handled most underage drinking cases in Milwaukee, and he later admitted that during the fifties he would often "not 'throw the book' at college students under 21 caught drinking" because he feared a conviction might irreparably harm the student's career. But winking at the law became a thing of the past when the judge and the university promised to control a problem that was aggravated by sixty-one taverns and "other beer selling establishments within ten square blocks" of the university. Twenty-three of these bars and grocery stores lined State Street, sixteen were on Wells Street, and fourteen on Wisconsin, making enforcement by the police

Wells Street, circa 1958. File 280

a troublesome proposition. The judge promised that henceforth he would inform the university of every violation, an action that would permit the deans of men and women to apply the student handbook's regulations against the offenders. The dean of men rued the fact that as a residential university Marquette had more alcohol-related problems than the University of Wisconsin-Milwaukee which, as a commuter school, left supervision of alcoholic consumption largely to parents.[51]

In dealing with violations of university regulations, the student affairs office tried for a time to treat male and female violators differently, setting up separate disciplinary boards in 1957. This approach lasted until 1962 when a single body was established "to minimize the 'double standard.'" Another strategy to head off trouble had the dean of men delivering a lecture on university rules during the women's freshman orientation. In the fifties and early sixties, the student affairs staff operated under the premise that students were mature enough to be guided through effective communication and that students would act correctly if they were reminded of right from wrong (as in the use of phony identification cards). Encounters between groups of students and police were relatively uncommon before the mid-sixties. For example, in 1961, after a brief, inconsequential run-in between police and students, the committee on student conduct formulated "regulations concerning student assemblies and respect for civil law" because no rules existed to manage these events. "'Unauthorized student demonstrations, rallies, parades, or other similar events will not be condoned by the University'" because training in good citizenship was one of the objectives of the university, the committee warned. Student protests were so unusual that the committee on student life actually discussed whether the university had an "obligation to aid students who were brought into court." Once guidelines were in place, they could be trotted out as needed. For instance, during the Cuban missile crisis in the fall of 1962, male students ran down Wisconsin Avenue carrying anti-Castro signs and an effigy of the Cuban leader. Father Floyd L. Stanton, vice president for student affairs, intervened, snatching signs and demanding student identification cards. If a similar incident had occurred just a few years later, it is doubtful whether a lone Jesuit would have been so persuasive.[52]

Questioning the prevailing social order was hardly popular among students in the late fifties and early sixties. America's global battle against communism called for solidarity, not individualism. In 1957, the College of Liberal Arts mandated three semester hours of American history or government in response to news that American prisoners of war during the Korean conflict who cooperated with their communist captors tended to be ill-informed regarding the country's political traditions. Two years later, the student senate went a step further, urging that all students take a mandatory class on communism. With funding from the Oscar Meyer Foundation, Marquette established an Institute for American Democracy in 1960.

Political figures appeared on campus infrequently. Senator Estes Kefauver, a candidate for the 1956 Democratic presidential nomination, came to Marquette in 1955. Instead of addressing the role of organized crime in labor unions—the headline-stealing issue for his Senate investigations—the Tennessean offered his thoughts on juvenile delinquency. During the 1957-58 school year, only one politician appeared at Marquette: Catholic congressman Eugene McCarthy of Minnesota. The most controversial visitor from this era was Dorothy Day, of the Catholic Worker movement, who spoke to small audiences in 1954 and 1958. As the 1960 presidential campaign neared, student interest in public affairs escalated. Senator John F. Kennedy, a Catholic vying for his party's presidential nomination, addressed a capacity crowd in Marquette's gymnasium in November 1959. A month later, Governor Nelson Rockefeller, who was challenging Vice President Richard Nixon for the Republican nomination, came to the Brooks Memorial Union. After his presentation, Rockefeller was sharply questioned about his support for the distribution of birth control information overseas. As the 1960 election drew near, a student poll endorsed Kennedy by a 54 to 46 percent, whereas the faculty supported the Massachusetts senator by a 67 to 33 margin over his challenger, Richard Nixon. The excitement generated by this race served as a harbinger of change. In February 1963, two hundred students attended a forum held in the union's faculty dining room. Facilitated by Father William Dooley of the philosophy department, participants asked polite but rather cynical questions regarding the purpose of their Jesuit education: Were students simply "wind-up Marquette doll[s]?" Were the faculty asking young people to be "'good Christian gentlemen,'" who followed instructions, instead of educated individuals who tackled complicated controversies with "'critical intelligence?'" Questioning well-established routines foreshadowed an age in which every facet of society came under close scrutiny and critical evaluation.[53]

STUDENT NUMBERS

The postwar surge of new college students altered American higher education forever. Families that only a generation earlier had dismissed the relevance of college now invested the family's future into post-secondary education. As the student survey during Marquette's self-analysis revealed, only 20 percent of the students had fathers who had attended college. Yet their offspring now treated four years of college as a natural extension of their formative development. With Milwaukee State Teachers College as the only other sizable educational institution in town, Marquette provided the most comprehensive curriculum—undergraduate, graduate, or professional—of any school in Wisconsin outside of Madison. (Renamed Wisconsin State College, Milwaukee in 1951, the former normal school did not become the University of Wisconsin-Milwaukee until 1956.) Located in the state's largest and most economically vibrant city, Marquette saw its enrollment jump from a wartime low of 3,081 enrollees in 1943 to a postwar high of 8,603 five years later. Registrations dropped by more than a thousand after the Korean War broke out in June 1950, but rose again in 1952. A new record (9,255) was reached in 1954; two years later more than 10,000 students attended the university. By 1960, this number soared past 11,000, climbing until 1962 when it paused at just under 12,000—nearly four times the number of students from nineteen years earlier. In 1962, the chronicler of the Jesuit community's annual history scrawled a pertinent question in his log: "Are we getting too big?"[54]

Brooks Memorial Union, September 1955. File 1285b.

Marquette's astonishing growth made it the largest Catholic university in the United States. Although other schools challenged this ranking, *America* (a Jesuit-produced magazine) confirmed the university's position for the 1957-58 school year. With 6,722 full-time students, Marquette surpassed Notre Dame by over 800 and, with 9,949 in total enrollment, it surpassed the University of Detroit by over 100. (Notre Dame won, however, when acreage was considered: 1,700 acres to 41.3 acres for Marquette.) Bragging rights could be challenged because each institution's figures included anomalies such as evening students, non-credit students, students at affiliated institutions (such as Park Air College at Saint Louis University), and even Jesuits in training at novitiates (such as the fifty-one novices in Oshkosh whom Marquette claimed credit for in 1957). However one measured the numbers, postwar Marquette had grown beyond anyone's expectations. Summer session figures also edged upward, from 1,900 in 1950 to 3,100 a decade later.

The key component to the school's growth after 1945 had been military veterans. In 1948, this segment of the student body topped off at an all-time high of 5,300. As late as 1951, 3,029 ex-servicemen were still enrolled at Marquette. The original G.I. Bill expired in July 1956. A second G.I. Bill of Rights (the Veterans' Readjustment Assistance Act) was passed in 1951 to assist Korean War vets. For these men and women, college classes had to begin by the summer of 1954 and be completed within seven years. Single veterans received monthly stipends of $110, whereas those with more than one dependent received $160. By 1956, there were only nine World War II servicemen still on campus but 1,521 Korean vets (seventeen of whom were female) as well as forty rehabilitation recipients. When Armistice Day was celebrated in 1956, a memorial Mass for the university's war dead still warranted front page coverage in the student newspaper. The university continued to deal with military matters throughout the fifties because of the 1948 draft law. University officials reminded first-year male students that they had to register within five days of their eighteenth birthday. Draft deferments were based on class ranking or an individual's score on the Selective Service College Qualification Test. The institution's well-established relationship with officer training programs was strengthened during the postwar period when the university added an Army ROTC unit (to the naval detachment) in 1951 and in the same year asked the Pentagon for an Air Force program.[55]

STUDENT ACTIVITIES

Marquette University's dealings with the U.S. government dated back to 1918 with the Student Army Training Corps and were reinforced with the assignment of a Navy ROTC unit in 1940. It took a new turn during the postwar period when the university applied for federal student-housing loans, first for O'Donnell Hall and later for Schroeder Hall. This relationship took on yet another dimension after Michael Shea became the first Warrior to receive an assignment as a Peace Corps volunteer in 1961. A mechanical engineering graduate, the former fullback was sent to California to prepare for work in Ghana. Brother Leo V. Ryan, CSV, an earnest proponent of interna-

Coventry play, 1951. File 1120.

tional service, held the position of Peace Corps coordinator at Marquette during the early sixties. Given their propensity to view international affairs through the lens of the Cold War, O'Hara Hall administrators warmly embraced the corps, agreeing to host admission exams and later a training site. Sixty-five volunteers from twenty-nine states came to Milwaukee during the summer of 1964 to attend an eleven-week training program before leaving for service in Brazil. A year earlier, the acting deputy director of the corps addressed one hundred students in the Brooks Memorial Union, heralding Marquette as the leading—not just a leading—university for involving its students in the Peace Corps. He lauded Brother Ryan for making the university's facilities available as a training center. By this time, nineteen Marquette students and alumni were in service, with another ten approved for training.[56]

Another student activity that achieved widespread recognition during this era was the Marquette University Players. Dramatic performances had been part of a Jesuit education in Milwaukee since the school opened. For some time, midyear literary exercises and end-of-the-year commencements had featured student plays and individual oratory. Dr. William Duffey had come to Marquette in 1925 from the University of Texas to invigorate the dramatic arts program (originally administered by the College of Music, later by the College of Liberal Arts, and finally by the School of Speech). The university's first theater was The Crow's Nest, located in the attic of Johnston Hall.

Performances were also presented in the speech building, the Marquette High School auditorium, and the medical school auditorium.

In 1951, Father John Walsh, SJ, a doctoral candidate in theater at Yale, arrived. Over the next decade and a half, he created a proud legacy that survives into the next century. One of his first productions took place on a flatbed truck parked in front of Gesu Church—with the temperature at twelve degrees below zero. This same play was redone in 1962—indoors this time—with the Columbia Broadcasting System hiring renowned thespian Helen Hayes to narrate the Ludus Coventry Medieval Mystery Play. Facilities for rehearsals and performances were always a problem at Marquette. Following the opening of Memorial Library in late 1953, drama students were assigned the library's old storage space in Bellarmine Hall. For one hundred and twenty dollars, the Marquette Players "purchased 126 theater seats, 22 gilded box seats, 37 mirrors, a red velvet curtain and carpeting" from the recently closed Davidson Theater, a venue that had hosted Marquette College events throughout the late nineteenth century. The newly refurbished facility in Bellarmine was then christened *Teatro Maria*. A 1962 production of Oliver Twist required seventy-eight performances to satisfy audience demands. The following year, Father Walsh created the Paul Claudel Theater in Grand-mora Apartments' inner courtyard for summertime productions. He left Milwaukee in

Marquette band joins parade honoring Milwaukee Braves. File 105.

1965. Nine years later, the Helfaer Theater opened, a stone's throw but a far cry from The Crow's Nest atop Johnston Hall.[57]

ATHLETICS

Decidedly less successful was the varsity football team. The mediocrity of the immediate postwar years plagued the Marquette eleven after the hiring of Lisle Blackbourn in 1949. As the team struggled on the field, the athletic board tried to justify the cost of athletic scholarships, an obligation made more onerous by rising tuition rates. More than once, the board considered sizable cutbacks in the athletic program. On the other hand, it also considered asking donors to support the lettermen. Caution prevailed, however, after William Conley (Father O'Donnell's "educational assistant") advised the board that the North Central Association probably would find this last suggestion academically unsound. So the administration took a completely different approach. In late 1955, the board replaced Conrad Jennings, the school's only athletic director in its history, with Laurence (Moon) Mullins, who came to Milwaukee from Kansas State. About a year later, Mullins negotiated a lease with the County Board of Supervisors to use Milwaukee County Stadium for the football team's home games. Mullins wanted to lure the region's football fanatics to the area's finest sports facility, still a relatively new stadium. The Green Bay Packers, facing similar attendance problems back home, adopted the same strategy. The County-Marquette contract was signed before the 1957 season. A prescient stipulation in the final agreement stated that should the Milwaukee Braves baseball team make the World Series in 1957, the Marquette football team would use the university's stadium on days when there might be a scheduling conflict. Not only did the Braves play in the series, they defeated the detested New York Yankees in seven games, winning the final contest at home. (At the university, an O'Hara Hall memorandum authorized supervisors to allow their employees to listen to the games on radio as long as the volume did not interfere with work.) While the streets of Milwaukee sang with joyous tumult in the days following the Braves' victory, Marquette's football team maintained a low profile in 1957 with its second winless season in a row. Its losing streak now reached twenty games over three seasons. The 1958 team broke the losing spell by winning two (of ten) games. Attendance during 1957's four home games totaled 31,044 in a facility that held nearly 50,000. In the following year, attendance at three home games slipped to 27,756. (Film footage and photographs taken during these games capture nearly empty stands.) So in 1959 the team returned to the university's stadium.[58]

The attendance problem was evident to everyone. In 1954, the *Marquette Tribune* investigated whether the lethargic performance of the football team resulted from a lack of "'enthusiasm or desire'" among students. Four years later, Bob Harlan (then sports editor of the *Tribune* and recently retired president of the Green Bay Packers) questioned whether "one of the best scholastic schools in the country" needed "big-time football" since it came at a price to individual student-athletes. Later in the same year, an editorial echoed this perspective when it observed that the students seemed uninterested, the alumni preoccupied with a "big-time football status," and the central administration in charge of everything.[59]

Within days after another dismal season in 1960 and after consultation with other Jesuit schools that had dropped football for similar reasons, Father John Holbrook, chairman of the athletic board, announced on December 9, 1960, that both football and track would be discontinued as varsity sports. The administration took this action only two days after the athletic board, on a four-to-three vote, recommended discontinuing the two programs. Football had incurred a $50,000 deficit and track a shortfall of $18,000. The administration explained that it had come to this decision quickly so that the coaches could find other jobs, the players could transfer to other schools in a timely manner, and recruiting could be curtailed immediately. Lisle Blackbourn, who had returned as coach after a stint with the Packers, was permitted to complete the remaining year of his contract. Athletic director Laurence Mullins lost his job the following year.

Although he was coincidentally out of town when the decision was announced, Father O'Donnell never flinched from defending his approval of this decision: non-academic activities were not going to operate on a deficit basis. He was not going to spend hundreds of hours on the road, trying to raise $30 million for The Greater Marquette Plan, and be vulnerable to questions regarding a fiscally unsound sports program. Unlike in 1912, there was no room for an appeal this time. Reactions among

1960 football team. Oversize file

students were surprisingly mixed, with some aghast and outraged, others willing to accept the decision as a reasonable decision, and yet another group preoccupied with Varsity Varieties and pre-Christmas exams. Several hundred students did charge down Wisconsin Avenue toward the courthouse and then reversed direction, heading back to the athletic building (the smaller of the Plankinton houses). Police restrained the crowd at points, arresting at least four individuals. Father Thomas Stemper, dean of men, failed to stop the protesters this time. But the demonstration lost its steam after Coach Blackbourn shrugged his shoulders when the protestors charged into his office. A "Football Forum," published in an early January 1961 issue of the *Tribune*, suggested that the student reaction remained divided at best.[60]

Also divided was the initial response to a new nickname for the university's sports teams. In 1953, the homecoming committee looked into the possibility of adopting a different moniker. The 1954 homecoming committee revisited the issue, an initiative that received the blessing of the administration, the athletic board and, ultimately, the student senate. Among the original words to replace Hilltoppers were Apostles, Explorers, Missionaries, Padres, Pères, Pilots, and a host of terms associated with Native American culture. When the word Warrior was first announced in the late spring of 1954, a *Marquette Tribune* editorial suggested it had been imposed by factions within the student body, especially the homecoming committee and the student government. The essay insisted that this nickname had not been accepted by the average student who asked why the Hilltopper—with its rich tradition—had been tossed aside in such a cavalier manner. By the following fall, the student body accommodated itself to the new nickname, although some continued to question the process. Seven years later, in March 1961, a fiberglass mascot, with the cartoonish image of a Native American named Willie Wampum, became tied to the Warrior moniker after a campus-wide naming contest. Also, during these years, the university cautiously broke with tradition and approved the first female cheerleaders. In January 1958, after reviewing what other Catholic universities had done on this matter, the administration permitted women to serve as cheerleaders as long as their uniforms consisted of high-necked sweaters and long skirts.[61]

CHANGE AT THE TOP

By 1962, "Red" O'Donnell, the kid from down the hill on Clybourn Street, was into his fourteenth year as Marquette's chief executive—the longest term in school history. In mid-February, he rose from his seat at the center of the head table in the Jesuit refectory, stepped to one side, and was replaced by Father William F. Kelley. In a move unique for Marquette, O'Donnell remained in Milwaukee, becoming the university's first chancellor. From this post, he could continue to oversee The Greater Marquette Plan.[62]

As for his replacement, William Kelley was born in Madison in 1914 and moved to Milwaukee's Story Hill community as a youngster. His father was a successful lumberman. Kelley attended Holy Cross Parish School until enrolling at Marquette University High School, from which he graduated in 1931 (the same year that Edward O'Donnell completed his course work at the university). These two young men from nearby Milwaukee neighborhoods met later that year in Florissant, Missouri, at St. Stanislaus Seminary, as novices in the Society of Jesus. Kelley subsequently earned both undergraduate and graduate degrees from Saint Louis University and obtained additional training in philosophy and theology before his ordination in 1944. Kelley's provincial then selected him for advanced training in higher education. The young priest was about to start his doctoral studies at the University of Chicago when the professor he intended to study with suddenly departed for a sabbatical leave. At the last minute, the provincial arranged to get Kelley into the University of Minnesota, where he completed his doctorate in 1950. He then started a series of assignments at Creighton University in Omaha, first as assistant to the president for public relations, then as dean of the College of Arts and Sciences, and finally as academic vice president. Kelley's next move was into the president's office in O'Hara Hall.[63]

Like his predecessor, Kelley understood that travel would consume a great deal of his time. (Because he preferred to go by rail rather than by air, Kelley maintained free passes on four railroad lines.) While on the road, the new president came to appreciate the benefits gained from Father O'Donnell's many years of "warming up the people who could give" to the university. Unlike his two predecessors, Kelley had not attended Marquette, but he felt fortified in soliciting support from donors because, as he later remarked, he was not "bluffing." Asking for financial support was "never easy," he observed, "but it wasn't impossible at all" because Marquette University had "living examples walking around in the hospitals as doctors and dentists and lawyers, all through Wisconsin." Given the frequency of fund raising events on his weekly calendar, the new executive tried to emulate his predecessor by finding the right people to care for the university during his absence. Kelley came to rely heavily upon Roy Kallenberger and Seb Helfer. Likewise, he drew upon advice from the board of governors because he believed these corporate leaders were "content to help … out and give the best knowledge they had from their experience, but I don't think they were yearning to run the university." For his chief academic lieutenant, Kelley replaced Father Drummond with a Jesuit from the College of Liberal Arts: John P. Raynor. A native of Omaha, Raynor had come to Milwaukee only two years earlier as a member of the education department. This choice would have a lasting impact upon the university.[64]

If change was in the air throughout the late fifties and early sixties, it was accomplished in an orderly fashion under the direction of "a steady hand," according to the *Marquette Tribune* in its depiction of the O'Donnell years. For the first time since the 1920s, the central administration controlled the timing of administrative reorganizations, property acquisitions, academic initiatives, and changes in student life, although powerful outside forces were threatening to disrupt this sense of control. These social and political pressures gained strength during the remainder of the1960s, ultimately imposing dynamic adjustments that tested America's national fabric.[65]

8

NEW DIRECTIONS AND POWERFUL DISRUPTIONS
1962-71

An avalanche of student unrest collided with governance issues to distinguish the late sixties at Marquette from the relative calm of the preceding decade. The significant but paced advances of the fifties, guided by the university's self-analysis, contrasted markedly with the unrelenting pressures of the next two decades. American college students in the late sixties refused to abide by the in loco parentis restrictions imposed upon previous generations. Rules were made to be questioned as well as broken. By the mid-seventies, neither America nor Marquette were the same. The nature of American higher education, from curriculum to contact with the local community, was thoroughly redefined. Each year during the late 1960s seemed to generate its own palette of unrest, with challenges at every level of authority from the nuclear family to O'Hara Hall to the White House.

CONTINUED PHYSICAL OVERHAUL

During the opening years of the sixties, before external forces introduced turmoil to the campus, Marquette's central administration went about its business of completing the physical plant's transformation. New construction focused upon classroom buildings and laboratories, especially for the natural sciences. A decisive moment came in 1965 during Father O'Donnell's visit at C. Frederic (Todd) Wehr's Libertyville, Illinois, estate. At one point while touring the property, the steel magnate turned to his guest (at the time Father O'Donnell was university chancellor, with responsibility to nurture potential donors) and asked how much it would cost to erect a new building at Marquette. Two million dollars, the Jesuit calmly replied. The conversation drifted off to other matters but several weeks later, Wehr returned to his earlier line of questioning, explaining that he wanted to honor his family, perhaps with a building for engineering. Father O'Donnell steered him toward the natural sciences, emphasizing research facilities and endowed professorships. Shortly thereafter, the university excitedly announced a gift of $2.2 million. Over the next eight years, portions of Wehr's money coupled with funds from The Greater Marquette Program and with government loans underwrote what became known as the Wehr Science Center. This three-building complex included a life sciences building (completed in 1962, three years before Wehr's gift but renamed to honor his family), the six-story Todd Wehr Chemistry building (occupied in 1966), and the William Wehr Physics building (named after Todd's brother and finished in 1973). This investment of nearly $8 million in the basic sciences represented Marquette's response to the Soviet Union's launch of Sputnik I (the world's first artificial satellite) in October 1957 and America's subsequent stampede to provide adequate

Wehr Science Center, with Life Science building at the rear on the right, the chemistry building on the left and the physics building to the right. File 313.

science education to protect the country's future. President John F. Kennedy fanned these flames with his promise to place a man on the moon by the end of the sixties.[1]

In the same year as Father O'Donnell's rewarding stroll with Todd Wehr, the university also announced plans for a "round library," part of an effort to upgrade the research facilities for the law school. Ground was broken in May 1967, and when completed, this curvilinear addition at the back of Sensenbrenner Hall cost $635,000. Within days of the law school's announcement, the administration unveiled plans for a language building on land southwest of the Gesu parish school and east of 14th Street. Seen as the first installment of a communication arts complex (similar to the Wehr Science Center), the language facility was expected to stand alongside a new home for the School of Journalism as well as a performing arts theater. Ground was broken for the $2 million language building in the spring of 1968; it was dedicated in April 1970. The trustees turned over naming rights to the president, who chose to honor Father Stanislaus Lalumiere, making this the third building named for the revered Jesuit. (The first had been General Winkler's residence—later O'Hara Hall—and the second a frame house on Michigan Street.) With its distinctive floor-to-ceiling "fisheye" windows and white stucco siding, this latest incarnation of Lalumiere Hall housed the sociology, anthropology, and political science programs as well as the foreign language department. As a reflection of the times, the administration permitted the students to determine the positioning of the building's north-facing sidewalks. Patterns of student-use determined the need for diagonal walkways northeast toward Carpenter Hall and the business administration building and northwest toward Brooks Memorial Union and the library.[2]

About the same time that the Lalumiere Hall project kicked off, a federal grant of nearly $500,000 permitted library administrators to address the growing need for additional space. With the development of three large residence halls, hundreds of students clamored for round-the-clock study areas. After decades of inadequate facilities in Johnston Hall, Bellarmine Hall, Canisius Hall, and other sites, the university's book collection had finally found a permanent home in Memorial Library in 1953. In the new addition, completed in 1971, Memorial Library's original design in the form of a cross was "filled in" at its corners. And just as the unexpected availability of federal funds facilitated the library addition, so did the appearance of a new donor gift crystallize the hazy dreams of a theater arts building (as part of the communications complex). Evan Helfaer, founder of Lakeside Laboratories and a valued university supporter, offered $1.6 million in 1972 to underwrite a facility that would replace *Teatro Maria*.[3]

Although academic construction tended to dominate this era, three projects, all initiated in 1964, addressed the ongoing shortage of student residences. Aging apartment buildings (including Nicolas, Bonifas, and Marian halls) had provided short-term solutions to the housing crunch. In early 1964, the university committed $800,000 to add two stories to Schroeder Hall, increasing its capacity from 590 to 750. Marquette administrators also purchased the La Salle Hotel, an eight-story building on Eleventh

LaSalle Hotel, later Cobeen Hall. File 335.

Street. This hotel, whose first floor lounge once featured performers such as Nat King Cole, was transformed into Cobeen Hall, a women's dormitory, at the pricey sum of $2.2 million. Upon completion of this renovation, the university shuttered Alumnae House, Lissette Lodge, and Xavier Hall. And just as the 1963-64 school year drew to a close, the university completed acquisition of an L-shaped strip of land near the northeast corner of Sixteenth and Wisconsin. By the following fall, federal authorities agreed to underwrite a twelve-story men's dormitory on the property. Construction of what was designated Dormitory #1 was delayed, however, as the university struggled to purchase the Louisiana Apartments, whose presence at the corner of this intersection presented design problems, specifically, how to build around it. Finally, in May 1966, demolition of the Louisiana apartments began and sixteen months later, as students prepared to move into the first six floors of Dormitory #1, law school alumnus and longtime university supporter Victor McCormick promised $2.5 million to the university, the institution's largest single gift to date. In appreciation for this beneficence and for his earlier purchase of a practice field for the football team, the university named the new residence hall in his honor. A year later, the school bestowed the title Founder of Marquette University upon Victor McCormick, an honor whose only other recipient was Todd Wehr.[4]

Two significant but unplanned additions to the campus were the Joan of Arc Chapel and a carillon. In July 1964, Marc B. Rojtman, a former Milwaukee industrialist then living in New York, donated a stone chapel thought to have been used by St. Joan of Arc in 1429. The daughter of renowned railroad magnate James J. Hill (who,

Dormitory #1, later McCormick Hall. File 915.

*On Michigan Street behind Gesu church & Johnston Hall are Jogues Hall on left
& second incarnation of Lalumiere Hall on right.* File 779.

Father Raynor blessing carillon. File 295.

coincidentally, had contributed to Marquette' first building campaign in 1916) had originally brought the chapel to the United States in 1927. Purchased in France, the chapel had been dismantled piece by piece and then reassembled on Long Island. Mr. and Mrs. Rojtman purchased this estate in 1962 and made a gift of the chapel to Marquette. Stone by stone, the 50-foot by 19-foot chapel was once again taken apart and shipped, this time to Milwaukee, where a cement foundation had been poured in a parking lot near Bonifas Hall. Reassembly began during the summer of 1965. Jogues and Lalumiere halls, two ramshackle houses west of Drexel Lodge, were torn down, and their foundations dislodged, crushed, and used as part of the facing for the new mall where the five-hundred-year-old chapel came to rest. Its dedication in May 1966 featured a procession led by the Marquette Players dressed in fifteenth-century costumes and a spokesman from the French embassy in Washington. The installation of a carillon in October 1967 enhanced the audile qualities of the campus. Hung in the Science Hall bell tower, these forty-eight bells (cast in France) were donated to Marquette by Mrs. John C. Dwan, a member of the board of regents.[5]

One downside of this buy-demolish-build era was the closure of a Jesuit ministry that predated the university in the Tory Hill neighborhood. Built in 1899, the Gesu parish school, occupying 62,000 square feet of land, had educated thousands of neighborhood children through boom and bust, two world wars, a depression, and a thorough transformation of Milwaukee's west side. By the mid-sixties, however, Marquette

Tory Hill neighborhood extends from upper left corner to lower right corner. To the far left is the original Red Arrow Park and behind Gesu, across Michigan Street, is St. Catherine's Home for Working Girls. File 209.

Central (later Marquette) Interchange, under construction, 1968. Tory Hill neighborhood has been removed. Copus Hall & Gesu parish school at center of photograph. File 895

administrators had their sights set on this property. Enrollment at the grade school had dwindled nearly 50 percent, from 435 students in 1939 to 234 in 1964. The demolition of the Tory Hill neighborhood inexorably hastened the migration of central city Catholics to the western edges of the city and into the suburbs. First the east-west expressway and then the north-south expressway (with its central interchange) destroyed hundreds of homes, replacing a vibrant residential community with an elevated curtain of concrete. Through real estate transactions in 1893, 1894, 1911, and 1944, Marquette had gained possession of both the school and the nuns' convent on Fourteenth Street. Edgy conversations in 1965 appraised the school's future in light of the university's master plan. Father James Corrigan, pastor of Gesu, pleaded for a revitalization of the parish school. Father Kelley fired back, asking tough questions regarding student numbers and the long-range intentions of the Sisters of Charity, instructors at the school since its opening. Sensing that the school's future was in doubt and facing staffing issues of their own, the sisters announced in early 1967 that they would no longer teach at Gesu after June 1968. Vague plans for a new Catholic school at Thirteenth and Kilbourn never materialized. Within months of the Gesu school's closing, the city began hounding the university to demolish the abandoned building. Wrecking companies eagerly bid to formally end Gesu's seven decades as a center of parochial education in Milwaukee.[6]

GOVERNMENTAL PARTNERS

Wrecking balls suspended from towering cranes became a common sight on the western edge of downtown Milwaukee during the fifties, sixties, and seventies. The primary benefactor of these demolitions was Marquette University. Land parcels were acquired and then followed by the demolition of mansions, coach houses, cottages, garages, gas stations, and mom-and-pop businesses. These vacant lots usually became temporary, makeshift parking lots until funds could be found for academic or residence halls. Slowly—much too slowly for university administrators—the near west side was remade and a discernible college campus began to unfold south of Wisconsin Avenue.

An unexpected partner in this era of tear down/build-up was the federal government. Beginning with the construction loan for O'Donnell Hall, Washington bureaucrats helped underwrite Marquette's master plan. Schroeder Hall, even before its two-story addition, carried a debt to the U.S. government in the form of a forty-year loan for $2.5 million at 2.75 percent. The chemistry building carried a loan of $1,634,000 for thirty years at 3.75 percent. (It also benefitted from a government grant of $700,000.) McCormick Hall was funded by a $3.7 million loan over fifty years at 3 percent. Lalumiere Hall was built with the aid of a $725,000 loan and a $562,000 grant. In each case, the university's direct expenditure was less than half of the total cost. By the late sixties, the university had spent nearly $4 million on its six largest projects and the federal government had invested $11 million through loans and grants. After decades of being on the opposite side of the church-state divide, Washington, D.C. suddenly became a generous provider of capital improvements at Marquette. In the absence of a sizable endowment, the university eagerly embraced this new friend. Then, unexpectedly, a different level of government—the city of Milwaukee, with no legacy of cooperation with Milwaukee's Jesuit university—became another partner.[7]

The 1949 National Housing Act, the country's most momentous piece of housing legislation in its history, envisioned a future in which every American family would be adequately sheltered. Public housing provided one avenue to realize this ambition. Another strategy involved redevelopment of what were designated blighted neighborhoods, especially those located near central business districts. To federal and local authorities, landscapes filled with aging, crumbling structures signified stagnation and economic decline. So municipal housing authorities were encouraged to draw upon their powers of eminent domain to acquire slum properties at market prices (with federal funds) and then to remove decrepit buildings (also with federal funds) before offering this vacant land to private developers. Entire neighborhoods were sacrificed for what was perceived to be the greater good. Thousands of families were displaced with promises of replacement housing—much of which was never built. Over the years, Congress repeatedly amended the 1949 housing act, increasing the allowable percentage of retail and commercial—that is, profitable—elements (such as convention centers, sports arenas, and shopping centers) at each site. The goal of decent housing for every American family languished as elected officials authorized more and more acres to be used in for-profit ventures. Educational institutions, however, were specifically proscribed from participation in urban renewal projects.

Marquette administrators had frequently complained about the costly process of accumulating parcels of sufficient size to construct dormitories and classrooms. When the city considered its own Red Arrow renewal project in 1957 (Red Arrow Park was located on a small parcel of land at Eleventh and Wisconsin), Father O'Donnell sent representatives to meet with Mayor Frank Zeidler, hoping that the school's ambitions might dovetail with the city's plans for the area. Zeidler rebuffed these visitors, explaining that federal law prevented Milwaukee from acting in the manner requested. Later when university officials shared blueprints of an "ultra-modern campus" with the faculty, administrators warned that these plans were only pipedreams unless land could be acquired quickly and inexpensively. As with many urban universities, Marquette had started well beyond the city's nineteenth-century downtown—in this case, on the hilltop. A century later, the central business district had enveloped the university. Meanwhile the local infrastructure had deteriorated and with it the quality of life.

Everything changed, however, ten years after the housing act of 1949. Section 112 of housing legislation Congress passed in 1959 reversed previous prohibitions against the participation of educational institutions and permitted urban renewal expenditures "for land acquisition, demolition, and relocation" by colleges and universities in collaboration with local authorities. The land in question had to be "adjacent to, or in the immediate vicinity" of the university. The property obtained through these grants had to "be retained for redevelopment or rehabilitation by the educational institution … for educational uses." The governmental body designated to oversee the acquisition and clearing of this land was the local municipality.[8]

At Father O'Donnell's direction, Roy Kallenberger and his assistant, Seb Helfer, prepared a campus master plan based on the school's history, objectives, and financial capabilities as well as current educational trends. In the process, the university's urban character was reaffirmed. For the third and last time, university officials decisively dismissed the notion of fleeing to the suburbs. Instead the master plan anticipated using Section 112 to provide for parking, academic facilities, and housing and recreational space for students. In March 1962, the board of trustees approved Kallenberger's outline for the future. The plan followed by one year the city council's decision to work with both the University of Wisconsin-Milwaukee and Marquette to augment "Milwaukee's pre-eminence as a higher educational center" through the 1959 housing act. On May 24, 1962, a new university president (Father Kelley), a relatively new mayor (Henry Maier elected in 1960), and their aides met in Brooks Memorial Union to discuss long-range campus improvements. One week later, Kelley formally asked Milwaukee to apply for federal urban renewal funds to redevelop the area from Clybourn to Wisconsin between Eleventh and Seventeenth streets as an academic zone, and the area from Wisconsin to Kilbourn as a mixture of parking, student housing, and university recreational facilities. The plan called for Washington to provide $11.2 million of the $15 million needed to acquire properties that the university did not already own

Aerial of Marquette neighborhood, looking south, before construction of I-94 from west. University buildings are numbered. Note Thirteenth Street as principal entranceway into Menomonee Valley. File 209

and to clear them for future development. The remaining $4 million (the local share of the project) would be covered by a credit of $3.2 million earned by Marquette's own investments during the preceding five years and, possibly, by $800,000 from the city. Milwaukee's portion, however, was expected to be reduced once the university purchased this cleared land from the city. The Marquette proposal was typical of urban renewal plans across the country.[9]

Two days after Father Kelley's formal request, the local alderman introduced a resolution authorizing the city's cooperation. Two city council committees held separate hearings later that month. WITI-TV, Channel 6, endorsed the plan, calling Marquette "a great asset to our city." A year later, station executives re-endorsed the plan in a second editorial. Eventually, the *Milwaukee Journal* lent its editorial support. On July 24, 1962, a unanimous common council approved the Marquette project and the mayor offered his support two days later. Enthusiasm swept the campus as expectations exceeded the realities of working within political bureaucracies. Seven months passed before the city delivered the "survey and planning" application to the regional urban renewal office in Chicago on the last day of February 1963. That July, the state legislature offered an unexpected assist when it stopped all new construction in the Marquette urban renewal zone. The common council passed a similar resolution. The intent of these laws was to block enhancements that might make federal authorities question the level of blight in the project area. These resolutions stopped the Catholic Knights Insurance Company (which was operating on its own time frame and for its own purposes) from moving ahead with plans to build a new high-rise at Eleventh and Wells to replace the recently sold Tower Hotel. The day after the state's intervention, federal authorities approved the survey and planning application and made $220,687 available for a study of Milwaukee's renewal area.[10]

Nearly a year passed before the city submitted the actual "loan and grant" segment of the project to federal authorities on May 22, 1964. Two and half months later, the Chicago regional office approved the proposal, forwarding it to the commissioner of urban renewal in Washington; he gave his conditional approval in mid-September, reserving $7,819,830 for the project. According to an account written by a Marquette insider, the entire "process took 4 years, three ulcers, 2 black eyes, 8 tons of patience and 3 novenas." Four months after federal approval, the Milwaukee Redevelopment Authority offered unanimous support for phase one. Additional hearings were held before the land commission and two city committees. Finally, on January 26, 1965, the full common council voted 17-0 to approve the first phase—exactly 960 days after Father Kelley's original announcement. (Within two weeks of the council's action, the university submitted its application for phase two.) The federal government provided final approval to the first phase on July 1, 1966, and by March 1967, the city and university signed the initial land contracts. The university paid $3,653,330 for about thirty-five acres of land whose market price was between $12.5 and $13.5 million. A second set of acquisitions took place in December 1968, and over the next twenty years, additional phases unfolded uneventfully, with one notable exception that will be discussed in Chapter Nine.[11]

THE VARIOUS PLAYERS

The masterminds behind this complex effort were Roy Kallenberger and Seb Helfer. A balding pipe-smoker in his forties, Kallenberger served as the university's director of physical plant in the sixties. He oversaw a small army of one hundred repair, maintenance, and general custodial staff. Between earning two engineering degrees at Marquette, Kallenberger had served in the navy during World War II. His second floor office in Drexel Lodge was layered in maps, building designs, and mounds of paperwork. His partner, Seb Helfer, returned to his alma mater in 1961 as a project planner. A graduate of the civil engineering department, Helfer was Marquette's point man with government officials. Decades later, Father Kelley still spoke highly of both men's talents and contributions.[12]

Kallenberger and Helfer needed to keep the government officials on track. They also needed to keep opponents at bay. In the beginning, a few local property owners refused to surrender their homes to the city and a landlord's association briefly objected to the project, fearing an increase in property taxes if so much land was removed from the tax rolls. Neighboring hospitals, in particular Mount Sinai, worried that they might have trouble improving their facilities because of the state and local freezes on construction. And Congressman Henry Reuss, usually a reliable friend of Marquette, questioned whether Milwaukee's west side was truly blighted as Congress had defined it in the

Roy Kallenberger on left and Seb Helfer on right. File 645.

1949 housing act. Anticipating expansion, the university had hired a real estate firm in the mid-fifties to photograph every piece of property in the nearby neighborhood not owned by Marquette. Snapshots of taverns, union halls, frame houses, mom-and-pop grocery stores, luncheon shops, and more taverns produced an album of buildings that would likely have been replaced in ten to twenty years regardless of urban renewal timetables. In light of how the words blight and slums were abused by metropolitan planners across the country in the fifties and sixties, the Marquette neighborhood was representative of mixed-use communities—usually adjacent to central business districts—that were replaced by freeways, sports stadia, shopping malls, and public housing projects. Why not by a university campus?[13]

To offset possible resistance within the general citizenry, Marquette's public relations staff asked one thousand individuals in late 1963 what they thought of the university. Responses provided exactly what the staff wanted: great respect for the university's contributions to Milwaukee and strong support for the school's urban renewal program. Although conclusive from Marquette's perspective, the survey had almost no effect upon elected officials. This exercise may have been too transparent.[14]

The most serious threats to the project came from three sources, including two Catholic institutions. As noted above, the Catholic Knights Insurance Company felt betrayed when state and city "no construction" zones blocked its plans for a high-rise at Eleventh and Wells. However, once the Marquette project had been approved in Washington, the papers signed in Milwaukee, and property acquisitions completed

Marquette neighborhood, south of Michigan Street, designated as blighted. File 255

over the next few years, opposition to additional improvements in the renewal zone diminished. Eventually, a new Catholic Knights building was built. Owners of St. Catherine's Home for Working Girls on Michigan Street across from Bellarmine Hall also had problems with the urban renewal project. The Sisters of Mercy provided lodging for unmarried, out-of-town, working women in a four-story apartment building that could hardly be described as blighted. The nuns earnestly worked to convince Marquette administrators (just as Gesu's pastor had) that their facility was compatible with the campus master plan. They too were unsuccessful. When the city made an offer to purchase the property, the nuns turned it down. University officials, especially Father Raymond McAuley, were troubled by a public spat between two respected Catholic institutions. Even more painful was the fact that several directors on St. Catherine's board were friends of the university. Seeking some middle ground, Marquette offered to substitute its option to purchase the Abbot Crest Hotel on Wisconsin Avenue in favor of the Sisters of Mercy or to assist in arranging a $500,000 loan to build at a new location. Eventually, the nuns obtained funding that allowed them to relocate the residence to Knapp Street on Milwaukee's east side.[15]

The principal non-Catholic group to protest the project was Protestants and Other Americans United for the Separation of Church and State (POAU), a national organization. This group included the Marquette project in a defamatory pamphlet that singled out Jesuits as manipulators who "ingratiated themselves with urban renewal officials" to insure "land grabs for ambitious Jesuit designs." Fordham and Saint Louis universities as well as Marquette were singled out for their "theft" of public property. The Marquette "case study" identified a "Fr. Henry McAnulty" as the university president who fraternized with the director of city redevelopment, permitting the school to gain "62 acres" free of charge. Silly inaccuracies regarding the president's name and the size of the project reflected on the publication's credibility. The annoyance that these inflammatory complaints generated was revealed in a heated letter sent by the urban renewal commissioner in Washington to POAU's executive director. In it, the federal official offered examples of court decisions upholding the use of government funds to assist sectarian institutions and cited examples of projects in the District of Columbia in which "Lutheran, Methodist, Baptist, Presbyterian, Catholic, and Bethel Tabernacle Pentecostal churches" had land made available to them. This distraction blew over in about five months.[16]

ABRUPT LEADERSHIP CHANGES

After Father O'Donnell became president in 1948, he developed a respectful association with the university's board of governors, a powerful group of corporate leaders favored by his predecessor, Peter Brooks. Until their deaths in the 1950s, men such as Frank Sensenbrenner and Harry Johnston had remained O'Donnell's confidants. But with their passing, O'Donnell turned to on-campus associates such as Father Drummond, Frank Casey, and Roy Kallenberger. The president limited the board of governors and a second group, the president's advisory council, to special projects such as fund-raising and long-term planning. He left academic policy, student life, and facilities development to his vice-presidents and administrative colleagues.

When Father Kelley assumed the presidency in 1962, he respectfully worked with his predecessor's board of governors but clearly preferred his own slate of advisors. Consequently, in March 1964, he elevated the board of governors en masse to "an honorary capacity" and replaced it with a board of regents, using terminology Father Fox had originally introduced in the 1920s. Kelley appointed seventeen men—and, notably, one woman—as regents. (The number was later increased to twenty-four.) For the first time, there were fixed, three-year terms. Regents were "to furnish the president of the university with an insight into the community, and the management skills and the economic counsel of a forum of distinguished citizens." The group established four working committees: finance, academic affairs, student affairs, and university relations. Although regents were to "take an active role in policy-making," the group's bylaws cautioned them that the board would "'not infringe on the responsibilities of the university board of trustees,' the legal entity of Marquette under its articles of incorporation." (At that moment, Fathers Kelley, McAuley, and Raynor served as trustees.) The board originally selected Norman R. Klug from the Miller Brewing Company as chairman, although he was soon replaced by George B. Hunt of the Milwaukee Dustless Brush Company. Mrs. John C. Dwan, who had donated the university carillon, was the first woman to hold such a prestigious office in school history. Ties to the Johnston family were maintained by including of Humphrey Desmond, Harry Johnston's son-in-law and publisher of the archdiocesan newspaper (a position he inherited from his father). Also serving on this board were executives from Gimbel Brothers department store, First Wisconsin National Bank, Northwestern Mutual Life Insurance Company, Marine National Exchange Bank, Marshall & Ilsley Bank, Allis-Chalmers Corporation, Joseph Schlitz Brewing Company, Pabst Brewing Company, and the Milwaukee Road.[17]

In the late summer of 1965, following widespread speculation within the Jesuit community, Marquette's academic vice president, John P. Raynor, succeeded Father Kelley as president. The provincial reassigned Kelley to oversee a national study of America's twenty-eight Jesuit colleges and universities. (The former president later moved to Creighton University where he spent many years in the development office.) With a school year about to start, the September 9 announcement caught the university community, if not the Jesuits, by surprise. Kelley's tenure in office—just over three and a half years—had been the shortest since early in the century. Historically, lay faculty had acquiesced to the provincial's choice of a president without a murmur. But from the moment of his arrival in Milwaukee, Father Kelley struggled to gain acceptance. He replaced a beloved leader (Father O'Donnell) who had elevated the status (and salaries) of the faculty during his fourteen years in office. Under O'Donnell, the university self-analysis and its academic blueprint had heralded a rejuvenated Marquette University, an institution that increasingly valued its lay faculty. Father Kelley had completed many of his predecessor's long-term plans for the school, but never received credit for putting his own stamp on these improvements. Even the building boom of the early sixties appeared to be little more than the fulfillment of his predecessor's ambitions.[18]

Beyond the point of whether he was as beloved as "Red" O'Donnell, the neighborhood rascal, William Kelley created his own problems. In an April 21, 1962, front page article in the *Marquette Tribune*, the new executive was cited for a 1950 article in which he had praised the motivations of "religious teachers" over that of "any other group of teachers." One week later, he delivered his first major address, in Washington, D.C. before the John Carroll Society. Seeking to counter critics (including *Time* magazine) who devalued Marquette's educational product because of the size of its student body, Kelley inadvertently denigrated the school's academic integrity (and the alumni's children) by insisting that "the mass production of intelligent followers" was "a good and solid function of a Catholic university." He spoke of the "hundreds and hundreds and hundreds of just solid, decent men and women working industriously and devotedly with their Marquette education to support handsome, and sometimes not so handsome, children [whom] they are leading along the ways of citizenship and morality and religion." "What have these ordinary educated people contributed in the way of 'ideas,' to the world of the intellect?" he asked. "Perhaps the answer lies here," he offered: "[W]e cannot all indulge ourselves in new ideas, new frontiers, constant voyaging to outer space. Someone has to hold the fort; prosaically, someone must be left to take care of the store." He repeated his earlier remark about Marquette graduates taking their lead from others: "And what of America's need for great Catholic intellectual leaders[?] I think that we might well ask with equal right where we are to procure the large numbers we need of Catholic intellectual followers. Every one cannot be … straining … for a scientific or cultural break-through…. Let us remember that if there are no followers, there can be no leaders." (Italics added in each instance.)

Kelley proceeded to explain that Johns Hopkins University and Harvard University, Massachusetts Institute of Technology and California Institute of Technology were not representative institutions: "What I am saying is that there is quite a considerable volume of splendid college education being provided for the preponderance of American young people that are not primarily research institutes." Critics of institutions that do not emphasize research, he suggested, do a disservice by focusing on "one facet of higher education, namely what they call the production of 'intellectuals.'" The only positive remark that Kelley offered on behalf of Catholic education referenced the replacement of "run-down, moldy, rather seedy looking plants of the earliest days in Catholic colleges" with "refreshing landscaped areas, dotted with well-planned buildings in integrated lay-outs."[19]

The president's designation of Marquette graduates as "followers" probably annoyed any alumnus who heard about the speech, but his dismissal of the university's intellectual stature and aspirations deeply rankled the faculty who certainly learned of his remarks. It is likely that Father Kelley had chosen this moment early in his presidency at a leading Catholic university to interject his own thoughts into the firestorm of debate triggered by John Tracy Ellis's 1955 speech before the Catholic Commission on Intellectual and Cultural Affairs (a speech that was later widely circulated as an essay). A renowned historian at Catholic University in Washington, D.C., Father Ellis carefully considered "the paucity of scholars of distinction" within Catholic America and the "impoverishment of Catholic scholarship in this country." He conceded that external forces had proscribed the development of great minds among American Catholics: poverty, anti-Catholic prejudice, and "even illiteracy." But he was equally blunt in his rebuke of the Church's self-imposed limitations which included the "lack of serious reading habits [among the faithful]," the hierarchy's inadequate "encouragement [of] intellectual concerns," and "the absence of a love of scholarship for its own sake." Because of its refusal to embrace an "intellectual apostolate," Catholic higher education by the mid-fifties perpetuated "mediocrity," Ellis concluded. Catholic education was a sad runner-up to its better financed, more ambitious secular counterparts. While he conceded the "danger of intellectual pride," Ellis warned of the opposite evil, "intellectual sloth." The reaction among American bishops and some Catholic educators over the next decade was downright hostile, hostile not only to Ellis's interpretations but also to his intentions. Six years after this speech, at Marquette's baccalaureate sermon, the Vatican's apostolic delegate to the United States (the pope's representative) still warned of those who would "'digress'" from past traditions in hopes of winning admiration from "'the intellectual circles of today.'"[20]

Students in classroom, 1965. File 325.

In 1962, Father Kelley, as Marquette's new president, finally had an opportunity to offer his own rejoinder to Ellis. He chose to dismiss a decade of hard work by administrators and faculty alike, Jesuits and lay people alike, to rebuild the university's graduate program from the dust bin of 1943 (when Marquette's doctoral programs had been shut down for some of the same inadequacies Father Ellis had identified) and to develop a scholarly attitude appropriate to a doctoral-granting institution. During their days in office, Fathers O'Donnell and Drummond had pushed to have new Marquette faculty hold terminal degrees (in most instances, a PhD) and maintain academic lives devoted to scholarship. Hundreds of new faculty members, hired during the fifties and sixties, proudly labored under this expectation. Now without warning, the institution's new executive proposed a strikingly different type of mission, a mission whereby Marquette faculty trained young adults to follow cutting-edge intellectuals and scientists from other institutions. Within days of Kelley's speech, the chairman of the biology department fired off a letter to Father President, insisting that "aspiring to excellence" should be the ambition of every student "no matter what his capacity." Only "a faculty which itself aspires to excellence in all scholarly functions can expect to inspire its students and elicit from each the best of which he is capable, be it true leadership or intelligent following," he insisted. To drive home his point, the chairman quoted from the "Principles of Marquette University on Scholarship and Research," a document promulgated in 1953 under Father O'Donnell. Grumbling among the faculty over Kelley's remarks persisted for decades to come.[21]

Marquette presidents had always spoken their minds. After all, they were not only the senior administrator on campus, but also the school's academic arbiter and moral guardian. Fathers Noonan and McCarthy, in particular, felt comfortable as pastors, providing social, political, and ethical advice from the president's chair. William Kelley had received his doctorate in education from the University of Minnesota and had been trained to appreciate the "big picture" in American higher education. His attempt to counter criticism of universities (including Marquette) whose enrollments had expanded to unimagined levels touched upon the debate over what University of California Chancellor Clark Kerr had labeled the "multiversity," postwar mega-size institutions with multiple missions. But in calling for the production of followers, not frontrunners at Marquette, Kelley unwittingly besmirched the school's image, a perception that dogged him for the rest of his tenure.

A month after his speech in Washington, Kelley clashed with thirty-seven faculty members over his approval of the committee on student life's refusal to allow an on-campus speech by someone who was depicted as too controversial. Despite this decision, the president insisted that the "spirit of free inquiry" reigned on campus and that there was "no University policy to be conservative or liberal or to follow any other label or 'ism.'" He engendered additional discontent in March 1964 when a group of faculty members accused him of endorsing in a letter to the alumni an informal survey of Marquette students published in the conservative periodical *National Review*. The local chapter of the American Association of University Professors insisted that the president's choice of words suggested there was only one university position on political and religious matters. Whether the association's interpretation of the letter was fair or not, this exchange underscored the tensions that prevailed during Kelley's three and a half years in office. His gruff demeanor contrasted sharply with his predecessor's. As one Jesuit noted, Father Kelley "had the hide of a pachyderm … he wasn't at all sensitive to anyone else[;] that's why he lasted only 3 years."[22]

His replacement, Father John P. Raynor, was not a Milwaukee native. Nor did he have extensive experience at Marquette. Raynor had attended parochial schools in Omaha (including Creighton Preparatory High School) before entering the Jesuit seminary in Florissant, Missouri, in 1941. He received his first two degrees from Saint Louis University and then a doctorate in education from the University of Chicago (where Father Kelley had originally intended to go). Raynor was ordained in 1954 and spent time as a high school teacher before beginning his doctoral studies. In 1960, he came to Marquette as an instructor in the department of education. Within a short time, he became assistant to the academic vice president and in June 1962, academic vice president.

Within days of his elevation to the presidency in 1965, Father Raynor startled the university community by appointing Arthur C. Moeller, dean of the College of Engineering and a layman, to succeed him as academic vice president. As a Jesuit remarked at the time, this had "never before [been] heard of in the U.S." and "How it will work remains to be seen." Raynor clearly had his predecessor's shaky relations with the faculty in mind when he explained that his choice of Moeller indicated "'the great emphasis we place on teaching *and research* as well as our traditional *teamwork* with laymen, who make up more than 90 per cent of our total faculty.'" (Italics added.) In contrast to his predecessor's characterization of Marquette's mission, Raynor lauded the "strong, stimulating, intellectual environment" at Marquette in his first interview with the student newspaper. He repeated the words *intellectual* and *intelligent* as he called for a strong faculty that would attract "brilliant students." A month later, at a presidential convocation held at the Milwaukee Auditorium, Raynor spoke of "troubled times," "very exciting times," and "'explosive'" times. He referred to the power of computers, the nation's war on poverty, and an unprecedented level of medical research, but reminded his audience (while drawing upon philosopher Jacques Maritain) that "Man cannot adequately possess wisdom unless the understanding of God plays a central role in the integrating of his conscious life. In a university like Marquette we are educationally rich because of the theocentric orientation of our heritage."[23]

SCHOOL OF MEDICINE'S FUTURE

Father Kelley embroiled himself during his first days on campus in controversy over his definition of a Marquette education. His successor devoted himself to the task of unraveling the university's Gordian knot: the fiscal viability of its medical school. Health care in the United States changed dramatically after 1945. Medical research reached unprecedented levels in the fifties and sixties, fueled by federal funds through agencies such as the National Institutes of Health. The Salk vaccine's startling victory over polio revealed just how much public health could benefit through the right combination of vision, technology, and money. In terms of medical education, Marquette's greatest deficiency was the absence of a university hospital. Cramer Hall was adequate for lectures, but the students' clinical work (as well as the private practice of faculty members) was dispersed across the metro area. For Father Fox in the 1920s, the answer had been a $1 million teaching hospital situated on the Schandein property, but the county had chosen to maintain a small emergency hospital and dispensary on these grounds. The Great Depression followed by World War II crushed ambitions related to a university medical center.[24]

Until 1955, that is, when a multimillion dollar bequest from Kurtis R. Froedtert triggered some fresh thinking on this matter. Froedtert had originally dreamed of a medical career before taking over the family malting business. Upon his death, he left more than half of his estate "to erect, establish, maintain and operate a non-sectarian hospital in the City of Milwaukee, Wisconsin, to be known as the 'Froedtert Memorial Lutheran Hospital' … with [a] definite preference to persons of the Lutheran faith." This stipulation seemed to preclude any connection between the new medical center and Marquette. But in his last years, Froedtert developed a close friendship with Father O'Donnell, even offering the university president use of his residence in Miami Beach. Mrs. Froedtert maintained these contacts after her husband's death in late 1951. The following year, the trustees of her husband's estate approached Father O'Donnell, quizzing him on how a Lutheran hospital might be associated with the Marquette University School of Medicine. In this action, the trustees had Mrs. Froedtert's full support.

These conversations became public knowledge in early 1955. Meanwhile the Froedtert trustees proceeded very cautiously, even as the trust grew in value. Then just as they finally seemed about to locate their hospital on the county grounds in Wauwatosa and expectations of a construction date mounted, the Lutheran Men of America entered the picture. An intersynodal organization dedicated to denominational interests, the association sued to block the use of Froedtert's money by a Catholic institution. After years of litigation, the association won its point when an out-of-court settlement blocked a direct relationship between the new medical center and Marquette.[25]

Meanwhile, similar conversations regarding the future of health care in southeastern Wisconsin were taking place elsewhere in town. Both the Greater Milwaukee Committee, the area's most powerful civic organization, and the County of Milwaukee appointed panels to look into this matter. In each instance, Marquette's School of Medicine—as the area's only medical educator—was seen as a central player. On campus, however, pressures were building because the university was ultimately, if not legally, responsible for the medical school's continuing deficits. Between1948 and 1964, the School of Medicine had balanced its annual budget only three times (by amounts of $10,000, $5,000, and $20,000) in the fiscal years of 1950-52. Shortfalls of $100,000 to $425,000 were common. Operational costs at the medical school rose from $225,000 in 1948 to $1,700,000 in 1964. In Father Raynor's first year in office (1965-66), tuition income provided 45 percent of the school's revenue. The endowment offered only 1.2 percent, with organized research providing 19.4 percent. Without a quick turnaround, the medical school's problems threatened the viability of the entire institution.[26]

Father Raynor approached the board of regents in October 1966, determined to act. He reminded the group about Dean John Hirschboeck's recommendations from two years earlier. According to the dean, the medical school had four alternatives: a legal merger with Marquette University, the sale of the medical school to the University of Wisconsin, the reduction of the Marquette University School of Medicine to a "two-year preclinical school" (while the University of Wisconsin "accepted total responsibility for existing and future clinical programs"), or the creation of a medical center that would handle all aspects of education, research, and service. The medical school's board of directors clearly preferred the last. Meanwhile, the school's deficit for its most recent fiscal year had reached $761,000. Its accumulated debt to the university totaled $3,271,048 and its current budget (for 1966-67) anticipated a deficit exceeding $1 million. Father Raynor reminded the university regents that public and private committees had looked into the region's health care needs but were making excruciatingly slow progress toward a resolution. Everyone supported the idea of a modern medical center on the county grounds, with the Marquette School of Medicine overseeing the educational—and probably the research—aspects of this institution. How to pay for such a complex, how to organize its administrative structure, how to involve local businessmen, and how to access federal and state money to fund the project (without violating the walls that separated church and state) were all duly considered in a round-table of comments. Two months later at a second meeting, the regents reviewed these same options.[27]

Every party in this debate held a position on the church-state dichotomy. The Lutheran Men of America stated its case decisively in the law suit brought against the Froedtert trustees. The County of Milwaukee had opposed Marquette's involvement in delivery of its health services dating back to the Schandein episode, despite the 1948 agreement to have the medical school become a participating affiliate at the county hospital. The State of Wisconsin had serious constitutional concerns about channeling public funds to Marquette. It even considered a new school of medicine at the University of Wisconsin-Milwaukee. Everyone agreed that a teaching hospital was desperately needed to serve the state's population center. In the Jesuit community, however, the church-state divide was seen from a very different perspective, as the priests envisioned the inclusion of religion at a new Milwaukee medical center, not its exclusion. Thus their draft of the statutes of affiliation for a future medical complex included "a Department of Religion in accordance with the mind of the American Medical Association," a Department of Medical Ethics with the chairman appointed by the university, and a chaplain to oversee a Newman Center, a Catholic activity center, such as the one that existed at the University of Wisconsin.[28]

Marquette "student mall," 1975. Cramer Hall, then used by Medical College of Wisconsin, on left. Elizabeth Plankinton mansion at top, east of Fifteenth Street. File 1267.

An abrupt resolution to these various conversations came on Saturday, September 30, 1967: all legal ties between the university and the medical school were severed. The medical school's board of directors reorganized itself through a series of charter amendments. The university president who, under the previous version, had been president of the medical school corporation was now replaced by a new president, attorney Louis Quarles, who explained the reasoning behind these moves: "[T]his step represents an important advance towards the earliest possible realization of a medical center complex for southeastern Wisconsin." Hereafter, no Jesuits would serve as ex officio members of the medical school's board of directors. Fathers Raynor and McAuley immediately resigned. The election of Marquette provost John Cowee as vice president of the new corporation represented the last administrative link to the university. Dr. Gerald Kerrigan, who had replaced John Hirschboeck as dean of medicine in 1965, lauded Marquette's half-century in medical education, noting that "more than half of all Wisconsin trained physicians are Marquette graduates."[29]

When this decision was formally presented to the university's board of regents ten days later, Cowee explained that a letter had already been sent to the attorney general of the State of Wisconsin regarding the use of state tax dollars for the services supplied by the faculty of Marquette School of Medicine, Inc. The state educational committee subsequently recommended support for the new institution but insisted that Wisconsin be granted the power to appoint a majority of the new board of directors. The directors of the new medical school brushed aside this demand, noting that the Marquette School of Medicine, Inc. was now a private, non-sectarian corporation. The state acquiesced and provided desperately needed funds. In October 1969, a unanimous Wisconsin State Supreme Court approved public funding for the privately run institution, releasing more than $3 million. The medical school subsequently repaid its debt to the university. In September 1970, three years after this all started, the word Marquette was dropped from the school's title as the new corporation became the Medical College of Wisconsin. Only one issue remained: the institution's relocation to new facilities in Wauwatosa.[30]

A NEW LEADERSHIP TEAM

The resolute manner evidenced by Father Raynor in resolving the long-simmering medical school problem revealed his willingness to confront difficult issues. Unlike his predecessor, Raynor favored rapprochement with the lay faculty, preferring to follow Father O'Donnell's lead. Raynor understood that laymen and laywomen had become essential to the operation of Jesuit universities in the late twentieth century. Ignoring this reality only delayed the laity's preparation for their new roles. Rather than be merely tolerated, they had to be prepared as missionaries for Jesuit education. This meant training. It ultimately meant responsibility and responsibility implied authority. Raynor's choice of Art Moeller as academic vice president within days of his own elevation to the presidency was a decisive statement. If Raynor had taken his time, bringing the engineering dean on board as academic vice president only after a lengthy period of reflection, the significance of this appointment would have been diluted, if not overlooked. Dispatch signified resolve. Yet by charter, in the absence of the president, a Jesuit had to be legally responsible for the institution. Therefore a new office of corporate vice president was created and assigned to one of the other two Jesuits from the board of trustees.[31]

Vice President Moeller reported directly to Father Raynor from September 1965 until June 1966 when Father McAuley was promoted from vice president for business and finance to the revived position of executive vice president. John Cowee replaced McAuley. This was notable because Cowee had not come up through the ranks at Marquette. He held a doctorate as well as a law degree and had been dean of the School of Business at the University of California, Berkeley before moving to Milwaukee. Seventeen months after becoming the vice president for business, Cowee was designated provost, with responsibility for all planning and policy development at the university. Roy Kallenberger, still deeply involved with the university's master plan, then became vice president for business and finance. In February 1968, Ed Simmons from the department of philosophy and acting dean of the graduate school since June 1967 became the university's first associate vice president for academic affairs. Two and a half years later, Quentin Quade, a political scientist who had replaced Simmons at the graduate school, was also named an associate vice president. After 1970, these two men divided supervision of the university's academic units and committees between them. Then, in 1971, Moeller, Simmons, and Quade all submitted their resignations. Father Raynor subsequently appointed Quade as academic vice president in March 1972. By this time, Father McAuley had resigned from his post as executive vice president, leaving Raynor and Quade at the top by early 1972. The stature of laymen at Marquette had now been confirmed.[32]

FACULTY GOVERNANCE

The appointments of these lay executives reflected the role that non-Jesuits filled at Marquette by the mid-sixties. In the absent of a sufficient number of duly trained Jesuits, Marquette had come to rely upon talented individuals who were neither members of the Society of Jesus nor in some cases congregants in the Roman Catholic Church. If the university's leadership were to come largely from the ranks of its own teacher-scholars in the future, faculty development had to be institutionalized. Lay vice presidents—and perhaps even a liberal arts dean someday—had to be trained to take on these responsibilities.

Art Moeller took a step in this direction when he resurrected a proposal left over from the O'Donnell days: reorganize the academic senate. The academic senate in 1966 remained a committee of deans and vice presidents. On the face of it, this arrangement provided a layman's voice in policy formation. Yet the sources for this voice were limited. In the late 1950s, Father O'Donnell had questioned whether rank and file faculty shouldn't serve on the academic senate. Instead, in 1961, he had established a committee on faculty (COF), with five of its thirteen members elected by the faculty and the remainder appointed by the president. Attempts to get Father Kelley to increase the elective proportion of this committee met with resistance at first, although by 1964 a bare majority of the committee—seven positions—had become elective. A faculty "voice" did not, however, constitute faculty governance.[33]

Moeller's suggestion in 1966 took this concept one step further, suggesting a role for the faculty on the body that advised the president on academic matters. Moeller proposed a new version of the senate with thirty-nine members, the majority of them from the faculty. Eighteen faculty representatives would be elected from the university's colleges and schools; two faculty members would be elected at large. All eight deans would be part of the senate as well as four senior administrators (in addition to the academic vice president who would serve as chair). The president would appoint four additional members from the university community. The senate would also have three student members, including the president of the student senate. A university-wide meeting of the faculty was called for January 17, 1967. In anticipation, the committee on the faculty proposed broadening the conversation to include "the whole issue of faculty participation as well as the particular proposal of the Vice President." The committee also asked whether future faculty assemblies should be held as a whole, or by college and school. Among the other questions it considered was: "Should students be members of whatever body is set up?" And should the faculty's governance role be limited to academic affairs or include matters such as student life, campus facilities, and the university budget?[34]

Nearly 250 individuals attended the January 17 meeting in the union ballroom. At the end of two-and-a-half hours, participants endorsed (by a voice vote) several resolutions suggested by the campus chapter of the American Association of University Professors (AAUP). They supported "a continuing consultative conversation" between the administration and the faculty in "all University undertakings, long-range or immediate, in order that the faculty's loyalty can be concretely realized and its responsibility as a full partner in the academic community fulfilled." They also approved faculty oversight of all "academic policies and procedures," including budgets. Departmental business was to be handled in "as democratic a manner as possible." By a tallied vote, they endorsed faculty control of "all academic policies" on matters such as curriculum, instruction, research, appointment, promotion, and dismissal. But they rejected, 123 to 94, a requirement that "formal advice and consent" be obtained from the faculty for "the selection of the higher all-University officers" as well as a statement that the faculty had "the right … to select their deans and directors, and … to elect their chairmen." A voice vote also endorsed the general notion that "an all-university senate" would determine "all-university policies, whether academic or not." The suggestion that students be allowed to participate in an all-university senate was defeated.[35]

Typical of timetables in the academy, these endorsements languished for two years. At a second all-faculty meeting held not long after the first, the COF decided to attend to its own reorganization, focusing upon elective versus appointed membership. Therefore, it was not until late in February 1969 that Vice President Moeller revisited the idea of a faculty-based academic senate when he appointed an ad hoc committee to look into the matter. To move the process along, he asked for a final report within two months and an interim report within two-and-a-half weeks. To insure that this schedule was met, he named his associate vice president, Ed Simmons, as chair and kept the size of this committee to seven: the chair and three members each from the current academic senate and the committee on faculty. Simmons and his committee delivered the interim report three days before the deadline. It called for a faculty majority on the academic senate and stipulated that no one could be appointed academic vice president without approval of a majority of the senate. Finally, the ad hoc committee favored creation of a second body, a university council, to serve the university president in the same way that the senate assisted the academic vice president: as an official advisory body. The Simmons report concluded that the committee on faculty might be meaningless at this point and therefore might evolve into a "faculty welfare committee."[36]

Conversations over these proposals were thoughtful, thorough, and lengthy. The ad hoc committee's final report was not delivered until August 1969. In the final version, the idea of a university council and of the COF's demise were dropped. This version also reduced the size of a reorganized academic senate, although the faculty retained a numerical majority. It also included three student members. The senate was seen as "a deliberative and legislative body with responsibilities for academic planning and policy of an all-University character, and with responsibilities for review of academic programs." Decisions of the senate were subject to the approval of the president and trustees, although the academic vice president was allowed to inform the president of personal objections to senate resolutions. Attached to this final version was a minority report that questioned the "legislative powers" of a new senate. In the months that followed, both the committee on faculty and the current academic senate debated this new report. Finally, on May 28, 1970, Father Raynor and Vice President Moeller issued a joint memorandum establishing a "reconstituted and reformed" academic senate with twenty-three members. Faculty representatives would make up a majority of twelve. The academic vice president was chairman. The senate was characterized "as a deliberative body with responsibilities for academic policy formulation of an all-University character, and for review and evaluation of academic programs and academic planning." Its recommendations were subject to the approval of the president and the trustees. The senate would also "evaluate and advise on all new appointments to major administrative positions in the academic area."[37]

The institutionalization of faculty authority over academic matters had taken twice as long (four years) as the School of Medicine's separation from the university. Father Raynor had sought to avoid his predecessor's troubles with the faculty while expanding its power. This had taken time, but the final product met most expectations. It was somewhat ironic that one of the first decisions of this reconstituted academic senate was to help find a replacement for Art Moeller, who resigned late in 1971. After Quentin Quade was chosen as his replacement, effective April 1972, the senate passed a Resolution of Appreciation, expressing appreciation for Moeller's role in guiding "an extraordinary increase in active participation by our students and faculty in all facets of academic life of the university." The outgoing vice president was lauded for his service "as an eloquent and tenacious spokesman for both the faculty and students" as well as for being a man who had been "open and accessible to faculty members and students alike." He was acknowledged for "his generous willingness to work hard, as hard as anyone at Marquette." The status of the university's new academic senate certainly verified these tributes.[38]

NEXT STEP: THE BOARD OF TRUSTEES

The formal inclusion of laymen (at this point, a gender-specific term was still accurate) in the senior administration and in the academic senate institutionalized two adjustments first considered during the O'Donnell years. John P. Raynor provided both developments with his own characteristic mark, especially in the appointment of Art Moeller as academic vice president. A third step in the laicization of the university's governance system went much further than anything Father O'Donnell had ever envisioned, and it bore Raynor's imprint in both design and execution. In a letter to the superior general of the Society of Jesus in March 1966 (seven months after assuming the presidency), Raynor justified his appointment of a layman (an "outstanding Catholic") to the second highest position on campus, the first non-Jesuit in Raynor's mind to hold such an assignment "at any institution of higher education run by the Jesuits in North America." Raynor also spoke of consultations with the faculty about general matters, of the School of Medicine's troubles, and of the restive nature of student life at American colleges. For the moment, he offered no hint of his next move.[39]

Among all the adjustments forced upon Catholic higher education after 1960, arguably the most consequential change was the transference of legal control over Catholic colleges and universities from members of religious orders to lay-dominated boards. As Alice Gallin, OSU, details, this process, while necessary, lacked a model for implementation. Each institution had to make its own way. As Gallin demonstrates, laicization seldom meant secularization, but it did mean that the Catholic identities of these schools were under review. For Jesuit schools, Saint Louis University took the lead at the direction of its president, Father Paul Reinert, who inquired into the permissibility of a lay board as early as 1965. About the same time that Saint Louis introduced a lay board two years later, news leaked to the local press that Marquette was considering a similar arrangement. Both Academic Vice President Moeller and Vice President for Business and Finance John Cowee were contacted late one night by both the *Milwaukee Journal* and the *Milwaukee Sentinel* to solicit their reactions to columns that the papers intended to run regarding laymen joining Marquette's board of trustees. Since its incorporation in 1864, Marquette College/University had been governed by three Jesuits. These men conferred degrees. They approved land acquisitions, bond sales, and capital campaigns. Only these priests could revise the corporation's bylaws. They might solicit advice from boards of governors and regents, from individuals such as

Frank Sensenbrenner and Harry Johnston, but they alone controlled Marquette University.[40]

   By the time Milwaukee's newspapers caught wind of a restructuring within the board of trustees, the university's board of regents had already discussed the matter. At a meeting on February 15, 1967, Father Raynor shared a proposal for an "adjustment in the Trustee structure." The regents needed to consider this matter because the university as "a private institution" with a "public trust … should have a broader base of support, public acceptance, public service, and also public governance." Raynor emphasized how this reincorporation would bring Marquette into "the mainstream of American higher education." He reassured the regents that this step was "not intended to make Marquette University a secular institution. The University will remain Jesuit, but will share control at every level, to bring it into conformity with good educational practice." He proposed expanding the board of trustees to fifteen members, with at least six Jesuits. The "appointment of the President, a substantial change in the character or resources of the institution, and future changes in the bylaws, would require a two-thirds concurrence of the fifteen Trustees," meaning that the six Jesuits could block a troublesome resolution. Matters such as budgets, duties of the corporate officers, and even the composition of the board would be decided by a simple majority. Future presidents would have to be members of the Society of Jesus, although at least one contemporary Jesuit trustee opposed this stipulation.[41]

   The regents considered this suggestion for the rest of the year. They seemed particularly concerned that a reorganization might be taken to mean that Marquette was becoming less Jesuit. Father Raynor worked to put these worries to rest. The regents proposed some changes in Father Raynor's design for the new board of trustees, and as a result, the number of trustees grew to twenty-nine members, with seven or eight Jesuits. The percentage of votes needed to effect major changes (such as redirecting the "aims and goals of the University") was raised to three-fourths (although if there were only seven Jesuits on the board instead of eight, they would not be able to block major changes). During the following year (1968), the superior of the Wisconsin province and the superior general of the Jesuits were consulted by telephone and in person. A final decision seemed to be imminent when certificates of appreciation were prepared for the impending dissolution of the board of regents.[42]

   On January 17, 1969, Father Raynor sent a letter to the faculty, staff, and administrators, announcing "a reorganization and expansion" of the board of trustees. He asked the Marquette community to keep this information confidential until a press conference could be scheduled. Without going into the new bylaws, the president explained that the "introduction of laymen into the governing structure at Marquette is an integral part of our development as a Jesuit University." The evolution of the institution demanded "active participation of both laymen and clergy, not only at the level of the faculty and administration, but also at the level of the Board of Trustees." He listed the advantages to this action, including the acquisition of "a wider spectrum of backgrounds, managerial experiences, and fields of interest."

At a press conference three days later, the new corporate charter became public. Both the president and the corporate vice president had to be Jesuits. There would be twenty-nine members on the expanded board: eight Jesuits and twenty-one lay people. The "expanding social, economic and cultural needs of the Milwaukee community" called for "an intensified response" from Marquette, the announcement read. That same afternoon, the new board convened for the first time. Among its members were several Jesuits from outside of Milwaukee: Fathers Gerard J. Campbell and Dexter L. Hanley from Georgetown University; Fathers Leo C. Brown and John W. Padberg from Saint Louis University; and, Father Ladislas M. Orsy from Fordham. Among the lay members were familiar names such as Lawrence G. Haggerty, Glenn L. Humphrey, Victor McCormick, and Robert A. Uihlein, Jr.[43]

Around the university, reaction was generally favorable. The faculty saw this change as a sign of the times, in accordance with the appointment of Art Moeller and the restructuring of the academic senate. One sore point for the faculty, however, was the absence of a single professional educator among the lay trustees. Ed Simmons, associate vice president for academic affairs and a member of the philosophy department, had already raised this point in a polite but pointed letter to Father Raynor during the summer of 1968. While conceding that he had not been completely "privy to discussion on the reconstitution of our Board of Trustees" (and therefore might not know for certain whether the matter had been thoroughly considered), Simmons worried that the makeup of the new board would mimic the board of regents; that is, it might be composed of "outstanding individuals, most of whom have made their mark in the world of business." Men of this ilk were certainly needed, Simmons acknowledged, but so were "men who have made their mark in the university world as well." The associate vice president pointed out that an academic organization was "a unique organization … unlike any other organization." How could those who had no experience "in terms of its innermost dynamics" insightfully address a world which they were not familiar with? The "non-university mind" must not dominate the new board of trustees, the philosophy professor respectfully submitted. Even if several of the Jesuits on the new board were "university men," he maintained, there was still a need for "some few laymen, either from our own faculty and administration or from the faculty and administration of other universities." Two weeks after Father Raynor announced the new trustee system, the university board of graduate studies, under the chairmanship of Quentin Quade, voted unanimously to "commend the administration" for the recent announcement regarding the trustees, but also to express its disappointment that the new board did not include "some representation from the faculty of Marquette University." Although they did not want to sound "ungracious," the graduate board felt that "distinguished teachers and researchers" who understood the world of "scholarship" needed to be appointed to the board to insure "the continued growth of Marquette as a center for teaching, research, and service." A year later, the committee on faculty chimed in, asking permission to provide names for additional trustees. In this instance, mention was made for the first time of introducing racial (but not gender) diversity to the board.[44]

Jesuit reactions were mixed. A treasured responsibility had been dropped into the hands of two dozen businessmen who had no legal obligation to shape their management decisions according to the teachings of St. Ignatius. In fact, Ignatius of Loyola was probably nothing more than a shadowy, if saintly, figure to most of them. And their commitment to the Catholic identity of Marquette University could not be guaranteed. The new board of trustees reordered the relationship of the university with the Society of Jesus. When three Jesuits legally controlled Marquette University, there was a straight-forward association between the school and the Society of Jesus, based on the religious vows taken by the trustees. Now, with twenty-one non-Jesuits constituting a significant majority of the new board, the vow of obedience no longer served as the glue that held Marquette University together.

Thus, in May 1967, nearly two years before Marquette's reincorporation was effected, the university's Jesuit community began to consider "Articles of Incorporation." Father Raynor explained to his confreres that a future restructuring of Marquette's board of trustees was necessary because of the "present inadequacies of merely three trustees, all Jesuits," the "philosophy and expectations of the North Central Association," "Federal relations," the "thrust" of the Second Vatican Council, and the "thrust of common sense." Shared governance referred not only to departments, colleges, and the general university, but also to "the level of board of control." A redefinition of the relationship between the local Jesuit community and a revised corporate body—still to be known as Marquette University, but no longer under the authority of the Society of Jesus—needed to be conveyed to both the provincial and to the superior general. Once the reincorporation took place in January 1969, the Jesuits not only did not control the university, they no longer had a legal relationship with the university. They were technically unemployed in the absence of formal contracts. The same men who had given their lives to the university ministry needed to regularize their situation at an institution that, for a century (1864-1969), had been their Society's responsibility. For the next year, the Jesuit community worked over various drafts of incorporation. When Father Raynor updated the new board of trustees on progress in June 1970, one lay board member insisted that "special attention be paid to retirement and pension provisions for present Jesuits as well as for those already retired who had given much service to the University." To have the well-being of older conferees become the object of contractual negotiations with lay trustees was just one indication of the considerable discomfort that some Jesuits experienced between 1967 and 1970.[45]

On September 11, 1970, the "Documents Pertaining to the Relationships of Jesuit Associates, Inc., and Marquette University" were completed. The Jesuit Associates, Inc. became "a Wisconsin nonprofit corporation," "auxiliary to" but not a replacement for "the Community, which is a regular, canonical, religious house of the Society of Jesus." The community was supported by the salaries and retirement benefits from the university, from Mass and pastoral stipends, and personal gifts. In addition to salaries, fringe benefits, and retirement accounts, the university agreed to provide "suitable on-campus living quarters." The rector of this religious community, once a title synonymous with presidential powers, was now "the canonical religious superior of the religious community" only. In exchange for these and other guarantees, the contract called for the Jesuit Associates to provide faculty members and administrators to the non-profit corporation known as Marquette University. In the months that followed, the trustees discussed the recruitment of Jesuits and any advantages these men might have over other applicants for faculty positions.[46]

ACADEMIC AFFAIRS

Marquette University's self-analysis in the mid-fifties was the most comprehensive review of the institution's assets and ambitions in its history. Only the advent of professional education between 1907 and 1910 and Father Burrowes's sequenced revisions of the *Ratio Studiorum*-based arts and sciences curriculum during the first decade of the twentieth century matched the significance of the self-analysis. By the end of World War II, the words *Ratio Studiorum* had largely disappeared from the vocabulary of Marquette faculty and students. Curricular adjustments were no longer accompanied by respectful bows to the past, to the *Ratio*, and increasingly, to Jesuit traditions. Instead, academic planning favored a corporate model first promoted by Father Fox in the 1920s, with adjustments precipitated by the highly competitive nature of American higher education.

Father Kelley, a year from his departure as president, directed Vice President John Raynor in September 1964 to prepare a new academic master plan to parallel the recently developed blueprint for campus facilities. The timing of this directive was shaped by an external force, the National Science Foundation's announcement that it would provide millions of dollars to a "selected number of universities" "to create 'centers of excellence.'" Marquette administrators wanted Milwaukee's Jesuit university to be among the elect. In a meeting with the board of regents, Father Raynor explained that an updated master plan was necessary to distinguish private institutions like Marquette from generously funded state schools. Sectarian schools needed to be energetic as well as ambitious. No longer could they rely upon congregants from their faith community to survive. Raynor was particularly worried about Marquette's ability to recruit first-rate faculty scholars in a market-driven system. Hence he welcomed the president's call to action.[47]

On September 11, 1964, Raynor directed all academic deans and directors to prepare, on an expedited schedule, "a master plan for the years 1965-75." He conceded that his timetable was driven by the National Science Foundation's call for proposals, with the aim of submitting an application by February 1, 1965. Roman Gawkoski, the university registrar, was appointed executive director for this undertaking. Uniform questionnaires were distributed and departments were instructed to have their reports completed within thirty days. A central steering committee consolidated all submissions. In remarks to the student newspaper, Raynor admitted that the science foundation's proposal was targeted at scientific centers of excellence, suggesting that the entire campus was undertaking a monumental exercise that might benefit only a handful of units. To Raynor, however, this exercise would update the 1950's self-analysis and provide an academic blueprint for the next capital campaign.[48]

An enormous amount of effort was expended over the next four months. Each department, college, school, and university office developed a report and each faculty member received a multi-page questionnaire to fill out. The board of graduate studies was so overwhelmed by the task that it addressed only the doctoral programs per instructions from the steering committee. Without similar guidance, the committee on faculty locked onto faculty salaries and fringe benefits. Even the vocabulary used in these reports created problems. In the College of Liberal Arts, evaluations referred to departments with the words good or solid. Father Gerard Smith, chair of the philosophy department, got into a heated exchange with the master plan's executive director over the value of imprecise terms when assessing scholarly communities: how could a department develop a strategic plan intended to move a unit from solid to good? A critical section of the master plan dealing with faculty compensation was still being revised as the February 1965 deadline passed. In April, a draft of enrollment projections was still being distributed for comment.[49]

Father Raynor's ascendency to Marquette's top post delayed the master plan even further. In October 1966, two years after the latest self-examination had kicked off, Art Moeller, as academic vice president, promised that "the first formal document emanating from the academic planning efforts of the University community will be made available for … review and suggestions." Moeller conceded that the new document would not contain "as some may have anticipated, a detailed summary of all the budgetary projections which were requested in the departmental academic planning materials. Rather it incorporate[d] major academic documents proposed in these original materials and establishe[d] criteria for the academic essentials which must be a part of one of these developments." The difficulty inherent in preparing a master plan amid the routine responsibilities of an academic year drove Father Raynor to reassign John Cowee (vice president for business and finance) to the new post of provost, with oversight of all long-term planning.[50]

In its final version, the master plan's priorities included a familiar list of ambitions for a research-minded university: additional doctoral programs, development of faculty research opportunities, enhancement of faculty salaries and fringe benefits, growth in library holdings, improved student financial aid packages, and additional construction. The context for this growth remained, however, the religious mission of Marquette, its ties to "all of creation and its Creator." Unique to this document was the linkage of Marquette's pedagogical product with the notion of service. A lengthy section titled "Commitment to Public Service" explored external applications of classroom learning. The entire university, not just its professional programs, was now characterized as a civic resource for all of Milwaukee. Individual colleges and schools spent the summer of 1967 fleshing out the details of what was characterized as resource delivery.[51]

For several departments, this emphasis upon service to the local community was timely and inspirational. In fall 1964, the department of education (Vice President Raynor's home unit) received permission to expand its already successful master of arts offerings (fifty degrees a year) by implementing two doctoral programs: a research-oriented doctor of philosophy degree (PhD) and a professional doctor of education degree (EdD). (Long a department in the College of Liberal Arts, education was later elevated to the status of a school in 1971.) Working with education and seeking to serve the Milwaukee community, the English and Spanish departments created MAs in teaching at the secondary level. The theology department also found the idea of service consistent with its future. In 1957, theology had fourteen students working on their master's degrees during summer sessions. Within a few years, a year-round master's degree was added, as was an undergraduate major. In 1963, a monumental step was taken with the addition of a PhD in religious studies. Spearheaded by the noted theologian, Bernard Cooke, SJ, this effort brought to culmination discussions sponsored by the Jesuit Educational Association to develop a theology doctorate outside the confines of seminaries and divinity schools. The need for professors of theology, whether lay or religious, at Catholic colleges far exceeded the pool of adequately trained instructors. When the idea of a central institute failed to gain traction, Marquette's president (Father Kelley) authorized Cooke to move ahead with a doctorate in religious studies, a title chosen to distinguish it as a scholarly discipline. Three nuns, each from a different order, received their Marquette doctorates in religious studies four years later, the first such PhDs ever awarded by an American Catholic university that was neither a seminary nor a divinity school. By this time, 174 students had received their master's degrees, and another 120 MA students and 49 doctoral students were working on their degrees. The faculty had grown from 9 full-time members in 1957 to 27 a decade later. In compliance with the university's new emphasis on outreach and service, a Center for the Study of Theology in Public Life was proposed in December 1967.[52]

For Marquette undergraduates, curricular changes during the sixties included subtractions as well as additions. The physical education requirement was dropped in 1962, replicating a trend among Jesuit schools. The fifteen-hundred freshmen who historically had filled the old gymnasium from eight in the morning until four in the afternoon now got their exercise largely through non-credit programs. Discontinuance of this graduation requirement undermined the mission of the physical education department, and by 1968, it was dissolved. The education department managed what remained of the for-credit classes and the dean of students handled recreational activities such as intramural sports.[53]

When completed, the new university's master plan triggered a re-examination of the liberal arts core required of every undergraduate. Ever since Marquette offered its first college classes in 1883, baccalaureate programs had been guided by the *Ratio Studiorum*. Philosophy, rhetoric, literature, history, and religion remained at the instructional heart of the university. The richness of each student's training in these subjects distinguished a Jesuit-educated graduate from others. From Burrowes to Fox to McCarthy to O'Donnell, no president had ever surrendered an inch on this point. Yet by the sixties, Milwaukee's Jesuit university was in a fierce competition with non-sectarian educational institutions across the country. No longer could Marquette recruit based solely on its reputation as a Jesuit institution.

The College of Liberal Arts undertook a review of its core requirements during the 1970-71 school year. Faculty committees proposed eliminating mandatory minors and the required class in speech (a mainstay of Jesuit education) while formalizing theology requirements at nine units, regardless of a student's religious affiliation. Although the faculty also suggested an upgrade of the fine arts program to the status of a department, the liberal arts dean quickly brushed aside this suggestion. In the late winter of 1972, Father Raynor approved a revised core that divided its required classes into Competency Requirements and Distribution Requirements, with English, foreign language, and mathematics classes assigned to the former, and classes in theology, philosophy, literature, history, natural science, and social science to the latter. The humanities, the traditional heart of a Jesuit education, were now thoroughly dissolved—at least in the minds of students if not the faculty—into the broader mix of the 128 units needed for graduation.[54]

The amalgamation of what was left of the *Ratio Studiorum* within a curriculum steeped in the natural and social sciences reflected the lay faculty's influence over academic matters after 1972. When adjunct faculty had questioned religious restrictions imposed upon the medical curriculum in 1919, Father Noonan had defiantly reminded dissenters that he was the ultimate authority on all instructional matters at Marquette University. Father McCarthy had unapologetically dismissed a faculty member for attending, outside of school hours, what the priest considered immoral political meetings. By the tumultuous sixties, however, the non-religious educational staff at Marquette viewed themselves as integral to the institution's purpose, not just employees. When Father Kelley was accused of belittling the academic integrity of the university in 1962, it was the lay faculty who dissented—openly and without apology. Before the sixties, differences of opinion would have been presented with a dose of deference to the religious whose congregations founded these institutions. By the end of the sixties, the lay faculty lost this hesitancy and became determined to have a structured say in the future of their institutions. Marquette happened to be in the middle of this reordering.

THE TIMES ARE, INDEED, CHANGING

Also searching for a voice in an era of outspokenness were America's college students, the younger siblings of the fifties's "silent generation." Although student protests at Marquette in the sixties were less violent than those at Columbia, Kent State, and the University of California, Berkeley, they forced university officials to re-evaluate the institution's oversight of those charged to its care. With peers confronting fire hoses in southern cities, high school classmates dying in Vietnam, and college roommates burning draft cards on street corners, students in the sixties insisted they were adults who deserved to be heard. The socio-political energy emblematic of the 1960s first appeared in the decade's opening year when a handful of collegians became thoroughly energized by John Kennedy's aspiration to seize the helm from a generation represented by their parents' favorite, Dwight D. Eisenhower. The younger set responded to JFK's calls to service, first enunciated in his inaugural address and later in programs such as the Peace Corps. Marquette students responded with particular enthusiasm to the latter. The emphasis in Marquette's 1967 master plan upon service to the local community embodied this spirit, this wish to make a difference by acting upon the moment. But Kennedy's horrific death traumatized the university community and the nation, derailing the optimism of the sixties. Disbelief deepened with each public murder: the president followed by Malcolm X, Martin Luther King Jr., and Robert Kennedy. The high expectations of the early part of this decade slammed against the ravages of personal violence. Dissent, anger, and finally systematic protest became routine, a style of expression fueled by dismay over racial injustice, the war in Vietnam, and even a patriarchal culture. The university's dismissal of young men who wore beards or young women who wore slacks in the student union seemed preposterous when crowds marched through the streets in opposition to the war, racism, and poverty or, on a much smaller scale, the library's service hours and Willie Wampum as the school mascot. Complaints became causes and the causes intersected, creating a cacophony of dissent. The burden of finding balance amid ceaseless unrest took its toll on Father Raynor and his aides. Raynor, in particular, proved more adept at handling crusades of his own choosing (such as the separation of the medical school or the incorporation of lay trustees) than spontaneous uprisings triggered by irate students and faculty.

At the outset of this decade, the committee on student life remained the most visible symbol of university authority over student behavior outside the classroom. With the approval of the vice president for student affairs and the university president, the CSL determined the regulations under which ten thousand Warriors were obliged to live. In the case of violations, the committee's options included expulsion, suspension, probation, official warning, fines, and removal for reasons of personality or health. In addition to handling disciplinary problems, the committee also served as the first layer of administration the student government encountered. The remarkable thing about the student senate's relationship with the committee, at least in the early sixties, was how respectful students could be.[55]

This civility was evidenced in a thirty-four-page document that the student government prepared early in 1966 following another disagreement over who controlled outside speakers on campus. Titled "The Marquette Report: Contributed with positive and mature concern for the present and future progress of our University," the report followed the administration's demand that every statement on student rights had to be accompanied by a statement on student responsibilities. The students politely agreed that "we seek first to understand for ourselves what Marquette ought to be and then to actualize this as much as possible." One faculty member was so taken with the thoughtfulness and thoroughness of this report that he characterized it as potentially "'the most important and most exciting event in Marquette history.'" For his part, Father Raynor created an ad hoc committee in September 1966 (eight months after the students delivered their position paper) to study the status and role of Marquette students. Two years later—a year beyond the president's original deadline—the ad hoc committee delivered its own report to the committee on student life, the academic senate, the committee on faculty, and the board of regents. The *Marquette Tribune* announced in the fall of 1968 that a new set of conduct procedures would be available by the following school year. Additional delays came after the office of legal counsel insisted upon reviewing a faculty committee's fourteen-page revision of the new student manual. Finally, in August 1969, Father Raynor approved new guidelines for student conduct—three and a half years after the students submitted their proposal. By this time, the civility (and patience) of the mid-sixties had evaporated, as evidenced by a December 1968 editorial in the *Tribune* that asked sarcastically "Is there really a Fr. Raynor?" after the president failed to follow-up on promises to meet with student councils from every school and college. In the past, no president would have tolerated such impertinence. The times had certainly changed.[56]

STUDENT CONDUCT

In the late sixties, the university's student affairs division faced a burdensome combination of old problems and new challenges. The Milwaukee police department contacted Marquette authorities on a weekly basis concerning underage drinking. The presence of advertisements for beer in the *Marquette Tribune* led to charges that the issue was being ignored by the dean of students. The situation became more troublesome in March 1972 after the state legislature passed an "age of majority" bill, lowering the legal drinking age to eighteen. Although this development may have alleviated certain difficulties with enforcement, it did nothing for the consequences of alcoholic consumption. And by the late sixties, a new concern had nudged its way into the student handbook: a section dealing with narcotics. The counseling and student health centers now offered assistance with "narcotics or other harmful or hallucinogenic drug[s]." With increasingly frequency, the *Tribune* featured stories of student arrests for drug possession.[57]

Housing regulations continued to be challenged: who was required to live in university housing, where could upperclass students reside, and how wide did the door have to be left open when a member of the opposite sex was present? By the 1964-65 school year, the university oversaw five men's dorms (Monitor, Nicolas, Noonan, Schroeder, and Stewart halls) and nine women's dorms (Alumnae House and Bonifas, Heraty, Highland, Marian, O'Donnell, Merritty, Carpenter, and Arden halls). The burden of supervising this number of students increased after the administration mandated that freshman and sophomores live in university housing; this requirement was expanded to include juniors in 1967. Adjustments in the rules for residential life became so routine that student handbooks were almost out of date by the time they were distributed. By the early seventies, the arrival of coeducational dormitories in Schroeder and Tower halls made some members of the student affairs office long for the innocence of an earlier era. The vice president for student affairs prepared a six-panel, question-and-answer brochure for parents, alumni, and the local community, titled "Coeducational Housing? '… Surely not at Marquette University.'" Letters written to Father Raynor and Art Moeller by parents, Jesuits, and Milwaukee residents vehemently protested this lapse in the pursuit of "moral excellence."[58]

   Etiquette at a Catholic university was also under assault. Male students at Marquette were still forbidden to grow beards in 1965. Moreover, they could not wear a hairstyle that was considered "effeminately long." When the student senate tried to challenge these restrictions through a series of resolutions (none of which were well received by the dean of students), an editorial in the *Milwaukee Sentinel* applauded Marquette authorities for serving "notice to the academic world that it will be no haven for the creeps and kooks who seem to be infesting American campuses in increasing numbers." The "reassertion of the old fashioned idea that a university is the master of the students" came as a welcome relief to the newspaper's editors. A year later, the issue switched to women's wardrobes. In May 1966, the dean of men issued a reminder that, with the return of warm weather to Milwaukee, shorts and blue jeans were not permitted in campus buildings or at social functions. The following year, the Associated Students of Marquette University passed a resolution asking that female students be allowed to wear slacks in the student union and in the library. In reply, the union manager warned that violators of the slacks rule would be refused food service and asked to leave. A "slack-in" was proposed. By the following fall, these rules had been quietly revised, allowing slacks after 6 p.m. on weekdays and all day on Saturdays. The student life office felt that faculty in particular were uncooperative in upholding the dress code. In an internal memorandum written in September 1967, the acting dean of men complained about the faculty's inconsistency in proscribing "any dress or attire which is provocative, suggestive, indecent, scandalous, lewd, lascivious or in just plain poor taste." Sorting out the sides on these matters could be a challenge in itself.[59]

STUDENT RIGHTS AND VISITORS FROM THE OUTSIDE

Crises on Marquette's campus may not have drawn the national media's attention but these protests certainly epitomized higher education's agitated state. Early in the decade, clashes often centered upon notions of personal freedom: how long one might wear his hair, whether one might wear slacks at the union, at what hour one was required to turn in on weekends, and—a bit more substantially—what students might publish in "their" newspaper. In the last instance, the central administration at Marquette had never hesitated to enforce its own views of propriety upon the *Tribune* staff. Father Fox had treated the paper as his personal publicity machine. Father Magee had ordered the dean of journalism to remove certain kinds of advertising that he considered unbecoming of a Catholic university. The tables were reversed in January 1956 when the student senate urged the administration to "set up an all-University editorial board for the *Marquette Tribune*," so that it might impose "'conclusive jurisdiction over the editorial policy … and advisory jurisdiction over the news content and the weight of the news.'" The senate worried that a small group of journalists assumed to speak for the entire student body—a notion the administration might have seconded over the years. A decade later, university officials proposed the formation of a university committee on student publications to advise the president and academic vice president regarding the "quality of all such student publications." For its part, the *Tribune* staff insisted upon abiding by its own set of guidelines, rules that held them "responsible" to a single individual: their faculty adviser. After all, the paper responded, it was their duty to "question and adversely criticize … the decisions by administrative officers of the University, committee and boards regulating the status and conduct of the faculty, students and employees of the University and of faculty, student, and employee organizations." The ground was set for edgier discussions of propriety.[60]

Before World War II, differences of opinion among students usually focused upon less controversial matters such as the role of varsity sports in university life or continued funding for certain types of student organizations (such as city and state clubs). Debates over larger issues such as the federal government's response to the Great Depression or American isolationism before Pearl Harbor simply did not take place within full view of the university community. In the years after the war, however, student voices grew louder and more insistent. For example, in 1948, the committee on student life authorized Marquette's student government to affiliate with the recently established National Student Association (NSA), if the latter would issue a statement on student responsibilities. At its founding, the national association had encountered factional strife between a group of leftists and a contingent of moderate Catholic students who ultimately prevailed. Despite this outcome, Marquette administrators remained wary of the association. When the group failed to issue a statement on student obligations, the university withdrew from the NSA in 1955, only to reconsider its action the following year. As a sign of the times, one Jesuit's unsubstantiated assertion that the NSA harbored communists successfully derailed further interest in the group. But by 1964, the Marquette student government once again looked into the matter; it invited commentary from various student groups regarding possible participation. Even though these opinions varied, the national association's condemnation of communism convinced the Marquette committee on student life to authorize participation. (Years later, it was revealed that the Central Intelligence Agency had secretly funded certain NSA activities after 1952.)[61]

Clashes between college students and university administrators in the early sixties frequently concerned the right of student organizations to invite outside speakers to campus. At Marquette, the Young Republicans touched upon this matter in January 1961 when they scheduled a speech by a former political science professor who had left Marquette on harsh terms. His intended topic was communism's threat to the United States, a subject well within his sphere of scholarly expertise. The committee on student life felt that the Young Republicans had acted out of turn by offering the invitation before receiving its permission. Therefore, when the Young Republicans approached the committee for approval, the CSL turned them down. At Father O'Donnell's request,

Student protest, undated. File 4.

however, the committee reconsidered its earlier decision and ultimately sanctioned the Young Republican's guest speaker. In a similar incident in late 1963, the Young Democrats came before the CSL, asking to invite a representative from their political party to speak, a presentation that would likely denounce the House Un-American Activities Committee. Following the precedent set in the Young Republicans' case, the committee on student life denied this latest request, with the dean of men going so far as to characterize the speaker as a "professional agitator" who had "no real foundation in education or politics." Members of the committee insisted that the Young Democrats were merely testing its resolve. Others worried that students were going to be exposed to ideas that were not approved by the university since the Democrat in question was said to have "close contacts with Communism." At nearly the same moment, the committee chastised the Young Republicans for inviting a University of Illinois professor who had depicted President Kennedy as a communist. Coming as it did less than three months after the president's assassination, the committee questioned whether this individual was the "type of speaker they want to bring to campus." Committee members also suggested this invitation was nothing more than an attempt by certain students to "'push'" authorities to the limits on free speech.[62]

The need for a speaker's policy was obvious. The committee on student life initiated a conversation on this matter in March 1964: who should make the final decision—outside of the president, of course—over guests from off-campus. The academic senate decided to join this conversation, although it took years before a policy was ultimately crafted by the central administration and a special ad hoc committee. The absence of such guidelines led to a divisive episode in February 1967 when the committee on student life rejected, by a 7-2 vote, the request to have poet Allen Ginsberg speak at Marquette. The student government immediately appealed the committee's decision to Father Raynor. Within days, the university president upheld the CSL's position, explaining that after consultation with the board of regents and senior administrators and after hearing from faculty and students alike, he agreed with the student life committee: "'the proposed appearance is not sufficiently compatible with the standards of propriety and the educational goals of the Marquette University community to warrant the official sponsorship you request.'" A group of students and faculty protested what they characterized as a denigration of "the[ir] right to bring speakers to … campus without interference from the Committee on Student Life … This restriction on our right of inquiry is intellectually stifling." A new group, the "Ad Hoc Committee for a Free Speaker's Policy," urged a letter-writing campaign to Father Raynor. The *Milwaukee Journal* published an editorial cartoon belittling the university's attempt to keep controversial speakers outside the walled fortress of the institution. Ultimately, Ginsberg spoke across town at the University of Wisconsin-Milwaukee. To protest what they insisted was a breach of free speech, about 150 Marquette students marched in seventeen-degree temperatures from the Joan of Arc Chapel to UWM to listen to the poet.[63]

Beatnik Allen Ginsberg may have been stopped from setting foot on Marquette's campus because of the sexual content of his writings, but other publicly prominent voices were heard. Less than a year after he attempted to block admission of African Americans to the University of Alabama, Governor George Wallace made a campaign swing through Wisconsin in April 1964 (after becoming a sudden entrant in the Democratic presidential primary). He denounced a proposed civil rights bill (which became law that summer) before an audience of 500 at the Marquette School of Medicine's auditorium. On this same trip, Wallace triggered national headlines by deftly mixing racism with law and order before a ferociously excited crowd at Serb Hall. Thirty ovations in forty minutes confirmed the growing appeal of his message. Six weeks later, Attorney General of the United States Robert F. Kennedy visited the city as Marquette's commencement-day speaker, with Father Kelley conferring an honorary degree upon the future presidential candidate. In 1966, Milwaukee native and astronaut James Lovell became the twenty-first recipient of the Père Marquette award in ceremonies at the student union. Three years later, his colleagues Neil A. Armstrong, Edwin E. Aldrin Jr., and Michael Collins received the first Père Marquette Discovery Medal, celebrating not only their recent moon landing but also the 300th anniversary of Father Marquette's exploration of the upper Midwest. Other national figures who visited the campus during these years included civil rights and antiwar activist Dick Gregory and pioneering feminist Betty Friedan.[64]

One of the most noteworthy of these incidents involving campus visitors is, ironically, one of the least-known. In October 1963, the committee on academic honors started to evaluate candidates for honorary degrees at the June 1964 commencement.

Apollo 11 astronauts come to Marquette to receive Père Marquette Discovery Award, November 1969. File 1075.

By its third session on October 16, twenty-nine names had been "retained ... for active consideration," including John A. McCone from the Central Intelligence Agency, Father John Courtnay Murray, SJ, A. Philip Randolph of the Railroad Porters' Union, President John F. Kennedy, and Dr. Martin Luther King Jr. Six days later, each committee member submitted his first five choices. Kennedy's name was on all five submissions, King's on four of five. The committee sent a memorandum to the university president on October 24 recommending Kennedy, King, and three others. In the weeks that followed, a confidential vetting of the King nomination took place. It is not clear if the university screened any of the other four nominees. The sources contacted regarding Dr. King had nothing but praise for him, although several unnamed associates of his were said to have questionable backgrounds. Three days before President Kennedy's assassination in Dallas, the committee chair wrote Father Kelley, urging him to move expeditiously to confirm the chief executive's availability in June.

Coincidentally, King visited Milwaukee two months later (January 1964) for a speech at the Auditorium. During a press conference at Mitchell Field, he lavished praise upon the Catholic Church's commitment to racial justice, applauding its willingness to back rhetoric with action. One week later, on February 3, Father Kelley formally invited the civil rights activist to attend Marquette's commencement on June 7 so that his "distinguished contribution to American life" might be recognized with a "Doctor of Humane Letters." King was lauded for his "salutary leadership of determined, peaceful, patriotic and legally sound improvement of racial understanding." The letter was mailed the next day. Unfortunately, it was sent to King's former address on Dexter Avenue in Montgomery, Alabama, and the envelope was returned two days later. Father Kelley's office obtained the correct address through contacts within the local African American community and a second invitation was sent to King. Because of prior commitments at Hebrew Union College and Connecticut Wesleyan College on the same day as Marquette's commencement, Dr. King declined Father Kelley's invitation. Attempts to switch his appearance to the previous day, for the Baccalaureate, proved futile. On February 18, Father Kelley wrote yet a third letter, expressing his disappointment at the scheduling conflict and suggesting that in the future "there will be an occasion when this can be accomplished."

Fourteen years earlier, at the height of the Cold War, Marquette had recognized J. Edgar Hoover with an honorary degree. By 1962, after repeated criticism by Martin Luther King regarding racism in the Federal of Bureau of Investigation, Hoover became consumed with destroying the civil rights leader's reputation. He ordered agents to follow King's every move, wiretap his conversations, and undermine his reputation whenever possible, including with President Johnson and New York Cardinal Francis Spellman. The FBI chief received word in March 1964 that King would soon be honored by Marquette, Hoover's honorary alma mater. FBI headquarters instructed its "Milwaukee agents to approach reliable contacts at Marquette with a confidential sample of the Bureau's worst allegations about King's private life and 'communistic connections.'" Unaware that the offer to honor King had been withdrawn three weeks

J. Edgar Hoover receiving honorary degree, 1950. File 690.

earlier, a local agent met with Father O'Donnell on March 10. The government official informed Marquette's former president and current chancellor that Dr. King was under the influence of "two known Communists" whom he refused to dismiss from his entourage. Moreover, the civil rights leaders's moral integrity was called into question. The university was told it could use this information however it wished, although "the source of our information should be withheld." Weeks later, after it became clear that King would not be coming to Milwaukee, the local FBI agent received a special commendation since the agency erroneously assumed it had blocked Marquette's celebration of the civil rights leaders. Documents similar to those turned over to university officials were later used by the FBI at the Vatican when the agency tried to prevent a meeting between King and the pope.

In 1976, news of the university's effort to recognize Martin Luther King twelve years earlier became public knowledge. At that time, the university's public relations office explained the scheduling conflict for the first time. More recently, the shadowy role of the FBI returned to the spotlight with the publication of the second volume of Taylor Branch's monumental study of the civil rights movement. Branch mistakenly credits the bureau with blocking Marquette's recognition of the civil rights leader. New evidence uncovered in the university's archives, confirms the authenticity of the scheduling explanation. For the want of a free Sunday on June 7, 1964, Marquette missed its opportunity to formally incorporate Martin Luther King into the university community. A final irony in this whole episode: Marquette's original invitation to King had been returned to Milwaukee, marked "Moved Not Forwardable." One day after this invitation had been originally sent to Alabama, King was nominated for the Nobel Peace Prize. Apparently, authorities in Sweden had an easier time locating him than postal employees in Montgomery.[65]

THE CAUSE FOR RACIAL JUSTICE

J. Edgar Hoover's vendetta against the Baptist minister from Atlanta was just one manifestation of the deep-seated sentiments evoked by the civil rights movement. The constitutional nudge provided by the 1954 Brown v. Board of Education case and the moral edge provided by the following year's bus boycott in Montgomery, Alabama, accelerated white America's rendezvous with justice. For some collegians, four black students from North Carolina A&T provided role models when they faced down Greensboro's racial divide at a Woolworth lunch counter in January 1960. Their refusal to leave until treated equally became a favorite strategy to showcase discrimination and to win precious air-time on the evening news. Caravans of buses carried civil rights proponents from town to town, testing freedom's options in communities long set in their ways. This media coverage, even when it covered deadly outcomes, allowed northern audiences to remain at arm's length from the struggles against Jim Crow. Yet with the legacy of the Interracial Study Club in the university's recent past, it was only a matter of time before someone brought this quest for justice closer to home.

Milwaukee's black population, remarkably small by the standards of other northern industrial cities, finally blossomed after 1960, just as the city's population reached an all-time high with 741,324 residents. In 1960, 62,458 African Americans represented 8.4 percent of the city's residents; by 1990, this number more than tripled to 191,255, representing 30.5 percent of the city's population. When Milwaukee neighborhoods immediately north of the Marquette campus started to undergo a racial transformation, the *Marquette Tribune* devoted dozens of columns to racial matters, including the treatment of black residents at nearby diners, barbershops, and theaters. Earnest young journalists broke into black and white teams to discover which landlords would rent to African Americans and which would not. Periodically, the paper interviewed black students, asking them about everyday encounters with prejudice at local venues as well as on campus. When pressed about similar issues at the university, officials in the student life office reaffirmed the university's policy on nondiscrimination in dormitory assignments. They did, however, agree to stop using photographs in matching potential roommates.[66]

The faculty also attended to segregated housing. Eighty-nine instructors signed an open letter to the state assembly and senate in January 1963, urging passage of legislation banning discrimination "in the rental and purchase of housing." A month later, the Marquette Faculty Association for Interracial Justice was formed. As civil rights protests in the South escalated, so too did support on campus for the endangered marchers. Seven hundred students and faculty gathered in front of Schroeder Hall in March 1964 on their way to join twice as many marchers from the University of Wisconsin-Milwaukee and the Congress on Racial Equality in front of the county courthouse to protest violence in Selma. During the summer, an audience of seven hundred nuns, priests, seminarians, and lay students attended an Interracial Justice Association panel discussion titled "The Integration Front This Summer." Lloyd Barbee, a local attorney and a fiery opponent of de facto segregation in Milwaukee public schools, was one of the speakers. A group of faculty members established the Negro Leadership Aid Program in 1962, underwriting classes at the university for more than four dozen African American adults. The Milwaukee Urban League and the Milwaukee Commission on Community Relations recruited the applicants; a faculty panel selected the recipients.[67]

Another new group, the Students United for Racial Equality (SURE), was formed in early 1965, aiming "'to promote justice in interracial relations … by involvement of the University community in study and other activities suitable to effectively accomplish this goal.'" Within months, three members were arrested for obstructing traffic during a protest. The following fall, Lloyd Barbee and his associates challenged the city's history of segregated schools by urging parents to refuse to send their children to the public school system and instead to enroll them in one of nearly two dozen "freedom schools." SURE provided staff support at several of these alternative schools, with assistance from at least a dozen Marquette faculty members. Tensions on campus mounted after the law school dean warned that the county district attorney "had rendered an opinion that such [a] boycott [of the public school system] is illegal and that participation therein by parents of children obliged by law to be in regular attendance at public or private schools is a misdemeanor." Anyone who assisted in the committing this crime, he noted, had also violated the law and, in the case of members of the legal profession, they had transgressed "the Canons of Professional Ethics of the American Bar Association." To SURE's dismay, the student senate refused to support

Student protest at rear of O'Hara Hall, November 1970. File 130.

the freedom schools. At the same time, another student group collected over four hundred signatures opposing the presence of a booth on campus to recruit Marquette students to work at the freedom schools. Father Richard Sherburne, dean of students, refused to block supporters of the alternative schools from furthering their cause. The priest assured the president of SURE that he and his associates were free "to decide for [them]selves … to participate in political and social action off-campus according to [their] best insights and responsible consciences."[68]

   Involvement by Marquette students in the civil rights cause intensified in March 1966 when SURE and another student organization, the Young Christian Students Association, joined Father James Groppi and his supporters in protesting the caucasian-only rule for membership in the Eagles Club. A national fraternal organization, the Eagles owned a clubhouse at Twenty-fourth and Wisconsin, just blocks west of the university. SURE members became even more agitated after discovering that the faculty bowling league used the club's facilities. At first, the bowlers insisted a contract forced them to use the clubhouse lanes. But by the fall of 1966, repeated run-ins with SURE prompted the bowling league to move its upcoming season to the Knights of Columbus building on Fifteenth Street. Another segment within the university community clashed with SURE over the 1966 Carnival after organizers for this annual event voted fourteen to zero to rent the Eagles' ballroom for their dance. A third Marquette group, students who were organizing the basketball tip-off dance, also decided (by a nine to seven vote) to rent space from the Eagles. Both the committee on student life and the student senate approved the venue choices for the Carnival and tip-off dances. In zero-degree weather, nearly two hundred members of SURE, the Young Christian Students, and the Young Democrats picketed the Carnival dance, to little avail. Earlier, some demonstrators had held a sit-in at Father Sherburne's office on the second floor of the student union, charging "that the 'intellectual, Christian spirit' was dead at Marquette." The administration took a neutral position on the Eagles' controversy, explaining that student groups were free to make their own choices although institutionally the university opposed racial discrimination. This effort to avoid offending either side in the controversy proved ineffective, triggering another protest. In the face of these repeated confrontations, the student senate reversed its position in the fall of 1967, directing all organizations to avoid dealing with the Eagles Club because of its racist policies. Troubled by the SURE sit-in and by the intensity of the protests in general, Father Sherburne resigned as dean of students, opening the door for the first layman to assume that position. Edward D. Kurdziel, an ex-marine, had formerly commanded the university's NROTC program.[69]

SURE remained the most outspoken civil rights representative at Marquette. Members marched to O'Hara Hall in March 1968 with a twelve-point petition calling for more scholarships for black students, more classes on black culture, and additional outreach programs in the local community. To press their demands, they entered upon a Lenten fast of bread, water, and tea. The poignancy of their sentiments came into sharper focus only a few weeks later following the assassination of Martin Luther King Jr. in Memphis, Tennessee. Two days after his death on April 4, eight hundred students attended a memorial Mass at Gesu church; Father Raynor concelebrated the Mass. That same day, the university announced an anonymous gift of $180,000 to "provide expenses for 20 Negro students for a four-year college education" at Marquette. A week earlier, before the murder of Dr. King, the university had established six scholarships "for underprivileged residents of the Milwaukee community" in honor of longtime civil rights champion, Father John P. Markoe, SJ.[70]

The violent death of Martin Luther King set the streets of America aflame; Marquette and Milwaukee could hardly avoid these outbursts. A month after the assassination, on the evening of May 8, two hundred students barricaded the doors of Brooks Memorial Union from the outside, preventing more than four hundred faculty and staff from leaving the annual Père Marquette dinner. The Milwaukee police arrived and arrested two students. Later that night, one hundred protestors gathered in the downstairs grill, threatening to stay unless the police released the arrested students. Eventually the group dispersed. The next day, Executive Vice President Raymond McAuley, SJ, delivered the administration's response: Marquette "will not allow disruptive demonstrations in normal operation of the University such as took place last night." McAuley acknowledged the right of students "to communicate, by lawful demonstration and protest, the positions which they conscientiously espouse on vital issues of the day." However, the "interference with processes or procedures of instruction, research, administration or other activities authorized to be conducted in University facilities … may result in suspension or expulsion of the offender from the University."

Rallies continued on a daily basis. The demonstrators, by now a fiery combination of black and white students, adopted the name, Respond, as they sought "to confront the ADMINSTRATION with [its] institutional racism." Their seven demands included one hundred scholarships for black students, more black history and culture courses, more black faculty and administrators, and an open speakers' policy. Respond set a deadline of May 17 to have its conditions met and when that date passed, twenty of the university's forty-nine black students withdrew, although most later reconsidered. Several faculty members threatened the same. Father Raynor released a statement expressing his appreciation for the overwhelming support he and his staff had received from other students and alumni for his refusal to give in to "militant students." At the same time, he authorized a Special Committee on Scholarship Programs and Courses in Black and Minority Cultures under the chairmanship of Ed Simmons. In a subsequent letter to alumni and to the parents of current students, the president reiterated his refusal to submit to "coercion," but outlined steps that the university, in keeping with its own traditions, had undertaken to address *Respond*'s concerns.[71]

The Simmons committee worked with dispatch. Its first meeting was held on May 21, less than two weeks after the Père Marquette incident. An interim report became available within a month. During the next thirty days, the committee searched for a director of the new Special Program for the Culturally Distinct Student. The administration considered forty-two individuals and selected Arnold Mitchem, who was already teaching a course on African American history at Marquette. He assumed the post on

Arnold Mitchem. File EOP.

January 15, 1969, eight months after the demonstration at Brooks Memorial Union. Not long thereafter, the Special Program for the Culturally Distinct Student dropped its problematic name, becoming the Educational Opportunity Program, a title it continues to bear. Even before Mitchem was hired, Gordon L. Berry, an administrator at Milwaukee Technical College, had joined the administration as assistant to the academic vice president, the first African American to work in the central administration. The Negro Leadership Aid Program, then seven years old, continued its quietly effective work, with twenty-five participants from the local community attending evening classes in the fall of 1968. Communications between African American students and the administration improved during the 1969-70 school year, as evidenced by an incident in November. A black student accused a faculty member of bias, but through Arnold Mitchem's adroit intercession, the matter was resolved without further conflict.[72]

VIETNAM COMES TO MILWAUKEE

Marquette students may have had no history of political protest before 1960, but they were quick learners. In 1961, the Young Republicans on campus first broached the right of students to invite any outside speakers they wished. About the same time, the *Marquette Tribune* began to link race relations on and around the campus with the national civil rights movement. In another demonstration of how local sentiment could intersect with national politics, hundreds of Marquette students paraded down Wisconsin Avenue at the height of the Cuban missile crisis in 1962, protesting the presence of a communist enclave ninety miles south of Florida. Homemade signs read "To Hell with Fidel." Father Floyd Stanton, vice president of student affairs, intervened; he snatched signs and demanded student identifications from those who refused to follow his orders to disperse. For religious and political reasons, Marquette students in the early sixties uniformly supported America's crusade against worldwide communism. Thus, in the fall of 1965, several hundred students signed a telegram supporting the presence of U.S. military personnel in the battle against communist insurgents in South Vietnam. An informal straw poll among three hundred students taken by the Young Democrats, Young Republicans, and Milwaukee's WISN-TV in late fall 1966 indicated only thirteen percent opposed the presence of American troops in Southeast Asia. In fact, a majority of those polled favored accelerating U.S. involvement—President Lyndon Johnson's preferred policy.

Sentiments shifted dramatically over the next year as casualties mounted. Opposition to the war grew so quickly that the administration distributed formal guidelines for student demonstrations in November 1967. Blocking "ingress or egress to any university building or office or classroom in a university building shall be fairly construed as obstructive," the document read. Such a confrontation exceeded the "right of a student to peacefully … demonstrate." Promulgation of these policies was timely, for a month later, protestors staged a sit-in at the dean of students' office, decrying Dow Chemical's recruitment session in Copus Hall because Dow was the manufacturer of napalm. Underscoring the civility of these early protests, demonstrators (including two Jesuit scholastics and two nuns) first appeared at O'Hara Hall to ask to sit-in at the president's office. Rebuffed, they calmly moved to the student union. In a flier, the organizers explained that their "non-violent, non-obstructive sit-in is meant to dramatize our disapproval of the decision-making process that has allowed Dow Chemical company to recruit on the Marquette campus." The protestors were particularly upset that the administration had failed "to consult with the faculty and students before making this decision," an "infringement" of their rights.[73]

Lines of polite demonstrators parading with inoffensive signs were soon a memory as differences over the Vietnam war escalated. By May 1968, the university issued a second set of rules, this time for "Faculty Participation in Disruptive Demonstrations." By then, a key target was the Reserve Officers Training Corps, a fixture at Marquette since before World War II. Yet, as late as February 1969, anti-war demonstrations at Marquette remained peaceful. A subcommittee of the student government sent a respectful note to the academic vice president, questioning the propriety of a military training program at a Christian university. Two weeks later, nine department chairs from the College of Liberal Arts endorsed this line of inquiry. A few days later, the student senate passed a resolution formally asking for a review of ROTC at Marquette. In response, Vice President Art Moeller asked the College of Liberal Art's curriculum committee to look into the legitimacy of for-credit ROTC classes. Coincidentally, on Tuesday, April 15, 1969, a senior army official arrived in Milwaukee to review Marquette's program. One hundred protestors marched through the old gymnasium (which the ROTC used on a daily basis) shouting for an end to the ROTC on campus. Plans to disrupt the general's inspection misfired when his review of the cadets was rescheduled for the morning instead of the afternoon. The next day, opponents of the war endorsed a statement demanding an end to Marquette's ROTC programs. A day later, on the seventeenth, dozens of demonstrators barreled past university security personnel in the gym as they made their way toward the naval ROTC offices. The Milwaukee police suddenly appeared—at the request of the university, according to law enforcement; not so, replied the administration. The demonstrators dispersed while the committee on faculty decided to look into the appropriateness of a ROTC program at a Jesuit and Catholic university. Another confrontation took place at the gym on April 22, 1969, as demonstrators attempted to prevent ROTC members from entering the gym for a drill. The dean of men confronted these protestors; ultimately they departed the building with Milwaukee police stationed just outside.[74]

About sixty students then strode from the gymnasium to the Joan of Arc Chapel, which they entered during the 4:00 p.m. Mass. Once inside, they locked the doors, securing them with a timber. Seven hours later, the police received a call from the Milwaukee Fire Department: they were headed to the chapel to investigate a bomb scare. After repeated warnings by the police that they needed to enter the building—warnings that may not have been heard by those inside—officers crashed through the doors, arresting sixty-eight individuals. Gathered outside of Joan of Arc was a second group,

Dow Chemical protest, December 1967. File 144

numbering between one and two hundred and consisting of a mixture of protestors, curious onlookers, and journalists. They were cordoned off to one side while the police and firefighters moved into the chapel. Later, about 150 individuals from this second group marched to O'Hara Hall where they protested into the early morning hours.

The following day, April 23, 1969, Father Raynor released a statement explaining the university's position on the Joan of Arc incident. That evening, opponents of the war in Southeast Asia assembled in the student union to consider their next move. A bomb scare broke up this meeting, although the gathering reassembled after law enforcement swept the building. The second session concluded after one in the morning with a request to meet with Father Raynor the following evening. Resolutions passed at that second meeting demanded amnesty for students arrested at the Joan of Arc Chapel incident, the resignations of Fathers Raynor and McAuley, and the termination of ROTC at Marquette. The next night, following the Père Marquette faculty dinner in the union ballroom, the president and a group of faculty members went downstairs to the grill where they meet with about eight hundred students. Several days of meetings followed. Another protest took place at the university tennis courts during a NROTC awards ceremony on the twenty-ninth and a peaceful assembly of protestors at the chapel followed in the early morning hours of the thirtieth. Meanwhile, the committee on the faculty moved ahead with its inquiry into the ROTC and the local chapter of the American Association of University Professors held an open forum attended by a crowd of seven hundred faculty and students. Defenders of the students arrested at the chapel prepared an eight-page, single-spaced statement on May 19 demanding due process for anyone facing either civil or university sanctions. Ultimately, seven seniors arrested at the Joan of Arc incident were cleared of university infractions; six students arrested at the gymnasium incident were suspended. A year later, charges against the chapel protestors were dismissed when the city's disorderly conduct ordinance was declared unconstitutional.[75]

Throughout the summer of 1969, drafts of a revised university policy on demonstrations shuffled across administrative desks in O'Hara Hall. The final version recognized the right of each student to demonstrate publicly in support of his or her cause or position. Others on campus, however, had every right to pursue their own "academic and vocational objectives without unreasonable obstruction or hindrance." The statement tried to draw a distinction between agitators who engaged in "clearly violent, unlawful, or otherwise disruptive activities" and others who participated "in [a] lawful demonstration and protest." Admitting that reasonable persons might disagree as to when one individual's protest infringed on a non-participant's rights, the new guidelines authorized any responsible university official—administrator or faculty member—to call for the dispersal of a crowd if the demonstration had "passed proper bounds." That same fall, the academic senate unanimously approved a review of Marquette's two officer training programs. It supported a reorganization of the curricula and urged closer ties between the military and other units in the College of Liberal Arts, especially the department of history. Almost a year later, a Special Committee on the Christian Character of Marquette University (chaired by the graduate dean, Quentin Quade) concluded that ROTC units were not inconsistent with the Catholic character of the university. The committee maintained that those who supported military training units and those who opposed them both represented the Catholic tradition and were not mutually exclusive. The committee agreed with the academic senate that curricular refinements needed to better situate ROTC within the university's academic community.[76]

Even as various committees hurried to develop enforceable guidelines for public dissent, no one could envision the escalation that would follow. On April 30, 1970, President Richard Nixon authorized American forces to invade Cambodia, a previously neutral nation, to pursue North Vietnamese troops and to disrupt the enemy's supply lines into South Vietnam. The nation's responses to this action varied. In New York City on May 2, construction workers assaulted a group of antiwar protestors with "bottles, cans, and clumps of asphalt." Six days later, as many as nine thousand counter-demonstrators, including building trades workers from the still-rising World Trade Center, confronted a thousand antiwar protestors at Federal Hall. At first the counter-demonstrators only seized control of the hall's front steps. But later, they roamed nearby streets, attacking anyone with long hair or a peace sign. Over seventy individuals were treated for "bruises, cuts, broken noses, and busted teeth." Before the day was over, the pro-war crowd had placed city hall under siege.[77]

On America's campuses, invading Cambodia triggered different but equally intense outbursts at over 700 colleges and universities. Hundreds of thousands of individuals, perhaps as many as two million nationally, engaged in protests that were often accompanied by violence to property. In Washington, Nixon called these street throngs "bums." Among the institutions affected was Kent State University in Ohio where protestors burned a ROTC building on May 2. The mayor declared a state of emergency; national guardsmen arrived to insure public safety. Organizers of the antiwar protest scheduled a protest for May 4. As the noon hour approached the next morning, just under a hundred guardsmen, carrying military-issue rifles chambered with live ammunition, concluded nearly an hour's effort of trying to disperse protestors who had gathered near the union. Now hundreds of students, perhaps several thousand, spilled out of classroom buildings heading to the union and across the campus. Some knew the protest had been banned; others—commuter students in particular—had no idea what was going on. Strained by the tensions of the past few days, the guardsmen discharged more than sixty shots within thirteen seconds, killing four students and wounding nine. Of those who died, the closest was 270 feet from the guardsmen, the farthest was 390 feet away.[78]

This time, the reaction was electrifying. This time rage mixed with fear. Even students previously unaffected by the antiwar movement were swept up in the emotions of the day. Some were in a fury over the death of innocent peers. Others worried that the armed might of the government could descend upon their campus at any moment. (As if to underscore the legitimacy of these fears, ten days later, law enforcement officers killed two black students at Jackson State University in Mississippi.) In the aftermath of Kent State, student leaders across the country called for protests and strikes. Rioters besieged ROTC facilities and seized university buildings. At some institutions, administrators canceled what remained of the spring term. Other colleges finished the semester, but with special memorials and truncated final exams. A few—a distinct minority—reacted minimally. Jesuit schools encountered the full range of experiences. At Fordham, where the Students for a Democratic Society (SDS) had inspired several years of sometimes violent occupations and confrontations, the Campus Center was burned to the ground in the aftermath of the Kent State killings. On the other hand, at Creighton in Omaha, the days of national unrest seem to have slipped by essentially unnoticed until the following fall when random gun shots targeted university buildings one evening and several bomb threats were reported.[79]

At Marquette on the day following the Kent State deaths, the student senate passed a resolution supporting a nonviolent strike. They also called for an all-day workshop to discuss recent events. In a move befitting a faith-based institution, they endorsed a three-day fast. Fliers circulated, calling for the university to condemn "the tragic and appalling crimes committed by the power structure." As part of the all-day workshop on May 6, Father Raynor celebrated a special Mass at 9 a.m. in Schroeder Hall. Two hours later, faculty members offered presentations on nonviolence; at noon, speeches focused on the history of American involvement in Southeast Asia. A huge rally began at one o'clock in front of Lalumiere Hall. Two thousand students later moved to Wisconsin Avenue, crowding both sides of the street. Police in riot gear stood by. Most students eventually returned to their daily routines, although vengeful acts continued. Fire bombs exploded at several points on the campus, causing minor damage.

Bomb scares became a familiar distraction during the days that followed. In one instance, a device that appeared quite authentic was found in McCormick Hall. Throngs of mournful and enraged students clashed with police and firefighters. Protestors barricaded Grandmora, the aging apartment building that served as home for the humanities departments. Others blocked access to the library and broke its windows as well as those in the chemistry and NROTC buildings. Sporadic street demonstrations led to the arrests of students on May 9. The school of journalism cancelled its year-end dinner. In response to a demand from the student body president to explain his position on the Kent State affair, Father Raynor prepared a letter expressing how appalled he was at the "violence and suffering, and the injustices man inflicts upon his fellow man." He deplored "the conditions which gave rise to the needless deaths at Kent State, and to the escalation of the war to Cambodia." In a separate communication to the university community, Raynor commended the "effective, nonviolent forms of expression" of Marquette students. He explained that final exams would proceed as scheduled with options for students who were "fearful and apprehensive about their personal safety." By the second week of May, with finals behind them, students drifted off to their summer destinations. Vice President of Student Affairs James Scott, who had prepared daily updates on the demonstrations, breathed easy for the first time in weeks. Law enforcement finally decamped from the campus.[80]

The committee on faculty spent a portion of the summer of 1970 in a forum, examining whether the central administration should be expected "to make a stand on publicly disputed issues." Participants failed to come to a final conclusion. They did endorse a student request for an October Moratorium prior to the upcoming, off-year November elections so that students could spend as much time as they wished involved with the political process. Vice President Moeller appointed his own committee, chaired by the dean of the law school, to look into the moratorium issue. This committee recommended that the administration turn down the student-faculty request for a moratorium. When the administration decided to follow this advice, it warned the faculty that there might be significant absences among students as the elections neared. When classes resumed in the fall of 1970, the campus was notably quieter, although late in September, scientist Edward Teller, an outspoken proponent of nuclear research for military purposes, was harassed after he delivered a speech in the chemistry building. Over a dozen bomb threats were reported during October and November, and one student suspect was arrested. But by the beginning of 1971, bomb threats tapered off significantly and some of the immediacy driving the student protests seemed to have diminished for the moment.[81]

Student protest, 1970. File 1144.

Student protest, undated. File 1144.

By the conclusion of the 1970-71 school year, Marquette had survived a remarkable decade. The organizational renovations instituted during Father Raynor's early years as president had been implemented with little controversy and considerable resolve. The medical school was on its way toward complete independence. Laymen served in the highest offices of the university. A lay board of trustees with unlimited powers now directed Milwaukee's Jesuit university. More controversial was the array of protests emanating from the student body. Across the country, university administrators learned to negotiate with their students on a face-to-face basis. At first, protests were seen as an annoyance. Later, they created frustration. Eventually, they became genuine challenges. Over the next decade, other crises arose. At Marquette, public safety became a vital concern. So too did worries over the institution's fiscal viability in the face of troublesome enrollment patterns. No longer the largest Catholic university in the nation, Marquette moved toward its centennial celebration in 1981 with less self-assurance than it had possessed at the opening of the 1960s.

9

SEARCH FOR A NEW ORDER
1960S-1981

The incessant drumbeat of protests, sit-ins, demonstrations, petitions, bomb threats, police sweeps, and press coverage during the late sixties and early seventies threatened to overwhelm Marquette's senior administrators—and their peers at comparable institutions. When Father Raynor moved into the president's first floor office in 1965 amid relative calm, he never envisioned the gathering storm. Consequently, he blithely set about addressing Marquette's longstanding troubles regarding the medical school's financial future and reordered the university's governance system: naming a layman to the academic vice presidency, creating a faculty-dominated academic senate, and reconstituting the board of trustees into a force beyond Jesuit control. He put his confreres on a contractual basis with the university. The new president might not have been so adventuresome had he foreseen what would transpire regarding outside speakers, student culture, the civil rights movement, ROTC, and the war in Vietnam. In coping with these unforeseen challenges, Raynor and his closest advisors turned cautious at the same moment that the faculty asserted their new governance powers and students insisted that yesterday's rules no longer made sense to them. Males let their beards and hair grow long whereas females wore short skirts and raised their voices on behalf of a standard of equality that administrators often found incomprehensible. The sexual behavior of undergraduates bedeviled the office of student affairs, even as public safety on campus became a daily concern. Enrollments stumbled, then soared, creating periods of uncertainty. Along the way came a centennial celebration that strove to focus on the promise of tomorrow, not the problems of yesterday.

ECONOMIC WOES

The social and political protests that pummeled Marquette (and American higher education in general) during the late sixties distracted the larger university community from a simmering crisis, one that threatened the school's fiscal well-being. Only the central administration appreciated the dangers of this situation. At the conclusion of his opening year as president in 1963, Father William Kelley proudly announced Marquette's first balanced budget in seven years. Truth be told, it was only the late Dr. John Heraty's bequest of $312,352 that prevented another deficit (of $250,000) at the conclusion of the 1962-63 fiscal year. The university rode a budgetary roller coaster during the next few years, with a deficit of $202,535 in 1963-64, followed by a surplus of $179,930; then came another deficit of $342,862, followed by a comfortable surplus of $364,679 in 1966-67 (the last year in which the medical school's finances were tied to the university's). The positive balance that year was distorted, however, because the administration switched the closing date for its annual budget cycle from the end of August to the end of June, insuring that the 1966-67 report covered only ten months. (July and August were notorious for having expenses surpass revenues.)[1]

Separating the medical school's balance sheet from the university's did not, surprisingly, improve matters. The university incurred yet another deficit in 1967-68, this time $777,154. A year later, the shortfall was $252,808. Annual statements never revealed these deficits, however, because the administration, with timely applications, assigned gifts from donors to balance the school's operating losses. For example, in the particularly troublesome year of 1971-72 (a decline in enrollment was compounded by a national wage/price freeze), the budget was more than a million dollars in arrears until $1,164,201 in gifts was used as current revenue. A vital factor in keeping the university solvent during these years was the generosity of the Jesuit community. In 1969-70, the year that the new lay trustees signed their first agreement with the Marquette Jesuit Associates, Inc., the religious community returned a $300,000 gift to the university at the end of the fiscal year. The community's largesse ranged between $275,000 and $311,000 over each of the next four years. In total, from September 1, 1966 to June 30, 1974, the Jesuits contributed $2.3 million to the university. Without this silent benefactor, the institution would have been in even more desperate straits.[2]

Marquette classroom, 1970-71. File 325.

Recurring debts forced operational changes. In 1969, Marquette terminated the 40 percent tuition discount granted to members of religious orders. In a press release, Father Raynor acknowledged the contributions that these priests and sisters (and, presumably, brothers) made to university life, but argued that the $141,000 loss in tuition dollars incurred by this discount contributed to a $750,000 deficit for 1967-68. The university also cut its cleaning staff by half, from ninety workers to fifty between 1970 and 1974. Daily custodial services were no longer available in most offices. The administration trimmed back the custodial staff once again in 1976, this time by another 25 percent. Three years earlier, the student health center closed its Heraty Hall nursing station (for after-hour and weekend emergencies) with expected savings of $8,000 per year.[3]

When fall enrollments did not meet budgetary expectations in the early seventies, mid-year corrections became routine. The deepest crisis occurred in the fall of 1971. At the recommendation of the vice president for business and finance, Father Raynor imposed a hiring freeze on all unfilled positions and ordered an under-expenditure of 1 percent in the current budget because of a $500,000 shortfall in tuition revenue. The university budget committee, in looking at "emergency or austerity measures," fretted over the institution's dependence upon tuition as well as the ebbing of faculty morale. In a letter to the faculty and staff, Vice President Art Moeller explained in painful detail the background of this crisis and its implications for the future. Anticipating another decline in enrollment, a joint letter from vice presidents Quentin Quade and Roy Kallenberger in July 1972 announced that the hiring freeze would remain in place. On everyone's mind were soaring instructional costs, triggered by runaway inflation. The 12.4 percent national inflation rate of 1974 doubled that of five years earlier. In the decade after 1973, America's cost of living increased an average of 8.2 percent per year, with the annual inflation rate still running at 11.3 percent in 1979. For employees, annual salary increases sometimes reached 7 or 8 percent. Yet these increases failed to keep up with rising costs even as escalating salaries wrought havoc on the university's bottom line. The budgeting process finally gained some stability during the 1974-75 fiscal year when the university introduced a five-year schematic: it started with the current year's figures for enrollment and expenditures and then projected trends forward for enrollments, salaries, and gifts.[4]

Spending cutbacks and modifications in the budgeting process helped right the fiscal ship. A surplus in the 1973-74 fiscal year doubled that of the previous year and the same occurred in the following cycle. A $256,626 excess of revenues over expenditures in 1976 allowed the administration to use that surplus for future needs. An even larger balance during the 1976-77 year allowed the administration to reassign $250,000 to the following year's budget and still make $273,000 available for current contingencies. By 1978, Marquette achieved its eighth consecutive year of balanced budgets. These improvements underwrote a university-wide vacation policy for non-faculty employees. What had previously been a haphazard jumble of personal agreements, with nary a nod to fairness, was now standardized: one to four years of employment earned three weeks of vacation; five or more years of service earned four weeks of vacation.[5]

Gifts from the Jesuit community and from individual donors were obvious factors in achieving fiscal stability by the late seventies, but Marquette students played a role as well. Tuition increased every other year during the 1960s, a key explanation for the roller coaster ride between surpluses (first year of an increase) and deficits (second year, without an increase) in the middle of that decade. After 1968, tuition charges rose annually. What began as $650 per year in 1958-59 rose to $1,450 a decade later. Tuition increased by at least a hundred dollars each year until 1974 when it jumped two hundred dollars. By 1977, it reached $2,900 per year, double the rate of 1968. In a survey of major private institutions completed in the mid-eighties, Marquette's tuition ranked twenty-seventh during the 1979-80 school year, near the bottom alongside Saint Louis University, Loyola University (in Chicago), and George Washington University. Marquette's tuition charge of $3,320 was two-thirds that of Harvard and M.I.T. By 1983, only Loyola cost less than Marquette, and both schools were well behind competitors such as Northwestern, Chicago, Notre Dame, Georgetown, Boston College, Fordham, and Saint Louis. As pricey as Marquette's tuition may have seemed to individual families, it was a bargain compared to rates at other private institutions.[6]

Supplemental funding during the sixties and seventies flowed primarily from three capital campaigns. The first effort was, of course, the Marquette Plan (later retitled the Greater Marquette Program), announced by Father O'Donnell in November 1960. The goal of $45 million by 1970 was to be met through $15 million from the federal government and faculty research grants, and two $15 million campaigns. The timing of the first installment in this campaign was interrupted when Father Kelley assumed the presidency in 1962 and, three-and-a-half years later, when John Raynor replaced Kelley. As with the university's earliest experiences in fund-raising, the Greater Marquette Program relied upon Milwaukee's industrial giants. Allis Chalmers, less than two decades from its own demise as the region's largest employer, contributed $375,000 and Briggs and Stratton offered $250,000. A.O. Smith, the automobile fabricator, provided $150,000. In total, as the first phase of the campaign drew to a close in late 1966, twenty-two corporations (identified as Group 1) had pledged nearly $2 million. The school's goal of $15 million had been exceeded by nearly $2.5 million. In total, corporations provided nearly a third of this sum ($5.45 million), with non-alumni donors offering another $3.5 million. Alumni, a constituency whose role would grow with time, added nearly $3 million, about 18 percent of the total. (In contrast, during the university's fund-raising effort that ended in 2005, alumni donated 34 percent, the most generous sector among all donors.) Even Lawrence Welk made his contribution in 1964 when he hosted a special concert at the Milwaukee Arena. (One of his daughters graduated from Marquette's Journalism College and married a medical school alumnus; his other daughter took classes in the liberal arts before transferring to Mount St. Mary in Los Angeles.)[7]

The second phase of the Marquette Plan was delayed until early 1969 and was re-named "ADVANCE—A Program for a Greater Marquette." It too started out as a five-year undertaking, with an expanded target of $30 million. Nearly half of these funds were earmarked for construction; almost $6 million was designated for student aid and student facilities, with more than $7 million for academic programs. ADVANCE was scheduled to conclude during the 1974 tercentenary of Father Marquette's second trip across the American Midwest. Key contributions came from Evan P. Helfaer and the Briggs and Stratton Foundation, both of whom provided $500,000. The Kresge Foundation offered $100,000 to renovate Johnston Hall. The growing importance of alumni-giving was evident in a detailed worksheet that listed Marquette graduates by city, with a list of their pledges. When ADVANCE concluded in late 1974, 25,043 donors had contributed $31.5 million. From this effort came Lalumiere Hall, Helfaer Theater, Helfaer Recreation Center, William Wehr Physics, and renovations to the law school, the dentistry school, and Johnston Hall.[8]

The final capital campaign undertaken before the school's centennial in 1981 began four months *before* ADVANCE's successful conclusion. Marquette's fiscal woes be-tween 1970 and 1973 made the trustees anxious and ultimately more assertive. After all, they had taken control of the university as recently as 1969, just as the budgetary woes intensified. Concern for the school's long-term financial prognosis steered them toward a strategy that would stabilize the school's future through an enhanced endow-ment. By October 1975, details of the lay trustees' first campaign became clearer: they wanted "realistic" goals, but a "reduced" solicitation schedule. They settled on a three-year effort with a goal of $40 million, and decided to minimize the role of local

Meeting of post-1969 Board of Trustees. Father Raynor, second from left. File 1345.

corporations and foundations during the first year, insisting that these companies had received sufficient attention during previous campaigns. Instead, national corporations and foundations as well as alumni would be the main targets of fund-raisers during the opening round. The need to get alumni more involved was obvious. According to one source, with a 21 percent participation rate, Marquette's graduates ranked in the middle of annual alumni-giving among all Jesuit colleges and universities in 1976-77. Regarding campaign goals, the trustees placed an emphasis on the endowment, a distinct departure from previous fund-raisers. Of the $40 million target, $25 million was originally earmarked for the endowment; $9 million was to go toward operating expenses and the remaining $6 million toward construction.

Trustees curiously chose to reuse the name of the Marquette Plan's first phase (1960-66) for its newest undertaking: the Greater Marquette Program (GMP). Former Gesu pastor Father James Corrigan directed the early phases of this latest effort as vice president for development and alumni relations. For chairman of the alumni effort, they turned to Father O'Donnell. Two-thirds of the way through, Father Bruce Biever, recently provincial of the Wisconsin Province, came aboard as vice president for university relations, a post that now included alumni relations, development, and public relations. Jim Sankovitz, previously vice president for university relations, became the first vice president for governmental relations, a sign of the central role that state and federal governments now played at Catholic universities. With academic development as the principal objective of this campaign, advancement developed a set of "General Guidelines for endowing Faculty Positions." Halfway through the campaign, six faculty chairs and professorships had been funded. The Allis-Chalmers Corporation endowed one in international affairs for $1 million and the Kimberly-Clark Corporation endowed another in engineering for $500,000. The Johnson Wax Foundation provided $255,000 for one research fellowship and two student scholarships. Eventually, twenty-four scholarships for students were established. The campaign's largest gift ($3.5 million) came from the Walter Schroeder Foundation in February 1978 to support massive renovations in Cramer Hall after the Medical College of Wisconsin departed for Wauwatosa. On April 21, 1980, a little after the original deadline for the Greater Marquette Program, Father Raynor announced that 23,194 alumni, corporations, foundations, parents, and other individuals had contributed $40,484,704, nearly $500,000 more than the original goal. Priorities had shifted, however. The president reported that more than $18 million was designated for capital improvements, with less than $10 million assigned to the endowment. Most of the remainder was applied to annual operating budgets.[9]

By the conclusion of the Greater Marquette Program, the university's endowment stood at $16 million, double the amount from five years earlier. Yet the financial exigencies of Catholic higher education were changing so rapidly that these new dollars failed to benefit the annual budget. In 1974, at the conclusion of the ADVANCE campaign, income from tuition had accounted for 54 percent of Marquette's annual revenues; monies from the federal government accounted for 9 percent and private gifts for 8 percent. Endowment income brought in 1 percent of the total. In the budget year (1980-81) following the conclusion of the Greater Marquette Program, tuition income still accounted for 54 percent of operating revenues and the endowment still contributed only 1 percent. But the federal portion had grown to 11 percent, one reason why Vice President Sankovitz produced an annual report on governmental sponsorship of research and programs.[10]

One final issue in the school's financial history during the late seventies and early eighties was the nascent debate over the presence of American corporations in the apartheid nation of South Africa. Hal C. Kuehl, chairman of the board of trustees, sent a memorandum in November 1978 to the chief executive officers of corporations in which the university owned stock. On behalf of the university's trustees, Kuehl requested that these businesses "adopt the Sullivan Principles or a superior policy"* and insisted that they "seek to improve communications with your black and other non-white work forces, including developing contacts with representatives of black or other non-white labor organizations, or other appropriate social structures." In an attached position paper, the university endorsed the free enterprise system as well as a "Catholic tradition" that held "the world's property and productive capacity exist[ed] for the material welfare of all mankind." The position paper conceded that corporate managers did not own the companies they oversaw, but held it in trust for the stockholders. Therefore, management could not accede to every demand, even from those who insisted American-owned companies withdraw from South Africa if the government did not terminate its racist practices. Marquette's statement labeled apartheid "unacceptable and repugnant." And if companies implemented apartheid, the university wanted them to discontinue this abhorrent policy. For the moment, however, trustees chose not divest the university of stock in companies that conducted business in South Africa, believing that divestiture would not "better the lives of those living under apartheid's injustice." Subsequently, the university developed a fund for black South African students; the first recipient graduated in the summer of 1981. Differences over economic involvement with South Africa continued to divide the university community throughout the eighties; students held a protest outside O'Hara Hall in 1985 and a 104-page proposal was submitted to the board of trustees four years later by the Marquette University Students Taking Action by Coming Together.[11]

MUSICAL CHAIRS—ACADEMIC STYLE

Balancing revenues and expenditures amid an overheated national economy nudged Father Raynor and others in O'Hara Hall into a cautious mode when anticipating new construction. During the decade before Marquette's centennial, the administration preferred to complete previously approved projects (including the school's urban renewal program) and remove obsolete facilities. A decade of nurturing development of Marquette's natural science center came to a welcome conclusion in November

---

* The Sullivan Principles, developed by a Philadelphia clergyman, asked American companies to treat their South African workers, regardless of color, as they would their American counterparts.

1973 when the William Wehr Physics building was dedicated, complementing the Wehr Life Sciences and Todd Wehr Chemistry buildings. Relocation of the physics and mathematics departments into the William Wehr facility triggered a chain reaction of spatial reassignments. The space that physics had occupied in Science Hall (soon renamed Marquette Hall) was turned over to the registrar, the College of Liberal Arts, and the Graduate School. The departure of mathematics from Nicolas Hall freed up room in that former apartment building for the School of Education. The space vacated by liberal arts in Johnston Hall provided room for speech and journalism. The university could now tear down speech's long-time home, the John Plankinton mansion on Fifteenth Street. (The adjoining house, built for William Plankinton and used for years by the athletic department, had been torn down in 1970.) Copus Hall also met its demise in this same parade of bulldozers. The three-story residence, with its signature turret, had housed journalism between 1950 and 1965 before the unit moved to the Alumnae House. The band subsequently occupied Copus Hall. Later, the university art museum and its adjoining park were built on this location.[12]

A contingent of Jesuits joined the liberal arts college in departing from Johnston Hall. In negotiating its contract with the Marquette Jesuit Associates, Inc. in 1970, the new board of trustees promised to provide suitable housing for the religious com-

Jesuit's room on fourth floor of Johnston Hall, 1973. File 718.

munity. Anticipating the shuffling of office space after the opening of the new physics building in late 1973, the trustees offered to move the Jesuits who lived in Johnston, Merritty, and Regis halls to Heraty Hall. In turn, this relocation displaced two hundred juniors and seniors who had used the former hotel for more than a decade. On January 17, 1973, Vice President of Student Affairs James Scott notified the female residents of Heraty that they would be evicted so that the university might provide appropriate accommodations for the Jesuits. A flurry of protests followed. An even more fascinating stir erupted among the uprooted Jesuits, some of whom questioned whether a communal consensus existed on the relocation to Heraty Hall. The *Marquette Tribune* took particular glee in reporting this fracture within the Jesuit ranks. By the time the sons of St. Ignatius occupied a renovated Heraty Hall (with its eye-catching white window treatments) in the fall of 1973, disagreements had been put aside and the new "Jes-Res" became a vital socio-spatial marker for the campus. For those Jesuits who worked at Gesu, the graduate school's move into Science Hall and the Marquette Players' 1974 relocation to the Helfaer Theater allowed them to take possession of Bellarmine Hall, eventually converting it into a parish center.[13]

The Varsity Theater and Cramer Hall also faced role changes during the seventies. Through the middle of the decade, the Varsity Theater remained just that, a movie house. Its proximity to Schroeder and McCormick halls and to the Jesuit commu-

Jesuit dining room in Johnston Hall basement, 1973. File 718.

nity (after 1973) coupled with the university's ownership of the building (since 1967) guided the management's choice of films (although it did present two x-rated movies during this period). In March 1976, during a week when *American Graffiti* was airing, the theater's manager suddenly announced that he would close the facility due to declining revenues. (At the time, the Varsity charged "a piddling $1.50 for most movies," according to the *Tribune*.) After extensive discussions, the central administration converted the Varsity to academic purposes, including the history department's memorable "Western Civ" courses. As for Cramer Hall, its future remained in a state of constant uncertainty because of acrimonious negotiations between Milwaukee County and the Milwaukee Medical Center (which included both the Medical College of Wisconsin and Froedtert Memorial Lutheran Hospital). Eventually, the medical college moved to the county grounds during mid- to late-1978. The Walter Schroeder Foundation then stepped forward with $3.5 million to renovate Cramer Hall. When it reopened as the Schroeder Complex, departments such as education, psychology, and physical therapy found a well-provisioned new home.[14]

One eyesore that met its demise during these years was the apartment complex known as Grandmora Hall, home to the English, history, philosophy, and theology departments. In one wing, both the fourth floor and the lower level (nicknamed "the catacombs") had been condemned by 1975; in addition, the building's fire escape ended twenty feet above ground and had no drop ladder. A grassy mall was originally planned for this conspicuous space along Wisconsin Avenue, but instead, another parking lot appeared. (The Katharine Reed Cudahy Building was built on this site in 1994.) Replacement space for the humanities departments, originally intended for the

Grandmora Hall, 1950s. File 625.

lot formerly occupied by Copus Hall, was instead built where the Gesu parish school once operated. Dedicated in May 1977, this brown-bricked, three-story structure was named in honor of Charles Coughlin, the longtime president of Briggs and Stratton Corporation, who had served on the university's board of governors from 1944 to 1964.[15]

Throughout the sixties and seventies, the university moved relentlessly to convert the retail and commercial landscape north of Wisconsin Avenue into a center for student life. Marquette purchased Dal's Drive-In and Sandwich Shop (formerly Sonny's five-cent hamburger shop) on the northeast corner of Thirteenth and Wisconsin in 1968. It was razed seven years later, about the same time that the university completed lengthy negotiations for the purchase of the adjoining Abbot Crest Hotel. Within a short time, this eight-story residential tower came tumbling down, allowing the entire corner—at first scheduled to become a parking lot—to be redeveloped into what the university called a "mini-park." The nearby retail block housing the University Store, Grebe's Bakery, and Cardijn Bookstore was acquired through a combination of gift and purchase in early 1968. A decade later, the trustees purchased the medical office building known by its address: 1212. Around the corner at Thirteenth and Wells, the National Super Market chain store was closed in 1973, only to be reopened for a brief time as Annie's Foods. The city subsequently demolished this structure in compliance with the Marquette urban renewal contract. This lot later became part of the Schroeder Hall intramural field.[16]

Miles away, another piece of Marquette's morphological memory vanished with nary an afterthought. By the mid-seventies, the university's club football team as well as its soccer and track teams no longer used the old football stadium. (Track and field had been reintroduced in 1963.) With the demise of the University of Wisconsin-Milwaukee's football program (which had rented Marquette's half-century-old facility for two seasons), only Marquette University High School played games at the site. A fire, probably set by vandals, during the summer of 1975 destroyed what was left of the press box. A year later, Roy Kallenberger notified the trustees that the stands had been declared "unsafe for public use." Demolition began in fall 1976. The site of magnificent gridiron triumphs in the twenties and thirties but only hard times after World War II was soon forgotten by a new generation of Warriors.[17]

Two significant but unscheduled additions came as a result of Evan Helfaer's generosity. A former University of Wisconsin tennis player who turned Lakeside Laboratories from a $500 company into a $14 million enterprise, Helfer became a financial angel for Marquette during the sixties and seventies. In 1967, he provided $500,000 for the president's discretionary use and $120,000 to equip the top two floors of the new chemistry building. Five years later, he contributed more than $1.5 million for a new theater and performing arts center. His fourth donation (of $2 million) funded the university recreational center. Sadly, Helfaer never saw more than the earliest stages of this construction because he died in February 1974.[18]

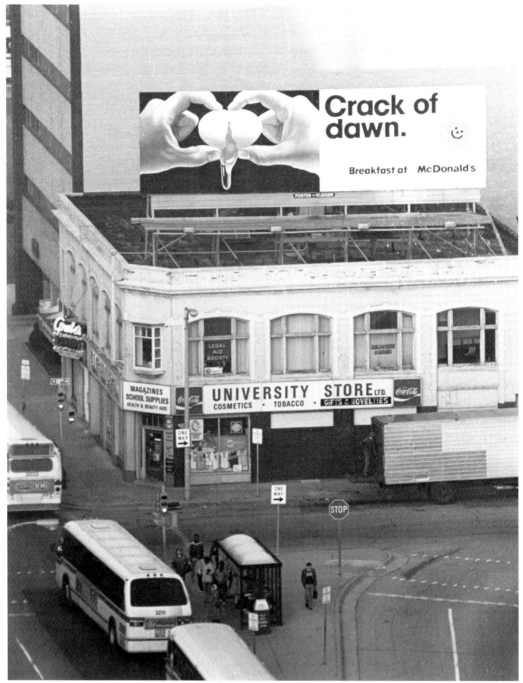

Northwest corner of Twelfth and Wisconsin, 1980s. File 260.

Another new university supporter was the Olin Foundation. After twenty years of discussions, Father Raynor finally convinced the foundation to provide $2.25 million in late 1973 to fund an engineering center. Positioned over what had once been Fifteenth Street, this stylish collection of offices, lecture rooms, and laboratories was dedicated in April 1978. Three years later, ground was broken for the last building planned

Ground breaking for Helfaer Theater, July 1973, with Copus Hall in background. File 662.

Helfaer Recreation Center under construction, July 1974. File 660.

before Marquette's fast-approaching centennial. A new home for the nursing college was scheduled to rise on a strip of land north of the gymnasium that had been used over time as a track stadium, tennis courts, and finally a parking lot. When the Milwaukee Medical College brought its nurses' training program to Marquette in 1907, the students had been housed in a Victorian residence across Ninth Street from Trinity/Marquette University Hospital. When a nursing curriculum returned to Marquette in 1936 (after a six year absence), these newest Hilltoppers took their course work at St. Joseph's Hospital on Forty-ninth and Burleigh. Marquette assumed financial as well academic control over the College of Nursing in 1971. But not until the construction of what became Emory T. Clark Hall could the college genuinely integrate its students and faculty with the rest of the university.[19]

Marquette undergraduates benefitted immensely from the improved academic facilities afforded by the Wehr Science Center and Olin Hall of Engineering. They clearly rejoiced in the special resources provided by the Helfaer Theater and the recreation center. But in truth, they probably spent more hours within the puzzle box of student housing options used by the university during the 1970s. The uncertainties of providing residential lodging for undergraduates were epitomized by Carmel Hall. A fire at the Society of Mount Carmel's seminary in Niagara Falls, Ontario, caused the order in 1968 to transfer its students to Marquette and into a three-story apartment complex on Seventeenth Street. This move came at the pinnacle of the American Catholic Church's richest era of religious vocations. Unprecedented numbers of nuns, brothers, and priests had to be educated, preferably at a Catholic university. But this move by the Carmelites came shortly before the Raynor administration terminated the university's tuition discount for members of religious orders. After a decline in their own vocations by the late seventies, the Carmelites moved their formation center to Chicago and sold Carmel Hall to the university for $550,000. Student affairs converted the building into thirty-nine apartment-style rooms for sixty-one students.[20]

Carmel Hall became the second apartment building acquired by the university during this decade, following the Abbotsford Apartments on Thirteenth Street in 1970. A very different sort of dormitory space was added to the mix in the fall 1974 when the university rented rooms for nearly seventy students at the Central YMCA, east of I-43. A crushing demand for campus housing had forced administrators to house students in the basement chapel of O'Donnell Hall, five lounges in McCormick and Schroeder halls, and in Merritty Hall after the Jesuits moved out. By 1976, Marquette students were using the top ten stories of the Y. Eventually, in 1993, after repeated denials of interest in another high-rise residential hall, the university purchased the YMCA outright.[21]

Meanwhile, the office of residential life had already turned to the Ambassador Hotel, at Twenty-third and Wisconsin, as an emergency shelter. Fifty-two students were assigned in 1976 to what was described as a "dream dorm." Within a few years, the university began to eye a neighboring business, the Holiday Inn-Central, which under the name of the Coach House Motor Inn had hosted the Beatles during their overnight

Coach House Motor Inn, later Mashuda Hall, 1964. File 9115.

stay in Milwaukee in 1964. Originally, the university intended to obtain a 3 percent loan from the Department of Housing and Urban Development to underwrite the purchase of the seven-story building. When the government turned down Marquette's application, the trustees proceeded on their own and bought what became Mashuda Hall in late 1979. Mashuda was actually the second Holiday Inn to serve Marquette students. In fall 1977, Marquette leased the nine-story Holiday Inn-Midtown at Twenty-sixth and Wisconsin to house 350 students in 170 rooms. Subsequently renamed West Hall, the residential tower was purchased in late 1980 despite its distance from the campus.[22]

The most memorable acquisition of this era also became the most distasteful episode of the Marquette urban renewal project. The third Plankinton mansion along Grand (Wisconsin) Avenue was built on the north side of the street in 1886 as a wedding gift from John Plankinton to his daughter Elizabeth. It sat vacant—despite its regal splendor: a rough-hewn limestone exterior, soaring turret, elegant wooden staircase, hand-carved banisters, and nine fireplaces— because Elizabeth's betrothed was said to have run off with a dancer from Minnesota. As a consequence, she wanted nothing to do with this magnificent reminder of her disappointment. The family eventually sold the residence, still unused, in 1896. Fourteen years later, the Knights of Columbus, a

Stratford Arms Hotel, later Heraty Hall, now Jesuit Residence, 1974.
Elizabeth Plankinton's mansion to left. File 718a.

Catholic organization, purchased it and later added a utilitarian service building on the mansion's north flank.

These buildings served as a clubhouse for meetings and included a bowling alley that was used by the Marquette faculty league. With the concurrence of the university and the Knights of Columbus, the property at 1492 Wisconsin Avenue was included in the Marquette urban renewal zone in the mid-sixties. Yet the city of Milwaukee delayed the final purchase, forcing the federal office of housing and urban development to order the city in 1973 to act promptly or lose its funding. For its part, the university made a strategic mistake when it obligingly extended the Knights' lease throughout the seventies. Finally, in late 1978, the university wanted to complete the acquisition of this land, which meant that the city had to clear the lot of its structures. At this point, an eclectic alliance of interests—historical preservationists, politicians, students, journalists, and local residents—succeeded in obtaining a judicial restraining order, blocking demolition. It was never clear whether the loudest voices opposing destruction of the Plankinton mansion constituted the entire opposition or whether they were the public face of a much larger constituency. These public outcries and the media's apparent delight in having anti-Marquette stories to report deeply troubled the administration. The city's failure to conclude its responsibilities under terms of the urban renewal agreement further incensed university officials. Finally in mid-October 1980, a bulldozer charged into the front stairway of the residence, commencing the demolition process. A decade later, a new student union replaced Elizabeth Plankinton's wedding gift.[23]

Most of the university's interactions with civil authorities were far more benign than those associated with the Knights of Columbus building. As various phases of the free-way interchange were completed alongside downtown Milwaukee, facilities manager Roy Kallenberger and project planner Seb Helfer developed a cordial relationship with the county expressway commission, quietly surrendering university property east of Tower Hall and at the southeast corner of the campus along Tory Hill. Then in April 1968, Father Raynor took a bold step, one that his predecessors would never have considered. He requested that the new central interchange be renamed for Milwaukee's Jesuit university. Surprisingly, this solicitation was granted and "The Marquette Inter-change" became part of the Milwaukee lexicon. Moreover, Milwaukee County—never supportive of Marquette's interests— approved a park in 1970 to honor the tercente-nary of Father Marquette's encampment along the banks of the Milwaukee River in 1674. The county park commission chose the site where Père Marquette was likely to have stayed, on the west bank of the river, north of Kilbourn Street. (Two decades lat-er, the park hosted President Bill Clinton's historic meeting with German Chancellor Helmut Kohl.) For its part, the university bestowed an honorary degree in 1976 upon Milwaukee's first county executive, John Doyne, a two-time alumnus of Marquette.[24]

ACADEMIC NON-PROLIFERATION

The fiscal clamps set in place by the central administration during the early seventies reduced custodial staff, eliminated contingency funds, and slowed the pace of new construction on campus. Operating with a dispassionate, corporate style of manage-ment favored by the new board of trustees, senior administrators eventually turned their budgetary shears upon the school's instructional program, especially graduate studies. In 1969, Vice President Art Moeller advised the trustees that "the next few years at Marquette will be marked by a concentration on academic consolidation and enrichment of existing programs." Moeller's attitude troubled at least one senior Jesuit who warned of "'major surgery on existing programs … [including] amputating en-tire programs, perhaps even entire colleges or schools'" in a move toward quality over quantity. Quentin Quade (Moeller's associate vice president) admitted in 1971 that "certain budget actions lately taken" had impacted graduate programs, though "[n]ever in its recent history has the university curtailed a graduate program on fundamentally economic grounds …. Graduate program curtailments at Marquette in recent years have been exclusively on academic grounds." For its part, the board of graduate studies in 1971-72 concluded that recent cuts in the academic budget had hindered doctoral programs for "the foreseeable future." Later that year when addressing the trustees, Quade conceded that the absence of new doctoral programs was linked to the admin-istration's sense of fiscal responsibility.[25]

Upon his promotion to academic vice president, Quade prepared a document, titled "Major Themes and Aspirations," in anticipation of the North Central Association's accreditation visit in February 1973. He spoke of the economic difficulties facing Marquette and how, following authorization of doctoral programs in chemistry and history, "a hold has been placed on further doctoral programming, and the result has inevitably been a kind of suspension for many departments." Quade admitted that this left the university's graduate offerings with a "lack of symmetry," but insisted that the "wisdom" of this strategy had been proven. Later, he acknowledged the university's need to ask a fundamental question: "Do we freeze the status quo or dismantle present doctoral programs?" The academic vice-president also wanted to investigate what he called a "'steady state'" approach to academic development. The trustees were clearly of the same persuasion. At a committee on finance meeting in December 1972, one trustee proposed "an in-depth study … to determine … what programs might have to be curtailed or eliminated."[26]

The tussle between academic innovations and budgetary constraints preoccupied senior administrators throughout the seventies. In his annual summary of academic affairs in 1974, Vice President Simmons admitted that "[n]ew programs are not ruled out, but they are being very carefully planned." In his next report, he explained that "achieving uniform excellence" came from "qualitative rather than quantitative growth" (better programs, not more) and he warned deans and directors that revenue gains from donor gifts would not underwrite "expansion and proliferation" of programs. Instead, these funds would be "aimed at uniform excellence in all that we do," that is, through qualitative development. Still, there was a limit to budget-cutting. Simmons dismissed suggestions that increasing faculty members' teaching loads would bring "relief to the budget situation." This "step in the direction of mediocrity" was, he explained, "not feasible at Marquette … a first-rate university." Father Raynor took a slightly different approach when he explained that the "whole idea of non-proliferation of programs, and then the pursuit of uniform quality" permitted the administration to "concentrate on [faculty] compensation."[27]

TAKING MEASURE OF EXCELLENCE

After achieving its immediate goals of bringing order to the university fiscal's condition and winning the university's first ten-year accreditation from the North Central Association in 1973, the central administration devoted what remained of that decade to defining qualitative rather than quantitative excellence. In preparing for the accreditation visit, the administration had hammered out a "self-understanding and self-definition." First and foremost, Marquette was Jesuit and "private, Christian, and Catholic." The second basic theme was its urban character; the university chose to be "of the city, not just in it." Furthermore, Marquette was dedicated to professional education, meaning that although it acknowledged "the centrality of the College of Liberal Arts," it proudly sponsored eight professional schools and colleges. Finally, Marquette's commitment to graduate education and scholarly research required on-going faculty development, constant improvements in library and research facilities, and a selective recruitment of students. If expanding academic programs was no longer an anticipated outcome, then excellence in what Marquette did choose to offer demanded the administration's and faculty's full attention.[28]

One measure of the university's recent successes became evident in 1970 when Phi Beta Kappa, "the nation's oldest and most prestigious liberal arts scholastic honor society," awarded Marquette a chapter. An exhaustive examination of the university's credentials preceded this distinction, including reviews of the undergraduate curriculum, characteristics of present students, performance of past graduates, and the faculty's stature. This stature was reinforced in 1975 when the university announced that three out of four faculty members now held doctoral degrees. As the liberal arts dean explained in a letter to his faculty, this level of terminal degrees had been attained through a rigorous recruitment process. Father Robert Gassert, dean for fifteen years, reflected upon "the many changes in academic climate that have occurred in this relatively brief period of time." He cited forming search committees, advertising nationally, and consulting with department colleagues as routine procedures in the recruitment process, in contrast to only a few years earlier when "there was little if any faculty involvement … and the appointment was simply made." The informal "old-boy" network had been modified, if not completely dismantled. Senior administrators kept the trustees informed of these improvements as well as with refinements in the promotion and tenure process. The university's statutes for promotion and tenure had been revised in 1969, and within a short time, were upgraded. In a 1972 memorandum, Quentin Quade confessed that "promotion and tenure are probably more difficult to achieve today than was the case when the Statutes were adopted." He also admitted that financial exigencies contributed to a more rigorous review of faculty promotions, but insisted that this was a healthier strategy than having the university freeze promotions or impose rank and tenure quotas. Four years later, Vice President Simmons conceded that certain faculty members probably experienced "discomfort" with the "more rigorous mode." Faculty now arrived at Marquette with scholarly ambitions that required the university to maintain its commitment to research. To Raynor, Quade, and Simmons, this commitment was symbolized by a new sabbatical leave program.[29]

Quade and Simmons submitted a detailed proposal for a sabbatical leave program to Art Moeller, the academic vice president, in the fall of 1969. Eight months later, their outline made its way to the academic senate. At the same time, a survey conducted by the committee on faculty indicated that two-thirds of the faculty heartily supported a sabbatical program. The senate's special committee on sabbaticals reported back in 1973 with the pointed observation that these new opportunities must benefit the university as a whole and not just the faculty. Guidelines for eligibility, the application process, funding, and departmental compensation were all addressed in detail. Referring to this document in his annual report, Vice President Simmons tied the sabbatical leave option to growth in the quality of the university's faculty. By September 1974, five years after his and Simmons's original suggestion, Quentin Quade (now executive vice president) formally presented the plan to Father Raynor.[30]

Development of faculty support for this program had been painless and procedures to implement it were developed without rancor. But the trustees needed a great deal of convincing. For one thing, they had to be educated on the intricacies of a research institution. There was no equivalent to sabbaticals in the corporate world. Annual bonuses and arbitrary dismissals, perhaps; released time for scholarly pursuits was quite another matter. In his first presentation before the trustees' subcommittee on educational policy and academic affairs, Quade insisted that sabbaticals were a "faculty enrichment; not merely a reward for faithful service." He reassured the trustees that the program would not be costly, if his guidelines were followed. In response, the trustees cautioned against "making the sabbatical program into a grant system," although they ultimately endorsed the proposal unanimously. The intensity of the trustees' new engagement with university matters was evidenced less than a year later when one member challenged the "validity and veracity" of an article that had appeared in the *Marquette Business Review.* His remedy for this alleged impropriety was to have the journal shut down. Quentin Quade deftly deflected this extreme suggestion by assuring the trustees' executive committee that the "factuality" of the article was under examination and that a stronger referee system would be put in place. As for the sabbatical leave proposal itself, the program was finally implemented in the fall of 1976. In announcing the first twenty-five recipients, Father Raynor extolled it as "one of the most important steps we can take to insure the quality of Marquette's educational product" for it enriched the faculty's scholarly life and increased "their capacity for excellent teaching." It also provided a vehicle for attracting accomplished scholars to Marquette.[31]

If improving the faculty's teaching prowess was an objective of the sabbatical leave program, then regular assessments of the university's instructional staff would be required. To provide input, the administration turned to the students. Even before protests became routine during the late sixties, a handful of energetic undergraduates had demanded the right to evaluate the instructors who graded their midterms, final examinations, and term papers. A handful of Marquette faculty introduced student evaluations as early as spring 1964. No academic unit mandated this, however. Each year the *Marquette Tribune*—and occasionally the student government—insisted upon formal student assessments, but nothing could be done without support from the faculty and administration. Even an attempt to develop a course description booklet in 1966 failed because of poor support among the faculty. Four years later, however, Vice President Art Moeller pushed this issue with the deans and department chairs, arguing that a student perspective was "an essential component of the [university's] evaluation program." A pilot program was introduced in the fall of 1970. Faculty were urged to make this evaluation of teaching effectiveness a "student project." Instructors were asked to leave the classroom while the forms were filled out. If they insisted on remaining in the room, they were warned to avoid giving the appearance of "'reading over'" the students' shoulders. The questionnaire rated instructors on eleven items, including

Science student at work in 1970. File 1260.

knowledge of subject, ability to motivate students, and attitude toward students. As this procedure became standardized, university committees routinely monitored the instrument. Faculty reactions varied, with one instructor maintaining that the "evaluation form is pure crap, and the revised evaluation form is pure crap. At least we have purity of essence." One academic unit suggested that student evaluations be divided into two clusters: questionnaires from A and B students and others from C and D students. The Marquette chapter of the American Association of University Professors jumped into the fray in 1973, criticizing the evaluation forms "as poor indicators of teaching effectiveness." Faculty disaffection with the design of student evaluations remained a sore point for decades. Yet in the same spirit that drove student interest in faculty evaluations, the committee on faculty worked with the academic vice president to develop an instrument whereby deans would be appraised by their faculty.[32]

This proclivity to judge others permeated individual academic units as well. One department particularly affected by this culture was theology. During the 1972-73 academic year, this unit—emblematic of the institution's religious character—was battered by differences over university, college, and department policies regarding the recruitment of Jesuits as faculty members: were they to be favored over lay people, even when their academic qualifications were not equal? Graduate students in theology were remarkably assertive—a sign of the times—writing challenging letters to every authority up the chain of command. Both the department and the committee on faculty were still working through this matter as late as 1975. Meanwhile, the department became embroiled in an even more difficult situation in 1973 after its former chairman, Quentin Quesnell, left the Society of Jesus. His departure raised another question: did a tenured faculty member who happened to be a Jesuit surrender this status upon resignation from the Society? The national office of the American Association of University

Father Thaddeus Burch, SJ at work in a physics laboratory. File 565.

Professors became involved by 1976, conducted its own investigation, and produced a report that claimed the university had mishandled Quesnell's academic rights. It censured Marquette. The administration's rebuttal, consistently maintained over the years, held that the priest understood the conditions of his employment through the Marquette Jesuit Associates, Inc. and knew that he surrendered tenure when he voluntarily left the Society of Jesus. At one point, the academic senate undertook its own inquiry into the matter. One outcome of the AAUP investigation was a survey of academic freedom at Marquette University. One hundred and eighty-two questionnaires (one-third of the total) were returned. Most respondents felt that faculty had as much freedom at Marquette as elsewhere; a strong majority had experienced no abridgment of their academic freedom; and a somewhat smaller majority had never heard of any colleagues' privileges being challenged. Eventually the heat of that moment dissipated, although the AAUP censure was not resolved until after the beginning of the new millennium.[33]

Far less controversial were the marginal adjustments made in the undergraduate curriculum during this era of academic "non-proliferation." The School of Speech became the College of Speech in 1973, permitting it to admit majors during the freshman year. During the following year, the university reclaimed the medical technology and physical therapy programs from the Medical College of Wisconsin. In the curricular separation of the medical school from the rest of the institution, these two departments had joined the medical college. However, for academic reasons, they returned to the university's direct supervision in late 1974. Other curricular changes in the seventies were low-key. An interdisciplinary minor in urban studies was added in 1975, and one year later, the interdisciplinary degree in social work was elevated to a full major. One academic enterprise that made significant strides during the seventies was the fine arts program. Under the direction of its new chairman, philosophy professor Curtis Carter, Marquette's fine arts committee established regular hours for Memorial Library's Marquette Room on Sunday afternoons in 1975. This space showcased the university's growing collection of paintings, sculptures, and rugs. By late in the decade, the fine arts committee had developed a full schedule of exhibitions and lectures. Their efforts to promote fine arts education at Marquette came to fruition in 1984 with the dedication of the art museum on land once occupied by Copus Hall. The Marquette University Women's Council spearheaded the $3 million fund-raising effort to underwrite this unique facility.[34]

A CATHOLIC, JESUIT IDENTITY

Just as the self-survey in the mid-fifties marked a pivotal moment for academic self-reflection, so too did the early seventies herald a span of time when members of the university community reconsidered the meaning of the school's Jesuit-Catholic mission. In the aftermath of the demographic, fiscal, cultural, and governance revolutions endured by American higher education during the sixties, Catholic institutions experienced over the next decade what acclaimed scholar Philip Gleason describes as an appraisal of a "taken-for-granted reality": their Catholic identity. Marquette joined other Catholic institutions such as Notre Dame in a rigorous self-analysis during the early seventies. Simply put, in Gleason's words: "why should a university, be it ever so good academically, exist as a *Catholic* university if its religious character [does] not somehow affect its mode of intellectual operation?" Less formal and less inclusive than the self-survey of the mid-fifties, Marquette's moments of reflection upon *Jesuit* and *Catholic* during the seventies proved to be timely and telling—considerations that shape the institution's self-image to this very day.

The university's intentions as a faith-based institution played a central role in developing a report for the North Central Association accreditation visit in 1973. Almost from the day that Father Raynor announced the reconstitution of the board of trustees in January 1969, senior administrators took measure of what *Jesuit* and *Catholic* would mean under an authority whose members might be neither. In March 1969, Ed Simmons, then associate vice president for academic affairs, prepared a thirteen-page discourse titled "Lay Witness: The Qualifications for Contemporary Impact" for a Jesuit Educational Association workshop. He wanted "to spell out the qualifications that the layman, as distinguished from the Jesuit, could and should bring to the Jesuit university community in order to have significant contemporary impact." Mostly, Simmons examined what was "essential to the Jesuit university as a Catholic institution of higher education." He later took collegial exception to remarks offered by Quentin Quade (then graduate dean), in an article on the future of Catholic higher education published in *America*, a Jesuit-produced magazine. To have two leading faculty members sparring over the laity's role in late twentieth-century Catholic higher education demonstrated just how quickly Marquette's Jesuit, Catholic character became the responsibility of non-Jesuits—and how critical faculty development would be in the future.[35]

This reflective state of mind intensified in the late spring of 1969 when Vice President Moeller asked a special committee to examine "'the implications of Marquette's religious commitments'" as well as the presence of a ROTC program at a Catholic university. The committee delivered its final report (later known as the Quade Report after its chairman) by the end of the year. As noted in the last chapter, the committee concluded that both those who supported ROTC programs at Marquette and those who opposed them represented established Catholic thought, with neither side possessing a superior moral position. Consequently, Marquette retained its affiliation with the armed forces. Marquette's proclivity for reflection upon its religious identity and for public demonstrations of this mission found further expression in the university's Program in Religion and Human Values in which the "Christian synthesis of faith and reason" was to be affirmed through a series of interdisciplinary courses, lectures, and visiting professorships. With its own Theology and Society Program, the theology department was central in this initiative, but other social sciences and humanities disciplines were expected to play equally vital roles.[36]

Another facet of this discussion on the future of Catholic education involved an assessment of the word *Jesuit*. After all, members of the Society of Jesus, like the lay staff, now signed employment contracts. By the end of the seventies, the dwindling presence of Jesuits on campus (about seven percent of the total faculty) became serious enough for the *Marquette Tribune* to run a series of articles identifying members of the Society. The newspaper admitted in 1977 that it was hard to discern Marquette's "Jesuitness." (The non-clerical garb some Jesuits wore may have made them unrecognizable to the average student.) Earlier, the central administration must have seen this coming. In the fall of 1970, Father Raynor had instructed the *Marquette University Magazine* to "carry a good, solid strong article on new Jesuit personnel at the University." On the occasion of naming Lalumiere Hall in 1971, Ed Simmons had spoken on "The Marquette Partnership of Jesuit and Lay." He made it clear that the university's lay employees had to embrace "a vision of Catholic higher education which admirably responds to the Christian thrust and, a fortiori, to authentically Jesuit aspirations." Simmons spoke wistfully of his own experiences at the College of Holy Cross (the Jesuit institution in Worcester, Massachusetts) where his application for a position in the philosophy department in 1952 had elicited an outburst from one Jesuit: "'What! A layman teaching philosophy at the Cross? Heaven forbid!'" He thanked Father Gerard Smith—the same man who had recruited women to the philosophy department—for his bravery in bringing Simmons to Marquette.[37]

One reflection of this attention to Marquette's "Jesuitness" appeared in the row over partiality toward Jesuits in the Department of Theology. In June 1971, Art Moeller issued a directive, drawn from the Quade Report, instructing university administrators to actively recruit Jesuits. Moreover, he added, in appropriate departments "the positive value of [a] Jesuit presence" should be considered when evaluating competing credentials. Lastly, university resources would be made available so that qualified Jesuits could be "recruited and appointed … regardless of whether there [was a] faculty vacancy … or an appropriate administrative position available." When Dean Robert Gassert, SJ, implemented this policy in the College of Arts and Sciences, tumult erupted in the theology department. Later in a May 1978 memorandum, Quentin Quade returned to "the important and delicate question of the import of the Catholicity of a prospective faculty or staff member." He referred to a recent directive that spoke of the need for recruiting faculty who understood "our nature." While this phrase technically referred to Jesuits, it also meant there should "be a sufficient number of Catholics on our faculty and staff so as to give some kind of 'moral guarantee' that we will continue to be true to the promises we make when we recruit students." Quade made it clear that he was not endorsing the recruitment of unqualified Catholics. But whether a candidate was Catholic should be "one of a host of factors which are pertinent to appointment." This perspective became part of the university's "Equal Employment Opportunity/Affirmative Action Policy" in late 1978 when the university reserved "its right to maintain its heritage and destiny as a Christian and Catholic witness in higher education."[38]

THE STUDENT VIEW OF *CATHOLIC* AND *JESUIT*

For Marquette students, the struggle to recognize and honor the school's religious identity came in other forms. The *Marquette Tribune* had published an article in the spring of 1964 that lamented the inadequate religious education received by the growing number of Catholics who chose to attend public universities. Marquette students were saved from this troubling circumstance because they could attend daily Mass, participate in annual retreats, and earn ten credits in theology. A little more than a year later, the *Tribune* revisited the issue of Catholicism on campus. Some students who were interviewed insisted they found their faith strengthened by attending the university; others understood how an individual could lose his or her faith by attending Marquette. Some thought the university culture was clearly Catholic, whereas others thought Marquette had become a secular institution. Jesuits such as Herbert Noonan and Raphael McCarthy would have been beside themselves at such a range of opinions. They would have been even more disturbed by a report in a 1973 *Tribune* editorial that claimed only 4 percent of the freshman class came to Marquette because of its "Catholic-Jesuit orientation."[39]

Yet it may not have been ambivalence that students demonstrated so much as confusion. Religious practices that had once been strictly controlled were now undergoing constant change. Liturgical refinements initiated during and after the Second Vatican Council (1962-65) baffled some young Catholics who had been raised in a time when rules were not just suggestions. The fine points of religious behavior guided one along the narrow footpath between everlasting salvation and eternal damnation. Eating even the smallest tidbit of food after midnight before receiving communion at Sunday morning mass was forbidden, no matter how difficult it might be for a diabetic who attended ten o'clock high Mass. Silent but anxious struggles to be sure that the communion host did not bump one's teeth as it melted created a frightful interlude on the return trip from the communion rail.

The certitude of this world had been shaken by the Vatican Council. In March 1963, Father Richard Sherburne, wearing the same vestments that priests had worn for generations, suddenly turned around and offered a "*Missa versus populum* (Mass facing the people) at Gesu church." A reporter from the archdiocesan newspaper who attended this service remarked how the congregants appeared less distracted, exhibiting a heightened level of participation. Three years later, instructions from Rome doused the fires of hell for those who ate meat on Friday. Refinements continued to revamp sacred habits from the past. In 1975, thirteen lay people distributed communion at weekend masses in the Joan of Arc Chapel. A year earlier, a brief furor had erupted over whether the host might be placed directly in the hands of communicants in defiance of archdiocesan dictates. Sunday afternoon Mass for Marquette students had been discontinued until the crisis was resolved and the traditional placement of the host upon a communicant's tongue was reintroduced.[40]

The superior general of the Society of Jesus, Father Pedro Arrupe, visited his Milwaukee confreres in April 1966, an honor heralded by the chronicler of the Jesuit community as "[o]ne of the greatest spiritual inspirations of this year." Five months later, Pope Paul VI chastised the Jesuits, accusing some of them of entertaining "'strange and sinister'" plans. Two years later, in 1968, even more controversy arose in the aftermath of *Humanae Vitae*, the pope's encyclical on contraceptive practices. For most students at Marquette, this directive reaffirmed long-understood teachings. For others, the defiant dismissal of Pope Paul's position by thirteen diocesan priests and Marquette faculty members underscored an evolving emphasis upon personal conscience. Between 1969 and 1975, the *Tribune* announced several times that Jesuits had resigned from the Society (including two former chairs of the theology department), heightening this confusion: what exactly did *Catholic* and *Jesuit* mean at Marquette University in the modern world? (The Society of Jesus in America lost more than a third of its members, dropping from over 8,000 to fewer than 5,000, in the twenty-five years after 1965.)

If faculty and administrators were grappling with the future of Marquette's mission, what was the everyday undergraduate to make of this fast-moving spiritual landscape? The moral implications of these changes became more bewildering because they came at a time during which all authority seemed open to challenge. It was therefore understandable that the student newspaper paid particular attention to a 1979 debate between Father Gregory F. Lucey, SJ, and Quentin Quade. Drawing from his doctoral dissertation on the state of Catholicity in contemporary Catholic higher education

Marquette visit by Reverend Pedro Arrupe, SJ, Father General of the Society of Jesus, 1966. File 718b.

(and using Marquette as his case study), Lucey worried about the university's ability to retain its Catholic mission in the future. He conceded the following: "Although Catholicity may be deeply embedded in the institutional character of the institution and dominant in the lives of a large portion of the faculty … in 1977 Catholicity was endangered by the internal dynamics of the institution. If observable patterns continue, by 1998 Catholicity as a distinctive character of the university will not have merely changed but will be lost." Quade was more sanguine, trusting that the right hiring

Mass in Joan of Arc Chapel, 1980s. File 265.

policies and proper faculty development could avoid the tragic outcomes that Lucey anticipated.[41]

Emblematic of these changes was the debate over annual retreats for every Catholic student. The Missouri and Wisconsin provinces of the Society of Jesus held a workshop in the summer of 1963 titled "Moral, Religious and Spiritual Formation of the Jesuit College Student." It recommended the continuation of a mandatory retreat, but also suggested that these spiritual exercises take place in a secluded environment, removed from everyday surroundings. By the following spring, the *Marquette Tribune* ran a two-part series urging a rethinking of the open retreat at Gesu which lacked the solitude needed for quiet reflection. The student senate deadlocked on a motion in 1966, requesting that the administration consider a new retreat policy. Frustrated, 1,900 undergraduates signed a petition asking for an end to mandatory retreats. This petition, supporting the discontinuance of a spiritual mainstay of Marquette since its days on the hilltop, provided evidence of just how much student attitudes had evolved—or devolved according to some. Opinions clashed, with one sociology professor voicing support for the traditional approach to retreats while Father Gerard Smith wanted an end to the compulsory tone of the retreat experience. New forms of Christian renewal were in place by the fall of 1966, providing students with five different options, including closed retreats and "Learning Christianity Week-ends." This step, taken with Father Raynor's approval, was newsworthy enough to generate a recounting in the *San Francisco Monitor* in February 1967.[42]

A new office of campus ministry assumed responsibility for Marquette's Catholic identity after 1970 when the president disbanded the committee on spiritual welfare. Instead of a single director and an advisory body, campus ministry had a full-time director and several other full-time and part-time associates, including a religious sister and a lay woman. A Lutheran pastor joined the team, with financial support from his own synod. As before, the director of campus ministry reported directly to the university president. In contrast to the director of spiritual welfare (a position established by Father O'Donnell in 1953), the new director received funding that covered salaries and operations.

During its earliest years, campus ministry was staffed by approximately a dozen individuals, not including dormitory and college ministers. Campus ministry oversaw daily Masses at Joan of Arc Chapel, Sunday Masses in the residence halls, prayer groups, weekend retreats, marriage preparation courses, Lenten services, and outside speakers. Two shortcomings facing this office were the inadequacies of its space in Merritty Hall and its separation from the Jesuit community. By the end of the seventies, the salary budget had doubled and clergymen from the Methodist and Episcopal faiths had been added to the staff. Non-Catholics as well as Catholics were now being served, as the ministry director urged every member of the Marquette community to be "a minister to everyone else." In 1978, the administration reassured the board of trustees that "an upsurge of religious concern and involvement on the Marquette campus" was evident within the student body.[43]

For Father Raynor, this resurgence revealed itself in several ways. During his 1979 state of the university address, the president lauded the principles of faith and justice demonstrated in programs such as the Thomas Merton seminar, the "Soup and Substance" dialogues, and, most notably, the Marquette University Community Action Program (MUCAP). The tradition of service, historically centered in the health science programs, had grown increasingly evident elsewhere on campus in the previous dozen years. In the winter of 1966, Pat Dolan, a Jesuit scholastic stationed at Marquette University High School, had urged Marquette students to imitate the social activism of Georgetown University students who volunteered their time and services throughout the District of Columbia. In support of this suggestion, Vice President Moeller approved a survey of student groups to measure their involvement in social action.

By the end of that school year, a constitution had been written and officers elected to guide a community action program. With offices in the basement of Grandmora Hall (the "catacombs"), MUCAP proceeded to contact faculty members in October 1966, asking for their support in recruiting volunteers to work "an hour, an afternoon, a weekend" in tutoring and recreational programs, at hospitals and county institutions. The organization wanted to make Marquette students aware of what was going on around Milwaukee and to draw upon their Christian obligations to "love, and serve." MUCAP foreshadowed many other service opportunities over the decades, among them the Institute on Poverty and Law (funded by the Educational Opportunity Program), the St. Boniface Teacher Assistance Program, the Marquette Action Program

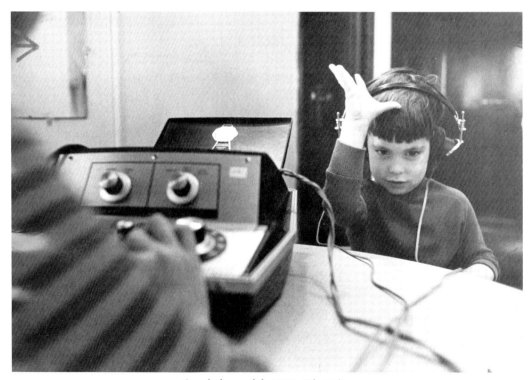

Speech therapy lab, 1970s. File 1245.

(an alternative spring break option), Students for Equal Education, and eventually Service Learning. During 1969, Marquette students participated in the local model cities program, one of the most ambitious initiatives of Lyndon Johnson's Great Society. Although MUCAP stumbled at times because its leadership constantly changed, it was reinvigorated in the early seventies when campus ministry assumed oversight. Service to others became a defining characteristic of undergraduate life at Marquette. A 1981 centennial news release depicted what *Catholic* meant at Marquette University: in addition to the Jesuits, the theology department, and the campus ministry office, the administration pointed to the volume of community service as evidence of the student body's religious convictions. Through these activities, the activism of the sixties lived on well beyond the school's centennial and into the new millennium.[44]

THE WORLD OF MARQUETTE STUDENTS

When the *Marquette Tribune* published the results of its unscientific poll in 1973 suggesting that as few as 4 percent of the undergraduates cared about the Jesuit-Catholic mission of Marquette, the future of the school's religious identity might have been called into question. Yet a more formal poll taken only four years later challenged any notion that Marquette's freshmen lacked a commitment to the school's religious character. Eight hundred and eighty-six members of the centennial class (those who would graduate in 1981 and, therefore, were first-year students in 1977) responded to a questionnaire. Fifty-seven percent agreed that Marquette's Catholic, Jesuit profile influenced their decision to enroll at the school. Ninety-six percent agreed with the statement: "[d]evelopment of moral and ethical character is an integral part of a college education." Nearly 97 percent affirmed that God was "a dynamic force" in their daily lives. A similar number believed that the Christian faith had "much to say about practical living," while 73 percent saw the ability to "help others in difficulty" as an "essential or important" objective of college (in contrast to 65 percent of all first-year college students across the country).[45]

These undergraduates were part of the fifth-largest student body in school history. The university's rapid expansion after World War II continued, somewhat unevenly during the Korean War, until the late fifties when Marquette became the largest Catholic university in the country. Enrollment reached 13,789 by 1965. Within eight years, this lofty figure plummeted 21 percent to under 11,000. It stagnated until 1975, offering an explanation for the school's fiscal woes in the late sixties and early seventies. If not for the wildly fluctuating numbers among continuing education students (especially Milwaukee public school teachers), these numbers would have been even more consequential for the school. By the mid-seventies, enrollments stabilized and then began to climb, reaching 13,932 by 1979. Thereafter the stated size of the student body declined—intentionally—because henceforth the registrar's office reported only for-credit students, excluding participants in the continuing education classes.[46]

These students experienced a university landscape that was dramatically altered from that which their predecessors had faced two decades earlier. Through the urban renewal

program, massive academic and residential structures, accompanied by expansive parking lots, replaced a congested panorama of low-rise frame houses and brick apartments.
Through the Central/Marquette Interchange, the federal government reworked the
west side of downtown. These concrete corridors created noisy, hard edges on two sides
of the campus. Even though at first glance the sight line along Wisconsin Avenue west
of Eighth Street may not have appeared threatening (given the fact that the north-
south expressway was below ground level at that point), Marquette was no longer in a
gentle transitional zone between Milwaukee's central business district and an upscale
residential district known as Grand Avenue. Downtown clearly terminated at Tenth
Street. Once upon a time, the Pabst brewery, St. Benedict's mission, and the county
courthouse sat a few city blocks east of Mt. Sinai Hospital. Now, the air space of the
freeway, tons of concrete roadways, and a torrent of speeding vehicles demarcated different sections of town. So too with Marquette and what had once been its neighbors
around Red Arrow Park, the Wisconsin Club, the public library, and the YMCA. To
the south, the obliteration of the Tory Hill neighborhood and its replacement with
a tangle of elevated roadways propped up on mighty pylons had created a dead zone
sheltering darkened parking lots.

   Juniors and seniors continued to live in an array of multi-family rental housing north
and west of the campus just as they had for decades. But the quality of life along these
streets had deteriorated. Once upon a time, thoroughfares such as Juneau, State, and
Highland had been the perimeter of student life. Now they were littered with bars,
empty lots, and abandoned buildings that made the area forbidding at best and dangerous at worse. For this reason, once the university acquired sufficient residential
space with the additions of Cobeen Hall and Carpenter Tower, it sold the complex
of women's residences along Highland Boulevard. Attending Marquette University,
according to one *Tribune* article, provided an education in the "Inner City." Traveling east of Thirteenth Street could be threatening on week nights as well as weekends.
Teenage gangs accosted Marquette students in the vicinity of the Abbot Crest Hotel
and the University Store. Variously identified as whites, blacks, Mexicans, and Puerto
Ricans, these individuals seemed to operate out of view of the police department. As
early as 1961, the student newspaper requested armed "gendarmes" to patrol the area
after 10:00 p.m. Chief Harold Breier insisted that nothing was amiss because nothing had been reported to his office. Consequently, the student board of governors at
Schroeder Hall delivered a formal complaint detailing recent incidents. A few months
later, the murder of a Marquette undergraduate heightened anxiety. At a hearing in the
district attorney's office, the confessed killer resembled Milwaukee's version of James
Dean: form-fitting white t-shirt, hair combed into a pompadour, and a cigarette dan-
gling from his lips. By the time he was given a life sentence in June 1966—eleven years
and three months before he would be eligible for parole—the streets had quieted sufficiently to elicit the curious observation from the head of Marquette two-man police
force that things were now "dead" on campus.[47]

By the following fall, no one was bored. Female and male gangs assaulted not only Marquette students, but also youngsters from the Wells Street Junior High School (now the Milwaukee Rescue Mission) and employees at both Mt. Sinai and St. Anthony's hospitals. Purses were stolen, nuns had to be escorted home, and one Sinai employee was raped. A student senate resolution, passed unanimously, asked the university administration to provide improved safety. The local alderman and the common council promised to look into the matter. Father Richard Sherburne, dean of students, asked for improvements to the area's street lighting. The university appointed Harold W. Grote, a veteran of the immigration and naturalization service, as its first director of security in December 1966, although it was still obvious that Marquette authorities viewed public safety as largely a municipal concern. Complicating matters was the criminal behavior of certain Marquette students. Two undergraduates tossed Molotov cocktails out of their Stewart Hall dormitory on Fifteenth Street in 1963. In the fall of 1965, nearly thirty male students appeared before the student conduct committee for violating the school's rules against alcohol. Vandalism and theft by unknown students was decried in a *Marquette Tribune* article one year later. Then, in the spring of 1967, a student was raped in her third floor apartment in Carpenter Tower by an individual unconnected with Marquette, a crime that came on the heels of another assault in Cobeen Hall. The police department finally added four extra patrol officers to the university area, which experienced a 16 percent drop in crime by the following fall. The university also hired its own residence hall guards to augment the surveillance provided by two private security firms. The university considered buying its own patrol car.[48]

Student government meeting, 1969. File 90.

The administration did not act decisively on these threats until a series of encounters in October 1974. In one, students returning from a party confronted a suspect who brandished a handgun. Three days later, a sexual assault took place near the Joan of Arc Chapel. The next month, the committee on student life held its first meeting of the new school year, specifically to consider public safety. The university established a women's physical safety task force. On her own, a journalism undergraduate started an escort service. When this effort did not prove successful, students in O'Donnell Hall formed their own all-night escort service. Near the conclusion of the 1974-75 school year, the student affairs office surveyed over two thousand students. Fear of physical assault was widespread: 88 percent anticipated an attack at some point during their stay in Milwaukee. The survey indicated that students remained unaware of any efforts by the office of campus security. Although respondents did not favor having Milwaukee police officers patrolling the campus, they did support increased surveillance by the police department in the surrounding area.[49]

Fears intensified during the fall of 1975 when these assaults continued despite foot patrols funded by the Federal Neighborhood Security Aids Program and another student-inspired escort service. The bursar's office on the first floor of Carpenter Tower was robbed at gunpoint just after noon on October 16, 1975. Since conventional lines of communication failed to generate a satisfactory response from O'Hara Hall, Marquette students delivered a petition to Father Raynor, representing the wishes of the student government, residence hall governments, and student organizations. It demanded "action rather than committees and reports." The central administration responded, but not in the way the students had anticipated. Quentin Quade, as executive vice president, wrote a letter to Marquette students on November 6 regarding safety and security. He acknowledged receipt of letters and petitions signed by hundreds of students, but advised "that they basically misportray the problem and are not productive of student and University welfare." Quade insisted that the number of incidents had actually declined from the previous year and that Milwaukee's crime statistics were among the lowest in urban America. While reassuring the students that the administration was as concerned for their safety as they were, he argued that protests and petitions were not what was needed; the administration wanted "specific ideas backed up by coherent arguments and evidence." Attached to his letter was a list of sixteen actions taken by the university during the preceding year to improve security around the campus. This message failed to assuage the student body, some of whom accused the administration of ignoring their fears. One student organization sold whistles to be used when an individual encountered danger. The office of student affairs finally assumed responsibility for the escort service, which now expanded to all residence halls. The work of campus security was eerily complicated after both the director and the acting director suffered heart attacks, one fatal.[50]

The following summer showed no improvement. Grebe's Bakery was robbed twice in three days during late June 1976; an optician's office in the 1212 building was the target of a similar incident. By the fall, crime reports became routine inserts in each issue of the *Marquette Tribune*. A few months after a new security chief was recruited from Northwestern University in the summer of 1976, the department of security was renamed the department of public safety, with responsibility for security and parking. The campus Organization of Women continued to sell whistles. University officials responded by upgrading outdoor lighting around residence halls, parking lots, and a few of the academic buildings.[51]

The administration's attention was distracted by the return of a nemesis from the sixties: bomb threats. In the fall of 1970, the university experienced nearly a dozen bomb threats during the semester following the Kent State protests. A Marquette student pleaded guilty to charges related to the evacuation of Lalumiere Hall. Another flurry of bomb threats struck the campus in the fall of 1973. (The following year the threat became far less threatening with the advent of streaking.) Yet in March 1976, just months after the students demanded that Father Raynor address safety on the streets, bomb scares emptied O'Donnell and Cobeen halls. Not long thereafter, six buildings, including the union, library, and recreational center, were evacuated on a single morning. The student affairs staff consulted with university public safety representatives as well as the Milwaukee Police Department. The university prepared a "Bomb Threat Policy and Procedure" manual. Then in the spring 1979, for the fourth time in the decade, another cluster of threats disrupted classes and examinations. This time, Raynor fired off a letter to the university community calling these actions "unchristian, immoral and criminal." He warned that expulsion and criminal charges awaited the perpetrators. In a follow-up letter to the faculty, Quentin Quade discussed the "administrative efforts [taken] to combat the current barbarism." Faculty replied with letters of their own, offering a variety of solutions. By early 1980, the campus scene had quieted somewhat. A report from the campus safety committee detailed what it saw as the reduced threat of violence during recent months. This report also contained the curious remark that the committee's biggest concern was finding new members.[52]

CHANGING WORLD FOR WOMEN

The well-being of female students and employees became a critical issue for the university community during the seventies. By distributing whistles as a public safety device and attending self-defense classes, women demonstrated personal responses to this problem. In addition, although the 1970s hardly constituted a era of gender equality at Marquette, the quest for equity did begin during this decade. Henceforth, gender justice warranted constant review.

In the mid-sixties, the *Marquette Tribune* still treated female students as a distinct, sometimes unfathomable, subset of the student body. And women themselves evidenced a lack of self-confidence. One female journalist reported in a 1966 article that a "majority of women interviewed [on campus] said that they definitely would not approve a female candidate [for president of the United States]." A freshman from medical technology acknowledged she preferred a male candidate "because I've been taught that the male sex is the dominant one." Later the same year, a regular column titled

Brooks Memorial Union lounge, 1975. File 155d.

Brooks Memorial Union grill area, 1974. File 155.

"The Marquette Woman" solicited faculty observations regarding female behavior in their classrooms. Stereotypes abounded, including that voiced by one instructor who thought the outstanding difference between the two sexes was that the "girls' penmanship" was better.[53]

These views may have been routine for 1966, but American society was on the verge of titanic realignments caused by the civil rights movement, the counterculture, the war in Southeast Asia, and ultimately feminism. In 1972, after almost twenty years of a co-educational student government at Marquette, a female successfully campaigned for student body president. Terri Nally, a junior in liberal arts, won 58 percent of the votes. The commander of Marquette's Army ROTC unit announced a little more than a year later that women would be admitted to his program. Two weeks later, freshman Kathy Nell, from Milwaukee, enrolled in the AROTC. These first steps reflected cultural changes taking place across the campus. A 1978 *Tribune* article discovered that 75 percent of the two hundred female undergraduates surveyed "considered themselves liberated and eighty-five per cent considered themselves career-oriented." In another essay published on the same day, a female reporter concluded there was no average Marquette woman because females at the university had a wide array of opportunities and interests from which to choose. This was particularly evident in a field such as engineering, where the first woman did not enroll until World War II, more than a third of a century after the college opened in 1908. In 1966, the *Tribune* was still asking the handful of female engineering students what it was like to be the only woman in class. Yet within a decade, the newspaper addressed the crumbling of gender barriers in engineering and the increasing job opportunities for women in this male-dominated profession.[54]

Attitudes followed by behaviors were changing so quickly that the Marquette University Organization for Women, a student-centered group instrumental in bringing safety issues to light, evolved into a more representative Marquette Council for Women in 1977. The latter retained its predecessor's concern for public safety but attended to new causes such as a women's resource center, a women studies program, and a day care center. In the early seventies, visitation rules in residence halls created a controversy after curfew hours were relaxed for men but not women. When Carpenter Tower became coeducational in 1972, James Scott, vice president of student affairs, was pressured to remove restrictions for female first-year students. Although university officials emphasized security concerns regarding these visitation restrictions, they were also worried about students' moral behavior. The student health center provided printed material and videotapes on birth control by the mid-seventies but, true to its Catholic identity, offered neither counseling nor contraceptive devices. (A Planned Parenthood office did open at Twelfth and State.) When Pope Paul VI reaffirmed Church teachings on premarital sex and homosexuality in 1976, some voices in the *Tribune* welcomed this confirmation of Catholic traditions, whereas others viewed the idea of sexual activity only within a marital context as unrealistic. However much certain faculty members might dissent from papal pronouncements, there were students who confidently stood by their Church's commitments, as evidenced by the formation of the Marquette Students for Life, a group formed in 1980 to oppose euthanasia, infanticide, and abortion.[55]

The alumnae had their battles to wage during this decade. The closing of Alumnae House as a residence hall in 1965 removed a landmark denoting an earlier generation's determination to improve life for its successors. To commemorate the conversion of Alumnae House into an academic facility, the Association of Marquette University Women (AMUW) honored Mildred Weil, resident manager from 1940 to 1965. Mabel Mannix McElligott, the true visionary behind this first dormitory, was similarly recognized in 1970. She had remained at Marquette following her resignation as dean of women to work alongside Father O'Donnell during his days as chancellor. By 1967, she was one of two Marquette women serving on the Wisconsin Governor's Commission on the Status of Women. McElligott ended four decades at Marquette in 1975 when she took a position at Milwaukee's Mount Mary College. The alumnae association itself, with a finely developed tradition of service to the university, resisted efforts to convert the group into an auxiliary organization in 1969. Also undergoing reconstitution during this era was the Faculty Wives Club, founded in 1922. It became the Marquette University Women's Club in 1973, opening membership to most women from the Marquette community. Finally, at the conclusion of the 1975-76 school year, Father Raynor appointed Joanne O'Malley Pier (a graduate of the nursing college) as the first female trustee. Three years later, Patricia B. Apple became the second, after chairing the Marquette Women's Council, which Father Raynor had created in 1975, to introduce "'a woman's point of view in Marquette's activities.'" The Women's Council led the subsequent drive to develop an art museum on campus.[56]

At the instructional and administrative levels of the university, change came more slowly. During a meeting of the Marquette chapter of the American Association of University Professors in 1976, several individuals decried the school's culture of "male chauvinism," citing the "lack of female membership on faculty committees" and the discrimination that nursing faculty often encountered. This issue was raised again two years later in remarks pointing to the absence of female administrators outside traditional fields such as dental hygiene and medical technology. As a counterpoint, Sister Mary Paton Ryan, then assistant dean of the liberal arts, insisted that "a woman definitely has an equal chance at becoming a dean of a Marquette college." A fellow religious on the Marquette staff, however, spoke out after the Vatican reaffirmed the Church's exclusion of women from the priesthood. Sister Elizabeth Dryer, then acting director of campus ministry, insisted the Church's credibility would suffer as a result of this ban. About this time, the *Marquette Tribune* ran a piece on a theology graduate student who spoke of her future as a Catholic priest.[57]

STUDENTS AND FACULTY OF COLOR

Women were not the only members of the university community searching for a representative role at Marquette. Upbeat articles in the *Star*, Milwaukee's black newspaper, during the mid-sixties conveyed the impression that race relations were improving at

Marquette compared to the rest of the city. Yet clashes over opening housing, desegregation of public schools, and use of the Eagles' clubhouse as well as repercussions from Martin Luther King's assassination suggested that all was not well in Milwaukee or at the university. The chairman of the Black Student Union and Father James Groppi (a local civil rights activist) took the occasion in late 1971 to criticize what they called a lack of commitment to racial justice on the part of Marquette's student body and the administration. The associate dean of students contributed to this criticism two years later, pointing to alleged discrimination in the hiring and promoting of minorities and women. In contrast, one student proudly anticipated becoming the first African American to graduate from the dental school in nearly two decades. Once the most integrated academic unit on campus, the dental school had not graduated a black student since 1958.[58]

By the mid-1970s, the trustees routinely received updates on the university's efforts to increase minority enrollment at Marquette. At the undergraduate level, there had been 219 students of color in 1970, representing 3 percent of the enrollment. By 1976, that number had grown to 578, representing nearly 9 percent. Agencies on campus seeking to improve the situation included the Educational Opportunity Program under Arthur Mitchem, the Upward Bound program with its pre-engineering and pre-health specialities, the American Indians Students office, and a minority affairs office

Students in mall between Memorial Library and Biltmore Apartments, 1978. File 1267.

in the School of Dentistry. The *Tribune* noted a drop in Marquette's minority student population by 1979 and the school's rather poor showing against local schools such as Concordia, the Medical College of Wisconsin, and the University of Wisconsin-Milwaukee. Yet in 1980 the trustees were informed that Marquette graduated nearly 39 percent of its minority students within a five-year period whereas the University of Wisconsin-Milwaukee graduated only 16 percent.[59]

As early as 1969, black students at Marquette demanded a minority cultural center. Two years later, twenty-three of the twenty-four students of color who responded to a survey endorsed the idea of a central gathering spot, with one-third expressing the need for "a place of communication" and a place that "would bring an end to alienation." (Interestingly, three-quarters of these respondents reported feeling a sense of alienation at some point in their time at the university but experienced it least in the residence halls.) When nothing happened, the Third World Union (TWU, a student group) seized control of the basement lounge in McCormick Hall in April 1972. Within weeks, the student affairs office and the TWU worked out an agreement to convert the teaching materials center (a former coffee shop on Wells Street east of Fourteenth) into a minority cultural center (later renamed the multi-cultural center). A director was hired, working with a $20,000 budget. By 1980, the center had become a rallying point for minority student organizations, including a chapter of the National Association for the Advancement of Colored People.[60]

An unproductive decade in the recruitment of black faculty led to a flurry of charges by critics and a proportionate volley of responses from the administration. These debates hinged on whether the university sincerely sought to hire faculty of color or paid this process only lip service. Critics pointed to the lack of cultural education at the university. To address some of these concerns, the trustees approved an affirmative action plan in October 1972. It guaranteed equal opportunity in "admissions, employment, retention, promotion, compensation, housing, and other activities without regard to race, color, religion, sex, or national origin." (A special section titled "Women's Equality" was included.) Responsibility for implementing these lofty goals was assigned to the newly created position of affirmative action officer. Attorney Joseph R. Thomas served in this capacity from 1975 to 1977; Rosemary Petranech handled the job for decades thereafter. Some in the university community viewed the administration's concomitant push to hire Jesuits and favor Catholics as clear violations of the spirit of this statement. Others were perturbed that recruitment of minorities was not a top priority. About the same time, Father Raynor established an Equal Opportunity Council, consisting of two students, three faculty members, three administrators, and two staff members, to provide continuing insight and advice on these matters. Its three subcommittees addressed the progress of women and minority groups as well as the hiring of professional administrative personnel.[61]

One place where race relations intersected with extramural affairs came with the decision to discard the school's sports mascot, Willie Wampum, the grinning depiction of an American Indian enthusiastically "swooshing" a tomahawk. In February 1971,

Willie Wampum. File 1380.

a group of Marquette students who were American Indians formally petitioned the student government to request discontinuance of the Willie Wampum image as well as the nickname *Warriors*. One week later, over two hundred students jammed into the basement of Schroeder Hall to witness the student government vote (16-9) in favor of this proposal. Petitions protesting the student government's action circulated within the audience even before the meeting ended. At the same time, the American Indian Information and Action Group (a group not affiliated with the university) sent a letter to the vice president of student affairs arguing that the current mascot was "an insult to our dignity and a perpetuation of the stereotype" that has cruelly depicted "our race as stupid and savage." Vice President James Scott then requested that the committee on student life, the athletic board, and the office of university relations (as liaison with the alumni) provide him with recommendations.

The committee on student life reported back on March 4, 1971. After reviewing "the thinking" of the student government, the athletic board, the athletic department, the American Indian students, and the Marquette Faculty Association for Interracial Justice as well as a petition signed by 539 students who opposed the retirement of Willie Wampum, the CSL concluded "that the distorted headpiece of Willie Wampum is disparaging to the American Indian; that pseudo-Indian dances are being performed by a non-Indian and the dances performed by Willie Wampum do not accurately portray the culture of the American Indian; and that the carrying and the use of a tomahawk by Willie Wampum projects an image of violence which is not in keeping with the concept of a Christian University." Less than a month later, Vice President Scott announced that the Willie Wampum mascot would "be retired," although the designation *Warriors* would be retained. The student government was asked to develop an adequate replacement for Willie Wampum. The American Indian students at Marquette submitted a proposal in 1978 to create a "First Warrior" symbol, not a mascot per se. A costume was designed, representing Native American tribes from across Wisconsin. Only authentic Indian dances were to be featured at basketball games. A 1980 *News and Views* newsletter detailed the authenticity of each element in the First Warrior's outfit. Yet differences over this matter continued, and in the 1984, the First Warrior symbol was dropped altogether. The Warrior nickname itself disappeared in November 1993, triggering a feverish and lengthy backlash. Ironically, on the very same day in 1971 that the administration terminated Willie Wampum as mascot, the *Marquette Tribune* announced that the trustees had decided to include students on two of its committees, a status long sought by the student government. The students would now serve as "staff members" without voting privileges.[62]

VARSITY SPORTS

Interest in Marquette's pigskin heritage had not completely disappeared following Father O'Donnell's decision to discontinue varsity football in late 1960. The athletic board periodically revisited this matter, even though students and alumni alike understood that Father O'Donnell had "whistled dead 68 years of intercollegiate football" based on cold, hard, fiscal facts. They also understood that a general de-emphasis in varsity sports prevailed among Jesuit colleges and universities after World War II as the ascendency of academics superceded extracurricular activities. Only eight of twenty-eight Jesuit schools sponsored football programs by 1965 and most of these eight had actually discontinued the sport at some point after 1945. When it returned, football was usually a non-scholarship, club sport. Consequently, in the most organized effort to revive football at Marquette after 1960, supporters favored the club style of play.[63]

The athletic board was familiar with inquiries regarding the return of intercollegiate football and recognized that any final decision rested with the president. As long as Father O'Donnell was the chief executive, it was unlikely he would reverse his earlier

First Warrior. File 1385.

decision. Shortly after Father Kelley became university president in 1962, however, the student body president approached the athletic board, asking them to reinstate football as a varsity sport. Two years later, a board member made the same request. This time, a subcommittee looked into the matter. Its final report, delivered to the athletic board in the spring of 1965, indicated that there was strong support within the student body (especially among the fraternities and sororities) to bring gridiron play back to Marquette. The *Tribune* tried to obtain a copy of this report but was rebuffed. The newspaper then published a series of articles examining football programs at other Jesuit institutions. A rally at the Marquette University stadium in early November, championed by former Hilltopper football star and one-time Chicago Bear John Sisk, drew 2,000 supporters. Even at this event, speakers acknowledged the priority that Jesuit administrators assigned to academic excellence, not to trophies earned on the playing field. Two months earlier, Father Raynor had replaced Father Kelley as president. The new executive was said to have an open mind on the issue but to be generally opposed because football "'values are not as great as the intellectual life of the student.'"

Six months later, the athletic board, the board of trustees (still three Jesuits), the dean of students (Father Sherburne), and the president were still considering a club football team. A key point for them was the financial support that this team might receive from the M-Club, an alumni group consisting of former lettermen. A minimum of $18,000 was needed to purchase uniforms and the other equipment. Another student rally was held in the fall of 1966, this time at the Brooks Memorial Union. Only 400 attended, one-fifth the number of students who had turned out the previous year. The athletic board refused to take any action in the absence of the $18,000 kick-off fund. Ultimately, the student government funded its own club team briefly, but when this program incurred a lingering debt of more than $3,000, the student government terminated support in 1972.[64]

On a more successful note, the basketball program finally catapulted out of the doldrums in the mid-1950s with the arrival of Coach Jack Nagle. The squad posted a 24-5 record in 1955 and was ranked eighth in the country. Nagle's teams suited up against well-respected competitors, including Louisville, Loyola of Chicago, Drake, Michigan State, and Notre Dame. In 1958, Ed Hickey, a coaching veteran from Creighton and Saint Louis universities, took over. His first team won twenty-three and lost only six. However, the coach's personal feud with Notre Dame athletic director Ed "Moose" Krause caused the long-running competition between these two midwestern Catholic schools to end in 1960. Hickey left after the 1964 season with a cumulative record of ninety-two and seventy.[65]

Although the basketball teams improved during the late fifties, the athletic board quietly ordered athletic director "Moon" Mullins to address the fact that the program did "not enjoy the respect it should" and that "inspiration and desire were, too often, lacking." The board was particularly concerned about the program's long-term future. It looked into the availability of Frank McGuire of South Carolina and John Wooden of the University of California, Los Angeles. In both instances, these renowned coaches found Marquette's offer of $12,000 per year for five years less than overwhelming. By early 1964, the board was once again in the market for a head coach, following the dismissal of Ed Hickey. It settled on Al McGuire, head coach at Belmont Abbey College in North Carolina, offering him a two-year contract. In announcing the board's decision, the *Marquette Tribune* noted that McGuire had big shoes to fill by following Hickey. A native New Yorker, a graduate of St. John's University on Long Island, and a three-year veteran of the National Basketball Association, McGuire came with a reputation for recruiting, although his last two teams at Belmont had compiled records of 8-16 and 8-15.[66]

Although he was not offered the athletic directorship—a position he had originally sought—McGuire quickly took command of the basketball program. In fall 1964, he asked the board to alter its policy—undoubtedly a Jesuit policy—forbidding the freshman team from traveling to other institutions for contests. A few months later, the board chastised McGuire for what was described as an "intemperate" use of his secondary title, "Assistant Athletic Director." The university's director of development penned a heated letter to his supervisor in 1968, complaining that he could get no cooperation from the athletic department in matters pertaining to public relations or fund-raising. The director cited the discontinuance of special ticket prices for local youth groups and a dismissive attitude toward Marquette's corporate supporters. By the late sixties, the athletic board worried that McGuire might be lured away by another college or by the National Basketball Association. As a sign of the times, senior administrators in O'Hara Hall assumed oversight of the coach's contract in the late sixties—a practice unfathomable in earlier times. Yet success on the basketball court softened these criticisms as well as any lingering regret over the fate of football at Marquette. Although McGuire's first team (8-18) fared only marginally better than Ed Hickey's last team (5-21), things turned around as early as his third campaign when the basketball team compiled a mark of 21-9. In 1970-71, his team remained undefeated until a heartbreaking one-point loss at the hands of Ohio State in the NCAA tournament. The 1973-74 team was runner-up as national champion to North Carolina State. By September 1976, throngs of students created a carnival-like atmosphere when they camped out overnight in front of Lalumiere Hall to obtain basketball tickets for what became a fairy-tale season.

McGuire startled the university community when he announced that he would retire at the conclusion of the 1976-77 season. (In January, the university announced that McGuire's assistant—and a candidate for the head coaching position in 1964—Hank Raymonds would take over after the current season.) The team stumbled at times, losing five home games, including contests to DePaul, Detroit, and Wichita State in a matter of five days during February. Still, the Warriors were invited to the National Collegiate Athletic Association's post-season tournament. In the opening rounds, the Warriors handled Cincinnati, reversing an earlier loss in the Queen City, squeaked past Kansas State by a point, overtook Wake Forest by fourteen, and UNC-Charlotte by two. In the finals, Marquette defeated the University of North Carolina by eight points

NCAA trophy, 1977. File 112

to win the national collegiate championship. The euphoria of this moment vanquished any lingering memory of the athletic board's preoccupation twenty years earlier with a basketball program that did "not enjoy the respect it should." McGuire's record of 295-80 at Marquette guaranteed that respect would not be a problem any time soon.[67]

Victorious men's basketball team, 1976-77. File 110e.

As remarkable as a national basketball championship may have been, the most significant athletic achievement for Marquette during the 1970s involved a triumph of an entirely different sort. In 1972, the U.S. Congress included Title IX in some general legislation on higher education. Title IX forbade sex discrimination at colleges and universities receiving federal aid. This mandate addressed housing, financial assistance, dress codes, and employment as well as athletics. By 1975, when President Gerald Ford approved implementation (under guidelines drawn up by the Department of Education), Marquette and hundreds of peer institutions had began to assess how these stipulations might affect matters such as faculty appointments. Anticipating that adjustments would also be forced upon the athletic program, university officials established a Committee on Women in Intercollegiate Athletics (with only one woman on the committee—a student) in late 1973. A year later, two women (one a student and the other a mathematics professor) became the first members of their sex to serve on the university's athletic board. Following President Ford's directive to begin enforcement, Marquette hired Tat Shiely as women's athletic coordinator. Funds were set aside to bring the varsity sports program into compliance—however slowly. Along the way, Title IX reinforced the "big dollar" spirit then infiltrating college sports. If the men's programs were to continue, comparable sums had to be available for scholarships, equipment, facilities, and travel for the women's teams. Television revenue became almost as vital as a winning tradition. Poor performances accompanied by poor attendance and support threatened more than coaches' reputations. By 1981, a few basics such as the lockers and weight-training rooms had been brought up to par at Marquette, but noticeable differences remained in many areas. Gender equity was not a task for a single season or even a single decade. Neither was it a matter of free choice. The federal government had imposed these standards upon Marquette and the rest of American higher education. University administrators came to recognize that federal authorities—and ultimately the courts—were now looking over their shoulders. Support from Washington had arrived bearing certain legal obligations.[68]

SPRINT TOWARD THE CENTENNIAL

The turmoil of the sixties and seventies, compounded by serious fiscal threats, ultimately took its toll upon the health of the university leadership. As mentioned earlier, two of the early directors of campus security suffered heart attacks. James Scott, vice president of student affairs during most of the late sixties and into the seventies, was sent by his doctors to bed with exhaustion. Father Raynor succumbed to cardiovascular disease in January 1978, prompting quadruple bypass surgery at St. Luke's Hospital. Following his return to the campus in mid-April, he adopted a rigorous walking regime as part of his recovery program. Yet a year later, a *Marquette Tribune* reporter observed that the school's chief executive looked "a decade older than his 55 years." That remark aside, Raynor pressed on toward the university's upcoming centennial.[69]

As early as the fall of 1976, the faculty had pushed the administration to create a Faculty Committee on Academic Excellence, with the priority of developing long-range plans for Marquette's second century. With Vice President Ed Simmons' approval, this committee took up preparations for the centennial celebration. In February 1978, the committee borrowed a page from Father O'Donnell's approach to Marquette's seventy-fifth anniversary by insisting that the "major orientation of the Centennial celebration should be academic, as befits an academic institution." Moreover, whatever was scheduled should be of high quality, with a "few outstanding projects and activities [rather] than a multitude of indifferent ones." Excessive glorification of the past should be avoided, thought the committee, and the future should be the focus of the celebration's events. Finally, the committee took the bold position that there should be no formal theme for fear of becoming too "gimmicky." (Turning aside this recommendation, the administration chose a centennial theme: "Faith. Knowledge. Justice.") The excellence committee also recommended that a textual connection should be developed between the fast-approaching centennial and the university's new logo. This logo had first been proposed in 1976, with plans to have it prominently displayed on identification markers placed at the edges of the campus. The first design was widely criticized, leading to a second approach that eventually found its way on everything from stationery to campus pylons.[70]

In contrast to the September 1955 to June 1956 schedule of the seventy-fifth anniversary, the Raynor administration hosted the centennial throughout the 1981 calendar year. Some of the points the president wanted to highlight were revealed in his September 1980 address to the Greater Milwaukee Committee's board of directors. After opening with a history of Marquette and a lengthy roll call of current statistics (on enrollment, degrees, alumni, budgets, and buildings), Raynor proudly listed the "stands" that his administration had taken in recent years against what he depicted, first, as the AAUP's "attempt to trample on religious freedom" (in the Quesnell matter) and, second, against internal pressure to divest Marquette of investments in South Africa, an action that Raynor claimed would have twisted the "University to be what it is not ordained to be." For the future, the university president spoke of "uniform excellence," a not-so-subtle endorsement of the non-proliferation policies of the past decade. To realize this goal, faculty and staff had to possess high qualities. Strong enrollments and an increased endowment were needed. Raynor promised that the upcoming accreditation visit from the North Central Association in 1983 would help define Marquette's long-range academic plans.[71]

A centennial planning committee had been established in 1978 under the leadership of Adrian M. Dupuis from the School of Education. The centennial committee put out a call for ideas. The final lineup of activities favored academic events. After an opening liturgy in mid-February 1981, a seminar, symposium, and lecture followed that same month. During March, the focus was on a week-long "Conference on Human Life," whereas several honors convocations dominated April. Symposia on student life, medieval philosophy, genetic engineering, and ethics and economics were rolled out in the fall. Without question, the highlight of that year's festivities was the conferring of the Père Marquette Discovery Award upon Mother Teresa of Calcutta on June 13, 1981, with 10,000 in attendance at the Milwaukee Auditorium and another 3,000 watching on closed-circuit television in the nearby Milwaukee Arena. A few months later, in presenting his 1981 state of the university speech, Father Raynor spoke excitedly about the recent events and how they reflected upon the university's achievements and status. Yet he abruptly turned to the matters at hand for 1982, reminding listeners that there was a time for reminiscing over an institution's accomplishments and there was time to get on with business. A new wave of freshmen, with improved Scholastic Aptitude Test scores, had arrived on campus only two months earlier and the endowment was three times what it had been seven years earlier. But the end of the postwar baby boom was anticipated for the rest of the 1980s, forcing universities to compete for a dwindling number of traditional-age undergraduates. The university's finances remained a concern in light of a possible decline in the enrollment. A new century of "uniform excellence" was awaiting Marquette University. It was time to move forward.[72]

A quarter of a century has transpired since Marquette's centennial in 1981. Challenges, similar to those that the university faced during its first century of operation, have revisited the institution during these past twenty-five years. For example, widely fluctuating enrollments associated with the end of the baby boomers' college years severely impacted universities across the country. At Marquette, student numbers dipped so dramatically by the early nineties that the university encountered severe financial stress in 1995 and 1996, leading to budget cuts, class cancellations, a 0 percent salary increase for one year, and the closure of East Hall for two years. Increasingly, the university relied upon donors to stabilize erratic tuition revenues. During his quarter of a century as president, John P. Raynor increased the number of contributors from under 8,000 to over 20,000. He concluded his tenure with the "Campaign for Marquette University: Beliefs in Action," which raised $131 million—more than $6 million above the original goal. As improbable as that sum may have seemed at the time, the university raised nearly two and a half times that amount in the "Magis" campaign between 1998 and 2005. Still, tuition revenue drives the institution's annual budget, a situation that a forthcoming campaign intends to address.

Father Raynor concluded his historic term as president in 1990, succeeded by Albert DiUlio, SJ. (Following in Father O'Donnell's footsteps, Raynor served as university chancellor until his death in 1997.) DiUlio burnished the "urban university" theme that had received so much attention in the late sixties but had later languished. In particular, he contested the steady deterioration of the local landscape. Just as the Raynor administration eventually came to understand that campus security was the university's responsibility (not solely the police department's), DiUlio and his staff concluded that Marquette would have to take the lead if there was to be any hope of a renaissance for the city's near west side. Amelioration of the physical conditions in this neighborhood could not be left to municipal authorities. With dramatic reductions in funding for the Department of Housing and Urban Development during the 1980s, local governments scurried to balance municipal budgets, reducing any inclination to invest in the inner city. Expanding upon the public-private partnership model promoted during the Carter presidency (and exemplified by Milwaukee's Grand Avenue Mall project), Father DiUlio organized a cooperative crusade among corporate and non-profit sponsors such as Ameritech and the YMCA to address the physical well-being of the areas surrounding Marquette. The Campus Circle project cost millions, renovated hundreds of housing units, and rehabilitated key commercial blocks, especially Wells Street. The outcome was a more secure environment for Marquette students, a landscape that enhanced recruitment and student life. The Avenue Commons proposal, a plan to convert Wisconsin Avenue between Eleventh and Sixteenth streets into a pedestrian mall, failed in 1995. Soon, thereafter, Father DiUlio resigned and was replaced in 1996 by Father Robert A. Wild who, years earlier, had served on the theology department faculty.

Marquette's sizable investment in neighborhood redevelopment caused on-campus construction to be scaled back. The university did add Katharine Reed Cudahy Hall in 1994 (on the site of Grandmora and Carpenter halls) to serve the school's information technology needs and the mathematics and computer science department. In 2004, land once occupied by Deaconess Hospital (acquired in 1985) became home to America's most modern dental school facility, allowing dentistry to vacate a relic left over from Henry Banzhaf's days as dean. The most significant structural addition to the campus in the past quarter of a century was the John P. Raynor Library on a footprint once used by Brooks Memorial Union and the Biltmore Apartments. Distinctive in design and purpose, the new library, with its signature "bridge" to Memorial Library, has become an academic showpiece for Marquette. Its use by the student body is unparalleled and its emphasis upon electronic-based learning unprecedented.

Everyday lives of Marquette students were dramatically altered in 1990 with the opening of Alumni Memorial Union on property once occupied by, among other things, the Knights of Columbus buildings. The incentive behind this project came from an anonymous $7.5 million challenge donation, which left the alumni responsible for the balance of construction costs. This vital center of student life has provided the university community with everything that Peter Brooks and Herbert Noonan envisioned for the Marquette Union back in 1920. The grounds around the new union have featured alumni gatherings, fund-raisers, satellite graduation ceremonies, and frisbee matches. Residential facilities expanded significantly after 1988, following the university's acquisition of Children's Hospital and its subsequent development into Humphrey Hall. Five years later, Marquette completed the purchase of the YMCA, facilitating the subsequent sale of West Hall.

The new union as well as venues such as the Annex (in the Campus Town development on Wells) have provided locations for fans of Marquette basketball to gather and watch their team play its way through four conferences. The university left its independent status behind in 1988 when the school joined the Midwest Collegiate Conference with the hope of gaining greater access to the NCAA post-season tournament. Two years later, Marquette helped establish the Big Midwest Conference and eventually played in Conference USA before joining the Big East Conference in 2005. During the early stages of the post-1981 era, selection to NCAA championship tournaments was hard to come by for Marquette athletes. The women's cross country team brought a national crown to Marquette in 1982, the first such honor since the 1977 men's basketball championship. The men's team returned to the "big dance" in 1993 after a ten-year absence and reached the final four a decade later. Women's athletics also migrated through a checklist of affiliations, from the Association for Intercollegiate Athletics for Women to the National Association of Intercollegiate Athletics and eventually to the NCAA. Both the women's and men's teams have benefitted immensely from the facilities provided by the McGuire Center, which was opened in 2003, two years after the

389

death of the legendary coach for which it was named. The odyssey of the university's nickname, from *Warriors* to *Golden Eagles* to *Gold* and back to *Golden Eagles*, stirred sufficient emotions to involve every alumnus at one time or another.

Through recent decades, the role of service has become a distinguishing feature of Marquette University, as it has at every Jesuit institution. The poignancy of this characteristic was driven home recently with the revelation that 10 percent of the 2006-08 United States Congress is Jesuit-educated. At Marquette, oversight of the university's commitment to public service has fallen largely to the laity, in the face of a dwindling number of Jesuits. The first generation of lay executives (Moeller, Quade, and Simmons) has been replaced by subsequent cohorts that include, at this moment, both a female provost and its first female chair of the Board of Trustees. This recent evolution of leadership at Milwaukee's Jesuit University underscores the centrality of programs for faculty and trustee development. The likelihood that a lay person will assume the top post by the 150th anniversary (a point repeatedly—and wisely—discussed by Father Wild) demonstrates how the faces will inevitably change, but each new generation of leaders must find its own way to sustain the school's Jesuit identity and its ultimate mission, as articulated by Father Leonard Batz in 1880: "the science of salvation." Eternal life gained through learning and teaching may not be as precise as any "science," but it must remain at the heart of Marquette University.

NOTES

ABBREVIATIONS USED IN NOTES

excomm   Executive Committee
MC   Marquette College
MJ   Marquette Journal
MT   Marquette Tribune

CHAPTER I

1 Scrapbook 15: October 1, 1905; Scrapbook 3: 1; Scrapbook 10: 20-21; Raphael N. Hamilton, *The Story of Marquette University* (Milwaukee: Marquette University Press, 1953), 15.

2 Steven M. Avella, *In the Richness of the Earth* (Milwaukee: Marquette University Press, 2002), 37-39.

3 Ibid., 37, 38, 43-49; Jon Teaford, *Cities of the Heartland* (Bloomington: Indiana University Press, 1993), 2-14; Gilbert J. Garraghan, *The Jesuits of the Middle United States* 3v (New York: America Press, 1938), 3: 351; Lee J. Bennish, *Continuity and Change* (Chicago: Loyola University Press, 1981), 18.

4 John Gurda, *The Making of Milwaukee* (Milwaukee: Milwaukee County Historical Society, 1999), 29-37.

5 Ibid., 42, 46, 48, 51, 56, 59-60; Avella, 25; Garraghan, 3: 350; Kathleen Neils Conzen, *Immigrant Milwaukee 1836-1860* (Cambridge: Harvard University Press, 1976), 14.

6 Avella, 55-56; Garraghan, 3: 351; clipping, May 20, 1939, Archives, D-2, Series 3, Box 1; Bennish, 18, 22-23; Herman J. Muller, *The University of Detroit* (Detroit: University of Detroit, 1976), 1.

7 Avella, 40, 56; Garraghan, 3: 352; "Marquette History," Archives, A-11, Series 1, Box 12; MT, May 25, 1939; Allan Farrell, *The Jesuit Code of Liberal Education* (Milwaukee: Bruce Publishing Company, 1938), 394; Robert I. Gannon, *Up To The Present* (Garden City: Doubleday & Company, 1967), 28; clipping, May 20, 1939, Archives, D-2, Series 3, Box 1.

8 Garraghan, 3: 352-55; Scrapbook 21: 61; Avella, 31, 40; "Marquette History," Archives, A-11, Series 1, Box 12; MT, May 25, 1939.

9 Garraghan, 3: 355-73; Avella, 5, 56; MT, May 25, 1939; Hamilton, 5; "Marquette History," Archives, A-11, Series 1, Box 12; "Brief History of Marquette University," Archives, D-5, Series 1, Box 1; Bennish, 23, 52; Muller, 2-3; http://eh.net; clipping, May 20, 1939, Archives, D-2, Series 3, Box 1.

10 Garraghan, 3: 372-81; "Marquette History," Archives, A-11, Series 1, Box 12; "Remember When," Archives, A-4.5, Series 10, File 1205; "Jesuits in Milwaukee," ibid., File 720; Avella, 51, 57; Scrapbook 21: 61; MT, May 25, 1939; clipping, May 20, 1939, Archives, D-2, Series 3, Box 1; Gerald McKevitt, *The University of Santa Clara* (Stanford: Stanford University Press, 1979), 23; Muller, 2-4.

11 Gurda, 60-61, 66, 116-17, 125; John Gurda, "The Church and the Neighborhood," 5, in Steven M. Avella, *Milwaukee Catholicism* (Milwaukee: Knights of Columbus, 1991); Avella, 51; Hamilton, 7; "Jesuits in Milwaukee," Archives, A-4.5, Series 10, File 720.

12 Garraghan, 3: 380-83; John G. LaVies, *Location and Detailed Description of Early Catholic Church Property* (Milwaukee, n.p., 1941), Sheet 65; Harry H. Heming, *The Catholic Church in Wisconsin* (Milwaukee: Catholic Historical Publishing Co., 1896), 331; Scrapbook 15: October 1, 1905; Scrapbook 21: 61; Hamilton, 7; Avella, 57.

13 Garraghan, 3: 383-84; MT, November 22, 1928; Scrapbook 10: 53-55; Scrapbook 15: October 1, 1905; Hamilton, 8-9, 12; Avella, 57; Heming, 331.

14 Garraghan, 3: 384-85; Hamilton, 9, 10; Avella, 57; Scrapbook 15: October 1, 1905; Scrapbook 21: 61; "Remember When," Archives, A-4.5, Series 10, File 1205; Heming, 332; "*Numen Flumenque*," Archives, A-4.5, Series 2, Box 1.

15 Garraghan, 3: 349, 368, 373, 385-86; Avella, 57-58; MT, May 6, 1948. My thanks to Professor Alison Barnes of the Marquette School of Law for clarifying the legal steps taken by Bishop Henni in his incremental transfer of the Hilltop to the Society of Jesus.

16 Michael F. Moloney, *Père Marquette: Inspiration for a Great University* (Milwaukee: Marquette University Press, 1956), 5-17; Hamilton, 6.

17 Garraghan, 3: 386-87; Hamilton,13.

18 Garraghan, 3: 385.

19 City Treasurer's Office, February 1, 1858 and October 1, 1870, Archives, A-5.1, Series 1, Box 13; Scrapbook 15: October 1, 1905; Garraghan, 3: 388; Scrapbook 21: 61; Board of Trustees minutes, March 31, 1864; ibid., May 3, 1864; http://eh.net; MT, September 30, 1964; Hamilton, 12-13; clipping, November 29, 1953, Archives, A-4.5, Series 10, File 495.

20 Anthony M. Orum, *City-Building in America* (Boulder: Westview Press, 1995), 50, 55; Gurda, 114, 117, 123-28, 164-69.

21   Gurda, 175-76; "Remember When," Archives, A-4.5, Series 10, File 1205; Garraghan, 3: 388.

22   Board of Trustees minutes, March 4, 1878; ibid., April 18, 1878; ibid., April 15, 1879; Scrapbook 10: 20-21; Scrapbook 15, October 1, 1905; Heming, 332-33; Hamilton, 13.

23   Avella, 58, 138, 151; Scrapbook 15: October 1, 1905; Scrapbook 10: 20-21.

CHAPTER 2

1   Anthony J. Kuzniewski, *Thy Honored Name* (Washington: Catholic University of America Press, 1999), 5-7; George Ganss, *Saint Ignatius' Idea of a Jesuit University* (Milwaukee: Marquette University Press, 1956), 9-17; Gerald McKevitt, *The University of Santa Clara* (Stanford: Stanford University Press, 1979), 56; Lee J. Bennish, *Continuity and Change* (Chicago: Loyola University Press, 1981), 28; Philip Gleason, *Contending with Modernity* (New York: Oxford University Press, 1995), 54.

2   Allan P. Farrell, *The Jesuit Code of Liberal Education* (Milwaukee: Bruce Publishing Company, 1938), 376-83; James Tunstead Burtchaell, *The Dying of the Light* (Grand Rapids: William B. Eerdmans Publishing Company, 1998), 564-66; *Company*, Summer, 2006, p. 5; John Francis Bannon, *The Missouri Province* (St. Louis: Missouri Province, 1977), 4-5.

3   Kuzniewski, 7; Ganss, 31, 44-80; Herman J. Muller, *The University of Detroit* (Detroit: University of Detroit, 1976), 22; McKevitt, 27, 56; Bennish, 44, 80; James M. Demske, *A Promise of Quality* (New York: Newcomen Society in North America, 1970), 10, 13.

4   McKevitt, 57-58, 108, 122; Nicholas Varga, *Baltimore's Loyola, Loyola's Baltimore* (Baltimore: Maryland Historical Society, 1990), 65; Muller, 25; Catalogue, 1885/86, 16-19.

5   The preceding paragraphs were drawn from the following sources: Michael W. Maher, "The Just Development of Mind and Heart: Jesuit Education at the Turn of the Century in Milwaukee, Wisconsin," in Thomas M. Lucas, ed., *Spirit, Style, Story.* (Chicago: Jesuit Way/Loyola Press, 2002), 403-425; Ganss, 31-34, 41-43, 44-53, 57-58, 202-17, 283-90; Farrell, 403; Fran Daly, "Magis," *Partners*, Summer, 2003, 17; Raphael N. Hamilton, *The Story of Marquette University* (Milwaukee: Marquette University Press, 1953), 21-25; Helen Lefkowitz Horowitz, *Campus Life* (Chicago: University of Chicago Press, 1987), 41; David H. Burton and Frank Gerrity, *Saint Joseph's College: A Family Portrait* (Philadelphia: Saint Joseph's College Press, 1977), 13; McKevitt, 56; Scrapbook 10: 20-21; Scrapbook 3: 1; Prefect's Diary, Archives, D-2, Series 3, Box 2, clipping, August 1881.

6   Scrapbook 3: 1; McKevitt, 40; Varga, 28; Muller, 21.

7   File folder with contracts, Prefect's Diary, Archives, D-2, Series 3, Box 1; Financial Diary, Archives, D-2, Series 3, Box 27, July 1, 1881; July 19, 1881; Prefect's Diary, Archives, D-2, Series 3, Box 2, clipping, August 1881; Scrapbook 3: 3; *Marquette's Silver Jubilee: A Memoir* (n.p.: n.p., n.d.), 10; photos of Marquette College, Archives, A-4.5, Series 10, File 885.

8   Horowitz, 5; *Marquette College, A Sketch*, Archives, A-11, Series 1, Box 10: 56-58; *Silver Jubilee*, 12-13, 98, 124; Prefect's Diary, Archives, D-2, Series 3, Box 2, September 5, 1881; McKevitt, 28; Muller, 26; Varga, 27.

9   Prefect's Diary, Archives, D-2, Series 3, Box 2, October 5, 1881; November 1881; February 17, 1882; March 1, 1882; June 10, 1882; June 12, 1882; February 5, 1883; May 10, 1883; September 17, 1883; November 12, 1885; September 26, 1886; December 5, 1890; October 12, 1891; November 20, 1891; *Silver Jubilee*, 41; "First Student," Archives, A-4.5, Series 10, File 590; Muller, 31; Varga, 85.

10   Prefect's Diary, Archives, D-2, Series 3, Box 2, December 15, 1881; *Silver Jubilee*, 98; Horowitz, 42.

11   Enrollment Statistics, 1881/82 to1886/87, Archives, A-6.4, Series 2, Box 1.

12   Prefect's Diary, Archives, D-2, Series 3, Box 2, September 5, 1881; September 4, 1882; Catalogue, 1881/82, 6-7; 1882/83, 7-9; MJ, December 1910; MC Diary, Archives, D-2, Series 3, Box 8, September 10, 1900; *Silver Jubilee*, 43; "Looking Back," Archives, A-4.5, Series 10, File 885; Burton, 8; Muller, 20-21, 27; McKevitt, 59.

13   Prefect's Diary, Archives, D-2, Series 3, Box 2, June 10, 1882; June 18, 1883; September 27, 1883; September 28, 1887; February 22, 1888; November 6, 1888; September 1, 1890; September 16, 1891; November 24, 1891; January 28, 1899; MC Diary, Archives, D-2, Series 3, Box 3, December 1896; January 24, 1899; June 27, 1899; *Silver Jubilee*, 41, 42; "Looking Back," Archives, A-4.5, Series 10, File 885; Varga, 52.

14 Prefect's Diary, Archives, D-2, Series 3, Box 2, January 10, 1886; December 31, 1886; January 3, 1887; February 10, 1899; October 17, 1899; MC Diary, Archives, D-2, Series 3, Box 8, December 16, 1903; January 20, 1904; MC Diary, Archives, D-2, Series 3, Box 3, December 8, 1898; February 9-11, 1899; September 17, 1909; October 27, 1911.

15 Prefect's Diary, Box 2, June 14, 1882; *Catalogue*, 1882/83, 7; MJ, June, 1905.

16 Catalogue, 1883/84, 23-24; 1884/85, 29-30; 1888/89, 39; 1893/94, 42; 1899/1900, 41, 43; 1900/01, 44-45; *Silver Jubilee*, 25-33, 40; *A Sketch*, 59, 61; Prefect's Diary, Box 2, October 12, 1883; MC Diary, Box 3, December 8, 1898; Scrapbook 21: 61; Kuzniewski, 62; McKevitt, 91.

17 Prefect's Diary, Box 2, November 22, 1894; *Silver Jubilee*, 36-37, 44, 52, 53, 59; Catalogue, 1884/85. 30; Scrapbook 5:66; Scrapbook 21: 61; Hamilton, 37, 387; MT, February 15, 1934.

18 Prefect's Diary, Box 2, October 25, 1897; *Silver Jubilee*, 48-49; Scrapbook 15: undated clipping in folder; November 7, 1903; MJ, February 1, 1906.

19 Scrapbook 5: 78, 81; Hilltop, 1926: 236; Prefect's Diary, Box 2, February 8, 1900; *Silver Jubilee*, 7, 51; Scrapbook 14: 9, 12, 77; Catalogue, 1899/1900, 44.

20 Catalogue, 1881/82, 18, 28; 1883/84, 25, 32; Scrapbook 10: 19; *Silver Jubilee*, 15-17, 40, 44, 127; Prefect's Diary, Box 2, p. 24ff; ibid., September 2, 1890; Scrapbook 3: 4, 16; MT, March 8, 1934; May 6, 1948, p. 11; "Public Quizzed," Archives, A-4.5, Series 10, File 401.

21 Catalogue, 1881/82, 16-20, 29; *Silver Jubilee*, 18-19; *A Sketch*, 58; Scrapbook 3: 4, 8a, 8b; Prefect's Diary, Box 2, p. 24ff.

22 Catalogue, 1882/83, 10, 20; 1886/87, 45; list of first graduating class including deaths, Archives, A-4.5, Series 10, File 590; *Silver Jubilee*, 42; MT, October 30, 1917; March 12, 1925; Prefect's Diary, February 1, 1888; Hamilton, 40.

23 Catalogue,1881/82, 15; 1885/86, 34-35; *A Sketch*, 60, 61; *Silver Jubilee*, 40; Prefect's Diary, Box 2, June 29, 1886; June 25, 1890; September 2, 1890; June 24, 1898; June 22, 1899; June 20, 1900; MC Diary, Box 3, June 21, 1901; June 22, 1902; June 21, 1903; Scrapbook 3: 16 and undated loose clipping regarding1886 commencement; Scrapbook 10: 8, 31, 51; Scrapbook 14: 12.

24 *Silver Jubilee*, 17, 41, 42-43; *A Sketch*, 58; Scrapbook 3: 57; MT, February 15, 1934.

25 Scrapbook 3: 10; *Silver Jubilee*, 22-23; Gilbert J. Garraghan, *The Jesuits of the Middle United States* (New York: America Press, 1938), 3: 452; Catalogue, 1884/85, 2; Scrapbook 14: 76; Prefect's Diary, Box 2, September 1, 1893; August 11, 1894; August 11, 1895.

26 Http://eh.net; Varga, 30-31; Burton, 8, 12; Muller, 1.

27 Financial Diary, Box 27, July 1, 1881; July 19, 1881; Board of Trustees minutes, April 18, 1878; May 4, 1878; April 15, 1879; January 7, 1881; *Silver Jubilee*, 41-42, 50; MT, March 8, 1934; Scrapbook 3: 57; Enrollment Statistics, 1887/88, Archives, A-6.4, Series 2, Box 1; Garraghan, 3: 452-53; Catalogue, 1898/99, 12; ibid., 1899/1900, 12; Hamilton, 19, 21; Bennish, 60. 63.

28 Financial Diary, Box 27, July 19, 1881; September 1, 1881; September 19, 1881; September 22, 1881; October 27, 1881; November 8, 1881; November 27, 1881; December 6, 1881; January 5, 1882; January 13, 1882; January 16, 1882; May 1, 1882; May 8, 1882; May 11, 1882; April 23, 1883; May 17, 1883; June 5, 1883; January 18, 1884; October 1, 1885; November 7, 1885; August 19, 1888.

29 Financial Diary, Box 27, October 6, 1881; November 5, 1881, February 26, 1882; MC Diary, Box 3, loose envelope; letter, January 19, 1927, Archives, C-9.1, Series 9c, Box 2.

30 Board of Trustees minutes, February 21, 1889; March 29, 1889; July 18, 1891; October 21, 1891; December 9, 1891; Financial Diary, Box 27, July 23, 1891; July 29, 1891; November 2, 1891; December 1891; November or December [uncertainty in original], 1891; Hamilton, 17, 47; MT, September 26, 1979, p. 2; Steven M. Avella, *In the Richness of the Earth* (Milwaukee: Marquette University Press, 2002), 215.

31 Board of Trustees minutes, February 17, 1892; May 4, 1892; June 22, 1892; November 10, 1892; April 27, 1893; February 11, 1895; September 17, 1898; November 3, 1898; November 18, 1898; Financial Diary, Box 27, February 1892; May 1892; May 13, 1892; May 16, 1892; May 21, 1892; May 26, 1892; undated entry regarding design plans, 1892; July 1892; undated entry regarding superintendent for construction, 1892; undated entry regarding lot distribution, 1892; October 1892; September 24, 1898; November 1898; November 5, 1898; MC Diary, Box 3, September 20, 1898; October 17, 1898; October 26, 1898; Scrapbook 10: 18, 19, 23, 38, 41, 52; Scrapbook 14: 38, 39, 43;

Scrapbook 15: 231; Harry H. Heming, *The Catholic Church in Wisconsin* (Milwaukee: Catholic Historical Publications Co., 1896), 333-34; Hamilton, 44.

32   Burton, 16; Bennish, 99; Muller, 47; Robert I. Gannon, *Up To The Present* (Garden City: Doubleday & Company, 1967), 101; *Silver Jubilee*, 34-35, 43-44; Prefect's Diary, Box 2, September 2, 1890; Catalogue, 1890/91, 40-41; Scrapbook 18, loose set of banquet programs for 1899 and 1902.

33   *Silver Jubilee*, 41, 47-48, 54; *A Sketch*, 60; Scrapbook 18: 2; Hamilton, 38-40, 49-52; www.aoc.gov.; *New York Times*, September 5, 2006, A16.

34   *A Sketch*, 56, 60-61; *Silver Jubilee*, 4, 20, 40; Garraghan, 3: 429-30, 452; Scrapbook 14: 47; Catalogue, 1882/83, 3; ibid., 1883/84, 3, 4; ibid., 1884/85, 3,9; ibid., 1887/88, 4; Bannon, 103-11; David P. Miros, "Rudolph J. Meyer and Saint Louis University: A Study of the Society of Jesus's Theological and Educational Enterprise at the Turn of the Century, 1885-1915," (Unpublished PhD dissertation, St. Louis University, 2005), 50

35   Garraghan, 3: 426-28, 429-35, 453; William B. Faherty, *Better the Dream* (St. Louis: St. Louis University, 1968), Chapter 8; Bannon, 103-11*; Silver Jubilee*, 43, 44, 45-46; Catalogue, 1885/86, 3, 34-35; 1889/90, 3; 1892/93, 3; Scrapbook 10: 1; Scrapbook 14: 54, 55; Scrapbook 19: 121; Scrapbook 3: 55; MT, October 27, 1927; photographs of college faculty, Archives, A-4.5, Series 10, File 717.

36   Garraghan, 3: 428, 431-32; Gleason, 52-54; McKevitt, 122-25; Faherty, 126, 189-90; Demske, 13; Miros, 66-70.

37   Ibid., 101-03, 110, 115, 119-20, 151ff; Faherty, 257-58; Farrell, 395; Hamilton, 22-24.

38   Kathleen A. Mahoney, *Catholic Higher Education in Protestant America* (Baltimore: Johns Hopkins University Press, 2003); Gleason, 30-32; MT, May 16, 1924; October 31, 1929; Gannon, 106-08; Varga, 154-55.

39   Enrollment Statistics, Archives, A-6.4, Series 2, Box 1, 1881/82 to 1905/06; *Silver Jubilee*, 124-29; *A Sketch*, 60; Varga, 140; McKevitt, 123.

40   Scrapbook 15: 159, 188, 189, 190, 192; *Silver Jubilee*, 24, 57; MC Diary, Box 8, November 15, 1904; Virginia A. Palmer, "The Normal School on Wells Street," in Thomas J. Jablonsky, ed., *Milwaukee Stories* (Milwaukee: Marquette University Press, 2005), 130-31.

41   Gleason, 96; Scrapbook 14: 69; Catalogue, 1901/02, 21-27, 45-47; Bennish, 104.

42   42. Catalogue, 1902/03, 8-12, 30.

43   Catalogue, 1903/04, 27-41; 1904/05, 34; 1905/06, 28; 1906/07, 26, 51, 55-74.

44   McKevitt, 150-152; Gannon, 79, 100; Muller, 76; Bennish, 105; Gleason, 56, 58; Peter McDonough, *Men Astutely Trained* (New York: Free Press, 1992), 59.

45   *Silver Jubilee*, 60-63; Scrapbook 18: 11, 18; Scrapbook 21: 61.

CHAPTER 3

1   The preceding discussion relied upon the following sources: Lawrence R. Veysey, *The Emergence of the American University* (Chicago: University of Chicago Press, 1965), Chapters 3, 5; George M. Marsden, "The Soul of the American University," in *The Secularization of the Academy*, edited by George M. Marsden and Bradley J. Longfield, (New York: Oxford University Press, 1992), 9-45; Julie A. Reuben, *The Making of the Modern University* (Chicago: University of Chicago Press, 1996), Introduction; Philip Gleason, *Contending with Modernity* (New York: Oxford University Press, 1995), 22-27; William P. Leahy, *Adapting to America* (Washington, D.C.: Georgetown University Press, 1991), Chapter 1; Peter McDonough, *Men Astutely Trained* (New York: Free Press, 1992), 12-13; Paul Westmeyer, *An Analytical History of American Higher Education*, 2 ed. (Springfield, Illinois: Charles C. Thomas Publisher, 1997), Chapter 4-6; www.registrar.wisc.edu/students/acadrecords/enrollment___reports.

2   Scrapbook 15: 230, 231; Raphael Hamilton, *The Story of Marquette University*. (Milwaukee: Marquette University Press, 1953), 110.

3   Scrapbook 15: 232, 238; Scrapbook 18: 12; Scrapbook 20: letter, September 10, 1945; ibid.: letter with attachment, November 29, 1945; Hamilton, 64-65.

4   MT, October 28, 1926, p. 6; October 30, 1952, p. 12; Scrapbook 15: 230, 232, 240, 261; Scrapbook 18: 17.

5   Scrapbook 17: 7; Board of Trustees minutes, June 29, 1906, Archives, A-2.1, Series 2, Box 1.

6 Board of Trustees minutes, April, 1907; Scrapbook 17: 17; Scrapbook 18: 28; MT, June 29, 1962, p. 2; Marquette College Diary, Box 3, July 5, 1907; August 15, 1907; August 19, 1907; Scrapbook 19a: 104; MJ, June 1907, pp. 134-35; photographs of Johnston Hall, Archives, A-4.5, Series 10, File 750.

7 Henry L. Banzhaf, "Growing up with Marquette University," *Milwaukee County Historical Quarterly* (Summer 1981), 50; Scrapbook 15: 232, 261; Scrapbook 17: 4, 27; William B. Faherty, *Better the Dream* (St. Louis: St. Louis University, 1968), 82-83, 212-15.

8 Norman H. Engbring, *An Anchor for the Future* (Milwaukee: The Medical College of Wisconsin, 1991), 7-9; Abraham Flexner, *Medical Education in the United States and Canada* (Boston: D. B. Updike, 1910), 318; Paul Starr, *The Social Transformation of American Medicine* (New York: Basic Books, 1982), 117; Scrapbook 17: 12, 27.

9 Board of Trustees minutes, May 4, 1907.

10 Board of Trustees minutes, May 11, 1907; May 14, 1907; August 15, 1911; Milwaukee Medical College, May 14, 1907, Archives, A-5.1, Series 1, Box 9; Scrapbook 17: 27; Scrapbook 18: 29.

11 Inventory, January 18, 1907, Archives, C-5, Series 1, Box 1; www.eh.net.

12 Description of the Seal of Marquette University, April 1926, Archives, A-1.1, Series 3, Box 5; MT, January 7, 1926, p. 3; December 18, 1930, p. 6; MJ, December 1906, pp. 47-48; March 1907, p. 74; June 1907, p. 137.

13 Scrapbook 18: 41; Catalogue, 1906/07, 108; Scrapbook 17: 24.

14 History of Marquette History Law School, Archives, D-5, Series 1, Box 1; Scrapbook 18: 41; Scrapbook 17: 38; Board of Trustees minutes, March 23, 1908; April 11, 1908; Michael J. Mazza, "The Rise and Fall of Part-Time Legal Education in Wisconsin, 1892-1924," *Marquette Law Review* (Summer, 1998), 1054, 1058-59; Hamilton, 83-84.

15 History of Marquette University Law School, Archives, D-5, Series 1, Box 1; Scrapbook 18: 36-38, 41-42; Scrapbook 17: 38; Hamilton, 84-85.

16 History of Marquette University Law School, Archives, D-5, Series 1, Box 1; Board of Trustees minutes, June 16, 1910; MJ, December 1910, p. 63; MT, February 6, 1920, p. 6; February 10, 1949; April 17, 1959; Hamilton, 85-86.

17 *Chicago Daily Tribune*, February 11, 1908, ProQuest Historical Newspapers; ibid., October 19, 1909, ibid.; MT, January 20, 1927, p. 1; September 21, 1933, p. 13; Scrapbook 21: 216; Enrollment Statistics, 1900/01 and 1907/08, Archives, A-6.4, Series 2, Box 1.

18 Board of Trustees minutes, February 26, 1908; Scrapbook 18: 50-51, 75; Scrapbook 17: 42; A Brief History of the College of Engineering, Archives, D-5, Series 1, Box 1; MJ, June 1912, p. 5.

19 Board of Trustees minutes, July 31, 1908; May 7, 1910; Scrapbook 18: 37, 38, 48, 50-51, 52, 57; Scrapbook 19: 1, 2; A Brief History of the College of Engineering, Archives, D-5, Series 1, Box 1; MJ, June 1912, p. 5; Hilltop, 1915, p. 14; MT, September 30, 1916, p. 1; clipping, June 29, 1961, Archives, A-8.5, Series 1, Box 3.

20 A Brief History of the College of Engineering, Archives, D-5, Series 1, Box 1; Scrapbook 18: 50-51; Scrapbook 19: 18; Scrapbook 20: 179; Scrapbook 21: 72-73; Scrapbook 23a: 4; MJ, June 1912, pp. 4-11; Hamilton, 90.

21 Scattered Data, p. 203, Archives, D-5, Series 1, Box 1; Scrapbook 19: 61, 63; MJ, December 1910, pp. 37-38; ibid., April 1911, p. 28; MT, November 19, 1953; Hamilton, 94, 97.

22 College of Journalism, pp. 1-4, Archives, D-5, Series 1, Box 1; Scrapbook 21: 56, 59; College of Journalism, Anniversary, 1910-60, Dean's Office, College of Communications, p. 1.

23 College of Journalism, pp. 4-7, Archives, D-5, Series 1, Box 1; MJ, April 1912, p. 42; ibid., October 1913, p. 46; Scrapbook 19b: 219; Scrapbook 21: 59; Scrapbook 23: 29-31, 36, 42, 44; Anniversary, 1910-60, 1-3. The Jesuit community was just as concerned with Father Copus' declining health. Vice-President's Diary, Arts and Sciences Department, Archives, unprocessed, October 21, 1914; November 2, 1914; December 14 & 17, 1914; January 3, 1915; May 13, 17, 18, & 19, 1915; June 4, 8, 12, & 14, 1915.

24 Scrapbook 19a: 152; Scrapbook 19b: 209; Scrapbook 23: March 1, 1916; ibid.: 231; Scrapbook 21: 46, 52; Scrapbook 19b: 251; MJ, December 1910, p. 35; October 1911, pp. 60-61; June 1912, pp. 31, 36-37; Map of Music College Location, Archives, A-5.1, Series 1, Box 13; Hamilton, 104; Photo of 1917 Conservatory Student Body, Archives, A-4.5, Series 10, File 971; MT, October 31, 1918, p.

4; October 18, 1945; Vice-President's Diary, Arts and Sciences Department, Archives, unprocessed, November 21, 1914; May 18, 1916; School of Embalming, Archives, C-5, Series 1, Box 1.

25   Herman J. Muller, *The University of Detroit* (Detroit: University of Detroit, 1976), 80-81; Robert I. Gannon, *Up to the Present* (Garden City: Doubleday & Company, 1967), 122, 147; Lee J. Bennish, *Continuity and Change* (Chicago: Loyola University Press, 1981), 112, 117, 123, 129; Nicholas Varga, *Baltimore's Loyola, Loyola's Baltimore* (Baltimore: Maryland Historical Society, 1990), 281; James M. Demske, *A Promise of Quality* (New York: Newcomen Society in North America, 1970), 18.

26   John S. Brubacher and Willis Rudy, *Higher Education in Transition* (New York: Harper and Row, 1968), 68-69; Susan L. Poulson and Loretta P. Higgins, "Gender, Coeducation, and the Transformation of Catholic Identity in American Catholic Higher Education," *Catholic Historical Review* 89 (July, 2003), 491; McDonough, 53.

27   Milwaukee Medical College, *Announcement for 1907-08*, p. 8; Department of Medicine, Marquette University, *Annual Catalogue and Announcement for 1908-09*, 10, 31-32; Helen Kean, "The History of Women in Jesuit Schools," JEA 1965 Workshop for Jesuit Student Personnel, Programs, and Services, pp. 3-4; electronic correspondence from Jeffrey J. Wenzler, August 18, 2005, regarding Saint Louis, Georgetown, and Loyola universities.

28   Women Graduates of MU, Archives, A-4.5, Series 10, File 1413; "First," clipping, ibid.; Catalogue, 1915, p. 62; MC Diary, Box 8, June 21, 1910; ibid., undated page following this entry backdating 1909 graduates; alumni card for Daisy Grace Wolcott, Archives; Engbring, 440.

29   Hamilton, 125.

30   Bulletin, Summer School, 1909; Hamilton, 125-26; Scrapbook 22: 148; letter and accompanying materials on Sister Generose from Sister Donna Marie Kessler, OSF, September 29, 2005.

31   Hamilton, 126-27; Bulletin, Summer School, 1910; College of Journalism, p. 4, Archives, D-5, Series 1, Box 1; Scrapbook 19: 58; MC Diary, Box 8, July 1911; June 25, 1912; June 27, 1912; June 28, 1912; Board of Trustees minutes, December 19, 1915; August 3, 1917; July 29, 1918; Catalogue, 1915, p. 62; Vice-president's Diary, Arts and Sciences Department, Archives, unprocessed, Summer Session, 1915; Summer Session, 1916; MJ, June 1911, p. 57; Scrapbook 19a: 160; Scrapbook 21: June 18, 1912; June 24, 1912; MT, January 23, 1930, p. 2.

32   Hamilton, 126-27; Register of Alumni, Archives, A-1, Series 1, Box 4; letter, May 20, 1911, ibid.; MC Diary, Box 8, November 6, 1911; Scrapbook 19a: 116, 118, 119, 169; Scrapbook 17: loose pages at front.

33   MC Diary, Box 8, July 6, 1911; Hamilton, 127; Bennish, 122-23; John Francis Bannon, *The Missouri Province SJ* (St. Louis: St. Louis University, 1977), 104.

34   Scrapbook 16: 50; Scrapbook 21: May 26, 1912; June 16, 1912; July 14, 1912; Scrapbook 31: July 25, 1918.

35   MJ, October 1912, p. 39; April 1916, pp. 25-26; MT, November 21, 1916, p. 3; January 29, 1917, p. 2; March 12, 1917, p. 8; April 23, 1917, p. 10; April 30, 1917, p. 4; Hilltop, 1915, pp. 45, 118.

36   MT, October 7, 1916, p. 1; January 18, 1917, p. 9; February 12, 1917, p. 9; Enrollment, 1916-17, Archives, A-6-4, Series 2, Box 1.

37   Bennish, 122-23, 126-27; Muller, 116, 117, 162; Demske, 18; Faherty, 316; Varga, 227; McKevitt, 285; Burton and Gerrity, 68.

38   MC Diary, Box 8, October 1909; October 2, 1911; October 3, 1911; MJ, October 1911, p. 41.

39   Enrollments, 1881/82 to 1910/11, Archives, A-6.4, Series 2, Box 1; Vice-President's Diary, Arts and Sciences Department, Archives, unprocessed, September 8, 10, 17, 1914; October 9, 1914; September 7, 1915.

40   Ibid., 1907/08 to 1910/11; Gannon, 133; Varga, 217.

41   Scrapbook 18: 39; Scrapbook 19a: 80, 194; Scrapbook 20: 99; Scrapbook 21: 55, 59, 71, 72, 78, 80, 89, 231; Scrapbook 23: 118, 248; Scrapbook 27: 79, 155; Scrapbook 31: 31;

42   Hamilton, 85. The Catalogues and Hilltops are the best sources for a list of the Jesuit Regents in any given year.

43   Board of Regents Charter, Archives, A-5.1, Series 1, Box 2; clipping, 1909, Archives, A-11, Series 1, Box 13; Scrapbook 18: 55; Scrapbook 19: 130.

44 Clipping, 1909, Archives, A-11, Series 1, Box 13; Scrapbook 18: 57; MJ, April 1910, pp. 5-9. Names of board members can be found in the Catalogues, occasionally in the Marquette Journal and some Hilltops. Because this board did not exist as part of the legal structure of the university, there seems to have been no inclination to faithfully identify its membership. The presence—or absence—of regents' names in university publications in any given year suggest which presidents made use of this body and which did not.

45 MJ, December 1911, pp. 5-33; MC Diary, Box 8, October 7, 1911; Marquette: Milwaukee's University brochure, Archives, A-1.1, Series 13, Box 1.

46 Engbring, 11-14; Flexner, 39, 81, 86, 109, 114, 117, 318-19; Starr, 118-20; Banzhaf, 51-53; MJ, June 1913, pp. 8-9.

47 Letter, February 13, 1911, Archives, C-5, Series 1, Box 1; letter, March 22, 1911, ibid.; MJ, October 1911, pp. 64-65.

48 Engbring, 14-17; Scrapbook 21: 163, 170-72, 176, 178-80, 200-01; Banzhaf, 53; Board of Trustees minutes, November 17, 1912; Hamilton, 75; MJ, June, 1913, p. 9; Hilltop, 1915, p. 94; Helen Lefkowitz Horowitz, *Campus Life* (Chicago: University of Chicago Press, 1987), 24ff.

49 Banzhaf, 53-56; Board of Trustees minutes, December 12, 1912; December 13, 1912; December 16, 1912; December 19, 1912; January 13, 1913; letter, December 17, 1912, Archives, A-2.1, Series 2, Box 1; agreement regarding personal property, January 13, 1913, Archives, A-5.1, Series 1, Box 9; agreement regarding MMC lease, January 13, 1913; Scrapbook 21: 202, 205-06, 209, 211, 213, 217; Engbring, 17.

50 Scrapbook 21: 223; MJ, February 1913, p. 45; June 1913, p. 9; ibid., December 1913, p. 68; February 1914, pp. 64-67; October 1914, pp. 54-55; October 1915, p. 29; map of WCPS property, Archives, C-5, Series 1, Box 1; MT, October 14, 1916, p. 1; April 30, 1917, p. 12; February 13, 1920; Robert Haukohl, "History of MU Dental School," 1939, Archives, Miller Research Files, Acc. 95.6, Box 1; Engbring, 17-19; Vice-President's Diary, Arts and Sciences Department, February 23, 1915; February 8, 1916, Archives, unprocessed.

51 MJ, April 1911, p. 47; October 1911, pp. 55-56; October 1914, p. 53; Scrapbook 18: 48, 75, 84, 130; Scrapbook 19a: 162, 164; Scrapbook 21: 83; Scrapbook 23: 247, 248.

52 Muller, 32; Bennish, 112; letter, September 24, 1914, Archives, A-5.1, Series 1, Box 13; Catalogue, 1915, 1, 39-51; Vice-president's Diary, Arts and Sciences Department, Archives, unprocessed, December 20, 1914; January 7, 1915; March 11, 13, 17, 1915; April 15, 17, 1915; May 17, 1915; May 22, 1915; June 15, 1915; June 17, 1915; August 29, 1915; September 1, 1915; November 25, 1915; February 11, 1916; April 3, 6, 1916; MT, July 12, 1956, p. 1; Hamilton, 111fn., 127-33.

53 Agreement, November 16, 1915, Archives, A-1.1, Series 13, Box 1; letter, February 18, 1916, ibid.; telegrams, February, 1916, ibid.

54 Information for Workers, Archives, ibid.; Talking Points, ibid.; Memo for Marshals and Captains, ibid.; Committee List, ibid.; *The Marquette Campaigner*, March 25, 1916, ibid.; Scrapbook 23: 158, 165, 169, 170, 172-200; Scrapbook 23a: loose clipping at front, p. 114, 129.

55 Scrapbook 23: 164, 170, 172; Vice-president's Diary, Arts and Sciences Department, Archives, unprocessed, March 11, 1916; photograph of tote clock, Archives, A-4.5, Series 10, File 495.

56 Scrapbook 23: 172-200; *The Marquette Campaigner*, March 25, 1916, Archives, A-1.1, Series 13, Box 1; Vice-president's Diary, Arts and Sciences Department, Archives, unprocessed, February 24, 25, 28, 1916; March 2, 16, 1916.

57 $500,000 in Two Weeks for New Buildings, ibid.; Talking Points, ibid.; letter, March 27, 1916, ibid.; MJ, April 1916, pp. 13-15; MT, September 30, 1916, p. 1; March 5, 1917, p. 12; Scrapbook 23: 207, 211; Vice-president's Diary, Arts and Sciences Department, Archives, unprocessed, March 18, 19, 1916.

58 MJ, October 1911, pp. 64-65; December 1911, pp. 52-53; Vice-President's Diary, Arts and Sciences Department, Archives, unprocessed, October 30, 1914; Marquette's Olympians, Archives, A-4.5, File 1039; Hilltop, 1915, pp. 166-167; MC Diary, Box 8, October 20, 1911; Catalogue, 1906/07, p. 86; ibid., 1907/08, p. 54; 1915, p. 57; Scrapbook 19: 57; Scrapbook 19a: 16, 86; MT, December 16, 1926, p. 11; January 27, 1927, p. 6; May 6, 1948, p. 8.

59   Scrapbook 16: November 22, 1908; Scrapbook 17: 41; Scrapbook 18: 27; Scrapbook 19: 98; Scrapbook 19b: 218; MT, December 14, 1916, p. 6; December 16, 1926, p. 11; January 6, 1927, p. 11; January 27, 1927, p. 6; May 6, 1948, p. 8; Hamilton, 112-13.

60   MT, December 16, 1926, p. 11; January 13, 1926, p. 11; Scrapbook 19: 119; Scrapbook 21: 238, 239; Scrapbook 23a: 2, 12; MJ, October, 1913, pp. 42, 50; Hamilton, 118; Vice-President's Diary, Arts and Sciences Department, Archives, unprocessed, January 18, 1915; March 21, 1915; November 18, 1915; Horowitz, 55.

61   MJ, June, 1914, p. 88; October, 1914, p. 61; Hilltop, 1915, p. 89; Vice-President's Diary, Arts and Sciences Department, Archives, unprocessed, September 22, 1914; October 2, 1914; To Whom It May Concern, Archives, C-9.1, Series 2, Box 1; Dear Dean, ibid.; clippings, October 21 & 22, 1915, Archives, C-9.1, Series 8, Box 2; Scrapbook 23: 28, 67, 68; Horowitz, 35.

62   MJ, October , 1912, p. 32; Hilltop, 1915, Club Section; Hilltop, 1916, Club Section; MT, September 30, 1966, p. 7. Also compare Catalogue, 1907/08, 51-54 with Catalogue, 1915, 54-57.

63   MT, February 20, 1930, p. 3; MJ, December 1911, p. 42; October 1915, p. 35; Hilltop, 1915, Fraternities section; Hilltop, 1916, Dances section.

CHAPTER 4

1   MT, May 21, 1917, p. 1; October 9, 1917, p. 3; October 23, 1917, p. 7; October 30, 1917, p. 10; January 24, 1918, p. 1; January 31, 1918, p. 1; April 18, 1918, p. 1; May 16, 1918, p. 1; October 3, 1918, p. 3; October 24, 1918, p. 4; December 12, 1918, p. 10; February 5, 1942, p. 1; Scrapbook 27: March 20, 1917; March 30, 1917; June 1, 1917; August 25, 1917; Raphael N. Hamilton, *The Story of Marquette University* (Milwaukee: Marquette University Press, 1953), 164; Philip Gleason, *Contending with Modernity* (New York: Oxford University Press, 1995), 73.

2   MT, February 26, 1917, p. 1; March 26, 1917, p. 2; April 23, 1917, p. 3; May 21, 1917, p. 1; October 9, 1917, p. 1; December 13, 1917, p. 7; February 7, 1918, p. 6; February 14, 1918, p. 1; March 14, 1918, p. 6; April 11, 1918, p. 7; May 30, 1918, p. 1; October 3, 1918, p. 2; clipping, June 14, 1918, Archives, A-1.1, Series 13, Box 1; Scrapbook 27: May 14, 1917; September 28, 1917.

3   Hilltop, 1918, pp. 7-27, 35-40; Hilltop, 1919, p. 5ff; Hilltop, 1920, "Men of Marquette Who Died in the World Struggle"; MT, October 3, 1918, p. 2; October 17, 1918, p. 1; October 24, 1918, p. 4; October 31, 1918, p. 2; December 5, 1918, p. 4; January 9, 1919, p. 1.

4   MT, October 3, 1918, p. 1; October 10, 1918, p. 1; October 24, 1918, pp. 2, 9; October 31, 1918, p. 2; November 7, 1918, p. 1; November 13, 1918, p. 11; November 28, 1918, pp. 1, 12; December 5, 1918, p. 1; Hilltop, 1919, pp. 178-81; Scrapbook 30: 81, 88, 101; brochure, Archives, A-1.1, Series 2, Box 12; Gleason, 73-75.

5   MT, May 14, 1917, p.1; December 20, 1917, p. 1; December 19, 1919, p. 3; October 15, 1920, p. 1; October 29, 1920, p. 1; March 25, 1921, p. 1; February 17, 1922, p. 1; Scrapbook 27: 123; Scrapbook 28: February 23, 1917; April 20, 1917; August 16, 1917; August 18, 1917; Scrapbook 29: loose clippings, 1917; March 9, 1917; March 16, 1917; Scrapbook 34: February 1, 1921; Scrapbook 35: October 13, 1921; October 14, 1921; February 12, 1922; Gleason, 78; Hamilton, 161, 162.

6   Ibid., 187; statement to Board of Trustees with handwritten remarks, November 23, 1919, Archives, A-1.1, Series 13, Box 1; letter, July 21, 1921, ibid.; letter, December 17, 1919, Archives, C-5, Series 1, Box 1; letter, December 17, 1919, ibid.; Scrapbook 30: 191; MT, May 12, 1922, p. 1.

7   Memorandum, undated, regarding Holy Name Church and School, Archives, A-5.1, Series 1, Box 3; MT, January 7, 1918, pp. 1, 8; February 6, 1919, p. 11; October 3, 1919, p. 2; Hilltop, 1920, p. 137.

8   Letter, May 9, 1913, Plankinton Family Papers, Box 2, Milwaukee County Historical Society; Board of Trustees minutes, July 31, 1908; January 22, 1917; Henry L. Banzhaf, "Growing Up With Marquette University," *Milwaukee History* (Summer, 1981), pp. 58-60; letter, June 30, 1916, Archives, A-5.1, Series 1, Box 11; letter, March 1, 1917, ibid.; letter, March 1, 1917, ibid.; letter, August 4, 1920, ibid.; letter, August 5, 1920, ibid.; letter, June 8, 1918, Archives, C-9.1, Series 3, Box 1; clippings, June, 1918, Archives, C-9.1, Series 8, Box 2; Scrapbook 30: 191.

9   Clipping, September 8, 1968, Archives A-4.5, Series 10, File 255; History of the School of Speech Building, ibid., File 1116; history, October 1, 1933, ibid.; MT, January 4, 1940, p. 8; October 2, 1941, p. 3; May 18, 1960, p. 6.

10   MT, March 13, 1919, p. 7; December 12, 1919, p. 4; February 18, 1921, p. 1; May 13, 1921, p. 1; June 3, 1921, p. 1; June 10, 1921, p. 7; October 28, 1921, p. 1; November 17, 1921, p. 11; Scrapbook 34: February 13, 1921; June 12, 1921; Board of Trustees minutes, June 23, 1921; August 15, 1921; August 27, 1921.

11   MT, April 23, 1920, p. 1; January 27, 1922, p. 1; March 31, 1922, p. 1; April 7, 1922, p. 1; May 19, 1922, p.1; September 29, 1922, p. 2; September 28, 1923, p. 8; November 16, 1923, p. 5; February 8, 1924, p. 1; February 22, 1924, p. 2; Scrapbook 30: 112, 132, 169; letter, June 7, 1923, Archives, C-9.1, Series 3, Box 1; Hamilton, 194, 250-51, 250 n.39.

12   Memorandum, January, 1925, Archives, A-1.1, Series 2, Box 8; letter, February 18, 1925, ibid.; letter, February 7, 1927, ibid.; letter, November 26, 1928, ibid.; Johnston dividend, undated, ibid.; memorandum, November 14, 1934, ibid.; report on administration of MU High, January 3, 1940, Archives, C-9.1, Series 9c, Box 5; letter, January 5, 1923, Archives, B-10, Series 4, Box 1; MT, March 26, 1925, p. 2; September 17, 1925, p. 2; September 24, 1925, p. 3; Hamilton, 198; Tim John, *The Miller Beer Barons* (Oregon, Wis.: Badger Books Inc., 2005), 168-69.

13   Hamilton, 189; letter, June 26, 1919, Archives A-1.1, Series 13, Box 1; letter, June 29, 1919, ibid.; MT, October 3, 1919, p. 1; October 17, 1919, p. 1; October 10, 1919, p. 1; October 31, 1919, p. 7; November 7, 1919, p. 6; November 28, 1919, p. 1.

14   Hamilton, 189; Gleason, 70-71.

15   Notice and response from Father Noonan, January 11, 1922, Archives, A-1.1, Series 13, Box 1; letter in Latin, February 25, 1922, ibid.; letter, July 21, 1922, ibid.; extract, August, 1922, ibid.; letter in Latin, September 15, 1922, ibid.; letter, July 25, 1922, ibid.; letter, July 26, 1923, ibid.; letter, August 4, 1923, ibid.; letter, September 15, 1922, Archives, A-5.1, Series 1, Box 11; speech, Archives, A-1.1, Series 2, Box 3; letter, September 29, 1922, Archives, C-9.1, Series 3, Box 1; Hamilton, 189; MT, January 13, 1922, p.1; September 29, 1922, p. 1; Scrapbook 35a: 1ff; Board of Trustees minutes, June 23, 1921; August 15, 1921; August 27, 1921. The depth of Father Noonan's hard feelings are revealed in his many letters to Henry Banzhaf over the course of the 1920s. Miscellaneous letters, Archives, C-9.1, Series 3, Box 1. Let me also express my appreciation to Father John Patrick Donnelly, SJ, a colleague in the Department of History, for his translations from Latin of several of abovementioned documents.

16   Letter, May 11, 1921, Archives, C-9.1, Series 3, Box 1; letter, May 31, 1921, ibid.; letter, July 16, 1921, ibid.; letter, exhibits, and schedules, September 28, 1921, Archives, A-5.1, Series 1.Box 3; current balance sheet, September 1, 1921, ibid., Box 13; appraisal certificate, May 10, 1921, ibid., Box 1;

17   Plant Assets and Liabilities, 1921-38, Archives, A-1.1, Series 2, Box 9.

18   MT, May 18, 1917, p. 1; October 2, 1917, pp. 1, 3; December 13, 1917, p. 1; Board of Trustees minutes, August 31, 1919; Gleason, 34-35; *Chicago Daily Tribune*, November 23, 1909, ProQuest Historical Newspapers.

19   MT, October 2, 1917, p. 3; October 9, 1917, p. 6; Board of Trustees minutes, July 13, 1918; Articles of Association, ibid., 1912-1923, p. 43.

20   MT, December 13, 1917, p. 1; January 10, 1918, p. 1; April 11, 1918, p. 1; May 9, 1918, p. 1; October 3, 1918, p. 1; November 14, 1919, p. 1; Endowment Fund brochure, Archives, A-4.5, Series 10, File 940; Medical Endowment Fund, Archives, A-1.1, Series 13, Box 1; Board of Trustees minutes, August 31, 1919; September 2, 1919; Scrapbook 29a: December 7, 1917; July 10, 1918; July 13, 1918; July 14, 1918; July 15, 1918; July 19, 1918; July 25, 1918; July 27, 1918; July 31, 1918; Hamilton, 174, 177.

21   Northern Michigan Land Co. Bonds, Archives, C-9.1, Series 9c, Box 3; letter, June 8, 1932, ibid.; Bill of Complaint, Archives, A-1.1, Series 13, Box 1; Board of Trustees minutes, December 3, 1918; resolution on following page; October 29, 1919; February 20, 1920; Hamilton, 178-79.

22   Northern Michigan Land Co. Bonds, Archives, C-9.1, Series 9c, Box 3; letter, June 8, 1932, ibid.; list of Town Treasurers, 1927, ibid.; lands owned by Marquette Land Company, ibid., Box 4; letter, August 31, 1922, Archives, C-9.1, Series 3, Box 1; Board of Trustees minutes, January 12, 1926; August 26, 1927; September 10, 1927; June 19, 1933; correspondence regarding Department of Forestry, Archives, A-1.1, Series 2, Box 2; for documentation regarding potential uses of this land, see letters and

reports between 1923 and 1933, ibid., Boxes 1-3; for a sample of responses to complaints, see March 18, 1935, A-1.1, Series 2, Box 8; for a series of letters from university presidents, see letters from 1935 to 1945, ibid.

23 Board of Trustees minutes, December 31, 1918; contract, February 26, 1921, Archives, A-1.1, Series 2.1, Box 1; letter, August 27, 1937, ibid.; Board of Trustees motion, undated, ibid.; letter, March 12, 1947, ibid.; clipping, undated, Archives, C-9.1, Series 8, Box 2; MT, March 4, 1921, p. 1; ibid., October 14, 1921, p.2; Scrapbook 34: February 28, 1921.

24 Letter, February 9, 1922, Archives, C-9.1, Series 3, Box 1; letter, February 11, 1922, ibid.; letter, July 21, 1922, Archives, A-1.1, Series 2.1, Box 1; letter, July 31, 1922, Archives, A-1.1, Series 2, Box 6; letter, July 31, 1922, Archives, C-9.1, Series 9c, Box 1.

25 Letter, April 19, 1923, Archives, A-1.1, Series 2, Box 7; statement, undated, ibid.; letter, January 21, 1924, ibid.; letter, February 26, 1924, ibid.; letter, July 5, 1924, ibid.; letter, September 24, 1930, ibid.; letter, September 24, 1930, ibid.; letter, April 9, 1923, Archives, C-9.1, Series 9c, Box 2; letter, January 30, 1924, ibid., Box 1; letter, January 31, 1924, ibid.; MT, April 27, 1923, p. 1; October 5, 1923, p. 3.

26 Letter, July 19, 1924, Archives, A-1.1, Series 2, Box 6; contract, July 25, 1924, ibid.; letter, August 6, 1924, ibid.; memorial to Archbishop Messmer, undated, Archives, A-4.5, Series 10, File 1413.

27 Report, April 18, 1926, Archives, A-4.5, Series 10, File 193; letter, April 26, 1926, ibid.; letter, May 4, 1926, ibid.; letter, March 31, 1926, Archives, A-1.1, Series 2, Box 9; letter, April 14, 1926, ibid.; letter, April 25, 1926, ibid.; letter, November 19, 1926, ibid.; letter November 20, 1926, ibid.; letter March 20, 1927, ibid.; letter March 23, 1927, ibid.; agreement, 1927, ibid.; William P. Leahy, *Adapting to America* (Washington, D.C.: Georgetown University Press, 1991), 82-83.

28 Announcement, February, 1929, Archives, A-1.1, Series 2, Box 6; letter, May 14, 1929, ibid.; letter, May 25, 1938, ibid.; letter, May 28, 1938, ibid.; letter, June 20, 1939, ibid.; newspaper clippings, ibid.; letter, July 24, 1928, ibid., Box 9; letter, August 14, 1928, ibid.; letter, September 14, 1928, ibid.; letter, July 7, 1929, ibid.; letter, May 2, 1934, ibid.; MT, April 7, 1927, p. 1; May 23, 1929, p. 1.

29 Report, February 27, 1922, Archives, A-4.5, Series 10, File 1335; letter, June 1, 1922, Archives, A-1.1, Series 13, Box 1; letter, September 21, 1922, Archives, C-9.1, Series 9c, Box 1; letter, June 21, 1922, Archives, C-9.1, Series 3, Box 1; letter, June 22, 1922, ibid.; letter, July 13, 1922, ibid.

30 Letter, September 29, 1986, Archives, A-4.5, Series 10, File 1335; Saga of Sisters in Milwaukee, undated, ibid.; History of the Hospital, undated, ibid.; MT, October 15, 1925, p.1; "The University Hospital," Departmental Reports, September, 1927, Archives, C-5, Series 1, Box 1.

31 Proceedings, Milwaukee County Board of Supervisors, Archives, A-11, Series 1, Box 17; MT, October 24, 1918, p. 10.

32 MT, January 20, 1927, p. 1; January 27, 1927, p. 1; February 3, 1927, p. 1; February 10, 1927, p. 3; February 17, 1927, p. 1; plan for the 500-bed Hospital on the Schandein Site, Archives, A-11, Series 1, Box 17; text of petition, ibid.; 22 Direct Questions pamphlet, ibid.; signature sheet, Archives, A-1.1, Series 3, Box 5; Scrapbook 40: 2, 4, 5, 7, 8, 9, 11, 13.

33 Marquette University Hospital Proposal, Archives, A-1.1, Series 3, Box 5; newspaper clipping, Archives, A-11, Series 1, Box 17; Schandein Site file folder, Archives, A-1.1, Series 3, Box 3; To the Citizens of Milwaukee, February 10, 1927, City Club of Milwaukee Collection, Box 10, UWM Urban Archives; press release, undated, ibid.; Scrapbook 37: October 13, 1925; Scrapbook 40: 8, 9, 11; Scrapbook 41: 1, 2,3, and loose page.

34 MT, March 3, 1927, p. 1; March 10, 1927, p. 3; March 17, 1927, pp. 1, 3; May 23, 1929, p. 1; clipping, March 9, 1927, Archives, A-11, Series 1, Box 17; map of County Supervisory Districts, ibid.; Schandein file folder, Archives, A-1.1, Series 3, Box 3; letter, April 13, 1929, Archives, A-1.1, Series 2, Box 4; Scrapbook 40: 14; Scrapbook 41: 7, 12.

35 MT, March 28, 1924, p. 1; letter, December 16, 1925, Archives, A-1.1, Series 2, Box 6; board of governors pamphlet, Archives, A-3.1, Series 1, Box 1; Scrapbook 41: 14.

36 Letter, August 26, 1927, Archives, A-1.1, Series 2, Box 6; Powers and Duties of Board of Directors, May 16, 1927, ibid.; Board of Governors statement, ibid.; clipping, September 18, 1927, Archives, A-11, Series 1, Box 13; Powers and Duties of the Board of Governors, ibid.; Board of Governors of Marquette University, Archives, A-5.1, Series 1, Box 2; MT, September 22, 1927, p. 1; Scrapbook 41: 14.

37   Letter, November 5, 1927, Archives, A-1.1, Series 2, Box 6; letter, November 9, 1927, ibid.; letter, December 11, 1928, ibid.; letter, December 22, 1928, ibid.; MT, May 12, 1927, p. 1; Why Marquette, Archives, A-11, Series 1, Box 13.

38   Letter, February 13, 1929, Archives, A-1.1, Series 2, Box 6; letter, February 16, 1929, ibid.; Gleason, 99.

39   Paul A. Fitzgerald, *The Governance of Jesuit Colleges in the United States, 1920-1970* (Notre Dame: University of Notre Dame Press, 1984), Chapter One; Robert I. Gannon, *Up to the Present* (Garden City: Doubleday & Company, 1967), 163; MT, November 10, 1922, p.1.

40   Gleason, 50; Herman J. Muller, *The University of Detroit* (Detroit: University of Detroit, 1976), 94; Nicholas Varga, *Baltimore's Loyola, Loyola's Baltimore* (Baltimore: Maryland Historical Society, 1990), 255; Gerald McKevitt, *The University of Santa Clara* (Stanford: Stanford University Press, 1979), 210; report of inspection of Marquette University, Archives, A-1.1, Series 2, Box 8; Standards of Accredited Colleges and Universities, ibid.; MT, May 6, 1921, p. 1. One additional result of the visit was the required renaming of all major academic divisions, except the Nurses' Training school, as colleges including Law and Dentistry. The new designations did not last very long, however. MT, April 27, 1923, p. 1.

41   Report of Inspection of Marquette University, Archives, A-1.1, Series 2, Box 8; Marquette University Libraries to 1954, Archives, Acc.99.54, Box 1; MT, December 20, 1923, p. 8; letter, September 10, 1924, Archives, A-1.1, Series 3, Box 5.

42   Letter, February 11, 1925, Archives, A-4.5, Series 2, Box 1; report, February 24, 1925, ibid.; letter, April 2, 1925, ibid.; Central Bureau of Information and Statistics, March 28, 1930, Archives, A-1.1, Series 3, Box 4; letter, undated, ibid.; MT, October 22, 1925, p. 2.

43   Central Bureau of Information and Statistics, March 28, 1930, Archives, A-1.1, Series 3, Box 4; report, August 9, 1926, ibid.; report, June, 1926, ibid., Box 5; letter, September 24, 1927, ibid.; memorandum, recorded March 19, 1929, ibid.; MT, January 13, 1927, p. 4; ibid., September 29, 1927, p. 7; Marquette University Libraries to 1954, pp. 1-7, Archives, Acc.99.54, Box 1; Marquette Libraries Chronology, 1881-1991, ibid.

44   Report, 1924-27, Archives, C-7, Series 1, Box 1; How to Secure a Master's Degree, Archives, A-11, Series 1, Box 9; clipping, March 29, 1925, ibid.; Curriculum for Graduate School, January 12, 1927, ibid.; Statutes for Graduate School, undated, ibid.; MT, October 27, 1922, p. 1; Hamilton, 248.

45   Report, 1924-27, Archives, C-7, Series 1, Box 1; MT, October 27, 1922, p. 1; ibid., February 23, 1923, p. 1.

46   MT, September 25, 1924, p. 2; October 22, 1925, p. 2; January 28, 1926, p. 3; January 12, 1928, p. 8; letter, March 23, 1928, Archives, A-1.1, Series 3, Box 4; personnel of College of Hospital Administration, ibid.; budget of College of Hospital Administration, 1927-28, ibid., circular letter, ibid.; Hamilton, 152, 272.

47   Correspondence regarding Professor O'Gorman recruitment, Archives, A-1.1, Series 3, Box 2; letter, January 22, 1924, ibid.; letter, February 20, 1924, ibid.; letter, August 9, 1924, ibid.; Status of the Department of Education, ibid.; letter and attachments, May 4, 1939, Archives, D-5, Series 1, Box 1; Milestones in the History of the College of Speech, Archives, Acquisition 95.6, Box 1; Chronological Listing of Major Events, College of Communication Files, Johnston Hall; Hamilton, 255; MT, September 28, 1923, p. 2; September 25, 1924, p. 3; October 22, 1925, p. 2; March 11, 1926, p.1; October 14, 1926, p. 4; January 12, 1928, p. 8; letter, March 23, 1928, Archives, A-1.1, Series 3, Box 4; personnel, ibid.; budget, 1927-28, ibid.; circular letter to Mothers General, undated, ibid.

48   Letter, August 11, 1924, Archives, C-9.1, Series 9c, Box 1; MT, May 29, 1923, p. 1; Catalogue, 1920; ibid., 1925; Patrick W. Carey, "Theology at Marquette University: A History," 4-5, Archives.

49   MT, December 8, 1922, p. 3; November 3, 1927, p. 1; University's Vision of the City, Archives, A-4.5, Series 2, Box 1; *Milwaukee Journal* and Marquette University, February 12, 1926, Archives, C-7, Series 1, Box 27; Scrapbook 38: June 8, 1926; Schandein file folder, Archives, A-1.1, Series 3, Box 3; speech, Archives, A-1.1, Series 2, Box 3; *Chicago Daily Tribune*, February 12, 1908, ProQuest Historical Newspapers; Hamilton, 211.

50   University's Vision of the City, Archives, A-4.5, Series 2, Box 1; MT, February 6, 1919, p. 1; February 13, 1919, p. 1; February 27, 1920, p. 3; April 21, 1922, p. 2; November 17, 1922, p. 9; Feb-

ruary 2, 1923, p. 1; March 9, 1923, p. 3; January 7, 1926, p. 2; May 27, 1926, p. 1; June 3, 1926, p. 3; May 19, 1927, p. 1; November 3, 1927, p. 1; clipping, May 10, 1926, Archives, A-11, Series 1, Box 13; tabulation showing school funds, ibid.

51   MT, February 16, 1928, p. 7; September 27, 1928, p. 1; November 8, 1928, p. 1; January 31, 1929, p. 3; letter, September 5, 1928, Archives, A-1.1, Series 3, Box 5; letter, February 11, 1929, Archives, A-1.1, Series 2, Box 3.

52   Enrollment, 1881/82 to 1957-58, Archives, A-6.4, Series 2, Box 6; MT, September 17, 1925; clipping, November, 1927, Archives, A-1.1, Series 13, Box 1.

53   Classification of Students by Religious Denominations, 1924-25, Archives, A-6.4, Series 4, Box 1; note, January 28, 1932, ibid.; Classification of Students by Religious Denominations, 1927-28, ibid.; Percentage of Non-Catholics in Student Body and Faculty, 1925-26, Archives, A-1.1, Series 3, Box 4.

54   Geographical Distribution of Students, 1926-27, ibid., Box 3; Occupations of Students' Parents and Guardians, 1926-27, ibid., Box 8.

55   Enrollment, 1881/82 to 1957/58, Archives, A-6.4, Series 2, Box 6; Women Students, 1926-27, Archives, A-11, Series 1, Box 4; letter, August 7, 1922, Archives, A-1.1, Series 3, Box 9; letter, August 10, 1922, ibid.

56   MT, October 9, 1917, pp. 3, 9; February 14, 1918, p. 11; February 28, 1918, p. 4; April 11, 1918, p. 3; October 17, 1918, p. 2; January 9, 1919, p. 3; January 16, 1919, p. 7; January 23, 1919, p. 8; April 24, 1919, p. 9; April 26, 1928, p. 6.

57   MT, September 28, 1923, p. 2; October 5, 1923, p. 2; December 14, 1923, p. 3; Hilltop, 1922, p. 32; Opportunities for Women, Archives, C-9.1, Series 6, Box 1.

58   MT, September 28, 1923, p. 6; October 9, 1924, p. 7; November 20, 1924, p. 1; March 18, 1926, p. 6; December 16, 1926, p. 1; June 2, 1927, p. 3; February 16, 1928, p. 1; clipping, November 4, 1926, Archives, A-11, Series 1, Box 1; clipping, October 27, 1927, ibid.; letter, March 12, 1924, Archives, C-9.1, Series 9c, Box 2.

59   Clipping, October 27, 1927, Archives, A-1.1, Series 1, Box 2; clipping, December 16, 1926, ibid., Box 20; clipping, November 8, 1928, ibid.; MT, September 25, 1924, p. 3; May 10, 1928, p. 1; Hilltop, 1925, p. 136; 1926, p. 128; 1927, pp. 148-49; 1929, pp. 130, 148-49, 254.

60   Geographic Distribution of Students, 1926-27, Archives, A-1.1, Series 3, Box 3; letter, April 6, 1929, ibid.; List of Foreign Students, April 22, 1927, Archives A-11, Series 1, Box 8; letter, October 8, 1924, ibid.; clipping, November 7, 1929, ibid.; clipping, October 4, 1934, ibid.; MT, October 7, 1916, p. 7; December 8, 1922, p. 4; January 26, 1928, p. 3.

61   "History of the Mission," St. Benedict the Moor Mission Annual, 1949, Father Stephen Eckert, O.M., Cap. Collection, Milwaukee County Historical Society; Steven M. Avella, "African-American Catholicism in Milwaukee: St. Benedict the Moor Church and School," Thomas J. Jablonsky, editor, *Milwaukee Stories* (Milwaukee: Marquette University Press, 2005), 140-41; Scrapbook 21: 90, 250.

62   Letter and attachments, October 16, 1923, Archives, C-9.1, Series 7, Box 1; report, September, 1925, ibid.; memorandum, December 11, 1925, ibid.; Richard D. Ralston, "American Episodes in the Making of an African Leader," *International Journal of African Historical Studies* (1973), 73, 75, 81, 85, 87; http://www.sahistory.org.za/pages/chronology/special-chrono/chronology__anc.html; Hilltop, 1915, p. 81; 1918, pp. 83, 111, 148; 1922, p. 98; 1923, pp. 94, 198; 1924, pp. 48, 55; 1925, pp. 54, 72; 1926, pp. 62, 73; 1927, p. 93; 1928, p. 63; MT, October 24, 1918, p. 6; November 24, 1922, pp. 8, 10; October 5, 1923, p. 11.

63   Hilltop, 1921, pp. 341-42; 1922, p.311; Scrapbook 36, August 20, 1924; MT, March 3, 1922, p. 9; October 13, 1927, p. 4; Joe William Trotter, *Black Milwaukee* (Urbana: University of Illinois Press, 1985), 41; Allan H. Spear, *Black Chicago* (Chicago: University of Chicago Press, 1967), 12; "Porgy and Bess (1934) by George Gershwin," http://www.classical.net/music/comp.1st/works/gershwin/porgy&bess.html; Nicholas M. Creary, "The Prophets and the Ivory Tower," Conference on the University and the City, Wayne State University, March 5, 1999. See also, letter, May 8, 1924, Archives, A-1.1, Series 2, Box 1; letter, May 27, 1924, ibid.

64   Information for Undergraduate Students, pp. 5, 7, 11-13, 16, 20-23, 34-35, Archives, A-8.1, Series 3, Box 1; Hilltop, 1922, p. 241; 1923, p. 452; 1924, p. 155; MT, March 5, 1917, p. 9; May 15, 1919, p. 7; October 1, 1920, p. 1; May 25, 1923, p. 1; September 28, 1923, p. 1; December 14, 1956, sec.2, p. 2.

65 Letter, October 6, 1923, Archives, A-1.1, Series 3, Box 9; letter, December 12, 1923, ibid.; letters, January 10, 1924, ibid.; Students Health Service Fund, July, 1925, ibid.; Students' Health Service Budget, 1925-26, ibid.; minutes, October 31, 1923, Archives, C-9.1, Series 9c, Box 1; MT, December 20, 1923, pp. 1, 6; March 7, 1924, p. 2; October 2, 1924, p. 1.

66 MT, May 14, 1920, p. 1; May 21, 1920, p. 1; May 28, 1920, p. 1; March 4, 1948, p. 8; April 9, 1953, p. 4; Hilltop, 1921, p. 91.

67 MT, August 10, 1920, p. 1; September 30, 1921, p. 4; September 30, 1921, p. 1; October 21, 1921, p. 1; March 24, 1922, p. 3; June 9, 1922, p. 2; September 29, 1922, p. 6; June 12, 1923, p. 3; September 25, 1924, p. 8; October 30, 1924, p. 1; November 6, 1924, p. 4; September 29, 1927, p. 2; September 20, 1928, p. 2; March 4, 1948, p. 8; April 9, 1953, p. 2; April 24, 1963, p. 4; Hilltop, 1921, pp. 213-214; 1924, pp. 155-57; letter, May 2, 1922, Archives, C-9.1, Series 3, Box 1.

68 MT, October 10, 1919, p. 6; October 1, 1920, p. 3; February 11, 1921, p. 1; March 25, 1921, p. 3; September 30, 1921, p. 1; October 21, 1921, p. 1; November 2, 1923, p. 12; November 10, 1927, p. 7; December 1, 1927, p. 2; February 5, 1964, p. 6.

69 Positions Secured through Employment Bureau, May 29, 1919, Archives, A-11, Series 1, Box 18; MT, October 1, 1920, p.6; December 17, 1920, p. 5; December 11, 1924, p. 6; January 13, 1927, p. 2.

70 MT, November 6, 1917, p. 6; Information for Undergraduate Students, p. 23, Archives, A-8.1, Series 3, Box 1; Hilltop, 1921, pp. 343-44.

71 Hilltop, 1924, pp. 166-69; photograph of 1925 Formal Prom, Archives, A-4.5, Series 10, File 1143.

72 Hilltop, 1922, p. 345; Fraternities and Sororities, Archives, A-11, Series 1, Box 9; Honor Societies, ibid., Box 8; MT, January 10, 1918, p. 12; September 30, 1921, p. 2; October 13, 1922, p. 5; November 3, 1922, p. 5; November 10, 1922, p. 4; November 9, 1923, p. 8; December 17, 1925, p. 6; March 5, 1942, p. 5.

73 MT, January 11, 197, p. 11; Hilltop Sport Mirror, April 7, 1927, Archives, A-11, Series 1, Box 2; Ye Kappa Beta Gamma Pledge, Archives, A-4.5, Series 10, File 1234.

74 Information for Undergraduate Students, pp. 24-28, Archives, A-8.1, Series 3, Box 1; journal clipping, December, 1939, Archives, C-1., Series 2, Box 1; Hilltop, 1923, p. 279; 1924, pp. 312ff; MT, November 21, 1919, p. 1; March 11, 1920, p. 6; April 30, 1920, p. 7; April 15, 1921, p. 7; October 19, 1923, p. 3; January 14, 1926, p. 1; September 22, 1927, p. 1; January 22, 1942, p. 3.

75 MT, May 5, 1922, p. 12; May 12, 1922, p. 7; September 25, 1924, p. 1; January 29, 1925, p. 1; summary of early affiliation, Archives, A-1.1, Series 3, Box 8; Hilltop, 1923, p. 278.

76 Hilltop, 1925, p. 241; 1927, p. 126; 1928, pp. 122-24; letter, November 4, 1925, Archives, A-1.1, Series 3, Box 8; expense analysis, 1925, ibid.; Report on Publicity through Radio, ibid.; letter, November 23, 1926, Archives, A-1.1, Series 2, Box 3; letter, June 16, 1927, ibid.; MT, September 24, 1925, p. 3; October 15, 1925, p. 9; November 25, 1925, p. 2; November 18, 1926, p. 3; May 5, 1927, p. 4; January 11, 1929, p. 6.

77 Manuel P. Servin and Iris Higbie Wilson, *Southern California and Its University* (Los Angeles: Ward Ritchie Press, 1969), 173.

78 MT, March 7, 1918, pp. 1, 8; December 12, 1918, p. 1; February 6, 1919, p. 11; February 13, 1919, p. 1; September 29, 1922, p. 14; November 24, 1922, p. 1; October 19, 1923, p. 1; October 26, 1923, p. 1; November 9, 1923, p. 1; Scrapbook 35b: 1; Hilltop, 1920, p. 137; photographs of gymnasium, Archives, A-4.5, Series 10, File 655; photograph of gymnasium and outside athletic field, ibid., File 280.

79 MT, September 30, 1916, p. 6; October 16, 1917, p. 1; October 16, 1924, p. 1; October 27, 1927, p. 11.

80 MT, December 2, 1921, p. 6; March 10, 1922, p. 9; October 6, 1922, p. 1; February 23, 1923, p. 1; March 9, 1923, p. 1; March 16, 1923, p. 1; January 18, 1924, p. 7; October 23, 1924, p. 1; October 15, 1925, p. 9; November 17, 1927, pp.1, 12; Hilltop, 1923, pp. 472-75; 1926, p. 161; letter, May 3, 1922, Archives, C-9.1, Series 9c, Box 1; Marquette Stadium 6% Bonds, ibid., Box 2; letter, August 18, 1933, ibid., Box 4; Marquette Stadium by Tom Kearney, Archives, A-4.5, Series 10, File 1255; Stadium Dedication, ibid.; New Marquette Stadium, ibid.; Marquette Stadium 6% Bonds, January 26, 1929,

ibid.; letter, April 4, 1924, Archives, B-2.1, Series 1, Box 1; letter, March 5, 1925, ibid.; photographs of stadium, Archives, A-4.5, Series 10, File 1255.

81   Hilltop, 1922, pp. 455-59; 1923, p. 188; 1924, p. 333; 1925, p. 171; 1927, p. 200; MT, November 5, 1925, pp. 12, 14; December 16, 1926, p. 11; January 6, 1927, p. 11; January 13, 1927, p. 11; January 27, 1927, p. 6; February 3, 1927, p. 9; February 10, 1927, p. 12; February 17, 1927, p. 9; October 3, 1928, p. 12; May 6, 1948, p. 8; "Bits About 'Em," Archives, A-4.5, Series 10, File 0095.

82   MT, January 18, 1917, p. 5; April 29, 1921, p. 1; May 23, 1924, p. 3; January 20, 1927, p. 4; May 6, 1948, p. 9; Information for Undergraduate Students, Archives, A-8.1, Series 3, Box 1, pp. 33-36; Handbook, Board in Control of Athletics, 1925, Archives, A-11, Series 1, Box 2; clipping, April 22, 1926, ibid.; Basketball Series, 1916/17 to 1929/30, ibid.

CHAPTER 5

1   MT, November 9, 1923, p. 3; January 19, 1928, p. 1; Scrapbook 42: 1, 2.

2   List of delegates, Archives, A-1.1, Series 3, Box 3; inauguration ceremonies, ibid., Box 4; inauguration address, ibid.; MT, March 8, 1928, p. 1; April 26, 1928, pp. 1, 3; May 31, 1928, p. 3.

3   Speeches, Archives, A-1.1, Series 3, Box 3; *Milwaukee Journal* clipping, January 15, 1928, Archives, A-11, Series 1, Box 8; *Milwaukee Sentinel* clippings, January 31, 1928, ibid.; MT, January 19, 1928, p. 1; February 2, 1928, p. 1; September 20, 1934, p. 15; Scrapbook 42: 4, 8, 9.

4   John Gurda, *The Making of Milwaukee* (Milwaukee: Milwaukee County Historical Society, 1999), 276-283; William E. Leuchtenburg, *Franklin D. Roosevelt and the New Deal* (New York: Harper and Row, 1963), 1-2, 19-21.

5   Letter with attachment, July 20, 1928, Archives, A-5.1, Series 2, Box 3; recapitulation, 1929-30, ibid.; recapitulation, 1930-31, ibid.; recapitulation, 1931-32, ibid.; recapitulation, tentative budget, 1932-33, ibid.

6   Letter, February 20, 1931, Archives, A-1.1, Series 2, Box 9; statement, December 10, 1931, ibid.; letter, March 12, 1931, ibid., Box 6; letter, April 4, 1931, Archives, C-9.1, Series 9c, Box 3.

7   See pertinent pages in Chapter Four; letter, September 21, 1922, Archives A-1.1, Series 3, Box 5; details of working plan, October 25, 1922, ibid.; letter, December 7, 1922, ibid.; letter, January 22, 1924, ibid.; letter, March 6, 1924, ibid.; letter to Dr. Carey, undated, ibid.; letter, August 24, 1929, ibid.; letter, March 29, 1924, Archives, A-1.1, Series 3, File Folder: Hospital (Old Trinity); letter, January 25, 1926, ibid.; letter, January 26, 1926, ibid.; letter, March 26, 1926, Archives, C-9.1, Series 9c, Box 2.

8   Statement, February 1, 1913 to July 31, 1928, Archives, A-1.1, Series 3, Box 5; report, 1912-1927, ibid.; MT, February 6, 1930, p. 1.

9   Letter, March 9, 1928, Archives, A-1.1, Series 3, Box 5; letter, March 16, 1928, ibid.; agreement, undated, ibid.

10   Statement, February 13, 1929, Archives, A-1.1, Series 3, Box 5; report, January 7, 1930, ibid.

11   Statement, January 29, 1930, ibid.; memorandum, undated, ibid.; letter, August 17, 1932, ibid., Series 2, Box 6; letter, May 4, 1937, Archives, A-5.1, Series 1, File: Hospital Annex Building; MT, April 3, 1930, p. 8; May 1, 1930, p. 3; May 8, 1930, p. 1; October 30, 1930, p. 3; Hilltop, 1930,pp. 70-71; File Folder: Music, College of, Archives, A-1.1, Series 3; letter, June 23, 1930, Archives, A-1.1, Series 3, Box 5; April 28, 1937, ibid.; letter, April 29, 1937, ibid.; letter, April 30, 1937, ibid.

12   Raphael N. Hamilton, *The Story of Marquette University* (Milwaukee: Marquette University Press, 1953), 282, fn.6; book count chart, in possession of B. Charaus; letter, undated, Archives, C-9.1, Series 9c, Box 5; memorandum, June 15, 1932, Archives, A-5.1, Series 1, Box 12; letter, December 5, 1938, Archives, A-1.1, Series 3, Box 5; note, undated, Archives, A-1.1, Series 3, File Folder: Association of American Colleges; letter, April 19, 1937, Archives, A-1.1, Series 13, Box 1.

13   MT, April 21, 1932, p. 3; contracts for 1932-33, Archives, A-5.1, Series 1, Box 12; memorandum, June 15, 1932, ibid.; salaries, 1932, Archives, D-2, Series 3, Box 21; memorandum, April 1, 1932, ibid.; letter, September 18, 1943, Archives, A-1.1, Series 3, Box 9; motion, June 9, 1932, Archives, A-1.1, Series 2, Box 6; letter, July 5, 1932, ibid.

14 Hamilton, 285; reviewer's comments, Father Steven M. Avella, June 2006; letter, January 9, 1933, Archives, C-9.1, Series 9c, Box 4; letter, July 14, 1933, Archives, A-1.1, Series 2, Box 6; letter, December 11, 1933, ibid.

15 Letter, undated, Archives, A-1.1, Series 2, Box 1; MT, September 21, 1933, p. 1.

16 Memorandum, January 24, 1933, Archives, A-1.1, Series 2, Box 9; memorandum, March 14, 1933, ibid.; letter, May 3, 1933, ibid.; letter, May 26, 1933, ibid.; total indebtedness list, ibid.; letter, April 7, 1933, ibid., Box 6; letter, February 21, 1934, Archives, C-9.1, Series 9c, Box 5; Hamilton, 283.

17 Report, August 8, 1929, Archives, C-9.1, Series 9c, Box 3; letter, March 23, 1939, Archives, A-1.1, Series 3, Box 5; Hilltop, 1943, p. 9.

18 MT, January 11, 1934, p. 1; October 3, 1935, p. 4; December 10, 1936, p. 1.

19 MT, December 10, 1936, p. 1; December 17, 1936, p. 1; biographical page, Archives, A-1.1, Series 3, Box 5.

20 MT, December 10, 1936, pp. 1, 12; March 4, 1937, p. 1; resolution, undated, Archives, A-1.1, Series 3, Box 3.

21 Report, August 8, 1929, Archives, C-9.1, Series 9c, Box 3; Norman H. Engbring, *An Anchor for the Future* (Milwaukee: The Medical College of Wisconsin, 1991), 71-72; statement, undated, Archives, A-1.1, Series 2, Box 6; letter, March 8, 1930, ibid.; letter, April 23, 1930, ibid.; MT, February 20, 1930, p. 14; September 17, 1931, p. 1; October 8, 1931, p. 3; Board of Trustees minutes, June 30, 1931; Board of Directors' Resolution, October 20, 1933, Archives, C-9.1, Series 9c, Box 4.

22 MT, October 8, 1931, p. 1; January 7, 1932, p. 1; September 15, 1932, p. 3; January 4, 1933, p. 2; clipping, December 15, 1932, Archives, A-4.5, Series 10, File 940; photographs, Archives, A-4.5, Series 10, Files 455 & 940; original costs and replacement values, 1946, Archives, A-5.1, Series 1, Box 1; brochure, Archives, C-5, Series 1, Box 1; Engbring, 72.

23 MT, December 5, 1929, p. 6; October 22, 1931, p. 5; March 7, 1935, p. 6; September 22, 1938, p. 1; October 6, 1938, p. 1; October 13, 1938, p. 3; December 8, 1938, p. 3; January 5, 1939, p. 1.

24 MT, December 5, 1935, p. 12; September 21, 1939, p. 3; Jesuit Bulletin clipping, Archives, D-5, Series 1, Box 1.

25 Letter, November 2, 1937, Archives, A-1.1, Series 2, Box 6; In Appreciation, ibid.; letter, November 19, 1940, ibid., Box 9; letter, October 19, 1940, ibid., Series 3, Box 9; letter, July 14, 1939, Archives, C-9, Series 9c, Box 5; statement by E. H. Kueger, ibid., Archives, C-9.1, Series 4, Box 1; resolution, April 24, 1939, Archives, A-5.1, Series 1, Box 2; *Jesuit Bulletin* clipping, Archives, D-5, Series 1, Box 1; Board of Trustees minutes, March 16, 1939; April 24, 1939; June 13, 1940; MT, September 21, 1939, p. 3; September 28, 1939, p. 1; February 22, 1940, p. 1; October 31, 1940, p. 1; November 27, 1941, pp. 9-12.

26 Report, Archives, A-1.1, Series 2, Box 8; MT, October 16, 1941, p. 4; Philip Gleason, *Contending with Modernity* (New York: Oxford University Press, 1995), 186-87.

27 Board of Trustees minutes, August 1, 1936; MT, March 19, 1936, p. 1; February 22, 1940, p. 2; Hilltop, 1937, pp. 26-27; Hamilton, 318-19.

28 MT, October 23, 1941, p. 1; November 13, 1941, pp.1,5; October 8, 1942, p. 2; November 12, 1942, p. 2; November 18, 1943, p. 1; Gleason, 156-57.

29 MT, October 8, 1942, p. 2; November 12, 1942; November 18, 1943; Gurda, 291, 294; letter, May 25, 1936, Archives, A-1.1, Series 2, Box 1; letter, November 9, 1937, ibid., Box 6; letter, November 18, 1937, ibid.; Gleason, 156.

30 Letter, December 1, 1922, Archives, C-9.1, Series 9c, Box 1; Hamilton, 310; MT, March 12, 1917, p. 1; March 26, 1917, p. 5; June 4, 1920, p. 1; February 18, 1921, p. 1; February 25, 1921, p. 1; March 4, 1921, p. 1; February 16, 1923, p. 4.

31 Letter to faculty, Archives, A-11, Series 1, Box 13; clipping, October 5, 1933, ibid.; letter with report, January 24, 1935, Archives, C-9.1, Series 9c, Box 5; MT, March 7, 1940, p. 3; April 4, 1940, p. 1; letter, June 6, 1944, Archives, A-1.1, Series 2, Box 7; memorandum #418, Archives, C-7, Series 1, Box 27; letter, March 3, 1938, Archives, A-1.1, Series 3, Box 8; memorandum #433, ibid.; policy statement, 1944, ibid.; Gleason, 204.

32 Memorandum, #120, Archives, C-7, Series 1, Box 27; memorandum # 121, ibid.; memorandum # 129, ibid.; memorandum # 141, ibid.; memorandum # 151, ibid.; memorandum # 152, ibid.; memo-

randum # 425, ibid., Box 4; list of fields, 1939-40, Archives, A-11, Series 1, Box 9; clipping, October 8, 1936, ibid.; Gleason, 100, 179, 191; MT, April 2, 1931, p. 8; March 7, 1935, p. 3; March 26, 1936, p. 1; thesis outlines, 1938, Archives, C-7, Series 1, Box 4.

33   Report, 1937-38, Archives, D-5, Series 1, Box 1; MT, September 21, 1939, p. 1.

34   Memorandum #56, Archives, C-7, Series 1, Box 27; letter, November 16, 1931, ibid., Box 3; letter, November 23, 1931, ibid.; telegram, November 14, 1931, ibid.; Hilltop, 1935, p. 11.

35   Letter, November 25, 1940, Archives, C-7, Series 1, Box 3; handwritten analysis of AAU report, ibid.; handwritten commentary on Hotel Pennsylvania stationary, ibid.; petition, ibid.

36   Letter, November 4, 1942, Archives, C-7, Series 1, Box 3; letter, November 20, 1942, ibid.; discussion of AAU recommendation, ibid.; pertinent passages, ibid.; survey on graduate school practices, ibid.; inspection by Dr. Payne, ibid., Box 4; letter, December 3, 1942, Archives, A-1.1, Series 2, Box 6; letter, February 9, 1943, ibid.; letter, March 15, 1943, ibid.; letter, May 7, 1943, ibid.; summary, JEA, January 18-21, 1943, ibid.; Gleason, 205-06.

37   Board of Graduate Studies minutes, April 13, 1943, Archives, C-7, Series 1, Box 5; letter, July 16, 1943, ibid., Box 4; handwritten notes, April 18, 1945, ibid.; typed version, ibid.; letter, September 1, 1943, ibid., Box 3; letter, October 9, 1944, Archives, A-1.1, Series 2, Box 6; letter, October 29, 1945, ibid.

38   Letter, June 21, 1942, contained in report of dean, Archives, C-7, Series 1, Box 3; Kenneth T. Jackson, *The Ku Klux Klan in the City, 1915-1930* (Chicago: Ivan Dee reprint, 1967), 156, 237; Todd Tucker, *Notre Dame vs. The Klan* (Chicago: Loyola Press, 2004); Gurda, 235-36.

39   Paul A. FitzGerald, SJ, *The Governance of Jesuit Colleges in the United States, 1920-1970* (Notre Dame: University of Notre Dame Press, 1984), 5-6, 21-22, 21-24; Gleason, 178-79.

40   Pamphlet on School of Medicine, Archives, C-5, Series 1, Box 1; advertisement, Archives, C-9.1, Series 6, Box 1; letter, May 12, 1924, Archives, A-1.1, Series 2, Box 5.

41   Letter, October 16, 1928, Archives, A-1.1, Series 3, Box 4; letter, February 26, 1927, Archives, C-9.1, Series 9c, Box 2; pamphlet, Archives, C-9.1, Series 6, Box 1.

42   Memorial, December 26, 1929, Archives, A-1.1, Series 2, Box 7.

43   List of faculty members, February, 1929, Archives, A-1.1, Series 3, Box 4; Classification of Teaching Staff by religious denominations, 1935-36 & 1942-43, Archives, A-6.4, Series 4, Box 1; list of Jesuits, Archives, A-1.1, Series 2, Box 7.

44   Letter, January 15, 1937, Archives, A-1.1, Series 2, Box 9; statement on treatment of Catholics and non-Catholics, ibid.; letter, September 18, 1941, ibid., Box 3; letter, May 27, 1942, ibid., Box 4; letter, May 28, 1942, ibid.; letter, June 3, 1942, ibid.; interview with Rev. Thomas Stemper, SJ, Archives, Miller Research File, Box 1; MT, November 10, 1922, p. 3; March 14, 1924, p. 1; December 15, 1932, p. 1; January 30, 1936, p.1; letter, February 27, 1923, Archives, A-1.1, Series 2, Box 1; letter, March 10, 1923, ibid.

45   MT, March 6, 1919, p. 2; March 27, 1919, p. 3; March 11, 1920, p. 1; March 11, 1921, p. 1; March 25, 1921, p. 2; April 6, 1923, p. 3; January 26, 1928, p. 1; March 8, 1934, p. 1; March 9, 1939, p. 1; March 12, 1942, p. 1; March 19, 1942, p. 1; March 13, 1947, p. 1; Hilltop, 1930, pp. 302-303; ibid., 1931, pp. 310-11; ibid., 1932, pp. 286-87; faculty retreat schedule, March 28-30, 1941, Archives, A-4.5, Series 10, File 565.

46   MT, May 27, 1937, p. 5; June 3, 1937, pp. 1ff; May 6, 1940, p. 1; November 21, 1940, p. 1; program, May 12, 1937, Archives, A-1.1, Series 3, Box 5; pamphlet in Honor of Jacques Marquette, SJ, ibid.; program, November 21, 1940, ibid., Box 4.

47   Enrollment table, 1882/83-1957/58, Archives, A-6.4, Series 2, Box 6; enrollment statistics, Archives, A-11, Series 1, Boxes 6 & 7.

48   Enrollment table, 1882/83-1957/58, Archives, A-6.4, Series 2, Box 6; enrollment statistics, Archives, A-11, Series 1, Boxes 6 & 7; MT, October 3, 1935, p. 1.

49   Survey sheet, Archives, C-9.1, Series 7, Box 1.

50   Announcement, September 4, 1930, Archives, A-11, Series 1, Box 9; magazine reprint, 1941, Archives, A-1.1, Series 3, Box 3; report to President, Archives, C-9.1, Series 6, Box 1; newspaper ad, ibid.

51   Handbook excerpt, Archives, C-9.1, Series 6, Box 1; cost of attendance, 1933-34, ibid.; pamphlet, ibid.; tuition and fees, Medical School, 1930-31, Archives, C-5, Series 1, Box 1; MT, March 24, 1970, p. 2.

52   Handbook excerpt, Archives, C-9.1, Series 6, Box 1; MT, November 27, 1929, p. 1; March 28, 1931, p. 8; September 17, 1931, p. 3; January 19, 1933, p. 2; November 9, 1933, p. 2; November 5, 1936, p. 6; student employment, Archives, A-11, Series 1, Box 18; information concerning part-time employment, ibid.; facts on college expenses, ibid.; letter, July 3, 1937, ibid., Box 14; *Marquette Alumni Bulletin*, November, 1937, p. 1.

53   Scholarships, 1924-25, Archives, A-11, Series 1, Box 18; scholarships, 1926, ibid., Box 17; Scholarships, 1931-32, ibid.; clipping, January 15, 1942, ibid.; letter, July 13, 1934, Archives, A-1.1, Series 3, Box 9; letters, July 19, 1934, ibid.; scholarships in Jesuit colleges, ibid.; K.C. Scholarships, ibid., Series 2, Box 8; MT, May 26, 1932, p. 1; October 3, 1935, p. 6; October 10, 1935, p. 7; October 24, 1935, p. 2; October 8, 1936, p. 1; Hilltop, 1935, pp. 11-12.

54   MT, February 15, 1934, p. 1; February 22, 1934, p. 1; September 20, 1934, p. 1; September 27, 1934, p. 2; February 7, 1935, p. 1; May 30, 1935, p. 1; June 6, 1935, p. 3; November 14, 1935, p. 7; May 7, 1936, p. 8; September 24, 1936, p. 7; September 25, 1941, p. 2; letter, October 1, 1934, Archives, A-1.1, Series 3, Box 7; letter, February 14, 1934, ibid.; letter, April 26, 1934, ibid.; memorandum, October 1, 1934, ibid.; letter, January 7, 1942, ibid.; letter, August 12, 1935, Archives, C-9.1, Series 9c, Box 5; Hilltop, 1934, p. 15.

55   MT, September 29, 1932, p. 1; November 3, 1932, p. 1; May 11, 1933, p. 1; Hilltop, 1933, 109.

56   Handwritten early history, Archives, A-11, Series 1, Box 19; broadcast schedule, December, 1927, ibid.; broadcast schedule, October, 1929, ibid.; broadcast schedule, June & July, 1931, ibid.; "Development of Station W.T.M.J.," *Marquette Engineer*, June, 1933, ibid.; clipping, May 11, 1939, ibid.; correspondence, budget sheets, programming information, Archives, A-1.1, Series 3, Box 8, Radio file; newspaper clippings, Archives, A-5.1, Series 1, Box 13; significant activities, station WHAD, ibid.; newsletter clipping, October 20, 1925, Archives, A-4.5, Series 2, Box 1; Board of Trustees minutes, May 10, 1934; MT, May 17, 1934, p. 1; May 11, 1939, p. 5; May 6, 1948, p. 5; May 2, 1962, p. 3; Hilltop, 1929, p. 105; 1931, p. 173; 1932, pp. 142-43; 1934, pp. 123, 131.

57   Questionnaire, December 1, 1938, Archives, A-1.1, Series 3, Box 4; Wenonah Eis, "An Analysis of Freshmen Women Students at Marquette University, 1939-40" (MEd thesis, Marquette University, 1940).

58   Randy D. McBee, *Dance Hall Days* (New York: New York University Press, 2000); Hilltop, 1928, p. 116; 1929, pp. 90, 98; 1931, p. 136; 1932, pp. 116-18; 1933, pp. 91, 95; 1937, p. 106; 1939, pp. 94, 102; Committee on Student Life minutes, October 16, 1933; January 28, 1936; January 17, 1939; April 4, 1939; May 2, 1939; April 22, 1941; MT, May 23, 1940, p. 5.

59   MT, September 20, 1928, pp. 3, 12; September 25, 1930, pp. 12, 13, 21; November 6, 1930, p. 8; September 24, 1931, p. 2; January 17, 1935, p. 3; October 17, 1946, p. 4.

60   MT, October 8, 1936, p. 4; October 29, 1936, p. 5; March 3, 1938, p. 6; clippings, 1933, Archives, A-4.5, Series 10, File 1348a; clipping, January 6, 1993, ibid.; photograph of Hopkins Hall, ibid.; photograph of students, ibid.

61   MT, January 14, 1937, p. 2; October 2, 1941, p. 6; October 23, 1941, p. 3; October 30, 1941, p. 4; February 15, 1945, p. 1; March 15, 1945, pp. 2,3; Hilltop, 1933, p. 195.

62   *A History of the Association of Marquette University Women, 1938-2000*, pp. 3-4; "Women of Marquette," Archives, A-4.5, Series 10, File 25, pp. 1-4; MT, September 28, 1939, p. 1; May 30, 1940, p. 3; October 2, 1941, p. 5; May 14, 1942, p. 5; December 21, 1944, p. 1; announcement, September, 1938, Archives, A-4.5, Series 10, File 26; photograph, ibid.; letter, April 25, 1940, Archives, A-1.1, Series 3, Box 9; Ruth Ann MacMahon, "History of the Marquette University Women's Residence Halls," (MEd thesis, Marquette University, 1964), pp. 6-9.

63   Rooming and Boarding list, July 1, 1943, Archives, A-11, Series 1, Box 8; MT, September 10, 1940, p. 1; September 19, 1940, p. 2; November 6, 1941, p. 1; September 7, 1944, p. 1; September 26, 1975, p. 7; photograph of Brooks Hall, Archives, A-4.5, Series 10, File 00150; clipping, ibid., File 865; photographs of Lisette Hall, ibid.; sketch of Alumni Hall, Archives, A-4.5, Series 10, File 1944; letter, November 31, 1941, Archives, A-1.1, Series 2, Box 8; Hilltop, 1938, p. 151; 1939, pp. 162, 165;

1942, p. 198; 1943, p. 176; Board of Trustees minutes, October 14, 1941; May 29, 1943; June 3, 1943; Hamilton, 352.

64   "Athletics and Physical Education," 1932, 1934, & 1939, Archives, A-11, Series 1, Box 2; clipping, October 14, 1926, ibid.; clipping, April 28, 1938, ibid.; MT, September 24, 1931, p. 7; May 30, 1940, p. 6; May 29, 1941, p. 1; June 5, 1941, p. 1; September 25, 1941, p. 6; October 23, 1941, p. 11; Hilltop, 1932, p. 240; 1933, pp. 188-89; 1934, pp. 108, 113, 117.

65   Minutes of Board of Trustees, October 27, 1933; letter, January 13, 1934, Archives, C-9.1, Series 9c, Box 5.

66   Athletic Board minutes, October 13, 1929, Archives, B-2.2, Series 1, Box 5; October 6, 1931, ibid.; May 14, 1932, ibid.; October 4, 1932, ibid.; July 19, 1937, ibid.; October 24, 1938, ibid.; November 30, 1938, ibid.; September 7, 1939, ibid.; May 14, 1940, ibid.; clipping, February 7, 1931, Archives, A-11, Series 1, Box 2; MT, November 20, 1930, p. 3.

67   MT, December 17, 1936, p. 1; December 11, 1941, p. 12; December 10, 1942, p. 1; Hamilton, 221-22.

68   Athletics and Physical Education brochures, 1932 & 1939, Archives, A-11, Series 1, Box 2; clipping, Archives, A-4.5, Series 10, File 95; Marquette's Olympians, ibid., File 1039; MT, October 2, 1930, p. 8; October 9, 1930, p. 9; April 6, 1933, p. 1; September 28, 1933, p. 7; January 10, 1935, p. 7; January 24, 1935, p. 6; October 10, 1935, p. 2; October 1, 1936, p. 10; June 6, 1940, p. 6; October 21, 1943, p. 4; November 11, 1943, p. 1; January 6, 1944, p. 1; May 6, 1948, p. 9; October 18, 1978, p. 9.

69   Marquette's Olympians, Archives, A-4.5, Series 10, File 1039; MT, May 10, 1928, p. 7; May 16, 1929, p. 7; March 10, 1932, p. 10; September 15, 1932, p. 9; January 26, 1933, p. 6; February 16, 1933, p. 9; March 16, 1933, p. 6; April 27, 1933, p. 7; September 21, 1933, p. 9; January 4, 1934, p. 7; January 25, 1934, p. 5; February 1, 1934, p. 6; February 8, 1934, p. 9; September 20, 1934, p. 9; September 20, 1934, p. 10; January 31, 1935, p. 6; September 24, 1936, p. 10.

70   Letter, May 5, 1939, Archives, A-1.1, Series 3, Box 4; MT, March 30, 1933, p. 4; July 22, 1943, p. 2; August 19, 1943, pp. 1, 2; August 26, 1943, p. 4; April 20, 1944, p. 2; May 25, 1944, p. 1; March 29, 1945, p. 4; May 17, 1945, p. 1; July 26, 1945, p. 2; Hilltop, 1933, pp. 62-63, 181-83; 1939, p. 32; 1941, pp. 56, 64, 68, 80.

71   Letter, April 23, 1938, Archives, A-1.1, Series 3, Box 4; letter, August 1, 1938, ibid.; letter, December 27, 1940, ibid.; letter, December 27, 1940, ibid.; letter to Rev. Kapusta, ibid.; letter, November 18, 1941, ibid.; letter, March 9, 1942, ibid.; letter, July 28, 1945, ibid.; MT, October 8, 1942, p. 2.

72   Enrollment, 1881/82 to 1957/58, Archives, A-6.4, Series 2, Box 6; MT, September 24, 1942, p. 1; October 8, 1942, p. 3; November 19, 1942, p. 1; December 17, 1942, p. 2; May 18, 1944, p. 3.

73   Marquette University and the War Effort, Archives, A-11, Series 1, Box 15; clipping, September 25, 1941, ibid.; clipping, February 11, 1942, ibid.; Hilltop, 1941, pp. 44-45; 1942, p. 28; 1944, pp. 92, 102; MT, January 9, 1941, p. 1; September 25, 1941, p. 2; February 19, 1942, p. 1; March 19, 1942, p. 3; April 16, 1942, p. 1; November 4, 1943, p. 3; April 19, 1945, p. 1; May 17, 1945, p. 1; Hamilton, 350-53; Gleason, 211-13.

74   Clipping, April 23, 1942, Archives, A-11, Series 1, Box 15; clipping, November 16, 1942, ibid.; clipping, July 15, 1943, ibid.; clipping, July 18, 1943, ibid.; clipping, March 7, 1943, Archives, A-4.5, Series 10, File 940; clipping, September 10, 1944, ibid., File 1005; MT, April 30, 1942, p. 7; July 29, 1943, p. 2; August 5, 1943, p. 2; August 12, 1943, p. 1; December 16, 1943, p. 1; August 16, 1945, p. 2; "Peace," brochure, *Historia Domus*, 1950-53; Hamilton, 350.

75   MT, February 5, 1942, p. 3; April 2, 1942, p. 3; October 1, 1942, p. 1; October 15, 1942, p. 1; October 7, 1943, p. 2; August 5, 1943, p. 1; December 2, 1943, p. 1, Special Gesu Insert; January 20, 1944, p. 1. January 27, 1944, p. 1; Hamilton, 358.

76   Letter, September 7, 1940, Archives, A-1.1, Series 2, Box 2; MT, January 15, 1942, p. 1; January 29, 1942, p. 1; May 14, 1942, p. 1; September 24, 1942, p. 1; October 8, 1942, p. 6; July 22, 1943, p. 3; September 30, 1943, p. 1; October 14, 1943, p. 1; October 21, 1943, p. 1; January 20, 1944, p. 1; February 3, 1944, p. 1; February 3, 1944, p. 4; July 13, 1944, p. 1; July 27, 1944, p. 1; November 9, 1944, p. 1; December 14, 1944, p. 1; January 4, 1945, p. 1; January 18, 1945, p. 1; May 10, 1945, p. 1; July 12, 1945, p. 8; Committee on Student Life minutes, April 15, 1941.

77   MT, October 15, 1942, p. 1; November 12, 1942, p. 3; August 5, 1943, pp. 4, 5; October 14, 1943, p. 5; February 3, 1944, p. 5; May 18, 1944, p. 2; August 3, 1944, p. 5; January 11, 1945, p. 1; Hilltop, 1943, p. 185.

78   MT, February 12, 1942, p. 3; December 18, 1942, p. 1; August 12, 1943, p. 1; September 30, 1943, p. 1; October 14, 1943, p. 1; August 3, 1944, p. 3; March 8, 1945, p. 1; April 5, 1945, p. 1; August 23, 1945, p. 1; list of Marquette servicemen, January 25, 1945, Archives, A-1.1, Series 3, Box 8; letter, December 5, 1945, ibid.; "Peace," brochure, *Historia Domus*, 1950-53.

79   MT, March 9, 1944, p. 1; March 16, 1944, p. 1; March 30, 1945, p. 1; William B. Faherty, *Better the Dream* (St. Louis: Saint Louis University, 1968), 322, 339-40; John Francis Bannon, *The Missouri Province* SJ (St. Louis: Missouri Province, 1977), 104. Father McCarthy became chair of the psychology department at Saint Louis University for three years until assuming the presidency of Regis College during the summer of 1947. He retired in 1953 and remained in Denver for the rest of life, dying in 1979 at the age of 90. MT, June 26, 1947, p. 1; September 5, 1979, p. 5.

CHAPTER 6

1   Enrollment, 1881/82-1957/58, Archives, A-6.4, Series 2, Box 6; MT, August 30, 1945, p. 1; September 27, 1951, p. 2; October 11, 1951, p. 2.

2   MT, September 20, 1945, p. 1; November 8, 1945, p. 1; November 15, 1945, p. 1; January 31, 1946, p. 1; July 18, 1946, p. 1; August 8, 1946, p. 1; September 19, 1946, p. 1; October 3, 1946, p. 1; January 30, 1947, p. 1; March 20, 1947, p. 1; July 31, 1947, p. 1; September 25, 1947, p. 1; October 2, 1947, p. 1; September 23, 1948, p. 1; February 17, 1949, p. 1; photographs of overcrowding, Archives, A-4.5, Series 10, File 170; clipping, January 31, 1946, ibid., File 106; brochure, Archives, A-1.1, Series 2, Box 12; Board of Trustees minutes, December 10, 1945.

3   Enrollment, 1881/82-1957/58, Archives, A-6.4, Series 2, Box 6; MT, July 20, 1944, p. 1; August 17, 1944, p. 1; September 7, 1944, p. 1; September 14, 1944, p. 1; November 23, 1944, p. 1; January 4, 1945, pp. 1, 4; January 11, 1945, pp. 1, 2; January 25, 1945, p. 1; February 1, 1945, p. 1; April 5, 1945, p. 3; March 21, 1946, p. 8; December 5, 1946, p. 2; list of discharged veterans, March, 1944, Archives, A-11, Series 1, Box 19; policy of educational institutions, ibid.; Armed Services edition, MT, April 1945: ibid. letter, August 30, 1948, Archives, A-1.1, Series 3, Box 3; Committee on Student Activities and Welfare minutes, May 30, 1944; September 5, 1944.

4   MT, November 23, 1944, p. 1; August 23, 1945, p. 7; September 6, 1945, p. 1; October 18, 1945, p. 2; November 29, 1945, p. 1; December 6, 1945, p. 1; March 14, 1946, p. 1; March 21, 1946, p. 2; April 14, 1949, p. 1.

5   Hilltop, 1946, opposite Dedication page; Marquette University and the Veteran, Archives, A-11, Series 1, Box 19; MT, December 13, 1945, p. 1; December 20, 1945, p. 1; April 18, 1946, p. 1; July 11, 1946, p. 2; July 25, 1946, p. 6.

6   Committee on Student Activities and Welfare minutes, April 10, 1945; Hilltop, 1946, p. 196; Marquette University and the Veteran, Archives, A-11, Series 1, Box 19; MT, November 22, 1945, p. 2; February 7, 1946, p. 1; April 11, 1946, p. 8; May 30, 1946, p. 2; April 24, 1947, p. 1; May 1, 1947, p. 1; September 25, 1947, pp. 3, 4; May 19, 1949, p. 3; November 3, 1949, section 2, p. 3; October 26, 1950, p. 12; April 15, 1951, p. 6.

7   MT, January 18, 1945, p. 1; September 19, 1946, p. 2; October 2, 1947, p. 3; November 13, 1947, p. 1; May 20, 1948, pp . 1, 4; Board of Trustees minutes, March 20, 1947; Hilltop, 1945, p. 27; *Historia Domus*, March 6, 1951.

8   O'Donnell Memoir, p.1, Archives, Miller Research Files, Box 1; MT, November 29, 1945, p. 3; May 20, 1948, p. 1; May 27, 1948, p. 2; April 9, 1953, section 2, p. 1; memorial, Archives, A-1.1, Section 2, Box 11; Board of Trustees minutes, May 19, 1948.

9   O'Donnell Memoirs, pp. 2-3, Archives, Miller Research Files, Box 1; clippings, Archives, A-1.1, Series 2, Box 9; drafts of obituaries, June 27, 1980 & October, 1985, Archives, A-4.5, Series 9, Folder 2; clipping, November 13, 1984, Archives, A-4.5, Series 10, File 260; brochure draft, ibid.; Board of Trustees minutes, August 16, 1948; MT, September 24, 1931, p. 4.

10   Program, October 19, 1948, Archives, A-1.1, Series 2, Box 9.

11   MT, January 31, 1946, p. 1; March 30, 1950, p. 7; board of governors' statutes, Archives, A-1.1, Series 2, Box 6; list of original board, May 17, 1951, ibid.; letter, June 16, 1937, ibid.; letter, July 17, 1939, ibid., Box 9; letter, July 18, 1940, ibid., Box 3; letter, July 20, 1940, ibid.; letter, August 26, 1941, ibid., Box 10.

12   Letter, December 27, 1938, Archives, A-1.1, Series 2, Box 6; board of governors powers, ibid.; clipping, January 12, 1939, Archives, A-11, Series 1, Box 13; MT, May 23, 1940, p. 1; Board of Trustees minutes, October 23, 1943.

13   MT, January 30, 1936, p. 4; January 28, 1937, p. 5; September 25, 1941, p. 7; August 3, 1944, p. 1; letter, August 13, 1937, Archives, A-1.1, Series 3, Box 5; letter, October 10, 1940, ibid.; compendium, undated, ibid.; letter, March 27, 1944, Archives, A-7, Series 3, Box 2; brochure, Archives, A-1.1, Series 2, Box 12; Board of Governor minutes, August 1, 1944; Board of Trustees minutes, August 1, 1944.

14   Letter, November 20, 1944, Archives, A-1.1, Series 3, Box 5; library fund list, ibid.; confidential report, March 7, 1945, ibid.; confidential report, December 5, 1945, ibid.; Board of Governors minutes, January 30, 1945; MT, December 7, 1944, p. 1; January 24, 1946, p. 1; February 14, 1946, p. 2; December 4, 1947, p. 5; Hilltop, 1945, p. 168.

15   O'Donnell Memoir, pp. 3, 6, Archives, Miller Research File, Box 1; building funds available, January 31, 1949, Archives, A-1.1, Series 2, Box 6; itemized account, ibid.; MT, September 22, 1949, p. 3; clipping, April 20, 1950, Archives, A-4.5, Series 10, File 255; The University brochure, ibid.

16   MT, June 23, 1949, p. 1; October 6, 1949, p. 1; O'Donnell Memoir, pp. 4-12, Archives, Miller Research File, Box 1; "Father O'Donnell Remembers," February, 1981, Archives, Marquette Today Scrapbooks; Peace Comes to Marquette Campus, Archives, A-4.5, Series 2, Box 1; What Will They Find Inside?, ibid.; Be Not Afraid of Greatness, ibid.; letter, March 28, 1951, ibid.; A Greater Marquette in a Greater Milwaukee, A-4.5, Series 10, File 952; clipping, June 16, 1949, Archives, A-4.5, Series 10, File 255; radio interview, February 27, 1949, Archives, A-1.1, Series 2, Box 3; The Milwaukee Letter, November 14, 1946, Archives, A-1.1, Series 3, Box 5.

17   Board of Governors minutes, December 2, 1948; February 24, 1949; April 28, 1949; August 4, 1949; August 24, 1949; December 13, 1949; letter, November 29, 1949, Archives, A-1.1, Series 2, Box 12; confidential report, December 13, 1949, ibid.; MT, May 19, 1949, p. 1.

18   MT, May 19, 1949, p. 1; June 30, 1949, p. 1; July 28, 1949, p. 1; September 22, 1949, p. 1; October 20, 1949, p. 1; November 23, 1949, p. 1; January 12, 1950, p. 8; August 3, 1950, p. 1; October 5, 1950, p. 1; October 12, 1950, p. 1; May 10, 1951, p. 1; June 7, 1951, p. 8; Historia Domus, January 10, 1950; October 10, 1950; notes for BOG, May 29, 1951, Archives, A-1.1, Series 2, Box 6; clipping, Archives, A-4.5, Series 10, File 281A; O'Donnell Memoir, pp. 17-19, Archives, Miller Research File, Box 1; "Father O'Donnell Remembers," Archives, Marquette Today Scrapbooks.

19   MT, October 7, 1943, p. 1; August 31, 1944, p. 3; September 14, 1944, p. 3; August 9, 1945, p. 2; February 14, 1946, p. 1; March 2, 1946, p. 2; October 14, 1948, p. 8; October 13, 1949, p. 7; September 28, 1950, p. 6; December 7, 1950, p. 1; December 14, 1950, p. 7; November 8, 1951, p. 1; November 29, 1951, p. 8; January 24, 1952, p. 1; March 6, 1952, p. 8; April 13, 1952, p. 8; May 1, 1952, p. 1; September 25, 1952, p. 6; June 25, 1953, p. 1; O'Donnell Memoirs, pp. 55-56, Archives, Miller Research Files, Box 1; Association of Marquette University Women, a Brief History, 5-6; Board of Trustees minutes, April 10, 1951; January 31, 1952; July 22, 1954; clippings, September 2, 1952, Archives, A-4.5, Series 10, File 255; Living and Learning, Archives, A-4.5, Series 10, File 695; photographs of Merrity Hall, Archives, A-4.5, Series 10, File 950; Historia Domus, December 11, 1950; clipping, back of p. 45, 1953.

20   MT, August 9, 1945, p. 2; October 4, 1945, p. 2; January 9, 1947, p. 1; January 30, 1947, p. 1; February 6, 1947, p. 1; March 27, 1947, p. 2.

21   MT, April 15, 1948, p. 6; September 23, 1948, p. 9; April 7, 1949, p. 3; April 21, 1949, p. 1; May 19, 1949, p. 2; May 26, 1949, p. 1; November 10, 1949, p. 8; December 1, 1949, p. 1; December 15, 1949, p. 1; February 9, 1950, p. 1; April 6, 1950, p. 1; April 20, 1950, p. 1; May 11, 1950, p. 1; May 18, 1950, p. 5; July 6, 1950, p. 1; September 21, 1950, p. 2; January 25, 1951, p. 1; March 29, 1951, p. 1; April 12, 1951, p. 1; May 3, 1951, p. 1; September 27, 1951, p. 9; November 21, 1951, p. 1; December 6, 1951, p. 1; December 13, 1951, p. 1; January 17, 1952, p. 1; March 6, 1952, p. 3; October 30, 1952, p. 12; January 8, 1953, p. 1; March 12, 1953, p. 12; June 4, 1953, p. 4; Historia

Domus, 1950-53, entry between pp. 32-33; May 1, 1951; April 16, 1952; May 19, 1952; December 4, 1952; December 11, 1952; January 13, 1953; March 28, 1953; May 18, 1954; letter & flier, May 18, 1950, Archives, A-1.1, Series 2, Box 11; O'Donnell Memoir, pp. 25-30, Archives, Miller Research File, Box 1; "Father O'Donnell Remembers," Archives, *Marquette Today* Scrapbooks.

22   MT, July 2, 1953, p. 4; September 17, 1953, p. 1; *Historia Domus*, May 1, 1953.

23   O'Donnell Memoir, pp. 23-25, Archives, Miller Research Files, Box 1; "Father O'Donnell Remembers," Archives, *Marquette Today* Scrapbooks; letter, September 15, 1949, Archives, A-1.1, Series 3, Box 3; MT, October 8, 1942, p. 1; October 29, 1942, p. 3; September 2, 1943, p. 3; May 4, 1950, p. 1; November 2, 1950, pp. 1,3; January 11, 1951, p. 1; March 1, 1951, p. 1; July 19, 1951, p. 1; December 3, 1953, pp. 1, 2,5; Board of Governors minutes, February 15, 1950; May 29, 1951; July 2, 1951; *Historia Domus*, July 19, 1951; April 16, 1952; May 19, 1952; Board of Trustees minutes, May 18, 1946.

24   MT, March 23, 1950, p. 1; May 25, 1950, p. 1; January 18, 1951, p. 3; April 12, 1951, p. 1; November 1, 1951, p. 12; March 13, 1952, p.1; May 29, 1952, p. 1; February 18, 1954, p. 9; May 13, 1954, sec.2, p.1; June 28, 1956, p. 1; clipping, Archives, A-4.5, Series 10, File 255; *Historia Domus*, May 26, 1952; O'Donnell Memoir, pp. 19-22, Archives, Miller Research File, Box 1; "Father O'Donnell Remembers," Archives, *Marquette Today* Scrapbooks.

25   Letter, July 10, 1953, Archives, C-1, Series 2, Box 1; titles of buildings, ibid.

26   Report, July 18, 1953, ibid.

27   Status of Financial Facts, Archives, A-2.1, Series 2, Box 1, Exhibit 1.

28   Ibid., Exhibits 3 & 3-A.

29   Ibid., Exhibits 5-10; Board of Governors minutes, December 28, 1946; Board of Trustees minutes, December 26, 1950.

30   MT, July 12, 1945, p. 5; March 21, 1946, p. 1; April 4, 1946, p. 2; September 19, 1946, p. 1; September 23, 1948, p. 2; September 15, 1949, p. 2; September 27, 1951, p. 1; January 17, 1952, p. 12; May 29, 1952, p. 2; September 25, 1952, p. 2.

31   Minutes, January 6, 1936, Archives, C-1, Series 1, Box 28; March 9, 1936, ibid.; January 15, 1940, ibid.; April 29, 1940, ibid.; Philip Gleason, *Contending with Modernity* (New York: Oxford University Press, 1995), 246-47; MT, October 22, 1942, p. 4.

32   MT, August 9, 1945, p. 1; October 5, 1950, p. 3; March 8, 1951, p. 1; October 4, 1951, p. 2; November 15, 1951, p. 3; February 28, 1952, p. 1; March 6, 1952, pp. 1, 3; October 29, 1953, p. 2; November 25, 1953, p. 1; January 7, 1954, p. 8; January 14, 1954, p. 8; February 18, 1954, p. 3; March 3, 1955, pp. 1, 12; November 11, 1959, p. 6; Bachelor of General Studies Degree, Archives, A-6.4, Series 1, Box 6; Board of Trustees minutes, January 26, 1952.

33   Letter, March 17, 1938, Archives, A-1.1, Series 3, Box 8; MT, July 31, 1947, p. 3; March 13, 1952, p. 9.

34   Letter, December 6, 1949, Archives, A-1.1, Series 3, Box 8; letter, November 20, 1950, ibid.; "A Talk with Father Gerard Smith, SJ," Archives, C-1, Series 2, Box 6; "Smith—A Common Name for an Uncommon Man," ibid.; clipping, 1955, ibid.; 1948 letters regarding Department, ibid., Box 1; MT, March 13, 1952, p. 9; January 10, 1952, p. 1; March 6, 1952, p. 1; contents, Beatrice H. Zedler Faculty Papers, Archives, C-1.12, Series 2, Box 1; obituary, *Milwaukee Journal Sentinel*, March 3, 2006. An example of just how feisty Father Smith could be was revealed in a 1951 letter in which he refused to cooperate with Dean Roach when the latter asked the chair to suggest laymen who might be laid off for budgetary reasons. Smith defiantly left it to his academic superior to decide who should be fired. Letter, February 5, 1951, Archives, A-1.1, Series 3, Box 8.

35   Labor College folder, Archives, A-1.1, Series 3, Box 5; R. Bentley Anderson, "Black, White, and Catholic," *Catholic Historical Review* (July 2005), 485; MT, November 4, 1946, p. 1; February 19, 1948, p. 2; March 18, 1948, p. 7; July 29, 1948, p. 1; September 23, 1948, p. 9; October 21, 1948, p. 2; February 3, 1949, p. 1; July 14, 1949, p. 1; October 4, 1951, p. 5; May 15, 1952, p. 2; October 8, 1953, p. 1; November 12, 1953, p. 9.

36   MT, February 21, 1946, p. 3; April 4, 1946, p. 1; October 9, 1947, p. 8; September 30, 1948, p. 12; June 30, 1949, p. 1; September 15, 1949, p. 3; March 9, 1950, p. 5; April 6, 1950, p. 1; May 15, 1952, p. 1; February 4, 1954, pp. 5, 12; March 25, 1954, p. 8; clipping, February 6, 1948, Archives, A-4.5, Series 10, File 940; clipping, July 19, 1951, ibid.; Board of Trustees minutes, January 26, 1952.

37   MT, September 20, 1945, p. 2; November 20, 1947, p. 1; February 5, 1948, p. 3; April 15, 1948, p. 3; April 29, 1948, p. 3; June 24, 1948, p. 1; February 10, 1949, p. 1; June 23, 1949, p. 2; January 26, 1950, p. 3; March 9, 1950, p. 7; October 5, 1950, p. 4; October 19, 1950, p. 1; November 9, 1950, p. 4; November 30, 1950, p. 4;

38   Student handbook, 1945, p. 4; MT, December 14, 1946, p. 2; February 27, 1947, p. 2; January 8, 1948, p. 1; April 8, 1948, p. 1; May 20, 1948, p. 3; November 18, 1948, p. 3; February 17, 1949, p. 1; January 17, 1952, p. 1; January 7, 1954, p. 4; letter and survey, February 12, 1948, Archives, A-1.1, Series 2, Box 6; letter, September 28, 1949, Archives, A-1.1, Series 3, Box 5; annual report of Sodality, 1945-46, Archives, A-1.1, Series 3, Box 9; letter and report, May 20, 1950, ibid.; Committee on Student Life minutes, January 12, 1951; January 18, 1951; May 25, 1951.

39   Report on Nuns, Archives, A-1.1, Series 3, Box 9; letter, June 18, 1948, ibid.; Patrick M. Carey, "Theology at Marquette University," 1996 ed., 15-17, Archives.

40   Jesuit Presence, Archives, A-4.5, Series 10, File 717; O'Donnell Memoir, p. 13, Archives, Miller Research Files, Box 1; letter, May 24, 1950, Archives, A-1.1, Series 2, Box 3; *Historia Domus*, September 14, 1950; May 16, 1951; November 12, 1951; September 8, 1953; Board of Trustees minutes, January 6, 1951; *Marquette Report*, October, 1953; Paul A. FitzGerald, *The Governance of Jesuit Colleges in the United States* (Notre Dame: University of Notre Dame, 1984), 110-20.

41   Letter and report, February 8, 1950, Archives, A-1.1, Series 2, Box 8; letter, September 19, 1950, ibid.; vocation lists, Archives, A-1.1, Series 3, Box 9; letter, December 10, 1949, ibid.; MT, January 14, 1954, p. 3; March 18, 1954, p. 4; July 1, 1954, p. 1; July 8, 1954, p. 1.

42   William B. Faherty, *Better the Dream* (St. Louis: Saint Louis University, 1968), 273, 323-24, 340-45; Anderson, 484-86; Gleason, 238-39; MT, July 26, 1945, p. 2; September 20, 1945, p. 3; December 5, 1946, p. 3; August 30, 1945, p. 2; July 25, 1946, p. 8; December 19, 1946, p. 2; May 15, 1947, p. 8.

43   MT, December 12, 1946, p. 2; January 9, 1947, p. 2; February 13, 1947, pp. 2, 4; March 13, 1947, p. 2; April 3, 1947, p. 2; April 24, 1947, p. 3; May 15, 1947, p. 8; June 26, 1947, p. 1; July 3, 1947, p. 3; July 10, 1947, p. 1; July 17, 1947, pp. 1, 2; July 24, 1947, p. 1; July 31, 1947, pp. 1, 2; October 9, 1947, p. 4; December 18, 1947, p. 8; January 15, 1948, p. 1; January 22, 1948, p. 4; February 5, 1948, p. 1; February 19, 1948, p. 5; February 26, 1948, p. 2; March 4, 1948, p. 2; April 8, 1948, p. 5; April 29, 1948, p. 4; May 27, 1948, p. 3; June 24, 1948, p. 2; July 29, 1948, p. 2; October 7, 1948, p. 8; November 4, 1948, p. 8; December 2, 1948, p. 1; December 9, 1948, pp. 1, 8; January 12, 1949, p. 4; February 10, 1949, p. 4; March 10, 1949, p. 2; March 17, 1949, p. 4; March 31, 1949, p. 4; April 7, 1949, p. 4; April 21, 1949, p. 4; July 7, 1949, p. 1; July 14, 1949, p. 2; July 21, 1949, pp. 1, 2; September 29, 1949, p. 2; October 27, 1949, p. 8; December 22, 1949, p. 1; February 2, 1950, p. 3; February 23, 1950, p. 2; April 20, 1950, p. 8; May 18, 1950, p. 4; November 9, 1950, p. 3; November 30, 1950, p. 12; December 7, 1950, p. 2; December 21, 1950, p. 8; January 11, 1951, p. 1; July 5, 1951, p. 4; October 25, 1951, p. 2; November 1, 1951, p. 1; February 26, 1953, section 2, p. 6; March 5, 1953, p. 5; November 19, 1953, p. 2; October 14, 1954, p. 4; Committee on Student Life, May 11, 1950; letters, March, 1949, Archives, A-1.1, Series 3, Box 4; letter, April 22, 1949, ibid., Box 9; letter, April 29, 1949, ibid.; Hilltop, 1948, p. 153. In 1958, the athletic board approved intercollegiate competition with Southern schools that practiced segregation as long as there were no restrictions on Marquette's use of "members of any race." Minutes, January 10, 1958, Archives, B-2.2, Series 1, Box 5.

44   MT, January 9, 1947, pp. 2, 4; February 12, 1948, pp. 1, 4; February 19, 1948, p. 1; March 18, 1948, p. 5; February 21, 1952, p. 1; December 4, 1952, p. 1; December 18, 1952, p. 2; April 23, 1953, p. 1; April 30, 1953, p. 1, 4; September 24, 1953, p. 1; October 15, 1953, p. 1; November 5, 1953, p. 4; January 14, 1954, p. 4; February 25, 1954, p. 1; March 4, 1954, p. 1; April 8, 1954, p. 1; *Historia Domus*, 1950-53, entry between pp. 33-34; Committee on Student Life minutes, January 25, 1952; February 25, 1954.

45   November 25, 1948, p. 1; MT, November 29, 1951, p. 1; March 20, 1952, p. 3; March 27, 1952, p. 1; October 1, 1953, p. 4; January 14, 1954, p. 4; March 25, 1954, p. 1; April 8, 1954, p. 3; March 15, 1957, p. 1; photograph, Archives, A-4.5, Series 10, File 1263; statement of problem, Archives, A-8.5, Series 1, Box 1; rules forbidding beer, ibid.; clippings, ibid.; letter, March 15, 1955, ibid.; Committee on Student Life minutes, March 21, 1952; March 28, 1952; October 10, 1952.

46   MT, August 8, 1946, p. 1; September 25, 1947, p. 6; September 23, 1948, p. 6; September 25, 1952, p. 9; February 12, 1953, p. 3; September 24, 1953, p. 8; Hilltop, 1948, p. 229; Committee on Student Life minutes, April 24, 1945; May 25, 1950; March 19, 1954.

47   MT, November 22, 1945, p. 1; December 11, 1947, p. 6; January 8, 1948, pp. 2, 5; March 11, 1948, p. 5; April 8, 1948, pp. 6, 7; March 23, 1950, pp. 3, 4; February 22, 1951, p. 8; December 6, 1951, p. 4; February 14, 1952, p. 1; February 21, 1952, p. 1; February 28, 1952, p. 2; March 11, 1954, p. 1; April 8, 1954, p. 2; photographs of proms, Archives, A-4.5, Series 10, File 1143.

48   MT, October 24, 1946, p. 3; October 30, 1947, p.1; October 13, 1949, p. 4; April 27, 1950, p. 1; October 4, 1951, p. 8; October 30, 1952, p. 2; photographs of floats, Archives, A-4.5, Series 10, File 680; Homecoming folder, Archives, A-1.1, Series 3, Box 5.

49   MT, February 21, 1946, p. 6; March 14, 1946, p. 6; December 22, 1949, p. 1; November 23, 1950, p. 4; football record, Archives, A-4.5, Series 10, File 595; Athletic Board minutes, February 26, 1946; October 14, 1946; March 14, 1947; September 8, 1947; December 9, 1947; November 8, 1948; December 17, 1948; January 24, 1949; February 17, 1949; March 21, 1949; December 14, 1949; letter, February 15, 1949, Archives, B-2.2, Series 1, Box 5; clipping, February 28, 1946, ibid.; Hilltop, 1946, p. 175; Board of Trustees minutes, June 7, 1945.

50   MT, July 31, 1947, p. 8; October 9, 1947, pp. 1, 7; October 30, 1947, p. 7; May 6, 1948, p. 10; May 13, 1948, p. 7; October 28, 1948, p. 7; January 13, 1949, p. 9; January 27, 1949, p. 6; February 17, 1949, p. 6; March 3, 1949, p. 6; July 21, 1949, p. 4; September 15, 1949, p. 7; February 9, 1950, p. 9; December 9, 1950, p. 9; March 15, 1951, p. 1; April 12, 1951, p. 10; January 10, 1952, p. 1; October 30, 1952, p. 9; November 13, 1952, p. 10; June 25, 1953, p. 1; March 11, 1954, p. 11; Athletic Board minutes, February 26, 1946; October 14, 1946; March 10, 1947; September 8, 1947; December 9, 1947; November 8, 1948; December 17, 1948; January 24, 1949; February 17, 1949; March 21, 1949; May 9, 1949; December 14, 1949; March 13, 1950.

51   Honorary degree recipients, 1908-1995, Archives, A-4.5, Series 10, File 690; O'Donnell Memoir, pp. 56-58, Archives, Miller Research Files, Box 1; MacArthur folders, Archives, A-1.1, Series 3, Box 6; Board of Trustees minutes, June 30, 1945; June 12, 1948; June 10, 1950; April 19, 1951; *Historia Domus*, 1951, insert, pp. 12-13; MT, June 14, 1945, p. 1; May 3, 1951, p. 1; photograph of J. Edgar Hoover, A-4.5, Series 10, File 400.

52   MacArthur folders, Archives, A-1.1, Series 3, Box 6; O'Donnell Memoir, pp. 58-61, Archives, Miller Research File, Box 1; *Historia Domus*, April 27, 1951; MT, May 3, 1951, p. 1.

53   Thomas C. Reeves, *The Life and Times of Joe McCarthy* (New York: Stein and Day, 1982), pp. 11-18; http://bioguide.congress.gov; letter, January 22, 1937, Archives, A-1.1, Series 2, Box 3; letter, February 8, 1949, Archives, A-1.1, Series 3, Box 2; letter, February 15, 1949, ibid.; February 25, 1949, ibid.; MT, February 20, 1930, p. 2; April 20, 1939, p. 1; February 8, 1940, p. 2; February 13, 1941, p. 2; July 31, 1947, p. 7; December 8, 1949, p. 8; October 26, 1950, p. 12; February 4, 1954, p. 3; Committee on Student Life minutes, January 18, 1952.

CHAPTER 7

1   O'Donnell Memoir, p. 89, Archives, Miller Research Files, Box 1.

2   MT, October 23, 1947, p. 3; May 6, 1948, pp. 1, 2, 3; September 18, 1952, p. 3; September 15, 1955, sec. 2, p. 4.

3   O'Donnell Memoir, pp. 64-77, Archives, Miller Research Files, Box 1; letter, July 31, 1953, Archives, C-1.16, Series 2, Box 1; letter, June 7, 1955, ibid.; *Marquette Today*, Fall, 1981, 5; MT, February 3, 1955, p. 1; June 2, 1955, p. 1; June 23, 1955, p. 1; September 15, 1955, p. 3; June 21, 1956, p. 4; *Historia Domus*, March 15, 1955; ibid., p. 33 insert; *Marquette Report*, December, 1954; March, 1955; June, 1955; November, 1955; January, 1956; April, 1956; The President's Report, Archives, A-1.3, Series 2, Box 1.

4   MT, April 5, 1956, p. 1; April 19, 1956, p. 1; *Historia Domus*, insert dated April 4, 1956; ibid., May 14, 1956; June 15, 1956; *Marquette Report*, April, 1956; O'Donnell Memoir, pp. 77-89, Archives, Miller Research Files, Box 1.

5   O'Donnell Memoir, pp. 89-90, ibid.; MT, April 8, 1954, p. 1; list of committee members, *Historia Domus*, p. 5 insert; ibid., April 3, 1954; *Marquette Report*, June, 1954; *Jubilee* article, July/August,

1956, Archives, C-1, Series 2, Box 6; *New York Times*, April 21, 1960; March 18, 1962; obituary, July 19, 1974, ProQuest Historical Newspapers.

6   *Historia Domus*, January 8, 1955; June 18, 1956; O'Donnell Memoir, pp. 90-92, Archives, Miller Research File, Box 1; letter, May 16, 1955, Archives, C-1, Series 2, Box 1.

7   Academic Senate minutes, November 15, 1955, Archives, C-7, Series 1, Box 1; ibid., November 11, 1957.

8   Ibid.; Administrator's Meeting minutes, January 25 & 26, 1961, Archives, A-4.1, Series 5, Box 1; MT, November 16, 1960, sec. 2, p. 7.

9   Report of President's Advisory Council, Archives, A-4.1, Series 3, Box 1; *Historia Domus*, insert dated June 20, 1957.

10   Administrative Committee and University Senate minutes, September 5 & 6, 1958, Archives, A-4.1, Series 5, Box 1; *Marquette Report*, October, 1953, Archives, A-1.3, Series 1, Box 1; MT, March 23, 1960, p. 3; February 13, 1963, p. 3; Academic Senate minutes, February 16, 1955, Archives, A-4.1, Series 5, Box 1; letter, November 7, 1952, *Historia Domus*, 1950-53, p. 31 insert; *Marquette Magazine*, v.1, #1, p. 2, ibid., 1960 Exhibit Envelope.

11   Academic Senate minutes, January 15, 1957, C-7, Series 1, Box 1; *Historia Domus*, October 1, 1960; Faculty Handbook, ibid., 1960 Exhibit G; John S. Brubacher and Willis Rudy, *Higher Education in Transition* (New York: Harper and Row, 1968), 181, 183, 322-23; 1940 Statement of Principles on Academic Freedom and Tenure, http://www.aaup.org/statements/Redbook/1940stat.htm.

12   Job descriptions for president, four vice presidents, and deans, C-7, Series 1, Box 1; Administrative Committee & University Senate minutes, September 5-6, 1958, ibid.; Academic Senate minutes, March 11, 1959, Archives, A-4.1, Series 5, Box 1; memorandum, September 20, 1961, ibid.; functions of boards, October 27, 1961, ibid.; memorandum, October 27, 1961, ibid.; governance survey, 1962, ibid.; memorandum, May 22, 1964, ibid.; election results, June 17, 1964, ibid.

13   MT, March 15, 1957, p. 1; March 12, 1958, p. 1; April 11, 1958, p. 1; April 17, 1959, p. 1; April 24, 1959, p. 1; September 25, 1959, p. 1; October 30, 1959, p. 5; Graduate Board minutes, March 28, 1963, Archives, C-7, Series 1, Box 6; memorandum, June 11, 1963, ibid.

14   MT, November 9, 1956, p. 1; December 7, 1956, p. 2; January 23, 1957, p. 1; March 14, 1958, p. 2; December 5, 1958, p. 1; July 26, 1963, p. 1; September 13, 1963, p. 1; September 20, 1963, p. 6; brochure, 1959, Archives, C-1, Series 1, Box 58; letter, April 30, 1962, ibid., Box 42; proposal, May, 1962, ibid.; letter, June 7, 1962, ibid.; letter, June 11, 1962, ibid.; letter, August 1, 1962, ibid.; report, November 13, 1962, ibid.; February 27, 1963, ibid.; letter, March 6, 1963, ibid.; letter, May 8, 1963, ibid.; programmatic developments, Archives, A-4.5, Series 10, File 1343; *Historia Domus*, September 13, 1963; ibid., p. 22 insert; *Marquette Today*, Fall, 1981, 5.

15   MT, January 11, 1956, p. 1; February 2, 1956, p. 1; November 2, 1956, p. 1; March 27, 1957, p. 1; September 18, 1957, p. 4; April 25, 1958, p. 2; December 12, 1958, p. 1; January 14, 1959, p. 1; November 13, 1959, p. 2; April 7, 1961, p. 3; *Historia Domus*, November 13, 1959; ibid., p. 24 insert; memorandum, July 26, 1960, Archives, C-1, Series 2, Box 1.

16   Letter, November 16, 1950, Archives, C-1, Series 2, Box 1; MT, March 26, 1953, p. 4.

17   Statement, October 12, 1954, Archives, C-7, Series 1, Box 5; agenda for UBGS meetings in 1954-56, ibid.; press release, September 21, 1957, ibid., Box 6; Graduate Board minutes, May 25, 1962, Archives, A-4.1, Series 5, Box 1; Graduate Board minutes, January 24, 1964, Archives, C-7, Series 1, Box 6; enclosure, June 8, 1956, Archives, C-1, Series 1, Box 121; MT, September 25, 1957, p. 1; March 20, 1963, p. 1; *Historia Domus*, September 15, 1957.

18   MT, February 2, 1956, p. 1; November 14, 1956, p. 1; April 10, 1957, p. 1; July 3, 1957, p. 1; November 6, 1957, p. 3; July 3, 1958, p. 4; July 10, 1958, p. 1; October 1, 1958, p. 2; October 31, 1958, p. 1; March 18, 1959, pp. 1,3; March 4, 1960, p. 2; October 5, 1960, p. 2; Administrators' Meeting minutes, November 13, 1961, Archives, A-4.1, Series 5, Box 1; Engineering College's Plan, September 1, 1959, Archives, Miller Research Files, Box 1; position paper, October 23, 1961, ibid.; Graduate Board minutes, March 2, 1962, C-7, Series 1, Box 6.

19   MT, September 15, 1955, p. 2; September 26, 1956, p. 5; September 26, 1958, p. 2; September 29, 1959, p. 4; September 20, 1961, p. 8; September 18, 1963, p. 1; JEA-Excerpts, May, 1958, Archives, C-7, Series 1, Box 1.

20   MT, May 13, 1959, p. 1; *Historia Domus*, May 13, 1959; May 18, 1959; list of recipients, Academic Vice-President's Office.

21   MT, May 21, 1953, p. 1; November 10, 1955, p. 11; March 18, 1959, p. 3.

22   Fiscal summary, 1945-72, Treasurer's Report, June 30, 1972, Archives, A-2.1, Series 4.1, Box 2; MT, March 14, 1958, p. 8.

23   Faculty salary totals, 1958/59 & 1959/60, Archives, C-7, Series 1, Box 1; five-year summary of athletic department, 1952/53-1956/57, Archives, A-5.1, Series 1, Box 13; scholarships to athletes, 1952/53-1956/57, ibid.; comparison of total expenses (provincial tax , student scholarships, & general administration), June 30, 1956 to June 30, 1957, ibid.

24   Revised budget, July 1, 1954 to June 30, 1955, Archives, A-5.1, Series 2, Box 3; budget, July 1, 1955 to June 30, 1956, ibid.; financial report, August 31, 1959, *Historia Domus*, 1960, p. 3 insert; projected deficits, January 25, 1962, Archives, A-4.1, Series 5, Box 1; MT, July 22, 1954, p. 1; December 15, 1955, p. 1; March 29, 1957, p. 1; July 18, 1957, p. 1; September 25, 1957, p. 1; July 23, 1959, p. 1; January 15, 1960, p. 2; January 18, 1961, p. 1; planning report, August, 1959, Archives, Miller Research Files, Box 1; newspaper clippings, Archives, C-5, Series 1, Box 2; article, "University Medical Center," ibid.; "Marquette University & Its School of Health Professions," Archives, A-4.5, Series 10, File 940.

25   General tuition, 1945 to 1972, Treasurer's Report, June 30, 1972, Archives, A-2.1, Series 4.1, Box 2; Academic Senate minutes, February 6, 1958, Archives, A-4.1, Series 5, Box 1; clipping, June 6, 1960, *Historia Domus*, 1960, Exhibit Envelope; MT, July 5, 1956, p. 1.

26   Report for the Board of Governors, September, 1956, Archives, A-3.1, Series 1, Box 1; 75th Anniversary Fund Campaign, January 23, 1957, Archives, A-5.1, Series 1, Box 13; cartoon, Archives, A-4.5, Series 10, File 255.

27   MT, November 16, 1960, sec. 2, p. 5; summary of proposed development program, March 2, 1959, Archives, A-4.1, Series 3, Box 1; clippings, November 16, 1960, *Historia Domus*, 1960, Exhibit Envelope; The Marquette Plan, ibid.

28   Ibid., clippings, November 16, 1960.

29   Administrative Committee minutes, April 20, 1961, Archives, A-4.1, Series 5, Box 1; memorandum, January 22, 1962, ibid.; memorandum, May 12, 1962, *Historia Domus*, 1961, p. 7 insert; MT, September 28, 1962, p. 6.

30   MT, September 13, 1963, p. 2; June 21, 1963, p. 1; Administrator's Meeting minutes, August 29-30, 1961, Archives, Miller Research Files, Box 1; Greater Marquette Program newsletter, October, 1963, *Historia Domus*, 1963, p. 24 insert; ibid., clipping, 1964, p. 7 insert.

31   MT, July 2, 1953, p. 1.

32   MT, January 14, 1954, p. 1; September 15, 1955, p. 6; January 19, 1956, p. 12; April 19, 1956, p. 2; clipping, September, 1958, Archives, A-4.5, Series 10, File 904; *Historia Domus*, March 27, 1957.

33   *Historia Domus*, handwritten notes, March 9, 1958; ibid., 1954, p. 6 insert; ibid., October 28, 1954; July 26, 1956; ibid., 1958, p. 6 insert; clipping, August 27, 1952, Archives, A-4.5, Series 10, File 255; clippings, February 20, 1955, ibid.; clipping, August 3, 1956, ibid.; university buildings, 1954, Archives, Miller Research File, Box 1.

34   Clippings, August 14, 1956, Archives, A-4.5, Series 10, File 305; clippings, June 30, 1960, ibid.; clippings, October 19, 1961 & October 28, 1961, ibid.; photograph, ibid.; clipping, February 25, 1962, Archives, A-4.5, Series 10, File 665; clipping, September 7, 1962, ibid.; Heraty Hall summary, ibid.; letter to stockholders, Archives, A-4.5, Series 10, File 718a; photograph, ibid.; *Historia Domus*, 1960, p. 8 insert; ibid., October 19, 1961; January 22, 1962; September 6, 1962.

35   Ibid., March 29, 1957; ibid., 1959, p. 20 insert; ibid., 1960, p. 17 insert; ibid., 1964, p. 11 insert; letter, October 7, 1957, Archives, C-1, Series 2, Box 1; clipping, March 20, 1957, Archives, A-4.5, Series 10, Files 255; clipping, July 28, 1957, ibid.; clipping, July 29, 1957, ibid.; clipping, 1957, ibid.; "MU Reveals" ibid.; building timetable, ibid.; clipping, October 5, 1960, Archives, A-8.5, Series 1, Box 3; photographs, Archives, A-4.5, Series 10, File 303; MT, October 20, 1955, p. 3; March 22, 1956, p. 5; January 18, 1957, p. 1; March 20, 1957, p. 1; May 3, 1957, p. 1; May 20, 1960, p. 6; April 15, 1964, p. 1.

36   Physical Growth and Change report, Archives, A-4.5, Series 10, File 910; clipping, February 6, 1963, ibid., File 255; *Historia Domus*, January 30, 1957; MT, February 24, 1961, p. 1.

37   O'Donnell Memoir, pp. 123-26, Archives, Miller Research File, Box 1; MT, September 19, 1956, p. 4; September 21, 1960, p. 1; Marquette President, March 30, 1954, Archives, A-4.1, Series 8, Box 7; *Historia Domus*, August 1, 1960; August 26, 1960.

38   *Marquette Report*, October, 1954; November, 1955; *Historia Domus*, November 12, 1951; September 8, 1953; August 15, 1955; ibid.,1961 summary; MT, September 15, 1955, p. 1.

39   Letter, November 16, 1949, Archives, A-1.1, Series 3, Box 4; ; *Marquette Report*, February, 1960; interview with Father Kelley, September 16-17, 1999; *Historia Domus*, September 6, 1957.

40   MT, February 18, 1954, p. 1; July 21, 1956, p. 1; *Historia Domus*, February 18, 1954; Hilltop, 1954, p. 18; 1956, p. 18 *Marquette Report*, November, 1955.

41   Hilltop, 1952, p. 16; 1953, p. 20; 1954, p. 18; clipping, 1950, Archives, A-1.1, Series 2, Box 9; MT, December 12, 1962, p. 1; letter, November 16, 1949, Archives, A-1.1, Series 3, Box 4; Proposals to Intensify the Public Relations Program, February 21, 1959, Archives, A-4.1, Series 3, Box 1; *Marquette Report*, January, 1954; October, 1954; College of Journalism, Golden Anniversary, p. 11; *Historia Domus*, January 3, 1953; December 10, 1962; May 10, 1963; December 9, 1963.

42   MT, June 26, 1952, p. 1; May 3, 1956, p. 1; July 31, 1958, p. 1; October 1, 1958, p. 2.

43   Duties of Jesuit Counselor, Permanent Committee, and Coordinator, September 1, 1953, *Historia Domus*, 1953, p. 49 insert.

44   MT, March 6, 1957, p. 1; March 21, 1958, p. 1; February 27, 1959, p. 1; February 15, 1961, p. 1; February 14, 1962, p. 6; Student Handbook, 1957-58, pp. unnumbered (chapel locations); ibid., 1960, p. 19.

45   MT, September 28, 1956, p. 2; January 9, 1957, p. 5; May 18, 1960, p. 6; May 19, 1961, p. 1; letter, October 10, 1955, Archives, C-1., Series 1, Box 18.

46   MT, September 25, 1957, p. 3; March 21, 1958, p. 3; July 24, 1958, p. 1; July 6, 1961, p. 4; clipping, June 22, 1958, Archives, C-5, Series 1, Box 2.

47   Survey and cover letter, May, 1955, Archives, A-8.5, Series 1, Box 4; MT, March 28, 1956, p. 1; April 15, 1956, p. 3.

48   MT, October 10, 1956, p. 1; October 18, 1957, p. 1; June 4, 1958, p. 1; September 25, 1959, p. 5; Student Handbook, 1956, p. 9.

49   Richard W. Cutler, *Greater Milwaukee's Growing Pains, 1950-2000* (Milwaukee: Milwaukee County Historical Society, 2001), 66; MT, October 19, 1950, p. 5; October 21, 1954, p. 1; January 11, 1956, p. 1; March 1, 1956, p. 1; October 5, 1956, p. 1; October 10. 1956, p. 4; October 31, 1956, p. 1; November 30, 1956, p. 1; February 1, 1957, p. 4; March 13, 1957, p. 2; November 15, 1957, p. 1; January 24, 1958, p. 3; February 19. 1958, p. 1; June 26, 1958, p. 1; October 8, 1958, p. 3; October 15, 1958, p. 1; November 5, 1958, p. 1; November 20, 1959, p. 6; January 8, 1960, p. 3; January 15, 1960, p. 6; February 17, 1960, p. 1; March 25, 1960, p. 1; September 16, 1960, p. 3; October 20, 1961, p. 6; March 20, 1963, p. 1; *Historia Domus*, September 6, 1960; clipping, September 16, 1960, Archives, A-4.5, Series 10, File 106.

50   MT, January 26, 1956, p. 4; March 5, 1958, p. 4; May 8, 1963, p. 1.

51   MT, November 28, 1956, p. 1; November 30, 1956, p. 1; May 1, 1957, p. 1; May 8, 1957, p. 1; October 9, 1957, p. 1; November 6, 1957, p. 1; December 18, 1957, p. 1; October 22, 1958, p. 1; November 7, 1958, p. 1; May 20, 1959, p. 5; January 27, 1960, p. 7; March 23, 1960, p. 1; May 11, 1960, p. 6; October 26, 1960, p. 6; March 15, 1961, p. 1; February 7, 1962, p. 1; April 11, 1962, p. 1; Committee on Student Conduct minutes, September 12, 1955; September 21, 1959; November 4, 1959; December 1, 1960; procedures and principles, Archives, A-8.5, Series 1, Box 1; Student Handbook, 1957-58, pp. 22-23; letter, October 31, 1960, Archives, B-2.1, Series 1, Box 2; clipping, November 11, 1960, ibid.

52   MT, October 18, 1957, p. 1; October 5, 1962, p. 1; Committee on Student Life minutes, December 1, 1960; November 29, 1961; *Historia Domus*, 1962, p. 23 insert; student regulations, October 30, 1962, Archives, A-8.5, Series 1, Box 1.

53   MT, December 2, 1954, p. 1; November 3, 1955, p. 1; December 1, 1955, p. 5; March 8, 1957, p. 5; February 12, 1958, pp. 1, 4; June 4, 1958, p. 5; May 22, 1959, p. 1; November 18, 1959, p. 3;

December 16, 1959, p. 1; October 21, 1960, p. 1; November 2, 1960, p. 1; November 4, 1960, p. 1; November 18, 1960, p. 1; February 15, 1963, p. 6; February 20, 1963, p. 1.

54   Enrollment, 1881/82-1957/58, Archives, A-6.4, Series 2, Box 6; *Historia Domus*, September 21, 1962; MT, September 28, 1950, p. 1; October 2, 1952, p. 1; October 1, 1953, p. 1; September 23, 1954, p. 1; September 28, 1956, p. 1; September 25, 1957, p. 1; October 1, 1958, p. 1; October 23, 1959, p. 1; October 21, 1960, p. 1; October 20, 1961, p. 1; October 17, 1961, p. 1.

55   MT, February 9, 1950, p. 2; March 9, 1950, p. 1; June 29, 1950, p. 1; July 20, 1950, p. 1; July 27, 1950, p. 1; October 19, 1950, p. 12; January 18, 1951, p. 1; February 22, 1951, p. 1; May 24, 1951, p. 3; July 26, 1951, p. 4; October 12, 1956, p. 3; November 7, 1956, p. 1; December 14, 1956, p. 1; January 30, 1957, p. 1; January 17, 1958, p. 1; January 21, 1959, p. 5; January 27, 1960, p. 2; June 23, 1960, p. 1; April 26, 1963, p. 2; *Historia Domus*, 1958-59, p. 1 insert; "The Veteran Returns," Archives, A-4.5, Series 10, File 1376; letter, September 2, 1955, ibid., File 510; Summary of Selective Service Regulations, August 30, 1957, ibid.

56   MT, May 12, 1961, p. 1; July 6, 1961, p. 1; October 10, 1962, p. 1; February 6, 1963, p. 1; May 8, 1963, p. 1; June 25, 1964, p. 1; O'Donnell Memoirs, pp. 132-34, Archives, Miller Research Files, Box 1.

57   In Search of a Theatre, College of Communication files; History of the Marquette Players, January, 1968, ibid.; MT, May 3, 1961, p. 6; October 24, 1973, p. 4.

58   Memorandum, February 18, 1955, Archives, B-2.1, Series 1, Box 1; memorandum, August 31, 1955, ibid.; letter, December 28, 1956, ibid.; memorandum & attachments, March 19, 1956, ibid.; memorandum, January 3, 1957, ibid.; time line of stadium negotiations, ibid.; letter, April 10, 1959, ibid.; letter, September 17, 1953, ibid., Box 2; memorandum, December 9, 1955, ibid.; Jennings affair, ibid., Series 1.1, Box 1; letter, August 9, 1955, ibid.; letter, August 19, 1955, ibid.; letter, December 30, 1955, Archives, B-2.2, Series 1, Box 5; memorandum, September 26, 1957, Archives, A-1.2, Series 4, Box 17; Athletic Board minutes, December 27, 1955; MT, April 15, 1954, p. 7; January 4, 1957, p. 7; February 1, 1957, p. 1; April 3, 1957; April 11, 1957; May 1, 1957, p. 7; November 12, 1957; May 28, 1958, p. 7; October 29, 1958, p. 4; November 12, 1959; November 23, 1958; November 26, 1958; April 15, 1959, p. 4; May 29, 1959, p. 4; May 25, 1960, p. 4; Statutes for Athletic Committee, October 29, 1958, Archives, B-2.2, Series 1, Box 5; Progress Report on Athletics, December 27, 1958, ibid.; Football, 1959/60, ibid.

59   MT, October 7, 1954, p. 11; May 2, 1958, p. 7; December 3, 1958, p. 6; December 17, 1958, p. 6.

60   O'Donnell Memoirs, pp. 117-23, Archives, Miller Research Files, Box 1; Athletic Board minutes, October 6, 1959; November 17, 1959; November 20, 1959; December 7, 1960; presidential statement, Archives, B-2.2, Series 1, Box 5; MT, December 9, 1960, p. 1; December 14, 1960, pp. 1, 2, 4; January 6, 1961, p. 6; September 15, 1961, p. 5; letters, January 27, 1961, Archives, B-2.1, Series 1.1, Box 1.

61   MT, May 27, 1954, p. 4; September 16, 1954, sec. 2, p. 3; October 21, 1954, p. 7; January 14, 1958, p. 1; March 8, 1961, p. 1; January 5, 1962, p. 1; January 12, 1962, p. 1; nicknames, Archives, A-4.5, Series 10, File 1387; photographs of Willie Wumpum mascots, ibid.; clipping, February 26, 1961, Archives, A-4.5, Series 10, File 310; photographs of cheerleaders, ibid.; letter, January 31, 1962, Archives, B-2.1, Series 1, Box 1; proposed report, May 13, 1965, Archives, B-2.2, Series 1, Box 5.

62   O'Donnell Memoirs, pp. 134-35, Archives, Miller Research Files, Box 1; MT, February 19, 1962, p. 1.

63   Press release of Kelley's appointment, Archives, A-4.5, Series 9; MT, February 19, 1962, p. 1; *Historia Domus*, February 18, 1962; February 19, 1962; interview with Father Kelley, September 16-17, 1999.

64   Ibid.; MT, June 22, 1962, p. 1.

65   MT, February 21, 1962, p. 3.

CHAPTER 8

1   O'Donnell Memoir, pp. 109-11, Archives, Miller Research Files, Box 1; *Historia Domus*, 1965, Exhibit B; February 8, 1965; April 30, 1965; June 6, 1965; June 11, 1965; Board of Trustees minutes,

April 15, 1965; Board of Trustees/excomm minutes, February 19, 1969; MT, June 24, 1965, p.1; July 14, 1971, p. 2; March 29, 1972, p. 8; News & Views, v. 1 #1; clipping, December 10, 1971, Archives, A-4.5, Series 10, File 159; building construction list, Archives, A-4.5, Series 10, File 165.

2   MT, December 3, 1965, p. 2; December 17, 1965, p. 8; January 6, 1966, p. 8; February 7, 1968, p. 3; March 27, 1968, p. 1; November 25, 1968, p. 1; September 12, 1969, p. 4; September 24, 1969, p. 2; September 22, 1971, p. 8; News & Views, April 1968; October 1968; April 1970; October 1971; *Historia Domus*, March 17, 1964; May 1, 1967; Board of Trustees minutes, February 14, 1968; building construction list, Archives, A-4.5, Series 10, File 165; chronology, Archives, A-4.5, Series 10, File 904.

3   MT, March 27, 1968, p. 1; December 4, 1968, p. 1; July 3, 1969, p. 1; February 25, 1972, p. 1; News & Views, October 1968; April 1970; building construction list, Archives, Series 10, File 165; chronology, Archives, A-4.5, Series 10, File 904; Board of Trustees/excomm minutes, July 25, 1969.

4   Ibid.; *Historia Domus*, 1964, p. 6 insert; February 26, 1964; May 12, 1964; August 31, 1964; October 21, 1964; January 8, 1965; undated entry regarding Alumnae House, etc., 1965; July 10, 1965; January 25, 1966; March 20, 1966; May 22, 1966; May 30, 1966; October 11, 1967; 1967, Exhibit K; Board of Trustees minutes, June 6, 1964; May 17, 1966; Board of Regents minutes, October 11, 1967; memorandum May 4, 1966, Archives, A-8.1, Series 1, Box 2; News & Views, November 1967; January 1968; October 1968; MT, December 15, 1965, p. 1; March 23, 1966, p. 2; May 25, 1966, p. 1; March 10, 1967, p. 3; October 13, 1967, p. 1; December 13, 1968, p. 1.

5   MT, July 2, 1964, p. 1; July 15, 1965, p. 1; July 29, 1965, p. 1; October 22, 1965, p. 1; June 1, 1966, p. 4; October 27, 1967, p.1; *Historia Domus*, July 10, 1965; 1966, Exhibit clippings; January 19, 1967; September 7, 1967; Board of Regents minutes, June 9, 1964; News & Views, October 1967.

6   Letter, January 29, 1965, Archives, A-1.2, Series 4, Box 5; memorandum, February 10, 1965, ibid.; letter, February 6, 1967, ibid.; *Catholic Herald Citizen* clipping, March 30, 1968, ibid.; memorandum, April 22, 1968, ibid.; memorandum, May 2, 1968, ibid.; "Gesu School" clipping, ibid.; memorandum, August 15, 1968, ibid.; memorandum, August 29, 1968, ibid.; clipping, May 4, 1968, Archives, A-4.5, Series 10, File 255; memorandum, November 13, 1968, File 620; *Historia Domus*, February 13, 1964.

7   Construction report, Archives, A-3.1, Series 2, Box 3; *Historia Domus*, August 31, 1964; September 27, 1964.

8   Policy summary related to Section 112 of 1949 Housing Act, Archives, A-7, Series 3, Box 2; letter, May 21, 1957, ibid.; MT, January 26, 1956, p. 1; February 6, 1957, p. 1; February 22, 1957, p. 1.

9   U.R. Program, Archives, A-7, Series 3, Box 1; remarks, July 23, 1962, ibid., Box 2; press release, May 24, 1962, Archives, A-4.5, Series 10, File 255; memorandum & case study, File 495; letter, June 11, 1962, Archives, A-4.6, Series 1, Box 1; memorandum & resolution, July 31, 1962, ibid.; *Historia Domus*, May 22, 1962.

10   Time table of events, Archives, A-7, Series 3, Box 1; U.R. Program, ibid.; WITI editorial, July 23, 1963, ibid., Box 2; summary report, ibid.; memorandum & case study, Archives, A-4.5, Series 10, File 495; memorandum, June 15, 1962, Archives, A-4.6, Series 1, Box 1; memorandum, June 19, 1962, ibid.; WITI editorial, June 26, 1962, ibid.; summary of committees' meeting, ibid., Box 2; *Historia Domus*, July 24, 1963; July 30, 1963.

11   Time table of events, Archives, A-7, Series 3, Box 1; U.R. Program, ibid.; summary report, ibid.; letter, July 14, 1967, ibid.; capital expenditures, November 6, 1969, ibid.; memorandum & case study, Archives, A-4.5, Series 10, File 495; MT, April 17, 1990, p. 6; *Historia Domus*, September 18, 1964; January 18, 1965; January 26, 1965; July 1, 1965; News and Views, October 1968; January 1971.

12   *Marquette University Magazine*, June 1961, pp. 2-9; clipping, , March 9, 1987, Archives, A-4.5, Series 10, File 495; MT, April 17, 1990, p.8; interview with Father Kelley, September 16-17, 1999.

13   Stop Higher Taxes, Archives, A-4.5, Series 10, File 495; letter, August 22, 1962, Archives, A-7., Series 3, Box 2; memorandum, September 5, 1962, ibid.; letter, October 18, 1962, ibid.; photo montage, Archives, A-4.5, Series 10, File 280; *Historia Domus*, 1966 Exhibit folder.

14   Survey, Archives, A-4.5, Series 10, File 255; MU Newsletter, November 15, 1964.

15   Board of Regents minutes, September 23, 1964; November 13, 1964; December 9, 1964; January 19, 1964; letter, December 20, 1962, Archives, A-7, Series 3, Box 2; photo, Archives, A-4.5, Series 10, File 1198; clipping, March 9, 1987, File 195; *Historia Domus*, September 30, 1964; January 6, 1965; January 11, 1965; October 24, 1966.

16 Letter, December 20, 1962, Archives, A-7, Series 3, Box 2; pamphlet, ibid.; letter, January 18, 1963, ibid.; clipping, September 22, 1962, Archives, A-4.5, Series 10, File 255.

17 Press release, March 15, 1964, Archives, A-3.1, Series 2, Box 1; Board of Regents list, 1965-66, ibid.; MT, April 23, 1965, p. 1; *Historia Domus*, April 23, 1965.

18 MT, September 17, 1965, p. 1; *Historia Domus*, 1965 Exhibit; Board of Trustees minutes, September 9, 1965.

19 MT, April 21, 1962, p. 1; May 2, 1962, p. 1; May 4, 1962, p. 4; clipping, April 29, 1962, Archives, A-4.5, Series 10, Father Kelley Files.

20 John Tracy Ellis, "American Catholics and the Intellectual Life," files of Father Steven Avella; Philip Gleason, *Contending with Modernity* (New York: Oxford University Press, 1995), 287-291, 304;

21 Letter, May 3, 1962, Archives, C-1, Series 1, Box 7; letter, May 7, 1962, ibid.; memorandum, May 7, 1962, ibid.

22 MT, May 25, 1962, p.1; March 4, 1964, p. 1; September 17, 1965, p. 7; text of interview with Rev. Thomas Stemper, SJ, Archives; clipping, March 5, 1964, Archives A-4.5, Series 10, File 565.

23 MT, September 17, 1965, pp. 1, 2; October 20, 1965, p. 4; *Historia Domus*, September 18, 1965; clipping, 1965 Exhibit folder.

24 Norman H. Engbring, *An Anchor for the Future* (Milwaukee: Medical College of Wisconsin, 1991), 166.

25 Ibid., 117; letter, March 10, 1951, Archives, A-1.1, Series 2, Box 6; letter, March 19, 1951, ibid.; letter, December 7, 1951, ibid.; Christmas letter, undated, ibid.; MT, February 24, 1955, p. 1; Administrative Council minutes, July 31, 1961, Archives, A-4.1, Series 5, Box 1; clipping, Archives, C-5, Series 1, Box 3.

26 Annual operating deficits, Archives, A-4.5, Series 10, File 940; clipping, March 20, 1964, ibid.; clipping, December 11, 1964, ibid., File 255; *Historia Domus*, 1964, p. 11 insert; p. 31 insert; 1967, p. 3 insert; Board of Regents minutes, October 27, 1965; MT, December 4, 1964, p. 1; Engbring, 172-75, 200-07.

27 *Historia Domus*, April 16, 1964; October 27, 1966; February 2, 1967; Board of Regents minutes, October 26, 1966; December, 14, 1966.

28 Clipping, January 14, 1967, Archives, C-5, Series 1, Box 3; *Historia Domus*, 1966, p. 2 insert.

29 Press release, September 30, 1967, Archives, C-5, Series 1, Box 1; *Historia Domus*, 1967 Exhibit folder; MT, October 4, 1967, p. 1.

30 Board of Regents Minutes, October 11, 1967, Archives, A-3.1, Series 2, Box 1; clipping, June 20, 1968, C-5, Series 1, Box 3; clipping, June 24, 1968, ibid.; clipping, June 26, 1968, ibid.; clipping, April 9, 1969, ibid., Box 2; clipping, July 25, 1967, Archives, A-4.5, Series 10, File 940; clipping, June 26, 1968, ibid.; clipping, May 11, 1969, ibid.; clipping, June 12, 1969, ibid.; clipping, July 14, 1969, ibid.; clipping, August 31, 1969, ibid.; clipping, October 4, 1969, ibid.; clippings, September 22, 1970, ibid.; clipping, September 23, 1970, ibid.; clipping, April 10, 1974, ibid.; MT, October 31, 1969, p. 2; September 23, 1970, p. 1; Board of Trustees minutes, December 21, 1968; Board of Trustees/excomm minutes, July 25, 1969; September 21, 1970.

31 Brief history of the office of vice president of academic affairs, May 22, 1969, Archives, A-4.1, Series 5, Box 7.

32 Ibid.; MT, September 16, 1966, p. 4; June 28, 1967, p. 1; November 15, 1967, p. 1; February 14, 1968, p. 1; July 18, 1968, p. 1; January 31, 1969, p. 1; February 13, 1970, p. 1; February 20, 1970, p. 1; February 27, 1970, p. 1; March 20, 1970, p. 1; October 30, 1970, p. 1; September 8, 1971, p. 1; September 10, 1971, p. 1; September 17, 1971, p. 1; December 10, 1971, p. 1; January 21, 1972, p. 1; March 8, 1972, p. 1; memorandum, October 29, 1970, Archives, A-4.1, Series 5, Box 2.

33 COF statement, February 20, 1969, Archives, A-4.1, Series 5, Box 7.

34 Memorandum, November 15, 1966, ibid., Box 1; memorandum to faculty, ibid., Box 7; MT, January 11, 1967, p. 1.

35 Minutes of general meeting, January 17, 1967, Archives, A-4.1, Series 5, Box 1; memorandum, February 20, 1967, ibid.; February 27, 1967, ibid.; recommendation to the President, March 10, 1967, ibid.; MT, February 1, 1967, p. 7.

36   Memorandum, December 10, 1968, Archives, A-4.1, Series 5, Box 7; memorandum, February 26, 1969, ibid.; statement , February 20, 1969, ibid.; draft interim report, March 12, 1969, ibid.; MT, February 7, 1969, p. 1; News and Views, February 1967; July 1967.

37   Memorandum, May 22, 1969, Archives, A-4.1, Series 5, Box 7; proposal, May 20, 1969, ibid.; memorandum, May 23, 1969; ibid.; membership proposal, June 26, 1969, ibid.; memorandum, July 30, 1969, ibid.; special meeting, COF, October 23, 1969, ibid.; recommendations, August 25, 1969, ibid., Box 2; academic senate minutes, October 17, 1969; October 31, 1969; May 13, 1970, ibid.; letter and minutes of COF meeting, October 27, 1969, ibid.; memorandum, May 28, 1970, ibid.; MT, September 12, 1969, p. 1; News and Views, April 1969.

38   Memorandum, November 1, 1971, A-4.1, Series 5, Box 2; resolution of appreciation, April 26, 1972, ibid.; letter, April 28, 1972, ibid.; Board of Trustees/excomm minutes, February 28, 1972; News and Views, March-April 1972.

39   Letter, March 22, 1966, files of Norbert Tlachac.

40   Alice Gallin, OSU, *Independence and a New Partnership in Catholic Higher Education* (Notre Dame: University of Notre Dame Press, 1996); memorandum, January 18, 1967, Archives, A-2.1, Series 1.1, Box 1; clippings, January 18, 1967, ibid.

41   Board of Regents minutes, February 15, 1967; memorandum, March 6, 1967, Archives, A-2.1, Series 1.1, Box 1; *Historia Domus*, May 16, 1967.

42   Board of Regents minutes, April 12, 1967; October 2, 1968; proposed amendment to Articles of Incorporation, April 15, 1967, Archives, A-2.1, Series 1.1, Box 1; summary of telephone call with provincial, May 23, 1968, files of Norbert Tlachac; certificate of appreciation, Archives, A-3.1, Series 2, Box 3.

43   Letter, January 17, 1969, Archives, A-2.1, Series 1.1, Box 1; press conference remarks, January 20, 1969, ibid.; trustee biographies, ibid.; clippings, January 21, 1969, ibid.; flow chart for university administration, Archives, A-2.1, Series 5.1, Box 4; Board of Trustees minutes, January 20, 1969; MT, January 22, 1969, p. 1.

44   Letter, July 25, 1968, Archives, A-3.1, Series 2, Box 3; university board of graduate studies minutes, February 6, 1969, Archives, C-7, Series 1, Box 7; MT, February 27, 1970, p. 1.

45   Text of interview with Rev. Thomas Stemper, SJ, Archives; confidential comments of Jesuit faculty to author; *Historia Domus*, 1967, Exhibit F; Board of Trustees/excomm minutes, April 18, 1969; June 23, 1970; conference draft, Archives, A-2.1, Series 1.1, Box 1; draft copy of foundation statements, ibid.

46   Jesuit Associates documents, September 1970, Archives, Miller Research Files, Box 1; clipping, December 16, 1970, Archives, A-4.5, Series 10, File 717; clipping, May 7, 1972, ibid.; essential documents of incorporation, ibid.; Board of Trustees minutes, May 19, 1971.

47   Presentation to Board of Regents, March 16, 1964, Archives, A-3.1, Series 2, Box 1; academic senate minutes, September 4, 1964.

48   Memorandum, September 11, 1964, Archives, A-6.4, Series 1, Box 3; *Historia Domus*, 1964, p. 24 insert; September 25, 1964; MT, September 30, 1964; MU Newsletter, September 25, 1964.

49   Memorandum, November 3, 1964, Archives, A-6.4, Series 1, Box 3; possible guidelines, November 3, 1964, ibid.; Graduate Board priorities, December 9, 1964, ibid.; rationale for priorities, December 28, 1964, ibid.; university-wide planning committee, ibid., Box 4; questionnaire, ibid.; memorandum, October 31, 1964, ibid.; draft of enrollments, April 8, 1965, ibid.; steering committee minutes, December 2, 1964, ibid.; January 20, 1965; March 24, 1965, ibid., Box 5; policies adopted, ibid.; Master Plan schematic, April 8, 1965, ibid.; memorandum, November 26, 1964, ibid., Box 6; graduate board minutes, November 11, 1964, Archives, C-7, Series 1, Box 7; criteria and priorities, November 16, 1964, ibid.; graduate board minutes, November 6, 1964, ibid., Box 8; letter, September 16, 1964, Archives, C-1, Series 2, Box 1; rexographed report, November 26, 1964, ibid., Box 2; letter, November 30, 1964, ibid.; memorandum, December 16, 1964, ibid.; letter, December 22, 1964, ibid.; College of Liberal Arts draft, ibid.; *Historia Domus*, June 10, 1965.

50   Memorandum, October 20, 1966, Archives, C-1, Series 1, Box 18; Board of Regents minutes, December 13, 1967.

51   Confidential draft, October 13, 1966, Archives, A-3.1, Series 2, Box 3; confidential draft, April 4, 1967, ibid.; various college and school drafts, July 1967, ibid.

52   MT, December 11, 1964, p. 1; June 20, 1969, p. 4; November 18, 1970, p. 1; memorandum, April 1, 1968, Archives, A-1.4, Series 1, Box 1; letter, July 1, 1968, ibid.; letter, July 3, 1968, ibid.; July 25, 1968, ibid.; education proposal, March 1970, Archives, A-4.1, Series 5, Box 2; initial operation plan, January 1971, ibid.; memorandum, February 9, 1971, ibid.; report of North Central Association visit, February 3, 1969, Archives, A-1.4, Series 1, Box 1; degree proposal, MA in Teaching English, Archives, A-4.1, Series 5, Box 1; degree proposal, MA in Teaching Spanish, ibid.; memorandum, February 11, 1966, ibid.; memorandum, March 12, 1968, ibid.; Patrick W. Carey, "Theology at Marquette University," second draft, 17-28; Board of Regents minutes, December 13, 1967; MT, July 12, 1967, p. 1.

53   MT, March 10, 1967, p. 2; July 5, 1968, p. 1.

54   MT, March 3, 1971, p. 1; March 4, 1971, p. 1; March 17, 1971, p. 4; March 18, 1971, p. 2; March 24, 1971, p. 1; March 31, 1971, p. 3; September 10, 1971, pp. 1, 6; January 21, 1972, p. 7; March 1, 1972, p. 1; March 3, 1972, p. 1; March 8, 1972, p. 1; March 15, 1972, p. 2; March 17, 1972, p. 6; memorandum, November 8, 1971, Archives, A-4.1, Series 5, Box 2.

55   Policies regarding committee on student conduct, Archives, A-8.5, Series 1, Box 1; types of disciplinary penalties, ibid.; MT, May 11, 1966, p. 1; May 13, 1966, p. 1; memorandum, December 6, 1971, Archives, C-7, Series 1, Box 3; memorandum, December 17, 1971, ibid.; public relations summary, 1968, Archives, A-11, Series 1, Box 12.

56   The Marquette Report, Archives, A-4.5, Series 10, File 95; MT, March 13, 1964, p. 1; November 3, 1965, p. 1; December 10, 1965, p. 1; January 12, 1966, p. 1; January 14, 1966, p. 1; March 11, 1966, p. 3; October 23, 1968, p. 1; December 11, 1968, p. 6; memorandum, September 9, 1966, Archives, A-4.1, Series 5, Box 1; memorandum, October 31, 1967, ibid.; student conduct procedures, 1969, Archives, A-4.1, Series 5, Box 2; memorandum, October 21, 1968, Archives, A-8.5, Series 2, Box 1; reaction of academic senate, ibid.; revised report, August 1969, ibid.; Board of Regents minutes, April 30, 1968.

57   MT, October 9, 1963, p. 1; February 26, 1965, p. 3; March 31, 1965, p. 2; May 6, 1966, p. 2; January 10, 1967, p. 1; February 25, 1970, p. 2; February 27, 1970, p. 2; March 8, 1970, p. 1; April 24, 1970, p. 3; October 7, 1970, p. 5; October 30, 1970, p. 1; March 22, 1972, p. 1; September 27, 1972, p. 6; December 6, 1972, p. 1; *Historia Domus*, 1967, Exhibit folder.

58   MT, May 1, 1964, p. 1; April 22, 1966, p. 6; March 3, 1967, p. 1; April 5, 1967, p. 1; May 24, 1967, p. 6; April 26, 1968, p. 1; April 22, 1970, p. 2; September 11, 1970, p. 1; November 13, 1970, p. 1; November 20, 1970, p. 4; March 10, 1971, p. 1; March 12, 1971, p. 1; September 3, 1971, p. 1; April 21, 1972, p. 1; *Historia Domus*, 1967, Exhibit C; memorandum, November 18, 1963, Archives, A-8.1, Series 1, Box 2; committee on student life minutes, April 21, 1965; Board of Trustees/excomm minutes, August 18, 1970; memorandum, June 19, 1964, Archives, A-8.1, Series 1, Box 2; yearly report, October 6, 1969, Archives, A-2.1, Series 5.1, Box 2; letter, February 28, 1970, Archives, A-8.5, Series 1, Box 2; letter, April 10, 1970, ibid.; intervisitation–problem areas, ibid; intervisitation–brief history, May 11, 1971, ibid.; letter, August 31, 1972, ibid.; memorandum, April 18, 1972, A-4.5, Series 10, File 500; brochure on coeducational housing, ibid.; letters of protest, ibid., File 695.

59   MT, October 20, 1965, p. 1; January 13, 1967, p. 1; May 3, 1967, p. 2; May 10, 1967, p.1; September 15, 1967, p. 1; *Historia Domus*, 1965, Exhibit I; 1965, Exhibit envelope; clipping, October 7, 1965, Archives, A-4.5, Series 10, File 90; memorandum, September 27, 1967, Archives, A-8.1, Series 1, Box 2; memorandum, May 23, 1966, ibid., Box 3.

60   Statement, January 5, 1956, Archives, C-7, Series 1, Box 1; statutes of committee on student publications, September 15, 1965, Archives, A-8.1, Series 1, Box 8; operating policies, September 16, 1965, ibid.

61   MT, April 20, 1966, p. 6; Gleason, 242-44.

62   Committee on student life minutes, January 12, 1961; February 2, 1961; November 13, 1963; January 29, 1964; February 12, 1964; February 18, 1964; MT, February 14, 1964, p. 1; February 21, 1964, p. 1.

63   Committee on student life minutes, March 4, 1964; handwritten notes on outside speakers, March 4, 1964, Archives, A-4.1, Series 5, Box 1; academic senate minutes, March 4, 1964; final draft of policy statement, April 10, 1964, ibid.; ad hoc committee's recommended speakers policy, ibid.; flier, February 1967, Archives, A-1.4, Series 1, Box 3; letter, February 19, 1967, ibid.; speakers policy, January

16, 1969, ibid.; clipping, May 14, 1972, ibid.; MT, February 8, 1967, p. 1; February 15, 1967, p. 1; February 17, 1967, p. 1; February 22, 1967, p. 1; February 24, 1967, p. 1.

64   MT, April 8, 1964, p. 1; May 13, 1964, p. 1; May 20, 1964, p. 1; June 25, 1964, p. 2; February 18, 1966, p. 1; February 25, 1966, p. 1; September 18, 1968, p. 1; October 3, 1969, p. 2; Michael W. Flamm, *Law and Order* (New York: Columbia University Press, 2005), 34-35; photograph of Robert Kennedy, Archives, A-4.5, Series 10, File 400; "Flames of Liberation" flier, Archives, A-1.2, Series 4, Box 16.

65   The letters, minutes, memoranda, envelopes, telegram, and clippings upon which this account has been constructed are located in the University Archives, Acc.#1990.78, Box L-6, Part I, President's Office. Also, press release, April 30, 1976, Archives, A-4.5, Series 10, File 690; clippings, ibid.; MT, February 5, 1964, p. 1; Taylor Branch, *Pillar of Fire* (New York: Simon and Schuster, 1998), 28, 245, 246, 483.

66   John Gurda, *The Making of Milwaukee* (Milwaukee: Milwaukee County Historical Society, 1999), 343, 386; MT, October 25, 1961, pp. 1, 6; October 27, 1961, pp. 1, 4; November 3, 1961, p. 6; November 8, 1961, pp. 1, 6; February 20, 1963, p. 1; May 17, 1963, p. 6; September 27, 1963, p. 2; April 3, 1964, p. 3; February 17, 1965, p. 1; March 24, 1965, p. 2; July 22, 1965, p. 1; September 17, 1965, p. 7; committee on student life minutes, October 31, 1961; November 15, 1961.

67   MT, January 6, 1963, p. 1; February 22, 1963, p. 1; March 1, 1963, p. 1; May 15, 1963, p. 6; March 17, 1964, p. 1; July 16, 1964, p. 1; July 23, 1964, p. 2; September 24, 1965, p. 2; October 15, 1965, p. 1.

68   Time line for student involvement, Archives, A-3.1, Series 2, Box 1; letter, October 11, 1965, ibid.; letter, October 13, 1965, ibid.; tentative draft #3, October 11, 1965, ibid.; MT, March 3, 1965, p. 1; October 20, 1965, p. 3; October 22, 1965, pp. 1, 12; *Historia Domus*, 1965, Exhibit envelope; clipping, October 26, 1965, Archives A-4.5, Series 10, File 1144; clipping, December 25, 1965, ibid., File 1290.

69   MT, March 18, 1966, p. 1; March 25, 1966, p. 1; September 16, 1966, p. 1; September 21, 1966, pp. 1, 4; September 28, 1966, p. 1; September 30, 1966, pp. 1, 4; October 5, 1966, p. 1; October 28, 1966, pp. 1, 2; December 7, 1966, p. 1; May 12, 1967, p. 1; May 24, 1967, p. 1; October 11, 1967, p. 1; October 18, 1967, p. 1; clipping, November 30, 1966, Archives, A-4.5, Series 10, File 1290; photograph, December 3, 1966, ibid.; clippings, December 3, 1966, ibid.; clipping, October 18, 1967, ibid.

70   MT, March 1, 1968, p. 1; petition, Archives, A-4.5, Series 10, File 1290; clipping, March 6, 1968, ibid.; letter, March 26, 1968, ibid.; draft release, March 26, 1968, ibid.; purpose of sit-in, April 3, 1968, ibid.; statement, April 25, 1968, ibid.; clipping, April 6,1968, ibid., File 1144; clippings on Father Markoe, 1967, File 130; clippings, Archives, A-4.5, Series 10, File 4; press release, April 6, 1968, Archives, A-1.4, Series 1, Box 1.

71   Clippings, May 9, 1968, Archives, A-8.5, Series 3, Box 1; statement, May 9, 1968, ibid.; photograph, May 9, 1968, ibid.; president's statement, June 1968, ibid., Series 1, Box 1; Respond Now flier, Archives, A-1.2, Series 4, Box 16; clipping, October 26, 1968, Archives 4.5, Series 10, File 130; clipping, June 11, 1968, ibid., File 25; MT, May 16, 1968, pp. 1, 7; May 22, 1968, pp. 1, 2; Arnold L. Mitchem, "Marquette University's Educational Opportunity Program," (Unpublished PhD dissertation, Marquette University 1981), pp. 9-11.

72   Memorandum, May 24, 1968, Archives, A-1.4, Series 1, Box 1; interim report, June 21, 1968, ibid.; confidential reflections, December 27, 1968, ibid.; job description, ibid.; memorandum, November 11, 1968, ibid.; statement, February 10, 1969, ibid.; draft of special committee, February 27, 1969, ibid.; memorandum, July 17, 1968, ibid., Box 3; memorandum, January 24, 1969, Archives, A-4.1, Series 5, Box 1; clippings, October 1968, Archives, A-4.5, Series 10, File 130; clipping, June 11, 1968, File 25; flier, Archives, A-1.2, Series 4, Box 16; MT, June 21, 1968, p. 1; September 6, 1968, p. 1; September 11, 1968, pp. 2, 3; September 20, 1968, p. 1; October 11, 1968, p. 1; December 18, 1968, p. 2; March 14, 1969, p. 1; November 5, 1969, p. 1; November 19, 1969, p. 8; January 30, 1970, p. 6; February 4, 1970, p. 6; Board of Trustees/committee on educational policy minutes, November 24, 1969; Mitchem, 9-29.

73   Clipping, October 25, 1962, Archives, A-4.5, Series 10, File 1265c; clipping, October 26, 1965, File 1144; Why We Protest, November 30, 1967, ibid.; clipping, December 9, 1967, ibid.; memoran-

dum, November 7, 1967, Archives, A-8.1, Series 1, Box 2; memorandum, November 20, 1967, ibid.; policy regarding demonstrations, A-8.5, Series 3, Box 4; MT, October 29, 1965, p. 1; November 9, 1966, p. 1; December 1, 1967, p. 1.

74 Memorandum, May 8, 1968, Archives, A-4.1, Series 5, Box 1; statement, May 9, 1968, ibid.; anti-ROTC fliers, Archives, A-1.2, Series 4, Box 16; chronology, July 10, 1969, Archives, A-2.1, Series 5.1, Box 2; memorandum, April 17, 1969, Archives, A-8.5, Series 3, Box 4; MT, April 18, 1969, p. 1. Seminar paper, Hannah Barnet, 2006.

75 Chronology, July 10, 1969, Archives, A-2.1, Series 5.1, Box 2; presidential statement, April 23, 1969, Archives, A-4.5, Series 10, File 1144; anti-ROTC coalition statement, April 24, 1969, ibid.; presidential statement, April 29, 1969, ibid.; reflection & suggested action, A-8.5, Series 3, Box 4; due process statement, May 19, 1969, A-8.5, Series 1, Box 1; MT, April 25, 1969, p. 1; April 30, 1969, p. 1; May 2, 1969, p. 1; May 1, 1970, p. 1.

76 Policy on demonstrations, July 16, 1969, Archives, A-2.1, Series 5.1, Box 2; AROTC and NROTC programs, September 17, 1969, ibid.; revised policy, July 23, 1969, ibid.; memorandum, July 28, 1969, Archives, A-4.1, Series 5 Box 1; policy on demonstrations, August 5, 1969, ibid.; policy on demonstrations, August 9, 1969, A-8.5, Series 3, Box 4; MT, March 20, 1970, p. 6.

77 Vincent J. Cannato, *The Ungovernable City* (New York: Basic Books, 2001), 448-51.

78 Philip Caputo, *13 Seconds* (New York: Chamberlain Bros., 2005), Chapter 2, 123-26; Maurice Isserman and Michael Kazin, *America Divided* (New York: Oxford University Press, 2004), 277-78.

79 Clipping, May 7, 1970, Archives A-4.5, Series 10, File 1144; Raymond A. Schroth, SJ, *Fordham, A History and Memoir* (Chicago: Loyola Press, 2002), 296-305; Dennis N. Mihelich, *The History of Creighton University, 1878-2003* (Omaha: Creighton University Press, 2006), 320.

80 List of rallies and demonstrations, May 19, 1970, Archives, A-4.5, Series 10, File 1144; fliers related to Kent State protests at MU, Archives, A-4.5, Series 10, File 1144; president's statement, May 10, 1970, ibid.; photos of protests, 1970, ibid.; chronology of disturbances, May 1970, Archives, A-8.5, Series 3, Box 1; final exam form for liberal arts, ibid.; memorandum, May 12, 1970, ibid.; student fliers, Archives, A-1.2, Series 4, Box 16; memorandum, May17, 1970, Archives, A-8.1, Series 1, Box 2; two memoranda, May 18, 1970, ibid.; memorandum, May 19, 1970, ibid.; MT, May 8, 1970, pp. 1, 3; May 14, 1970, p. 1; September 9, 1970, p. 1.

81 MT, July 23, 1970, p. 2; September 30, 1970, p. 2; memorandum, June 30, 1970, Archives, A-4.1, Series 5, Box 2; policy statement, June 26, 1970, ibid.; memorandum, November 13, 1970, Archives, A-1.2, Series 4, Box 2; bomb threat policy, March 25, 1971, ibid.; Board of Trustees/student affairs committee minutes, December 2, 1970.

CHAPTER 9

1 *Historia Domus*, 1964, p. 4 insert; MT, February 1, 1967, p. 1; January 31, 1968, p. 1; April 23, 1969, p. 1; consolidated report for year ended June 30, 1967, Archives, A-3.1, Series 2, Box 3.

2 MT, April 23, 1969, p. 1; April 8, 1970, p. 1; October 23, 1970, p. 1; December 9, 1970, p. 1; November 17, 1971, p. 6; comparative statement, 1971 and 1972, Archives, A-5.1, Series 2, Box 3; memorandum, October 8, 1971, ibid.; memorandum, July 1, 1974, ibid., A-2.1, Series 5.1, Box 1.

3 Press release, June 18, 1969, Archives, A-4.5, Series 10, File 1348; News and Views, September 13, 1974; April 2, 1976; MT, September 10, 1969, p. 7; April 18, 1973, p. 1.

4 Memorandum, September 13, 1971, Archives, A-5.1, Series 2, Box 3; budget committee minutes, October 1, 1971; September 28, 1972, ibid.; memorandum, January 19, 1973, ibid.; memorandum, October 4, 1971, ibid., A-7, Series 3, Box 1; memorandum, November 8, 1971, ibid., C-1.1, Series 2, Box 2; memorandum, July 1, 1972, ibid., C-1, Series 1, Box 10; memorandum, March 6, 1974, ibid.; Board of Trustees/committee on finance minutes, October 10, 1973, ibid., A-2.1, Series 5.1, Box 4; memorandum, July 1, 1974, ibid.; Board of Trustees/educational policy and student affairs committee minutes, November 12, 1971; News and Views, January 23, 1976; January 14, 1977; MT, January 21, 1972, p. 8; March 7, 1973, p. 1; October 26, 1977, p. 1; James T. Patterson, *Restless Giant* (New York: Oxford University Press, 2005), 7-8, 65, 127.

5   Annual Reports, 1972/73 through 1981/82, Archives, A-1.3, Series 2, Box 3; News and Views, March 5, 1976; November 10, 1978; Board of Trustees/excomm minutes, September 26 1973; September 18, 1974; MT, October 12, 1973, p. 7; November 25, 1975, p. 1.

6   MT, January 16, 1976, p. 1; January 28, 1976, p. 1; January 19, 1977, p. 1; comparative tuition amounts, Archives, A-2.1, Series 4.1, Box 1.

7   MT, November 16, 1960, p. 1; September 18, 1964, p. 1; March 1, 1967, p. 1; March 2, 2006; pledges by December 31, 1966, Archives, A-3.1, Series 2, Box 3; pamphlet, Greater Marquette Program Progress, author's possession; *Historia Domus*, 1967, p. 2 insert; ibid., p. 4 insert.

8   Letter, January 22, 1969, Archives, A-4.5, Series 10, File 495; donor list by area, December 31, 1972, ibid., A-2.1, Series 5.1, Box 1; News and Views, September 13, 1974; December 11, 1974; MT, January 24, 1969, p. 1; January 29, 1969, p. 1; June 20, 1969, p. 1; July 10, 1969, p. 10; September 22, 1971, p. 1; November 8, 1972, p. 6.

9   Board of Trustees/excomm minutes, October 2, 1975; November 11, 1975; November 16, 1977; Board of Trustees/executive and development committees' minutes, December 2, 1975; various clippings, memoranda, guidelines, minutes, Archives, A-2.1, Series 5.1, Boxes 1 & 2; memorandum, April 18, 1980, Archives, A-2.1, Series 1.1, Box 2; GMP update, November 30, 1979, Archives, A-2.1, Series 2.1, Box 3; minutes, December 14, 1979, ibid., B-10, Series 8.1, Box 7; various clippings, Archives, A-4.5, Series 10, File 494; News and Views, December 30, 1975; December 14, 1976; July 22, 1977; July 21, 1978; MT, October 3, 1975, p. 1; January 23, 1976, p. 2; June 28, 1978, p. 1; November 7, 1979, p. 1; April 23, 1980, p. 1.

10   Chart IV, Economic Indicators, attached to Trustee Digest, November 1, 1981; report #6 on dependency on governmental programs, March 17, 1980, Archives, A-2.1, Series 4.1, Box 1; report #7 on dependency on federal, state and local government support, February 25, 1981, ibid.; News and Views, April 21, 1980.

11   Board of Trustees/excomm minutes, July 19, 1978; memorandum and position paper, November 1978, Archives, A-2.1, Series 1.1, Box 2; Trustee Digest, May 1, 1981; various documents on divestiture, Archives, A-4.5, Series 10, File 497; clipping, October 18, 1985, File 1260; clipping, October 30, 1990, ibid.

12   MT, July 6, 1973, p. 4; July 13, 1973, p. 1; November 14, 1973, p. 1; September 18, 1974, p. 3; February 7, 1975, p. 8; September 17, 1975, p. 2; September 26, 1975, p. 2; October 21, 1977, p. 1; clipping and photographs, Archives, A-4.5, Series 10, File 425; Board of Trustees/excomm minutes, January 23, 1974.

13   Memorandum, January 17, 1973, Archives, A-4.5, Series 10, File 720; photos, File 718; clippings and photograph, File 665; clipping and photographs, File 1170; MT, October 12, 1966, p. 3; January 26, 1973, p. 1; February 28, 1973, p. 1; October 5, 1973, p. 1; October 31, 1975, p. 8; February 6, 1978, p. 2; Board of Trustees/excomm minutes, December 6, 1972; July 20, 1977.

14   MT, March 13, 1974, p. 1; March 15, 1974, p. 1; April 5, 1974, p. 1; April 10, 1974, p. 1; September 10, 1975, p. 1; February 4, 1976, p. 5; March 26, 1976, pp. 1, 6; June 23, 1976, p. 2; April 28, 1976, p. 2; February 22, 1978, p. 1; October 8, 1980, p. 2; News and Views, June 18, 1976; March 10, 1978; Board of Trustees/excomm minutes, July 16, 1975; Norman H. Engbring, *An Anchor for the Future* (Milwaukee: Medical College of Wisconsin, 1991), 306-08.

15   Clippings, Archives, A-4.5, Series 10, File 625; MT, February 28, 1975, p. 7; October 31, 1975, p. 1; April 28, 1976, p. 1; February 11, 1977, p. 2; March 4, 1977, p. 1; April 6, 1977, p. 1; May 6, 1977, p. 1; News and Views, November 14, 1975; May 14, 1976; November 5, 1976; May 6, 1977; April 20, 1979; Board of Trustees/excomm minutes, April 13, 1977.

16   Clippings, Archives, A-4.5, Series 10, File 255; photograph, File 3; MT, October 17, 1973, p. 1; April 25, 1975, p. 3; May 7, 1975, p. 1; September 3, 1975, p. 1; October 8, 1975, p. 1; October 8, 1975, p. 1; October 15, 1975, p. 10; November 5, 1975, p. 5; January 16, 1976, p. 1; March 31, 1976, p. 6; July 7, 1976, p. 1; September 1, 1976, p, 2; April 5, 1978, p. 1; April 29, 1977, p. 1; March 31, 1978, p. 3; April 19, 1978, p. 7; September 20, 1978, p. 1 ; March 28, 1979, p. 1; November 21, 1980, p. 1; News and Views, July 16, 1976; May 20, 1977; September 29, 1978; Board of Trustees/excomm minutes, July 17, 1974; April 12, 1978.

17   MT, February 7, 1975, p. 1; August 29, 1975, p. 3; Board of Trustees/excomm minutes, July 21, 1976; August 18, 1976; clippings, Archives, A-4.5, Series 10, File 1255; News and Views, September 10, 1976.

18   MT, July 6, 1973, p. 1; February 5, 1974, p. 1; September 8, 1976, p. 7; News and Views, April-May, 1973; May 1974; January 17, 1975; January 31, 1975; clippings, September 4 & 6, 1974, Archives, A-4.5, Series 10, File 159.

19   MT, December 10, 1975, p. 1; May 5, 1976, p. 2; March 9, 1977, p. 1; March 11, 1977, p. 1; September 2, 1977, p. 1; February 17, 1978, p. 3; April 21, 1978, p. 6; March 19, 1980, p. 1; November 21, 1980, p. 1; April 1, 1981, p. 6; October 9, 1981, p. 9; News and Views, August 27, 1976; November 5, 1976; April 7, 1978; October 10, 1980; November 21, 1980; Board of Trustees/excomm minutes, June 22, 1971; July 16, 1975; April 11, 1979; academic senate minutes, December 4, 1974.

20   MT, July 11, 1968, p. 1; September 13, 1972, p. 3; July 25, 1979, p. 1; clippings, Archives, A-4.5, Series 10, File 296; Board of Trustees/excomm minutes, April 11, 1979.

21   MT, August 30, 1974, p. 1; September 3, 1975, p. 1; April 23, 1976, p. 1; June 23, 1976, p. 3; Board of Trustees/excomm minutes, May 27, 1970.

22   MT, September 8, 1976, p. 1; July 6, 1977, p. 1; September 21, 1979, p. 1; October 10, 1979, p. 1; October 26, 1979, p. 1; December 5, 1979, p. 1; September 24, 1980, p. 1; clipping, October 3, 1979, Archives, A-4.5, Series 10, File 695; Board of Trustees/excomm minutes, July 20, 1977; April 11, 1979; July 16, 1980; News and Views June 18, 1976; July 22, 1977; September 1, 1978; October 27, 1978; "September 4, 1964," This Week in Marquette History, Week of September 3, 2006.

23   Board of Trustees/excomm minutes, August 3, 1978; Board of Trustees/committee on buildings and grounds minutes, May 1, 1974; clipping, July 19, 1978, Archives, A-2.1, Series 5.1, Box 1; Trustee Digest, February 1, 1980; clipping, October 28, 1978, Archives, A-4.5, Series 10, File 90; clippings and photographs, File 1116; photographs, File 771; clipping, March 14, 1973, File 159; MT, April 6, 1973, p. 1; October 31, 1973, p. 1; July 26, 1978, p. 1; September 29, 1978, p. 1; October 27, 1978, p. 7; November 29, 1978, p. 1; September 11, 1979, p. 1; August 31, 1979, p. 6; February 6, 1980, p. 1; February 15, 1980, p. 1; February 29, 1980, p. 1; March 19, 1980, p. 1; April 11, 1980, p. 1; August 27, 1980, p. 3; September 10, 1980, p. 1; September 26, 1980, p. 1; October 15, 1980, p. 1; October 22, 1980, p. 4; March 20, 1981, p. 5; October 21, 1981, p. 1; News and Views, September 1, 1978; September 14, 1979; October 12, 1979.

24   Letter, November 19, 1963, Archives, A-7, Series 3, Box 2; letter, April 30, 1968, ibid., Box 1; MT, November 6, 1970, p. 1; News and Views, April 30, 1976.

25   Statement to Board of Trustees committee on educational policy and student affairs, September 23, 1969; Board of Trustees/committee on educational policy and student affairs minutes, December 13, 1972; educational policies, philosophy, and objectives, ibid., A-2.1, Series 2.1, Box 2; memorandum, October 28, 1969, Archives, C-1, Series 1, Box 10; memorandum, November 9, 1971, Archives, C-7, Series 1, Box 7; university board of graduate studies minutes, November 18, 1971, ibid.

26   Major themes, September 18, 1972, Archives, A-4.1, Series 5, Box 2; position paper, April 19, 1972, ibid., A-2.1, Series 5.1, Box 2; Board of Trustees/committee on educational policy and academic affairs minutes, April 5, 1973; Board of Trustees/committee on finance minutes, December 6, 1972.

27   Survey of academic developments, July 1, 1973-June 30, 1974, Archives, A-2.1, Series 5.1, Box 3; review of academic developments, July 1, 1974-June 30, 1975, ibid.; memorandum, July 16, 1975, ibid., A-6.4, Series 1, Box 2; memorandum, July 17, 1975, ibid., A-4.1, Series 5, Box 3; academic senate unapproved minutes, October 29, 1980; ibid., A-4.1, Series 5, Box 5; New and Views, November 7, 1980.

28   News and Views, September 1973; major themes and aspirations, August 8, 1973, A-1.4, Series 1, Box 1; revised draft, September 18, 1972, Archives, A-4.1, Series 5, Box 2; statement, September 15, 1975, ibid., A-6.4, Series 1, Box 2.

29   MU Report, Fall 1970, Archives, General Information Files, File 1090; chronology, Archives, A-4.5, Series 10, File 904; report to liberal arts faculty, May 11, 1978, ibid., C-1, Series 1, Box 28; memorandum, October 16, 1972, ibid., A-4.1, Series 5, Box 3; memorandum, May 7, 1975, ibid.; memorandum, January 21, 1980, ibid., Box 5; statement, January 22, 1981, ibid.; Trustee Digest, February 1, 1979; review of academic developments, July 1, 1975-June 30, 1976, ibid., A-2.1, Series 5.1, Box 3; MT, November 22, 1972, p. 1; May 4, 1973, p. 6; June 29, 1973, p. 2; October 3, 1975, p. 2.

30   Memorandum, October 24, 1969, Archives, A-4.1, Series 5, Box 2; memorandum, June 30, 1970, ibid.; COF agenda, March 4, 1971, ibid.; preliminary proposal, ibid.; academic senate minutes, March 5, 1971, ibid.; report of special committee, April 3, 1973, ibid., Box 3; survey of academic developments, July 1, 1973-June 30, 1974, Archives, A-2.1, Series 5.1, Box 3; memorandum, September 9, 1974, ibid.; MT, May 1, 1970, p. 1; October 20, 1972, p. 1; April 13, 1973, p. 3; March 6, 1974, p. 2.

31   Board of Trustees/committee on educational policy and academic affairs minutes, October 9, 1974; News and Views, October 25, 1974; February 20, 1976.

32   MT, May 1, 1964, p. 6; January 14, 1966, p. 1; January 6, 1967, p. 1; October 27, 1972, p. 2; March 14, 1973, p. 1; February 18, 1977, p. 1; memorandum, November 17, 1970, Archives, A-4.1, Series 5, Box 2; memorandum, April 1, 1971, ibid.; instructions and evaluation form, 1971, ibid.; ASMU course and teacher evaluation proposal, January 31, 1972, ibid.; memorandum, to academic senate, undated, ibid.; academic senate minutes, October 25, 1972; March 31, 1976; report of special committee, Archives, A-4.1, Series 5, Box 3; memorandum, September 4, 1973, ibid.; memorandum, September 11, 1973, ibid.; memorandum, September 20, 1973, ibid.; memorandum, September 24, 1973, ibid.; memorandum on evaluation of academic administrators, undated, ibid.; memorandum, January 11, 1980, ibid., Box 5; letter, February 23, 1972, Archives, A-8.5, Series 1, Box 1.

33   Various materials pertaining to theology department, Archives, C-1, Series 1.1, Box 8; various materials pertaining to theology department, ibid., A-4.1, Series 5, Box 3; academic senate minutes and related materials, February 26, 1975, Archives, A-4.1, Series 5, Box 3; AAUP report, February 20, 1976, ibid.; letter, February 27, 1976, ibid.; MT, March 21, 1973, p. 4; September 7, 1973, p. 1; September 12, 1973, p. 1; September 14, 1973, p. 2; October 12, 1973, p. 1; January 17, 1975, p. 3; April 9, 1975, p. 1; January 28, 1976, p. 1; February 26, 1976, p. 7; March 17, 1976, p. 1; April 14, 1976, p. 1; April 14, 1976, p. 1; June 30, 1976, p. 1; April 28, 1978, p. 6; March 7, 1979, p. 7; November 21, 1980, p. 3.

34   MT, September 26, 1973, p. 1; October 15, 1975, p. 4; November 25, 1975, p. 1; March 26, 1976, p. 2; February 2, 1979, p. 9; memorandum and proposal, Archives, C-1, Series 1, Box 120; News and Views, October/November, 1973; April 25, 1975; March 19, 1976; February 20, 1981; A History of the Friends of the Haggerty Museum of Art, 1999.

35   Philip Gleason, "A Half-Century of Change in Catholic Higher Education," *U.S. Catholic Historian* (2001), 4, 11.

36   Essay, March 1969, Archives, A-2.1, Series 5.1, Box 2; final report, December 10, 1969, Archives, A-8.1, Series 1, Box 1; working paper for special committee, 1969, Archives, A-2.1, Series 5.1, Box 2; draft of values program, July 23, 1970, ibid., A-4.1, Series 5, Box 2; MT, May 14, 1969, p. 1; October 31, 1969, p. 4.

37   MT, November 18, 1977, pp. 5, 6, 8; April 19, 1978, p. 2; memorandum, October 12, 1970, Archives, A-4.5, Series 10, File 720; speech, September 19, 1971, ibid., G-1, Series 2, Box 4; Gregory Francis Lucey, "The Meaning and Maintenance of Catholicity as a Distinctive Characteristic of American, Catholic Higher Education: A Case Study," (Unpublished PhD dissertation, University of Wisconsin-Madison, 1978), 250.

38   Jesuit presence policy, June 22, 1971, Archives, C-1, Series 1, Box 119; correspondence and other materials regarding Jesuit preference policy, ibid.; memorandum, May 8, 1978, ibid., A-4.1, Series 5, Box 4; academic senate unapproved minutes, September 20, 1978, ibid.; affirmative action statement, October 1978, ibid.; MT, October 3, 1975, p. 1; October 10, 1975, p. 7.

39   MT, May 6, 1964, p. 6; October 27, 1967, p. 3; October 31, 1973, p. 6.

40   Clipping, March 16, 1963, Archives, A-4.5, Series 10, File 1183; clippings regarding student mass, File 265; MT, November 22, 1966, p. 1; October 15, 1975, p. 1.

41   MT, September 11, 1968, p. 6; December 3, 1969, p. 1; October 10, 1975, p. 1; April 6, 1979, p. 3; April 18, 1979, p. 4; clipping regarding Father Cooke, undated, *Historia Domus*, 1965, Exhibit folder; ibid., annual summary, 1966, Exhibit folder; clipping, November 25, 1966, ibid., p. 36 insert; Gleason, "Half-Century of Change," 10, 12; Lucey, 255.

42   Position statement, 1963, Archives, C-1, Series 2, Box 5; letter, May 16, 1966, ibid.; letter, March 14, 1966, ibid., Box 1; MT, April 17, 1964, p. 6; October 9, 1964, p. 6; February 11, 1966, p. 1; February 23, 1966, p. 1; May 3, 1967, p. 3; Christian renewal programs, 1966-67, Archives, A-4.5, Series 10, File 1183; clippings, ibid.

43   Campus Ministry History, Office of Mission and Identity; letter, August 28, 1970, Archives, A-4.5, Series 10, File 265; programs and clippings, ibid.; MT, March 13, 1970, p. 1; September 16, 1970, p. 6; March 31, 1978, p. 2; April 5, 1978, p. 1; April 7, 1978, p. 1; April 12, 1978, p. 1; Trustee Digest, October 1, 1978.

44   MT, March 2, 1966, p. 3; May 11, 1966, p. 1; October 7, 1966, p. 4; September 18, 1968, p. 7; March 8, 1968, p. 4; May 10, 1968, p. 1; February 21, 1969, p. 4; December 10, 1969, p. 6; December 12, 1969, p. 6; September 16, 1970, p. 2; January 23, 1974, p. 2; October 8, 1975, p. 2; October 22, 1976, p. 1; News and Views, November 9, 1979; letter, October 1, 1966, Archives, A-4.5, Series 10, File 903; statement concerning MUCAP, August 15, 1967, ibid.; Catholic character of Marquette, April 1981, File 720; clipping, October 13, 1992, File 1379a; report, Office of Student Affairs, October 6, 1969, Archives, A-2.1, Series 5.1, Box 2; letters, clippings, and chronology of MU's involvement with anti-poverty programs in Milwaukee, 1963-65, Archives, C-1.12, Series 2, Box 9.

45   Freshman survey, Archives, A-4.1, Series 5, Box 4.

46   Enrollment figures, 1957/58 to 1981/82, Archives, A-6.4, Series 2, Box 6.

47   MT, April 7, 1961, p. 6; December 18, 1966, p. 1, 6; May 19, 1965, p. 1; February 1, 1966, p. 2; clippings, May 1965, Archives, A-4.5, Series 10, File 1147; ibid., August 1965 and June 1966, File 1265c; clipping, File 904.

48   MT, October 14, 1966, p. 1; October 19, 1966, p. 1; October 21, 1966, p. 1; October 26, 1966, p. 1; November 4, 1966, p. 1; November 11, 1966, p. 6; December 14, 1966, p. 1; April 7, 1967, p. 1; April 19, 1967, p. 1; April 26, 1967, p. 1; November 8, 1967, p. 2; clipping, October 14, 1966, Archives, A-4.5, Series 10, File 1147; clipping, October 25, 1966, ibid.; clippings, April and September, 1967, ibid.; clippings, April 25 & 26, 1963, File 1265c; student conduct committee report, first semester 1964-65, Archives, A-3.1, Series 2, Box 1.

49   MT, October 30, 1974, p. 1; November 20, 1974, p. 1; December 6, 1974, p. 1; February 26, 1975, p. 5; Board of Trustees/committee on students affairs minutes, May 7, 1975.

50   MT, August 29, 1975, p. 1; September 17, 1975, p. 1; September 26, 1975, p. 1; October 1, 1975, p. 1; October 10, 1975, p. 7; October 17, 1975, p. 1; October 22, 1975, p. 1; October 24, 1975, p. 6; November 5, 1975, p. 7; November 12, 1975, pp. 1, 8; November 19, 1975, pp. 2, 6; January 28, 1976, p. 1; February 25, 1976, pp. 1, 2; February 27, 1976, p. 1; March 19, 1976, p. 1; April 23, 1976, p. 7; May 5, 1976, p. 2; letter, November 6, 1975 attached to News and Views, November 14, 1975; memorandum, November 7, 1975, Archives, A-4.5, Series 10, File 1147; clippings, November 1975, ibid.; Board of Trustees/committee on student affairs minutes, February 23, 1976; summary report, office of students affairs, 1975-76, Archives, A-2.1, Series 5.1, Box 4.

51   June 23, 1976, p. 1; July 21, 1976, p. 1; September 10, 1976, p. 1; September 15, 1976, p. 1; September 17, 1976, p. 1; September 22, 1976, p. 2; October 1, 1976, p. 1; October 6, 1976, p. 1; December 10, 1976, p. 1; March 2, 1977, p. 5; March 11, 1977, p. 2; News and Views, March 21, 1980.

52   MT, January 30, 1970, p. 1; October 9, 1970, p. 2; November 2, 1973, p. 3; March 6, 1974, p. 1; March 26, 1976, p. 1; March 31, 1976, p. 2; April 2, 1976, p. 1; September 24, 1976, p.1; memorandum, October 26, 1976, Archives, A-1.2, Series 4, Box 2; bomb threat policy, November 1976, ibid.; letter, April 19, 1979, ibid.; handwritten letter, April 1979, ibid.; memorandum, April 24, 1979, ibid.; memorandum, April 25, 1979, ibid.; memorandum, April 26, 1979, ibid.; memorandum, May 3, 1979, ibid.; board of graduate studies minutes, April 20, 1979, Archives, C-7, Series 1, Box 7; letter, April 24, 1979, Archives, A-4.5, Series 10, File 1265c; letter, April 25, 1979, ibid.

53   MT, March 9, 1966, p. 4; October 26, 1966, p. 7.

54   Clipping, May 30, 1872, Archives, A-4.5, Series 10, File 90; MT, October 5, 1966, p. 7; August 24, 1973, p. 2; September 5, 1973, p. 2; October 22, 1975, p. 7; January 26, 1977, p. 3; April 14, 1978, pp. 7, 8.

55   MT, February 28, 1973, p. 7; August 24, 1973, p. 1; September 17, 1975, p. 2; October 15, 1975, p. 1; October 29, 1975, p. 6; November 7, 1975, p. 1; November 14, 1975, p. 3; November 25, 1975, p. 3; January 23, 1976, p. 1; February 4, 1977, p. 3; May 6, 1977, p. 5; October 7, 1977, p. 1; October 3, 1979, p. 1; clipping, October 30, 1980, Archives, A-4.5, Series 10, File 255; clipping, May 9, 1973, ibid., File 1260; News and Views, February 22, 1980.

56   Clippings, May and June, 1965, Archives, A-4.5, Series 10, File 25; clipping, February 4, 1970, ibid.; clipping, 1966, ibid.; clipping, December 18, 1969, ibid.; MT, April 7, 1967, p. 7; May 2, 1975,

p. 3; June 23, 1976, p. 1; News and Views, October/November, 1973; April 25, 1975; June 20, 1975; April 21, 1978; January 12, 1979.

57   MT, November 17, 1976, p. 8; February 11, 1977, p. 7; February 18, 1977, p. 1; April 14, 1978, p. 6; October 26, 1979, p. 2.

58   Clipping, June 26, 1965, Archives, A-4.5, Series 10, File 130; clipping, June 18, 1966, ibid.; MT, September 24, 1971, p. 1; October 15, 1971, p. 1; November 30, 1973, p. 1; December 5, 1973, p. 1; February 22, 1974, p. 2; September 6, 1978, p. 1; April 11, 1979, p. 4;

59   Racial characteristics of students, 1975-77, Archives, A-8.1, Series 4, Box 18; Trustee Digest, September 1, 1976; August 1, 1977; June 1, 1980; MT, September 21, 1977, p. 1; December 7, 1977, p. 5; January 19, 1979, p. 1.

60   Clipping, November 5, 1969, Archives, A-4.5, Series 10, File 130; clipping, January 30, 1980, ibid.; survey, ibid., A-8.1, Series 4, Box 18; goals for Multi Cultural Center, 1982-83, ibid., Box 15; MT, September 24, 1975, p. 3; April 28, 1972, p. 1; May 5, 1972, p. 1; September 21, 1973, p. 2; September 29, 1976, p. 1; August 29, 1980, p. 1; October 29, 1980, p. 9.

61   MT, November 12, 1971, p. 1; July 9, 1975, p. 1; September 28, 1977, p. 1; December 7, 1977, p. 7; July 5, 1978, p. 1; November 14, 1979, p. 1; November 29, 1979, p. 1; April 11, 1980, p. 3; October 29, 1980, pp. 7, 8; November 5, 1980, p. 4; April 22, 1981, p. 7; affirmative action program, Archives, A-4.5, Series 10, File 8; clipping, January 22, 1975, ibid.

62   MT, February 10, 1971, p. 1; February 17, 1971, p. 1; February 24, 1971, p. 3; March 4, 1971, p. 1; April 2, 1971, p. 1; letter, February 10, 1971, Archives, A-1.4, Series 1, Box 3; letter, February 19, 1971, ibid.; press release, February 25, 1971, ibid.; CSL report, March 4, 1971, ibid.; letter, April 1, 1971, ibid.; various materials on Warriors name, ibid., A-4.5, Series 10, File 1387; News and Views, February 22, 1980; clipping, Archives, A-4.5, Series 10, File 90; letter, November 3, 1993, File 25.

63   MT, October 27, 1965, p. 6; October 6, 1982, p. 10.

64   Athletic board minutes, November 5, 1962; December 10, 1964; May 13, 1965; October 14, 1965; May 12, 1966; September 15, 1966; November 9, 1966; MT, October 27, 1965, p. 6; October 29, 1965, p. 8; November 3, 1965, p. 6; November 10, 1965, p. 1; March 11, 1966, p. 5; October 5, 1966, p. 2; April 2, 1976, p. 1.

65   MT, November 12, 1982, p. 13; schedule, 1955-56, Archives, A-4.5, Series 10, File 95; *Marquette Basketball Media Guide*, 2004-05.

66   Athletic board minutes, March 7, 1957; April 1, 1958; March 30, 1964; April 11, 1964; April 20, 1964; MT, April 15, 1964, p. 5.

67   Athletic board minutes, September 9, 1964; January 20, 1966; May 11, 1967; October 19, 1967; March 6, 1968; March 18, 1969; April 8, 1969; September 24, 1969; October 1, 1969; November 5, 1969; December 3, 1969; December 17, 1969; June 27, 1972; March 20, 1974; August 5, 1975; February 22, 1977; memorandum, January 4, 1968; memorandum, March 31, 1969, Archives, A-1.2, Series 4.1, Box 29; memorandum, April 7, 1969, ibid.; memorandum, September 17, 1969, ibid., Box 6; *Marquette Basketball Media Guide*, 2005-06; MT, September 24, 1976, p. 8; January 19, 1977, p. 8; January 28, 1977, p. 1; March 30, 1977, pp. 1, 8, 9; April 1, 1977, p. 1; Hilltop, 1977, pp. 54-55; seminar paper, Andrew Sharos, 2006.

68   Athletic board minutes, November 1, 1973; February 13, 1974; March 20, 1974; January 20, 1976; February 10, 1976; March 24, 1976; November 29, 1977; December 12, 1978; February 20, 1979; April 3, 1979; September 11, 1979; clipping, June 8, 1975, Archives, A-4.5, Series 10, File 565; memorandum, April 28, 1981, Archives, B-2.2, Series 1, Box 8; News and Views, November 8, 1974; MT, August 29, 1975, p. 8; September 12, 1975, p. 1; April 14, 1978, p. 6; March 28, 1979, p. 11; March 30, 1979, p. 5; February 6, 1981, p. 7.

69   MT, January 25, 1978, p. 1; April 18, 1979, p. 5; April 29, 1979, p. 4; News and Views, February 10, 1978; April 21, 1978.

70   MT, July 14, 1976, p. 1; September 22, 1976, p. 1; December 1, 1976, p. 1; October 12, 1977, p. 1; December 2, 1977, p. 1; August 31, 1979, p. 3; March 19, 1980, p. 1; April 25, 1980, p. 1; letter and recommendations, February 14, 1978, Archives, A-4.1, Series 5, Box 4; academic senate minutes, October 27, 1976; February 14, 1978.

71   Address, Trustee Digest, 1980 folder; MT, October 29, 1980, p. 2.

72 News and Views, January 12, 1979; February 9, 1979; October 26, 1979; February 22, 1980; March 7, 1980; April 18, 1980; January 9, 1981; February 20, 1981; address, October 22, 1981, Archives, Miller Research Files, Box 1; academic senate minutes, April 10, 1978; May 5, 1981; MT, September 18, 1981, p. 7; October 23, 1981, p. 1; Trustee Digest, July 1, 1981.

AFTERWORD
1 University timetable, Archives; MT, November 19, 1997, pp. 3-7.
2 *National Catholic Reporter,* January 19, 2007, p. 5.

INDEX

Student enrollment, 33-34, 35, 57-58, 70, 73, 75, 86-87, 96, 131, 134-35, 173, 182, 195-96, 201-03, 243, 269-71, 367

Student finances/employment, 30, 141-42, 183-85, 251, 340

Student health, 139-40, 265

Student housing, 37, 141-42, 184, 189-91, 203, 204, 212, 213, 214, 266, 315-16, 344-45, 350-51, 373, 388

Student organizations/activities, 37-38, 101-02, 142-145, 185-89, 198, 228-31, 271-74

Student safety, 367-71

Student unions, 136, 140-41, 142, 189, 204, 212, 214-15, 229, 231, 388

Students' Army Training Corps (SATC), 105-106, 107, 111

T

Taft, William Howard, 36, 97, 236
Teller, Edward, 333
Theology, 248, 312, 358-59
Thomas, Joseph R., 376
Timmerman, Lawrence J., 124, 240
Tomkiewicz, Gabriella, 84
Toy, Charles, 98, 256
Trainor, Dennis, 32
Trinity/Marquette University Hospital, 69, 70, 92, 93, 122, 148, 158-159, 350
Trostel, Gustav J. A., 90
Truman, Harry, 234

U

Uihlein, Joseph, 77, 93
Uihlein, Robert, 207, 209, 231
Uihlein, Robert, Jr., 308
Urban identity, 162-63, 311, 365-67, 387
Urban renewal, 287-93, 351-53, 367-68

V

Van Hise, Charles R., 90

Vogel, Fred, 94

W

Walker, George, 14, 15
Wallace, George, 319
Walsh, John, 273-74
Ward, Eber Block, 24
Webster, William C., 77
Wehr, C. Frederic (Todd), 279, 281, 283
Wehr, William, 279
Weil, Mildred, 374
Welk, Lawrence, 236, 340
Wellman, John D., 253-254
WHAD, 145-47, 153, 185-86
Wild, Robert A., 9, 387, 389
Williams, Elijah, 138
Williams, Katherine, 80, 82
Wilson, Woodrow, 103, 107
Winkler, Frederic C., 112, 114, 131, 166, 281
Winter, Tex, 232
Wolcott, Daisy, 80
Women, 75, 79-85, 120-22, 135-37, 370, 371-74, 381-83
Wooden, John, 380
World War I, 103-06
World War II, 195-200

X

Xavier University, 16, 17, 45, 49, 52, 54, 58, 79, 84, 85
Xuma, A. B., 138

Z

Zedler, Beatrice, 221, 223
Zeidler, Carl, 208, 231, 236
Zeidler, Frank, 240, 288
Zuercher, Joseph, 206, 258